THE NATIONAL SECURITY CONSTITUTION

This book addresses the various ways in which modern approaches to the protection of national security have impacted upon the constitutional order of the United Kingdom. It outlines and assess the constitutional significance of the three primary elements of the United Kingdom's response to the possibility of terrorism and other phenomena which threaten the security of the state: the body of counter-terrorism legislation which has grown up in the last decade and a half, the evolution of the law of investigatory powers, and (to the extent relevant to the domestic constitution) the law governing international military action and co-operation. On the basis of this, it demonstrates that national security as a good to be protected and promoted in contemporary Britain is reflected not merely in the emergence of a discrete body of law by which it is protected at home and abroad, but that the concern with national security has leaked into other areas of public law—areas which are not directly linked to terrorism and legal response to it, but which become (whether by accident or design) implicated in these endeavours, with significant and potentially grave consequences for the constitutional order generally. A renewed and strengthened concern for national security since 9/11 has, it is argued, dragged into its orbit a variety of constitutional phenomena and altered them in its image, giving rise to what we might call a national security constitution.

Volume 4 in Hart Studies in Security and Justice

Hart Studies in Security and Justice

Series editor: Liora Lazarus

The interplay between security and justice has always featured prominently in legal scholarship, but it has taken on a particular urgency since the new Millennium. The new scholarly questions that arise are theoretical, doctrinal and empirical, cutting across a range of traditional sub-disciplines within the legal academy. They address some of the most pressing legal issues of our time, such as the legal status of the 'the war on terror', the nature of states of exception, targeted killing, preventive pre-trial detention, mass surveillance and the numerous other threats that security poses to human rights, the rule of law and liberal democracy.

The purpose of this series is to engage with security and justice scholarship broadly conceived, and to promote a sophisticated and complex understanding of the important challenges it faces. The series is inclusive, promoting new and established scholars from a range of disciplines. It covers doctrinal, empirical, historical and theoretical work, as well as studies which focus on domestic, comparative and international dimensions of emerging security and justice fields. The series also strives to promote the most inclusive range of politics and methodologies, scrutinizing received wisdom and established paradigmatic approaches, and promoting an intellectual dialogue between its authors and the wider field of law as a whole.

Recent titles in this series:

Surveillance, Privacy and Trans-Atlantic Relations
Edited by David Cole, Federico Fabbrini and Stephen Schulhofer

Parliament's Secret War
Veronika Fikfak and Hayley J Hooper

Permanent States of Emergency and the Rule of Law
Alan Greene

The National Security Constitution

Paul F Scott

•HART•
OXFORD • LONDON • NEW YORK • NEW DELHI • SYDNEY

HART PUBLISHING

Bloomsbury Publishing Plc

Kemp House, Chawley Park, Cumnor Hill, Oxford, OX2 9PH, UK

HART PUBLISHING, the Hart/Stag logo, BLOOMSBURY and the Diana logo are trademarks of Bloomsbury Publishing Plc

First published in Great Britain 2018

A catalogue record for this book is available from the British Library.

Library of Congress Cataloging-in-Publication data

Names: Scott, Paul, 1985- author.

Title: The national security constitution / Paul F Scott.

Description: Oxford ; Portland, Oregon : Hart Publishing, 2018. | Includes bibliographical references and index.

Identifiers: LCCN 2017056847 (print) | LCCN 2017057313 (ebook) | ISBN 9781509911028 (Epub) | ISBN 9781509911011 (hardback : alk. paper)

Subjects: LCSH: National security—Law and legislation—Great Britain. | Terrorism—Prevention—Law and legislation—Great Britain. | War and emergency legislation—Great Britain.

Classification: LCC KD6000 (ebook) | LCC KD6000 .S37 2018 (print) | DDC 344.4105/32516—dc23

LC record available at https://lccn.loc.gov/2017056847

ISBN: HB: 978-1-50991-101-1
ePDF: 978-1-50991-103-5
ePub: 978-1-50991-102-8

Typeset by Compuscript Ltd, Shannon
Printed and bound in Great Britain by CPI Group (UK) Ltd, Croydon CR0 4YY

MIX
Paper from responsible sources
FSC® C013604

To find out more about our authors and books visit www.hartpublishing.co.uk. Here you will find extracts, author information, details of forthcoming events and the option to sign up for our newsletters.

ACKNOWLEDGEMENTS

This book was started during a period of research leave from the University of Southampton and completed (mostly) during my first year back teaching at the University of Glasgow, where I had previously completed my PhD. Many colleagues at Southampton encouraged and assisted me while I worked on the early pieces of research which later revealed themselves as aspects of the bigger story that I attempt to tell in this book—particularly Mark Telford and Emily Reid, who were also, and continue to be, wonderful friends. John Coggon continued to store food on his desk even after realising that I would happily help myself to it, and ensured that I (mostly) did not have to drink alone. Matt Nicholson talked to me about justiciability in the heady days when every new judgment was hundreds of pages long and represented a leap forward in the law of act of state. Back in Glasgow, Adam Tomkins read the proposal for what became this book, queried some of the comma usage, and encouraged me to expand it beyond its already ambitious scope. Had he read it slightly more carefully, he would probably have told me not to write the book at all. Chris McCorkindale and Marco Goldoni kept me ticking over intellectually, and provided a welcoming and much needed sense of community.

Marta read and commented on every aspect of this book, which would certainly not exist were it not for her efforts on this front and many others. When I completed my PhD, I wrote in the acknowledgements that '[i]t has long since become clear to me that whatever merit I might have as a person I owe entirely to my mother and my father, and for that I thank them'. I don't imagine that they ever read those words (or, indeed, that many others did). Though the sentiment still holds true, it is now necessary to add another person to that list.

CONTENTS

Introduction: The Constitution and National Security

I. The United Kingdom's Constitutional Order

The most distinctive features of the contemporary British constitution are well-known: first, an order which is uncodified and partially unwritten, reliant upon conventional rules (enforced politically rather than legally) in order to guide the exercise of legal powers whose substance is often undemocratic; second, an omnipotent legislature, capable—at least as a matter of law—of legislating without reference to any standards of morality or legal limitations which would act, more or less successfully, as a proxy for them; third, an electoral system which has usually resulted in an executive which commands a large majority in Parliament, which as a result often appears incapable of effecting the ongoing accountability upon which the Westminster model of government is predicated; fourth, courts which are not only incapable of striking down the enactments of the legislature, but are simultaneously limited in their institutional capacity to adjudicate upon, and to enforce their will against, the executive of the day; fifth, a system of human rights protection which is deliberately weaker than equivalents elsewhere, reliant on interpretation and declaration to avoid unsettling the traditional balance of power between the institutions of state, and so reflecting the traditional British preference for political over legal mechanisms of constitutional accountability even as the efficacy of those political mechanisms is too often left unconsidered; sixth, a territorial division of power whose only consistent quality is its instability. Taken together, these features both give rise to and reflect an order that, though remarkably stable over the long term, is susceptible to sudden and dramatic change both on its surface and, increasingly, at deeper and more fundamental levels.

In the past, the great evolutionary forces of the constitution included the torrid struggle between the Crown and Parliament, from which much of our modern constitutional settlement continues to flow: the doctrine of parliamentary sovereignty and, in particular, the subordination of the Crown to the Crown-in-Parliament, which enjoys the right to regulate its succession and ultimately to abolish it; the exercise by a parliamentary executive of powers which were once the monarch's; the progressive limitation of the Crown's prerogative powers; the financial privilege of the Commons. A second of the historic forces giving rise to evolution is the growth of formalised democracy in the period beginning with Earl Grey's Reform Act of 1832. On one hand, many of the distinctive features of the modern constitution—the most important of the conventions which emerged in order to add a democratic veneer to the (less than democratic) legal base, for example, and the almost total subordination of the upper chamber to its popular counterpart—result more or less directly from the subsequent expansion of democracy. More generally, however, the expanded democratic element of the constitution entered into an important and yet poorly understood dialectic with the emergent administrative state, the one prompting and in turn being prompted by the other. In the absence of a deliberate break with the centuries of accumulated law, practice and variegated tradition—a moment of constitutional renewal presumably given effect via the exercise, by 'the people', of a constituent power which the UK's constitution has historically been unable to recognise to it—these forces continue to scar the constitutional landscape which we encounter today, even if awareness of the geological processes which created that landscape ebbs and flows.

In recent decades, on the contrary, the equivalent forces remain present to the senses and vital to an understanding of how the constitution has come to be as it is. Within the relevant time-frame, a variety of such forces are prominent. Some are at least partly endogenous, being the product of a political environment which the constitutional ordering has created or to the existence of which it has at least contributed. Amongst these we might number, for example, the internationalisation of politics in the post-war twentieth century. This internationalisation is represented most obviously by the formation of what became in time the European Union, British accession to which in the early 1970s began a process of legal evolution which is ongoing to this day even as the method—and in fact the possibility—of undoing the effect of EU membership on the domestic constitution and the associated legal order(s) is contested on all sides. It is evident too in the creation of the Council of Europe, guardian of the European Convention on Human Rights and Fundamental Freedoms, to which the UK has been a signatory since inception, and which was partially transposed into domestic law by the Human Rights Act 1998. A second, related but broader, theme involves the judicialisation of the constitution: the assertions and reassertions of a judicial right to control the legality of executive action even where Parliament appears to have granted to it a broad discretion (a wholly unfettered discretion facilitates arbitrariness, and opposition to the arbitrary exercise of power is the golden thread which runs through the history of public law) and perhaps even—*in extremis*—to control the lawfulness of Parliament's legislation itself. Both positions reflect, it seems, a belief in the inability of political mechanisms to limit executive and legislative action such that they must be supplemented, if not supplanted, by mechanisms enforced, and if necessary devised, by courts of law. Only where the domestic political constitution has been threatened by courts alien to the UK's constitution have the domestic courts sought to defend it, warts and all, from those who invariably privilege its legal aspects over their political counterparts. A third theme—logically posterior—is that of resistance to the increased prominence of (legal) human rights mechanisms within the constitution. As the courts' familiarity with and fondness for individual rights has increased, suspicion of those mechanisms has often shifted from the left of the political spectrum to its right, the constitutional order in this way sowing the seeds of a possible future realignment of a scheme of human rights protection which has not yet existed for even two decades. A fourth is the introduction of devolution—demand for which was in many ways a feature of the constitution's inability to accommodate the uptick in nationalist sentiment to which its own failings had in the past contributed—and the frequent amendment of which has been a function of the failure of devolution to close off these conversations, which it has often instead encouraged and amplified by producing new divergences between politics within the devolved institutions and at Westminster, and new forums in which those differences are made manifest.

Other features of the political context are, however, wholly or almost entirely exogenous: the constitutional order comes to reflect new values, new priorities, not because of anything that has been done by or within it, but because the world beyond has changed and so too—as a result of political decisions, social pressures, media perspectives which operate within political processes, both formal and informal—must it. In recent years, far and away the most prominent of these exogenous factors has, this book contends, been the renewed and expanded focus upon the needs of national security following on from the terrorist attacks on New York and Washington on 11 September 2001 and which has been shaped by a variety of other specific attacks or broader trends in the years since. Many of the legal rules which are most prominent in this work are the direct result of those attacks and later evolutions (or apprehended evolutions) of the nature of the threat to the UK and its people. We have seen, in short, the emergence and the strengthening—at times, the dominance—of a 'national security constitution' which overarches the constitutional order as described above; which comprises new bodies of law created in response to emerging and evolving threats, pre-existing bodies of law which have been newly and explicitly deployed in service of the often all-encompassing exigencies of national security, and bodies of law which on the surface have little or nothing to do with national security but which have been, slowly but inexorably, pulled into the orbit of that theme, and which come to be reconceptualised as part of, or even subsumed within, this new national security constitution. It is on this phenomenon—on these overlapping and interlocking bodies of law—which the present work focuses.

II. The National Security Constitution

The purpose of this book is to account for and explore the changes in the constitutional order which have taken place as a result of the dominance of national security as a policy priority within the contemporary UK: to first of all analyse, from a constitutional perspective, those new, renewed, and repurposed legal rules which directly and unambiguously reflect the predominance of national security in the contemporary political environment, and then, secondly, to consider the ways in which the wider constitution has come to be impacted—indirectly, and at times inadvertently—by that predominance. The book's methodology is, least by the standards of contemporary public law work, unsophisticated. Public law in the UK has for many years been characterised by a turn to theory which began in the early 1990s and which remains influential to this day. The public law scholar cannot content him or herself with a familiarity with the relevant legal rules and their political context, as might once have been the case; indeed, very often the key effect of the turn to theory has been to wrest public law from that political context. Instead, discussion around public law takes place with reference to a vast range of theoretical work, some indigenous to the discipline, some imported from other parts of the academy. This work has done much to enhance the study of the UK's constitution, not least by forcing those who study it to reflect upon and then articulate their own assumptions as to, most obviously, the role of the state, and its appropriate relation to the individual; the question of the extent to which the right can be separated from the good, and how that distinction should be reflected in arrangements of governance; the inter-relation between law and politics in the constitution, and the extent to which it should (and can) be reconfigured. Nevertheless, there have been costs: a portion of that literature is prone to advancing arguments which are broad and sophisticated, purporting to shed new light on the UK's constitution in particular or public law (or 'constitutionalism') in general, but which are only weakly grounded in the legal rules to which they ostensibly relate and which do not balance out the indulgence of starting from a point other than the basic constitutional landscape with a willingness to end there; to use the insights gleaned to work towards reshaping it. This work seeks to do the opposite. It begins in every case from direct consideration of the relevant legal position, augmented by the standard sources of constitutional scholarship: parliamentary materials, legal commentary, and so on. Where it seeks to theorise it does so lightly, seeking never to become unmoored from the law from which it began. For this, I make no apology. A fundamental truth of academic work is the importance of one's priorities. Even within the relatively well-defined world of contemporary public law, there is far more legislation enacted, far more cases decided, than any one person could usefully engage with. And the greater the number of people who are writing about things other than legal developments, the more likely it is that those developments and their effects will go unconsidered at appropriate length. This is true of certain of the issues dealt with in the current work: in the UK, national security law has yet to emerge—as it has in the US—as a discipline in its own right. Even then, considerations of space mean that much of relevance is not discussed in this book in the requisite detail, and in some cases at all.

It must be emphasised too that the overarching argument offered by this book is a descriptive one. In many cases, reason will be offered for thinking that the changes which have taken place—both deliberate and inadvertent—are to be regretted. This is, though, by no means the case for all of those developments addressed herein. On the contrary, many are the result of judicious attempts to ensure that the necessary evolution of the constitution takes place in the way which does the least possible to unsettle its rules, institutions and values. More generally, where the pursuit of national security ends reaches further into the constitutional landscape than was previously the case, that fact is often in large part the consequence of there having been formalised in law (and, by extension, in constitutional law) processes and actions which would previously not have taken place, or would have happened without legal authority. That is, what is presented here as the emergence (or acceleration) of a national security constitution is in many ways the consequence of developments which are themselves, from the point of the rule of law—or, if that is too diffuse a value, the bare commitment to legality—unambiguously positive. Even where that is true, however, we must not assume that the wider consequences of desirable change are necessarily to be welcomed. It will be argued, at several points, that some act or development which was admirable (or simply and obviously necessary) in the context in which it took place has had consequences which we might nevertheless regret.

A third preliminary point concerns the scope of the material under consideration, defined—of course—with reference to the dual concepts of 'national security' and 'constitution'. The language of national security is relatively new; older statutes spoke instead of the 'defence of the realm', the language pushing to the foreground the link between the imperative of protecting a territory and the identity of that territory's Sovereign. National security has never been the subject of statutory definition and for much of the twentieth century various features of the constitutional order ensured that the courts were not called upon to consider the question too frequently, or with particular care. What emerges from the relevant case law is less a sense of what national security is than of who it is for: that national security is the province of the executive is constantly reaffirmed, as is the fact that accountability for the executive's action in that domain is primarily political, to Parliament, rather than legal, to the courts, which will therefore exercise the lightest of touches in reviewing actions in this domain.[1] That idea is evident also in the following passage from the decision of the House of Lords in *Rehman*, the last national security case of the pre-11 September era, which is notable also for the broad, pragmatic definition of 'national security' offered by Lord Hoffmann:

> ... there is no difficulty about what 'national security' means. It is the security of the United Kingdom and its people. On the other hand, the question of whether something is 'in the interests' of national security is not a question of law. It is a matter of judgment and policy. Under the constitution of the United Kingdom and most other countries, decisions as to whether something is or is not in the interests of national security are not a matter for judicial decision. They are entrusted to the executive.[2]

'National security', as used in the present work, mirrors that definition: it is 'the security of the United Kingdom and its people', and includes both the internal and external security of the state. It tracks, crucially, those concepts as they are understood and invoked by those with constitutional responsibility for national security, and so does not seek to second-guess in the abstract the claim that this or that phenomenon is relevant to the concept of national security. Several points follow from this. The first is that this book treats, say, the phenomena of domestic counter-terrorism and military action abroad—much of which is or purports to be aimed at ensuring security at home—as part of a single whole, rather than focusing on one to the exclusion of the other. The second is that without needing to define the concept of 'national security' in any greater detail than does Lord Hoffmann, we are able to make use of the implicit distinction between those measures taken, and those powers which exist, for national security purposes, and those designed to combat 'ordinary' crime, which does not threaten the security of the UK and its people. Time and again we find that the former are broader and more intrusive than are the latter. To begin from a subjective understanding of the concept of national security allows for a starting point which is suitably attuned to the reality we must confront—one which does not require us to reject out of hand, based on mere definitional disagreement, the relevance of legal rules and practices which make up the UK's response to threats to its national security—but without depriving us of the capacity for critical treatment of that empirical legal reality.

Our second concept—that of the constitution—need not cause difficulty. Many of the defining features of the constitutional order of the UK cited above can in fact be traced back, more or less directly, to the first and most consequential: the uncodified and partially unwritten nature of the constitution. Though this deprives us of the most obvious of starting points—the constitutional document, or Constitution—from which we would inevitably, elsewhere, begin, the absence of that starting point must in the circumstances

[1] See, most significantly, *R v Halliday, ex parte Zadig* [1917] AC 260, *Liversidge v Anderson* [1942] AC 206, *Chandler v Director of Public Prosecutions* [1964] AC 763, *R v Secretary of State for the Home Department, ex parte Hosenball* [1977] 3 All ER 452, and *R v Secretary of State for the Home Department, ex parte Cheblak* [1991] 2 All ER 319.

[2] *Secretary of State for the Home Department v Rehman* [2001] UKHL 47, [50].

of a work such as the present one count as an advantage. We can range widely and freely across that body of law and practice which relates the distribution and exercise of public power, focussing on functional concerns and avoiding the temptation to reify, as might be done in certain other jurisdictions, the text of that document, and to risk being distracted by disputes as to the proper method of its interpretation. And so the present work deals primarily with the classic trinity of questions to which a constitutional order must offer answers—what are the institutions of the state? how do they relate to each other? how do they relate to the individual?—without being in any way fenced in by them.

What should be emphasised, finally, is that in speaking of a 'national security constitution' I mean to suggest neither that the focus upon national security is a new one, nor that the modern era is unique in seeing national security impact upon the constitutional order. Neither claim would be even superficially plausible. National security, though not always under than name, has always been central to the task of government. Indeed, the twin domestic and international dimensions of security are in many accounts some of the very few ends in pursuit of which public power might legitimately be employed; they represent not an addendum to but the irreducible minimum of the state's role, to which all other tasks are in theory and often in practice necessarily secondary or subordinate. If national security is more prominent as a policy end now—and that itself may be an illusion based upon the public knowledge, in the modern era, of information which would once have been part of the *arcana imperii*—that should not be taken to suggest that it was not similarly vital in previous decades, even if the specific threats which were apprehended differed in important ways; ways which in turn impact upon the manner in which the constitution comes to reflect national security needs. And, again: the idea that the manner in which national security is protected and pursued might be reflected in the relationship between Parliament and executive as it appears at a particular point in time, or the relationship between citizen and state, is by no means a new one. If national security is the primary purpose of the state, and the constitution the body of rules and practices by which the state pursues its purposes, the constitution, we can see, must always have contained a national security dimension; or, rather, must always have been capable of being understood through a national security lens. What has happened, therefore, is not the emergence of a wholly novel phenomenon, nor the identification of a new perspective from which an existing phenomenon might be described. Instead, there has been, this book contests, an intensification not only of the importance of national security to the domestic policy agenda, but with that, and at least partially as result of it, a broadening and a deepening of the work done by the concept of national security within the constitution: the national security dimension of the constitution has grown, and the extent to which one can make sense of the constitution through a national security lens is greater than it has been for many decades, perhaps ever.

III. Structure

The book is divided into two parts. In the first I consider the law of the national security constitution as it has evolved in recent decades and with reference, in particular, to its constitutional implications. This discussion takes place under three headings, to each of which a chapter is devoted: counter-terrorism, investigatory powers, and what I call 'the military constitution'. The second part of the book shifts its focus from these topics to what I describe as the 'themes' of the national security constitution. Here, we consider not those legal frameworks which directly address the threat to national security, but those changes to the broader constitutional order which are derivative of or consequential upon the renewed focus upon national security in contemporary social and political activity. Here I argue that the contemporary constitution tends, due to the contingent but nevertheless evident centrality of national security as an end of government in the modern era, towards a 'national security constitution' in which, in its most extreme form, little or nothing would be untouched by the exigencies of national security. It is not any part of the argument of the book to suggest that we have already arrived at that particular destination: there is much of the constitution which does not (yet) bear the marks of national security, albeit that fewer of its aspects meet that description than might be immediately realised. Nor, crucially (I emphasise again) is it argued that the process by which national security comes to influence and condition aspects of the constitution other than those explicitly designed in order to further those ends is a new one, which began in 2001 and represents a break with an impliedly prelapsarian past. Such a narrative would be unsustainable. Constitutions are frameworks of governance, implementing some vision—however implicit, however poorly articulated, however contested—of the public good, while leaving room, and creating processes for, the resolution of conflicts as to what the public interest, to the extent not already reflected in the constitution, demands. In this first sense, the public interest a constitution protects will always and everywhere include some consideration of the *salus populi*, even where such thing is not—as it might once have been—the *suprema lex*. That is, constitutions bear necessarily the imprint of national security concerns. They do so in the first place merely by existing and so constituting a group of people, and the territory they occupy, as a polity distinct from all others, and entitling some amongst them to act on behalf of those people and to speak for them on an international plane. They do so similarly in the very fundamental distinction they encode between insiders and outsiders—those who are granted a higher status by law and those who, without citizenship, relate to the state in a necessarily different, less secure fashion, than do its own citizens. Relations between legislatures and executives, between both of those and courts, will always and everywhere reflect some sense that the executive bears responsibility for the protection of national security, in relation to which the other parties can expect to play, whether formally or otherwise, a lesser role than in other areas of policy. So too will a constitutional order always provide for some level of secrecy as to the activities of government, its capacities and its strategic thinking. All of these things are, it goes without saying, clearly identifiable within the constitutional order of the UK from its earliest days, and certainly long before the turn of the millennium.

What is argued therefore is not that the national security constitution as described herein is a novelty, but instead that the prominence of national security concerns has increased, having both spread and deepened, penetrating areas of the constitution which are not explicitly implicated in the pursuit of national security ends; areas which, though they were never previously immune from its influence, have been acted upon by national security more explicitly and to a greater degree than was previously been the case. We are, however, dealing with a change rather than a mere continuation of a prior trend: the process described has accelerated significantly over the last two decades, and if it continues at that pace may ultimately give to the constitutional order a fundamentally different nature.

The themes I address are four, each understood broadly: they are citizenship, justiciability, secrecy and sovereignty. In relation to this final theme, I show how the internationalisation of national security works to undermine the process—its constitutionalisation—charted in earlier chapters. It must again be emphasised that these themes are not exhaustive of the changes which are evident in the constitution: others might have been chosen, though few of these demonstrate change of the same degree and, potentially, consequence as those addressed.

IV. The National Security Council

Finally, because it is significant, and because there is no other obvious place for a consideration of it, it is worthwhile to take a moment here to discuss the constitutional body most relevant to national security as a whole: the National Security Council, a Cabinet committee which is 'the main forum for collective discussion of the government's objectives for national security and about how best to deliver them in the current financial climate.'[3] The immediate origins of the Council lie in the 2010 general election. Both of the main parties were committed to the appointment of a National Security Advisor, and though Gordon Brown had introduced a Cabinet committee ('National Security, International Relations and Development') with related responsibilities, William Hague (foreign secretary in the Coalition) claimed that the government after 2010 had 'inherited a structure of government that had no effective mechanism for bringing together strategic decisions about foreign affairs, security, defence and development or to align national objectives in these areas.'[4] The NSID committee was therefore, in conjunction with the launch of a Strategic Defence and Security Review, replaced with the NSC, which seeks to 'bring together foreign, defence, security, resilience and intelligence policy under the auspices of one committee and secretariat structure in a way which was not a feature of earlier arrangements.'[5] The Council includes the Prime Minister and the relevant Cabinet Ministers; other Ministers, as well as the Chief of the Defence Staff,[6] the Chief of the Joint Intelligence Committee,[7]

[3] 'National Security Council': www.gov.uk/government/groups/national-security-council.

[4] William Hague, 'Britain's Foreign Policy in a Networked World' 1 July 2010. This narrative of discontinuity is challenged by Joe Devanny, 'Co-ordinating UK Foreign and Security Policy: The National Security Council' (2015) *The RUSI Journal* 20, 21, on the basis that the NSC's key departure from prior arrangements is to be found 'in the use to which it has been put, the frequency of its meetings, and the investment of prime ministerial time in driving its processes'. The longer pre-history of the NSC is canvassed in Joe Devanny and Josh Harris, *The National Security Council: National Security at the Centre of Government*, Institute for government (2014).

[5] Devanny and Harris (n 4) 10.

[6] The professional head of the UK's armed forces. The CDS sits on the Defence Council and the Defence Board, and is the Chair of the Chiefs of Staff Committee, of which are members also the Vice-Chief of the Defence Staff and the professional heads of each of the branches of the armed forces: the First Sea Lord and Chief of the Naval Staff, the Chief of the General Staff (the head of the Army) and the Chief of the Air Staff.

[7] The JIC is a much older body, originally a sub-committee of the Committee of Imperial Defence, members of which are to 'bring to the attention of their ministers and departments, as appropriate, assessments that appear to require operational, planning or policy action.' 'Joint Intelligence Committee': www.gov.uk/government/groups/joint-intelligence-committee.

The Butler Review into the role of intelligence in the Iraq war observed that there was 'a strong case for the post of Chairman of the JIC being held by someone with experience of dealing with Ministers in a very senior role, and

and the heads of the three security and intelligence agencies (MI5, MI6 and GCHQ) attend when necessary.[8] Distinguishing it from its spiritual predecessor, the Council's secretary is the National Security Adviser.[9] Ministerial sub-committees of the Council focus on specific issues, including 'threats, hazards, resilience and contingencies', 'nuclear deterrence and security' and 'matters relating to cyber programmes and policy development.'[10] The associated National Security Secretariat 'provides coordination on security and intelligence issues of strategic importance across government' and as of 2014 comprised five directorates: the Civil Contingencies Secretariat, Foreign Affairs, Security and Intelligence, the Office for Cyber Security and Information Assurance, and the Computer Emergency Response Team UK.[11]

Considering the work of the NSC, the Joint Committee on the National Security Strategy observed that while it welcomed the introduction of the NSC in order to 'to give strategic direction to the Government's national security agenda', it was unconvinced 'that the NSC has successfully maintained its strategic focus' but rather, had strayed often into operational territory.[12] This loss of focus was accompanied by—if it did not cause—a lack of imagination in the selection of topics for discussion by the NSC: the Joint Committee noted specifically the NSC's 'failure to discuss the national security implications of either the Eurozone crisis or the possibility of Scottish independence'.[13] A related and persistent complaint about the work of the NSC has been the dominance of foreign policy questions within its work, linked by some commentators to the recruitment as National Security Adviser of a series of individuals whose previous experience had been mostly or entirely in the Foreign and Commonwealth Office.[14] Moreover, the limited information in the public domain about the work of the Council has made it difficult to assess the nature and significance of that work, and the Joint Committee has requested 'regular confidential oral briefings on the work of the Council.'[15] A further recommendation was that the NSC meet regularly, including when Parliament is not in session.[16] What emerges most clearly from those considerations of the NSC and its work which have taken place in the still-short period since its creation, however, is the contingency of its position within the

who is demonstrably beyond influence, and thus probably in his last post.' Report of a Committee of Privy Counsellors, *Review of Intelligence on Weapons of Mass Destruction* (HC 2003–04, 898), [597]. The current Chairman is Charles Farr, formerly Director of the Office for Security and Counter-Terrorism.

[8] One weakness of the NSC which has been identified is the inadequate level of military expertise, with the Chief of Defence staff the only member representing the armed forces: House of Commons Defence Committee, *Decision-making in Defence Policy* (HC 2014–15, 682), [98].

[9] Currently Mark Sedwill, previously the UK's Ambassador to Afghanistan and Permanent Secretary at the Home Office. The NSA is also the accounting officer for the single intelligence account, from which the security and intelligence agencies are funded.

[10] 'National Security Council' (n 3).

[11] Devanny and Harris (n 4) 27.

[12] Joint Committee on the National Security Strategy, *First Review of the National Security Strategy 2010*, (2010–12, HL 265, HC 1384), [83]. See also Defence Committee (n 8) [107]–[112], making the same point.

[13] ibid [86].

[14] ibid [87]–[88] and Devanny and Harris (n 4) 29–30.

[15] Joint Committee on the National Security Strategy, *The next National Security Strategy* (2014–15, HL 114, HC 749), [54].

[16] ibid [55].

executive's national security endeavours. Though judged by many to have been 'remarkably effective',[17] it seems clear that a weaker Prime Ministerial commitment to the Council and its work might quickly threaten the place it has established for itself within the national security constitution.[18] Though the Prime Minister at the time these observations were made, David Cameron, has since been replaced by one with a long-standing involvement in, and evident concern for, national security matters, it is by no means clear that that pattern will be repeated in future, particularly if national security issues fade from prominence in light of, say, the currently ongoing Brexit process. In such a scenario, the (perhaps surprisingly recent) creation of an institution which brings the full range of national security questions together at the heart of government may, in effect, be undone.[19] What this book shows, however, perhaps above all else, is that any such change would do little to undermine the prominence of national security within the wider constitutional order.

[17] Devanny and Harris (n 4) 45. See also Devanny (n 4) 22, and the Joint Committee on the NSS: 'We agree with the assessment of the National Security Adviser that in providing a regular forum for all relevant Ministers, including those not traditionally considered to have a voice in security affairs, the NSC has been a valuable addition to the machinery of government' Joint Committee on the National Security Strategy, *National Security Strategy and Strategic Defence and Security Review 2015* (2016–17, HL 18, HC 153), [107]. See also Defence Committee (n 8) [86]: 'One of the main benefits of the NSC is that national security is now given priority in a formal setting.' Other strengths identified are the NSC's inter-departmental design, the provision of an 'auditable trail for decision-making', and the opportunity to challenge military advice and MoD decision-making ([86]–[92]).

[18] Devanny and Harris (n 4) 45–6.

[19] The Joint Committee argued, in light of this risk, that the government 'should consider creating a ministerial post within the Cabinet Office with oversight of national security', which would 'strengthen the leadership on national security at the centre of government, a function which is currently fulfilled by the Prime Minister.' Joint Committee on the National Security Strategy (n 15) [109].

1

The Counter-Terrorism Constitution

I. Introduction

At the heart of the national security constitution in its modern form stand those powers which address, directly and explicitly, the threat of terrorism. Here, not only is there a significant body of law to consider, but that body of law is rapidly and constantly evolving: the law of counter-terrorism in the middle of the century's second decade was very different from that which was put in place by the Terrorism Act 2000. This first chapter considers the evolution of that law, providing an overview of the background to the legal position, followed by a discussion of the key developments since the attacks of 11 September 2001, showing how the approach to counter-terrorism has shifted in response to changing patterns of national security threats (or at least changing perception as to the nature of those threats) and considering certain specifically constitutional themes which recur within the modern law of counter-terrorism. The most important point which emerges from this chapter, however, is one which cannot be made directly within it, but must be made elsewhere in this book: that the law of counter-terrorism upon which this chapter focuses, though it is the most direct constitutional response to modern threats to national security at home, constitutes only a small fraction of the national security constitution.

Though in beginning from a consideration of the law of counter-terrorism we are addressing that element of our broader subject which enjoys the highest public (and academic) profile, to focus only upon the law of counter-terrorism would be to miss the number of other ways in which the constitution promotes and otherwise reflects the ends of national security. One point to make is that in considering the counter-terrorism constitution, we are always in the domain of exceptionalism. Even where the law is stable over time, even where the powers are widely used, the law of counter-terrorism necessarily presents itself as something exceptional, a body of law which implements powers or limits rights in ways which would not otherwise be accepted because it responds to a phenomenon which exists outside the mainstream of those activities which the law is required to address. Were it otherwise—were terrorism understood by lawmakers to be a phenomenon capable of accommodation within the normal criminal and civil law—there would be no counter-terrorism law. In what follows, that claim to exceptionalism acts as the background to certain critical observations made about the law in this area, but it should not thereby be assumed that it is in any way endorsed. There is good reason to believe not only that terrorism is not an exceptional phenomenon requiring an exceptional legal response, but—further—that there does not exist a group of activities which can be usefully categorised, at least as a matter of law, as a single phenomenon of 'terrorism'.[1]

[1] See, eg, Alan Greene, 'Defining Terrorism: One Size Fits All?' (2017) 66 *ICLQ* 411.

II. CONTEST and the Joint Terrorism Analysis Centre

The government's approach to terrorism is underpinned by 'CONTEST: The United Kingdom's Strategy for Countering Terrorism', published for the first time in 2006 and reissued, following occasional revision, in 2011. The strategy, the aim of which is 'to reduce the risk to the UK and its interests overseas from terrorism, so that people can go about their lives freely and with confidence', is organised around four 'workstreams': **Pursue** ('to stop terrorist attacks'); **Prevent** ('to stop people becoming terrorists or supporting terrorism'); **Protect** ('to strengthen our protection against a terrorist attack)'; and **Prepare** ('to mitigate the impact of a terrorist attack').[2] The second of the four has been the subject of the most sustained attention, as a result of the perceived anti-Muslim bent of many of the projects which take place within the workstream.[3] Otherwise, what is most striking about CONTEST strategy is the level of generality at which the key commitments are formulated, and how little work they are therefore able to do in determining the specific steps taken in order to combat the threat of terrorism. That is, though the various legal issues and regimes described in the chapter can all easily be numbered under one or the other of these headings, the specific form that they take and the manner in (and time at) which they are reformed or amended, appears to be causally connected to CONTEST in only the loosest of ways.

The key institution of the counter-terrorism constitutional order is the Joint Terrorism Analysis Centre (JTAC), established in 2003, which is the body which 'pulls together all the available intelligence on the Islamist threat, analyses it and produces short-term assessments of the level of threat and longer-term assessments of terrorist networks, capabilities and trends.'[4] JTAC enjoys a certain level of prominence as the body which sets the 'threat level'—the threat posed to the UK by international terrorism on one hand and Northern Irish terrorism on the other—changes in the former of which are widely reported and often result directly in changes to the experience of travellers and other sections of the public.[5] JTAC, though it is 'self-standing' and comprises representatives of over a dozen separate bodies and agencies, is based within MI5's headquarters. Its head is accountable to the Director General of MI5, and reports periodically to the JTAC Oversight Board. The creation of JTAC is widely seen to have been a positive development (Hennessy notes that it has 'spawned a number of imitators across the developed world')[6] and it may well be true

[2] HM Government, *CONTEST: The United Kingdom's Strategy for Countering Terrorism* (July 2011).

[3] HM Government, *Prevent Strategy*, Cm 8092 (2011). For criticism, see Open Society Justice Initiative, *Eroding Trust The UK's Prevent Counter-Extremism Strategy in Health and Education* (2016), concluding (at 15) that Prevent 'creates a serious risk of human rights violations' and 'is flawed in both its design and application, rendering it not only unjust but also counterproductive.'

[4] Intelligence and Security Committee, *Report into the London Terrorist Attacks on 7 July 2005*, Cm 6785 (2006).

[5] The ISC, in its report on the London attacks of 2005, recommended 'a greater transparency of the threat level and alert state systems as a whole, and in particular that more thought is given to what is put in the public domain about the level of threat and required level of alert ... We do not expect detailed JTAC reports or sectoral threat levels to be made available, but the Government should consider what messages about the general level of the threat or alert state could usefully be conveyed.' ISC (n 4) [H].

[6] P Hennessy, *The Secret State: Preparing For The Worst 1945–2010* (London, Penguin, 2010). See also the Report of a Committee of Privy Counsellors, *Review of Intelligence on Weapons of Mass Destruction* (HC 2003–04, 898) ('the Butler review') [134].

that the quality of analysis has improved as a result. It is nevertheless clear that very little of JTAC's work leaves any obvious mark upon the legal record.

III. The Role of the Criminal Law in Counter-Terrorism

One of the key features of the legal response to terrorism is, of course, the criminal law. There exist, and have existed for many decades, a large (and growing) number of criminal offences which specifically relate to terrorism, as well as an unquantifiable number which might be committed by people recognised—in law or merely informally—as terrorists. Some of the terrorism offences are intuitively justified; others are far broader than can be justified and only selective enforcement prevents the law being brought into dispute—perhaps rendered farcical—by their existence.[7] Some are prosecuted with relative frequency; others rarely or not at all.[8] There is also a special power of arrest under section 41 of the Terrorism Act 2000, to which a longer permissible period of pre-charge detention than usual applies.[9] Though this chapter makes reference to some of the relevant offences at certain points, they are not its focus. For one thing, the offences in question (mostly) raise issues which are not relevant to a consideration of national security from a constitutional perspective. There are, of course, exceptions—see, for instance, the consideration of public interest immunity and in camera trials in Chapter 5—but the primary issues to which the various relevant offences give rise are better addressed by criminal lawyers. That there remains a counter-terrorism constitution to consider in this chapter is the result of a variety of factors. A first is that the criminal law can respond only to acts which have already taken place (even if those acts are preparatory to some act which might take place in future). The legal response to terrorism seeks, alongside that possibility, to pre-empt terrorist acts; to put in place mechanisms which prevent them from taking place at all. Related to this is the criminal standard of proof: though—as we shall see—the legal threshold for the various mechanisms under discussion here varies, each is by definition lower than the 'beyond reasonable doubt' standard used in the criminal law, and some are much lower indeed.

[7] See, eg, ss 57 and 58 of the Terrorism Act 2000. The former makes it an offence for a person to possess 'an article in circumstances which give rise to a reasonable suspicion that his possession is for a purpose connected with the commission, preparation or instigation of an act of terrorism.' The latter provides that a person commits an offence if 'he collects or makes a record of information of a kind likely to be useful to a person committing or preparing an act of terrorism'. One commentator has described these provisions as 'ill-thought-through offences that oscillate between criminalising silence in suspicious circumstances, criminalising conduct that can in fact be shown to be connected, however remotely or indirectly, to future acts of terror, and conduct that may conceivably increase the risk of such acts being committed.' Antje Du Bois-Pedain, 'Terrorist possession offences: curiosity kills the cat?' (2009) 68 *CLJ* 261, 363.

[8] The Home Office publishes, on a quarterly basis, statistics relating to the use of counter-terrorism powers: see, eg, Home Office, *Operation of police powers under the Terrorism Act 2000 and subsequent legislation: Arrests, outcomes, and stop and search, Great Britain, quarterly update to December 2016*, Statistical Bulletin 04/17 (March 2017). The most commonly charged terrorism offence in the period since 9/11 is preparation of terrorist acts under s 5 of the Terrorism Act 2000: see David Anderson QC, *The Terrorism Acts in 2015 Report of the Independent Reviewer on the Operation of the Terrorism Act 2000 and Part 1 of the Terrorism Act 2006* (December 2016), [9.3].

[9] The length of that detention has varied over time and been the subject of frequent political dispute: for an overview, see Alexander Horne and Gavin Berman, *Pre-Charge Detention in Terrorism Cases*, House of Commons Library Standard Note SN/HA/5634 (15 March 2012).

This alone does not explain the discrepancy: after all, the criminal standard of proof applies generally, and there is no sense in which too few offences are successfully prosecuted in the contemporary United Kingdom. More important within the specific context of terrorism is the law governing the use made within the legal process of material acquired via the interception of communications (what is usually described as 'intercept evidence', and which by statute includes the content of intercepted communications but also 'secondary data' or 'communications data' associated with those communications).[10] The relevant rules as found in the Regulation of Investigatory Powers Act 2000 (RIPA) provided that 'no evidence shall be adduced, question asked, assertion or disclosure made or other thing done in, for the purposes of or in connection with any legal proceedings' which disclosed intercept material in circumstances suggesting that it originated in one of a number of acts, or which tended to suggest that such acts had taken place.[11] For present purposes, the most important of those acts was 'the issue of an interception warrant' but also included within the categories of acts which were not to be disclosed in this way were unlawful interception by one of a number of identified agents of the state, the making of an application for a warrant, and 'the imposition of any requirement on any person to provide assistance with giving effect to an interception warrant.'[12] The basic position therefore effectively prevented the use of intercept evidence though without directly forbidding it: if the material could be adduced in a manner which did not suggest that it originated in any of the relevant acts (or that such acts had otherwise taken place) then it could be used. This rule was subject to a number of exceptions, the most important of which permitted the material to be used before various specialist bodies (the Investigatory Powers Tribunal, the Special Immigration Appeals Commission etc),[13] subject to limitations preventing the disclosure of the relevant material to the non-state party (or parties) and their ordinary counsel (rather than special advocates).[14] Communications data could be adduced in legal proceedings where to do so did not suggest the issue of an interception warrant; as, for example, where it was acquired under the separate powers in RIPA governing the acquisition of such data. An equivalent scheme to that in RIPA is now contained in the Investigatory Powers Act 2016 (IPA).[15]

The effect of these regimes is to allow intercept material to be disclosed (and relied upon) in those specialist tribunals which are required (or empowered) by statute to employ 'closed material procedures', as long as doing so does not lead that material being disclosed to those (including the person on whom the measures etc are imposed) outside of the national security framework. As discussed in Chapter 5, however, such procedures are not available in the context of criminal law; their use therein would represent a clear (and inherent) breach

[10] For the definition of 'communications data' see Regulation of Investigatory Powers Act 2000, s 21(4) and for that of 'related communications data', see s 20. These concepts are discussed in Ch 2.

[11] RIPA 2000, s 17(1). See, before this, Interception of Communications Act 1985, s 9. This provision was much-litigated: see *R v Preston* [1994] 2 AC 130 and *Morgans v DPP* [2001] 1 AC 315. In his report on terrorism discussed below, Lord Lloyd suggested that it was 'essential' that s 9 be amended so as to permit the use of intercept evidence in criminal trials.

[12] RIPA 2000, s 17(2).

[13] The list of exceptions is found in RIPA 2000, s 18(1).

[14] RIPA 2000, s 18(2).

[15] Investigatory Powers Act 2016, s 56 and Sch 3. At the time of writing, these provisions have not yet been brought into force.

of natural justice which, though it could as a matter of law be authorised by Parliament, would often be incompatible with the European Convention on Human Rights. Intercept evidence can therefore be used to demonstrate the necessity of imposing some civil measure upon persons suspected of involvement in terrorism (and in rebutting any challenge to that imposition) but not in trying them for terrorism or terrorism-related offences. This does not, though, mean that intercepted material plays no role in the criminal justice system, merely that its role is necessarily indirect rather than direct: either because the use of some civil mechanism acts as a trigger bringing certain terrorism offences into play (as is the case, most obviously, with proscription) or because, as is true more generally, the civil mechanisms are backed up by criminal sanctions. In this way, the criminal law makes a secondary, derivative use of the intercept evidence which might be used directly in imposing (and resisting challenges to) the civil mechanisms with which this chapter is mostly concerned, the additional step of remove permitting this use to take place without disclosing the use made of intercept powers.

Two points might be made about the rules governing the use of intercept evidence. The first is that this is perhaps the most considered question in the legal system: a number of reviews of the position have taken place in the period since the enactment of RIPA, and those reviews have mostly concluded that intercept material should—in principle—be made admissible if a way can be found to reconcile, at acceptable cost, the legal requirements which would have to be met in order to ensure that the fairness of trials was not compromised with the operational requirements of those who carry out intercept.[16] No change has been implemented however, and it seems highly unlikely that that position will change in the short or medium term, given the range of practical hurdles and the cost of overcoming them. The second is that there are no equivalent rules relating to the material gathered via 'equipment interference': the various forms of computer (and other) hacking which might be carried out (now) under the Investigatory Powers Act 2016.[17] Given that such practices appear to take place in a large number of criminal investigations, it is perhaps the case that the possibility of making use of evidence acquired via equipment interference will create a situation in which prosecutions which would previously have been impossible cease to be so. Notable in this regard is that the powers newly created (or regularised) by the 2016 Act—not only equipment interference—have not seen their product subject to the same sort of restrictions as applied to intercept material under RIPA and are replicated in the IPA.[18]

[16] See, most recently, Secretary of State for the Home Department, Intercept *as Evidence*, Cm 8989 (2014). A summary of previous reviews and their findings is contained at Annex C. A fuller consideration is found in the *Report of the Privy Council Review of Intercept as Evidence*, Cm 7324 (2008). See also David Ormerod and Simon McKay, 'Telephone intercepts and their admissibility' (2004) *Crim LR* 15.

[17] See the discussion in Ch 2. One reason for the absence of any such rules in the past was presumably that to legislate for the exclusion (on the model of ss 17 and 18 of RIPA) would have required the state to acknowledge that equipment interference was taking place, something that was not avowed until shortly before the Investigatory Powers Act 2016 was enacted.

[18] IPA 2016, s 56 and Sch 3 (which identifies the various exceptions to the basic rule).

IV. Counter-Terrorism Law up to and Including the Terrorism Act 2000

A. Before 2000

Before 2000, the law of counter-terrorism in the UK reflected very strongly the fact that the primary threat of terrorism in the modern UK was that which emanated from Northern Ireland, starting from the Prevention of Terrorism (Temporary Provisions) Act 1974, enacted in the immediate aftermath of the Birmingham pub bombings of 21 November that year and introducing a package of measures which were in their combination—the Home Secretary who introduced them noted—'unprecedented in peacetime' and yet 'fully justified to meet the clear present danger'.[19] Northern Ireland had seen the introduction of internment, under both the Civil Authorities (Special Powers) Act (Northern Ireland) 1922—and then, following the imposition of direct rule, the Northern Ireland (Temporary Provisions) Act 1972—which would last until 1975, accompanied by a derogation from the European Convention of Human Rights in recognition of the incompatibility of internment with, at least, Article 5 of the Convention.[20] At the time of the 1974 Act, it was governed by the Northern Ireland (Emergency Provisions) Act 1973, which introduced significant powers of arrest and detention, created various offences against public order and public security, and suspended the right to trial by jury for a number of offences, replacing it with the 'Diplock courts' recommended by the eponymous judge in order to deal with the perceived problem of intimidation of jurors in the province.

The 1974 Act made it an offence to belong to or to support in a variety of ways proscribed organisations, or to wear clothing or other items which suggested membership or support of such an organisation.[21] It introduced a system of 'exclusion orders' available in order to prevent acts of terrorism designed 'to influence public opinion or Government policy with respect to affairs in Northern Ireland.'[22] Such orders might be made against non-citizens, preventing them from entering the UK.[23] Equally, however, they might be made against a UK citizen, in which case they prevented that person from entering Great Britain.[24] No such order could be made, however, against those ordinarily resident in Great Britain.[25] The effect was to create the possibility of excluding those living in Northern Ireland and suspected of involvement in terrorism from the mainland, without concern for travel in the opposite direction. Also introduced were new powers of removal for those subject to

[19] HC Deb 25 November 1974 vol 882 col 35. An excellent account of the circumstances of the enactment of the 1974 Act is found in David Bonner, 'Responding to Crisis: Legislating Against Terrorism' (2006) 112 *LQR* 602. This was not, though, the first terrorism legislation: see before it, for example, the Explosive Substances Act 1883.

[20] See *Ireland v United Kingdom* (1979–80) 2 EHRR 25 and David Bonner, 'Of outrage and misunderstanding: Ireland v United Kingdom—governmental perspectives on an inter-state application under the European Convention on Human Rights' (2014) *LS* 47.

[21] Prevention of Terrorism (Temporary Provisions) Act 1974, ss 1 and 2.

[22] PTA 1974, s 3.

[23] ibid, s 6.

[24] ibid, s 3(3).

[25] ibid, s 3(4).

such orders, as well as new 'border' controls for those entering Great Britain from Northern Ireland.[26] The 1974 Act was periodically revised—in 1976, 1984 and 1989[27]—and both it and its successors were subject to annual renewal. Expanded versions of the powers contained in the 1974 Act were implemented on each occasion, including, after 1976, a power to exclude persons from Northern Ireland itself.[28] The 1984 Act expanded the powers to reflect the growing threat from what is described in this area as 'international terrorism'; that is, that which takes place or relates to places and people beyond the confines of the UK.[29] Throughout this period, 'terrorism' was defined as 'the use of violence for political ends including any use of violence for the purpose of putting the public or any section of the public in fear.'[30]

V. The 2000 Act and the Definition of Terrorism

Towards the end of 1996, Lord Lloyd of Berwick completed a major report on counter-terrorism law,[31] prompted by the prospect of peace in Northern Ireland and seeking to address the question of whether there would continue to be a need for specific counter-terrorism legislation in the event of 'lasting peace' there. Answering in the affirmative,[32] he nevertheless concluded that some of the most controversial legal tools which had evolved in the Northern Ireland context—amongst them the Diplock courts, internment, exclusion orders—would cease to be necessary were such peace to emerge.[33] No longer would there be two separate statutory regimes for dealing with terrorism,[34] nor would the relevant law be 'temporary' and therefore subject to annual renewal.[35] A single statute would suffice, and was eventually enacted several years later (after the conclusion of the Good Friday Agreement) as the Terrorism Act 2000. The most important feature of the 2000 Act, which covered much of the same ground as did those statutes it replaced, was the expanded definition of terrorism it contained, replacing one which had been criticised, Lord Lloyd noted, for being simultaneously too broad ('because it covers trivial as well as serious acts of violence')

[26] ibid, s 8.

[27] Prevention of Terrorism (Temporary Provisions) Act 1976; Prevention of Terrorism (Temporary Provisions) Act 1984; Prevention of Terrorism (Temporary Provisions) Act 1989.

[28] Prevention of Terrorism (Temporary Provisions) Act 1976, s 5.

[29] See Prevention of Terrorism (Temporary Provisions) Act 1984, s 12(3)(b) and, before that, the Suppression of Terrorism Act 1978, which gave effect to the European Convention on the Suppression of Terrorism and gave extra-territorial ambit to a number of specified offences (not specifically terrorist offences).

[30] See Prevention of Terrorism (Temporary Provisions) Act 1974, s 9(1) and Prevention of Terrorism (Temporary Provisions) Act 1989, s 20(1).

[31] Lord Lloyd of Berwick, *Inquiry into legislation against terrorism*, Cm 3420 (1996).

[32] Lloyd (n 31) [5.15]. This point has mostly been uncontroversial in the modern legal context, but in a speech to the Criminal Bar Association, Max Hill QC (then recently appointed Independent Reviewer of Terrorism Legislation) called into question the distinction between crime and terrorism: 'The point of principle is that terrorism is crime, and all terrorists are criminals. As such, they should be arrested, charged and brought before the courts, and the more that can be done under general criminal legislation the better.' Lecture to the Criminal Bar Association (19 September 2017). This of course would not obviate the need (if such need is accepted) for civil mechanisms focused upon the pre-emption of terrorist acts rather than their punishment.

[33] Lloyd (n 31) [16.4], [16.8], [16.13].

[34] ibid [5.21].

[35] ibid [17.6].

and too narrow ('because, being limited to political ends, it might be said not to apply to acts of terrorism perpetrated by single issue or religious fanatics').[36] The definition whose scope he sought to replicate was that employed by the FBI, which referred to 'the use of serious violence against persons or property, or the threat to use such violence, to intimidate or coerce a government, the public, or any section of the public in order to promote political, social or ideological objectives.'[37] In the consultation paper which led eventually to the 2000 Act, the government demurred from certain aspects of this, most notably the reference to 'social' objectives, which risked bringing within the legal concept of terrorism acts which did not seek to 'to disrupt or undermine the democratic process'.[38] Moreover, as had been noted by Lord Lloyd himself, acts such as the disruption of vital computer systems were not caught by the definition, and the government took the view that they should be.[39]

Reflecting these points of disagreement, the 2000 Act, as enacted, defined terrorism as the 'use or threat' of certain action which is 'designed to influence the government or to intimidate the public or a section of the public' and which is 'made for the purpose of advancing a political, religious or ideological cause'.[40] The 'actions' in question were far broader than the previous definition (which referred only to violence), including alongside action which 'involves serious violence against a person' also that which 'involves serious damage to property', 'endangers a person's life, other than that of the person committing the action', 'creates a serious risk to the health or safety of the public or a section of the public' or 'is designed seriously to interfere with or seriously to disrupt an electronic system.'[41] Similarly broad were the statutory references to persons or property (which apply without regard for where the persons or property are situated); those to 'the public', which includes 'the public of a country other than the United Kingdom'; and, finally, and perhaps most astonishingly, those to 'the government', which means 'the government of the United Kingdom, of a Part of the United Kingdom or of a country other than the United Kingdom.'[42] Taken together, these points ensure that action is 'equally criminal whether it is intended to take place in the UK or elsewhere',[43] and that the various criminal offences relating to terrorism capture conduct which is aimed at 'countries which are governed by tyrants and dictators'.[44] The definition was amended by the Terrorism Act 2006, so as to place attempts to influence international organisations on an equal footing to those to influence 'the government';[45] it was amended again by the Counter-Terrorism Act 2008, in order to include within it—alongside acts done for political, religious or ideological ends—those done to advance a 'racial' cause.[46] Following these amendments, though not as

[36] ibid [5.22]. For an overview of the issues surrounding giving terrorism a distinct legal reality, see Ben Saul, 'Terrorism as a legal concept' in G Lennon and C Walker (eds), *Routledge Handbook of Law and Terrorism* (London, Routledge, 2015). The influence of the UK's legal conception of terrorism is considered by Kent Roach, 'The migration and derivation of counter-terrorism' in the same volume.

[37] Lloyd (n 31) [5.23].

[38] Home Office, *Legislation Against Terrorism: A consultation paper*, Cm 4178 (1998), [3.16].

[39] Home Office (n 38) [3.16].

[40] Terrorism Act 2000, s 1(1).

[41] ibid, s 1(2).

[42] ibid, s 1(4).

[43] Government reply to Lord Carlile's Report on the Definition of Terrorism, Cm 7058 (2007), [13].

[44] *R v F* [2007] EWCA Crim 243, [32].

[45] Terrorism Act 2006, s 34.

[46] Counter-Terrorism Act 2008, s 75.

a result of them, the Independent Reviewer of Terrorism Legislation concluded the definition to be 'remarkable by its breadth.'[47] One recommendation which would have (on paper, at least) limited the definition—the substitution of 'intimidate' for 'influence' in relation to the effect an act must be designed to have on governments (bringing, in this way, governments in line with the public)—was made by Lord Lloyd in 2007 but never implemented.[48] The very broad definition therefore remains and causes difficulty, in particular, in terms of the range of conduct which it captures (and, in the field of criminal law, the significant prosecutorial discretion thereby created).[49]

In *R v Gul*,[50] the Supreme Court was required to determine whether the definition of 'terrorism' in the 2000 Act operates 'so as to include within its scope any or all military attacks by a nonstate armed group against any or all state or inter-governmental organisation armed forces in the context of a non-international armed conflict?'[51] The context was a challenge to the conviction of Mohammed Gul for offences under section 2 of the Terrorism Act 2006, which prohibits the dissemination of terrorist publications. The publications in question were videos, uploaded onto the internet by the appellant, some of which showed attacks on coalition forces in Iraq and Afghanistan and 'were accompanied by commentaries praising the bravery, and martyrdom, of those carrying out the attacks, and encouraging others to emulate them.'[52] The Supreme Court answered the question which had been posed in the affirmative, noting however that the definition of terrorism within the 2000 Act is, 'at least if read in its natural sense, very far reaching indeed', such that 'on occasions, activities which might command a measure of public understanding, if not support, may fall within it: for example, activities by the victims of oppression abroad, which might command a measure of public understanding, and even support in this country, may well fall within it.'[53] Though the Supreme Court found 'unattractive' the use of prosecutorial discretion to manage the breadth of the relevant powers—noting that such a device 'risks undermining the rule of law'[54]—it suggested that it would be improper for a court to 'cut down' the 'natural, very wide, meaning of the definition' found in statute,[55] while nevertheless suggesting that concerns expressed by the Independent Reviewer (who had said the definition was 'remarkably broad—absurdly so in some cases') merited 'serious consideration' and that a legislative narrowing of the definition consistent with the need

[47] David Anderson QC, *Report on the Operation in 2010 of the Terrorism Act 2000 and of Pt 1 of The Terrorism Act 2006* (2011), [3.2].

[48] Lord Carlile of Berriew QC, *The Definition of Terrorism*, Cm 7052 (2007), [86(11)].

[49] Some of the discretion which would otherwise exist is curtailed by statutory requirements that the DPP consent to the bringing of most prosecutions and, more particularly, that the Attorney General consent to prosecutions relating offences committed outside the United Kingdom 'or for a purpose wholly or partly connected with the affairs of a country other than the United Kingdom': Terrorism Act 2000, s 117 (as amended). See also Terrorism Act 2006, s 19, which imposes an equivalent requirement. Though note the Supreme Court's caveat to this point: 'the prosecutorial discretion was never intended, and as far as we can ascertain, it has never been suggested that it was ever intended, to assist in the interpretation of legislation which involves the creation of a criminal offence or offences.' *R v Gul* [2013] UKSC 64, [35].

[50] *R v Gul* [2013] UKSC 64.

[51] [2013] UKSC 64, [8].

[52] ibid, [2].

[53] ibid, [29].

[54] ibid, [36].

[55] ibid, [38].

to protect the public would be 'welcome'.[56] The significance of these conclusions derives from the manner in which the definition of terrorism percolates through the law in this area: as the court noted, its extreme breadth effectively grants 'unusually wide discretions to all those concerned with the application of the counter-terrorism law, from Ministers exercising their power to impose executive orders to police officers deciding whom to arrest or to stop at a port and prosecutors deciding whom to charge'.[57] The effect of the Court's decision, one observer said, was to send 'a strong signal that the definition of terrorism in section 1 of the 2000 Act is unsatisfactory'.[58] Nevertheless, that definition persists and the aspect of it highlighted by the facts of *Gul* is likely to be more prominent as the boundaries between terrorism and armed conflict become increasingly blurred.

The implications of the definition's scope are demonstrated most clearly by the decision in *Miranda*,[59] concerned with the exercise of powers under Schedule 7 of the 2000 Act to stop and search the applicant (the spouse of a journalist who had been in contact with Edward Snowden) in pursuit of materials leaked by Snowden. The powers in question are designed to be used in order to determine whether a person is concerned in terrorism; here, the Divisional Court held that the purpose of stopping Miranda ('to ascertain the nature of the material which the claimant was carrying and if on examination it proved to be as was feared, to neutralise the effects of its release (or further release) or dissemination')[60] fell within the Schedule 7 powers as properly understood. The Court of Appeal accepted some important limitations on the definition of terrorism, holding that each of the categories of action employed in the definition imports—even where it is not immediately apparent from its terms—a mental element.[61] It remains the case, however, that the publication of material might constitute an act of terrorism, including where a person knows (or is reckless as to the fact that) 'it creates a serious risk to the health or safety of the public or a section of the public.'[62] The effect of this, it has been argued, is that the publication of a newspaper article arguing against vaccination on religious or political grounds would, if 'it were judged to create a serious risk to public health, and if it was designed to influence government policy,' constitute terrorist action.[63] And, again, this conclusion flows through the legal order, potentially rendering the newspaper which published such an article and its employees subject to proscription, asset-freezing, and TPIMs.[64] The associated broad discretion is replicated also, and is more objectionable precisely because the majority of civil mechanisms are imposed by or on the application of political actors, rather than an independent prosecuting authority. And though the Court of Appeal issued a declaration of incompatibility as regards the stop power (on the basis that it lacked adequate safeguards

[56] ibid, [34].
[57] ibid, [34].
[58] Alan Greene, 'The Quest for a Satisfactory Definition of Terrorism: *R v Gul*' (2014) 77 *MLR* 780, 793.
[59] *R (Miranda) v Secretary of State for the Home Department* [2016] EWCA Civ 6.
[60] *R (Miranda) v Secretary of State for the Home Department* [2014] EWHC 255 (Admin), [27].
[61] [2016] EWCA Civ 6, [53]–[56].
[62] ibid, [55].
[63] David Anderson QC, *The Terrorism Acts in 2013 Report of the Independent Reviewer on the Operation of the Terrorism Act 2000 and Part 1 of the Terrorism Act 2006* (2014), [4.19].
[64] Anderson, *Terrorism Acts in 2013* (n 63) [4.21].

against its arbitrary exercise in relation to journalistic material),[65] it upheld the decision of the High Court that the particular stop at issue was lawful.

Parliament has, however, shown no sign of desiring to constrict the definition and so undermine the 'apparent "operational necessity" for a broad malleable definition which section 1 currently provides.'[66] If the boundaries of the counter-terrorism constitution are identified by reference to the statutory definition of terrorism, through which all of the relevant law flows, a first (if unoriginal) observation must be that the phenomenon is a broad one; broader than was historically the case, and broader too than would seem to justified upon any intuitive account of what terrorism is and why we might be justified in addressing it a as a single, discrete legal phenomenon. Alan Greene has argued that the unsatisfactory nature of the definition of terrorism in UK law is owed in large part to the fact that a single definition is employed, which must constitute a lowest common denominator, capable of capturing all of the conduct that the relevant authorities may wish to deem terrorism.[67] Greene's suggested response—the introduction of multiple definitions for use in relation to different powers—does not, however, address either the inflationary imperative evident from any consideration of the development of counter-terrorism law over time, nor the fact that the breadth of any given definition is a function of a much more deep-rooted disagreement about the extent to which particular individuals and types of behaviour pose a threat to the state which justifies the deployment of its coercive apparatus. Though legal definitions of terrorism are a useful way of teasing out the specifics of conceptual disagreement, they are its symptom rather than its cause. Multiple definitions of terrorism would fragment that disagreement; they would not overcome it.

VI. Obsolete Counter-Terrorism Mechanisms

Though the 2000 Act represented a broad and substantial overhaul of counter-terrorism law intended to meet the needs of a new era in the history of national security in the UK, it was never intended that it would meet all count-terrorist needs which might arise in future. In his 1996 report, Lord Lloyd had said that new legislation 'should be confined to what is needed in the way of permanent legislation to meet the foreseeable terrorist threat' and should not attempt 'to cater in advance for emergencies, which may take a form which cannot now be foreseen.'[68] Nevertheless, it seems unlikely that those in Parliament who enacted the 2000 Act after a careful process lasting several years anticipated that they would be required to deal with such an emergency so soon afterwards.

[65] [2016] EWCA Civ 6, [108]–[117]. The compatibility of the Schedule 7 power more generally with the ECHR is considered below.

[66] Greene (n 58) 793.

[67] Greene (n 1).

[68] Lloyd (n 31) [19].

A. Detention

The attacks of 11 September 2001 were met, little more than three months later, with the Anti-Terrorism, Crime and Security Act 2001. Though the Act covered a considerable amount of ground,[69] we can focus here upon the immigration and asylum powers contained in Part IV, which reflected the situation created by the decision of the European Court of Human Rights in *Chahal v United Kingdom* in 1996.[70] *Chahal* was a challenge to the compatibility with the ECHR of the deportation of a Sikh separatist to India, on the basis that the presence of the applicant was unconducive to the public good, on national security grounds and for political reasons related to the fight against international terrorism. The Strasbourg Court's decision had both a procedural and substantive element. The former is considered in Chapter 5 in the context of the procedural innovations of the national security constitution prompted by the decision in *Chahal*. The substantive element of the decision related to the applicant's claim that to deport him to India would put him at risk of treatment in breach of Article 3 of the Convention, which provides that '[n]o one shall be subjected to torture or to inhuman or degrading treatment or punishment.' The Strasbourg Court accepted this, finding that there was 'a real risk of Mr Chahal being subjected to treatment contrary to Article 3 if he is returned to India' and so he could not be returned there without violating Article 3.[71] The effect of its decision was that when the UK came to address the threat of terrorism posed by non-nationals living in Britain, it could not in many cases simply deport them back to their country of origin: to do so where there was a real risk of treatment contrary to Article 3 would amount to a violation of the Convention. Nor could it simply derogate from the provisions of the Convention: though Article 15 permits the parties to it to derogate from the Convention in the context of 'war or other public emergency threatening the life of the nation', that provision excludes certain of the Convention's provisions, including Article 3. The solution adopted was a system whereby the Secretary of State could designate persons as 'suspected international terrorists'. Such persons could then be detained pending their deportation even though their 'removal or departure from the United Kingdom' was prevented—temporarily or indefinitely—by 'a point of law which relates wholly or partly to an international agreement'.[72] The result was a regime of indefinite detention without trial for those who could not, as a result of the Strasbourg Court's decision in *Chahal*, be deported to their home jurisdiction.[73]

[69] On that statute generally, see Adam Tomkins, 'Legislating against Terror: the Anti-terrorism, Crime and Security Act 2001' [2002] *PL* 205, and Helen Fenwick, 'The Anti-Terrorism, Crime and Security Act 2001: A Proportionate Response to 11 September?' (2002) 65 *MLR* 724.

[70] *Chahal v United Kingdom* (1996) 23 EHRR 413.

[71] (1996) 23 EHRR 413, [107].

[72] This was a variation of the previous approach under Sch 3 of the Immigration Act 1971, which—in accordance with the decisions in *R v Governor of Durham Prison, ex parte Hardial Singh* [1984] 1 WLR 704 and *Tan Te Lam v Superintendent of Tai A Chau Detention Centre* [1997] AC 97—permitted detention pending deportation only for as long as was reasonably necessary to carry out the deportation.

[73] The legal dispute over the system was mirrored in a rhetorical dispute as to whether what was introduced by the 2001 Act was functionally equivalent to the regimes of internment which had operated during the two World Wars, and in relation to which two decisions of the House of Lords—*R v Halliday, ex parte Zadig* [1917] AC 260 and *Liversidge v Anderson* [1942] AC 206—stood as testament to the dangers of excessive judicial deference to the executive in the field of defence of the realm. On the topic, see generally: AWB Simpson, *In the Highest Degree Odious Detention without Trial in Wartime Britain* (Oxford, Oxford University Press, 1995).

No such provision for detention was made as regards UK nationals: connecting the detention to deportation meant that it could only be applied to those who were, by virtue of their immigration status, liable to such deportation. The UK approach to counter-terrorism, once confined to acts of violence related to the political situation in Northern Ireland, was now characterised most acutely by measures which were unavailable as against UK nationals, reflecting very obviously not only a shift from a concept of national security to one of international security, but also now, perhaps, the subsuming of the former within the latter. Because the regime was assumed to be incompatible with the right to liberty under Article 5 of the Convention on Human Rights (which permits, however, 'the lawful arrest or detention … of a person against whom action is being taken with a view to deportation or extradition'), the UK chose to derogate from that provision. This it did by, on the international plane, informing the Secretary General of the Council of Europe of the measures taken and the reasons for taking them and, as a matter of domestic law, 'designating' the derogation order under section 14 of the Human Rights Act, rendering the statutory formulation the 'Convention rights' as defined in section 1(1) of that statute subject to the derogation.[74]

The number detained under the 2001 Act was small: 17 persons had been certified under section 21 by the time the legality of the scheme was finally determined. The scheme was challenged, starting in the Special Immigration Appeals Commission and ending up before a panel of nine judges in the House of Lords, which ruled in December 2004.[75] One strand of the challenge to Part 4 (and the associated derogation order) was that the conditions of a legitimate derogation from the Convention on Human Rights under Article 15 were not met. The first of those conditions is, as noted above, that there exist a 'war or other public emergency threatening the life of the nation'. Of nine judges in the House of Lords, eight accepted that this requirement was met. Representative of their reasons for doing so are those offered by Lord Bingham, who emphasised not only that the interpretation given to that phrase by the Strasbourg Court was wide enough to encompass the situation in which the UK found itself post-11 September, but also the political nature of the decision, in relation to which a court should be very slow indeed to disagree with the judgement of the executive:

> The more purely political (in a broad or narrow sense) a question is, the more appropriate it will be for political resolution and the less likely it is to be an appropriate matter for judicial decision. The smaller, therefore, will be the potential role of the court. It is the function of political and not judicial bodies to resolve political questions … The present question seems to me to be very much at the political end of the spectrum.[76]

[74] Human Rights Act 1998 (Designated Derogation) Order 2001 (SI 2001/3644). Sch 3 to the 1998 Act was modified by the Human Rights Act 1998 (Amendment No. 2) Order (SI 2001/4032) to include the text of the derogation (later removed by the Human Rights Act 1998 (Amendment) Order (SI 2005/1071). Though 'Convention rights' is defined by s 1, that provision makes reference to 'the Convention', defined in turn by s 21 of the 1998 Act to mean 'the Convention for the Protection of Human Rights and Fundamental Freedoms, agreed by the Council of Europe at Rome on 4th November 1950 *as it has effect for the time being in relation to the United Kingdom*' (emphasis added).

[75] *A v Secretary of State for the Home Department* [2004] UKHL 56. The challenge to Pt 4 of the 2001 Act had succeeded in SIAC ([2002] HRLR 1274) but the Home Secretary's appeal had been unanimously allowed by the Court of Appeal ([2002] EWCA Civ 1502).

[76] [2004] UKHL 56, [29]. The only judge to hold that this first condition was not met was Lord Hoffman, who indulged in a slightly unfortunate rhetorical grandstanding at odds with both earlier and later decisions of his own

The determinative issue was therefore the requirement in Article 15 that any derogation be limited to what is 'strictly required by the exigencies of the situation,' understood to mean not only that the measures taken were necessary, but also that they were proportionate in the sense familiar from Convention jurisprudence. In holding (by seven to one) that the measures taken were disproportionate, the House of Lords highlighted two features of the legislative scheme: first, the discrepancy already mentioned whereby the nature of the scheme—specifically, its grounding within immigration law—forced it to exclude from its purview UK nationals, whose rights were thereby left intact regardless of any threat they might pose to national security.[77] This was particularly powerful given that it was no part of the government's claim that the threat to national security post- September 11 derived solely from non-nationals. If national security did not require that they be detained indefinitely, it could not require that non-nationals be so detained; there was a discrimination between nationals and non-nationals in their enjoyment of Article 5, such as to breach Article 14 (the prohibition against discrimination in the enjoyment of the Convention rights) from which no derogation had taken place. Second, however, was the nature of the detention in Belmarsh prison, which became for the purposes of the ATCS Act a 'prison with three walls' from which those who were able to find a third country willing to accept them were able to leave at any point (and from which some in fact did leave, to countries as close to the UK as France).[78] This anomaly, which significantly undermined the claim that the measure was necessary in the interests of national security was itself again a side-effect of the fact that detention was tied to the frustrated desire to deport rather than some free-standing legal regime. The derogation therefore could not have been 'strictly required by the exigencies of the situation', while the regime of detention pending deportation unjustifiably discriminated between nationals and non-nationals.[79] The outcome was that the derogation order was quashed, and the relevant provision of the 2001 Act declared incompatible with Articles 5 and 14 of the Convention. In line with the treatment of Parliament's sovereignty by the modern regime of human rights (which gives courts no powers to strike down or otherwise deprive of its validity a provision of primary legislation incompatible with the ECHR) the regime remained in force until repealed by Parliament, and replaced—by virtue of the Prevention of Terrorism Act 2005—by a system of control orders.

The decision in the *A* case was considered to represent a major victory for individual freedom in the British constitution—such as to be reckoned alongside the great case of *Entick v Carrington*[80]—and, more strikingly, to represent a break with the predominant

in the area of national security. 'This is a nation,' he said, 'which has been tested in adversity, which has survived physical destruction and catastrophic loss of life'. Al-Qaeda, unlike Hitler, did not 'threaten our institutions of government or our existence as a civil community': [96].

[77] See, eg, [2004] UKHL 56, [68].

[78] [2004] UKHL 56, [2] and [81].

[79] John Finnis has argued, with some justification, that the decision in *A* was incorrect in not considering how the regime under the 2001 Act might be read down in accordance with s 3 of the Human Rights Act: 'Nationality, Alienage and Constitutional Principle' (2007) 123 *LQR* 417. Given the nature of the concessions—which Finnis describes—made by the Attorney General on behalf of the Government, however, it is difficult to see how the House of Lords might have arrived at the conclusion Finnis defends.

[80] See the comments of David Feldman in 'Proportionality and Discrimination in Anti-Terrorist Legislation' (2005) 64 *CLJ* 271. Further contemporary perspective is provided by the case notes by Tom Hickman, Stephen Tierney, David Dyzenhaus and Janet Hiebert published at (2005) 68 *MLR* 654ff.

pattern of excessive judicial deference to (or, perhaps, obsequiousness in the face of) executive invocations of the needs of national security.[81] Where Parliament had been content to acquiesce in a scheme of detention that did not represent a proportionate or even rational response to the threat of terrorism as it emerged in the era of Al-Qaeda dominance, the courts did not do so. That they derived their legal right to do so and perhaps also their confidence to make use of that right from the enactment by Parliament itself of the 1998 Act does not wholly negate the importance of the decision in *A*. Nevertheless, the record of the courts in terms of their willingness to stand up to claims as to what national security requires and in favour of those values and principles over which national security has too often trampled, should not be judged solely by reference to decisions like that in this case, where the courts have the opportunity to take a high-profile stand and deploy the grandest of rhetoric in the knowledge that the words will echo in the law books for years to come. As we will see elsewhere in this book, the record of the courts must account also for its decisions in less glamorous cases, where the implications for the liberty of the individual—or the rule of law, or the democratic process—are less obvious, but no less great. Even if, that is, we accept that the decision in *A* (and, perhaps, those in other similar cases relating to those legal mechanisms which stand or have stood at the heart of the state's response to the threat of terrorism) is the great victory it has been claimed to be, that does not itself suffice to look favourably upon the role played by the courts within the wider national security constitution, which has been decidedly mixed, and occasionally appalling.

But the decision of House of Lords must be judged not only by its constitutional significance—the question of what role it reflects for the court within the national security constitution—but also on its own terms. From that perspective, one point of ongoing significance stands out, relating to the correctness of the decision to quash the order, made under the Human Rights Act, by which the derogation was 'designated'. As noted in the text above, section 14 of the Human Rights Act permits the Secretary of State to designate a derogation by order. Though such an order is called a 'derogation order', it does not constitute a derogation and has no effect on the lawfulness or validity of the derogation itself, which is a device which sounds only in international law. Nor does the provision limit in any way which derogations might be designated: most importantly, it imposes no rule that the designation of a derogation is limited to situations in which the derogation fulfils the criteria laid down in Article 15 of the ECHR. It is therefore unclear why it is that the disproportionality of the measures taken (and the fact that they were not 'strictly required by the exigencies of the situation') justified the House of Lords quashing the derogation order. And, of course, in the event that it did not do so, the designation order would have continued to have effect, excluding the rights in respect of which it was made from the 'Convention rights' for the purposes of section 1 HRA, and (it seems) preventing the House of Lords from finding that the 2001 Act was incompatible with Article 5 (unless the failure of the derogation order to address Article 14 was held to allow the courts to make a finding

[81] Adam Tomkins, 'National security and the role of the court: a changed landscape?' (2010) *LQR* 543, 544 notes the view that the post-*A* case law reflects something of a regression to the national security mean ('the relative enlightenment of Belmarsh, which, despite its great promise, appears in turn to have been followed by a series of cases that, even if they do not return us to the twentieth-century position, can hardly be seen as continuing to shine, or even much to reflect, Belmarsh's 'beacon of light"'), though contests that view in part by reference to the decisions of the lower courts.

of incompatibility regardless of the derogation order). Some of this complexity is noted by Lord Scott of Foscoe in his judgment,[82] but has never been adequately resolved and has the potential to become relevant once more, given contemporary proposals to derogate from the Convention in respect of future armed conflict abroad.[83]

B. Control Orders

The legislative response to the declaration of incompatibility made by the House of Lords was the Prevention of Terrorism Act 2005, which introduced the device known as the control order, a civil order imposed on individuals suspected of involvement in terrorism and backed by criminal penalties.[84] Control orders originally existed in two (potential) forms: one of these was the 'derogating' control order which, unlike its 'non-derogating' counterpart, was capable of implementing conditions up to and including a 24-hour curfew (effectively house arrest) on a person; conditions which were acknowledged to be incompatible with the Article 5 right to liberty under the Convention of Human Rights and whose imposition would therefore have require a (further) derogation from that provision by the UK.[85] In recognition of its more intrusive status, a derogating control order would be made not by the Secretary of State but by a court on application by the Secretary of State.[86] In the event, no derogating control order was ever made under the 2005 Act, avoiding a situation in which the courts were required to again pronounce upon whether the conditions for a lawful derogation from the ECHR were met (a question the answer to which might have differed if asked about the circumstances in 2005 rather than those in 2001, when the first derogation was made). A control order could be made where the Secretary of State had 'reasonable grounds for suspecting that the individual is or has been involved in terrorism-related activity' and considered it 'necessary, for purposes connected with protecting members of the public from a risk of terrorism, to make a control order imposing obligations on that individual'.[87] The standard for the making of a control order—reasonable suspicion—was lower than applied to the certification of a person under Part IV of Anti-terrorism, Crime and Security Act 2001 (ATCSA 2001), which was that of reasonable belief. The obligations which could be imposed were any considered to be 'necessary for purposes connected with preventing or restricting involvement by that individual in terrorism-related activity' and specifically included restrictions on movement, employment, possession of certain articles, the controlee's contact with certain persons, and much more,[88] all of it overseen by an intrusive system of monitoring to which the controlee was required to submit.[89] Control orders could, in short, create a personalised

[82] [2004] UKHL 56, [148]–[150].
[83] Discussed in Ch 3.
[84] The criminological basis of the control order is discussed by Lucia Zedner, 'Preventive Justice or Pre-Punishment? The Case of Control Orders' (2007) 60 *Current Legal Problems* 174.
[85] Prevention of Terrorism Act 2005, s 4.
[86] PTA 2005, s 4.
[87] ibid, s 2(1).
[88] ibid, s (1)(3) and (4).
[89] ibid, s 4(4)(n) and (6).

regime of restrictions, backed by criminal sanctions, which entered into almost every detail of a person's life. Perhaps the most significant of all possible restriction was that which 'relocated' a person subject to a control order, requiring him to live in a particular place some distance from his ordinary place of residence, with a view to disrupting those networks of communication and interaction considered to represent a threat to national security. This practice—usually characterised by its opponents as a form of 'internal exile' and used in almost half of all control order cases[90]—became the subject of particular distaste, being described by the reviewer of counter-terrorism powers as 'utterly inimical to traditional British norms'.[91]

Those obligations which might be imposed on any given person were those considered 'necessary for purposes connected with preventing or restricting involvement by that individual in terrorism-related activity'[92] where 'terrorism-related activity' meant 'the commission, preparation or instigation of acts of terrorism,' or the facilitation or encouragement thereof, or conduct giving 'support or assistance to individuals who are known or believed to be involved in terrorism-related activity'.[93] Where the involvement in terrorism-related activity seemed to have involved the commission of a terrorism offence, the Secretary of State was required—before making the control order—to 'consult the chief officer of the police force about whether there is evidence available that could realistically be used for the purposes of a prosecution of the individual for an offence relating to terrorism'[94] and then to notify the same chief office that the control order had been made,[95] at which point he was under an obligation to keep under a review the investigation of the controlee's conduct 'with a view to his prosecution for an offence relating to terrorism'.[96] Except in urgent cases, the Secretary of State required the permission of the court to make even a non-derogating control order,[97] which the court could give unless it determined that the Secretary of State's decision that there were grounds to make the order was 'obviously flawed'.[98] The court was then to give direction for a hearing on the order 'as soon as reasonably practicable after it is made'.[99] This meant that control orders could be—and in practice were—imposed without any notice having been given to the person subject to them.[100] Controls orders had a maximum duration of 12 months, but could be renewed an unlimited number of times.[101] The same was true of the substantive powers contained in the 2005 Act: they were to expire after 12 months but could be continued in force for up to 12 months at a time by secondary legislation.[102]

[90] David Anderson QC, *Control Orders in 2011: Final Report of the Independent Reviewer on the Prevention of Terrorism Act 2005* (2012), [3.35].

[91] Lord Macdonald of River Glaven QC, *Report on the Review of Counter-Terrorism and Security Powers*, Cm 8003 (2011), [22].

[92] Prevention of Terrorism Act 2005, s 1(3).

[93] ibid, s 1(9).

[94] ibid, s 8(2). Though see *Secretary of State for the Home Department v E* [2007] UKHL 720.

[95] ibid, s 8(3).

[96] ibid, s 8(4).

[97] ibid, s 3(1).

[98] ibid, s 3(2)(b).

[99] ibid, s 3(2)(c).

[100] As was explicitly permitted by s 3(5) of the 2005 Act.

[101] PTA 2005, s 2(4).

[102] ibid, s 13.

The 2005 Act was a subject of a number of important decisions about the use of (and limits to) secret processes, some of which are discussed in Chapter 5 of this book.[103] The most important of the substantive judgments was that given by the House of Lords in *JJ*,[104] where the control order challenged imposed an 18-hour curfew on the controlees, obliging them to wear electronic tagging devices and to subject to police searches of the premises at any time. It was held by a 3-2 majority in the House of Lords that such conditions collectively amounted to a deprivation of liberty contrary to Article 5 of the ECHR and that there was therefore no power to impose such conditions under the provisions permitting 'non-derogating' control orders. Lord Brown of Eaton-under-Heywood sought to provide some certainty as to where acceptable controls on liberty lapsed in deprivations thereof, suggesting the 'acceptable limit to be 16 hours', such a regime being best understood as 'one which restricts the suspect's liberty of movement rather than actually deprives him of his liberty'.[105] Though technically obiter, this remark guided the future use of control orders, and no curfew longer than 16 hours was imposed after the decision in *JJ*. And in *AP*[106] it was held that a control order might, by reference to conditions within it which were themselves proportionate restrictions on the Article 8 right to a private and family life, be rendered a deprivation of liberty under Article 5. The Supreme Court there recognised the possibility that a control order involving a 16 hour or even 14 hour curfew might be regarded as a deprivation of liberty, but for that to be the case 'the other conditions imposed would have to be unusually destructive of the life the controlee might otherwise have been living.'[107] Control orders, however, were replaced soon afterwards, and a third phase of the post-11 September counter-terrorism constitution—that which remains in force today—was entered.[108]

VII. Current Counter-Terrorism Mechanisms

A. TPIMS

The 2010 coalition agreement between the Conservative and Liberal Democrat parties promised to 'urgently review Control Orders, as part of a wider review of counter-terrorist legislation, measures and programmes'.[109] This pledge resulted in the enactment of the Terrorism Prevention and Investigation Measures Act 2011 (TPIM), which abolished the

103 See also Ed Bates, 'Anti-terrorism control orders: liberty and security still in the balance' (2009) 29 *LS* 99.
104 *Secretary of State for the Home Department v JJ* [2007] UKHL 45.
105 [2007] UKHL 45, [105].
106 *Secretary of State for the Home Department v AP* [2010] UKSC 24.
107 [2010] UKSC 24, [4].
108 For a retrospective overview of the control order system, see Anderson (n 90).
109 HM Government, *The Coalition: our programme for government* (2010), 24.

system of control order, replacing them with the eponymous device.[110] The conditions to be met if a TPIM was to be imposed were that:

(a) "the Secretary of State reasonably believes that the individual is, or has been, involved in terrorism-related activity";

(b) that some of the activity in question is "new terrorism-related activity" (meaning that it occurred since a TPIM was last imposed);

(c) that "the Secretary of State reasonably considers that it is necessary, for purposes connected with protecting members of the public from a risk of terrorism, for terrorism prevention and investigation measures to be imposed on the individual";

(d) "the Secretary of State reasonably considers that it is necessary, for purposes connected with preventing or restricting the individual's involvement in terrorism-related activity, for the specified terrorism prevention and investigation measures to be imposed on the individual."[111]

'Terrorism-related activity' was originally defined to mean, first, 'the commission, preparation or instigation of acts of terrorism' or (second) the encouragement or (third) facilitation thereof.[112] It also included, however, 'conduct which gives support or assistance to individuals who are known or believed by the individual concerned to be involved in conduct falling within' those three categories. The effect was that a TPIM could be imposed on a person who supported someone who encouraged acts of terrorism (and so who was, himself, at two steps away from the acts of terrorism themselves). On the recommendation of the Independent Reviewer of Terrorism Legislation (IRTL),[113] however, this definition was tightened, so that only conduct supporting or assisting the commission, preparation or instigation (rather than supporting or assisting the encouragement or facilitation thereof) is 'terrorism-related activity'.[114] Also altered was one of the criteria for the imposition of a TPIM, which now requires that the Secretary of State 'is satisfied, on the balance of probabilities' is or has been involved in such activity, rather than having only to 'reasonably believe' such a thing.[115] The IRTL's recommendation, however, had been that the standard which now applies the Secretary of State applied in fact to the court;[116] this (more demanding) recommendation was not acted upon.[117]

[110] Some comparison between the two regimes is found in Clive Walker and Alexander Horne, 'The Terrorism Prevention and Investigation Measures Act 2011: one thing but not much the other?' [2012] *Crim LR* 421. In another contribution, the same authors compare the processes by which the control order and TPIM legislation was enacted, arguing that the latter 'was the more rewarding experience' but that the quality of the process does not have a strong causal effect upon the substance of the resulting legislation: Alexander Horne and Clive Walker, 'Lessons learned from political constitutionalism? Comparing the enactment of control orders and terrorism prevention and investigation measures by the UK Parliament' [2014] *PL* 267, 286–7.

[111] Terrorism Prevention and Investigation Measures Act 2011, s 3.

[112] TPIM Act 2011, s 4(1).

[113] David Anderson QC, *Terrorism Prevention and Investigation Measures in 2013: Second Report of the Independent Reviewer on the Operation of the Terrorism Prevention and Investigation Measures Act 2011* (2014), [6.12]–[6.16].

[114] Counter-Terrorism Act 2015, s 20(2).

[115] CTA 2015, s 20(1).

[116] Anderson (n 113) [6.16]–[6.18].

[117] David Anderson QC, *Terrorism Prevention and Investigation Measures in 2014: Third Report of the Independent Reviewer on the Operation of the Terrorism Prevention and Investigation Measures Act 2011* (2015), [3.9].

As with non-derogating control orders, TPIMs are imposed by the Secretary of State (though the permission of the court is needed, except in cases of urgency, and cannot be given if the decisions of the Secretary of State in relation to the above criteria are 'obviously flawed'),[118] though with 'reasonable belief' having replaced 'reasonable suspicion' as the relevant standard. An application for permission to impose measures may be heard ex parte, without notice, and without the prospective subject of the TPIM having any right to make representations.[119] An individual on whom a TPIM is imposed nevertheless has a right to a 'review hearing', to be held 'as soon as reasonably practicable' after a 'directions hearing', itself to be held within seven days of the imposition of the TPIM.[120] At the review hearing, the court must—applying principles of judicial review—decide whether the conditions for the making of a TPIM 'were met and continue to be met', and may quash the TPIM or measures made under it or order its variation, as appropriate.[121] Other key differences between the TPIMs and the control orders which preceded them are the time-limited nature of TPIMs as opposed to control orders (their maximum duration is two years,[122] and a further TPIM can be imposed only if there is evidence of 'new' terrorism-related activity since the imposition of the original measure);[123] the absence of powers of relocation within the new statutory regime; and generally softer conditions in the former as opposed to the latter as regards, for example, overnight residence and the right to use phones and computers. Nevertheless, the measures which might be included in a TPIM are in many cases extremely intrusive, and overall not noticeably less so than was the case with control orders. The Independent Reviewer of Terrorism Legislation observed that the variations between the two 'render TPIMs more rights-compliant than control orders, and less likely to be a focus for community grievance' as well as underlining 'the need for alternative strategies to contain the risk from those believed to be dangerous terrorists, especially once TPIMs have expired.'[124] If this was true, it is unfortunate that one of the most important of the liberalising changes—the removal of provision for forced relocation—was effectively undone by the Counter-Terrorism and Security Act 2015, which added to the measures which might be imposed as part of a TPIM a requirement that the individual live in a locality considered appropriate by the Secretary of State (though with the proviso that, if at the time of the measure's imposition, there are premises that are the individual's own residence, a residence further than 200 miles from it could be specified by the Secretary of State only if the individual agreed to it).[125] The decision to reintroduce these measures was in large part a function of the insufficiency of exclusion zones (measures prohibiting individuals from entering certain areas) which, it had transpired, 'do nothing to prevent a subject from meeting harmful associates on his home patch for the purposes of terrorist plotting, facilitating an abscond or simply maintaining links and networks.'[126]

[118] Terrorism Prevention and Investigation Measures Act 2011, s 6.

[119] TPIM Act 2011, s 6(4).

[120] ibid, ss 8 and 9.

[121] ibid, s 9.

[122] ibid, s 5.

[123] ibid, s 3(2) and (6).

[124] David Anderson QC, *First Report of the Independent Reviewer on the Operation of the Terrorism Prevention and Investigation Measures Act 2011* (2013), 4.

[125] Counter-Terrorism and Security Act 2015, s 16.

[126] Summary conclusion from a 'secret and unpublished' report carried out by the Independent Reviewer of Terrorism Legislation on locational constraints under TPIMs and submitted in September 2014 (available at: https://terrorismlegislationreviewer.independent.gov.uk/relocation-relocation-relocation/).

As the name suggests, one element of the move to replace control orders with TPIMs was the idea that the latter were intended to facilitate investigations leading to criminal prosecutions, with the legislative change accompanied by extra resources for that purpose, and related statutory duties put in place. Before making an application to the court for permission to impose a TPIM on an individual, the Secretary of State is required to consult the police as to 'whether there is evidence available that could realistically be used for the purposes of prosecuting the individual for an offence relating to terrorism'; where a TPIM notice has been served, the police come under a duty to 'secure that the investigation of the individual's conduct, with a view to a prosecution of the individual for an offence relating to terrorism, is kept under review throughout the period the TPIM notice is in force' and report on that review to the Secretary of State.[127] In its post-legislative scrutiny, however, the Joint Committee on Human Rights observed that it had found no evidence that 'TPIMs have led in practice to any more criminal prosecutions of terrorism suspects', confirming its earlier suspicion that 'the replacement for control orders were not 'investigative' in any meaningful sense.'[128] It suggested on that basis that 'TPIMs should be referred to as Terrorism Prevention Orders, or something similar, to reflect the reality that their sole purpose is preventive, not investigative.'[129] What stands out, however, is that TPIMs did not for a period appear to be playing a significant role within the national security constitution. Within a few years of their introduction, the number in force dwindled significantly—partly as a result of the two year expiration date and the fact that measures cannot be re-imposed unless there exists evidence of terrorism-related activity in the period since measures were last imposed, but also as a result (it was said) of the government's 'strong record of prosecuting terrorists in recent years ... the Government's successful deportation of some high profile terrorist suspects and ... the productive use of other means of disruption'.[130] At the time of the Independent Reviewer on Terrorism Legislation's 2014 report (published in March 2015) only a total of 10 people had ever been subject to TPIMs (9 of them having been previously subject to control orders and transferred onto the new regime when it was introduced) and only one person was still subject to a TPIM, no new measures having been imposed in that year.[131] Already before then the Joint Committee on Human Rights had stated its 'distinct impression that, in practice, TPIMs may be withering on the vine as a counter-terrorism tool of practical utility.'[132] Although the IRTL had noted that the 'sparing use' of TPIMs was 'no cause for regret' given that they are a tool of last resort, this pattern began to reverse somewhat subsequently, with a Home Office review in late 2016 noting that there were, at the end of August 2016, six TPIMs in force,[133]

[127] Terrorism Prevention and Investigation Measures Act 2011, s 10.

[128] Joint Committee on Human Rights, *Post-Legislative Scrutiny: Terrorism Prevention and Investigation Measures Act 2011* (2013–14, HL 113, HC 1014), [35]. For a consideration of the reasons for that failure, see Helen Fenwick, 'Redefining the role of TPIMs in combatting 'Home-grown' terrorism within the widening counter-terror framework' (2015) *EHRLR* 41, in which the author argues that the objectives of prevention and investigation are inevitably in conflict.

[129] JCHR (n 128) [35].

[130] Anderson, *Terrorism Acts in 2013* (n 63) [6.4].

[131] David Anderson QC, *Terrorism Prevention and Investigation Measures in 2014: Third Report of the Independent Reviewer on the Operation of the Terrorism Prevention and Investigation Measures Act 2011* (2015), [1.10].

[132] JCHR (n 128) [15].

[133] Home Office, *Memorandum to the Home Affairs Committee Post-Legislative Scrutiny of the Terrorism Prevention and Investigation Measures Act 2011*, Cm 9348 (2016), [37].

and the regular quarterly Ministerial statement required by the 2011 Act,[134] made in December 2016, saw that figure increased to seven.[135]

The Secretary of State's power to impose TPIMs was originally due to expire five years after the 2011 Act came into force. That sunset could be postponed by secondary legislation made under the Act after consultation with the IRTL, the Intelligence Services Commissioner, and the Director-General of MI5 and the power to do so has been exercised;[136] the sunset will now take place, unless further postponed, in 2021. Though TPIMs remain on the statute book, however, they have become in many ways less relevant as a result both of success in deporting and prosecuting suspected terrorists and changing patterns of terrorism—most obviously the emergence of the Islamic State (which, unlike traditional terrorist groups, enjoys—or enjoyed—control of significant territory)—which are addressed by distinct counter-terrorism mechanisms, some of them considered in Chapter 4. Alongside the tense dialectical interplay of domestic and international legal regimes at their point of intersection in the Human Rights Act, which has influenced both the emergence of TPIMs as the most flagship counter-terrorism measure and the location of the line which TPIMs must walk in trading off the needs of security and those of liberty, the UK's response to the threat of terrorism is therefore subject to a second evolutionary force. The changing foreign policy environment in part precipitated by the UK's foreign misadventures—the invasions of Afghanistan and, more importantly, Iraq—has in that way doubled back upon itself, coming now to influence the domestic aspect of the state's response to threats to its security. What is notable, however, is how much more stable are certain other elements of the counter-terrorist environment than are these mechanisms which operate at the forefront of the counter-terrorism constitution. That is, though TPIMs remain available and in use, albeit only in a small handful of cases, many of the less prominent elements of the counter-terrorism constitution as it has existed since 2000 have proven remarkably resilient, indicating—perhaps—a greater appropriateness to the ongoing (rather than transient) needs of national security, and a better balancing, at the time of their enactment, of the needs of security and the relevant individual rights.

B. Proscription

It was noted above that the proscription of terrorist organisations was a central element of the response to the threat of terrorism in Northern Ireland.[137] Proscription was (re)written into the Terrorism Act 2000, extending it, for the first time, beyond those organisations concerned in terrorism in Northern Ireland to those concerned in international terrorism.[138] It did so notwithstanding the government's acknowledgment that the 'practical and policy difficulties involved in drawing up and then maintaining an up to

134 Terrorism Prevention and Investigation Measures Act 2011, s 19.

135 Amber Rudd, HC Deb 15 December 2016, volume 618 col 64WS.

136 Terrorism Prevention and Investigation Measures Act 2011 (Continuation) Order (SI 2016/1166).

137 For an overview, see C Walker, *The Prevention of Terrorism in British Law*, 2nd edn (Manchester, Manchester University Press, 1992).

138 Terrorism Act 2000, Pt II.

date list of international and domestic groups to be covered would be formidable.'[139] The relevant portion of the Act has survived the various shifts in the national security landscape which have taken place since then. Section 3 of that Act provides that organisations listed in a Schedule to it (or which operate under the same name as one therein listed) are proscribed, and empowers the Secretary of State to add or remove organisations from the Schedule, though 'only if he believes that it is concerned in terrorism',[140] meaning that it 'commits or participates in acts of terrorism ... prepares for terrorism ... promotes or encourages terrorism, or ... is otherwise concerned in terrorism.'[141] Though the basic condition has remained unchanged since 2000, the provision was amended in 2006 to state that the third of these possibilities includes the situation in which the activities of the organisation 'include the unlawful glorification of the commission or preparation (whether in the past, in the future or generally) of acts of terrorism' or 'are carried out in a manner that ensures that the organisation is associated with statements containing any such glorification.'[142] Glorification is unlawful if there are persons who may become aware of it 'could reasonably be expected to infer that what is being glorified, is being glorified as' conduct to be emulated, or of a type which should be emulated, 'in existing circumstances'.[143] Unlike in relation to several of the powers discussed above, there is no judicial involvement in the proscription process; though Parliament must approve orders proscribing additional organisations, it has never withheld the required approval. On the possibility that this reflects Parliamentarian's relative ignorance of the national security context (as well, presumably, as a political deference to the judgement of the executive), it has been suggested that the Intelligence and Security Committee of Parliament (which can be given access to sensitive material) be involved in the process.[144] The threshold for prescription is—in the absence of a requirement of necessity—lower than is the case for comparable powers, and there is no limit on the duration of an organisation's proscription.

It has long been accepted, however, that the proscription regime is limited in its effect, working mostly to 'inform the public, and especially sympathisers with organisations, as to what is banned and therefore should not be joined' and providing—in the form of prosecuting membership of a proscribed organisation—'a useful way of dealing with lower level activity'.[145] This is particularly true of those organisations and actors which pose the most high-profile threat in the modern day: proscription laws are 'difficult to apply to the flexible networks of al-Qaeda inspired terrorism in the 21st century, let alone to the "lone wolf" who is part of no network at all.'[146] And in practice, the Secretary of State does not proscribe all organisations which meet the statutory criteria but has from the beginning been

[139] Home Office, *Legislation Against Terrorism: A consultation paper*, Cm 4178 (1998), [4.16].

[140] TA 2000, s 3(4).

[141] ibid, s 3(5).

[142] ibid, s 3(5A).

[143] ibid, s 3(5B).

[144] David Anderson QC, *The Terrorism Acts in 2011: Report of the Independent Reviewer on the Operation of the Terrorism Act 2000 and Part 1 of the Terrorism Act 2006* (2012), [4.52].

[145] Lord Carlile of Berriew QC, *Report on the Operation in 2008 of the Terrorism Act 2000 and of Part 1 of the Terrorism Act 2006* (2009), [51].

[146] David Anderson QC, *The Terrorism Acts in 2010: Report of the Independent Reviewer on the Operation of the Terrorism Act 2000 and Part 1 of the Terrorism Act 2006* (2011), [4.17].

committed to exercising the discretion created by the statute with reference to the following five factors:

> (a) the nature and scale of the organisation's activities; (b) the specific threat that it poses to the United Kingdom; (c) the specific threat that it poses to British nationals overseas; (d) the extent of the organisation's presence in the United Kingdom; and (e) the need to support other members of the international community in the global fight against terrorism.[147]

In reality, there are many elements of the use of the proscription power which are objectionable, even beyond the statutory scope. The most obvious is captured by the fifth of the discretionary factors, which sees the power used as an 'inexpensive tool of foreign policy', with organisations proscribed even though they do not or cannot represent a threat to the UK. In this context, the proscription of such organisations 'may be aimed at securing influence with the government of a country in which the organisation is active, or at demonstrating UK solidarity with an important ally. Conversely, it is sometimes feared that to deproscribe such an organisation might cause offence to a friendly country whose territory or whose nationals have been threatened by it in the past.'[148] This is objectionable even if the friendly countries in question are democratic, rights-respecting states. Often, however, they are not, and it has been claimed that in some cases, accusations of the use of violence (justifying proscription) have been made against internal political opposition, for what are effectively propaganda purposes.[149] Though those accusations may be correct, proscription also impacts 'on the lives of individuals and communities who share the ethnicity and the political aspirations (though not the violent methods) of such groups.'[150] The need to use the power sparingly is underlined also by the fact that the act also creates a series of criminal offences relating to, broadly, membership of or support for proscribed organisations.[151] These are amongst the most commonly charged terrorism offences.

More so even than the excessively broad criteria for proscription, the key problem with the regime under the 2000 Act is the difficulty of achieving deproscription. The 2000 Act permits the organisation (or any persons affected by its proscription) to apply for an order removing it from Schedule 2.[152] Very few such applications have ever been successful, and the government has never delisted an organisation on its own initiative. Given that proscription is—unlike related measures—temporally indefinite, the overall effect is that deproscription almost never in fact takes place. An appeal against an application which has been refused lies to a body called the Proscribed Organisations Appeal Commission (POAC),[153]

[147] Lord Bassam, HL Deb 16 May 2000, vol 613 col 252, cited in Anderson (n 144) [4.6].

[148] Anderson, *Terrorism Acts in 2011* (n 144) [4.38].

[149] 'The UK is said to be the only country in the world that proscribes the Baluchistan Liberation Army. I am told, but have not been able independently to verify, that the fact of UK proscription has been referred to by the Pakistan Government to justify military action or reprisals taken against Baluch "terrorists"': Anderson, *Terrorism Acts in 2011* (n 144) [4.47].

[150] Anderson, *Terrorism Acts in 2011* (n 144) [4.44].

[151] Terrorism Act 2000, ss 11–13. David Anderson has described the consequences: 'The appearance of an organisation on that list is a trigger for certain criminal offences under sections 11-13 TA 2000, notably support for a proscribed organisation, which carries a maximum sentence of 10 years, active membership (2 years) and uniform offences (6 months). The financial resources of the organisation become terrorist property for the purposes, of Part III TA 2000, and an investigation of those resources is a terrorist investigation for the purposes of Part IV.' Anderson, *Terrorism Acts in 2011* (n 144) [4.9].

[152] TA 2000, s 4.

[153] ibid, s 5 and Sch 3.

mandated to allow the appeal if it considers the decision to refuse delisting flawed 'when considered in the light of the principles applicable on an application for judicial review',[154] and with the power to order the Secretary of State to delist the organisation in question. POAC, which sits as a commission of three people (one of whom must hold or have held high judicial office, with the others not judges)[155] is empowered to carry out the same sort of the closed material procedure as was introduced in the Special Immigration Appeals Commission in 1997,[156] and it is not clear that a wholly separate body is required to carry out challenges to proscription, particularly in light of the small amount of work done by POAC. The only successful endeavour for deproscription, was that of the Peoples Mojahadeen Organisation of Iran (PMOI), which had been added to Schedule 2 in 2001.[157] Following two unsuccessful applications to the Home Secretary for delisting (predicated upon the abandonment by the PMOI of its previously violent means), a third was made by a group of Parliamentarians. That too was unsuccessful, but the refusal to make a delisting order was successfully appealed to the POAC.[158] When the Home Secretary applied, unsuccessfully, for permission to appeal, the Court of Appeal held that an organisation which has:

> temporarily ceased from terrorist activities for tactical reasons is to be contrasted with an organisation that has decided to attempt to achieve its aims by other than violent means. The latter cannot be said to be "concerned in terrorism", even if the possibility exists that it might decide to revert to terrorism in the future.[159]

Here, there was no 'reliable evidence that supported a conclusion that PMOI retained an intention to resort to terrorist activities in the future.'[160] Two aspects of the Court of Appeal decision are notable. The first relates to the standard of review employed, which the Secretary of State argued was more intensive than justified in the circumstances: by failing to employ the *Wednesbury* unreasonableness standard of review, POAC had effectively, it was said, substituted its own conclusion for the decision of the Secretary of State.[161] The Court of Appeal rejected this, holding that POAC 'approached its task correctly in subjecting the applicant's decision to intense scrutiny, thereby carrying out a review according to the principles of judicial review that apply where a decision affects fundamental human rights.'[162] This is a welcome conclusion, which departs from the approach normally taken in the context of national security judicial review. That it is arrived at explicitly on the basis of the appropriate standard of review rather than—as would have been perhaps more plausible—on the basis that the question is one of precedent fact,[163] is particularly

[154] ibid, s 5(3).

[155] ibid, Sch 3, para 4(3).

[156] It was held in *R (Kurdistan Workers' Party and others) v Secretary of State for the Home Department* [2002] EWHC 644 (Admin) that it was not appropriate to challenge proscription by way of judicial review, notwithstanding that the available remedies were significantly more restricted than are available in the Administrative Court.

[157] By the Terrorism Act (Proscribed Organisations) (Amendment) Order 2001.

[158] *Lord Alton of Liverpool v Secretary of State for the Home Department* PC/02/2006 (30 November 2007). For discussion see Tomkins (n 81) 559–563.

[159] *Secretary of State for the Home Department v Lord Alton of Liverpool* [2008] EWCA Civ 443, [38].

[160] [2008] EWCA Civ 443, [53].

[161] POAC had been clear, however, that it would have arrived at the same decision even if applying the *Wednesbury* standard: PC/02/2006, [327].

[162] [2008] EWCA Civ 443, [46].

[163] Nathan Raiah, 'Reviewing Proscription under the Terrorism Act 2000' (2008) 13 *Judicial Review* 187.

attractive. A second point relates to an observation made by the Court of Appeal which is particularly significant in light of the consistent refusal of applications for delisting (in the PMOI case, as in all others):

> It is a matter for comment and for regret that the decision-making process in this case has signally fallen short of the standards which our public law sets and which those affected by public decisions have come to expect.[164]

Not only has the pattern of refusal continued since these remarks were made, but various recommendations of the Independent Reviewer of Terrorism as to improvements which might be made to the delisting process have not been taken up: some, such as the introduction of a requirement that proscription be not merely justified but also necessary, were rejected;[165] another, a process of deproscribing groups whose listing was no longer justified, was begun but abandoned due to a loss of political will, with no groups having been delisted as part of it.[166] Instead, the situation is as follows:

> No evidence is collected for the purpose of determining whether a proscribed group remains "concerned in terrorism", thus saving Ministers from the embarrassment of maintaining the proscription of groups which do not satisfy the statutory test. Groups seeking deproscription, or sympathetic figures prepared to act on their behalf, must themselves take the initiative to request it.[167]

As the IRTL has noted, however, this creates an intolerable situation:

> The issue of legality is however basic and non-negotiable. It is not a factor to be weighed against others, but an overriding requirement. If an organisation is found after careful review not to satisfy the current threshold, then it is not enough to label it a "difficult case" and leave the proscription in force. Either the organisation must be deproscribed, or the threshold must be changed in such a way as to render its continued proscription lawful.[168]

The proscription regime has maintained its relevance even as other mechanisms have variously been introduced, repealed, or allowed to 'wither on the vine'. In July 2016, for example, 84 organisations were listed in Schedule 2 to the 2000 Act (an increase, since July 2011, of 22).[169] And, unlike the mechanisms discussed above, the proscribed organisations regimes has always been, and continues to be, used also in the context of the Northern Ireland: of the 84 organisations listed in March 2015, 14 were Northern Irish.[170] Here, unlike elsewhere in the counter-terrorism landscape, there is therefore a strikingly ecumenical approach to combatting terrorism, even if some of that can be ascribed to the fact that it would take 'almost eccentric courage' for a Home Secretary to prune the list of proscribed organisations of his or her own accord,[171] and particularly given the sensitivities associated

164 PC/02/2006, [57].

165 HM government, *The Government Response to the Annual Report on the Operation of the Terrorism Acts in 2011 by the Independent Reviewer of Terrorism Legislation*, Cm 8494 (2013).

166 Anderson, *Terrorism Acts in 2013* (n 63), [5.8].

167 ibid, [5.9].

168 David Anderson QC, *The Terrorism Acts in 2012: Report of the Independent Reviewer on the Operation of the Terrorism Act 2000 and Part 1 of Terrorism Act 2006* (2013), [5.30].

169 Anderson, *Terrorism Acts in 2015* (n 8) [5.4].

170 ibid.

171 C Gearty, *Civil Liberties* (Oxford, Oxford University Press, 2007), 158, quoted in Anderson, *Terrorism Acts in 2013* (n 63) [5.10].

with the listing and delisting of Northern Irish organisations, notwithstanding the years which have passed since the Good Friday Agreement. No Northern Irish organisation has been deproscribed while the 2000 Act has been in place, notwithstanding that some appear to no longer exist.[172]

One innovation of note in the practice of proscription was the decision in late 2016 to proscribe National Alliance,[173] a domestic far-right political group. Until that point in time no such organisation was proscribed, and the IRTL had noted that though he believed this 'to be the result not of oversight but of careful consideration' the matters was 'a sensitive one in Muslim communities' and the law should not be seen to be applied in a discriminatory fashion.[174] He therefore recommended that if there are 'far-right terrorist organisations in the UK that can be said to meet the statutory requirement for proscription, their possible proscription should be considered according to the same discretionary criteria as have been applied to UK organisations concerned in al-Qaida related terrorism.'[175] In carrying out the proscription—several years later—of National Action, the Home Secretary, Amber Rudd, described it as a 'racist, antisemitic and homophobic organisation which stirs up hatred, glorifies violence and promotes a vile ideology' and which 'has absolutely no place in a Britain that works for everyone.'[176] Nevertheless, while the fundamental and significant flaws in the proscription system continue to exist, it hardly matters that the powers are exercised in a way which appear more balanced than before: though the necessity and proportionality of the regime have been repeatedly reasserted, as has the existence of comparable regimes in other states, a system which is capable of being operated with so little regard to basic notions of legality and (to the extent the two diverge) fairness, should not exist at all.

C. Stop and Search

The 2000 Act provided for powers of arrest, detention, search and seizure in connection with terrorism, most of which include requirements of reasonable suspicion of a sort familiar to the criminal law.[177] Amongst these powers, however, were those under section 44 which permitted a police officer to authorise (with the confirmation of the Secretary of State, and for periods of up to 28 days) the stopping and searching either of vehicles (including their drivers and passengers) or of pedestrians where it was considered expedient for preventing acts of terrorism.[178] Though the power could be exercised only for the purpose of searching for articles which 'could be used in connection with terrorism' (a formulation whose breadth undermines its ability to provide a meaningful limitation

[172] See, eg, Lord Carlile of Berriew QC, *Report on the Operation in 2007 of the Terrorism Act 2000 and of Part I of the Terrorism Act 2006* (2008), [68]. Red Hand Commando, one of the proscribed organisations, applied for delisting in Autumn 2017—the first such application by a Northern Ireland organisation under the 2000 Act. At the time of writing a decision is awaited, though the relevant individuals would be sensible not to get their hopes up.

[173] Given effect by the Terrorism Act 2000 (Proscribed Organisations) (Amendment) (No. 3) Order 2016/1238.

[174] Anderson, *Terrorism Acts in 2011* (n 144) [4.16].

[175] ibid [4.62].

[176] Home Office, 'National Action becomes first extreme right-wing group to be banned in UK' (16 December 2016).

[177] Terrorism Act 2000, ss 40–43.

[178] TA 2000, s 44.

on the power's use), it did not require the possession of grounds for suspecting the presence of such articles. Nor, of course, does the formulation of the power require that there be any suspicion that any particular person or group of persons detained under it have committed any offence. In practice, these powers were very widely used in the years following 2001: in 2008/09, for example, 255,700 persons were searched under the powers,[179] and there was an ongoing authorisation in respect of the Metropolitan Police's entire force area until 2009. The powers were also consistently used to a disproportionate degree in relation to those from minority ethnic backgrounds, and became a well-document source of friction between the police and certain communities.[180] Suspicionless stop and search on this basis was challenged all the way to the House of Lords in *Gillan v Commissioner of Police for the Metropolis*,[181] where it was held that the fleeting nature of the detention carried out under the powers (as against, in that particular case, individuals travelling to a demonstration taking place outside an arms fair) meant that there was no deprivation of liberty for the purposes of Article 5 of the Convention on Human Rights; they could not be regarded 'as being detained in the sense of confined or kept in custody, but more properly of being detained in the sense of kept from proceeding or kept waiting' according to Lord Bingham.[182] Nor was Article 8 of the Convention engaged by what had been done, Lord Bingham 'inclining' to the view that 'an ordinary superficial search of the person and an opening of bags, of the kind to which passengers uncomplainingly submit at airports, for example, can scarcely be said to reach' the level at which the Convention right is engaged.[183] Even if it did represent an interference with Article 8, it was one which was proportionate to the legitimate aim being pursued, and so was justified in accordance with paragraph 2 of Article 8.[184]

On application by the same individuals to the Court of Human Rights in Strasbourg,[185] however, it was observed there that the applicants 'were obliged to remain where they were and submit to the search and if they had refused they would have been liable to arrest, detention at a police station and criminal charges' and that 'this element of coercion is indicative of a deprivation of liberty within the meaning of Article 5.'[186] The Strasbourg Court rejected the analogy with the search of baggage at airports, noting that in such a case the traveller knows that a search will take place and can choose not to subject himself to it. Under the 2000 Act powers, on the contrary, a person 'can be stopped anywhere and at any time, without notice and without any choice as to whether or not to submit to a search.'[187] As such, there was an interference with Article 8, and in fact the question of whether it was, as Lord Bingham had suggested, a proportionate one, did not arise, for it was not 'in accordance with the law' for the reason that 'the powers of authorisation and confirmation as well as those of stop and search under sections 44 and 45 of the 2000 Act are neither sufficiently

[179] David Anderson QC, *Terrorism Acts in 2010* (n 146) [8.17].

[180] See Tufyal Choudhury and Helen Fenwick, *The impact of counter-terrorism measures on Muslim communities*, Equality and Human Rights Commission Research report 72 (2011), Ch 4.

[181] *Gillan v Commissioner of Police for the Metropolis* [2006] UKHL 12.

[182] [2006] UKHL 12, [25].

[183] [2006] UKHL 12, [28].

[184] ibid, [29].

[185] *Gillan and Quinton v United Kingdom* (2010) 50 EHRR 45.

[186] (2010) 50 EHRR 45, [57].

[187] ibid, [64].

circumscribed nor subject to adequate legal safeguards against abuse.'[188] The requirement of 'expediency' rather than necessity mean that the proportionality of the measure was never considered, while the broad geographical scope and infinitely-renewable nature of authorisations meant that there was no 'real check' on their use both counted in favour of such a conclusion.[189] So too, most pressingly, did the breadth of the discretion effectively granted to individual police officers and the consequent possibility that the powers in question would—as seemed to be the case—be exercised disproportionately against certain minority groups.[190] In the aftermath of the decision, a remedial order was made under section 10 of the Human Rights Act,[191] followed by amendments contained in the Protection of Freedoms Act 2012. The new powers are more circumscribed than those which they replaced: authorisations of suspicionless stop and search of persons and vehicles are now permitted only where a senior police officer reasonably suspects that an act of terrorism will take place, and reasonably considers that the authorisation is necessary to prevent such an act, and of no greater geographical or temporal scope than is required.[192] Provision was also made requiring the publication of Codes of Practice relating to the powers of stop and search under the 2000 Act, both with and without suspicion.[193]

The other set of powers which have attracted the attention of the courts are those under Schedule 7 of the 2000 Act,[194] which applies only to 'ports' (including airports and hoverports)[195] but goes further than the suspicionless stop and search powers at issue in *Gillan*. Officers may question any person at a port (or in the 'border area')[196] who is believed to be entering or leaving Great Britain or Northern Ireland (or, now, travelling within them by air) in order to determine 'whether he appears to be' a terrorist.[197] No grounds for believing that a person is a terrorist are required,[198] and a person being questioned under Schedule 7 must, amongst other things, 'give the examining officer any information in his possession which the officer requests'.[199] Where an 'examination' can last up to one hour,[200] persons stopped under schedule 7 can also be 'detained'. Originally detention could be for up to 9 hours,[201] during which period a person could be searched, as could 'anything which he has with him, or which belongs to him, and which the examining officer reasonably believes has been, or is about to be, on a ship or aircraft'.[202] Anything given over

[188] ibid, [87].
[189] ibid, [80]–[81].
[190] ibid, [83]–[87].
[191] Terrorism Act 2000 (Remedial) Order 2011 (SI 631/2011).
[192] TA 2000, s 47A.
[193] The changes made to the regime of counter-terrorism stop and search—as well as the question of who deserves credit for them—are discussed in John Ip, 'The Reform of Counterterrorism Stop and Search after *Gillan v United Kingdom*' (2013) 13 *HRLR* 729.
[194] Like many powers discussed here, a modern incarnation of a regime whose roots are much older: see Walker (n 137) Ch 9.
[195] Terrorism Act 2000, Sch 7, para 1(2).
[196] ibid, para 4.
[197] TA 2000, Sch 7, para 2. As with other elements of the 2000 Act, these powers are successors to powers first introduced in the PTA 1974.
[198] TA 2000, Schedule 7, para 2(4).
[199] ibid, para 5.
[200] ibid, para 6A.
[201] ibid, para 6(4) (now repealed).
[202] ibid, para 8.

to or found by the officer in accordance with the Schedule 7 powers may be detained for examination for up to 7 days,[203] or indefinitely if he believes it may be needed in relation to criminal proceedings or proceedings or the making of a deportation order.[204] Fingerprints and DNA samples may be taken.[205] These powers are heavily used: in 2015/16, more than 28,000 examinations took place (with around 1,800 lasting longer than an hour) and around 1,800 persons detained.[206] Though the number of examinations has declined sharply over time (in 2009/10, by comparison, over 87,000 examinations took place) the number of detentions is rising (in 2009/10, fewer than 400 persons were detained under Schedule 7).[207]

Schedule 7 has been amended in a number of ways since the 2000 Act was introduced. The Protection of Freedoms Act 2012 placed a six-month limit upon the retention of fingerprints and DNA samples (subject to certain exceptions).[208] The Anti-social Behaviour, Crime and Policing Act 2014 made a number of changes, including shortening the period for which a person could be detained (to six hours),[209] prohibiting intimate searches of those detained,[210] and granting such persons the right (in most cases) to have someone informed and to access a solicitor.[211] Periodic review of detention under Schedule 7 was also required.[212] Alongside these liberalising changes, however, was one which introduced the power to make and retain copies of anything given to, found by, or examined under the Schedule (a change which, it must be recognised, gave a more solid legal footing to practices which were already common).[213] This power is frequently used in order to download data from electronic devices in the possession of those stopped.[214] In 2015/16, the number of devices downloaded was 4,300,[215] and it has been reported—based on documents leaked by Edward Snowden and which predate the institution of a clear legal power—that material downloaded in this way was (and presumably still is) routinely passed to GCHQ.[216] Finally, the Schedule creates a number of criminal offences, including that of wilfully failing 'to comply with a duty imposed under or by virtue of this Schedule',[217] and there is no statutory bar on the use of admissions which are made in the context of questioning

[203] ibid, para 11.
[204] ibid, para 11A.
[205] ibid, para 10.
[206] Anderson, *Terrorism Acts in 2015* (n 8) [7.9].
[207] ibid.
[208] TA 2000, Sch 8, para 20G.
[209] TA 2000, Sch 7, para 6A.
[210] ibid, para 8(4).
[211] TA 2000, Sch 8, para 7A. This change was prompted by the decision in *R (Elosta) v Metropolitan Police Commissioner* [2013] EWHC 3397 (QB).
[212] TA 2000, Sch 8, part 1A.
[213] TA 2000, Sch 7, para 11A.
[214] Anderson, *Terrorism Acts in 2012* (n 168) [10.65]–[10.80].
[215] Anderson, *Terrorism Acts in 2015* (n 8) [7.11].
[216] 'This mobile phone data is downloaded from people stopped at UK ports (i.e. sea, air and rail). It includes anything stored on a target's phone, although only phonebooks, sms and call events are currently databased …' The document also states that' unless substantial traces are found against that person, mobile phone downloads are deleted' and so the database into which it is entered is very unlikely to be a 'bulk personal dataset' for the purposes of the Investigatory Powers Act 2016 (on which see Ch 2). Notable also is the claim made, under the heading of 'Legalities', that '[t]he data is legally volunteered under s.7 and s.8 of TACT (Terrorism Act 2000), although the person will not be directly told their phone is downloaded.' The reference is presumably to schedules, rather than sections; the weakness of the account of the law is presumably reflected in the later creation of a legal basis for the practice: 'Phantom Parrot GCHQ', an undated document published by *The Intercept* (23 September 2017), and available at https://theintercept.com/document/2017/09/23/phantom-parrot-gchq/.
[217] TA 2000, Sch 7, para 18.

under Schedule 7 being used in subsequent criminal proceedings. These offences have been deployed against persons who refuse to give over passwords demanded during the course of a Schedule 7 detention.[218]

There has also been significant litigation associated with the powers. One important case—*Miranda*—is discussed above, and established that Schedule 7 was incompatible with Article 10 of the European Convention on Human Rights because of its failure to provide adequate safeguards against the arbitrary exercise of the powers in relation to journalistic material.[219] The other leading decision is that of the Supreme Court in *Beghal v DPP*,[220] in which the appellant had been charged with failing to comply with a duty imposed on her by Schedule 7, having refused to answer a variety of questions posed to her during an examination. The Supreme Court rejected the claim that Schedule 7 was incompatible with Article 8 of the ECHR, resisting an analogy drawn with the decision of the Strasbourg Court in *Gillan and Quinton* on the basis that the geographic scope of the Schedule 7 powers is limited; that being stopped at a port represents a lower level of interference with one's rights (and is one to which the citizen is accustomed);[221] and that there were significant differences in how the two sets of powers were being used in practice (in particular, there was no evidence of a discriminatory use being made of the Schedule 7 powers).[222] The effect of these distinctions was that lesser safeguards were required in order to protect against the arbitrary exercise of power and so to ensure compatibility with the ECHR; here, sufficient safeguards (including judicial review and the work of the IRTL) existed.[223] The interference with the qualified Convention rights was proportionate to what was achieved by it in terms of the legitimate aim it pursued. The decision is notable for the forceful dissenting judgment given by Lord Kerr, who rejected the premise that the public being accustomed to being stopped at ports was relevant to the lawfulness of the regime:

> Firstly, being subject to border controls such as the requirement to provide proof of identity and entitlement to enter is an entirely different matter from being required to answer questions about one's movements and activities. As this case shows, these questions can be quite detailed and, more importantly, if they are not answered, the person of whom they are asked faces criminal sanction. Secondly, and more importantly, whether people in this country are accustomed to intrusion when they move through ports of entry or exit does not bear on the question of whether the circumstances in which the Schedule 7 powers may be exercised are too widely drawn to satisfy the test of "in accordance with law". Put shortly, an unfettered power which may be arbitrarily or capriciously used does not become legal just because people generally do not take exception to its use.[224]

[218] See the case of Muhammad Rabbani, international director of the NGO Cage, an 'in independent advocacy organisation working to empower communities impacted by the War on Terror' who was charged with wilfully obstructing or seeking to frustrate a search or examination under Schedule 7 and convicted in September 2017: Owen Boycott, 'Campaign group chief found guilty of refusing to divulge passwords' *The Guardian* (25 September 2017).

[219] *R (Miranda) v Secretary of State for the Home Department* [2016] EWCA Civ 6.

[220] *Beghal v DPP* [2015] UKSC 49.

[221] 'The public in this country has historically enjoyed the right to free movement about the streets and the power to stop and search is … a substantial intrusion on it … By contrast, those who pass through our ports have always been adjusted to border controls, including the requirement to identify oneself and to submit to searches and answer questions in aid of general security. The potential importance of intercepting, detecting and deterring terrorists at border points is generally recognised.' [2015] UKSC 49, [38].

[222] [2015] UKSC 49, [42].

[223] ibid, [43].

[224] ibid, [101].

Though the Code of Practice prohibited the use of the power solely on the grounds of a person's ethnic or religious characteristics, there was no mechanism by which it could be ensured that this did not happen and, anyway, this provision was compatible with the use of the powers being guided by those factors as one amongst many.[225] As well as the Schedule 7 regime therefore making space for arbitrary exercise of the stop and search powers, the nature of those powers was such as to make it impossible for the proportionality of any specific interference with qualified Convention rights to be assessed:

> The examining officer does not have to explain why he or she chose a particular individual for the exercise of the Schedule 7 powers. Indeed, he or she does not have to have a reason (in the sense of a rationalised conclusion) for the exercise of the power, since it is unnecessary to have any form of suspicion. A purely instinctive impulse based on nothing more than a feeling that something relating to terrorism might be disclosed by the exercise of the powers is enough to permit recourse to them. In those circumstances, an examination of whether the powers have been used proportionately is simply unfeasible.[226]

It is not clear that Lord Kerr's interpretation of the relevant law is compatible with a suspicionless stop and search power of any kind; indeed, he notes 'the absence of any articulated reason' for any such power, and the fact that such absence 'makes its justification on the basis that it strikes the right balance problematic.'[227] Nevertheless, in light of the long-standing testimonials to the utility of Schedule 7 given by, most importantly, the IRTL, it is unlikely that the executive would tolerate it being limited in the same way as were the section 44 powers after *Gillan and Quinton*. It is nonetheless likely that the issues in *Beghal* will eventually be considered by the European Court of Human Rights.[228] If that Court repeats, in some future case, the rejection of the decision of the UK's highest court, the stage is set for another clash between the two regimes, and the further unsettling of the dialectic which has powered so much of the counter-terrorism constitution's evolution. On that point, however, it must be noted that the broader context within which such a dispute would arise is rather different from that which prevailed in the early post-11 September interaction between the two regimes, when the Human Rights Act was freshly minted, and the government in power committed to its preservation notwithstanding its frequent palpable frustration with the effects of specific decision of both the domestic courts and of that in Strasbourg. Now, not only is the future of the Human Rights Act in doubt, but so is the underlying membership of the UK of the Council of Europe up for grabs; transient frustrations have been replaced by an outright hostility (encapsulated by the comparatively trivial issue of the right of prisoners to vote). Very likely as a result of that changed context, the Strasbourg Court has shown a significant and at times rather unedifying hesitation to make decisions which might provoke the UK; a repeat of *Gillan and Quinton* seems for that reason—almost regardless of the merits of the point—rather unlikely.

[225] ibid, [103]–[104].
[226] ibid, [106].
[227] ibid, [128].
[228] An earlier application to the Strasbourg Court regarding Sch 7 was declared admissible, but later withdrawn: *Malik v United Kingdom* (App 32968/11).

D. Asset-Freezing

The final topic which we consider in the context of the contemporary counter-terrorism constitution is that of asset-freezing. The first point to note is that the law here is significantly more diffuse than is what has been described so far: while the proscription regime has been in place in its current form since the 2000 Act, and the regimes of detention pending deportation, control orders and TPIMs were enacted sequentially, the law of asset-freezing regimes has mushroomed over time, with new regimes augmenting (rather than replacing) what came before. The Terrorism Act 2000 contains powers relating to 'terrorist property' ('money or other property which is likely to be used for the purposes of terrorism (including any resources of a proscribed organisation'), the 'proceeds of the commission of acts of terrorism' and the 'proceeds of acts carried out for the purposes of terrorism'),[229] and a number of offences: fund-raising for terrorism,[230] financing terrorism etc.[231] It also obliges those who, in the context of their employment, believe or suspect that one of the offences has been committed, to communicate that belief to the police;[232] other persons are empowered—notwithstanding restrictions on disclosure—to communicate a suspicion or belief that any money or other property 'is terrorist property or is derived from terrorist property'.[233] The Anti-Terrorism, Crime and Security Act 2001 goes further, permitting the making of 'freezing orders'; an order which 'prohibits persons from making funds available to or for the benefit of a person or persons' who are specified in them.[234] These latter can be made where the Treasury reasonably believes that either 'action to the detriment of the United Kingdom's economy (or part of it)' or 'action constituting a threat to the life or property of one or more nationals of the United Kingdom or residents of the United Kingdom' has been or is likely to be taken by a person or persons who are all either foreign governments or residents of some other state.[235] Freezing orders under the 2001 Act must be affirmed by each House of Parliament within 28 days of their being made or they cease to have effect,[236] and can last up to a maximum of two years.[237]

In practice, only a small number of orders have been made under the 2001 Act. The breadth of the power to make freezing orders is demonstrated by the fact that the majority of those that have been made have related not to the assets of terrorists or other threats to national security as generally conceived, but rather to assets belonging, or related, to the Icelandic national Bank Landsbanki—the intention being to prevent funds being transferred out of the UK and back to Iceland after the bank entered receivership.[238]

[229] Terrorism Act 2000, Pt III.
[230] TA 2000, s 15.
[231] ibid, s 17.
[232] ibid, s 19.
[233] TA 2000, s 20. See Peter Binning, 'In safe hands? Striking the balance between privacy and security, antiterrorist finance measures' (2002) 6 *EHRLR* 737.
[234] Anti-Terrorism, Crime and Security Act 2001, s 5(1).
[235] ibid, s 4(2).
[236] ibid, s 10.
[237] ibid, s 8.
[238] Landsbanki Freezing Order (SI 2008/2668), Landsbanki Freezing (Amendment) Order 2008 (SI 2008/2766), Landsbanki Freezing (Revocation) Order (SI 2009/1392).

Though Walker and Lennon have agreed that the order in question was lawful under the 2001 Act, they argued that it nevertheless constituted 'a dangerous use of the legislation that was all but inevitable due to the failure to address concerns raised at the time of enactment and in a subsequent review regarding its scope.'[239] The only other order to have been made thus far relates to the assets of Andrey Lugovoy and Dmitri Kovtun, two Russians believed to be responsible for poisoning Alexander Litvinenko with polonium in London in 2006.[240] Though, again, there is no doubt as to the lawfulness or appropriateness of that order, the fact that it has little to do with terrorism as ordinarily understood similarly suggests that the powers are out of place in the statute in which they are found.[241]

These powers were on the statute book soon after the attacks of 11 September. When, however, a variety of sanctions prescribed by the United Nations were given legal effect in the UK, this was done not via these provisions—with their attendant safeguards—but instead via two orders made under the authority of the United Nations Act 1946.[242] Section 1 of that statute permits the making of Orders in Council in order to apply measures which themselves give effect to a decision by the UN Security Council under Article 41 of the UN Charter (which permits 'measures not involving the use of armed force' in order to 'to maintain or restore international peace and security'). Though Orders made under section 1 are laid before Parliament,[243] Parliament has no ability either to scrutinise or to amend them. There is no room here to consider the sanctions regime as it operates at the UN level; it suffices to note that the regime is both draconian in substance and procedurally deficient.[244] That the orders by which that regime was given effect in domestic law shared some of the relevant characteristics proved fatal to them, when they were challenged in the Supreme Court in *Ahmed*.[245] The principle of legality means that the courts will hold a statutory provision to successfully override fundamental rights only if it is suitably explicit in doing so: 'general or ambiguous words' will not suffice.[246] The 1946 Act, it is plain, contains only such words, with nothing in it explicitly permitting the executive to override fundamental rights of any sort, and certainly not of the right to property, which the common law holds so dear.[247] For that reason, the two orders were held to be ultra vires the statute under whose authority they had been made, and were quashed: one in whole, the other only in part.[248] As with other invocations of the principle of legality, the emphasis was placed on the ability of that rule to safeguard rather than undermine the

[239] Genevieve Lennon and Clive Walker, 'Hot money in a cold climate' [2009] *PL* 37, 37.

[240] Andrey Lugovoy and Dmitri Kovtun Freezing Order 2016 (SI 2016/67).

[241] Tomkins (n 69) 206 is therefore incorrect in his decision not to discuss the powers in question in his critique of the 2001 Act because they 'are not particularly controversial, and … do seem to be reasonably closely related to the events in the United States of September 11, 2001'.

[242] The Terrorism (United Nations Measures) Order 2006 and the Al-Qaida and Taliban (United Nations Measures) Order 2006.

[243] United Nations Act 1946, s 1(4).

[244] For discussion, see Andrew Hudson, 'Not a Great Asset: The UN Security Council's Counter-Terrorism Regime: Violating Human Rights' (2007) *Berkeley Journal of International Law* 204.

[245] *HM Treasury v Ahmed* [2010] UKSC 2.

[246] *R v Home Secretary, ex parte Simms* [2000] 2 AC 115, 131.

[247] See, eg, P Scott, 'Entick v Carrington and the legal protection of property' in A Tomkins and P Scott (eds), *Entick v Carrington: 250 Years of the Rule of Law* (Oxford, Hart Publishing, 2015).

[248] [2010] UKSC 2.

constitutional processes of political accountability. 'Nobody should conclude,' said Lord Phillips, 'that the result of these appeals constitutes judicial interference with the will of Parliament. On the contrary it upholds the supremacy of Parliament in deciding whether or not measures should be imposed that affect the fundamental rights of those in this country.'[249]

As has (too) often happened elsewhere, however, Parliament's response was such as to suggest it did not consider itself slighted by the failure to make use of the alternative, specific, authority it had enacted. Judgment in *Ahmed* was given on 28 January 2010, and the Supreme Court refused, on 4 February, to suspend the effect of its decision. Six days later Parliament enacted the Terrorist Asset-Freezing (Temporary Provisions) Act 2010, deeming the Orders in question to have been validly made under and within the power conferred by the 1946 Act, and retrospectively deeming 'valid, lawful or effectual' anything done under the Orders in the period between their quashing and the enactment of these temporary provisions.[250] That statute was superseded later that year by the Terrorist Asset-Freezing etc. Act 2010, which imposes financial restrictions upon 'designated persons'—either those listed in a list provided for by a specified EU Regulation[251] or those designated by the Treasury under the Act.[252] Designation may be interim or final, the former lasting for up to 30 days or until it is replaced by a final designation, which lasts for up to a year but may be renewed annually for an indefinite period.[253] Though in both cases designation requires that the Treasury consider it 'necessary for purposes connected with protecting members of the public from terrorism that financial restrictions should be applied in relation to the person',[254] the threshold is higher for the making of a final designation (reasonable belief of involvement in terrorism related activity)[255] than for the making of an interim designation (reasonable suspicion).[256] Even this higher standard, however, falls short of the 'balance of probabilities' test recommended by the JCHR in its consideration of the Bill.[257] In either case, designation should be notified to the person in writing (though there is no statutory requirement to give reasons) and, unless certain exceptions apply,[258] the Treasury must 'take steps to publicise the designation generally'.[259] The upshot is that there is no role for either Parliament or the courts in the making of a designation, creating a contrast with both the proscription regime on one hand and those of control orders/TPIMs on the other. There is, however, a right of appeal to the High Court or Court of Session against a decision to make, vary or renew, or to not vary or revoke, a designation.[260] Other decisions can be challenged on judicial review principles.[261]

[249] [2010] UKSC 5, [157].
[250] Terrorist Asset-Freezing (Temporary Provisions) Act 2010, s 2(2).
[251] Art 2(3) of Council Regulation (EC) No 2580/2001.
[252] Terrorist Asset-Freezing etc. Act 2010, s 1.
[253] ibid, ss 3 and 4.
[254] ibid, ss 2(1)(b) and 6(1)(b).
[255] ibid, s 2(1)(a).
[256] ibid, s 6(1)(a).
[257] *Legislative Scrutiny: Terrorist Asset-Freezing etc Bill (Second Report)*, (2010–11, HL 53, HC 598), [1.8].
[258] Terrorist Asset-Freezing etc. Act 2010, ss 3(2)–(4) and 7(2)–(4).
[259] ibid, ss 3(1)(b) and 7(1)(b).
[260] ibid, s 26.
[261] ibid, s 27.

Where a person is designated under the 2010 Act, significant restrictions come into play. It is an offence to do the following things where one knows or has reasonable cause to suspect the connection with a designated person:

> deal with funds or economic resources owned, held or controlled by a designated person;
>
> make funds or financial services available (directly or indirectly) to a designated person;
>
> make funds or financial services available to any person for the benefit of a designated person;
>
> make economic resources available (directly or indirectly) to a designated person;
>
> make economic resources available to any person for the benefit of a designated person.[262]

Finally, it is an offence to 'make economic resources available (directly or indirectly) to a designated person' if one 'knows, or has reasonable cause to suspect' the involvement of the designated person and 'that the designated person would be likely to exchange the economic resources, or use them in exchange, for funds, goods or services.'[263] Some minor exceptions exist, while the prohibitions do not apply at all to acts done under licence from the Treasury.[264] It is an offence to 'intentionally participate in activities knowing that the 'object or effect' of those activities is to circumvent the prohibitions, or to enable their contravention.[265] Though undoubtedly an improvement upon the prior regime, TAFA 2010 nevertheless shares the fundamental characteristic (and therefore flaw) of other pre-emptive mechanisms relating to property: asset-freezing thereunder creates 'effects equivalent to punishments for criminal offences' but it is 'imposed via a standard of proof and a procedure falling far short of the fair trial standard'.[266]

The pattern over the years has been that of a sharp decline in the number of persons subject to designation under the 2010 Act: the Independent Reviewer of Terrorism Legislation gives a figure of 162 Treasury designations at the start of 2008 and 38 in September 2011.[267] Though there was some turnover of designees, the number had fallen to 33 in September 2014.[268] The most recent quarterly report, made in March 2017 (and giving figures for the period ending 20 September 2016) named 14 designated individuals (and another 10 designated by the EU under Council Regulation (EC) 2580/2001) and 7 organisations (plus 22 on the EU list).[269] Part of the reason for the decline is a policy whereby individuals subject to asset-freezing measures on the part of either the UN or the EU are not subject to designations in domestic law which duplicate their effect.[270] Another element is that the test of necessity is not met where individuals are imprisoned for long periods.[271] Given also that some of the designations are in respect of individuals based

[262] ibid, ss 11–14.
[263] ibid, s 15.
[264] ibid, s 17.
[265] ibid, s 18.
[266] Adam Tomkins, Helen Fenwick and Liora Lazarus, 'Terrorist asset-freezing: Continuing flaws in the current scheme' (2011) 25 *International Review of Law, Computers & Technology* 117, 127.
[267] David Anderson QC, *Fourth Report on the Operation of the Terrorist Asset-Freezing Etc. Act 2010* (2015), [2.12].
[268] Anderson (n 267) [2.14].
[269] *Operation of the UK's Counter-Terrorist Asset Freezing Regime: 1 April 2016 to 30 June 2016*, HC Deb 28 March 2017, vol 624 cols 9-11 WS.
[270] ibid.
[271] On the necessity test, see *C v HM Treasury* [2016] EWHC 2039 (Admin).

overseas (on whom the freezing of assets in this jurisdiction may have little direct effect), the effect was that—in late 2014—only three persons at liberty in Britain were the subject of Treasury designations.[272] As with TPIMs, this (relative) withering must be welcomed—in many ways, the freezing of assets is even more intrusive than are the restrictions on physically liberty which TPIMs impose, and approaches in some cases a sort of civil death.

Not only, though, did victory in the Supreme Court not bring to an end the sanctions regime in domestic law: it would not have done so even if the 2010 Acts had never been enacted. The reason for this is that the sanctions lists drawn up at the UN level (as were those dealt with by the Supreme Court) were not only incorporated into domestic law; they were incorporated into EU law by Council Regulation (EC) No 881/2002, which implements a regime of asset freezing for EU law that sits alongside that under Council Regulation 2580/2001 (that those listed in which are automatically 'designated persons' for the purposes of the 2010 Act).[273] When the Orders made under the 1946 Act were struck down, regulations 'in effect reproducing the controls previously imposed under the 1946 Act'[274] were made under the 1972 Act instead.[275] These new regulations encompassed those who had successfully challenged the freezing of their assets in the Supreme Court, rendering the victory hollow. The 1972 Act regime was (indirectly) litigated, again to the Supreme Court, by one of those who had successfully challenged the freezing of his assets under the 1946 Act in the *Ahmed* case. What was directly challenged was the decision of the Foreign Secretary to remove a 'hold' which the UK had placed upon the designation of the appellant (a Mr Youssef) by the United Nations Sanctions Committee. The case—which failed at all levels—raises interesting questions as to the domestic legal basis of the sanctions to which Youssef was now subject. It is a principle of domestic law that interferences with legal rights must be justified by some legal authority, and the question arose of where the relevant authority was found for the vast interference with property rights represented by the freezing of Youssef's assets; here, it was argued that the Secretary of State, by removing the hold on Youssef's designation, had effectively interfered with his assets by virtue of the Royal prerogative, which it was claimed was unlawful—the prerogative's ability to ground a lawful interference with property being now very limited, and usually requiring compensation.[276] In the Supreme Court, the answer offered to this contention was that the interference with property 'was directly and specifically authorised by regulation 881, which was given legislative effect in this country by the European Communities Act 1972' and that the combination of the two 'provides ample statutory authority to satisfy the *Entick* principle.'[277] It was noted, however—without elaboration—that '[n]o issue has been raised as to the effectiveness' of the 1972 Act for the purpose of giving effect to

[272] Anderson (n 267) [2.20].

[273] On the EU dimension of asset-freezing, see Jørn Vestergaard, 'Terror Financing—Asset Freezing, Human Rights and the European Legal Order' (2011) 2 *New Journal of European Criminal Law* 175. The due process issues associated with the UN sanctions regime caused particular difficulty for the EU courts called upon to address the relationship between that regime and EU law: see, most importantly, *Kadi v Council of the European Union* (C-402/05 P) [2009] 1 AC 1225 and the voluminous commentary on that decision.

[274] *Youssef v Secretary of State for Foreign and Commonwealth Affairs* [2016] UKSC 3, [3].

[275] The Al-Qaida and Taliban (Asset-Freezing) Regulations (SI 2010/1197) and later, superseding these, the Al-Qaida (Asset-Freezing) Regulations 2011 (SI 2011/2742).

[276] On which see *Burmah Oil Company Ltd v Lord Advocate* [1965] AC 75.

[277] [2016] UKSC 3, [34].

the regulation.[278] This is, it would seem, a reference to the point by which victory had been secured in *Ahmed*: whether the language of the enabling Act (there, the 1946 Act; here, the 1972 Act) was capable of grounding secondary legislation which interfered with fundamental rights, or whether its wording was 'general and ambiguous' and so incapable of doing so.

In the High Court, it had been held—unconvincingly—that the principle of legality was not relevant, because in deciding 'whether to support or oppose the designation of an individual by the Sanctions Committee, the Foreign Secretary is not exercising a power derived from an Act of Parliament' but rather is 'acting on behalf of the Government in its capacity as a member of an international body, the Security Council.'[279] In the Court of Appeal, the principle of legality had been invoked by name, but treated by the Court as coextensive with the argument that 'the Prerogative conferred no power on the Secretary of State to bar the appellant from access to funds or other economic resources, because it lacked the authority of legislation'.[280] The answer to that, of course, is the one given by the Supreme Court: there does exist legislation which grounds the interference with property: the 1972 Act. The Court of Appeal then acknowledged and simultaneously dismissed the genuine difficulty here (representing an instantiation of the principle of legality properly understood), noting that there 'might be an argument upon the question whether the general words of the European Communities Act 1972, by virtue of which the Regulation has the force of law in the UK, are sufficient to authorise the EU legislature to empower or require the Secretary of State to deprive an individual of access to any economic resources' but that 'no such argument has been run in this or any case, and it would plainly not be appropriate to canvass it now'.[281] This is unfortunate, for had the point been taken up by the Court of Appeal (or, following its signalling of the point, before the Supreme Court) it seems that the best understanding of the legal position is that the general power to make regulations which is found in the 1972 Act is insufficiently explicit to ground regulations which interfere with fundamental rights, particularly to the extent demonstrated by the regulations at issue here. The principle of legality is one of the strongest legal weapons in the common law armoury: it was the basis of a victory in *Ahmed* which should be more well-known, more celebrated than it is, in which the courts struck—in the field of national security—a rare victory for the common law and, through it, the political organs of the constitution. That it played no real role in the *Youssef* litigation shows that the weaknesses of the common law constitution remain intact and, perhaps, that where *Ahmed* is the exception, such weaknesses are the rule. The question which arises, of course, is whether or not that weakness is the fault of the courts.

So far, we have considered three asset-freezing regimes: those under the 2001 and 2010 Acts, and that given effect by secondary legislation under the 1972 Act (perpetuating, effectively that previously given effect by secondary legislation under the United Nations Act 1946). There is a fourth regime, contained in Schedule 7 to the Counter-Terrorism Act 2008, whereby the Treasury may give 'directions' to the financial sector as a whole (or particular

[278] ibid.
[279] *R (Youssef) v Secretary of State for Foreign and Commonwealth Affairs* [2012] EWHC 2091 (Admin), [53].
[280] *Youssef v Secretary of State for Foreign and Commonwealth Affairs* [2013] EWCA Civ 1302, [25].
[281] [2013] EWCA Civ 1302, [26].

persons or category of person operating therein)[282] in relation to non-EEA states where at least one of three conditions is met:

> first, where the "Financial Action Task Force has advised that measures should be taken in relation to the country because of the risk of terrorist financing or money laundering activities" being carried out in or by the country in question;
>
> second, where the Treasury believes that "there is a risk that terrorist financing or money laundering activities are being carried on" in or by the country and that this "poses a significant risk to the national interests of the United Kingdom";
>
> third, where the Treasury reasonably believes that the "development or production of nuclear, radiological, biological or chemical weapons in the country" (or of anything which facilitates such development or production) "poses a significant risk to the national interests of the United Kingdom".[283]

Amongst the requirements which a direction may impose (upon those operating in the financial sector) in relation to transactions or business relationships with a country or those operating in it are: reporting or monitoring requirements, requirements to 'undertake enhanced customer due diligence measures' or, most importantly, to not do (or to cut off) business with the country or those operating in it (either in relation to specific transactions or generally).[284] The requirements imposed by directions must be proportionate to the risk which justifies them.[285] Directions expire a year after being made,[286] and must be contained in an order which, if it is to require persons to limit or cease doing business, must be made under the affirmative procedure.[287] They can be challenged in the High Court on judicial review principles.[288]

In 2009 a direction was made under Schedule 7 requiring all those operating in the financial sector to not do business with two institutions: the Islamic Republic of Iran Shipping Lines and Bank Mellat.[289] The latter, said the accompanying Ministerial statement, had 'provided banking services to a UN listed organisation connected to Iran's proliferation sensitive activities, and been involved in transactions related to financing Iran's nuclear and ballistic missile programme.'[290] This order was quashed by the Supreme Court on both substantive and procedural grounds.[291] As regards the first, it was held by Lord Sumption that 'the distinction between Bank Mellat and other Iranian banks which was at the heart of the case put to Parliament by ministers was an arbitrary and irrational distinction and that the measure as a whole was disproportionate' because 'once it is found that the problem is not specific to Bank Mellat but an inherent risk of banking, the risk posed by Bank Mellat's access to those markets is no different from that posed by the access which comparable

[282] Counter-Terrorism Act 2008, Sch 7, paras 1 and 3.
[283] ibid, para 1(2)–(4).
[284] ibid, paras 10–14.
[285] ibid, para 9(6).
[286] ibid, paras 15(5) and 16(4).
[287] ibid, para 14(2).
[288] CTA 2008, s 63(3).
[289] Financial Restrictions (Iran) Order 2009 (SI 2009/2725).
[290] HC Deb 12 Oct 2009, vol 497 col 2WS.
[291] *Bank Mellat v HM Treasury (No 2)* [2013] UKSC 39.

banks continued to enjoy'.[292] Moreover, the common law duty to give notice and so permit the making of representations applied here, but had not been complied with.[293] The basis of the successful challenge in *Bank Mellat* was reflected in two further and two consecutive directions made under the Schedule 7 power: both were made to all persons operating in the financial sector and directed them not to do (or to cease doing) business with all banks incorporated in Iran, and branches and subsidiaries thereof, wherever located.[294] While the first direction expired automatically in accordance with the 2008 Act, the second order was revoked,[295] equivalent measures having been introduced at the EU level.[296] These events, however, demonstrate the limits of an approach to proportionality founded upon inequality or discrimination. In the early years of the modern national security constitution, when the House of Lords was assessing the proportionality of Part IV of the ATCSA 2001 and the related derogation from the Convention, various of the Law Lords were careful not to give the impression that the disproportionality they identified in the treatment of foreign nationals suspected of involvement in terrorism might be remedied simply by subjecting British nationals to an equivalent regime of indefinite detention. The *Bank Mellat* cases show why they were correct to be fearful of that possibility: an injustice (if that is what it was) is no less unjust because meted out equally to a number of parties.

The most important point to make about the constitutional position of asset-freezing is therefore that it is difficult to establish that position. There are four regimes, which vary along every significant axis, including (but not limited to) the following: the threshold for making use of the relevant powers; their implications for those in respect of whom they are exercised and those whose might deal with such persons; the frequency with which they are used; whether or not they have an international dimension, or are entirely a creation of domestic law. This is not acceptable: such incoherence—even if not deliberate, but merely the consequence of decisions taken for sensible reasons at particular points in time—creates unnecessary obstacles to understanding and, in turn, accountability. Indeed, perhaps the most significant point about the multiplicity of asset-freezing regimes is the fact that only one of the four discussed here falls within the jurisdiction of the Independent Reviewer of Terrorism Legislation.[297] It is not at all clear why that should be so, and the gap in the review of counter-terrorism review means that appropriate consideration of the question of whether or not the various regimes are all necessary does not appear to take place. Notable in this regard is that, almost a year after the EU referendum of 2016 (and a matter of hours before the purdah regime for the 2017 general election kicked in) the government published a consultation paper relating to changes to the sanctions regime which, it argued, would become necessary as a result of the then-impending Brexit process.[298] Though this

[292] [2013] UKSC 39, [37].

[293] [2013] UKSC 39, [38]–[49].

[294] Financial Restrictions (Iran) Order 2011 (SI 2011/2775) and Financial Restrictions (Iran) Order 2012 (SI 2012/2904). Bank Mellat had applied to have both orders set aside, with legal argument focusing upon the extent of disclosure required by Article 6 of the ECHR: See *Bank Mellat v Her Majesty's Treasury (No 4)* [2015] EWCA Civ 1052.

[295] By the Financial Restrictions (Iran) (Revocation) Order 2013/162.

[296] By Council Regulation (EU) No. 1263/2012, amending Regulation (EU) No. 267/2012.

[297] David Anderson, 'The independent review of terrorism legislation' (2011) *EHRLR* 544, 549.

[298] HM government, *Public consultation on the United Kingdom's future legal framework for imposing and implementing sanctions*, Cm 9408 (2017).

is—of course—a shambolic procedure to be adopting, it is evident from the consultation document that the government intends to make use of this opportunity (which might be better deemed a pretext) in order to make substantive alterations to the asset-freezing regime. The effect is likely to be a regime of asset-freezing which is both broader and more complex than the already unedifying picture painted in this section.

VIII. Themes of the Counter-Terrorism Constitution

In this final section, I draw out certain themes of the counter-terrorism constitution as emerges from the consideration of the specific powers which exist within it.

A. The (F)utility of the Common Law

The first point perhaps makes itself, and relates to the general absence of the common law from the picture that has thus far been painted. When resistance emerges to this or that initiative of the state, that resistance is (far) more likely to be grounded in the European Convention of Human Rights than it is in the common law, with its values and principles and standards of review. On one hand, this is easily explained: the common law (still) recognises as its fundamental overarching doctrine the sovereignty of Parliament, and any possible departure from that position will come in a context very far removed from that of national security generally, and counter-terrorism specifically. It is therefore true that a suitably explicit provision of primary legislation will trample over any obstacle the common law might erect. Nevertheless, what is striking in the case law described above is how infrequently it does so. Perhaps the best example of common law principle standing in the way of the government's counter-terrorist efforts is *Ahmed*, where the principle of legality was invoked in holding that the terms of the United Nations Act 1946 were not sufficiently explicit to ground interference with fundamental rights. Even there, however, the government's response was to effectively replicate the impugned secondary legislation with new measures made under the European Communities Act 1972. Though the courts have noted the possibility that that statute might be similarly incapable of providing the requisite authority, nothing has yet been done to give effect to that observation. This is disappointing: if the government believes that certain steps are necessary to counteract the threat of terrorism, it should be willing to make that case to Parliament and request explicit authority to take those steps. If it is unwilling to do so, it is reasonable to question whether the powers in question are truly necessary; though there need not be absolute transparency regarding the nature of the threat, the form of the state's response to that threat should be clearly set out in statute and given Parliament's approval. The courts should insist upon this, always and everywhere, not only because (as is often the case elsewhere) to do so buttresses the political constitution which the executive might wish to sidestep, but because too often in the context of national security it suits political actors to absent themselves; to not know, and not confront, what is being done in their name. Such abdication of responsibility should not be permitted, and the insistence upon the principle of legality and analogous rules of construction ensures that Parliament and its component parts must at least go through the relevant motions and—if they so desire—perhaps even argue on the terrain of substance itself. The requirement of a clear and explicit authority, endorsed within the political process, also provides a hook upon which what I have called elsewhere the informal political constitution might hang its efforts to resist particular measures—the media, the public, and the various NGOs who take an interest in these matters are able to insert themselves into the political process only if such processes in fact take place.

An extension of this point is the general absence within the counter-terrorism constitution (at least as it reaches the appeal courts) of the common law grounds of review. Again, the basic reason for this absence is self-evident: insofar as the relevant rules and regimes are contained within primary legislation, the standard judicial triad of illegality, irrationality and procedural impropriety has no bite. Though the majority of these regimes give considerable authority to the executive to act via orders or secondary legislation, all of which are vulnerable to such review, the varying standard of substantive review which characterises modern administrative law, particularly in combination with an approach to deference which ebbs and flows, will potentially see such measures subjected to only very light review. Nevertheless, the embracing of the proportionality standard where common law fundamental rights are at issue should require the courts to address more directly the implications for individuals of those measures taken in the field of counter-terrorism, and the balance struck by those measures in particular cases. We have seen some examples of this in action: the *Bank Mellat* case, for example, in which the grounds of the successful challenge, both procedural and substantive, were traditional common law grounds. And yet too often, the common law standards are passed over in favour of specifically ECHR/HRA or EU law measures. This is unfortunate, and does not seem to have been reversed to any great degree by the judicial insistence on the priority of the common law which is reflected—by no means exclusively—in the judgment of Lord Reed in *Osborn v Parole Board*.[299] The judgment of the House of Lords in *A v Home Secretary* was treated as representing a historic break in the relations between the courts and executive in the field of national security; there, however, the court identified their right to arrive at the conclusion that it did (in the face of claims that it violated the separation of powers) specifically by reference to the mandate given them by Parliament in the form of the 1998 Act. The true shift, therefore, is represented by cases such as *Ahmed* and *Bank Mellat* in which common law principle is brought to bear by the court on the executive's counter-terrorism efforts. Only when that use of the common law has been normalised—as appears to not yet have happened—then it will be possible to talk of a new era in the relationship between the courts and the executive in the national security constitution.

B. Law's Dialectic: The Domestic Courts and the Strasbourg Courts

The second theme which emerges is the fraught dialectic in which domestic law stands with the Strasbourg Court. As we have seen, in certain areas of the counter-terrorism constitution (and this is equally true of several of the other issues discussed in the present work), the evolution of the counter-terrorism constitution, and the specific forms into which it has

[299] *Osborn v Parole Board* [2013] UKSC 61.

resolved itself over time, is a function of the influence of the ECHR and the decisions of the Strasbourg Court. The picture here is more complicated, however, than one in which the domestic law must simply keep up (or fail to) with the evolving interpretation of the ECHR by the Court of Human Rights. As seen, for example, in the judgment of Lord Reed in *Osborn* mentioned in the previous section, there are three 'bodies' of law operating within the process by which the Convention prompts the evolution of the legal order, and three parties to the process. The first such body is what has become known (misleadingly) as 'domestic' law; that is, all domestic law other than the Human Rights Act 1998. If Lord Reed's injunction is taken seriously, then the first step of any court deciding a question of law should be to determine what will result from the application of 'domestic' law. If what results would be a breach of the ECHR, then the court should consider whether it is appropriate to develop or extend that common law into the gap which it has identified between the domestic status quo and the requirements of the Convention. Only if to do so is, for one reason or another, impossible should the courts apply the Convention on Human Rights in the various manners in which the Human Rights Act requires or permits them to do so. And in deciding what are the requirements of the Convention, the courts appear to have stepped back from the strict and inflexible approach of keeping pace with Strasbourg—'no more but certainly no less'—articulated in *Ullah*.[300] Instead, there exists the possibility that they will interpret it as requiring something less than what Strasbōurg has asserted that it does (though only in exceptional circumstances, where Strasbourg has—for example—made a decision 'inconsistent with some fundamental substantive or procedural aspect of our law')[301] or that the domestic courts will continue the logical progression of the Strasbourg jurisprudence beyond where that body has as yet had the opportunity to do so. Given that the Convention sounds also (in fact primarily) in international law, the domestic courts' understanding of what it requires in some given situation is subject to the possibility that the Strasbourg Court will disagree, and that there will therefore arise in international law an obligation on the UK to 'abide by the final judgment of the Court in any case to which they are parties'. In many cases, it will do so by legislating to bring 'domestic' law into conformity with the Convention, or making use of the procedure found in section 10 of the Human Rights Act.

There are therefore three parties—the domestic courts, the domestic legislature, and the Strasbourg Court—and three legal regimes—'domestic law', the Convention as interpreted by the domestic courts, and as interpreted by Strasbourg—at play. The overall effect is to create a complex and fast-moving evolutionary dynamic which has been particularly evident in the context of counter-terrorism; far greater, it must be noted, than before the transposition of the ECHR into domestic law, when the dialectic involved only 'domestic' law and the Strasbourg Court's interpretation of the Convention. Though the dialectic does not always operate in the same direction, the general tendency is towards a greater level of individual liberty (and, conversely, restraint on the state), which has worked to shape the counter-terrorism constitution in a number of ways—most obviously the shift away from detention pending deportation and the specific form of the controls orders (and later

[300] *R (Ullah) v Special Adjudicator* [2004] UKHL 26. See the discussion in R Masterman, 'Deconstructing the Mirror Principle' in R Masterman and I Leigh (eds) *The United Kingdom's Statutory Bill of Rights: Constitutional and Comparative Perspectives* (Oxford, Oxford University Press, 2013).

[301] *Manchester City Council v Pinnock* [2010] UKSC 45, [48].

TPIMs) which replaced it. Nevertheless, here as elsewhere we see the limits of legal control upon national security measures. The nature of the endeavour, the fact that it reflects a body of knowledge and expertise possessed by the courts rather than the executive—all this means that it will usually be easier to challenge measures taken on national security grounds from a formal rather than a substantive point of view. It is striking from this point of view that the most significant substantive victory of (or achieved through) the courts was one in a case—the *Belmarsh* case—where the disproportionality derived not from a failure of evidence as to what was and was not required by the exigencies of security, but rather to a logical incoherence visible on the face, as it were, of the 2001 Act. This in turn suggests something about the interconnection between legal and political constitutional processes: a measure which did not share this incoherence may or may not have been compatible with the Convention, but to enact it in law—to constitute indefinite detention without trial as a national security rather than an immigration measure—would have been politically difficult and perhaps impossible.

C. The Role of the Independent Reviewer of Terrorism Legislation

The final point to be made is one which is (mostly) specific to the counter-terrorism constitution, and relates to the role in this area of the Independent Reviewer of Terrorism Legislation, whose reports have been cited numerous times in this chapter and who offers a particularly effective form of oversight for the content of (and use made of) counter-terrorism law.[302] The IRTL is a form of 'hybrid' institution,[303] one which marries features of both legal and political institutions so as to perform a role for which neither the courts nor Parliament (the paradigm of legal and political institutions respectively) are suited; such institutions are often found in areas in which—as a previous IRTL has noted in relation to the reviewer's work—'potential conflicts between state power and civil liberties are acute, but information is tightly rationed.'[304] That is, the IRTL is a legally-qualified figure, with

[302] The position of the IRTL derives from an observation made by Lord Jellicoe in one of the ad hoc reports on the terrorism legislation, in which he observed that the debates on renewal which took place annually had not usually enjoyed the necessary Parliamentary time and recommended a move to a full periodic re-enactment. The government instead instituted an annual review by an independent reviewer—some who was not a judge but 'a person whose reputation would lend authority to his conclusions, because some of the information that led him to his conclusions would not be published.' The review was not of the substance of the law as such, but rather 'the use made of the statutory powers relating to terrorism': quoted in David Anderson QC, 'The Independent Review of Terrorism Laws' [2014] *PL* 403, 405–6. The reviewers were, in turn, Sir Cyril Phillips, Viscount Colville QC and John Rowe QC (406). The next reviewer, Lord Carlile of Berriew QC, was famously asked to take up the role on the morning of September 11 2001, shortly before the planes hit the World Trade Centre in New York and the UK, like the US, entered a new national security era. See also J Blackbourn, 'Independent Reviewers as Alternative; an Empirical Study from Australia and the UK' in FF Davis and F de Londras (eds), *Critical Debates on Counter-Terrorism Judicial Review* (Cambridge, Cambridge University Press, 2014).

[303] Another institution which might be so categorised is the Joint Committee on Human Rights, which considers (a subset of) legal issues but within the political process. It too has been prominent in this area of policy: see, eg, A Tomkins, 'Parliament, human rights and counter-terrorism' in T Campbell, KD Ewing, and A Tomkins (eds) *The Legal Protection of Human Rights: Sceptical Essays* (Oxford, Oxford University Press, 2011), and A Kavanagh, 'The Joint Committee on Human Rights: A Hybrid Breed of Constitutional Watchdog' in M Hunt, H Hooper and P Yowell (eds), *Parliaments and Human Rights: Redressing the Democratic Deficit* (Oxford, Hart Publishing, 2015).

[304] Anderson (n 302) 421. Other institutions of this sort include the various Commissioners who have worked in the field of investigatory powers (now replaced by a single Investigatory Powers Commissioner under the Investigatory Powers Act 2016).

access to security cleared material, required to produce annual reports on the operation of certain counter-terrorism statutes (in the round, rather than in the context of specific uses of the relevant powers, as would be the case for a court), but possessed also of a 'roving' jurisdiction which distinguishes him (the IRTL has always been a man) even further from the role played by courts in our (adversarial) system. As a former holder of the post has noted:

> By accepting review of this kind, Ministers make it harder for themselves to use the age-old brush-off: "If you had seen what I have seen …". The Independent Reviewer *has* seen what they have seen and, unconstrained by the disciplines or loyalties of office, has every reason—unless he has gone rogue or gone native—to tell it as it is.[305]

This is not to say that the role is without its flaws. The most important, perhaps, is that there is—in law—no such thing as the IRTL, but rather a series of statutes which require that there takes place independent review of particular frameworks (not necessarily by the same person) and a person appointed (contingently, rather than out of legal obligation) to carry out not only those reviews, but others which might appear necessary.[306] One result of this is that there the IRTL is owed no duty of cooperation by those who possess relevant information (as is the case, for example, with the various Commissioners which have existed and exist under the investigatory powers and intelligence services legislation).[307] Nor, for the same reason, is there any statutory security of tenure of a sort which those Commissioners (sometimes) enjoy, nor requirement that the individual who carries out the review enjoy any particular level of legal experience (even if in practice the role has always been carried out by an eminent legal figure).

Another important limit on the effectiveness of the role is that its scope is fundamentally incoherent: not only does it not cover all of the relevant legislation, but distinctions are implicitly drawn between related powers, so that—to take only the most grievous anomaly—there is a requirement of independent review of the asset-freezing regime under TAFA 2010, but not of those under ATCSA 2001, or the CTA 2008. The reviewer may also produce reports other than those required by statute (whether 'at the request of the Secretary of State or on the reviewer's own initiative'); though reports of this sort have 'invariably been laid before Parliament' there is no requirement that this happen.[308] Appointment to the role was previously by the Home Office and took place on an informal (and 'indefensible') basis;[309] the Home Office must therefore have enjoyed the ability to choose a candidate it considered to be relatively sympathetic to the counter-terrorism efforts of the state. The situation has changed somewhat with the classification of the IRTL as a public

305 Anderson (n 302) 403.

306 Albeit that now the role of IRTL is acknowledged by the order in council which classified it as a public appointment (on which see below).

307 See, eg, IPA 2016, ss 235(2)–(7). David Anderson QC noted that he 'has experienced no attempt to deny access to sensitive material, and no attempt to control or to monitor the range of people to whom he speaks' and that '[w]ere any such attempt to be made, it could be effectively met by recording it (or threatening to record it) in a report which the Secretary of State is under a statutory duty to lay before Parliament, and which—particularly if it is critical—may well be of interest to the media.' David Anderson QC, 'The independent review of terrorism legislation' (2011) *EHRLR* 544, 548.

308 Anderson (n 307) 545.

309 Anderson (n 302) 410. See also Anderson (n 307) 548: the role is 'in the sole gift of the Home Secretary; and other than the bald requirement that the reviewer be independent, there are no statutory limits on her discretion.'

appointment, meaning that the process now sees 'a panel … draw up a list of appointable candidates by an open, fair and merit-based process, from which Ministers will choose.'[310] This move does not, of course, exclude the possibility of such considerations factoring into the decision-making process at the final stage, and the possibility of unilateral renewal of the IRTL's position leaves open the possibility—identified in relation to the prior method of appointment—that 'a reviewer might be perceived to be influenced by the desire to be appointed to a second term'; no method of appointment or reappointment would suffice however to counter the related danger that the fulfilment of the role might be influenced by 'the desire for additional preferment once the term of office is complete.'[311]

Nevertheless, the IRTL has been a uniquely well-informed and consistently high-quality observer of, and commentator on, the counter-terrorism landscape (and, later, also on questions of investigatory powers) without which the scope for achieving oversight of the content of the state's counter-terrorism powers, and accountability for the use to which they are put, would be greatly diminished. As to the ability of the IRTL to make a practical difference to the shape of the counter-terrorism constitution, however, empirical consideration of the point suggests that the reviewer's recommendations are significantly more likely to be adopted where they involve the preservation of the status quo, indicating—perhaps—the limits of even the most well-informed and conscientious party's ability to influence such matters.[312] This is not, though, in any sense an indication of the role's futility: in a parliamentary democracy it is inevitable that political processes will be the ultimate determiner of policy—as much on matters counter-terrorism as on anything else—and if that involves the rejection of the recommendations made by the IRTL, then so be it; better that the recommendations are rejected than that they are never made at all. The political constitution is stronger for it.

IX. Conclusion

More than 15 years after the attacks of 11 September 2001, the counter-terrorism constitution has—in its core form—taken on a number of distinctive characteristics. The first is that it reflects, inevitably but strikingly, the changed character of the apprehended terrorist threat, not only by incorporating where it previously did not a concern for international issues (and so contributing to a theme we will have cause to examine at length in Chapter 7), but in often allowing that concern to eclipse the forms of terrorism with which it—until not so long ago—concerned itself uniquely. The second, a continuation though not a consequence of this first, is the interplay of the domestic and the international regimes in determining the evolution of the counter-terrorism regimes. At crucial moments the body of international norms incorporated into domestic law by the Human Rights Act has been employed to condemn key planks of the legislative response to terrorism; at others, it has been the international apparatus which oversees those norms which

[310] Anderson (n 302) 410.

[311] Anderson (n 307) 548.

[312] Jessie Blackbourn, 'Evaluating the Independent Reviewer of Terrorism Legislation' (2014) 67 *Parliamentary Affairs* 955.

has made that call when the domestic courts would not or could not. The point should not be overstated, however: the replacement of control orders with TPIMs considered above, was not prompted by anything said or done by the European Court of Human Rights, but by the ebb and flow of domestic politics, which continues to take place within a loose, flexible, and unpredictable framework whose mark the law will often bear more clearly than it will any sort of legal (or rationalist, or technocratic) influence. Third, we might divide the counter-terrorist constitution into two layers. On the upper layer sit those grand set-pieces of the counter-terrorism landscape: indefinite detention pending deportation, control orders, TPIMs. Such mechanisms, though they may well be necessary at the time of their implementation (or at least honestly and reasonably believed to be) are as much political gestures as anything else, a way by which the state signals that it takes seriously the threat the public apprehends and will push the boundaries of legality, practicality, perhaps morality, in responding to it. Whatever the proximate cause of their demise, several of these mechanisms have been reasonably short-lived, and yet it seems unlikely that the threat to which they responded was in each case so transient as to justify their introduction at one point in time and yet have faded away (in law, or as a matter of practice) so soon afterwards. On the lower level sit those mechanisms which, reflecting the essential rather than contingent elements of the threat of terrorism, are more long-term, more stable, than those which are more likely catch the attention of the eye of the public and the superior courts. In seeking to understand the counter-terrorism constitution, we must be as attentive to this lower layer as to its upper counterpart. And in seeking to understand the national security constitution as a single phenomenon, we must move beyond counter-terrorism altogether. We do so now through a consideration of the state's investigatory powers.

2

Investigatory Powers and the Constitution

I. The Constitution and Investigatory Powers

The body of law addressed in the first chapter is that which concerns national security most directly. Like the acts which it seeks to prevent or to punish, counter-terrorism law is high-profile and dramatic, liable to capture the public imagination and the interest of the press. From a purely quantitative perspective, however, such powers pale into something approaching insignificance when compared to the day to day use of the investigatory powers now provided for, mostly, by the Investigatory Powers Act 2016. This chapter addresses these powers insofar as they speak to questions of national security, considering in particular the powers to intercept communications and acquire communications data, and powers relating to what are known as bulk personal datasets, both before and after the enactment of the 2016 Act. In doing so, the chapter speaks to certain fundamental constitutional themes, both historic and contemporary. Amongst these are the common law's approach to the rule of law and its implications for the way in which powers of investigation must be regulated; the influence, particularly acute in this area, of the European Convention on Human Rights (ECHR) and its evolving doctrine; the division of labour as between judicial and ministerial figures; the balancing of political and legal mechanisms of accountability; the distinction which the relevant law draws—at times only implicitly—between what the state does at home and what it does abroad, or to citizens at home versus those abroad; the relationship between the state and its citizens, and the way in which broad powers of data collection and retention threaten to reshape that. Relevant also, however, is the question of secrecy[1]—many of the difficulties associated with securing accountability for the use of the powers discussed in this chapter derive from the fact that in order to be effective (so we are told), the specific capabilities of the state must, like the particular manner in which they are used, remain secret. Nevertheless, it has become clear—in part as a result of the Snowden disclosures of 2013—that too much was kept secret; that in certain cases investigatory powers were derived from statutory provisions sufficiently ambiguous or obscure that the practices allegedly authorised by them were effectively secret, with no possibility of legal or political accountability for their use. Viewed from a generally constitutional point of view—rather than viewed, as it as often is, through the specific lens of privacy—the regulation of investigatory powers in the UK reveals itself to be a mix of the

[1] On which see principally Ch 5.

good and the bad. Though there has been, by virtue of the 2016 Act, a significant expansion of the statutory powers available to the executive—in particular the making available of so-called 'bulk' powers—that statute in part codifies and in part makes manifest practices which were already taking place. To that extent, it must be welcomed. Nevertheless, there remains excessive fragmentation of investigatory power, while several of the bulk powers (including those which must count as most intrusive) are, by virtue of their 'foreign focus', probably beyond the reach of the ECHR and so subject to only those relatively few restrictions imposed by the 'domestic' constitutional order.

In considering investigatory powers, I focus in particular upon the following questions: the nature of the powers (as in what actions they permit); their scope (in terms of which bodies can exercise them, and for what purposes); the identity of those who can permit their use; the breadth of the powers (whether 'targeted', 'thematic' or 'bulk'); whether they are 'foreign-focused' (in that they are unavailable in relation to persons or property in the British Islands,[2] or communications which are 'internal', in that they are both sent or received from a place outside of those Islands); whether material collected is subject to limits upon its examination, and what those limits are. One further distinction is crucial in making sense of the law which applies in this area and its evolution: that between content and metadata. Though the latter is reflected in a number of separate legal concepts, the basic distinction can be made with reference to the classic case of interception of a telephone call: the words spoken are the content; the details as to the numbers the call was made from and to, and how long it lasted, are examples of metadata. The basic approach, we shall see below, has long been that of treating the collection of metadata as being less intrusive than is the interception of communications—and so available to a wider range of bodies, under less restrictive conditions. Three developments regarding metadata are worth highlighting already at this stage: first, the evolution of the specific legal concepts used to identify metadata, and consequent shifting of the content/metadata boundary; second, the imposition of obligations on private bodies to generate and retain metadata which they would not otherwise possess, in order that it might be later acquired for investigatory purposes; third, the progressive challenging of the implied hierarchy whereby metadata is presumed—even in an era of ubiquitous electronic communications—to be less intrusive than is the interception of communications, particularly given the possibility of quickly and accurately aggregating such data.[3] In relation to the last of these developments, it suffices for now to note that—as stated by a former Director of the National Security Agency—'[w]e kill people based on metadata'.[4] Except for the occasional drawing of a contrast with investigatory powers of national security relevance, I do not here address the powers of the

[2] The usual formulation employed in this context. By virtue of the Interpretation Act 1978, Sch 1, this term refers to 'the United Kingdom, the Channel Islands and the Isle of Man.'

[3] See, eg, (in the American context) SM Bellovin, M Blaze, S Landau and SK Pel, 'It's Too Complicated: How The Internet Upends Katz, Smith, And Electronic Surveillance Law' (2016) 30 *Harvard Journal of Law & Technology* 1, 2: 'In this digitized, Internet Protocol ("IP")-based communications environment, the once stable legal distinction between content and non-content has steadily eroded to the point of collapse …'. See also, Nóra Ni Loideain, 'EU Law and Mass Internet Metadata Surveillance in the post-Snowden era' (2015) 3 *Media and Communications* 53, 54–5.

[4] Quoted in Ni Loideain (n 3) 54. The 'we' is of course the United States—as discussed in Chs 3 and 7, however, it should not be assumed that US efforts on this front take place entirely without the involvement of the UK.

'ordinary' police,[5] though these of course might also be relevant to national security ends given that, as we have seen, the criminal law has been one tool amongst many by which the threat of terrorism has been addressed in recent decades. Nor do I address in detail the powers of surveillance (whether 'directed' or 'intrusive')[6] or the use of 'covert human intelligence sources'[7] (both regulated under Part II of the Regulation of Investigatory Powers Act 2000), though both are available for the purpose, amongst many others, of protecting national security.

II. The Rule(s) of Law

The nature of national security law is such that it is in practice very difficult for any actor—courts, Parliament, NGOs—to challenge executive claims as to what substantive powers are necessary. For that reason, the formal elements of the relevant powers, those which fall most obviously under the heading of the rule of law, are generally the most direct focus of legal challenge. Here, I consider the common law rule of law, and the manner in which the presence in domestic law of the European Convention on Human Rights complicates that issue.

A. The Common Law Rule of Law and its Limits

The approach to the regulation of investigatory powers in the UK (to use the term anachronistically) has always been heavily influenced by the common law's approach to the rule of law, whereby the executive must have authority for any of its actions which interfere with the legal rights—as recognised in public or private law—of the individual. Usually identified as authority for this proposition is *Entick v Carrington*,[8] in which the search and seizure of John Entick's property by the King's messengers was held unlawful because no legal authority for the issue of a warrant for seditious libel could be identified. This places public authorities in the same basic position as private individuals, justifying to that extent Dicey's insistence that the rule of law—which in his understanding required the legal equality of public and private actors—was achieved in England, even if Dicey failed to account for

[5] Alongside the Regulation of Investigatory Powers Act 2000 and the Investigatory Powers Act 2016 (both discussed in this chapter) see the Police and Criminal Evidence Act 1984 and the Police Act 1997. It emerged, at the time of the recent reform of the law of investigatory powers that the 1997 Act, enacted in response to the decision of the House of Lords in *R v Khan* [1996] 3 All ER 289, was being used to authorise 'computer network exploitation' (or 'hacking' or, now, 'equipment interference') by the police. That possibility is now limited—though not entirely extinguished—by s 14 of the 2016 Act.

[6] See the Regulation of Investigatory Powers Act 2000, Pt II and the Covert Surveillance and Property Interference Code of Practice (December 2014).

[7] See the Regulation of Investigatory Powers Act 2000, Pt II and the Covert Human Intelligence Sources Code of Practice (December 2014).

[8] *Entick v Carrington* (1765) 2 Wils 275, (1765) 19 St Tr 1029, and P Scott, '*Entick v Carrington* and the Legal Protection of Property', in A Tomkins and P Scott (eds), *Entick v Carrington: 250 Years of the Rule of Law* (Oxford, Hart Publishing, 2015).

those special immunities of which the Crown could avail itself.[9] To this bare requirement of legality, the common law routinely adds, in the context of certain rights and principles recognised as fundamental, a further requirement that the statutory authority be suitably unambiguous—a requirement reflected by Lord Camden's comment that, in relation to the interference with Entick's property which had taken place, 'one should naturally expect that the law to warrant it should be clear in proportion as the power is exorbitant'[10]—in order that the courts can be certain that the implications of the statutory power for those fundamental rights were fully understood by the Parliament which enacted them, and endorsed upon that basis.[11] Legal accountability in this way bolsters the constitution's processes of political accountability in a way that the dichotomisation of political and legal decision-making in recent years has often obscured.[12]

The converse of the claim that legal authority is required where an interference with legal rights takes place is, of course, that where there is no such interference, there is no requirement of legal authority.[13] Within the requirement of legality, there therefore exists a triggering condition, whereby legal authority must be identified if and only if the act being done constitutes an interference with the legally protected interest of the individual.[14] This requires an understanding of what constitutes an interference, a point upon which considerable uncertainty is betrayed by the variety of formulations used in the literature: some talk of plain, unqualified 'interference', others of 'wrongful', 'coercive', or 'tortious' interference. Some use instead the language of the executive acting 'unlawfully'. Part of the linguistic confusion stems from the fact that two separate phenomena are being addressed by these formulations, which differ in important respects. One is where the executive uses its legal powers to change the normative legal position of a private individual by, for example, entering into a contract—whether of, say, sale or employment—with that individual. The other is where the individual has a prima facie negative right against interference by public authorities—whether recognised in private law, as in *Entick*, or in public law, as is the case for an increasing range of interests—and the legal authority is an authority which allows the public authority in question to overcome that prima facie restriction on its acting.

The (ultimately unsuccessful) attempt to identify the necessary legal authority for the grant of a search warrant in *Entick* gives a second, partly subsidiary but also more wide-reaching, example of the common law's commitment to the rule of law. One of the bases identified in argument before Lord Camden, Chief Justice of the Common Pleas, for the existence of the power to issue warrants for search and seizure of seditious material was that it was 'necessary for the ends of government to lodge such a power with a state officer.'[15] To this Camden replied that 'the common law does not understand that kind of reasoning,'

[9] AV Dicey, *Introduction to the Study of the Law of the Constitution*, 8th edn (Indianapolis, Liberty Fund, 1982) 114. Elements of those immunities are considered in Chs 3 and 6.

[10] (1765) 19 St Tr 1029, 1065–6. Some of these points I have already made in Paul F Scott, 'General Warrants, Thematic Warrants, Bulk Warrants: Property Interference for National Security Purposes' (2017) 68 *NILQ* 99.

[11] *R v Secretary of State for the Home Department, ex parte Simms* [2000] 2 AC 115, 131.

[12] A point made in *Simms* itself: 'the principle of legality means that Parliament must squarely confront what it is doing and accept the political cost.' [2000] 2 AC 115, 131.

[13] See, most famously, *Malone v Commissioner of Police of the Metropolis (No.2)* [1979] Ch 344.

[14] For discussion of this point, see Scott (n 8), as well as the chapters by Tomkins and Endicott in the same volume.

[15] (1765) 19 St Tr 1029, 1073.

noting also that the constitutional battles of the seventeenth century had seen such claims rejected by the ultimately victorious Parliamentary side, with the judges who decided the *Case of the Ship-Money* 'impeached for holding, first, that state-necessity would justify the raising money without consent of parliament; and secondly, that the king was judge of that necessity.'[16] Understood in its strongest form—as the claim that the law does not vary with the needs of the state, amongst which we would now number prominently those of national security—this rejection by Lord Camden of the state necessity argument exemplifies a second way of understanding the common law's commitment to the rule of law, over and above the requirement of legality with which *Entick* is most strongly associated.

A third theme from *Entick* is also relevant to the modern constitutional position of investigatory powers. In *Entick*, the warrant issued by Lord Halifax named the individual at whom it was directed. Other cases decided in the same period and raising the same issues, however, were centred on warrants which were general, in the sense of failing to identify the specific individuals to whom they related and instead, typically, citing only the 'authors, printers, or publishers' of some allegedly seditious publication.[17] Such general warrants are problematic in that they require those executing the warrants—rather than the person issuing it—to decide for themselves whether or not there exists sufficient evidence against particular individuals to justify executing the warrant.[18] This means that the issuing authority—in the case of the warrants in question here, a Minister rather than a judge—is not him or herself required to assess the weight of evidence against any particular individual or individuals. But warrants of the sort at issue in *Entick* and the various cases related to it are general also in a second sense, in that they justify interferences with property which is unrelated to the criminal wrong, the doing of which is the basis of the warrant's very existence. In *Entick*, the point is made by Lord Camden in the following terms:

> Nor is there pretence to say, that the word "papers" here mentioned ought in point of law to be restrained to the libellous papers only. The word is general, and there is nothing in the warrant to confine it; nay, I am able to affirm, that it has been upon a late occasion executed in its utmost latitude: for in the case of Wilkes against Wood, when the messengers hesitated about taking all the manuscripts, and sent to the secretary of state for more express orders for that purpose, the answer was, "that all must be taken, manuscripts and all." Accordingly, all was taken, and Mr. Wilkes's private pocket-book filled up the mouth of the sack.[19]

Both forms of generality are at issue in the modern regulation of investigatory powers, though to the extent that general powers are clearly and explicitly authorised by statute, there is of course no violation of the rule(s) in *Entick*.

Two final points: first, in the general warrants cases that the warrants at issue were given by Lord Halifax, one of the King's ministers. If there had been a legal basis for the warrant

[16] (1765) 19 St Tr 1029, 1073.

[17] See *Wilkes v Wood* (1763) Lofft 1, 98 ER 489 and *Money v Leach* (1765) 1 Bl 555, 96 ER 320.

[18] See on this point Lord Mansfield's observation in *Money v Leach* 96 ER 320, 323, that 'it is not fit, either upon reasons of policy or sound construction of law, that, where a man's being confined depends on an information given, it should be left to the officer to ascertain the person.' See also Blackstone, *Commentaries on the Laws of England*, IV, 288: 'A *general* warrant to apprehend all persons suspected, without naming or particularly describing any person in special, is illegal and void for it's uncertainty; for it is the duty of the magistrate, and ought not to be left to the officer, to judge of the ground of suspicion.'

[19] (1765) 19 St Tr 1029, 1065.

in question, this lack of independence would have caused no further difficulty and much modern national security law continues to afford the right to grant warrants permitting highly intrusive acts to executive rather than judicial actors. One question to which we must pay attention is the extent to which that practice—which differs from the position in relation to ordinary search warrants[20]—is now legally problematic in a way which it would not have been in late eighteenth-century England. Second, the general warrants cases repeatedly reaffirm, with great eloquence, the importance of one's private papers, which are seen almost as a window into the soul, and so worthy of the highest protection which the law might offer. It is therefore striking that many of the powers discussed here would seem by any standard to be even more intrusive than is the search and seizure of one's papers in late eighteenth-century England. This is potentially true not only of powers to intercept communications, but also of at least some powers relating to metadata, particularly that generated by a mobile phone which one carries with oneself at all times, betraying one's location, one's habits, the identities of one's contacts and so on.[21]

B. The ECHR Dimension

Entick v Carrington captures certain key themes of the common law rule of law which have not merely remained relevant to the modern regime of investigatory powers, but which in fact become increasingly relevant in the context of the process by which such powers have become (have been forced to become) more explicit and more expansive in recent years. As an understanding of the rule of law which coexists with the doctrine of parliamentary sovereignty, however, and the traditionally limited recognition by the common law of individual rights beyond those necessary for the functioning of a system of commodity exchange, the common law's ability to protect against executive power has often been limited. Much of that limitation was overcome with the enactment of the Human Rights Act, transposing a number of the rights under the European Convention on Human Rights into domestic law. Now, it is unlawful for public authorities to act incompatibly with the Convention Rights thus transposed,[22] which will in most cases be the case where an interference with such a right lacks a suitable legal basis. Crucially, amongst these rights is a right to a private and family life of a sort which the common law did not traditionally recognise and in whose absence it became necessary (as in *Entick*) to protect the right to privacy via the right to property, recognised not (as would now often be the case) as a freestanding and overarching public law right but as one of those private law rights which, in accordance with the Diceyan account of the rule of law, can be enforced equally as against public actors.[23] With the introduction of the Human Rights Act, therefore, domestic courts were required to consider the detail of investigatory powers in far greater detail than had previously been the case.

[20] Under, most importantly, the Police and Criminal Evidence Act 1984.

[21] See, making that case at length, SB Wicker, *Cellular Convergence and the Death of Privacy* (Oxford, Oxford University Press, 2013).

[22] Human Rights Act 1998, s 6.

[23] Dicey (n 9) 114.

Article 8 of the ECHR protects the right to 'private and family life, his home and his correspondence'. Much if not all surveillance activity will therefore represent an interference with the right(s) protected thereunder. The basic rule, as with other interferences with Article 8 (and indeed the other qualified rights), is that to be compatible with the Convention, the interference must then be justified: it must take place 'in accordance with the law', in pursuit of one of the specified legitimate aims ('the interests of national security, public safety or the economic well-being of the country … the prevention of disorder or crime … the protection of health or morals … the protection of the rights and freedoms of others') and the interference must be 'necessary in a democratic society'. It is this third requirement—interpreted as imposing a requirement of proportionality—which does most of the work in the ordinary Article 8 case law. This is not the case where investigatory powers are concerned. Instead, much of the case law turns on the compatibility of the surveillance regime with the 'in accordance with the law' requirement, which is understood as imposing not only a requirement that the interference have a basis in domestic law, but also the requirements that the law be 'accessible' and the interference 'foreseeable'.[24] In the specific context of secret surveillance, the Court of Human Rights recognises that this 'cannot mean that an individual should be able to foresee when the authorities are likely to intercept his communications so that he can adapt his conduct accordingly'.[25] Nevertheless, the risks of arbitrariness in the exercise of powers are heightened where the exercise of those powers is secret, and so 'domestic law must be sufficiently clear in its terms to give citizens an adequate indication as to the circumstances in which and the conditions on which public authorities are empowered to resort to any such measures.'[26]

In addition, the court emphasises—using the language of the rule of law—the need to ensure that those who exercise secret powers do not enjoy an unfettered discretion and, therefore, requires that the relevant domestic law 'indicate the scope of any such discretion conferred on the competent authorities and the manner of its exercise with sufficient clarity to give the individual adequate protection against arbitrary interference.'[27] In the leading case on the matter—*Weber and Saravia v Germany*, from which these dicta are taken—the Court identified six factors which constitute 'minimum safeguards' and which the relevant law must identify if the individual is to be adequately protected against the possibility of arbitrary interference. These are, in language reflecting the context—interception of communications—in which they were made:

> the nature of the offences which may give rise to an interception order; a definition of the categories of people liable to have their telephones tapped; a limit on the duration of telephone tapping; the procedure to be followed for examining, using and storing the data obtained; the precautions to be taken when communicating the data to other parties; and the circumstances in which recordings may or must be erased or the tapes destroyed.[28]

[24] In a classic formulation of the requirements the first means that 'the citizen must be able to have an indication that is adequate in the circumstances of the legal rules applicable to a given case'; the second implies that 'a norm cannot be regarded as a "law" unless it is formulated with sufficient precision to enable the citizen to regulate his conduct: he must be able—if need be with appropriate advice—to foresee, to a degree that is reasonable in the circumstances, the consequences which a given action may entail.' *Sunday Times v The United Kingdom* [1979] ECHR 1, [49].

[25] *Weber and Saravia v Germany* (2008) 46 EHRR SE5, [93].

[26] (2008) 46 EHRR SE5, [93].

[27] ibid, [94].

[28] ibid, [95].

Though the case law is not always unambiguous on the matter, the same requirements apply to circumstances in which the interference does not involve the interception of (the contents of) communications but only the acquisition of metadata: information about the communication other than its contents.[29] This contrasts with the domestic law position, which has always reflected a hierarchy within which the possibility of acquiring communications data is recognised to a far wider range of parties than is that of intercepting communications, and the requirements which must be met in order to do so lawfully are far less stringent. The *Weber* requirements would also seem to apply equally regardless of whether the communication is 'internal' (both the sending and receiving parties are inside the state) or 'external' (only one party is inside the state and the other is outside it). No jurisprudence of the Strasbourg Court exists on the application of the Convention to wholly external communications (where both sending and receiving parties are outside the territory of the state whose authorities carry out the interception) though such a situation raises immediately the question of whether the individuals in question are within the jurisdiction of the High Contracting Party for the purposes of its Article 1 obligation to 'secure to' them the Convention rights.[30] Finally, the *Weber* requirements appear to apply equally to powers which are (in the contemporary terminology) 'targeted' (aimed at a person or specified category of persons) and those which are 'bulk' (aimed at a large number of people many of whom are understood to be of no interest, actual or potential, to the security services). Though the majority of the bulk powers in the UK have a 'foreign focus' (in that they relate to external communications or to persons or property located outside of the jurisdiction), not all do. As things stand, therefore, it is at the stage of determining the proportionality of interference that the bulk nature of the powers will be factored in to the question of compatibility with the ECHR.

There are, however, suggestions in more recent case law of the Strasbourg Court that more demanding requirements might be imposed: that it may be the case that an authorisation must identify the specific persons whose communications are to be intercepted,[31] and that the authority which grants it 'must be capable of verifying the existence of a reasonable suspicion against the person subject to surveillance measures'.[32] If these are—or become—general requirements which surveillance measures must meet if they are to be compatible with Article 8, many of the powers discussed below will likely fall foul of them.

[29] Though *cf Malone v United Kingdom*, suggesting a distinction between interception and 'metering' of telephone calls: (1984) 7 EHRR 14, [84].

[30] The Investigatory Powers Tribunal has held that 'a contracting state owes no obligation under Article 8 to persons both of whom are situated outside its territory in respect of electronic communications between them which pass through that state.' *Human Rights Watch v Secretary of State for Foreign and Commonwealth Affairs* [2016] UKIPTrib15_165-CH, [60]. Nor was the argument that persons in other Convention states within the UK's jurisdiction (based upon the 'espace juridique' line of reasoning employed by the Strasbourg Court) successful: 'This contention, if correct, would radically alter the nature of the obligation undertaken by a contracting state: it would impose an obligation in respect of all persons within the jurisdiction of any contracting state. Such a construction of Article 1 would go well beyond any conceivable construction permitted by public international law and is inconsistent with the careful incremental approach of the ECtHR, when dealing with issues which may not have been fully foreseen by those who negotiated the Convention.' ([55]). For discussion, see L Raible, 'Human Rights Watch v Secretary of State for the Foreign and Commonwealth Office: Victim status, extraterritoriality and the search for principled reasoning' (2017) 80 *MLR* 510. This topic is discussed in Ch 3, in another context.

[31] *Zakharov v Russia* (2016) 63 EHRR 17, [264].

[32] ibid, [260].

Alongside these emergent requirements (if that is what they are) which apply primarily to bulk powers, the Court has also suggested that the party authorising the use of surveillance measures may require a certain level of independence from the executive and, though the party in question need not be a judicial actor, supervision of their use by a 'politically responsible member of the executive, such as the Minister of Justice, does not provide the necessary guarantees' of independence.[33] Though this was a finding not of the Grand Chamber but a mere Chamber of the Court, and though it was made in the context of bulk powers, it is a requirement which—again, assuming its development and wider adoption within the jurisprudence of the Court—would be incompatible with regimes of investigatory powers as they have traditionally existed in Britain, whether bulk or targeted. It is perhaps not surprising, therefore, that the Investigatory Powers Act 2016 seeks to pre-empt any such development by introducing a judicial role into aspects of the regime where one was previously lacking, in the form of the 'double lock' discussed below.

III. Investigatory Powers

Against that background of the common law and ECHR, I consider here the constitutional issues raised by three sets of powers: those relating to the interception of communications, those relating to the acquisition of communications data, and those relating to the retention and use of 'bulk personal datasets'.[34] The first two powers exist (now unambiguously, but not newly) in both 'targeted' and 'bulk' forms. The first category describes powers in relation to which the person or property against whom they are to be used must be specified in the warrant authorising them. The degree of specification required, however, is variable and at times contested: in certain cases, the bar is sufficiently low that the powers are better conceptualised as being 'thematic', in that the specific persons or property need not be identified by name, but can be described by reference, for example, to some category to which they belong. Bulk powers are those which can be used (subject to requirements of, for example, necessity and proportionality) against groups of persons some of whom are of no interest to the investigating bodies. Material acquired by virtue of bulk powers is, in light of this, usually subject to limits on its examination; limits which prevent them from being used in order to bypass the additional requirements of specification which apply to the use of targeted powers. The final set of powers—relating to 'bulk personal datasets'—by definition exist only in a bulk form.

A. Interception of Communications

The interception of communications has by far the longest history of the powers considered herein, but that history is unedifying, serving as a case study of the secrecy, offences against

[33] *Szabó and Vissy v Hungary* (2016) 63 EHRR 3, [77].

[34] A fourth set of powers—relating to 'equipment interference', including what we would normally call 'hacking'—are not considered for reasons of space: for a full consideration of those powers, see Scott (n 10).

the rule of law, and failures of accountability which the modern regime of investigatory powers seeks belatedly to avoid.[35]

i. Interception of Communications Prior to the ECHR

The traditional approach to the interception of communications is in considerable tension with the rule of law ideal outline above. Two reports shed light on the matter. The first, published in 1844 by the 'Secret Committee on the Post Office', was a response to the realisation by the Italian political exile Giuseppe Mazzini that post addressed to him was being opened.[36] In investigating the matter, the Committee began from the premise that the law at the time it was produced was the same as that found in a statute of 1711.[37] Though it had been charged with inquiring into 'the State of the Law in respect of the Detaining and Opening of Letters at the General Post-office, and into the Mode under which the Authority given for such Detaining and Opening has been exercised' it preferred, rather absurdly, not to discuss the 'purely legal question, how far the Statute of Anne, in recognizing the practice, on the part of the Secretaries of State, of issuing Warrants to open Letters, rendered it lawful for the Secretaries of State to issue such Warrants.'[38] The committee instead offered a detailed history of the practice, which concluded that, though few specific incidents of post's interception were known, 'no reasonable doubt can be entertained that the Governments of the different Monarchs who reigned between 1660 and 1711, had frequently recourse to the practice of opening Letters.'[39] Only with the Statute of Anne, however, was the practice recognised in statute, and even then only in oblique terms. That Act makes it an offence, inter alia, 'wittingly, willingly or knowingly to open detain or delay or cause procure or suffer to be opened detain or delay' any letter entrusted to the postal service 'except by an express Warrant in Writing under the Hand of One of the Principal Secretaries of State.'[40] This is as much legal authority as can be identified for the practice. Like many of the powers later identified, the authority it provides is negative in form; an exception to a prohibition rather than a positive and explicit power, and would seem to imply that the opening of mail was not otherwise unlawful. This perhaps goes some way to explaining the grant of a postal monopoly around this time: only if the Crown alone

[35] For considerations of that history—albeit not from a legal perspective—see P Fitzgerald and M Leopold, *Stranger on the Line: Secret History of Phone Tapping* (London, Bodley Head, 1987).

[36] The Secret Committee on the Post-Office, *Report* (1844) ('Secret Committee'). A second report on the same issues was carried out by an equivalent committee of the House of Lords, which noted that the power 'appears to have been exercised from the earliest period, and to have been recognised by several Acts of Parliament' and that the Committee had not found 'any other authority' for the detention or opening of letters at the post Office: *Report from the Secret Committee of the House of Lords relative to the Post Office* (7 August 1844).

[37] The report identifies it as 9 Anne c 10; other sources suggest that it is instead 9 Anne c11.

[38] Secret Committee (n 36) 3.

[39] ibid 7.

[40] 9 Anne c 11, s 41. The Act employed very similar wording to a Proclamation of 25 May 1663, which appears to be the first (if similarly oblique) reference to the power in question. The General Post Office was established by Charles II in 1660, upon the restoration of the Monarchy. For a consideration of this topic in the context of the seventeenth century, see A Marshall, *Intelligence and Espionage in the Reign of Charles II, 1660–1685* (Cambridge, Cambridge University Press, 1994), esp Ch 2: 'One of the best ways in which [seditious ideas] could be transmitted was through correspondence. The best means to control such correspondence therefore was a government-sponsored agency. The suppression or absorption of rival postal agencies by the state in the period goes some way to proving this.'

controlled the postal service could it use it to intercept communications.[41] Though its data is acknowledged to be incomplete, the Committee identified only a very small number of warrants that were issued: no more than seven in a single year between 1712 and 1798, and no more than 28 in any single year in the half-century leading up to the Committee's work, giving an average of just over eight a year, with an average of two persons named in each warrant (though how many of each persons' letters were inspected on the authority of any warrant the Committee could not say).[42] Some of these warrants were general warrants: the Committee notes that '[a]mong the Warrants there are 8, applied each to some particular object but not restricted to any definite number of persons' and quotes, amongst others, the following example:

> Secretary the Duke of Newcastle to the Postmaster-general, Sept. 20, 1745: To open and detain all (such) Letters, Packets, or Papers, printed or otherwise, as shall come to the General or other Post-office, suspected to contain matters of a dangerous tendency; and to transmit them to the office of the Secretary of State.[43]

Similarly general warrants were issued in a number of cities throughout the 1810s, reflecting outbreaks of 'intestine commotion'.[44] The Committee denied, however, having seen evidence of the most 'general' practice which had been alleged: the sending of entire mail bags full of post to the Home Office for inspection.[45] Some of the warrants seemed to it to have been dubious in their purpose, being 'issued on grounds which would now be considered highly objectionable, and would not be sanctioned by recent practice.'[46] One example, issued in 1741 at the request of an unnamed person, permitted that person's eldest son to open and inspect any letters written by his youngest son to either of two women 'one of whom that youngest son had imprudently married.'[47] Warrants issued in the nineteenth century were divided by the Committee into two categories. The first was that of warrants in pursuit of criminal justice. The second we can call national security warrants; those 'issued for the purpose of discovering the designs of persons known or suspected to be engaged in proceedings, dangerous to the State, or (as in Mazzini's case,) deeply involving British interests, and carried on in the United Kingdom or in British Possessions beyond the seas.'[48] These latter were issued by the Home Secretary 'of his own discretion',[49] with no formal records kept; only in 1937, it seems, did the Home Secretary begin to issue formal warrants.[50] In 1951, the Home Office issued guidelines to the Metropolitan Police and Customs and Excise which identified the conditions which must be met before an interception warrant

[41] See the Proclamation of 1657, cited in the *Report of the Committee of Privy Councillors appointed to inquire into the interception of communications* (1957) ('Birkett'), [31]: setting up a Post Office was 'the best means to discover and prevent many dangerous and wicked designs which have been and are daily contrived against the peace and welfare of the Commonwealth …'.
[42] Secret Committee (n 36) 11.
[43] ibid, 12.
[44] ibid, 13.
[45] ibid, 15.
[46] ibid, 12.
[47] ibid.
[48] ibid, 14.
[49] ibid, 15.
[50] Secretary of State for the Home Department, *Interception of Communications in the United Kingdom: A Consultation Paper*, Cm 4368 (1999), [2.1]. See also Birkett (n 41) [41].

would be issued by the Home Secretary. These were that the offence at issue must be 'really serious', that '[n]ormal methods of investigation must have been tried and failed, or must, by the nature of things, be unlikely to succeed if tried' and '[t]here must be good reason to think that an interception would result in a conviction'.[51]

The second of the reports which shed light on the historical practices of intercepting communication was carried out by a Committee of Privy Councillors, headed by Norman Birkett (later a Lord of Appeal in Ordinary), which reported in 1957.[52] The catalyst for the report was an incident in which the Metropolitan Police had intercepted the telephone calls of one Billy Hill. Transcripts of Hill's telephone calls with his Barrister, Patrick Marrinan, had been shown to the Bar Council following the conclusion of Hill's trial, with Marinnan consequently barred from practice.[53] In the Birkett report, however, there is perhaps even less clarity than in the 1844 report as to the source of the power to intercept telephone calls. The executive had argued that the power was an instantiation of a prerogative right to intercept communications, an argument which was undermined by the absence of any reference to it in Chitty's great work on the prerogative.[54] To the claim that the executive was making an argument of state necessity of the sort rejected in *Entick*, it was replied that the power in question was a 'limited, strictly governed use of the Secretary of State's warrant.'[55] The Committee accepted that view which had earlier been taken as to the authority (such as it was) for the interception of post, noting that subsequent statutes had contained analogous provision and extended also to telegrams.[56] As to the interception of telephone calls, however, it was required to go further. It considered a number of views as to the source of the power. First, that the interception of such calls was the exercise of a prerogative which power to intercept communications which, in line with the decision in *In re a Petition of Right*,[57] should be recognised as encompassing modern developments and so include the power to intercept telephone calls.[58] Second, that the necessary authority might be found in the Telegraph Act 1868, interpreted in line with an 1880 decision that a telephone conversation is a 'telegraphic communication'.[59] And, third, the view that the Post Office had, until 1937, been entitled, as the operator of the telephone network, to intercept calls, it not being unlawful for it to do so.[60] Ultimately, however, Birkett offered a deeply unsatisfactory account of the law, which involved endorsing none of the arguments advanced. Its conclusion was that:

> The power to intercept letters has been exercised from the earliest times, and has been recognised in successive Acts of Parliament.

[51] ibid, [2.2].

[52] Birkett (n 41). See Fitzgerald and Leopold (n 35) 119–32.

[53] The tale is told in D Vincent, *The Culture of Secrecy: Britain, 1832–1998* (Oxford, Oxford University Press, 1999), 186–194.

[54] J Chitty, *A Treatise on the Law of the Prerogatives of the Crown: And the Relative Duties and Rights of the Subject* (London, J Butterworth & Son, 1820).

[55] Birkett (n 41) [25].

[56] ibid, [39].

[57] *In re a Petition of Right* [1915] 3 KB 659.

[58] Birkett (n 41) [42].

[59] ibid, [44]–[46]. The case in question is *Attorney General v Edison Telephone Co of London Ltd* (1880–81) LR 6 QBD 244.

[60] Birkett (n 41) [49].

> This power extends to telegrams.
>
> It is difficult to resist the view that if there is a lawful power to intercept communications in the form of letters and telegrams, then it is wide enough to cover telephone communications as well.[61]

The difficulties with this are myriad. First is the fact that the rule of law requirement exemplified by the decision in *Entick* suggests that it is not sufficient for a power to be 'recognised': the law must be 'found in our books', and if 'it is not to be found there, it is not law.'[62] Nor is it sufficient to show that it has been 'exercised since the earliest times'. This too recalls *Entick*, where one of the potential bases identified for the grant of general warrants by the King's Ministers was the history of practice since the revolution of 1689. Rejecting this, Camden CJ identified the revolution as having 'restored this constitution to its first principles' and 'no more'.[63] Neither the length of time for which the practice had been carried out nor the fact that the courts had never condemned it sufficed to establish its existence:

> With respect to the practice itself, if it goes no higher, every lawyer will tell you, it is much too modern to be evidence of the common law; and if it should be added, that these warrants ought to acquire some strength by the silence of those courts, which have heard them read so often upon returns without censure or animadversion, I am able to borrow my answer to that pretence from the Court of King's-bench which lately declared with great unanimity in the Case of General Warrants, that as no objection was taken to them upon the returns, and the matter passed *sub silentio*, the precedents were of no weight.[64]

With regards to the first of these points, the issue of interception of letters might be distinguished from the grant of general warrants by virtue of the fact that, where the latter was traceable back only to 1689 (or a little before)—a period of 100 years or so before the decision in *Entick*—the Secret Committee is able to point to a far longer history, of (at least) several hundred years. The second point applies, however, with even greater force here: that the practice had never been identified as unlawful could be attributed not (as in *Entick*) to the fact that the courts were never asked to rule upon them,[65] but the fact that knowledge of the practice was so limited that no one was in a position to challenge it. The second step in its argument is logical on its face—the provision in the Post Office Act 1953, which was the relevant statute at the time of the Birkett report, recognising the power of interception used the term 'postal packet', which was defined within the Act to include telegrams[66]—but is undermined by its reliance on a false premise.

The third step ('It is difficult to resist the view that if there is a lawful power to intercept communications in the form of letters and telegrams, then it is wide enough to cover telephone communications as well') is the most interesting, and—as the hesitant phrasing suggests—the most problematic. On one hand, there is a certain logic, not least in terms

[61] ibid. [51].
[62] (1765) 19 St Tr 1029, 1066.
[63] ibid, 1068.
[64] ibid.
[65] Camden notes, in one of the best lines from a judgment which abounds in them, that 'it would be strange doctrine to assert that all the people of this land are bound to acknowledge that to be universal law, which a few criminal booksellers have been afraid to dispute'. (1765) 19 St Tr 1029, 1069.
[66] Post Office Act 1953, s 87(1).

of the fact that while the interception of a letter involves an interference with property, the interception of a telephone call (like the interception of a telegram, and as would prove significant in later case law) does not. The latter is therefore, in at least this sense, less intrusive than the former and the power to do a more intrusive thing might seem, *a fortiori*, to permit the doing of an analogous but less intrusive act. On the other, however, the alleged statutory basis is now weaker: the language of 'telegraphic communication' might once have been interpreted to apply to telephone calls, but the case for interpreting the language of 'a telegram' (the formulation employed in the 1953 Act) to do so is less sure. We have, then, a body with no particular authority to answer legal questions offering a deeply unconvincing account of the legal basis of telephone tapping in the mid-twentieth century UK. Though it considered that the making of transcripts of intercepted telephone conversations available to the Benchers of Lincoln's Inn was a mistake, the more general system of interception was given a clean bill of health, with only relatively minor changes considered.[67] Where it was left to Parliament to consider whether legislation might be introduced to make unauthorised telephone tapping an offence, no suggestion was made of implementing a statutory regime (with attendant safeguards) for lawful tapping. With the enactment of the Post Office Act 1969, that institution ceased to be a department of state, and was no longer under the control of a Minister of the Crown. The 1969 Act contained a provision equivalent to that found in prior legislation recognising the power of interception,[68] again saving the power without ever expressly creating it or clarifying its underlying nature. The 1969 Act further provided that it was to be a defence for a person charged with various offences under older statutes to prove that the act 'constituting the offence was done in obedience to a warrant under the hand of a Secretary of State.'[69]

The Birkett report, however unsatisfying in its conclusions on the interception of telegrams and telephone calls, at least addressed such matters. Left entirely unaddressed by it was the question of the interception of what we would now call external communications; those sent or received by persons outside of the UK. The authority for such interception was found in section 4 of the Official Secrets Act 1920, which permitted the Secretary of State, where it appeared to him to be 'expedient in the public interest' to grant a warrant requiring those who control wired or wireless telegraphy systems used to send or receive telegrams to or from outside the UK 'to produce to him … originals and transcripts, either of all telegrams, or of telegrams of any specified class or description, or of telegrams sent from or addressed to any specified person or place.' Though the statutory basis of this powers is preferable to the fuzzy (and perhaps non-existent) basis of the power to intercept internal communications (as, indeed, is the clarity of the provision, which would suffice to fulfil its intended purpose even in the context of more stringent modern approaches to statutory interpretation), the power was of course remarkably broad: such warrants could easily be more general than anything the eighteenth century seems to have known.[70] This seems to have been the first statutory recognition of a power of intercept of external communications; though later enactments have maintained both the underlying distinction between

[67] Birkett (n 41) [153]–[169]. One member of the Committee dissented from some of its conclusions.

[68] Post Office Act 1969, s 80.

[69] Post Office Act 1969, Sch 5, para 1(1).

[70] Albeit that, unlike the seventeenth century general warrants, a warrant of this sort could only catch communications; a person's private papers, uncommunicated to others, could not be acquired using this power.

internal and external communications and much of the astonishing breadth evident in the 1920 Act, they also impose limits on the possibility of examining the material acquired via external warrants. The 1920 Act contained no such limits, with the effect that it was wholly lawful to grant warrants permitting the acquisition of all telegrams being sent into or out of the UK without requirements of suspicion, and without any requirement that national security (or even the fight against 'ordinary' crime) be at stake, and then to sift through those telegrams in order to find those sent to, or by, any person or group of person, for any reason or for none. The 1920 Act provided that 'the expression "telegram" shall have the same meaning as in the Telegraph Act, 1869, and the expression "wireless telegraphy" shall have the same meaning as in the Wireless Telegraphy Act, 1904' meaning, on the logic considered above, that they were available not only in relation to telegraphy, but also to telephony. The powers under the 1920 Act existed, in plain language and in the open, for several decades without—it seems—attracting significant attention. When a description of their use was published by the journalist Chapman Pincher in 1967, the Prime Minister Harold Wilson accused the publication of having taken place in breach of D-Notices (as they were then called) and later went on to reject the verdict of a Committee of Privy Councillors charged by him with investigating the matter.[71]

This overview gives a sense of the key features of the regime by which the state's investigatory powers were regulated in the UK historically. Often, there was no authority at all: powers were recognised by law rather than created by it, and where there was direct legal authority, it was often obscure and in some cases effectively hidden in plain sight, with no public understanding of the use that could be—and in fact was—made of the powers in question. Secondly, in demonstrating propriety and at times even legality, there was a strong reliance on the historic provenance of the powers, as though the mere passage of time might suffice to remedy the defects of the legal structure. Third, there was a remarkable lack of publicity: only where some public scandal caused the question of the interception of communication to attract the attention of the political community and the press was any sort of light shed upon what was happening and under what authority it was being done. This suggests, very strongly, that the sort of political oversight which is often relied upon in order to make good the defects of processes of legal accountability was simply impossible. If no one knew what powers the executive possessed and what use was being made of them, they could not hope to carry out effective scrutiny of these powers. And even where the basic outline of powers could be known, much of the relevant detail as to their use and implications was kept secret: powers existed in a strange and inherently unsatisfactory no man's land where they were theoretically knowable, but never meaningfully known.

The legal turning point was the Interception of Communications Act 1985, which had as its proximate cause—the White Paper which preceded it makes clear[72]—the decision of the European Court of Human Rights in *Malone v United Kingdom*,[73] a judgment which brings together a number of issues considered so far in this chapter. Malone had been prosecuted for handling stolen property; during the trial the prosecution had admitted that his telephone calls had been intercepted. When he launched a challenge to the legality

[71] See the discussion in Ch 5.

[72] Home Office, *The Interception of Communications in the United Kingdom*, Cmnd 9438 (1985).

[73] (1985) 7 EHRR 14.

of that warrant,[74] Megarry V-C in the Chancery Division advanced an orthodox reading of *Entick v Carrington*, whereby the reason that legal authority had been required for the search and seizure of John Entick's property was that such acts involved a trespass against property; here, the tapping having been carried out by the Post Office, there had been no such trespass.[75] The claimant was left arguing that a person making a telephone call had a property right in the electrical impulses, an argument swiftly disposed of by the Court.[76] Nor was Megarry V-C willing to recognise a common law right to privacy, interference with which would act to trigger the requirement of legal authority.[77] Though the decision in *Malone* might be regretted for any number of reasons, it seems to have represented the correct understanding of English common law at the relevant point in time. Its effect was that, even in the absence of clear legal authority of a sort which the 1920 Act provided for the interception of 'external' communications, the tapping of the telephone was lawful as a matter of English law: earlier inquiries into the matter had, it now seemed, misunderstood the legal position, trying to identify a legal basis for an act which had none, because it did not require one. Little wonder that their efforts were so unconvincing. In the Court of Human Rights, however, it was held that the interception of telephone calls was an interference with the Article 8 right to a private a family life, which was therefore required—if it was not to violate the ECHR—to be justified in accordance with the criteria for a justified interference contained in paragraph 2 of Article 8.[78] Amongst these requirements is that any interference takes place in accordance with the law, interpreted by the Strasbourg Court to include a requirement of foreseeability, which differs where—as here—the interference takes place in secret:

> The requirement of foreseeability cannot mean that an individual should be enabled to foresee when the authorities are likely to intercept his communications so that he can adapt his conduct accordingly. Nevertheless, the law must be sufficiently clear in its terms to give citizens an adequate indication as to the circumstances in which and the conditions on which public authorities are empowered to resort to this secret and potentially dangerous interference with the right to respect for private life and correspondence.[79]

While accepting that the interception of domestic communications was lawful under domestic law, the Court held that 'it cannot be said with any reasonable certainty what elements of the powers to intercept are incorporated in legal rules and what elements remain within the discretion of the executive' and that 'the law of England and Wales does not indicate with reasonable clarity the scope and manner of exercise of the relevant discretion conferred on the public authorities.'[80] Particularly problematic was the Post Office Act 1969's explicit saving of prior practices, which provided no clarity as to what exactly those modes of operation were, and whether or not they were founded in law: exactly the questions which Birkett had failed to answer.[81] Malone's Article 8 rights had therefore been

[74] *Malone v Commissioner of Police of the Metropolis (No. 2)* [1979] Ch 344.
[75] [1979] Ch 344, 355–6.
[76] ibid, 357.
[77] ibid.
[78] *Malone v United Kingdom* (1985) 7 EHRR 14, [64]. See, before *Malone*, *Klass v Germany* (1978) 2 EHRR 214.
[79] (1985) 7 EHRR 14, [67].
[80] ibid, [79].
[81] ibid, [69]–[79].

violated, and in a fashion which meant that the regime of interception as a whole was operating in a manner incompatible with the Convention. No longer could the interception of communications take place on the shoddy and uncertain basis which had until now been identified for it.

The Malone litigation had also prompted political interest in the status of the law on interception and the use of the powers. A 1980 White Paper had brought up to date the position since Birkett, laying out the conditions under which interception warrants might be applied for by the Police, Customs and Excise, and the Security Service, but not proposing any change to the system as it then operated.[82] Where Birkett had declined to give statistics for the number of interception warrants granted,[83] an exception was here made in recognition of the fact that there existed a fear that 'technological changes have made it much easier to intercept telephones and that interception is now on a much greater scale' than at the time of Birkett.[84] They showed that though the number of warrants granted for the opening of mail was in decline, the number of telephone interception warrants signed by the Home Secretary had risen from 129 in 1958 to over 400 in each year of the 1970s.[85] In 1981, Lord Diplock, who had been appointed to the position of what would later become the Interception of Communications Commissioner (but which at this stage was a non-statutory role) produced a report which was the fruit of direct observation of the process of granting warrants and dealing with their fruits, concluding that the procedures were 'working satisfactorily and with the minimum interference with the individual's right of privacy in the interests of the public weal.'[86] Moreover, while *Malone* was being considered in Strasbourg, British Telecommunications, which had been spun out of the Post Office by the British Telecommunications Act 1981 (which also permitted the private provision of public telecommunications services), was heading towards privatisation under the Telecommunications Act 1984. No longer would there be a monopoly provider in conjunction with whom interception could take place.[87]

ii. The Interception of Communications Act 1985 and RIPA

By comparison with what followed it, the Interception of Communication Act 1985 was a model of simplicity: twelve sections and two short schedules. It introduced legal authority for the interception of both internal and external communications, repealing the provision of the Official Secrets Act 1920 under which the latter had previously taken place. The key features of the interception regime it implemented are shared with the Regulation of Investigatory Powers Act 2000 (RIPA) and the Investigatory Powers Act 2016 (IPA), discussed below, and so need not be considered in detail here. Reflecting its proximate cause, the 1985 Act stood up to many of the ECHR-based challenges to it launched in the

[82] Home Office, *The Interception of Communications in Great Britain*, Cmnd 7873 (1980).

[83] On the basis that it would 'greatly aid the operation of agencies hostile to the State if they were able to estimate even approximately the extent of the interceptions of communications for security purposes': Birkett (n 41) [121].

[84] Home Office (n 72) [25].

[85] Home Office (n 72) Annex.

[86] Lord Diplock, *The Interception of Communications in Great Britain*, Cmnd 8191 (1981), 6–7.

[87] See Fitzgerald and Leopold (n 35) 9.

subsequent decade. In *Campbell Christie v United Kingdom*,[88] the applicant (the General Secretary of the Scottish Trades Union Congress) challenged the lawfulness of the interception of telexes sent to him by trade unions based in Eastern Europe. Assessing the admissibility of the complaint to the European Court of Human Rights, the Commission concluded that the interference with Article 8 had taken place 'in accordance with the law', rejecting arguments to the contrary based upon the failure of the statute to define key terms (including 'national security' and 'economic well-being') and the absence of adversarial argument as to interpretation when the Interception of Communications Tribunal (created by the 1985 Act) investigated complaints. The other criteria of a justified interference being fulfilled, the alleged interference was not a violation of the ECHR. That position was upheld in later cases on similar facts.[89] The 1985 Act, however, left important gaps in the regulation of interception of communications. One such gap was demonstrated by the Strasbourg Court's decision in *Halford v United Kingdom*,[90] relating to the interception of the phone calls of the Assistant Chief Constable of Merseyside Police during a period when she was involved in a sex discrimination case against the force. Here, crucially, two sorts of phone calls were at issue: those on her home telephone and those on her work telephone. The latter not being made over a public telecommunication network (the only form of telephone system whose interception was provided for by the 1985 Act), the interference with her Article 8 rights did not take place in accordance with the law, and so represented a violation of her Convention rights.[91]

A series of criminal cases in the domestic courts were similarly affected by this anomaly,[92] while certain developments in technology and its use had rendered the legislation inadequate.[93] And though its decision was not made until many years after the 1985 Act had been superseded by RIPA, the European Court of Human Rights eventually found that the regime for the interception of external communications was incompatible with Article 8 of the Convention.[94] The Court noted the breadth of the power to intercept external communications but also the generality of the descriptions which might be employed in a certificate justifying the examination of material collected thereunder, which the applicants had claimed 'were formulated in general terms and related only to intelligence tasks and priorities, such as, for example, "national security", "preventing or detecting serious crime" or "safeguarding the economic well-being of the United Kingdom"'.[95] Many of the details regarding, for example, the internal arrangements which were required by the statute to be in place and which were also necessary in order to comply with the *Weber* criteria were not publicly available even though they had later been made so within the Code of Practice issued under the subsequent RIPA regime.[96] The regime did not indicate 'with sufficient

[88] 21482/93 (unreported) 27 June 1994 (admissibility decision). See also *Preston v United Kingdom* (24193/94) 2 July 1997 (admissibility).

[89] See, eg, *Matthews v United Kingdom* (28576/95) 16 October 1996 (admissibility).

[90] (1997) 24 EHRR 523. See also *Copland v United Kingdom* [2007] ECHR 253.

[91] See also *Taylor-Sabori v United Kingdom* (2003) 36 EHRR 17.

[92] See, eg, *R v Effik* (1994) Crim LR 832.

[93] See Home Office, *Interception Of Communications In The United Kingdom: A Consultation Paper* (1999) Cm 4368, [3.4]–[3.7].

[94] In *Liberty v United Kingdom* (2009) 48 EHRR 1.

[95] ibid, [65].

[96] ibid, [68].

clarity, so as to provide adequate protection against abuse of power, the scope or manner of exercise of the very wide discretion conferred on the State to intercept and examine external communications' and was therefore not compatible with Article 8.[97]

By that time, however, the relatively straightforward 1985 statute had been replaced by RIPA, whose opacity (particularly after a decade and a half of amendment) was remarkable, and which regulated not only the interception of communications (as the 1985 Act had done) but also a variety of other powers, some of which are discussed further below. Though the framework was more complicated, the key features of the 1985 Act's interception regime were retained: the same three part test for the use of the powers; a distinction between the interception of internal communications (which required a certain degree of specification of the warrants' target)[98] and that of external communications (which did not);[99] a broad definition of 'person'—found amongst the interpretation provisions—which made possible warrants that were 'thematic' rather than truly targeted;[100] a provision indemnifying the intercept of internal material when necessary to carry out an external warrant;[101] a provision limiting the selection for examination of material obtained in pursuit of an external warrant so as prevent it from being used to evade the restrictions on the availability of targeted warrants as regards persons in the British Islands.[102] The powers were used extensively: the report by the Interception of Communications Commissioner for 2015 shows that over 3,000 interception warrants were issued in that year, up by 9% on the previous year; of these warrants, approximately two thirds were given for purposes relating to serious crime, with one third given for national security reasons.[103]

Both elements of the RIPA interception framework were ultimately challenged before the courts; that governing interception of internal communications before the Investigatory Powers Tribunal and later the Court of Human Rights.[104] In both cases, it was held to be compatible with Article 8 of the Convention. The Court of Human Rights held that, taken together with the Code of Practice issued under it (of which there was no equivalent in relation to the 1985 Act), RIPA fulfilled the *Weber* requirements, and that there was 'no evidence of any significant shortcomings in the application and operation of the surveillance regime'.[105] It emphasised too the safeguards offered by the existence, under RIPA, of

[97] ibid, [70].

[98] Regulation of Investigatory Powers Act 2000, s 8(1), which required a warrant to 'name or describe either (a) one person as the interception subject; or (b) a single set of premises as the premises in relation to which the interception to which the warrant relates is to take place.'

[99] RIPA 2000, s 8(4) and (5).

[100] RIPA 2000, s 81. A 'thematic' warrant is one which applies to a group of persons united by some common theme, such as membership of a group or participation in some endeavour. In the case of RIPA, s 81 provided that '"person" includes any organisation and any association or combination of persons', meaning that a single warrant could meet the requirements of specification imposed on 'internal' warrants without in fact identifying by name the individuals whose communications were to be intercepted. For discussion of thematic warrants in another context, see Scott (n 10).

[101] RIPA 2000, s 5(6).

[102] RIPA 2000, s 16. This was in addition to general safeguards found in s 15, which required *inter alia* that the disclosure of intercept material was limited as far as possible both in in terms of the extent of its disclosure and the number of persons to whom it was disclosed.

[103] Sir Stanley Burton, *Report of the Interception of Communications Commissioner: Annual Report for 2015* (HC 2016–17, 255), [6.37]–[6.42].

[104] *Kennedy* (IPT/01/62 and IPT/01/77) and *Kennedy v United Kingdom* (2011) 52 EHRR 4.

[105] (2011) 52 EHRR 4, [169].

an Investigatory Powers Tribunal (IPT) (in which those who believed their communications to have been intercepted could seek a limited legal redress, with no restrictions on standing) and an Interception of Communications Commissioner (responsible for carrying out annual reviews of the interception regime).[106] The regime for the interception and examination of external communications was challenged before the IPT along with the processes for data sharing between UK and US authorities in the post-Snowden period. The IPT rejected the claim that technical evolution since the enactment of RIPA had rendered the internal/external distinction unfit for purpose. In order to do so, however, it had to consider the government's understanding of 'external communications' which, it now became clear, included communications sent from computers inside the British Islands to servers located abroad, and included within the concept many things—such as a Google search—which it may not have been immediately obvious was any sort of communication at all.[107] Similarly, it held that the safeguards imposed by RIPA upon the examination of material collected under a bulk warrant were sufficient to ensure the regime was in accordance with Article 8.[108] The relevant arrangements, it said, 'are sufficiently signposted, in the Statute, in the Code, in the Commissioner's reports, and as now recorded in this judgment.'[109]

This latter judgment highlights a phenomenon central in particular to the recent (post-Snowden) case law: alongside what was revealed (or suggested) to have taken place within the field of investigatory powers, the resulting litigation has prompted the disclosure of internal ('below the waterline') arrangements which govern the processes by which interception material or its equivalent is dealt with, but which were found neither in RIPA nor in the relevant Code of Practice. Though in the case of external interception under RIPA, this belated disclosure made no difference to the issue of Article 8 compatibility,[110] certain points can be made about it. The first is the fact that it was ultimately disclosed (in full or in gist) suggests that much of it could have been disclosed at some earlier point with no adverse consequences. The second is that the UK's response in this field is always and everywhere ultimately reactive: all changes are made belatedly, in response to some external stimulus, with no attempt ever made to make the scope of its powers clear to the public, nor what might be done with the material collected in the exercise thereof. Though it represents an improvement in this state of affairs (in the form of a largely, if not wholly exhaustive regime of investigatory powers) the Investigatory Powers Act 2016 can be seen to represent a continuation of this responsive approach. Like the reviews leading to it,[111] it seems certain that it would not have been enacted were it not for the Snowden revelations. One question, then, is whether the 2016 Act represents the end of this process of belated disclosure and

[106] RIPA 2000, ss 57 and 58 and ss 65–70. Each institution had predecessors in the 1985 Act.

[107] Witness statement of Charles Farr in case IPT/13/92/CH (16 May 2014), [126]–[141].

[108] *Liberty v GCHQ (No 1)* [2015] 3 All ER 142. Though communications data associated with the material collected might be subject to fewer safeguards than is the content of the communications, that difference 'is justified and proportionate by virtue of the use of that communications data for the purpose of identifying the individuals whose intercepted material is to be protected.'

[109] [2015] 3 All ER 142, [140].

[110] *Liberty v The Secretary of State for Foreign and Commonwealth Affairs* [2015] 3 All ER 212, [12].

[111] David Anderson QC, *A Question of Trust: Report of The Investigatory Powers Review* (2015); Intelligence and Security Committee, *Privacy and Security: A modern and transparent legal framework* (HC 2015, 1075); Royal United Services Institute, *A Democratic Licence to Operate: Report of the Independent Surveillance Review* (2015).

reform: though it is clear that the substance if not the gist of many of the arrangements which are 'below the waterline' will remain there, what else might remain hidden in plain sight even after the 2016 enact brought into focus much which was scattered across the statute book. As it stands, however, the RIPA question is not yet closed: an application to the Court of Human Rights in which the IPT's conclusions on these matters will be tested remains outstanding.[112] As before, however, domestic law has moved on: even if the Court of Human Rights ultimately finds the RIPA regime to be incompatible with domestic law, it will represent a condemnation of a past which has already been transcended. In this area of law, perhaps more than any other, the relationship between the law and the Convention on Human Rights demonstrates a strange, almost Hegelian, dynamic in which the applicable law is (and for the most part can be) understood only at the point at which it no longer applies.

iii. Interception under the Investigatory Powers Act 2016

The 2016 Act introduces a new regime for the interception of communications, one which exemplifies many of the key features of contemporary investigatory powers. This section will outline the relevant power and consider some of those features, most of which apply to the majority of the 'targeted' power under the Act. Three forms of targeted warrant exist, though we will consider only two here: the targeted interception warrant and the targeted examination warrant.[113] The former permits the interception of communications and the obtaining of 'secondary data' from communications; the latter the examination of material intercepted in accordance with a bulk interception warrant. The definition of 'secondary data' employed here is, however, crucial. Where RIPA had employed in this context the concept of 'related communications data', defined in such a way that only metadata was included within it, the definition of 'secondary data' in the IPA shifts the boundary into the domain of content. That is, 'secondary data' is defined to mean both (a) any 'systems data' ('any data that enables or facilitates, or identifies or describes anything connected with enabling or facilitating, the functioning of … a telecommunication system')[114] 'which is comprised in, included as part of, attached to or logically associated with the communication'[115] and (b) 'identifying data' which is 'comprised in, included as part of, attached to or logically associated with the communication', is 'capable of being logically separated from the remainder of the communication, and 'if it were so separated, would not reveal anything of what might reasonably be considered to be the meaning (if any) of the communication, disregarding any meaning arising from the fact of the communication or from any data relating to the transmission of the communication.'[116] 'Identifying data' is defined in turn to mean 'data which may be used to identify, or assist in identifying, any person, apparatus, system or service' or 'which may be used to identify, or assist in identifying, any event' or 'which may be used to identify, or assist in identifying, the location of any person, event or thing.'[117]

[112] *10 Human Rights Organisations v United Kingdom* (application 24960/15).

[113] The third is a 'mutual assistance warrant', which governs the making of a request for assistance to a foreign partner or conduct giving effect to such a request made to the UK: see IPA 2016, s 15(4).

[114] IPA 2016, s 263(4).

[115] ibid, s 16(5).

[116] ibid, s 16(6).

[117] ibid, s 261.

The effect is this: though 'secondary data' which is systems data is true metadata, in that it forms no part of the content of the communications intercepted, that which is 'identifying data' would seem to breach the conceptual divide. Even if, therefore, we accept the (heavily contested) notion that metadata is less intrusive than content, the IPA would—to this extent at least—appear to assimilate some content with metadata, though the requirement that a particular piece of data 'would not reveal anything of what might reasonably be considered to be the meaning (if any) of the communication' makes it difficult to know where exactly the boundary will be drawn in practice. And, of course, the language of 'interception'—as well as the chronological manner of this story's telling in the present work—should not mislead as to the scope of these powers, which apply to 'telecommunication systems'; that is, 'a system (including the apparatus comprised in it) that exists (whether wholly or partly in the United Kingdom or elsewhere) for the purpose of facilitating the transmission of communications by any means involving the use of electrical or electromagnetic energy.'[118]

Where in RIPA the provision which permitted ostensibly targeted warrants (to use that term anachronistically) in a 'thematic' way was found in the general interpretation provision, the 2016 Act is transparent as to this possibility: though a targeted warrant—whether for interception or examination—may refer to 'a particular person or organisation' or 'a single set of premises', it may also relate to 'a group of persons who share a common purpose or who carry on, or may carry on, a particular activity', 'more than one person or organisation, or more than one set of premises, where the conduct authorised or required by the warrant is for the purposes of a single investigation or operation'.[119] Though the terms of these provisions are such that they do not permit the granting of 'general' warrants, nor should they not permit the granting of 'bulk' warrants (where the communications of persons who are of no interest to the security services are also intercepted), this is obviously far broader than a genuinely targeted warrant, and will permit the interception (or examination) of communications sent or received by persons who are not named, nor otherwise personally identified, within the warrant. In keeping with the intrusiveness of the interception of communications, those who can apply for such a warrant are limited to the heads of the Security and Intelligence Agencies, the Director of the National Crime Agency, Police Chief Constables, the Commissioners of HMRC, and the Chief of Defence Intelligence.[120] A warrant may be granted (subject to requirements of proportionality, and to the requirement that there exist suitable safeguards against disclosure)[121] only where the Secretary of State considers it necessary on one of three standard grounds: 'in the interests of national security', for the 'purpose of preventing or detecting serious crime' or 'in the interests of the economic well-being of the United Kingdom so far as those interests are also relevant to the interests of national security' with this last purpose being limited to situations in which 'the information which it is considered necessary to obtain is information relating to the acts or intentions of persons outside the British Islands.'[122] The extent of disclosure of intercept material as well as the number of people to whom disclosure takes place, as well

[118] ibid, s 261(13).
[119] ibid, s 17(2).
[120] ibid, s 18(1).
[121] ibid, s 19(b) and (c).
[122] ibid, s 20.

as the extent of copying, must be kept to the minimum necessary.[123] Special safeguards apply to warrants designed to intercept communications sent to or from members of the various legislatures,[124] to material subject to legal privilege,[125] to confidential journalistic material,[126] and to the source of journalistic material.[127]

One other difference between interception under the IPA as compared to its predecessors—which applies not only to the granting of an interception warrant but to most other warrants under the IPA—is that a warrant may be issued only where (except in cases of urgency) the decision to do so has been approved by one of the new Judicial Commissioners whose roles were created by the IPA in order to work with the new Investigatory Powers Commissioner (IPC).[128] The Judicial Commissioners (JCs)—like the IPC—must be persons who hold or have held 'high judicial office'.[129] Here, as elsewhere, they are tasked by the IPA with reviewing the relevant conclusions that a warrant is indeed necessary on the grounds identified, and that the conduct authorised by it is proportionate to what it seeks to achieve.[130] This 'double lock' is one of the major innovations of the 2016 Act, introduced in order to counter suggestions that the new statute gave to the executive excessive power and, as it was suggested above, to head off any development within the jurisprudence of the Court of Human Rights that would have the effect of requiring warrants for interception (and equivalent interferences) to be approved by a person independent of the executive and, perhaps, specifically a judge. Nevertheless, the Judicial Commissioner is not an equal partner in the 'double lock' system, but rather reviews the decision of the primary decision maker. In doing so, the JC is to 'apply the same principles as would be applied by a court on an application for judicial review'[131] (while also considering the relevant questions with sufficient care so as to uphold the general duties regarding privacy which are contained in the 2016 Act).[132] At the time of writing, one major question regarding the IPA is how the JCs will approach this task, and what will be understood by the reference to principles of judicial review:[133] if, as seems likely, the JCs take a traditional common law approach, checking only for any unreasonableness in the conclusions of the primary decision-maker, then the double-lock risks collapsing into a purely cosmetic

[123] ibid, ss 53 and 54.
[124] ibid, s 26.
[125] ibid, s 27.
[126] ibid, s 28.
[127] ibid, s 29.
[128] ibid, s 227(1)(b).
[129] ibid, s 227(2).
[130] ibid, s 23(1)
[131] ibid, s 23(2)(a).
[132] ibid, s 23(2)(b).
[133] The case cited most frequently in favour of the claim that the statutory formulation was such as to require the JCs to separately satisfy themselves that the conditions for the granting of a warrant are met is one relating to control orders, in which the Court of Appeal, while bound by House of Lords authority to the effect that the imposition of a control order was not equivalent to the determination of a criminal charge, nevertheless accepted that it was 'a pre-condition to the making of a control order under section 3 that there must be reasonable suspicion that the controlled person has been engaged in terrorism-related activity' and that 'the obligations that may be imposed under a non-derogating control order, while falling short of infringing Art 5 of the Convention, can nonetheless impact severely on both civil and Convention rights.' It therefore accepted that the requirements of Art 6 could be satisfied only 'if the court made its own independent assessment of whether the requirements for imposing the control order were satisfied.' *Secretary of State for the Home Department v MB* [2006] EWCA Civ 1140, at [47]–[65].

exercise, which may prevent it from curing any incompatibility with the ECHR deriving from the primary decision-maker's lack of independence. Any refusal to approve the decision to grant a warrant must be accompanied by written reasons;[134] where a JC has refused approval, it may nevertheless be sought from the IPC him or herself.[135] Where a warrant has been issued without the approval of a JC due to the urgency of the situation, a JC must be informed and the decision approved before the end of the third working day after the day on which it was issued; if it is refused, the warrant ceases to have effect.[136] In such a case, the person to whom the warrant was addressed must 'so far as is reasonably practicable, secure that anything in the process of being done under the warrant stops as soon as possible' and the JC may order that any material collected under it be destroyed or otherwise place conditions upon its retention or use.[137] What was done in the period before the JC refuses to approve the decision to grant a warrant is nevertheless lawful.[138]

iv. Bulk Interception

The Investigatory Powers Act 2016 institutes a regime for the bulk interception of external communications, which shares key features with the previous regimes—under the 1985 and 2000 Acts—and with the other bulk powers found in the 2016 legislation. A bulk interception warrant permits—in the first place—the 'interception in the course of their transmission by means of a telecommunication system, of communications described in the warrant' and the selection of those communications for examination obtained under the warrant'.[139] Such a warrant can be granted only by the Secretary of State and only on the application of the heads of an intelligence service:[140] the bulk variant is in this way more limited than is the targeted version. The grounds upon which a warrant might be given are the same as for targeted interception warrants (where necessary in the interests of national security, for the purpose of preventing or detecting serious crime, in the interests of economic well-being), but in the bulk context the grounds relating to serious crime and economic well-being can make a warrant necessary only alongside national security and not on their own.[141] A requirement of proportionality applies,[142] as does a requirement of approval by a Judicial Commissioner.[143]

The bulk nature of the warrant is reflected not only in the relatively limited availability of the warrants, but also by the special requirements relating to examination of material acquired thereunder: a bulk interception warrant must identify a series of 'operational purposes' for which the material acquired under the warrant might be examined, and the Secretary of State must therefore be satisfied also that each of the specified operational purposes 'is a purpose for which the examination of intercepted content or secondary data

[134] IPA 2016, s 23(4).
[135] ibid, s 23(5).
[136] ibid, s 24.
[137] ibid, s 25.
[138] ibid, s 25(8).
[139] ibid, s 136(4).
[140] ibid, s 138(1).
[141] ibid, s 138(1)(b).
[142] ibid, s 138(1)(c).
[143] ibid, s 138(1)(g).

obtained under the warrant is or may be necessary' and that 'the examination of intercepted content or secondary data for each such purpose is necessary on any of the grounds on which the Secretary of State considers the warrant to be necessary.'[144] The question of operational purposes is therefore crucial to the use which is made of material collected under the authority of a bulk warrant. It must be emphasised, against that background, that the concept of an 'operational purposes' imposes only a vanishingly weak limit upon the selection of material for examination. The operational purposes identified within a bulk interception warrant must be contained on a list of operational purposes maintained by the heads of the intelligence services.[145] Additions to this list must be approved by the Secretary of State.[146] The list must be passed to the Intelligence and Security Committee quarterly, and be reviewed by the Prime Minister at least annually.[147] The only substantive limitation upon the operational purposes which might be included upon the list, however, is that the Secretary of State can approve their inclusion only if 'satisfied that the operational purpose is specified in a greater level of detail' than the grounds upon which a bulk interception warrant might be made.[148] This is a remarkably lax standard given the generality with which those grounds—most prominently, 'the interests of national security'—are formulated. It seems that it will do very little indeed to limit the examination of material acquired under a bulk warrant, particularly in light of the fact that the relevant provisions explicitly permit a bulk intercept warrant to specify all of the operational purposes contained on the list.[149]

Though limited to 'overseas-related communications' (those either sent, or received, or both sent and received, by individuals outside of the British Islands)[150] a bulk interception warrant also authorises 'any conduct which it is necessary to undertake in order to do what is expressly authorised or required by the warrant', including—most importantly—the interception of communications which are not overseas-related, being both sent and received by persons inside the British Islands.[151] Here the issue of examination becomes relevant again: were it lawful to acquire massive quantities of communications under a bulk warrant and sift through them for the communications of persons within the British Islands, then the requirements of specification imposed upon the granting of targeted warrants might easily be evaded. The 2016 Act therefore imposes a further restriction upon the selection for examination of the material (analogous to those found in its 1985 and 2000 predecessors)[152] which prevents the selection of material for examination if 'any criteria used for the selection of the intercepted content for examination are referable to an individual known to be in the British Islands at that time' and 'the purpose of using those criteria is to identify the content of communications sent by, or intended for, that individual.'[153] This prevents the selection of material in such a fashion even where to do so is necessary

[144] ibid, s 138(1)(d).
[145] ibid, s 142(3).
[146] ibid, s 142(6).
[147] ibid, ss 142(8) and (10).
[148] ibid, s 142(7).
[149] ibid, s 142(5).
[150] ibid, ss 136(2) and (3).
[151] ibid, s 136(5).
[152] ICA 1985, ss 3(2)–(4) (which permitted specification of an address in the British Islands where the Secretary of State considered that 'the examination of communications sent to or from that address is necessary for the purpose of preventing or detecting acts of terrorism'; RIPA 2000, s 16.
[153] IPA 2016, ss 152(3)(a) and (4).

for one of the operational purposes specified in the warrant and otherwise necessary and proportionate.

There are nevertheless multiple ways in which the material acquired via a bulk interception warrant might be lawfully examined. The first is where that prohibition is not breached: that is, the material is selected using factors referable to individuals who are known to be outside (or, at least, not known to be inside) the British Islands, or the purpose of selecting material for examination using criteria referable to a person known to be inside the British Islands is something other than that of identifying the content of communications from or to that individual; to select, for example, communications which refer to such a person, but are not sent by or received by him. Subject only to requirements of necessity and proportionality (as well as those—weak—limits imposed by the 'operational purposes') this is a power of tremendous breadth. In practice, it may well be that the only meaningful limit is that of technical capacity; the question of just what proportion of worldwide communications (including internet traffic) the intelligence services can capture at any point in time. The second means of examination (to which the necessity, proportionality and operational purpose requirements also apply) is where there is in place a 'targeted examination warrant',[154] a device which is mostly equivalent to a targeted interception warrant, and which is subject to the same requirements of specification (including the possibility of being thematic rather than truly targeted). The third is during a 'grace period' of sorts when a person in respect of whom material is selected for examination enters the British Islands (or after it becomes known that the belief that he or she was outside the British Islands is mistaken): here, where there exists a 'written authorisation' from a 'senior officer', the selection of material for examination on the basis of criteria referable to that person can continue until the fifth working day after the person to whom the warrant is addressed becomes aware of the change of circumstances.[155]

The availability of bulk interception warrants under which vast quantities of communications might be intercepted and—subject to the limitations discussed—examined is always liable to be controversial, given the instinctive sense (also reflected in the law) that the content of communications is particularly intrusive. Nevertheless, the existence of bulk interception warrants should be equally concerning for another feature, unrelated to content. That is, bulk interception warrants permit not only the interception of (overseas-related) communications, but also the obtaining of 'secondary data' from such communications.[156]

[154] ibid, s 152(3)(d).

[155] ibid, ss 153(3)(c) and (5)–(8).

[156] IPA 2016, s 137. This is not new, and of the equivalent powers in RIPA, the Intelligence and Security Committee noted the following:

> We were surprised to discover that the primary value to GCHQ of bulk interception was not in reading the actual content of communications, but in the information associated with those communications. This included both Communications Data (CD) as described in RIPA (which is limited to the basic "who, when and where" and is described in greater detail in Chapter 6), and other information derived from the content (which we refer to as Content-Derived Information, or CDI), including the characteristics of the communication ***. While CDI is not what might be most obviously understood to be content, under RIPA it must be treated as content, not CD. Examination of CDI therefore requires the same Ministerial authority as examination of content.

ISC (n 111) [80]. At least some of what the ISC called 'CDI' will be 'secondary data' for the purpose of the IPA 2016.

And obtaining secondary data from a communication includes not only acts done when the communication is in the course of transmission, but also 'at any time when the communication is stored in or by the system (whether before or after its transmission).'[157] 'Secondary data' is subject to the same enigmatic definition as was discussed above in the context of targeted interception: we are not, that is, in the realm of pure metadata, which can be meaningfully and strictly distinguished from content. The reason for which this second function of bulk interception warrants is relevant, and the reason for which its uncertain, but possibly quite broad, scope must be understood, is that the most important of the rules limiting examination of the data—the prohibition on selecting it for examination by reference to criteria referable to individuals known to be in the British Islands, and the consequent need for a targeted examination warrant to overcome that prohibition—do not apply to the examination of secondary data, which is limited only by the 'operational purposes' rules and the requirements of necessity and proportionality.[158] The more that is encompassed within that legal category, therefore, the more material from which the security services can select for examination, including by criteria referable to persons who they know to be in the British Islands. It serves to remember, at this point, that though the purpose of a bulk intercept warrant must relate to 'overseas-related' communications (whether their interception or the obtaining of secondary data associated with them), if it is necessary to intercept non-overseas-related communications or to obtain secondary data associated with such communications in order to fulfil that purpose, the IPA permits that conduct. It may well be, therefore, that though the distinction between interception and other forms of surveillance, and between bulk interception and targeted interception, is predicated upon an assumption that the content of communications is more sensitive than is data about those communications, that the truly outrageous element of the bulk intercept power under the 2016 Act is what is done to, and with, the secondary data obtained in accordance with a bulk interference warrant, including that relating to communications which are both sent and received in the British Islands.

B. Communications Data

Alongside powers of interception, which permit certain organs of the state to acquire communications, are those which permit the acquisition of communications data (separately from their acquisition as an adjunct of the interception of communications, as was permitted under RIPA, and is now permitted by the IPA).[159] Communications data is again a form of metadata, the usual shorthand way of defining which is as the 'who, where, when, what and how' of a communication and, from a negative point of view, everything about a communication other than its content.[160] The relevant powers were put in place by RIPA (with their absence in the 1985 Act being one of the reasons the enactment of RIPA was

[157] IPA 2016, s 137(2)(b).

[158] ibid, s 152(1)(c), which unlike the other safeguards on examination, refers only to intercepted material and not also secondary data.

[159] RIPA 2000, s I5(1)(d) and (6)(b); IPA 2016, s 15(2)(b) and 16. In the later statutory scheme, communications data is subsumed for this purpose within a broader category of 'secondary data'.

[160] For its statutory definition, see now IPA206, s 261(5).

considered necessary)[161] and later superseded by the 2016 Act.[162] Relatively little need be said about such powers, in and of their own right,[163] however, as it is only in its bulk form that communications data becomes a matter special to the domain of national security.[164] Targeted communications data can be acquired by a vast number of public authorities, including—for example—the Food Standards Agency and the Competition and Markets Authority,[165] and for a range of purposes over and above the three which justify interception, amongst them public safety, public health, tax collection, and the purpose of 'preventing death or injury or any damage to a person's physical or mental health, or of mitigating any injury or damage to a person's physical or mental health.'[166] Moreover, here the authorisation is not granted by either Minister or judge, but rather by a 'designated senior officer' of the relevant body itself, who can grant authorisations relating to investigations and operations on which he or she is working only in exceptional circumstances, and who—again, except in exceptional circumstances—must consult a 'single point of contact' within the body before granting any authorisation.[167] The degree of specification required by an authorisation is far lower than is the case for an interception warrant.[168]

Certain types of communications data authorisations are, however, subject to greater limitation, including those which relate to 'internet connection records' and those granted for the purpose of identifying or confirming the source of 'journalistic information'.[169] The very fact that such limitations exist, however, reinforces the basic point that the IPA shares the long-standing assumption about communications data—that its acquisition is less intrusive than is the interception of the communications itself; that it is less of an interference of one's privacy for the state to learn who one contacted, and when, and how for long, and whether that was a one-off contact or one of a large number of communications, than for it to learn what was said during the course of the conversation. This assumption has been strongly contested in recent times, as the quantity and quality of metadata generated as part of the process of communication (and by digital communications in particular) has increased.[170] Moreover, it seems clear that as a matter of practice, greater reliance is placed upon communications data than is placed upon the interception of communications, such

[161] The RIPA powers to acquire communications data were originally limited to a similar set of bodies as was empowered to request interception warrants. More public authorities were added to the list of those who might acquire communications data by a series of orders made by the Secretary of State under RIPA s 25 (1), starting with the Regulation of Investigatory Powers (Communications Data) Order 2003 (SI 2003/3172).

[162] IPA 2016, Pt 3.

[163] The powers are used on a massive scale: 761,702 items of communications data were acquired by public authorities during 2015, but an item of data is 'a request for data on a single identifier or other descriptor' and so '30 days of incoming and outgoing call data in relation to a mobile telephone would be counted as one item of data'. 50% of data was subscriber information, with just 2% service use information. 83% of items of data related to telephony, and 14% to internet identifiers. 5% of the items of data were acquired by the SIAs: Burton (n 103) [7.23]–[7.38].

[164] On the use of communications data by the SIAs, see Intelligence and Security Committee, *Access to Communications Data by the Intelligence and Security Agencies*, Cm 8514 (2013).

[165] The powers are enjoyed by a very large number of 'relevant public authorities', which are listed in IPA 2016, Sch 4.

[166] IPA 2016, s 21(7).

[167] ibid, s 76.

[168] ibid.

[169] ibid, ss 62 and 76.

[170] See, eg, the materials cited at n 3.

that it 'has had a significant role in every counter-terrorist operation MI5 has run in the past decade.'[171]

Nevertheless, everything within the regime for acquiring communications data continues to reflect that assumption, even as the relevant legal regimes have not merely been used to exploit the increased availability of such data but actively required the generation and retention of more data than is necessary for the functioning of a communication system. RIPA divided communications data into three categories, 'assumed to be in descending order of intrusiveness': 'traffic data' (which 'identifies the person, apparatus, location or address to or from which a communication is transmitted, and information about a computer file or program that has been accessed or run in the course of sending or receiving a communication'), 'service use information' (which relates to 'the use of a particular telecoms service' and 'subscriber data' ('all other information that the service provider holds about the person that uses the service').[172] The IPA supplants these, defining 'communication data' (in the telecommunications context) as either 'entity data'[173] or 'events data'[174] which falls into one a number of complex categories, including that of data which 'is (or is to be or is capable of being) held or obtained by, or on behalf of, a telecommunications operator and … is about an entity to which a telecommunications service is provided and relates to the provision of the service' and that of data which is 'comprised in, included as part of, attached to or logically associated with a communication (whether by the sender or otherwise) for the purposes of a telecommunication system by means of which the communication is being or may be transmitted'[175] This chain of definitions is complex, and was widely criticised during the passage of the 2016 Act. Given, though, that the powers to acquire this data are not limited to traditional data telecommunications companies, but 'telecommunications operators'—defined so as to include those who offer in the UK 'any service that consists in the provision of access to, and of facilities for making use of'[176] a 'telecommunications system' (defined as in relation to interception)—the range of data that might be acquired under these powers is vast. It seems clear, for example, that these powers permit the acquisition of—say—data regarding the masts to which a phone was connected at various times, and for how long, and much more, or even an individual's location as derived from GPS signals. The effect is that, though we technically remain outside the realm of content (communications data, the IPA also provides, 'does not include any content of a communication')[177] communications data is defined so as to include data about people and their activities which more closely resembles the content of a communication than it

[171] David Anderson QC, *A Question of Trust: Report of the Investigatory Powers Review* (2015), [7.43]–[7.45]. See also ISC (n 156) [18]–[23].

[172] Anderson (n 171) [6.6].

[173] IPA 2016, s 261(3): 'any data which (a) is about (i) an entity, (ii) an association between a telecommunications service and an entity, or (iii) an association between any part of a telecommunication system and an entity, (b) consists of, or includes, data which identifies or describes the entity (whether or not by reference to the entity's location), and (c) is not events data.'

[174] IPA 2016, s 261(4): 'any data which identifies or describes an event (whether or not by reference to its location) on, in or by means of a telecommunication system where the event consists of one or more entities engaging in a specific activity at a specific time.'

[175] IPA 2016, s 261(4).

[176] ibid, s 261(10).

[177] ibid, s 261(5).

does the traditional metadata associated with, say, telephone calls. Seen in this light, the gulf between interception and the acquisition of communications data, in terms of both their availability and the safeguards which apply, seems impossible to justify.

i. Data Retention

The element of the topic of communications data which has appeared most urgent in recent years, however, relates not to the acquisition of the communications data by the various state actors who are permitted to do so, but to the requirement that it be (generated and) retained in the first place, which raises important issues of European law. The reason for which there exists separate retention requirements is, in essence, that telecommunications providers will only collect and retain for themselves certain categories of data necessary for their commercial use, most obviously subscriber information.[178] Often, however, the relevant data may relate to a period prior to the making of the authorisation—prior, in the paradigmatic example, to the point at which some individual became known to the security services or the police or so on—and so, even though an authorisation to acquire communications data is able to also require the relevant telecommunication provider to obtain data, it may not in fact exist.[179] Retention requirements solve this problem by requiring certain types of data to be kept for specified periods so as to ensure that if, for example, a person detonates a bomb at some point in time, his or her communications data for some specified period leading up that act are available for acquisition by the relevant authorities, and details of how he or she was in contact with, and when, can be retrieved.

The retention regime in the UK has evolved rapidly over time. Following the 11 September attacks, and within the Anti-Terrorism, Crime and Security Act 2001, there was introduced a regime permitting the making of voluntary Codes of Practice,[180] by which telecommunications providers would retain data which they were not legally required to retain. The 2001 Act also permitted the making of orders which would permit the giving of directions requiring the retention of communications data, and which could potentially be given to communications providers generally.[181] This power, which was never used, acted as a fall back in the event that the voluntary arrangements were proving insufficient, and automatically expired two years after the passing of the Act.[182] No requirement of proportionality was imposed by statute on the power to make such an order, while the voluntary nature of the scheme which was implemented allowed it to evade those requirements, which would have applied to any attempt to implement related requirements under RIPA itself. Later retention requirements derived ultimately from EU law. The Data Retention Directive[183] (DRD) was adopted on the basis of Article 95 EC,[184] which creates competence to adopt

[178] And these categories will diminish as, eg, itemised billing ceases to matter in the context of mobile phone contracts which do not limit the use made of the phone qua phone.

[179] See also ISC (n 164) [24]–[30] identifying other gaps in the availability of communications data, some of which relate to retention.

[180] Anti-Terrorism, Crime and Security Act 2001 (ATCSA), ss 102–3. See the Retention of Communications Data (Code of Practice) Order 2003 (SI 2003/3175).

[181] ATCSA 2001, s 104.

[182] ibid, s 105.

[183] Directive 2006/24/EC.

[184] Now Article 95 TFEU.

harmonising measures relating to the functioning of the internal market. It required—creating, in this respect, exceptions to the e-Privacy Directive[185]—that Member States introduce measures requiring the retention of specified communications data for between six months and two years, as well as 'measures to ensure that data retained in accordance with this Directive are provided only to the competent national authorities in specific cases and in accordance with national law', subject to requirements of necessity and proportionality.[186] The DRD was given effect in the UK by two sets of regulations made under section 2 of the European Communities Act 1972,[187] but was the subject of a preliminary reference to the Court of Justice of the European Union (CJEU) regarding its compatibility with the European Charter of Fundamental Rights (CFR) in the *Digital Rights Ireland* case.[188] Though the immediate effect of the CJEU's decision in *Digital Rights Ireland*—in which it invalidated the DRD for reason of its incompatibility with Articles 7 and 8 of the CFR—was clear, its wider implications were not. And so when, the UK having taken the view that it was necessary to replace the Regulations made under the 1972 Act with the Data Retention and Investigatory Powers Act 2014 (DRIPA), the compatibility of that Act with the CFR that statute was itself questioned, the domestic courts struggled to make sense of the implications of *Digital Rights Ireland*.

At first instance, the High Court took the view that the nature of the question the CJEU had been asked to decide in *Digital Rights Ireland* was such that 'a domestic statute in the identical terms would have had the same failings', and that the standards it had identified related not only to the regime under which data was retained, but also that under which it was accessed.[189] 'The solution to the conundrum,' in the High Court's view, 'and the *ratio* of Digital Rights Ireland, is that legislation establishing a general retention regime for communications data infringes rights under Articles 7 and 8 of the EU Charter unless it is accompanied by an access regime (laid down at national level) which provides adequate safeguards for those rights.'[190] It identified certain of the CJEU's observations as amounting to mandatory requirements of EU law. Two of those are particularly significant: first, 'legislation establishing or permitting a general retention regime for personal data *must* expressly provide for access to and use of the data to be strictly restricted to the purpose of preventing and detecting precisely defined serious offences or of conducting criminal prosecutions relating to such offences'; second, 'access by the competent national authority to the data retained *must* be made dependent on a prior review by a court or an independent administrative body whose decision seeks to limit access to the data and their use to what is strictly necessary for the purpose of attaining the objective pursued, and which intervenes following a reasoned request of those authorities.'[191] Not being in accordance

[185] Directive 2002/58/EC.

[186] Directive 2006/24/EC, Art 3. The categories of data to be retained are found in Art 5.

[187] The Data Retention (EC Directive) Regulations (SI 2007/2199) and the Data Retention (EC Directive) Regulations (SI 2009/859).

[188] *Digital Rights Ireland Ltd v Minister for Communications, Marine and Natural Resources* (C-293/12) [2015] QB 127. For commentary, see Orla Lynskey, 'The Data Retention Directive is incompatible with the rights to privacy and data protection and is invalid in its entirety: Digital Rights Ireland' (2014) 51 *Common Market Law Review* 1789.

[189] *R (Davis) v Secretary of State for the Home Department* [2015] EWHC 2092 (Admin), [83].

[190] [2015] EWHC 2092 (Admin), [89].

[191] [2015] EWHC 2092 (Admin), [91].

with these requirements, DRIPA was—to the extent it was incompatible with EU law—to be disapplied. The Court of Appeal, on the other hand, took the view that it would be 'surprising' if the CJEU 'had intended to lay down definitive mandatory requirements for an access regime which lies outside the scope of EU law save to the extent that it is incidentally relevant to the retention regime.'[192] This conclusion was buttressed by the fact that the requirements it was alleged to have identified would be more demanding than those under the ECHR as currently interpreted.[193] The Court of Appeal therefore made a preliminary reference to the CJEU, in its response to which the CJEU went even further than *Digital Rights Ireland* had suggested, holding not only that access to stored data required prior judicial authorisation and should be restricted to serious crime purposes,[194] but also suggesting that even in that limited context a regime involving 'general and indiscriminate retention' is contrary to the CFR.[195]

In the meantime, however, further rules regarding retention were introduced in the Counter Terrorism and Security Act 2015, which amended DRIPA so as to extend its retention requirements to include the data necessary in order to match a given IP address with the specific device which was using that address as a particular point in time.[196] The 2015 Act, however, excluded from the definition of the data whose retention might be required data which 'may be used to identify an internet communications service to which a communication is transmitted through an internet access service for the purpose of obtaining access to, or running, a computer file or computer program.'[197] And, as the Court of Appeal had suggested when making its preliminary reference, the matter remains significant because—despite the expiration of DRIPA at the end of 2016[198]—the Investigatory Powers Act contains new powers to require the retention of communications data to go with the new powers of acquiring such data.[199] The power in question can be exercised by the Secretary of State (with the approval of a Judicial Commissioner) where he considers it necessary and proportionate for one or more of those purposes for which communications data can be acquired under the provisions noted above.[200] A retention notice may be valid for up to 12 months and can be framed tremendously broadly, being permitted to:

(a) relate to a particular operator or any description of operators;
(b) require the retention of all data or any description of data;
(c) identify the period or periods for which data is to be retained;
(d) contain other requirements, or restrictions, in relation to the retention of data;
(e) make different provision for different purposes;
(f) relate to data whether or not in existence at the time of the giving, or coming into force, of the notice.[201]

[192] *R (Davis) v Secretary of State for the Home Department* [2015] EWCA Civ 1185, [76].
[193] [2015] EWCA Civ 1185, [115].
[194] *Tele2 Sverige AB and Watson* (Joined Cases C-203/15 and C-698/15) EU:C:2016:970 (21 December 2016), [102].
[195] EU:C:2016:970, [112].
[196] Counter Terrorism and Security Act 2015, s 21.
[197] CTSA 2015, s 21(3), inserting a new definition into DRIPA.
[198] DRIPA 2014, s 8(3).
[199] IPA 2016, Pt 4.
[200] ibid, s 87(1).
[201] ibid, s 87(2).

Not only are the powers to require retention permanent where those in DRIPA were temporary, but they go substantively beyond those of DRIPA in a number of ways—most importantly, in requiring the retention of internet connection records (ICRs) by service providers.[202] A similar power had been contained in the abortive Communications Data Bill in 2013,[203] which foundered in the face of belated Liberal Democratic opposition. This was the data which the 2015 Act excluded, a record of all of those websites visited by the user of a particular device, and though restrictions apply to the access of ICRs requirements over and above those associated with other forms of communications data, it is nevertheless the case that the generation of ICRs carries with it a significant threat to the privacy of the individual; not only when they are accessed by some public authority, but also when stored by one's Internet Service Provider and at risk of nefarious access or disclosure. The power to require the retention of ICRs was therefore called by the Independent Reviewer of Terrorism Legislation the 'most substantial new power in the Act'.[204] It is in recognition of that intrusiveness that additional limits apply to the making of an authorisation for obtaining data that is ('or can only be obtained by processing') an ICR.[205] The basic effect of these is firstly to prevent local authorities from acquiring ICRs,[206] and secondly to permit other public authorities to match a known use of a relevant service to an unknown person, or vice versa.[207]

As noted above, however, significant elements of this regime (at the very least) are threatened by the CJEU's interpretation of the CFR. First of all, the purposes for which an authorisation to access communications data can be granted under the IPA are not limited to serious crime, but to 'preventing or detecting crime or of preventing disorder' and to a variety of other purposes, most of which can safely be assumed to be even less likely to meet the standard set by the CJEU: public health, public safety, tax collection etc.[208] Moreover, access to communication is not authorised by a judge, but—as discussed above—by a person internal to the relevant public authority (of whom there exist a large number, few of whom would be thought to pursue ends whose importance is on a par with preventing and detecting serious crime). To a certain extent, however, these difficulties might be overcome by suitable amendments limiting the grounds upon which data can be accessed and introducing procedural protections similar to those which exist in the context of the interception of communications (though the scale upon which access to communications data takes place would introduce significant practical difficulties). The claim that 'general and indiscriminate retention' of communications data is contrary to EU law, however, is much

[202] The statutory formulation employed is 'relevant communications data', specified to mean 'communications data which may be used to identify, or assist in identifying, any of the following … (a) the sender or recipient of a communication (whether or not a person), (b) the time or duration of a communication, (c) the type, method or pattern, or fact, of communication, (d) the telecommunication system (or any part of it) from, to or through which, or by means of which, a communication is or may be transmitted, or (e) the location of any such system'. For the avoidance of doubt, however, the IPA specifies that the 'expression therefore includes, in particular, internet connection records.' For the definition of ICR, see IPA 2016, s 62(7).

[203] On which, see the Joint Committee on the Draft Communications Data Bill, *Draft Communications Data Bill* (2012–13, HL 79, HC 479).

[204] David Anderson QC, 'The Investigatory Powers Act 2016—an exercise in democracy' (3 December 2016).

[205] IPA 2016, s 62.

[206] ibid, s 62(1).

[207] ibid, s 62(2)–(5).

[208] ibid, s 61(7).

more difficult to address, for it would seem to prevent the data from ever being collected in the first place, meaning that unless it was known in advance what data might be required, it would not be possible to collect it: the internet connection records of a terror suspect which predated his or her coming to the attention of the security services could not be accessed on this account, because they would not exist. Though the CJEU in *Watson* softened the blow somewhat by holding that retention 'based on objective evidence which makes it possible to identify a public whose data is likely to reveal a link, at least an indirect one, with serious criminal offences' is compatible with EU law,[209] this formulation contains difficulties of its own, and it is not clear why it is less objectionable to retain the data, say, only of Muslim internet users (in relation to whom one might marshal 'objective evidence' of a greater propensity to engage in certain forms of serious crime) than that of all internet users. The example given by the CJEU itself—that of 'using a geographical criterion where the competent national authorities consider, on the basis of objective evidence, that there exists, in one or more geographical areas, a high risk of preparation for or commission of such offences'[210]—verges on the nonsensical. It can be expected that the compatibility of the IPA regime of data retention will be challenged on this basis at the earliest opportunity, and notwithstanding the UK's intention to leave the EU, it seems highly unlikely that the law as it stands can fairly be considered to be in accordance with EU law in the meantime. Indeed, the Investigatory Powers Tribunal, in a case discussed in the following section, has already made a further reference to the CJEU on the interpretation of *Watson*.[211] Given that it decided not to request an expedited hearing,[212] it is possible that the UK will have ceased to be a member of the EU before the matter is resolved.

ii. Bulk Communications Data

The RIPA powers to acquire communications data were not limited by any requirement that the authorisation under which the communications data is acquired specify the person whose data was to be acquired thereunder: RIPA required only that an authorisation specify 'the conduct … that is authorised and the communications data in relation to which it is authorised.'[213] Nor were any such substantive limitations contained in the relevant Codes of Practice. Subject, therefore, to the statutory requirements of necessity and of proportionality that restrict the making of such authorisations, an authorisation might validly permit the acquisition of communications data in bulk (what we can call bulk communications data or 'BCD') even where the data in question related to a person in the UK; where it was in no sense 'foreign focused'. Only in the process leading to the enactment of the BCD did it become clear, however, that this was not the sole power by which BCD might be acquired; that a second such power was contained in the Telecommunications Act 1984, section 94 of which empowered the Secretary of State to give various directions to those, no longer under his control, who would be running the telecom system after privatisation.[214] Two sorts of

209 EU:C:2016:970, [111].
210 ibid.
211 *Privacy International v Secretary of State for Foreign and Commonwealth Affairs* UKIPTrib IPT_15_110_CH. The details of the reference are discussed below.
212 UKIPTrib IPT_15_110_CH, [74]–[77].
213 RIPA 2000, s 23(1).
214 Telecommunications Act 1984, s 94.

direction were made possible by the 1984 Act as enacted, capable of being given to anybody who was the Director or operator of a public telecommunications network (or an 'approved contractor').[215] The first permitted the Secretary of State to give persons (following consultation with them) 'such directions of a general character as appear to the Secretary of State to be requisite or expedient in the interests of national security or relations with the government of a country or territory outside the United Kingdom.'[216] This is an astonishingly broad power, not explicitly restricted even to the field of telecommunications, nor related to the pursuit of national security interests strictly defined. The second power was that to give directions (in pursuit of the same end(s), and again after consultation) 'to do, or not to do, a particular thing specified in the direction.'[217] Persons to whom directions were given were required by law to give effect to them notwithstanding any other duties under which they were placed by the 1984 Act.[218]

The Act also instituted a particularly pernicious regime of secrecy as to the directions: though the basic rule was that copies were to be laid before Parliament, there was an exception where the Secretary of State held the view that 'disclosure of the direction is against the interests of national security or relations with the government of a country or territory outside the United Kingdom, or the commercial interests of any person.'[219] The Secretary of State was similarly entitled, on the same basis, to notify persons that nothing done under section 94 was to be disclosed.[220] The cumulative effect was to permit directions of astonishing generality to be given for reasons not necessarily related to national security, of which neither Parliament nor the wider public would ever come to know, on the basis of a power which stood outside of the relevant national security frameworks. The provision was later modified to—most notably—introduce requirements of necessity and proportionality and to include OFCOM amongst those to whom directions might be given.[221] There remained, however (and in contrast with the RIPA power) no time limit upon directions given under section 94, nor provision for the issuing of a Code of Practice governing the acquisition of communications data on the authority of section 94. In practice, no directions made under section 94 appear to have ever been made public: though the power existed in the statute books (and occasional nods were made towards it) what (if any) use was in fact made of it remained entirely unknown. In his review of the investigatory powers framework, David Anderson QC identified section 94 as containing one of the non-RIPA investigatory powers, and noted that '[t]here is little or nothing in the public domain that explains how frequently

215 ibid, s 94(8).
216 ibid, s 94(1).
217 ibid, s 94(2).
218 ibid, s 94(3).
219 ibid, s 94(4).
220 ibid, s 94(5).
221 By the Communications Act 2003. The Joint Committee on the Draft Bill recommended that '[b]efore undertaking a technical revision of section 94 of the Telecommunications Act 1984, the Government should ask itself the prior question of whether such broad powers are either required or compatible with Convention rights'. Joint Committee on the Draft Communications Bill, *Draft Communications Bill* (2001–02, HL 169-I, HC 876-I), [141]. The government in its response gave some indication of the power's use: 'Directions which have been issued in the past have dealt with matters including aspects of emergency planning, adherence to appropriate standards in the security vetting of staff, where that is necessary, and sensitive operational matters considered necessary for protecting national security, some of which were issued in the aftermath of the events of 11th September 2001': Department of Trade and Industry and Department of Culture, Media and Sport, *Government's Response to the Report of the Joint Committee on the Draft Communications Bill*, Cm 5646 (2002), [55].

(if at all) they are used.'[222] Nor was there any general oversight by the usual means. Some oversight of 'one particular set of Directions' which were made at the request of GCHQ took place first by the Interception of Communications Commissioner (between 2004 and 2006) and later by the Intelligence Services Commissioner (between 2006 and 2015). Such oversight, however, applied not to the giving of Directions but only to the access of data acquired thereunder.[223] In March 2015 the position changed: the Interception of Communications Commissioner disclosed that he taken on (on a non-statutory basis) the role of reviewing section 94 Directions.[224] This new role resulted in a report on the use of section 94 which was able to provide a greater level of detail as to the use which was being made of the provision,[225] but was hampered by certain factors, including that the nature of the statutory framework was such that there was no requirement of record keeping, and that much of the information which could be pieced together could not be disclosed without violating the secrecy provisions of the 1984 Act.[226] There were therefore clear incentives to making use of the 1984 Act rather than RIPA, and the claim that the preference was in fact because, unlike RIPA, section 94 allowed for the functioning of normal constitutional processes of political accountability entirely fails to convince.

In a challenge to the collection of BCD under section 94 which followed its avowal, the claimants argued that the RIPA regime was the only one by which communications data might lawfully be acquired by the security services. The IPT rejected that claim with reference to the saving provisions of subsequent statutes, culminating in that found in RIPA, by which:

> Nothing in any of the provisions of this Act by virtue of which conduct of any description is or may be authorised by any warrant, authorisation or notice, or by virtue of which information may be obtained in any manner, shall be construed—
>
> (a) as making it unlawful to engage in any conduct of that description which is not otherwise unlawful under this Act and would not be unlawful apart from this Act;
>
> ...
>
> (c) as prejudicing any power to obtain information by any means not involving conduct that may be authorised under this Act.[227]

There were, therefore, 'two lawful routes' by which BCD might be acquired.[228] The IPT nevertheless held that the regime had not—prior to November 2015—been in accordance with Article 8 of the ECHR. The reason for this was the inadequate oversight of the power which had existed before that point and, in particular the fragmented nature of that (non-statutory) oversight which had in fact been carried out by the Commissioners.[229] In the 'absence of the necessary oversight and supervision by the [Interception of Communications

[222] Anderson (n 171) [6.20].

[223] See the explanation in Sir Stanley Burton, *Report of the Interception of Communications Commissioner: Review of directions given under section 94 of the Telecommunications Act (1984)* (HC 2015–16, 33), [2.1(i)].

[224] Sir Anthony May, *Report of the Interception of Communications Commissioner* (HC 2014–2015, 1113), s 10.

[225] Burton (n 223).

[226] Burton (n 223) [11.6].

[227] RIPA 2000, s 80.

[228] [2016] UKIPTrib 15_110-CH, [57].

[229] ibid, [80].

Commissioner], the secondary roles of the [IPT] and the ISC were no replacement.'[230] Issues regarding the proportionality of the acquisition of BCD were left for later determination; the question is, of course, crucial to the compatibility of the BCD powers found now in the 2016 Act with the Convention Rights. Also left undecided in the original judgment was the question of compatibility with EU law, which later prompted a further reference to the CJEU. That reference asks, first, whether or not EU law applies to the activities of the SIAs as regards BCD (its acquisition and use for national security purposes) and, if so, whether or not the e-privacy Directive (and the specific requirements identified in *Watson*) apply to such activities. In case the invitation to the Luxembourg Court to back down from the strident position adopted in *Watson* was not clear enough, the IPT asked, finally: should the *Watson* requirements apply, 'to what extent, taking into account the essential necessity of the SIAs to use bulk acquisition and automated processing techniques to protect national security and the extent to which such capabilities, if otherwise compliant with the ECHR, may be critically impeded by the imposition of such requirements.' This framing makes very clear the belief that a reading of EU law which applies not only the Directive but also the specific requirements articulated by the Court of Justice is potentially harmful to the UK's national security endeavours, going as it does beyond the requirements so far imposed by the ECHR. Though—as noted above—the question may not be answered before Brexit comes to pass, the reference captures the possibility that while the law of investigatory powers is probably capable of complying, however belatedly and however grudgingly, with the requirements of the ECHR, EU law as currently interpreted poses a possibly existential threat to this element of the national security constitution.

The section 94 power was first used 'at scale' following the 11 September attacks, with its use 'extended' following the London attacks of July 2005 so as 'to respond to the domestic terrorist threat'.[231] The only useful information as to the number and nature of directions issued is that found in the IOCC's 2016 report, which confirms that MI6 did not make use of section 94, but that there were 23 directions in force which fell within the scope of the review,[232] all of which had been given by either the Home or Foreign Secretaries, on the request of either MI5, GCHQ, the 3 SIAs acting together, or the Metropolitan Police Service's Counter Terrorism Command.[233] All were given for national security purposes (rather than the alternative purpose for which directions might lawfully have been given under section 94).[234] Of the 23, 15 related to BCD, all of which related specifically to 'traffic data';[235] that is, 'data that may be attached to a communication for the purpose of transmitting it and could appear to identify the sender and recipient of the communication,

[230] ibid.

[231] HM Government, *Operational Case for Bulk Powers* (November 2015), [9.7]. The implication of course being that it was used between the enactment of the 1984 Act and September 2001, though in a comparatively limited fashion.

[232] The scope of the review is explained in Burton (n 223) [2.5] but is not amenable to concise restatement. Suffice it to say that Directions given on behalf of Ofcom and the department of Business, Innovation and Skills are excluded, while included are Directions given on behalf of the SIAs and similar, even where they do not relate to BCD.

[233] Burton (n 223) [7.1]–[7.5].

[234] ibid [7.3]. The alternative basis is the 'interests of … relations with the government of a country or territory outside the United Kingdom.'

[235] Burton (n 223) [8.34].

the location from which and the time at which it was sent, and other related material.'[236] The report notes, however, that GCHQ had previously had in place a direction relating to 'subscriber information'—'data held or obtained by the provider of a communications service in relation to a customer and may be the kind of information which a customer typically provides when they sign up to use a service'[237]—but that the requirement ceased following an 'internal review' shortly before the use of section 94 was first avowed.[238] That timing seems perhaps other than coincidental, and it must be likely that the 'secret' nature of the section 94 power and the associated absence of political scrutiny (whether by Parliament, the IOCC, or the wider public) contributed to it having remained in place for some unknown period prior to the internal review which brought to light its (unspecified) inappropriateness. The number of occasions on which BCD was accessed was much higher: the report gives the figures, relating to MI5 in 2015, of more than 20,000 access requests being made, these relating to more than 120,000 items of communications data.[239]

Section 94 is to be repealed by the 2016 Act, and there will in future exist only a single regime for the acquisition of bulk communications data.[240] A BCD warrant is one which requires a specified telecommunications operator to obtain and/or disclose communications data specified in the warrant or which authorises the selection for examination or disclosure of communications data obtained under the warrant.[241] The new regime limits the making of a BCD warrant to the same grounds upon which bulk interference warrants might be granted;[242] the same requirements of necessity and proportionality;[243] the same requirements relating to the operational purposes for which the BCD might be examined;[244] and the same requirement of approval by a Judicial Commissioner.[245] They may only be made on the application of a head of the intelligence services and are granted by the Secretary of State.[246] Though the same rule—that the warrant also authorises any conduct 'which it is necessary to undertake in order to do what is expressly authorised or required by the warrant'[247]—that provision does less work here, given that there is no requirement that the main purpose of a BCD warrant be the acquisition of communications data relating to overseas-related communications. As such, though the examination of material acquired under a BCD warrant is limited to the operational purposes laid out specified in the warrant (and a requirement of proportionality),[248] there is no prohibition on the selection of material for examination using criteria referable to persons known to be in the British Islands, nor—in turn—any need for a targeted examination warrant to overcome such prohibition. As with the targeted acquisition of communications data,

[236] ibid [8.3]. The relevant definition of 'traffic data' in RIPA 2000 is found in s 22(6).
[237] ibid.
[238] ibid [8.35].
[239] ibid [8.70].
[240] On the utility of the power, see David Anderson QC, *Report of the Bulk Powers Review* (August 2016), Ch 6.
[241] IPA 2016, ss 158(5) and (6).
[242] ibid, s 158(1).
[243] ibid, ss 158(1)(a) and (b).
[244] ibid, s 158(1)(c).
[245] ibid, s 158(1)(e).
[246] ibid, s 158(1).
[247] ibid, s 158(7).
[248] ibid, s 172.

perhaps the most objectionable feature of this regime will be its interaction with the retention notices for which the 2016 Act provides: telecommunications providers will likely be required to generate vast quantities of data—some of it at least as intrusive as the content of communications—in order that it might then be acquired under a BCD warrant and selected for examination via a process subject to only very weak legal restrictions.

C. Bulk Personal Datasets

Alongside bulk communications data, a second bulk power—similarly lacking any requirement of a foreign focus—was also avowed only at the point at which the government was about to place it upon a new and much more explicit statutory basis: the power to acquire, retain and use 'bulk personal datasets' (BPDs). BPDs are datasets which contain personal information about a large number of individuals; they might contain details of travel, for example, or financial affairs, and are acquired by the SIAs via a range of means: either the processing of data acquired via one of those investigatory powers described above, by theft (possibly authorised by a warrant or authorisation under the Intelligence Services Act 1994), or by purchase on commercial terms. The legal regime governing their retention and use was challenged in the IPT alongside that contained in section 94 of the 1984 Act, and the same conclusion arrived at: the regime governing the use of BPDs by the SIAs was historically incompatible with the 'in accordance with the law' element of Article 8 ECHR, but the incompatibility was (to the extent it was based upon that requirement, at least) remedied by a combination of improvements made to the oversight regime and disclosures made as part of the litigation process.[249] Unlike the section 94 regime, however, no challenge was brought to the domestic legality of the use of BPDs.[250] This failure is unfortunate, for it is not clear that the BPD regime as a whole had—before the enactment of the IPA 2016—a suitably solid basis in domestic law. Prior to the coming into force of the 2016 Act no statute gave clear authority for any of this; there were only a number of more or less obviously related provisions scattered across the statute book. The most significant of these are what are (now) referred to as the 'information gateway provisions' of the Security Service Act 1989 and the Intelligence Services Act 1994 which state that (taking the provision relevant to MI6 as our example) the Chief of MI6 'shall be responsible for the efficiency of that Service and it shall be his duty to ensure … that there are arrangements for securing that no information is obtained by the Intelligence Service except so far as necessary for the proper discharge of its functions and that no information is disclosed by it except so far as necessary' for the proper discharge of its functions of related ends.[251] Amongst these functions is that of 'obtain[ing] and provid[ing] information relating to the actions or intentions of persons outside the British Islands.'[252] The most important feature of the gateway provision is its negative status: it does not explicitly empower the doing of anything, but instead imposes a duty to ensure that certain things do not happen.

249 [2016] UKIPTrib 15_110-CH.
250 ibid, [64].
251 Intelligence Services Act 1994, s 2(2).
252 ISA 1994, s 1(1)(a).

The implication is that without this provision there would be no restrictions upon the power of MI6 (and, given that there exist in relation to them equivalent provisions, also MI5 and GCHQ) to obtain or disclose information.[253]

Drawing on the discussion above regarding the common law's commitment to the rule of law, it will be seen that this assumption is—broadly—correct. That is, the common law rule of law requires the existence of legal authority only for acts which have legal effects; which conflict with some public or private law right of a (natural or legal) person or which have the effect of altering the normative legal position of such persons. Because simply acquiring, retaining and disclosing information on BPDs does not interfere with any (common law) public or private law right of the individuals to whom the data relates, there is no requirement that the security services possess positive legal authority for doing so; it is therefore legitimate for the information gateway provisions to take the negative form which they do (the implication being that, before the 1989 and 1994 Acts were put in place, there were no limits on the purposes for which BPDs might be obtained and disclosed).[254] The situation resembles—albeit on a bigger scale—that in *ex parte C*,[255] where it was held that the Department of Health's maintenance of a list of persons considered unsuitable to work with children was lawful. Though the judgment of the court discusses the third source (or common law) powers of the Crown, the better view is that this is an example of what Adam Perry calls the Crown's 'ordinary powers': those things that can be done without any legal authority at all.[256] This is not to say, however, that the relatively complacent treatment of the domestic legality of BPDs by the IPT is entirely justified. One example suffices to demonstrate why a more thoroughgoing treatment would have been justified. It is clear that though the range of BPDs held by the security services are acquired in a variety of ways: some are stolen, some acquired via the use of investigatory powers of the sort on which this chapter focuses, while others are purchased. This last category raises an interesting question: for the executive to be capable of contract (in employment or so on) it must have some legal basis for doing so, because the making of a contract alters the legal position of those party to it. This presents little difficulty in the case of the central government departments which are emanations of the Crown: the Crown is (or is, at least, usually taken to be) a corporation sole, with all of the legal capacity of a natural person of capacity, including the capacity to make contracts. The security services, though under the authority of various secretaries of state, however, are not emanations of the Crown, and it is not clear from where their legal right to make contracts (including those for the purchase of BPDs) would derive; of which explicit power they might represent a necessary implication. It is for this reason unfortunate that the point was not pressed in the IPT, and that Tribunal forced to offer a fuller account of the powers of the SIAs in relation to BPDs.

[253] As indeed, had been decided by the Commission in *Hewitt and Harman v United Kingdom* [1989] ECHR 29, where it was held that the gathering and storing of the information regarding the applicants—the General Secretary of the NCCL and a Labour MP respectively—as had been revealed by MI5 whistle-blower Cathy Massiter, was incompatible with Article 8 because not in accordance with the law: the closest thing to a legal basis enjoyed by MI5 (the so-called Maxwell-Fyfe Directive) did not have the force of law.

[254] See Ian Leigh and Laurence Lustgarten, 'The Security Service Act 1989' (1989) 52 *MLR* 801, 825. The Data Protection Act contains a number of exemptions for personal data where it is certified by the Secretary of State that 'exemption … is required for the purpose of safeguarding national security.' Data Protection Act 1998, s 28.

[255] *R v Secretary of State for Health ex parte C* [2000] 1 FLR 627.

[256] Adam Perry, 'The Crown's Administrative Powers' (2015) 131 *LQR* 652.

Moreover, to the common law implications of BPDs must be added those of the Human Rights Act 1998 (the introduction of which postdates the facts of *ex parte C*, and whose outcome it would presumably alter) and, in particular, Article 8 of the ECHR. Here too, however, the IPT's treatment is only partial, focusing on the forms and quality of the oversight to which the BPD regime had been subject over time, which was variable and mostly inadequate. When formal oversight was introduced by the *Intelligence Services Commissioner (Additional Review Functions (Bulk Personal Datasets) Direction 2015*, it was only continuing prior, informal, oversight by the Intelligence Services Commissioner. Though the IPT concluded, therefore, that the oversight of BPDs had been adequate since 2010, the regime was in accordance with the requirements of Article 8 only since March 2015, when details of it were revealed in the ISC's Privacy and Security Report, at which point (it would seem) the use being made of the datasets became sufficiently foreseeable.[257] The effect was that not only could there be no effective legal accountability for the use of these powers (one cannot challenge a practice which one does not know takes place), but the possibility of political accountability was greatly diminished by the informal basis of the Commissioners' work and the secrecy surrounding it. The IPT did not address the question of the suitability, from the ECHR point of view, of the legal basis of the BPD regime. In *Esbester* the Commission had held the 1989 Act to be capable of grounding justified interferences with the Article 8 rights of the applicant, in the course of which it accepted that the relevant interference 'had a valid basis in domestic law, namely, the Security Service Act 1989 which placed the Security Service on a statutory footing for the first time.'[258] Had the Commission focussed more directly on the language of the 1989 Act, however, it may have come to see that though the Security Service was given a legal basis, the collection by it of information was not; or at least was given such a basis in such an oblique fashion as to not meet the most fundamental of the 'in accordance with law' requirements.[259] Even assuming the Commission's conclusions in *Esbester* to have been correct (at least at the time at which they were arrived), they relate to the acquisition and holding of data regarding individuals of interest to the SIAs. They do not relate to the acquisition or use of the *bulk* data with which the current work is concerned (which by definition includes information relating to those of no interest to the SIAs). Such use was—as noted above—avowed only in March 2015, with the publication of the Intelligence and Security Committee's report on the investigatory powers regime as a whole.[260] There is reason for believing, therefore, that on the best understanding the historic incompatibility of the retention and use of BPDs was not limited to the quality of the oversight, but was rather more fundamental.[261]

[257] [2016] UKIPTrib 15_110-CH, [101].

[258] *Esbester v United Kingdom* [1993] ECHR 64 (admissibility). *cf* Ian Leigh and Laurence Lustgarten, 'Employment, Justice and Détente: The Reform of Vetting' (1991) *MLR* 613, 630-3 and *Leander v Sweden* (1987) 9 EHRR 433 (discussed by Leigh and Lustgarten). The case is also discussed in: Security Services Commissioner, *Report of the Commissioner for 1993*, Cm 2523 (1994).

[259] Argument before the Commission focused primarily on the question of whether the imprecision of 'national security' prevented the law from achieving sufficient foreseeability.

[260] ISC (n 111) 55–7.

[261] See HM Government, *Operational Case for Bulk Powers* (November 2015), Ch 10, in which it is said that 'analysis of BPD by the security and intelligence agencies is a critical part of their response to the increasingly complicated and challenging task of defending the UK's interests and protecting its citizens in a digital age.'

The relevant provisions of the 1994 Act remain as they were when they originally came into force. What has changed, however, has been the addition to the landscape of a number of other provisions relevant to the acquisition and use made of BPDs, over and above that imposed by section 6 of the Human Rights Act (for the purposes of which the SIAs are public authorities). The Counter-Terrorism Act 2008 contains provisions which permit persons to 'disclose information to any of the intelligence services for the purposes of the exercise by that service of any of its functions' and permit the SIAs to disclose information received by them for the purpose of any of their functions for the purpose of the proper discharge of their respective functions or for other specified purposes, which in all three cases include 'criminal proceedings.'[262] These powers of disclosure to and disclosure by the SIAs override any duty of confidence owed by the disclosing person, as well as 'any other restriction on the disclosure of information (however imposed).'[263] Only two (sets of) limits exist to these powers over and above those imposed by the reference to the functions of the SIAs (and the requirements of necessity and proportionality which they reflect):[264] those found in Part 1 of RIPA,[265] and those found in the Data Protection Act 1998.[266] The latter are not as much of an obstacle as might be assumed, however. Under the Act, each of the SIAs is a data controller in relation to data which it holds which is 'personal data', and so are required to comply with the various data protection principles, a requirement which places significant limits upon what can be done with the data, and how. Nevertheless, the DPA contains a number of exceptions—which apply not only to the SIAs but to all data controllers—including one which provides that personal data are exempt from provisions including the DPP 'if the exemption from that provision is required for the purpose of safeguarding national security.'[267] That requirement is established conclusively by a certificate signed by a Minister of the Crown which certifies that 'exemption from all or any of the provisions mentioned in subsection (1) is or at any time was required for the purpose there mentioned in respect of any personal data.'[268] Finally, the use which might be made of this data is limited by the Official Secrets Act 1989.

The 2016 Act again assumes either that no legal authority is (at common law) required to retain and examine BPDs or that whatever authority is required is contained in the 1989 and 1994 Acts: the power to do so is created not positively but negatively, by providing that '[a]n intelligence service may not exercise a power to retain a bulk personal dataset

[262] Counter-Terrorism Act 2008, s 19.

[263] CTA 2008, s 19(6). They apply 'without prejudice to any rule of law authorising the obtaining, use or disclosure of information by any of the intelligence services': s 20(3).

[264] CTA 2008, s 20(2).

[265] Which, most importantly, impose restrictions on the use that might be made of intercepted material, so as to protect against the disclosure of the fact of interception.

[266] A broadly equivalent regime is contained in the Data Protection Bill introduced into the House of Lords in 2017 (HL Bill 2017-19 [66]). The Bill will—if enacted—make provision intended to ensure UK compliance with the General Data Protection Regulation (Regulation (EU) 2016/679) when it comes into force in May 2018, even after UK exit from the EU, but National security is outside the scope of EU law and so processing for that purpose is not encompassed by the GDPR. The stated intention is therefore for the relevant parts of the Bill to comply also with the Personal Data Protection Convention ('Convention 108') which is currently being 'modernised'. The Bill also contains a provision—cl 107—governing transfer of personal data outside the UK.

[267] Data Protection Act 1998, s 28.

[268] DPA 1998, s 28(2). A certificate can be reviewed on judicial review principles by the Tribunal which, if it finds that 'the Minister did not have reasonable grounds for issuing the certificate' may quash it: ss 28(4) and (5).

unless the retention of the dataset is authorised by a warrant under this Part' and that '[a]n intelligence service may not exercise a power to examine a bulk personal dataset retained by it unless the examination is authorised by a warrant under this Part.'[269] No direct definition of BDP is given, but the statute describes the circumstances under which one of the SIAs will retain a BPD: it does so if it 'obtains a set of information that includes personal data relating to a number of individuals'; the set's nature 'is such that the majority of the individuals are not, and are unlikely to become, of interest to the intelligence service in the exercise of its functions'; after initial examination the set is retained by the SIA 'for the purpose of the exercise of its functions' and 'the set is held, or is to be held, electronically for analysis in the exercise of those functions.'[270] No warrant is therefore required for holding a dataset in a non-electronic format, for holding it in such a format otherwise than for analysis, or for holding datasets which contain mostly data relating to persons of interest to the agency. The IPA provides for two types of warrants to obtain, to retain, and to examine, bulk personal datasets. The first is a 'specific BPD warrant',[271] which permits the retention (and examination) of a single specified dataset (and which therefore ensures that the acquisition in question is directly and individually authorised). The second is a 'class BPD warrant',[272] which permits the retention (and examination) of datasets which fall within the category specified in the warrant, the individual acquisition of which need not be authorised by—or even notified to—the Minister. Both types of warrant are subject to the now-standard triple test, whereby the warrant may be issued only if the Secretary of State considers it necessary for the purposes of national security, the prevention or detection of serious crime, or (insofar as also relevant to the interests of national security) in the interests of the UK's economic well-being, and considers that 'the conduct authorised by the warrant is proportionate to what is sought to be achieved by the conduct'.[273] They must also have been approved by a Judicial Commissioner (except, in the case of specific BPD warrants, in situations of urgency),[274] and are required to contain certain information, including—in the case of class warrants—a 'description of the class of bulk personal datasets to which the warrant relates'.[275] Where a warrant authorises examination of the BPD, it must also specify, from amongst a list maintained by the heads of the intelligence services,[276] the operational purposes for which the data contained in the BPDs may be selected for examination,[277] though the same points as to the weakness of this obstacle as made above apply also here.

Certain BPDs may not, however, be retained or examined on the basis of a class BPD warrant:[278] these include BPDs consisting of or including 'protected data' (defined in a manner which resembles an amalgam of the definitions of 'secondary data' and

[269] IPA 2016, s 201.
[270] ibid, s 199.
[271] ibid, s 200(3)(b).
[272] ibid, s 200(3)(a).
[273] ibid, ss 204 (class BPD warrants) and 205 (specific BPD warrants).
[274] ibid, ss 203(3)(e) and 205(6)(e).
[275] ibid, s 204(2)(a).
[276] ibid, s 212(5).
[277] ibid, s 204(2)(b).
[278] ibid, s 202.

'protected material' discussed in the context of interception warrants, and so is broader than each individually),[279] BPDs consisting of, or including, 'health records'[280] or a substantial proportion of which consists of 'sensitive personal data',[281] and BPDs the nature (or circumstances of acquisition) of which are such that its retention raises 'novel or contentious issues' which should be considered by the Minister and a Judicial Commissioner via an application for a specific warrant.[282] For such BPDs, a specific warrant is required, and the Secretary of State may impose further conditions which must be met 'before protected data retained in reliance on the warrant may be selected for examination on the basis of criteria which are referable to an individual known to be in the British Islands at the time of the selection.'[283] Warrants may last for up to six months, and be renewed an indefinite number of times.[284] No warrant is, however, required where the BPD was obtained under a warrant or authorisation issued or given under the Act—including, for example, where it is obtained via equipment interference, or via new powers to acquire communications data.[285] If an intelligence service comes into possession of a BPD otherwise than in pursuit of powers under the 2016 Act, the statute specifies that—unless the retention of the BPD is authorised by an extant class warrant—a specific BPD warrant must be sought either within three months (if the set was created in the UK) or within six months (if created outside it).[286] The Secretary of State must also ensure that arrangements are in place to ensure that examination of BPDs take place only where necessary for one of the operational purposes specified in the warrant which authorises examination, and 'the selection of any such data for examination is necessary and proportionate in all the circumstances.'[287] There is therefore no direct or even secondary judicial control of the examination of BPDs.

In reviewing the draft Investigatory Powers Bill, the ISC expressed strong concern about the manner in which apparent considerations of practicality were being allowed to override privacy concerns, and recommended that class BPD warrants be removed from the Bill altogether.[288] This did not happen. The limitations discussed above, however, on the

[279] ibid, s 203.

[280] Defined in s 206 to mean records (or copies thereof) which '(a) consists of information relating to the physical or mental health or condition of an individual, (b) was made by or on behalf of a health professional in connection with the care of that individual, and (c) was obtained by the intelligence service from a health professional or a health service body or from a person acting on behalf of a health professional or a health service body in relation to the record or the copy.'

[281] Defined in s 202(4) to mean personal information of the kind mentioned in s 2(a)–(f) of the Data Protection Act 1998.

[282] IPA 2016, s 202(3).

[283] ibid, s 207.

[284] ibid, s 213.

[285] IPA 2016, s 201(1). The SIAs can apply—under s 225(3)—to have that rule displaced by a direction from the Secretary of State, at which point it will be necessary for the retention and examination of the BPD to be authorised by either a specific or class BPD warrant. The direction can (subject to certain limitation, such as are contained in s 225(6) and which prevent the disapplication of the prohibition on disclosing intercept in legal proceedings) remove or modify any 'associated regulatory provisions' which applies to the dataset: ss 225(5) and (14). Such a direction requires the approval of a Judicial Commissioner, applying judicial review principles: s 225(7) and (8).

[286] IPA 2016, s 220. The ISC had objected to the equivalent provisions of the draft IP bill, which allowed BPDs acquired in this way to be held (but not used) indefinitely without a warrant: Intelligence and Security Committee, *Report on the draft Investigatory Powers Bill* (HC 2015–16, 795), [19] and [G]. It recommended time limits of one month for the retention without a warrant of UK-sourced BPDs, and six months for the retention without a warrant of overseas-sourced BPDS.

[287] ibid, s 221.

[288] ISC (n 286) [17]–[18] and [F].

use of class BPD warrants in relation to 'protected information' and 'health records' and in circumstances raising 'novel or contentious' issues were themselves added at the prompting of the Chairman of the ISC,[289] and go some way to dampening objections to the availability of such warrants.[290] Previously the ISC recommended that the reform of investigatory powers bring together all of the relevant statutory powers, so as to create a comprehensive and exhaustive regime.[291] Again, this was not done, and the relevant provisions of the 1989 and 1994 Acts—the information gateway provisions, as well as those authorising property interference domestically and a broader category of interferences outside the British Islands—remain in place, and are in fact widened to some uncertain extent by amendments made by the 2016 Act.[292] The negative definition of the powers to acquire and retain BPDs eliminate—or at least should be interpreted as eliminating—any scope for arguing that the 1989 and 1994 Acts constitute a second legal route permitting such acquisition and retention, or even that the common law rule of law operates in such a way that there is no requirement for legal authority at all. As with BCD, the proportionality of the interference with Article 8 occasioned by the BPD powers remains to be determined by the IPT.[293] Analysis of that question will—the Tribunal indicated—be influenced by the review of bulk powers carried out by the Independent Reviewer of Terrorism Legislation, where it was concluded that 'BPDs are of great utility' to the security services, principally in terms of the 'identification and development of targets'.[294] Relevant also to the assessment of proportionality is that while in some situations alternative methods would be capable of producing equivalent results, these methods would be 'slower, less comprehensive or more intrusive.'[295] In other situations, however, the IRTL concluded, 'no practicable alternative to the use of BPDs exists.'[296]

IV. Conclusion

The regime of investigatory powers impacts upon constitutional issues in a number of ways, but the opposite is also true. That is, though it has taken far longer than should have

[289] The limitations were added to the Bill during its passage through the House of Lords, having been suggested during the Committee stage in the House of Commons by Dominic Grieve QC MP, Chair of the Intelligence and Security Committee: HC Debs, 7 June 2016, vol 611 col 1049.

[290] Eric King and Daniella Lock, from whom I take this point, note that a third restriction suggested by Grieve, whereby a limit would be placed on the number of BPDs which might lawfully be acquired under a single class warrant, was not implemented, and so 'provisions regarding class warrants fall short of meeting the standard, as laid out by the ISC.': See Eric King and Daniella Lock, 'Investigatory Powers Bill: Key Changes Made by the Lords', *UK Constitutional Law Blog* (1 December 2016).

[291] ISC (n 111) [XX].

[292] See IPA 2016, s 251, amending s 3 of the Intelligence Services Act 1994 so as to allow GCHQ to 'make use of' (in addition to 'monitor' and 'interfere with') electromagnetic and other emissions, and amending s 5 of the 1994 Act, so as to permit MI6 and GCHQ to apply for property interference warrants for the purposes of preventing and detecting serious crime within the British Islands.

[293] BPDs formed no part of the reference to the CJEU made by the IPT which was noted above in the context of the acquisition of bulk communications data under the Telecommunications Act 1984.

[294] David Anderson QC, *Report of the Bulk Powers Review* (August 2016), [8.33].

[295] Anderson (n 294) [8.35].

[296] ibid, [8.36].

been the case (and the interventions not only of the Strasbourg Court, but also of a rogue military contractor), the regime now is for the most part in accordance with the common law's fundamental approach to the rule of law: there is, for all those powers of which we are aware, statutory authority. In most cases, the statutory authority is sufficiently explicit to justify what we understand to be the actions for which it will be identified as authority. The higher standards imposed by the ECHR have—through a process of whistleblowing and strategic litigation for which the organisations who have brought the various challenges deserve great credit—managed to drag from the government a far greater level of detail as to the nature of the use of the powers than would otherwise have entered the public domain, albeit leaving much of the key information 'below the waterline' and making public only a gist of the relevant procedures. Here too, however, accountability for unlawful use of the various powers has come only late in the day, as the era of ad hoc and at times secret investigatory powers has (it would, at least, appear) given way to one which is more rational, more coherent, and more realistically knowable to the public. For this reason alone, it would be foolish to assume that we are now aware of all of the relevant practices or even the statutory powers which ground (or fail to ground) them. More broadly, the number and scope of the powers in question are now such that it would be similarly foolish to think of them as a tool which might be used only against some small, aberrant subset of the UK population: they can and will be used, even if only in their bulk form, in such a way as to collect the data of many of those who read this book. In democratic constitutional orders, the relationship between citizen and the state is not a purely static one: instead, the power exercised by the state works to construct the subjectivity of the citizen who then operates within formal and informal political processes. We may, I suggest, be approaching the point at which a significant role in the construction of individual subjectivity is played by the law and practice of investigatory powers; those who participate in the political process are not merely their possible targets, but also their products.

3

The Military Constitution

I. Introduction

National security is, as it is normally discussed in constitutional literature, a primarily domestic policy aim, focussed on those threats which arise within, or are otherwise aimed at, the territory of the UK and the people, property and institutions found there. There is, however, an obvious and substantial sense in which it is an international and extra-territorial endeavour. I have already considered—in the context of both counter-terrorism and investigatory powers—examples of legal rules which derive ultimately from the international plane, or whose shape reflects the influence of international legal instruments or co-operation between states. A later chapter will consider more generally how that element of the topic has come to dominate in recent years and decades; how the national security constitution has tended towards an *inter*-national security constitution. In this chapter, however, we concern ourselves with the law which governs the UK's response to external threats to its security, whether posed by foreign states or, as is increasingly common, by non-state actors.[1] One caveat must be entered: the topic of what I call 'the military constitution' is a major one, to which a single book could not do justice, never mind a single chapter. In choosing what questions (and which elements of those questions) to consider here I am guided by considerations of contemporary significance: the topics addressed are, for the most part, those which have been most relevant to the unfolding of events (or, conversely, to which events have been most relevant) in the period since the 11 September attacks. With that said, we must nevertheless insist on the centrality of this chapter's topic to the broader theme: the national security constitution encompasses a military dimension which too often escapes notice from those whose focus is domestic rather than international; artificial boundaries are drawn as between different sorts of threats to national security which are part of the same constitutional picture, with traditional disciplinary divides working to obstruct a full (or fuller) understanding of that picture.[2]

[1] Space precludes a full consideration of the use of military force within the UK: for a starting point, see Michael Head, 'Calling out the troops and the Civil Contingencies Act: some questions of concern' [2010] *PL* 340. More general considerations of the use of military power within the state itself are offered in A Babington, *Military Intervention in Britain: From the Gordon Riots to the Gibraltar Incident* (London, Routledge, 1990) and PJ Rowe and CJ Whelan (eds), *Military Intervention in Democratic Societies* (London, Croom Helm, 1985). And see now Ministry of Defence, *UK Operations: The Defence Contribution to Resilience and Security*, Joint Doctrine Publication 02, 3rd edn (2017). An earlier edition of the same document is discussed by Head; the newer edition is more measured in the legal claims it makes.

[2] See, eg, the debate on the withdrawal of troops from Afghanistan which took place in 2012, in which the Armed Forces Minister stated that '[w]e are in Afghanistan for one overriding reason: to protect our own national

II. The Place of the Military in the Constitution

Control of the Armed Forces had been a central feature of the struggle between Crown and Parliament in the lead up to the English civil war, with Charles I refusing assent to a Militia Bill which would have transferred control over the Armed forces to Parliament and the latter responding by promulgating it as an ordinance and declaring that 'the People are bound by the Ordinance for the Militia, though it has not received the Royal Assent.'[3] In turn, one of the Nineteen Propositions sent by Parliament to Charles I in 1942 was that the King 'rest satisfied with that course that the Lords and Commons have appointed for ordering of the militia, until the same shall be further settled by a Bill; and … recall [his] Declarations and Proclamations against the Ordinance made by the Lords and Commons concerning it.'[4] Charles' response was to describe the Ordinance as representing the erection of 'an upstart Authority without Us (in whom, and only in whom, the Laws of this Realm have placed that power) to command the Militia.'[5] Following restoration, Parliament acknowledged in the Militia Act 1661 that 'the sole supreme government, command, and disposition of the militia and of all forces by sea and land and of all forts and places of strength is and by the laws of England ever was the undoubted right of His Majesty and his Royal Predecessors, Kings and Queens of England' and that 'both or either of the Houses of Parliament cannot nor ought to pretend to the same'. The Convention Parliament of 1660 disbanded the Militia: the King consented, for he too 'had some reason to dread a standing army.'[6]

Reflecting this history, the Bill of Rights 1689 forbade 'the raising or keeping of a standing Army within the Kingdom in time of Peace unless it be with the Consent of Parliament.'[7] This saw the emergence of a practice whereby Parliament consented to the keeping of a standing Army via the annual passage of a Mutiny Act which determined both the size of the force in question and the rules of military discipline which applied to it.[8] These rules were codified into the Army Act 1881 and their continuation in force was ensured until 1955 by the passage of an annual statute which modified the 1881 Act where necessary. The Army Act 1955 permitted the annual extension of its provisions by Order

security by helping the Afghans take control of their own', the UK's strategy there being 'designed to enable the country effectively to manage its own security and prevent its territory from ever again becoming a safe haven for international terrorism.' HC Deb 7 November 2012, vol 552 col 241-2WH. This claim was met by a request, from Paul Flynn MP, that the Minister 'tell us precisely what the threat to our constituents is from the Taliban in Afghanistan'.

[3] Journal of the House of Lords iv, 646 (15 March 1642). The Militia Ordinance was passed on 5 March 1642. The text can be found in SR Gardiner (ed), *Constitutional Documents of the Puritan Revolution 1625–1660*, 3rd edn (Oxford, Oxford University Press, 1906), 245–7; the King's proclamation condemning the Ordinance (27 May 1642) is at 248–9.

[4] 'The Nineteen Propositions Sent by the Two Houses of Parliament to the King at York' in Gardiner (n 3) 249–54, Art 9.

[5] Charles I, 'His Majesties Answer to the Nineteen Propositions of Both Houses of Parliament', in JL Malcom (ed), *The Struggle for Sovereignty: Seventeenth-Century English Political Tracts, vol 1* (Indianapolis, Liberty Fund, 1999), 117.

[6] FW Maitland, *The Constitutional History of England* [1908] (Cambridge, Cambridge University Press, 2008), 326.

[7] Bill of Rights 1689, Art 6. The words 'in time of peace' of course imply that in war Parliament's consented is not needed. This does not, however, obviate the need for Parliament to grant the relevant supply.

[8] See WS Holdsworth, A *History of English Law* (London, Methuen & Co, 1937), vol X, 377–401.

in Council, with parliamentary approval required after five years[9] and—along with the Air Force Act 1955 and the Naval Discipline Act 1957—created the regimes of military discipline which persisted for the second half of the twentieth century. The current practice is for an Armed Forces Act to be passed every five years,[10] though the scope of the Act varies depending on the extent of the changes being made to the organisation of the forces. The Armed Forces Act 2006, for example, effected a major reorganisation of military law as put in place by the three aforementioned enactments, harmonising the powers of summary discipline across the three services, and creating a unified Services Prosecuting Authority for the prosecution of more serious offences. That Act provides for its own expiry one year following its enactment,[11] and though it could be extended for up to a year at a time by Order in Council (passed using the affirmative procedure) its date of expiry could not by Order be put back beyond the end of 2011.[12] By contrast, the Armed Forces Acts 2011 is comparatively short, effecting the continuation of the authorisation for the existence of a standing army via a new section substituted into the 2006 Act, though with the date beyond which its expiry could not be postponed now the end of 2016.[13] The 2016 Act makes an equivalent substitution, giving statutory authority for the continuation of the authorisation until the end of 2021.[14]

Notwithstanding this harmonisation of the applicable systems of military discipline, the legal bases of the services continue to vary, with the other services not subject to the requirement of annual renewal. The Royal Air Force derives its existence from the Air Force (Constitution) Act 1917, which permits the Monarch 'to raise and maintain a force, to be called the Air Force, consisting of such number of officers, warrant officers, non-commissioned officers, and men as may from time to time be provided by Parliament.'[15] The Navy, however, is not encompassed by these statutory rules and is instead still 'maintained by virtue of the prerogative.'[16] Within the executive, defence is a function of the Ministry of Defence, formed in 1964 out of the amalgamation of the Admiralty, the War Office, the Air Ministry, and the Ministry of Defence,[17] with the functions of the Ministry of Aviation Supply added in 1971.[18] The Ministry is headed by a Secretary of State (supported by a number of other ministers) who chairs the Defence Council—in which legal powers are vested by both statute and Letters Patent—which includes also the various ministers in the Ministry of Defence, the key civil servants, and the six most senior military figures (the Chief of the Defence Staff, the Vice-Chief of the Defence Staff, the First Sea Lord and Chief of Naval Staff, the Chief of the General Staff, the Chief of the Air Staff, and

[9] Army Act 1955, s 226(4) and (5).

[10] The effect of placing the time limit on the renewal of the Act by secondary legislation is to ensure that a full Parliamentary debate must take place at least every five years.

[11] Armed Forces Act 2006, s 382. The same applies to what remains in force of the earlier enactments.

[12] ibid s 382 (3) and (4).

[13] Armed Forces Act 2011, s 1.

[14] Armed Forces Act 2016, s 1.

[15] Air Force (Constitution) Act 1917, s 1.

[16] Public Administration Select Committee, *Taming the Prerogative: Strengthening Ministerial Accountability to Parliament* (HC 2003–04, 422) [9]. The navy had not attracted the sort of political suspicion that had a standing army: Blackstone called it England's 'greatest defence and ornament … an army, from which, however strong and powerful, no danger can ever be apprehended to liberty.' Blackstone, *Commentaries*, I, 405.

[17] Defence (Transfer of Functions) Act 1964.

[18] By the Ministry of Aviation Supply (Dissolution) Order 1971 (SI 1979/719).

the Commander of the Joint Forces Command)[19] and the Director General of Finance at the Ministry of Defence. The Defence Council includes as sub-committees three services boards (the Admiralty Board, the Army Board and the Air Force Board) which meet annually. In practice, everyday decisions are made by a Defence Board, comprising of the Secretary of State, the Minister for Defence Procurement, the Permanent Under-Secretary, the Chief and Vice-Chiefs of Defence Staff, the Director General of Finance and four non-executive members.[20] The organisational structure of defence was the subject of significant reform following the publication of a report by Lord Levene in 2011,[21] which made 53 recommendations aimed at producing 'a model for running Defence that ensures that the whole is more than the sum of its parts and which has affordability at its core.'[22] Notwithstanding that several of the recommendations aimed at simplifying the defence framework, the decision-making structure retains considerable complexity.[23]

One further point is worth making here, before turning to some of the legal and constitutional issues pertaining to the military. Though certain questions—principally those discussed in the present chapter—have attracted considerable attention in recent years, the general tendency has been to write the armed forces out of the constitutional picture. Where once they were discussed as standard in major works on public law, treatment in contemporary textbooks is often thin or non-existent. The reasons for this change are not hard to discern: in the constitutional struggles of the seventeenth century, Parliament's victory was almost total, and memories of wars which impact upon life in the UK are fading. War is something which happens elsewhere, whose effects are felt mostly by others, and so on. Perhaps more important still is that there is broad alignment of political and military opinion on the most important issues of the day. Though dissent is often heard, mostly regarding resourcing, the political neutrality of the armed forces is taken for granted,[24] and the principle of its civilian control so-well established, it seems, as to barely merit consideration. As such, the precise nature—as well as the quality—of political control in this sphere is of little interest and (as the previous paragraph makes clear) rather complex. And though questions about the governance and conduct of the armed forces arise more persistently in Northern Ireland, the low-key but pervasive othering of the province in British political discourse allows it to exist in a parallel world, the details of which do not resonate in the

[19] A 'confusing aspect of the structure within the MoD is that the [Chief of the Defence Staff] does not command the Chiefs'; that is, '[t]here is no chain of command from the CDS down to the Chiefs. The CDS works directly to the Secretary of State and likewise the Chiefs work directly to the Secretary of State.' House of Commons Defence Committee, *Decision-making in Defence Policy* (HC 2014–15, 682), [79].

[20] A helpful overview of the organisation in previous times is found in WR Anson, *The Law and Custom of the Constitution—Part II: The Crown*, 2nd edn (Oxford, Oxford University Press, 1896), Ch 8.

[21] Lord Levene of Portsoken KBE, *Defence Reform An independent report into the structure and management of the Ministry of Defence* (June 2011).

[22] Lord Levene (n 21) 5. One of the key effects of the Levene reforms was 'to diminish further the roles' of the Chiefs, who lost their places on the Defence Board and are now 'jointly represented by the Chief of the Defence Staff': Defence Committee (n 19) [69]–[70]. The Chiefs do, though, 'have the right to put their thoughts directly to the Prime Minister or the Secretary of State' [74].

[23] See the conclusions in Defence Committee (n 19) [118]: 'The changes that have been introduced … the Levene reforms, have clarified and improved the structures of decision-making' but they have 'not yet addressed fundamental problems in the process of decision-making.'

[24] As outlined in the Queen's Regulations for the Army (1975) (as amended).

mainstream of constitutional thinking. Little wonder, therefore, that there is a preference for singling out for consideration instead the specific question of the exercise of the war prerogative and—in particular—the basic decision to deploy the armed forces. Though this tendency is understandable (and largely replicated here), it is—I suggest—to be resisted. One does not need to go too far back in British history to find, at Curragh in 1914, a section of the armed forces willing to disobey orders in pursuit of a constitutional vision at odds with that of the government.[25] And as the Labour Party has shifted political direction in recent years—with a leadership that remains opposed to the Trident nuclear weapons system—persistent whispers, carefully channelled into appropriate outlets, have suggested that the principle of civilian control might not be as dependable as is often assumed.[26] This alone makes the question of the governance of the military more important than the modern constitutional literature would seem to allow. Beyond that, however, constitutional scholarship which excludes consideration of the armed forces likely excludes also a variety of other institutions which are similarly central to public power and its exercise. Talking—as often happens—about the relationship between the courts and the executive, or the executive and Parliament, while thinking only of the Prime Minister, the Cabinet and perhaps the Civil Service, reflects a very meagre conceptualisation of politics, one which risks not only misrepresenting but in fact misunderstanding the constitutional reality of the contemporary UK.

III. The Use of Force in Constitutional Law and Practice

This section considers the law and practice governing the use of military force abroad as a matter of domestic law. There are two elements to this in the general constitutional literature. One is the strict legal position, discussed in its constitutional context below.[27] The second reflects the emergence of the conventional rule requiring parliamentary assent to the use of force.[28] The argument offered here is that the focus upon Parliament's role obscures certain other elements of the constitutional picture which are equally important and in some cases work to undermine the democratic control created by the emergence of the convention in question: amongst these issues are the international law element to

[25] For an account which puts it in its constitutional context, see G Dangerfield, *The Strange Death of Liberal England* [1935] (Stanford, Stanford University Press, 1997) 269–81.

[26] See most strikingly the story published by the *Sunday Times* in September 2015 which quoted a serving general as suggesting that the armed forces would take 'direct action' in the event that Jeremy Corby became Prime Minister: 'you would face the very real prospect of an event which would effectively be a mutiny': Tim Shipman, Sean Rayment, Richard Kerbaj and James Lyons, 'Corbyn hit by mutiny on airstrikes' *The Sunday Times* (20 September 2015).

[27] The leading account of the war prerogative is R Joseph, *The War Prerogative: History, Reform, and Constitutional Design*, (Oxford, Oxford University Press, 2013).

[28] On which, see James Strong, 'Why Parliament Now Decides on War: Tracing the Growth of the Parliamentary Prerogative through Syria, Libya and Iraq' (2015) 17 *British Journal of Politics and International Relations* 604; Philippe Lagassé, 'Parliament and the War Prerogative in the United Kingdom and Canada: Explaining Variations in Institutional Change and Legislative Control' (2017) 70 *Parliamentary Affairs* 280. See also HJ Hooper and V Fikfak, *Parliament's Secret War* (Oxford, Hart Publishing, forthcoming).

the use of force, which limits the use of force whether or not Parliament is willing—as a matter of domestic constitutional practice—to accept it; the limited ability of Parliament—for reasons of knowledge, expertise and secrecy—to scrutinise the use of force, and consequent likelihood that the use of force will be determined in practice by considerations of domestic political practice of dubious relevance to the matters; the deployment of special forces, which takes place in secret and is not covered by any convention—whether actual or potential—regarding parliamentary involvement.

A. The War Prerogative

Though the legal bases of the services vary, the power to make war is distinct and in relation to all three of the services it has been generally accepted that it is the prerogative which governs their 'deployment and use overseas … including involvement in armed conflict' alongside the power to declare war and the 'use of the armed forces within the United Kingdom to maintain the peace in support of the police.'[29] The most important writer on the prerogative, Joseph Chitty, described this as including 'the exclusive right to make war or peace, either within or out of his Kingdom' and 'to grant or refuse a capitulation or truce.'[30] Chitty argued, against Blackstone, that 'it seems that no public declaration, or formal proclamation of war is, by law, absolutely necessary to render it the duty of the king's subjects to consider and treat as an enemy any foreign power against whom war has in point of fact been resolved upon and commenced by his Majesty.'[31] The fact of such a declaration is now similarly irrelevant in international law, and no formal declaration of war has been made by the UK since the Second World War.[32] Amongst the rights incidental to the prerogative, Chitty counted the King's position at the head of the Army and Navy, noting that he alone was 'entitled to order their movements, to regulate their internal and arrangements, and to diminish or, during war, increase their numbers.'[33] Within the contemporary constitution, one important part of that claim is no longer true: with a small number of exceptions,[34] the prerogative is exercised not by the Monarch personally

[29] Public Administration Select Committee, *Taming the Prerogative. Strengthening Ministerial Accountability to Parliament*, (HC 2003–04, 422), [9]. See also Thomas Baty and John Hartman Morgan, *War: Its Conduct and Legal Results*, EP Dutton and Co (1915), Ch 4.

[30] J Chitty, *A Treatise on the Law of the Prerogatives of the Crown: And the Relative Duties and Rights of the Subject* (London, J Butterworth & Son, 1820), 43.

[31] Chitty (n 30) 44

[32] 'The last time there was a declaration of war was in 1939. It is not necessary to make a declaration of war these days. Since then, we have been involved in a number of armed conflicts. The existence or not of a legal state of war is nowadays irrelevant for most purposes of international law. The application of what used to be called "the law of war" and the status of prisoners of war depends upon the existence of an armed conflict, which is a factual situation and not a question of a declaration of a state of war. Whether there is a state of war might still be relevant for certain purposes of domestic law: for example, as regards the application of certain private contracts referring to war. Apart from that … a formal declaration of war is not necessary.' The Attorney General (Lord Goldsmith), HL Deb 19 February 2003, vol 644 col 1139.

[33] Chitty (n 30) 44. See also on those incidental powers Joseph (n 27) 117–24, where the author notes that many of them have over time been moved onto a statutory basis.

[34] The exceptions are sometimes called the 'political prerogatives'—the granting of Royal Assent, the appointment of a Prime Minister and other ministers, the prorogation of Parliament etc.

(and even where the Monarch does exercise the prerogative powers, their use is almost always circumscribed by convention),[35] but by the Prime Minister and other ministers in the name of the Crown. This is equally true for the war prerogative, including the management of the armed forces.

Nevertheless, even this democratic evolution left the power to make war in a constitutional position which might be thought unsatisfactory for, though it was accepted by the courts that the King 'hath no prerogative, but that which the law of the land allows him'[36]—and thus that they were entitled to adjudicate upon the existence and scope of the prerogative—this rule was historically accompanied by an unwillingness to review the use to which a legally-recognised power was put,[37] justifying Blackstone's claim that the King was, in his exercise of the powers, 'irresistible and absolute'.[38] That claim no longer holds, in light of a series of decisions of the English courts which have established that the reviewability of a power is a function of its subject matter rather than its source in law, and which have seen even the power to manage (if not to deploy) the armed forces subject to oversight by the courts in some circumstances.[39] A fuller discussion of justiciability is found in Chapter 6. I take that discussion to have the following implications for the war prerogative: the power generally is justiciable if, and to the extent that, there is some legal question for the courts to determine, either at common law or statute, albeit that the standard of review is likely to be as light-touch as imaginable in the context of the majority of the acts done thereunder.[40] Many such acts will, however, be non-justiciable in the strict sense by virtue of the doctrine of Crown act of state; even these, however, will be justiciable where statute empowers (or requires) the courts to rule upon them. The one element of this which requires further consideration is that of whether there is a legal question for the courts to determine in the first place: that is, does the war prerogative necessarily have any legal effect? If not, it is not clear—for the reasons discussed in Chapter 4 in relation to passports—that it is properly designated a prerogative at all. To the extent that the war prerogative is used to ground the destruction or requisition of property, there is no difficulty here. What of the decision to declare war itself? A convenient answer is provided by the Supreme Court in the *Miller* case,[41] where that Court explains the two sets of circumstances in which the prerogative can have domestic legal consequences: the first where the exercise of the prerogative inherently

[35] The exception is the grant of a small number of honours in relation to which the Sovereign enjoys unfettered discretion, and—perhaps—certain of the political prerogatives which might, it is argued, be exercised at the monarch's discretion in extreme circumstances. Where it is argued that this is a constitutionally correct account, such powers are sometimes designated the 'reserve powers' of the Monarch.

[36] *The Case of Proclamations* (1611) 12 Co Rep 74.

[37] See, eg, *China Navigation Company v Attorney General* [1932] 2 KB 197.

[38] Blackstone, *Commentaries on the Laws of England*, I, 244.

[39] *R v Ministry of Defence*, ex parte Smith [1996] QB 517. See also Joseph (n 27) 124–44.

[40] Though see, most clearly, *Campaign for Nuclear Disarmament v Prime Minister* [2002] EWHC 2777 (Admin), [59(iii)]: 'In my view it is unthinkable that the national courts would entertain a challenge to a Government decision to declare war or to authorise the use of armed force against a third country. That is a classic example of a non-justiciable decision.' Note though that the question of whether the Kingdom is at war is a factual, rather than a legal question: 'If the King says by an Act of State that the Commonwealth of countries over which he reigns is at war with a particular state, it is at war with that state, and the certificate of the Secretary of State is conclusive.' *R v Bottrill, ex parte Kuechenmeister* [1947] 1 KB 41, 50.

[41] *R (Miller) v Secretary of State for Exiting the European Union* [2017] UKSC 5,

affects legal rights, and the second where 'the effect of an exercise of prerogative powers is to change the facts to which the law applies':

> Thus, the exercise of the prerogative to declare war will have significant legal consequences: actions which were previously lawful may become treasonable (as in *Joyce v Director of Public Prosecutions* [1946] AC 347), and some people will become enemy aliens, whose property is liable to confiscation.[42]

Not only: as discussed elsewhere in this book the prerogative to intern and deport enemy aliens under the prerogative appears to persist.[43] The key contemporary implication of the power to go to war being found in the prerogative is that it is—as a matter of law—exercisable at the discretion of the executive of the day, without any formal safeguards or procedural limitations. Any accountability has been political and almost inevitably after the fact, though this does not exclude that a King (or now a Prime Minister) would choose not to go to war for fear of the political consequences of doing so (both within and outside of Parliament, and as part of the informal political process), in which case the accountability is anticipatory and may be effective despite leaving no clear trace on the historical record.

B. Reforming the War Power

In 2006, a report of the House of Lords Constitution Committee concluded that 'the exercise of the Royal Prerogative by the Government to deploy armed force overseas is outdated and should not be allowed to continue as the basis for legitimate war-making in our 21st century democracy' and that '[t]here is a need to set out more precisely the extent of the Government's deployment powers, and the role Parliament can—and should—play in their exercise.'[44] There are, however, many ways in which those factors might be set out. That recommended by the Committee was that 'there should be a parliamentary convention determining the role Parliament should play in making decisions to deploy force or forces outside the United Kingdom to war, intervention in an existing conflict or to environments where there is a risk that the forces will be engaged in conflict'.[45] The creation of a convention would presumably be effected via declaration: though statutes have been used to give

[42] [2017] UKSC 5, [53]. See also *Amin v Brown* [2005] EWHC 1670 (Ch), in which Mr Justice Lawrence Collins in the Chancery Division held that 'the disability of alien enemies is part of the rules of English law relating to the traditional laws of war, and that there is no warrant for extending it to modern armed conflict not involving war in the technical sense.'

[43] See Ch 4.

[44] House of Lords Constitution Committee, *Waging war: Parliament's role and responsibility* (HL 2005–06, 236-I) [103]. The Public Administration Select Committee had in 2004 recommended that the government consult on the future of the prerogative powers, and that the consultation should include proposals 'for legislation to provide greater parliamentary control over *all* the executive powers enjoyed by Ministers under the royal prerogative' including the powers relating to military action: PASC (n 29)[60] (emphasis added). Before and after that report, and prompted most directly by the vote in Parliament prior to the 2003 war in Iraq, several private members' bills had been introduced with a view to place the war power on a statutory footing and require that it be made use of only with the consent of Parliament. One of these, the Military Action Against Iraq (Parliamentary Approval) Bill (presented by Tam Dalyell) was unable to proceed through the House of Commons because 'Queen's consent' (needed because the Bill affected the Queen's prerogative powers) was not given (though it is unclear whether it was refused, or whether Dalyell was unwilling to request it). See now, Cabinet Office, *Guide to Making Legislation* (April 2017), Ch 18.

[45] HLCC (n 44) [108].

convention a legal basis and to 'recognise' them as conventions, where the intention is to create a convention, the preferred mechanism has normally been via a declaration, often in the form of a resolution of the House of Commons.[46] The suggestion was later taken up by the government, following consultation,[47] in the White Paper on 'The Governance of Britain',[48] which contained a draft 'war powers' resolution.[49] The preference for this method of proceeding, it was said, reflected '[t]he uncertain nature of military deployments' and the 'likelihood that the lead up to each conflict or potential conflict situation would not necessarily conform to any pattern'. It would 'define a clear role for Parliament in this most important of decisions, while ensuring our national security is not compromised by the introduction of a less flexible mechanism.'[50]

The Committee, in endorsing the convention route, implicitly rejected placing the question on a statutory footing, but provides a useful overview of the arguments against such a path, some of which apply to any parliamentary involvement, regardless of its legal status, but some of which bite exclusively on the statutory approach.[51] These latter included 'a lack of clarity in identifying those deployments to which legislation would apply' and that 'the legislation could open the door to judicial review, appeal and challenge in a way that might have adverse operational consequences.'[52] The first of these difficulties could probably be overcome with careful drafting, though to do so would involve acknowledging openly that (as discussed further below) there are forms of military intervention of which the public is not informed and which could not therefore readily be disclosed to Parliament in order that Parliament might endorse or reject them. The second is strictly correct: even if the war prerogative is currently non-justiciable in the strict sense, the inclusion of a requirement for parliamentary approval in a statute would suffice to render that element of the matter justiciable (overcoming any countervailing considerations either of subject matter or of parliamentary privilege). Nevertheless, the courts would in that scenario be acting in accordance with an implied mandate from Parliament, and unless the standard of review was specified in the statute, would likely review Parliament's actions with only the lightest of touches. Nor, in the absence of statutory mandate, would they likely be willing to provide a remedy which purported to inhibit the conduct of war. To these we might add a third difficulty: almost every claim that the deployment of armed forces should be (or in fact already is) subject to parliamentary authorisation recognises an exception to the convention (whether actual or hypothetical) where military action is urgent. To frame such an exception in statute would be difficult, and the exception would have the potential to undermine entirely the basic rule. In the event, though a convention to the effect that Parliament must approve the deployment of troops appears to have emerged, it has done so organically and hesitantly, rather than via unilateral declaration.

[46] For a critique of this 'soft law' approach to constitutional reform, see Aileen McHarg, 'Reforming the United Kingdom Constitution: Law, Convention, Soft Law' (2008) 71 *MLR* 853.

[47] Ministry of Justice, *The Governance of Britain—War powers and treaties: Limiting Executive powers*, Cm 7239 (2007).

[48] Ministry of Justice, *The Governance of Britain—Constitutional Renewal*, Cm 7342-I (2008).

[49] Ministry of Justice (n 48) Annex A.

[50] ibid, [215].

[51] HLCC (n 44) [81]–[84].

[52] HLCC (n 44) [82].

C. The War Powers Convention

Where a convention is argued to have emerged organically, the standard view, first elaborated by Jennings but recently applied by the Upper Tribunal,[53] holds the test for its existence to have three parts: first, persons must act in a certain way (there must, that is, be practice consistent with the alleged convention);[54] second, they must do so not merely out of habit but out of a belief that such conduct is obligatory; third, there must be a reason for that conduct to be obligatory.[55] As regards the first element, Parliament traditionally had a very limited role in the authorisation of use of force, reflecting that in law force can be employed without its assent.[56] Parliament was nevertheless often given the opportunity to debate the use of force: sometimes on the substantive question, but often on a motion to adjourn (and so with no opportunity to endorse or condemn military action) and usually after the fact.[57] Only with the war in Iraq in 2003 does Parliament's involvement become direct and prospective, with Parliament endorsing the use of military force on a substantive motion two days prior to its commencement, though after the deployment of troops had begun.[58] There had been no parliamentary approval of the use of force in Afghanistan two years earlier, and in the years following the only substantive motion on which that question was debated was one tabled not by the government but by the Commons Backbench Business Committee, in 2010.[59] The House of Commons later approved, however, the extension of that force to Syria in December 2015,[60] having two years earlier defeated a motion laying the ground for (but not yet approving) the use of force there.[61] There is therefore now a body of relevant practice: both positive, where the deployment of troops has been preceded by the grant of parliamentary approval, and negative, where the withholding of such approval has seen plans for military intervention postponed or abandoned.

The practice has not, however, been consistent even in the relatively short period in question: though Parliament approved the use of force in Libya (as approved by UNSC Resolution 1373) in March 2011,[62] military action had in fact begun several days earlier. This inconsistency occurred notwithstanding that it was in the specific context of the Libya intervention that the existence of the convention (applicable 'except when there is an

[53] *Evans v Information Commissioner* [2012] UKUT 313 (AAC), [75]: 'for the purposes of the present case, the answer to the question we posed above is that a particular constitutional obligation will be a constitutional convention if the Jennings test is met.'

[54] It need not, however, be a substantial body of practice—Jennings notes that '[a] single precedent with a good reason may be enough to establish the rule.' I Jennings, *The Law and the Constitution*, 5th edn (London, University of London Press, 1967) 136.

[55] Jennings (n 54) 134–6.

[56] For an exploration of the historical practice and the reasons for it, see Joseph (n 27) 45–79.

[57] An overview is provided in Claire Mills, *Parliamentary approval for military action*, House of Commons Library Briefing Paper 7166 (12 May 2015). See also the consideration in Peter Rowe, *Legal Accountability and Britain's Wars 2000–2015* (Routledge, 2016) Ch 4.

[58] HC Deb 18 March 2003, vol 401 col 911.

[59] HC Deb 9 September 2010, vol 515 col 569.

[60] HC Deb 2 December 2015, vol 603 col 499.

[61] The motion voted on included that the House believed that 'every effort should be made to secure a Security Council Resolution backing military action before any such action is taken, and notes that before any direct British involvement in such action a further vote of the House of Commons will take place'. HC Deb 29 August 2013, vol 566 col 1425–6.

[62] HC Deb 21 March 2011, vol 525 col 806.

emergency and such action would not be appropriate') was acknowledged by the Leader of the House of Commons,[63] from where it found its way into the 2011 edition of the Cabinet Manual.[64] Gavin Phillipson suggested that though the government appeared to have recognised the convention, these events demonstrate 'it did not appear to regard itself as bound to obtain the assent of Parliament *before* commencing military action …'[65] Moreover, when military assets were deployed in Mali in early 2013, there was no debate and no Parliamentary vote. The Leader of the House reaffirmed in that context the government's commitment to the convention but distinguished the situation in Mali from those which the convention encompasses on the basis that 'the role of British troops [in Mali] is clearly not a combat role and it is not our intention to deploy combat troops.'[66] In this context, it is the Syria vote of 2013 rather than anything which went before which marks the turning point: not only because the government held a vote before using force, but also because in that example (unlike in relation to Iraq) Parliament in that instance 'was given a real choice without the pressure of a major deployment having already taken place.'[67] That the government then lost the vote was, therefore, merely the icing upon the constitutional cake.

As to third part of the Jennings' test ('did the actors in the precedents believe that they were bound by a rule'),[68] the question is potentially fraught, it being difficult to disaggregate the doing of something out of a sense of constitutional propriety on one hand and out of political convenience (or necessity) on the other. Here, however, the question appears to be answered by the government's acceptance of the convention's existence (albeit that we therefore involve ourselves in something of a paradox: the convention exists because the government accepts its existence). Jennings himself, however, placed the greatest emphasis upon the normative question—is there a reason for the rule? He noted in particular that a 'whole string of precedents without such a reason will be of no avail, unless it is perfectly certain that the persons regarded them as bound by it'.[69] This leaves us in a further, and more concerning, logical bind: that is, it would seem—notwithstanding the prior inconsistency of practice, and the uncertain and perhaps unprincipled scope of the convention—that it is, to use Jennings' words, 'perfectly certain' that the government regards itself as bound by the convention and that it therefore can and should be understood to exist regardless of whether there is a reason for it. In this context, however, that conclusion is not necessarily a welcome one, for the normative underpinnings of the convention are weak, and possibly self-defeating.

[63] HC Deb 10 March 2011, vol 524 col 1066: 'A convention has developed in the House that before troops are committed, the House should have an opportunity to debate the matter. We propose to observe that convention except when there is an emergency and such action would not be appropriate. As with the Iraq war and other events, we propose to give the House the opportunity to debate the matter before troops are committed.' Later, the Foreign Secretary pledged that the Government would 'enshrine in law for the future the necessity of consulting Parliament on military action': HC Deb 21 March 2011, vol 525 col 799. No such law was ever enacted.

[64] The Cabinet Manual (2011), [5.38].

[65] Gavin Phillipson, "Historic' Commons' Syria vote: the constitutional significance: Part I', *UK Constitutional Law Association Blog* (19 September 2013). See also 'Part II—the way forward', *UK Constitutional Law Association Blog* (29 November 2013).

[66] Phillipson (n 65).

[67] ibid.

[68] Jennings (n 54) 136.

[69] ibid.

D. The Normative Element

The basic normative underpinning of the argument for parliamentary involvement in the decision to exercise the war prerogative is intuitive and, superficially at least, attractive: Parliament (or rather the House of Commons)[70] is, for all its flaws, the closest thing the UK constitution has to a formal repository of democratic sentiment. Its endorsement of the decision to go to war lends that decision a legitimacy which it can never enjoy while it is purely a function of an executive-decision making process which may in reality be the decision of the Prime Minister alone; or, perhaps worse, the decision of the Prime Minister acting under the influence not of the electorate but of domineering foreign allies. The case for parliamentary (more precisely, House of Commons) involvement has been made eloquently elsewhere, and there is little need to repeat it here.[71] Howsoever the convention was formulated, it would certainly be capable of meeting the standard set by Jennings' requirement that there exists a reason for a convention to exist: such a convention would bridge the gap between the mediaeval approach to the war power which remains embedded in strict law and the modern reality of democratic politics. Better, it would do so without fettering the executive in its conduct of war: the substance of the convention could be sufficiently flexible to allow for urgent military responses, and would ultimately be subject to only political rather than legal mechanisms of enforcement. If the sanction for a breach of a convention is imposed by political organs and political actors (most likely the House of Commons) then a considerable level of deference to the decision-making of the executive (as to both whether the convention has been breached and whether the breach was justified) can be anticipated. Nevertheless, there are several reasons for believing that the normative element of the position is weaker than often supposed. We should not be, that is, too quick to incorporate parliamentary oversight of the use of the war prerogative within a whiggish account of the democratisation of the constitutional order: the conduct of war has special features which might justify excluding it from such process.

The first reason to be sceptical about the involvement of Parliament is the extent to which the decision to go to war is reliant upon knowledge and expertise that is likely to be possessed by a small number of members of the House of Commons, most of them members of the executive which proposes to do so in the first place. Though information has at times been shared with members of the opposition on 'Privy Council terms' the content of the briefings cannot then be discussed on the floor of the House, leading to the suggestion that briefings of this sort are 'used strategically by the government to tacitly remove certain questions or issues from the political agenda.'[72] Two possible consequences are identifiable, assuming (as we can) that the executive is unwilling to disclose the entirety of the intelligence it possesses to the chamber as a whole. The first is that the motion authorising the use of military force is voted upon in ignorance of the relevant material (or, at least, comparative ignorance). In such a case, whatever the outcome is, something is potentially lost—either

[70] The war powers convention thus stands as further evidence of the primacy of the House of Commons over the Lords (to which it has no application). It joins the list of matters which will need to be rethought in the unlikely event that the reform of the upper chamber is ever completed.

[71] Though arguing for a statutory implementation of a requirement of parliamentary approval (along with associated procedural innovations), see Joseph (n 27) Ch 6.

[72] Hayley J Hooper, 'Voting on Military Action in Syria: Part II', *UK Constitutional Law Blog* (1 Dec 2015).

because a compelling case for military intervention is not acted upon, or a weak case is. The second, and more likely, is that the information is mediated via some person or body and potentially distorted in the process.[73] In the context of the Iraq war, the case for war was made by reference to two dossiers—the 'September Dossier'[74] and the 'February Dossier'[75] (the so-called 'dodgy dossier')—which were later shown to be flawed in a number of ways.[76] Rosara Joseph has suggested two possible mechanisms for overcoming the difficulties caused by the inability of Parliament to access the relevant information: a public interest test along the lines of that found in freedom of information legislation (though 'with a more explicit focus on the relevance of the particular information to democratic deliberation about proposed policies or actions') and the establishment of a joint committee which would have access to all of the relevant information and report on that information to Parliament as a whole.[77] Whether or not such mechanisms would be capable of solving the problem in question, it must be underlined that the war powers convention has taken hold without any moves having been made to ensure Parliament has access to the relevant material. And all of this of course assumes that whatever information is made available will play a significant (perhaps determinative) role in the decision of individual parliamentarians to endorse (or not) military action. At least as likely, however, is that the decision is made not on the basis of a reasoned consideration of the evidence, to which each representative contributes a variety of more or less subjective intellectual and moral considerations, but on some other basis: unthinking loyalty to the party line, perhaps, or some other similarly crude political calculation; maybe an acquiescence to the public mood (perhaps as influenced or otherwise mediated by the fourth estate). Democratic involvement in the decision to go to war must be considered in light of a realistic assessment of the quality of the democratic process, both in the abstract and in the circumstance of this particular decision.

The second difficulty is that the question of domestic constitutional propriety of the exercise of the war prerogative exists alongside, and as a matter of law pales into insignificance in relation to, the international law position. That position is easily stated: there is a general prohibition on the use of force, both in customary international law and in Article 2 of the UN Charter, which provides that all members 'shall refrain in their international relations from the threat or use of force against the territorial integrity or political independence of any state, or in any other manner inconsistent with the Purposes of the United Nations.' Two basic exceptions to that prohibition exist: the first where the Security Council of the United Nations, in accordance with Article 42, chooses to 'take such action by air, sea, or land forces as may be necessary to maintain or restore international peace and security.' The second is recognised (though not established) by Article 51 of the Charter, which provides that 'nothing in the present Charter shall impair the inherent right of individual or collective self-defence if an armed attack occurs against a Member of the United Nations,

[73] See the discussion of this issue in Joseph (n 27) 197–201. And see also Hooper and Fikfak (n 28).

[74] HM Government, *Iraq's Weapons of Mass Destruction: The Assessment of the British Government* (September 2002).

[75] HM Government, *Iraq—Its Infrastructure of Concealment, Deception and Intimidation* (January 2003). The name by which the document is known reflects the date at which it was first issued to journalists.

[76] See principally the Report of a Committee of Privy Counsellors, *Review of Intelligence on Weapons of Mass Destruction* (HC 2003–04, 898) ('the Butler review').

[77] Joseph (n 27) 187–201.

until the Security Council has taken measures necessary to maintain international peace and security.' Such measures 'shall not in any way affect the authority and responsibility of the Security Council under the present Charter to take at any time such action as it deems necessary in order to maintain or restore international peace and security.' This recognises the right to use force in circumstances of individual or collective self-defence to respond to an armed attack.[78] Alternatively, states may consent to the use of force in their territory.[79] In the context of the conflicts in which the UK has participated in recent decades, questions of international legality have played a major role; the most important—by far—relating to the legality of the war in Iraq.[80]

And it is not merely the case (which it is) that international law represents a separate (and logically prior) regime whose requirements must be satisfied before war is lawful and to which the domestic constitutional arrangements are of no relevance. Rather, it may be that the co-existence of two legal-constitutional regimes, and associated concerns and questions, works to obstruct the proper functioning of both. On one hand, Murray and O'Donoghue have argued that:

> Democratic domestic assemblies should … be wary of becoming the predominant governance point for authorizing military force, on the principled basis that doing so would undermine UN institutions and on the pragmatic basis that legislators are ill-equipped to assess whether a use of force is legitimate under the tests currently in circulation. Relying upon domestic assemblies to provide the sole necessary authorization point for certain uses of force might appear to offer a means to unblock international institutional processes—but this course turns away from international constraints upon the use of force and opens the door to new forms of unilateralism.[81]

If we are concerned to preserve the integrity of the international law regime governing the use of force, therefore, we must be careful not to conflate the legality of the use of force in international law with the question of whether force should be used by the UK. Equally, however, if parliamentary debate is focussed only upon the question of whether military action is lawful, then—as Veronika Fikfak has noted—there are obscured 'the questions that are purely domestic in nature' such as 'what is the risk to military troops, what are the economic and budgetary implications of waging a war or the potential long term effects of intervention, what is the opinion of the home public and finally, what is the direct British interest?'[82] A complicating factor as regards this second point is that the content of the legal advice given by the Attorney General as to the international law basis of military action is in no way immune from politicisation. The Chilcot report found that in the context of the 2003 Iraq war a fuller account of the legal advice offered by the Attorney General, Lord Goldsmith—who was initially hesitant as to the ability of UNSCR resolution 1441 to revive the authority to use force found in UNSCR 678, dating from the first Gulf War, but later took the position that the 'better view' was that it did—should have been provided

[78] As under Art 5 of the NATO Treaty.

[79] For a critique of this rule, see Ashley S Deeks, 'Consent to the Use of Force and International Law Supremacy' (2013) 54 *Harvard International Law Journal* 1.

[80] See, now, the discussion of the question in Report of a Committee of Privy Counsellors, *The Report of the Iraq Inquiry* (HC 2015–16, 264) ('the Chilcot report'), s 5.

[81] CRG Murray and A O'Donoghue, 'Towards Unilaterialism? House of Commons Oversight of the Use of Force' (2016) 65 *ICLQ* 305, 341.

[82] Veronika Fikfak, 'Voting on Military Action in Syria', UK Constitutional Law Blog (28 November 2015). See also Hooper and Fikfak (n 28).

to Cabinet, which was 'being asked to confirm the decision that the diplomatic process was at an end and that the House of Commons should be asked to endorse the use of military action to enforce Iraq's compliance' and 'should have been made aware of the legal uncertainties.'[83] This point is a more direct threat to the logic of the convention than are concerns about the information available to Parliament. While they posit the convention as potentially ineffective, the interaction of the domestic and international regimes suggest it is in fact counter-productive: each regime works to undermine the effect of the other, such that the existence of the convention may ultimately make it more, rather than less, likely that the United Kingdom goes to war.

Finally, it is important to note the political (and geo-political) context within which this debate has emerged in the UK and other western democracies, and which is reflected in the assumption, which pervades this discussion, that a key benefit of the convention will be to limit the frequency with which military force is used by the UK. Notwithstanding the rhetoric, simultaneously empty and dangerous, of the 'war on terror', much of the military action taken since 11 September—and certainly that which has proven most controversial—has been related only weakly (if at all) within the public mind to domestic national security interests: indeed, it was the perceived abuse of such considerations within the context of the Iraq war which contributed to its current position in the UK's public discourse as the paradigm of a dishonest war, one which continues to cast a long shadow over military action of any sort. The constitutional disputes discussed herein would, it is submitted, look very different if recent wars had been wars of clear necessity. In a certain sense, then, when an argument has been made that a convention should exist whereby Parliament is required to consent to the use of force, what has really been meant is that the UK should not involve itself in the sorts of wars which it has undertaken in recent decades. The same point might be made by reference to the popularity of the wars in question, except that (notwithstanding the vast popular opposition which mobilised against it) even the Iraq war—the paradigm of unpopular and unnecessary military intervention, which will for years to come cast a shadow over any military action the UK might undertake—enjoyed considerable public support at the time it began.[84] This point matters in particular because if questions of process are acting as a proxy for questions of substance, it is important to have a realistic sense of the substance: involving Parliament in the decision-making process will not lead to less war if war is popular. It would appear not to be at the moment, but the practice of justifying semi-permanent constitutional change by reference to the contingent political environment which prevails at a particular point in time is a dangerous one, and the future operation of the convention which has become established will not necessarily reflect the context in which it developed.

E. Special Forces

Two particular issues must be considered over and above the general question of the war prerogative. One, the use of drones to carry out targeted killing on and off the battlefield,

[83] Chilcot (n 81) s 5, [954].

[84] The issue of public opinion in relation to military intervention is discussed in B Clements, 'Public Opinion and Military Intervention' (2013) 84 *Political Quarterly* 119.

brings together a number of issues already discussed or considered in the following section—including the position in international law and under the ECHR—and will be discussed in the final section of the chapter. The second—the regulation of the use of Special Forces—can more conveniently be considered here, given that it does not (necessarily, at least) raise issues of law over and above those which apply to armed force generally, but is nevertheless distinctive from the point of view of domestic constitutional practice. In the UK, 'Special Forces' includes both the Special Air Service (SAS) and the Special Boat Service (SBS), along with supporting units.[85] As with 'ordinary' forces, they are managed and deployed as an exercise of the prerogative. No information is given of the use to which Special Forces are put ('[w]e never comment on the disposition of our special forces anywhere in the world and that will remain our policy')[86] and they are the subject, along with the security and intelligence services, of one of the standing DSMA-Notices.[87] In response to a 2016 question asking whether he would 'assess the potential merits of appointing a committee of parliamentarians to oversee the operations and budget of special forces, similar to the functions of the Intelligence and Security Committee in respect of the intelligence services', the Secretary of State for Defence replied as curtly as possible: 'No.'[88] Financial scrutiny is also limited: the National Audit Office had, it was noted in 2016, not conducted an audit of the UK's Special Forces in the previous seventeen years.[89] Nor are the rules of engagement under which they operate made public.[90] All members have, since 1996, been obliged to sign a confidentiality agreement,[91] which presumably goes beyond the requirements imposed generally by the Official Secrets Act. One former member was served with a court order in 2008 preventing him from making disclosures about the rendition of captured Iraqi and Afghan combatants to torture.[92] The convention which now exists whereby Parliament must authorise the use of force cannot logically encompass, therefore, the deployment of Special Forces. Though the convention as acknowledged by the government and reflected in the Cabinet Manual does not make that exception explicit, the exclusion of Special Forces was always the intention of those arguing for the introduction of a mechanism to regulate the exercise of the war prerogative.[93] As a result of the government policy of not commenting on Special Forces, the quantity of information in the public domain regarding their work is limited (with the resulting gap often filled by work of dubious reliability). It is known, however, that Special Forces were active in Northern Ireland during the Troubles,[94]

[85] For background, see A Finlan, 'The (Arrested) Development of UK Special Forces and the Global War on Terror' (2009) 35 *Review of International Studies* 971.

[86] Defence Secretary Philip Hammond, quoted in J Moran, 'Time to Move Out of the Shadows? Special Operations Forces and Accountability in Counterterrorism and Counter-Insurgency Operations', (2016) 39 *UNSW Law Journal* 1239, 1246.

[87] On which see the discussion in Ch 5.

[88] WQ41980, asked 5 July 2016 and answered 11 July 2016.

[89] Moran (n 86) 1251.

[90] ibid 1252.

[91] I Cobain, *The History Thieves: Secrets, Lies and the Shaping of a Modern Nation* (London, Portobello Books, 2016) 97.

[92] Richard Norton-Taylor, 'Court gags ex-SAS man who made torture claims' *The Guardian* (29 February 2008).

[93] See Ministry of Justice (n 48) [217]: 'The Government proposes that for any conflict decision involving the Special Forces or other members of the UK Forces, where their only purpose is assisting the activities of the Special Forces, prior approval would not be required.'

[94] Ruth Jamieson and Kieran McEvoy, 'State Crime by Proxy and Juridical Othering' (2005) *British Journal of Criminology* 504.

and in a variety of 'end of Empire' contexts, while reports of Special Forces' work have emerged in the last decade in places such as Somalia, Libya, Yemen, Afghanistan, Iraq and Syria.[95] A 1969 Ministry of Defence publication notes that Special Forces undertake 'the collection of information on local insurgents, ambush and harassment of insurgents, sabotage, assassination and demolition, border surveillance, limited community relations and liaison with, and organisation, training and control of, friendly guerrilla forces operating against a common enemy'.[96] While the role of the armed forces as a whole has evolved significantly over the decades since that precis was produced, it is clear that the Special Forces in many cases continue to undertake tasks which either would not or could not be carried out by their regular counterparts.

It is therefore concerning that as parliamentary oversight of the armed forces generally and the use of force in particular has developed over time, the use to which Special Forces are put appears to have expanded.[97] One observer has identified amongst the reasons for this that such forces 'may be employed where conventional operations are not possible, due to legal restrictions, or political or civil society opposition' and quotes a leaked Ministry of Defence document suggesting that the public have a 'more robust attitude' to the losses incurred by Special Forces than by regular forces (though one would hope that political opposition to the use of military force would be based on considerations broader than the possible loss of life incurred on the UK side).[98] Not only: in recent years elements of the regular armed forces have been acting alongside the Special Forces as the 'Special Forces Support Group', in which case they are subject to the same policies regarding disclosure as apply to the Special Forces themselves. If the question which determines the rules of disclosure is whether or not the unit is acting act under the operational command of the Director of Special Forces,[99] then there is a clear and strong incentive to broaden that command to encompass as much as possible. As it grows, the scope for political accountability (inside and outside of Parliament) rather than expanding, in fact diminishes, tending always towards zero. This trend shows no sign of slowing, and the 2015 National Security Strategy and Strategic Defence and Security Review announced the intention of the government to 'more than double our current planned investment in Special Forces equipment to enhance their ability to operate and strike globally in the most hostile environments on their own or with our closest allies, and in particular to enhance their counter-terrorism capabilities.'[100] And not only are Special Forces excluded from the emergent convention as to the exercise of the war prerogative: it appears to be the case that they have in recent years been deployed even in circumstances in which Parliament has explicitly withheld consent.[101] The use of Special Forces in these ways works to undermine the advances which have been made in terms of democratic accountability for the use of military force, potentially rendering the

[95] See Emily Knowles and Abigail Watson, *All Quiet on the IS Front? British secret warfare in an information age* Remote Control (2017) 19–21.

[96] Quoted in Jamieson and McEvoy (n 94) 508.

[97] See Finlan (n 85) 976–81 and Moran (n 86) 1241–5.

[98] Moran (n 86) 1240.

[99] As was the case with the convention proposed in 2008: see Ministry of Justice (n 48) Annex A, s 4(2) of the draft war powers resolution.

[100] HM Government, *National Security Strategy and Strategic Defence and Security Review 2015 A Secure and Prosperous United Kingdom*, Cm 9161 (2015), [4.45].

[101] Knowles and Watson (n 95) 21.

advances made elsewhere in terms of democratic oversight of the use of force moot. Indeed, it seems highly likely that there exists a causal connection between the government's acquiescence to the existence of the convention governing the exercise of the war prerogative and the expansion in the use of those forces which are specifically excluded from both the scope of that convention and all other forms of formalised political scrutiny.[102]

Though there is some way to go, the UK is moving towards a situation in which the norms and practices governing the use of force have been entirely upended. Major military interventions are becoming public property: though the executive continues to have formal control, it is required to justify itself to an ever-greater degree to the public at large, and now to seek the specific consent of Parliament to go to war. Both such developments necessitate the provision of sufficient information to persuade the relevant constituencies, though of course the ability to persuade is rather different from the ability to ground a reasoned conclusion. Though these developments can be welcomed, at least at the headline level, for their democratic credentials, they are accompanied by an expansion in the use of Special Forces: not only are these not governed by the emergent convention regarding the use of the war power (to the point that the government is willing to deploy them even in circumstances in which Parliament has specifically declined to authorise the use of force) but even the minimal democratic oversight historically associated with the use of force is excluded in relation to those forces. As the constitution evolves in a democratic direction, the underlying practices thrust us back in time, with the effect that the evolution in question may prove to be of merely theoretical significance. If it is correct that, as suggested above, the greater political oversight of the use of force has been accepted precisely because of these significant limits to its practical effect, it becomes easier to make sense of the significant hostility evinced towards parallel developments in the legal domain, the most important of which are the result of the expanding extra-territorial jurisdiction of the European Court of Human Rights. These developments are less easily evaded or otherwise undermined than are those in the political domain.

IV. Legal Accountability for the Use of Force Abroad

The use of military force must take place in accordance with those elements of international law which precisely govern it, but also with the body of domestic law, including public law, private law,[103] and—in particular—the Human Rights Act 1998 (HRA). Many of the special issues raised by the application of domestic law to national security endeavours involving military force abroad are canvassed in Chapter 6, on justiciability. That matters encompassed by the Human Rights Act are justiciable skips over, however, the prior question of what matters are so encompassed: that is, if the Human Rights Act provides remedies for

[102] Analogous to the process described in R Hirschl, *Towards Juristocracy The Origins and Consequences of the New Constitutionalism* (Cambridge MA, Harvard University Press, 2007), whereby the cession of political power by elites is accompanied by the imposition of legal limits upon the use of that power.

[103] The extent to which English law will govern torts committed as part of military action abroad is a function of the Private International Law (Miscellaneous Provisions) Act 1995, s 11 of which provides that 'the applicable law is the law of the country in which the events constituting the tort or delict in question occur.'

violations of (most of) the substantive rights contained in the European Convention on Human Rights, to what extent do those rights bite upon the pursuit of military action abroad? That is the first of the questions considered in this section, with reference to the terms of the HRA and ECHR themselves and, most significantly, the jurisprudence of the Strasbourg and domestic courts in the period encompassing the military action in Iraq and Afghanistan. It should be noted, however, that there is no *a priori* limitation of the Convention and, indirectly, the HRA to the pursuit of military action. It is conceivable that the Convention rights might equally apply to other forms of action by UK public authorities abroad. In practice, however, and for reasons which will be discussed below, there is a very close relationship between the pursuit of military action abroad and the ability of an individual to invoke the rights under the ECHR. It is therefore reasonable to treat—with suitable caution—the question of the ECHR's extraterritorial jurisdiction as a facet of the military constitution.

A. The ECHR Jurisprudence on Extra-Territoriality

The European Convention on Human Rights requires, by virtue of its Article 1, those states which are parties to it to 'secure to everyone within their jurisdiction the rights and freedoms defined in Section I' of the Convention, which comprises Articles 2 to 18 of the Convention, including both the unqualified rights and the qualified rights found within those provisions and the associated provisions regarding, for example, the right not to be discriminated against in one's enjoyment of those substantive rights and derogations from the Convention.[104] The Convention does not therefore impose obligations on High Contracting Parties to it which are universal in scope, but instead limits their obligations (and, indirectly, the possibility of claiming to be the victim of a violation of the Convention) via the reference to 'jurisdiction'. The Court of Human Rights for much of its history treated this as a territorial limitation, stating—for example—*in Soering v United Kingdom* that:

> Article 1 ... sets a limit, notably territorial, on the reach of the Convention. In particular, the engagement undertaken by a Contracting State is confined to "securing" ... the listed rights and freedoms to persons within its own "jurisdiction." Further, the Convention does not govern the actions of States not Parties to it, nor does it purport to be a means of requiring the Contracting States to impose Convention standards on other States.[105]

The twenty-first century, however, has seen the jurisdiction recognised to the contracting state by the ECHR expanded. In *Bankovic v Belgium*,[106] the applicants alleged violations of the Convention rights arising out of the bombing of the studios of Radio Televizije Srbije (the Serbian public broadcaster) as part of the air strikes carried out in the Federal Yugoslav Republic in 1999. The respondent states argued that the applicants (victims of the bombing and their relatives) were not within their jurisdiction for the purpose of the ECHR. Accepting that the ordinary meaning of Article 1 was such that 'the jurisdictional

[104] Discussed in Ch 1 in relation to the UK's response to the 11 September attacks.

[105] *Soering v United Kingdom* (1989) 11 EHRR 439, [86].

[106] *Bankovic v Belgium* (2007) 44 EHRR SE5.

competence of a state is primarily territorial',[107] the Court nevertheless noted that jurisdiction might be established on some other basis, which must however be 'exceptional and requiring special justification in the particular circumstances of each case'.[108] The correctness of such an interpretation was evidenced in particular by the *travaux préparatoires* of the Convention.[109] Though the Court had in earlier judgments recognised the possibility that one such exceptional justification was in the circumstances of military action, when a Party to the Convention exercised, as a consequence of such action 'effective control' of territory other than its own,[110] it held here that there was not any 'jurisdictional link' between the victims of the acts in question and the respondent states.[111] The ability of the ECHR to apply outside the territory of the contracting state was limited, in particular, by the fact that it could apply only where the entirety of the rights could be secured: to 'divide and tailor' the rights according to circumstance would render the reference to jurisdiction in Article 1 'superfluous and devoid of any purpose.'[112]

When these issues were disputed in the domestic courts in the years following the invasion of Iraq, the House of Lords noted that though the parties agreed that 'the Convention's reach is essentially territorial and that there are exceptions to the basic principle of territoriality' (citing *Bankovic* for both propositions), 'there is complete disagreement as to the width, nature, rationale and applicability of the exceptions.'[113] The case, *Al-Skeini*, involved Article 2 and 3 claims brought by the relatives of persons who had died in Iraq while under occupation. Five claims related to individuals shot by British troops; one to an individual, Baha Mousa, who died in British custody within a military prison.[114] On the basis of an extensive review of the ECHR and other jurisprudence, the Divisional Court held that the first five deaths did not come 'within any possible variation of the examples of acts by state authorities in or from embassies, consulates, vessels, aircraft, (or, we would suggest, courts or prisons) to which the authorities repeatedly refer.'[115] Baha Mousa's position was different:

> He was not just a victim, under however unfortunate circumstances, of military operations. He was not, as we understand the matter, a prisoner of war. He was, prima facie at any rate, a civilian employee. He was arrested by British forces on suspicion of involvement with weapons hidden in the hotel where he worked as a receptionist, on suspicion therefore of involvement in terrorism. He was taken into custody in a British military base. There he met his death, it is alleged by beatings at the hands of his prison guards. The death certificate referred to "cardio-respiratory arrest: asphyxia".[116]

To acknowledge this death as occurring within British jurisdiction was entirely compatible with even a very narrow reading of the exceptions to the basic territoriality rule.[117]

[107] (2007) 44 EHRR SE5, [57].
[108] (2007) 44 EHRR SE5, [59].
[109] ibid, [61].
[110] See, eg, *Loizidou v Turkey* (1995) 20 EHRR 99.
[111] (2007) 44 EHRR SE5, [80].
[112] ibid, [73].
[113] *R (Al-Skeini) v Secretary of State for Defence* [2007] UKHL 26.
[114] On Baha Mousa's death, see AT Williams, *A Very British Killing: The Death of Baha Mousa* (London, Jonathan Cape, 2012).
[115] *R (Al-Skeini) v Secretary of State for Defence* [2004] EWHC 2911 (Admin), [284].
[116] [2004] EWHC 2911 (Admin), [286].
[117] ibid, [287].

This conclusion was upheld on appeal by both the Court of Appeal and the House of Lords, the latter holding that the obligation to uphold the rights under the Convention existed only where the state was in effective control of an area such as to enable it to provide to those in that area the full package of rights thereunder; in the circumstance of the occupation of Iraq, that standard was not met and so no such obligation arose.[118] When, however, the case came before the Court of Human Rights,[119] it purported to reaffirm the basic approach of *Bankovic* (that extra-territorial jurisdiction is exceptional and based upon 'effective control') while in reality endorsing a looser model of jurisdiction, according to which the exercise of some public powers was sufficient to establish a jurisdictional link that brought the deaths of all of the claimants—and not just within Baha Mousa—within the UK's jurisdiction for Convention purposes.[120] During the period between the removal of the previous regime, and the introduction of the provisional authority, the Court held, 'the United Kingdom, through its soldiers engaged in security operations in Basrah during the period in question, exercised authority and control over individuals killed in the course of such security operations, so as to establish a jurisdictional link between the deceased and the United Kingdom for the purposes of Article 1 of the Convention.'[121] An inquiry was set up into the death of Baha Mousa;[122] a second was later charged with investigating the conduct of British soldiers following the 'Battle of Danny Boy' in Iraq in May 2004 (the 'Al-Sweady Inquiry'),[123] the latter finding the vast majority of the accusations of mistreatment to be without merit.[124] Later, the Iraq Historic Allegations Team (IHAT) was introduced in order to sift allegations of mistreatment.[125] In order to meet the obligations of the UK under Article 2 of the ECHR, the Iraq Fatality Investigations were set up in 2014 in order to follow up on investigations which have been carried out by IHAT where no criminal charges are being brought: as of mid-2017 six investigations had been concluded and a seventh was underway. The direct legal accountability made possible by the extra-territorial application of the ECHR in this way results, indirectly, in alternative forms of redress which would not otherwise be available. Law acts as a gateway through which extra-legal accountability enters the picture.

Three bases for establishing extra-territorial jurisdiction are identified by the Strasbourg Court in *Al-Skeini*. One is where the contracting party 'as a consequence of lawful

[118] See, eg, [2007] UKHL 26, [79]–[83].

[119] *Al-Skeini v United Kingdom* (2011) 53 EHRR 589.

[120] See Marko Milanovic, 'Al-Skeini and Al-Jedda in Strasbourg' (2012) 23 *EJIL* 121, 127–133. Milanovic suggests, 129, that 'the Court's disavowal of Bankovic is half-hearted at best. Its conceptual foundation—that the extraterritorial application of the ECHR can only be exceptional and needs to be justified by reference to general international law—remains.'

[121] (2011) 53 EHRR 589, [149].

[122] See Rt Hon Sir William Gage, *The Report of the Baha Mousa Inquiry*, (HC 2011–12, 1452-I).

[123] Sir Thayne Forbes, *The Report of the Al Sweady Inquiry: Volume I* (HC 2014–15, 818-I).

[124] Sir Thayne Forbes, *The Report of the Al Sweady Inquiry: Executive Summary* (HC 2014–15, 819) [740]: 'the work of this Inquiry has established beyond doubt that all the most serious allegations, made against the British soldiers involved in the Battle of Danny Boy and its aftermath and which have been hanging over those soldiers for the last 10 years, have been found to be wholly without foundation and entirely the product of deliberate lies, reckless speculation and ingrained hostility.'

[125] The disbanding of IHAT (and the handing over of remaining caseload to the Royal Navy Police) was announced in 2017, following the striking off of the lawyer—Phil Shiner—who had brought many of the relevant case for professional misconduct related to claims arising out of the *Al-Sweady* and related cases.

or unlawful military action … exercises effective control of an area outside that national territory'.[126] Here, the *Bankovic* injunction against division of the Convention rights holds good: the state which exercises such control 'has the responsibility under Article 1 to secure, within the area under its control, the entire range of substantive rights set out in the Convention and those additional Protocols which it has ratified.'[127] A second is based upon the notion of '*espace juridique*', and applies where 'the territory of one Convention State is occupied by the armed forces of another', in which event the occupying state is responsible for securing the rights under the Convention within the occupied territory.[128] The third—the most amorphous and therefore most important—is where there exists 'state agent authority and control'; this encompasses not only the acts of diplomats or consular agents, as well as the exercise of public power by a party to the convention outside its own territory, but also the 'use of force by a State's agents operating outside its territory may bring the individual thereby brought under the control of the State's authorities into the State's Article 1 jurisdiction.'[129] Though the prior cases had all involved an individual in the custody of the contracting party, the Court rejected the notion that such custody was a *sine qua non* of such jurisdiction: what was decisive was 'the exercise of physical power and control over the person in question.'[130] It is this final formulation which has both opened the doors to an extraterritorial jurisdiction far broader than was recognised in *Bankovic* and yet still radically uncertain.[131] Crucially, however, the Court explicitly accepted that for the purpose of 'state agent authority and control', the indivisibility of the Conventions rights which had been insisted upon in earlier case law does not hold: instead, a contracting party exercising authority and control over an individual is obliged to 'secure to that individual the rights and freedoms under Section 1 of the Convention that are relevant to the situation of that individual.'[132] The Court of Human Rights has adopted its *Al-Skeini* approach also in subsequent decisions.[133]

Though the Strasbourg Court failed to explain (or even acknowledge) its departure from the approach taken in *Bankovic*, its decision in *Al-Skeini* has been treated as having established a new method of establishing jurisdiction. In *Smith*,[134] the ECHR judgment in *Al-Skeini* was considered authoritative, and as demonstrating—in the words of Lord Hope—that 'extraterritorial jurisdiction can exist whenever a state through its agents exercises authority and control over an individual'.[135] The question of jurisdiction has thus ceased to be a purely spatial but has assumed alongside that a personal dimension. In *Smith* the result of the Strasbourg Court's new account of jurisdiction was that British soldiers

[126] (2011) 53 EHRR 589, [138].

[127] ibid.

[128] ibid, [142].

[129] (2011) 53 EHRR 589, [136]. Perhaps the key difficulty with the schema offered in *Al-Skeini* is that that this third category appears to conflate territorial jurisdiction (of a sort which seems addressed by the first exception and which is generally less controversial) with a personal model which would appear to distinct, in that it is capable of being established even where there is not territorial control whatsoever.

[130] (2011) 53 EHRR 589, [136].

[131] For commentary, see Max Schaefer, 'Al-Skeini and the elusive parameters of extra-territorial jurisdiction' (2011) *EHRLR* 566.

[132] (2011) 53 EHRR 589, [137].

[133] Eg, *Hassan v United Kingdom* [2014] ECHR 9936; *Jaloud v The Netherlands* (2015) 60 EHRR 29.

[134] *Smith v Ministry of Defence* [2013] UKSC 41.

[135] [2013] UKSC 41, [49].

serving in Iraq were within the UK's jurisdiction for Article 1 purposes. Such conclusion followed not only from the decision in *Al-Skeini* but also from logic whereby if British soldiers were the jurisdictional link between the UK and those over whom it exercised control, they themselves could not be outside that jurisdiction: 'an occupying state cannot have any jurisdiction over local inhabitants without already having jurisdiction over its own armed forces'.[136] The instant effect was to permit to proceed to trial the claim that Article 2 of the Convention had been breached by the Ministry of Defence as a result of its failure 'to take measures within the scope of its powers which, judged reasonably, it might have been expected to take in the light of the real and immediate risk to life of soldiers' who had died on patrol.[137]

Alongside these, however, another element of the decision in *Smith* has become entangled with the expansion of extra-territorial jurisdiction. Some of the claimants brought common law claims in negligence relating to the training of soldiers and the procurement of the equipment upon which they were relying in Iraq. There can be no common law liability relating to things done in the course of combat—this is the rule of 'combat immunity'.[138] The Ministry of Defence argued, however, that combat immunity should be recognised as applying beyond the actual conduct of hostilities; that it should 'be given a sufficiently broad scope to cover all acts or omissions that are alleged to have caused death or injury in the course of combat operations.'[139] The majority in the Supreme Court declined to take such an approach, holding that it would represent an extension of the doctrine of combat immunity for which there was no prior authority.[140] While this element of the decision in *Smith* is a superficially conservative one—holding the immunity to its traditional scope—it is not clear that the distinction between the conduct of hostilities and events preparatory to it is sufficiently robust to keep the courts from entering of the domain from which combat immunity has traditionally excluded them. For that reason, the common law element of *Smith*—which, unlike the point about the extra-territorial application of the ECHR, is the doing of the domestic courts alone—has come to be treated as an aspect of the same growing, and allegedly intolerable, judicialisation of warfare as is represented by decisions such as that in *Al-Skeini* and which must be addressed together with the ECHR question if that process is to be reversed.[141]

In subsequent case law upon Article 1 of the ECHR, one particular question has come to represent most clearly the contested boundary of jurisdiction under that instrument: whether or not the use of force against a person by itself suffices to bring that person within the state's jurisdiction for ECHR purposes. The dispute is brought out clearly by the disagreement between the High Court and the Court of Appeal in *Al-Sadooon*, relating to the use of force against individuals in Iraq, but when Britain was not an occupying power (in which case *Al-Skeini* had confirmed that the ECHR applied) and when the individuals were not in British custody. In the High Court, Leggatt J cast doubt on the principle that the

[136] ibid, [50].
[137] ibid, [10].
[138] *Mulcahy v Ministry of Defence* [1996] QB 732.
[139] [2013] UKSC 41, [83].
[140] ibid, [92].
[141] See Richard Ekins, Jonathan Morgan and Tom Tugendhat, *Clearing the Fog of Law: Saving our armed forces from defeat by judicial diktat* (Policy Exchange, 2015), Ch 3.

extra-territorial use of force against a person was sufficient to bring him within the scope of the Convention, but held that where such a principle had been established it is 'impossible to say that shooting someone dead does not involve the exercise of physical power and control over that person':

> Using force to kill is indeed the ultimate exercise of physical control over another human being. Nor as it seems to me can a principled system of human rights law draw a distinction between killing an individual after arresting him and simply shooting him without arresting him first, such that in the first case there is an obligation to respect the person's right to life yet in the second case there is not.[142]

The 'essential principle' he therefore identified was that 'whenever and wherever a state which is a contracting party to the Convention purports to exercise legal authority or uses physical force, it must do so in a way that does not violate Convention rights.'[143] The implications of this holding are significant, as are the public policy arguments against it: even if the only relevant Convention right (once those rights are divided up into those which do and do not apply in a given case) is Article 2 in its negative form—being the duty not to engage in unlawful killing—the effect of this finding would be to open the door to claims for damages in respect of those killed by British troops. Such policy considerations are very apparent in the decision of the Court of Appeal allowing an appeal against this element of the High Court's decision, concluding that 'in laying down this basis of extra-territorial jurisdiction the Grand Chamber required a greater degree of power and control than that represented by the use of lethal or potentially lethal force alone.'[144] If the decision was to be made to apply the Convention to those against whom force was used without prior power or control, then the Strasbourg Court (rather than a domestic court) would have to make that decision.[145] Absent a future decision of the Strasbourg Court which confirms Mr Justice Leggatt's reading of *Al-Skeini* (or which makes explicit what *Al-Skeini* merely implies), the result is that there will be difficult and at times almost certainly unprincipled distinctions to be drawn between situations in which persons against whom force is used are, as a result of some prior degree of control, considered to be within jurisdiction, and those in which they are not. As Leggatt J notes, the effect may be to incentivise (at least from the point of view of the Convention) an approach to engagement which errs on the side of lethal force, where to take some lesser action is to risk bringing the persons against whom force is used within the scope of the Convention. Even the narrower view of the Court of Appeal ultimately prevails, however, the effect of the ECHR's case on this point is that much which is done by British troops during military action abroad will now be governed by the Convention and, in turn, the HRA.[146]

[142] *Al-Saadoon v Secretary of State for Defence* [2015] EWHC 715 (Admin), [95].

[143] [2015] EWHC 715 (Admin), [106].

[144] *Al-Saadoon v Secretary of State for Defence* [2016] EWCA Civ 811, [69].

[145] [2016] EWCA Civ 811, [70].

[146] It might once have been conceivable to pursue an approach to jurisdiction under the HRA different from that which has been taken by the Strasbourg Court. The *Al-Jedda* litigation, discussed below, would seem to preclude that possibility.

B. The ECHR and the UN Charter

A second question about international law which requires consideration relates to the relationship between the Convention and the UN Charter, and in particular those provisions within Chapter 7 which govern the use of armed force by the United Nations and its Members. Article 24 grants to the Security Council 'primary responsibility' for 'the maintenance of international peace and security', while Article 25 provides that '[t]he Members of the United Nations agree to accept and carry out the decisions of the Security Council in accordance with the present Charter'. The question arises as to the situation in which a Member of the UN, in carrying out these decisions, is required to act incompatibly with alternative provisions of international law and, in particular, that body of law (international human rights law, or 'IHRL') which protects individual rights. On its face, such a situation is governed by Article 103 of the Charter, which provides that '[i]n the event of a conflict between the obligations of the Members of the United Nations under the present Charter and their obligations under any other international agreement, their obligations under the present Charter shall prevail.' The specific effect of these provisions in the context of the occupation of Iraq was canvassed in the English courts in relation to Hillel Al-Jedda, a naturalised UK citizen of Iraqi origin.[147] Al-Jedda was detained in Iraq in 2004 and brought proceedings challenging his detention, which was alleged to represent a breach of Article 5 of the ECHR and so a violation of the rule, in section 6 of the Human Rights Act 1998, which prohibits public authorities from acting in breach of the Convention rights.[148] The House of Lords—having first dismissed the argument that the actions of the forces operating in Iraq were attributable to the United Nations itself and therefore outside the scope of the ECHR (to which the UN is not a party)[149]—held that the obligation of Members to carry out the Security Council's decisions prevailed, by virtue of Article 103, over their obligations under the ECHR. Notwithstanding that on its face the relevant Security Council Resolution (UNSCR 1546) was couched in the language of authorisation rather than obligation, the UK was required to detain individuals where necessary for 'imperative reasons of security' and so Al-Jedda's Article 5 rights were overridden by it. Determinative here were, in the judgment of Lord Bingham, three factors. The first was certain provisions of the Hague and Geneva Conventions, taken by Lord Bingham to show that 'there is a power to intern persons who are not protected persons'.[150] This power segues almost imperceptibly into an obligation, on the logic that 'if the occupying power considers it necessary to detain a person who is judged to be a serious threat to the safety of the public or the occupying power there must be an obligation to detain such person.'[151] Second, it is effectively impossible for the UN to employ mandatory rather than permissive language in

[147] It was believed, at the time of the relevant litigation, possessed dual UK-Iraqi nationality, though that, as discussed in Ch 4, was later contested.

[148] *R (Al-Jedda) v Secretary of State for Defence* [2005] EWHC 1809 (Admin) and *R (Al-Jedda) v Secretary of State for Defence* [2006] EWCA Civ 327.

[149] *R (Al-Jedda) v Secretary of State for Defence* [2007] UKHL 58, [5]–[25].

[150] [2007] UKHL 58, [32].

[151] ibid. Protected persons are those—including civilians, prisoners of war, and the sick—who enjoy the protection of international humanitarian law.

this context. Though it can and does do so elsewhere, 'language of this kind cannot be used in relation to military or security operations overseas, since the UN and the Security Council have no standing forces at their own disposal and have concluded no agreements under article 43 of the Charter which entitle them to call on member states to provide them.'[152] The third reason is that it would be inappropriate to give the term 'obligations' a 'narrow, contract-based, meaning' in the context of an organisation charged with maintaining global peace and security taking action to that end.[153] Under Article 25, quoted above, UN Members have agreed to 'accept and carry out' the Security Council's decisions and those states which contributed to the 'multi-national force' in Iraq in this way 'became bound by articles 2 and 25 to carry out the decisions of the Security Council in accordance with the Charter so as to achieve its lawful objectives' and so the UK was in turn 'bound to exercise its power of detention where this was necessary for imperative reasons of security' for '[i]t could not be said to be giving effect to the decisions of the Security Council if, in such a situation, it neglected to take steps which were open to it.'[154]

This negation of Article 5 by the incompatible provisions of Resolution 1546 was not, however, total but took place only to the extent of the incompatibility between the UK's duties under the former and Al-Jedda's rights under the latter. As it was put by Lord Bingham:

> ... there is a clash between on the one hand a power or duty to detain exercisable on the express authority of the Security Council and, on the other, a fundamental human right which the UK has undertaken to secure to those (like the appellant) within its jurisdiction. How are these to be reconciled? There is in my opinion only one way in which they can be reconciled: by ruling that the UK may lawfully, where it is necessary for imperative reasons of security, exercise the power to detain authorised by UNSCR 1546 and successive resolutions, but must ensure that the detainee's rights under article 5 are not infringed to any greater extent than is inherent in such detention.[155]

The immediate claim under Article 5 therefore failed, though due only to the mandatory nature of the general duties under Resolution 1546 and of the specific act of detaining Al-Jedda, which was assumed to be 'necessary for imperative reasons of security'.[156] That the correctness of this conclusion was perhaps the subject of a certain nagging doubt is suggested by Lord Bingham's unnecessary invocation of a 'power or duty' to detain when, he had held, only the latter was at issue.[157]

The claimant, having been released from detention shortly after the House of Lords gave judgment, made an application to the Court of Human Rights claiming breach of Article 5.[158] The Strasbourg Court agreed with the House of Lords that his detention was

[152] [2007] UKHL 58, [33].
[153] ibid, [34].
[154] ibid, [34].
[155] ibid, [39].
[156] ibid, [39].
[157] Keir Starmer has criticised the decision of the House of Lords, noting of Lord Bingham's reasoning discussed in the text that '[b]ridging the gap between an *authorisation* to use all necessary measures, including a power of internment, and an *obligation* to intern sufficiently robust to trigger Art.103 of the UN Charter was no mean feat': 'Responsibility for troops abroad: UN mandated forces and issues of human rights accountability' 2008 *European Human Rights Law Review* 318, 335.
[158] *Al-Jedda v United Kingdom* (2011) 53 EHRR 23.

attributable not to the UN but to the UK,[159] but departed from its conclusions as to the effect of Resolution 1546. It did so on the basis of a principle of interpretation akin to that known in domestic law as the principle of legality: 'in interpreting its resolutions, there must be a presumption that the Security Council does not intend to impose any obligation on Member States to breach fundamental principles of human rights' and so '[i]n the event of any ambiguity in the terms of a Security Council Resolution, the Court must therefore choose the interpretation which is most in harmony with the requirements of the Convention and which avoids any conflict of obligations'.[160] Here, the language was not such as to unambiguously communicate an intention to place UN Members participating in the MNF 'under an obligation to use measures of indefinite internment without charge and without judicial guarantees, in breach of their undertakings under international human-rights instruments including the Convention'—in particular because it makes no reference to interment—and in the absence of such an intention, it was to be assumed that the UNSC intended those Members to comply with their obligations under international rights instruments.[161] As there was no binding obligation to intern individuals, there was no conflict between the UNSC Resolution and the ECHR on which the terms of Article 103 might bite; the violation of Article 5 ECHR was therefore exactly that, and not undone by the supervening effect of the UN Charter.[162]

The decision of the Strasbourg Court in *Al-Jedda* created a point of dispute with the domestic courts which remained unresolved for several years afterwards, until a further round of civil claims against the UK government began to emerge in the courts, some of which were accompanied by claims under the Human Rights Act 1998 which revived the issue as to the relationship of the legal basis of the occupation of Iraq (if not the UN Charter as a whole) and the ECHR. *Al-Waheed* involved claims brought by several hundred Iraqi civilians seeking damages for unlawful detention by British forces in Iraq under Article 5 of the ECHR as incorporated into domestic law by the HRA 1998.[163] Many of these claims related to detention which took place after the coming into force of Resolution 1546, the relationship of which to the ECHR was the subject of the House of Lords' decision in *Al-Jedda*, on the basis of which the only possible course of action was for the claims to be dismissed. In view, however, of the Strasbourg Court's disagreement, a certificate was granted under the Administration of Justice Act 1968, allowing a direct appeal to the Supreme Court.[164] Alongside *Al-Waheed*, a related issue was raised in the *Iraqi Civilians* case,[165] where it was concluded that two other, earlier, UN Security Council Resolutions—1483 and 1511—placed the UK under a duty to detain individuals when it was considered necessary

[159] *cf Behrami v France* (admissibility) (2007) 45 EHRR SE10. For discussion of this question, see Starmer, (n 158); Kjetil Mujezinovic Larsen, 'Attribution of Conduct in Peace Operations: The 'Ultimate Authority and Control' Test' (2008) 19 *EJIL* 509; Russell Buchan, 'UN peacekeeping operations: when can unlawful acts committed by peacekeeping forces be attributed to the UN?' (2012) 32 *LS* 282.

[160] (2011) 53 EHRR 23, [102].

[161] ibid, [105].

[162] See Milanovic (n 120) 136–9.

[163] *Al-Waheed v The Ministry of Defence* [2014] EWHC 2714 (QB).

[164] [2014] EWHC 2714 (QB), [17]–[20].

[165] *Iraqi Civilians v Ministry of Defence* [2014] EWHC 3686 (QB). A number of related tort claims (governed by Iraqi law) were held by the Supreme Court to be subject to the Iraqi law on limitation periods (and therefore possibly out of time): *Ministry of Defence v Iraqi Civilians* [2016] UKSC 25.

to do so for imperative reasons of security, but that the duty in question did not override the UK's obligations under Article 5 of the ECHR. On the contrary, 'the UNSCRs required the duty to be performed consistently with the UK's obligations under article 5 (as those obligations applied in a situation of international armed conflict).'[166] This conclusion therefore charted a course between the divergent decisions of the House of Lords and the Court of Human Rights in *Al-Jedda*, though was facilitated by the availability by that point of the new line of reasoning endorsed in *Hassan* (discussed in the next section), whereby it was now possible to say that there was no necessary inconsistency with Article 5 of the ECHR in detaining a person who was considered to pose a threat to security.

C. IHRL and IHL

Overarching these disputes are more fundamental questions about the relationship between the ECHR (and the broader body of law, IHRL, to which it belongs) and the law of war (international humanitarian law, or 'IHL').[167] As the reach of the ECHR has expanded beyond the territory of contracting states—such that it will often apply to military acts—it has entered the domain of IHL, which is almost invariably more tolerant of certain acts and capable of providing a lower level of procedural protection: to apply IHRL to circumstances governed by IHL is therefore—it is claimed—to impose on the conduct of war limitations which are fundamentally incompatible with it. *Al-Jedda* had been decided on the basis that the ECHR and the relevant Security Council Resolutions could not be reconciled. Was that true? The question was considered by the Strasbourg Court in *Hassan v United Kingdom*,[168] in which the UK government, rather than arguing that Article 5 was displaced by the UN Charter (the argument which had failed in *Al-Jedda*) instead requested that the Strasbourg Court disapply or otherwise modify the operation of Article 5 in light of the powers of detention which the UK enjoys under international humanitarian law, particularly the Third and Fourth Geneva Conventions, which provide a legal basis for (and dictate procedure with respect to) the interment of civilians and combatants.[169] The Court emphasised its practice, based upon the Vienna Convention, of interpreting the ECHR 'in harmony with other rules of international law of which it forms part', including the body of international humanitarian law and the relevant Conventions.[170] And though it rejected the claim that no jurisdiction exists for the purposes of Article 1 where IHL applies,[171] it accepted the UK's contention that 'the lack of a formal derogation under Article 15 does not prevent the Court from taking account of the context and the provisions of

[166] [2014] EWHC 3686 (QB), [32].

[167] A topic far bigger than this short section can hope to represent: see, eg, Alexander Orakhelashvil, 'The Interaction between Human Rights and Humanitarian Law: Fragmentation, Conflict, Parallelism, or Convergence?' (2008) 19 *EJIL* 1; Christian Tomuschat, 'Human Rights and International Humanitarian Law' (2010) 21 *EJIL* 15.

[168] *Hassan v United Kingdom* 38 BHRC 358.

[169] The relevant provisions of the Third and Fourth Geneva Conventions are listed at 38 BHRC 358, [33]: key amongst them are Arts 43 and 78 of the Fourth Geneva Convention.

[170] 38 BHRC 358, [77].

[171] ibid.

international humanitarian law when interpreting and applying Article 5 in this case'.[172] The requirements of the Convention were to be interpreted against the relevant background of IHL, such that a new ground of justified deprivation of liberty was effectively recognised by it: deprivation of the liberty of civilians posing a threat to security in the context of international armed conflict as long as that deprivation of liberty was compatible with IHL and 'in keeping with the fundamental purpose of Article 5(1), which is to protect the individual from arbitrariness.'[173] Article 5 remained relevant also procedurally, though was to be interpreted in a way which took into account 'the context and the applicable rules of international humanitarian law'.[174] In the specific context of the case, no violation of the applicant's Article 5 rights was therefore found.[175] Though this approach represents a victory for the UK's government—as well as those who seek to secure the position of IHL as the *lex specialis* applying to war—its effect is limited by the differential development of IHL in different contexts. In international armed conflicts (IACs) between sovereign states—to which *Hassan* related, the applicant being the brother of an Iraqi being detained by British forces during active hostilities between the coalition and Iraq—IHL provides a legal basis for detention. In relation to non-international armed conflicts (NIACs), where one or more of the parties is not a sovereign state but an organised armed group, however, IHL does not explicitly offer such a basis: the relevant provisions of the Geneva Conventions regulate the treatment of detainees without empowering that detention in the first place.

The issue was considered by both the High Court and Court of Appeal in the case of *Serdar Mohammed* (it having been joined in the latter with *Rahmatullah*), relating to conflict between the UK (and its allies, including Afghanistan) and the Taliban in the territory of Afghanistan itself.[176] The claimant, detained by UK forces for several months, alleged violation of his Article 5 rights, which would be established unless there was a lawful and non-arbitrary basis for detention: no such basis could be found in the relevant UNSCR, IHL, or the domestic law of either Afghanistan or the UK. Even the requirements of Article 5 had been modified by the existence of a NIAC, the procedural safeguards required by IHL were absent. A violation of Article 5 was therefore found.[177] In the Supreme Court, *Mohammed* was joined with *Al-Waheed*,[178] discussed above, with the Court tasked with determining whether there existed a legal basis for detention (in the case of Waheed, at all; in that of *Serdar Mohammed* in excess of the 96 hours permitted by the detention policy of the International Security Assistance Force which led the operation in Afghanistan) and if so whether Article 5 of the ECHR should be read in light of that power of detention. The majority held that, whether or not such a power was found within customary international

[172] ibid, [103].

[173] ibid, [105].

[174] 38 BHRC 358, [106].

[175] ibid, [108]–[111].

[176] *Mohammed v Ministry of Defence* [2014] EWHC 1369 (QB); *Mohammed v Secretary of State for Defence* [2015] EWCA Civ 843.

[177] See the Court of Appeal's summary of its decision at [2015] EWCA Civ 843, [8]. See also Jane M Rooney, 'A legal basis for non-arbitrary detention: Mohammed v Secretary of State for Defence' [2016] *PL* 563, calling for a domestic legislative response to the decision in order to provide a legal basis for detention in the context of NIACs with sufficient procedural protection in order to render that detention non-arbitrary.

[178] *Mohammed v Secretary of State for Defence* [2017] UKSC 2.

law, detention was permitted by the relevant UNSCRs where necessary for imperative reasons of security.[179] Detention was not limited to detention pending delivery to the Afghan authorities and was not limited to detention for up to 96 hours: 'the United Kingdom was entitled to adopt its own detention policy, provided that the policy was consistent with the authority conferred by the relevant Security Council Resolutions, ie provided that it did not purport to authorise detention in circumstances where it was not necessary for imperative reasons of security.'[180]

The next point to be decided was whether the logic of the Strasbourg Court's decision in *Hassan* applied equally to the context of detention in a NIAC. The Supreme Court held that it did: the subparagraphs of Article 5(1) which specify the permitted grounds of interference with the right to liberty are not exhaustive and so 'where the armed forces of a Convention state are acting under a mandate from the Security Council to use all necessary measures, article 5(1) cannot be taken to prevent them from detaining persons for imperative reasons of security'.[181] While the procedural protections of Article 5 continue to apply, they may require adaptation, which is permissible 'provided that minimum standards of protection exist to ensure that detention is not imposed arbitrarily'.[182] The minimum standards in question are initial and regular subsequent reviews of the detention's appropriateness by an impartial body employing a fair procedure.[183] Though Mohammed's detention was held not to be covered by the relevant exceptions to Article 5 (in part because for most of the relevant period he was being held for intelligence exploitation), it was compatible with Article 5(1) in that he was being detained for imperative reasons of security, as permitted by the applicable SCR. What the Supreme Court held, however, was that because he did not have an effective means of challenging his detention (the reviewing body was not independent and there was no provision for the detainee's participation) there had been a violation of Article 5(4) for which the UK was liable.[184]

The effect of the decision of the Supreme Court is to resolve—in part—one of the key problems cause by the extra-territorial application of the ECHR in and since *Al-Skeini*. Together with the earlier decision of the Court of Human Rights in *Hassan*, it shows there will often be a limited power to detain both in IAC and NIAC; the latter without the UK having had either to legislate or to attempt (probably in vain) to promote the rapid evolution of IHL to fill the gap left by the limited application of the provisions of the Geneva Convention permitting detention. There are, however, several reasons for believing that we have not heard the last of this debate. One is that the Court of Human Rights may well disagree that its own decision in *Hassan* is equally capable of application to the context of NIAC; that the modification of Article 5 in light of the law of war requires a more explicit basis for detention than the Supreme Court was able to identify here. The second is that

[179] For a critique of the assimilation of UNSCRs with the Geneva Conventions as a rule of international law permitting detention in the Supreme Court's judgment, see Admas Habteslasie, 'Detention in times of war: Art 5 of the ECHR, UN Security Council Resolutions and the Supreme Court decision in Serdar Mohammed v Ministry of Defence' (2017) *EHRLR* 180.

[180] [2017] UKSC 2, [38].

[181] ibid, [68(2)].

[182] ibid, [68(3)].

[183] ibid.

[184] ibid, [104]–[109].

there may not always be a relevant UNSCR providing the authority for detention which the Supreme Court considered to be provided by the Resolutions relevant to the detention of Mohammed and Al-Waheed. A third is that even though such authority exists, it will still be necessary where detention is challenged to convince a court that it was necessary for the purposes of imperative security. Fourth, the question of what procedural protections must apply if detention is to not merely have a legal basis but also be non-arbitrary is an open one.[185] And, finally, this discussion addresses only the Article 5 point: ECHR claims based on acts done as part of military action abroad are often based on other provisions of the Convention.

D. Derogation in Respect of Military Action Abroad

The confluence of circumstances describe in the preceding sections—the inconsistent willingness to attribute military action to the UN or to allow the UN Charter to trump the ECHR, the unwillingness to limit the applicability of the ECHR in order to leave the floor to IHL and, underlying all of this, the expansion of the concept of jurisdiction under Article 1 of the Convention to encompass situations which would previously be entirely excluded from—has prompted concerns about the judicialisation of warfare; the application to it of legal regimes enforceable by individuals before domestic and international courts (with one of them, the European Court of Human Rights, well-known for its expansive and evolutive approach to the interpretation of the relevant instrument) and, moreover, legal regimes which are not designed for the regulation of armed conflict. This narrative of judicialisation has become entangled with a renaissance of political constitutionalism in the UK. Where the political constitutionalism of JAG Griffith and his successors, however, was a phenomenon which reflected clear left-wing priorities and was born, in part, out of a belief that the imposition of legal limits upon the political organs (primarily the legislature, but also—at least in the early years of the phenomenon—the executive) reflected a desire to prevent the pursuit of broadly progressive ends,[186] a reorientation has taken place. That is, the respective centres of gravity have shifted—a result, perhaps, of a post-Thatcherite consensus on some, if not all, economic questions on one hand, and the reconceptualisation by the judiciary of their own role in the years leading up to and beyond (and now because of) the enactment of the Human Rights Act—such that regardless of which political party is in power, the now-standard picture which emerges is a of a judiciary which is more liberal (and perhaps, on occasion, also more progressive) than the political branches, and so likely in many cases to prove more of an obstacle to the executive's intentions than is Parliament. On one telling, what has been taken place has been a shift from a political constitution to a mixed constitution.[187] Better, though, to think of a constitution which—on an institutional

[185] See Rooney (n 177).

[186] See, most importantly, JAG Griffith, 'The Political Constitution' (1979) 42 *MLR* 1. Though the thread of political constitutionalism which had most purchase in the discipline was that aimed—as was Griffith's Chorley lecture—at rights-based limitations upon legislative action (in the form of the incorporation of the ECHR into domestic law), Griffith (unlike many of his inheritors) was similarly concerned about the implications of subjecting, as the courts had done and continued to do, the executive to greater legal control in the 60s and 70s.

[187] See Adam Tomkins, 'What's left of the political constitution?' (2013) 14 *German Law Journal* 2275.

level—was always mixed, but in which old certainties about the relative positions of those institutions have been upended.[188]

In relation to several of the phenomena which have prompted the emergence of this new political constitutionalism, it is not clear what remedial action might be taken. Where the complaint is about overreach in particular judgments, the response often amounts to what seems little more than a call for 'better' decision-making. In the specific context of the judicialisation of the military constitution, however, a series of more formal responses have been commended.[189] The first would address the reduction in the scope of common law combat immunity by restoring the Crown's immunity in tort vis a vis its own troops by making an order under the Crown Proceedings (Armed Forces) Act 1987, which removed the limited immunity preserved by the Crown Proceedings Act 1947 but provided that it might be restored by secondary legislation if 'necessary or expedient' because of 'any imminent national danger or of any great emergency that has arisen' or 'for the purposes of any warlike operations in any part of the world outside the United Kingdom or of any other operations which are or are to be carried out in connection with the warlike activity of any persons in any such part of the world.'[190] This course of action would, however, extend the immunity beyond where it had stood prior to the decision of the Supreme Court in *Smith*, discussed above. Alternatively, a statutory 'restoration' of the doctrine of combat immunity may be possible. As regards the priority given to IHRL in circumstances in which IHL is considered to be the more appropriate body of law, it has also been argued that the UK should promote the development of IHL, particularly as it relates to non-international armed conflict, in order that it is able to occupy the space which IHRL has in recent years often come to fill; no longer, it is argued, will the absence of clear IHL rules regarding the conduct of NIAC be used to justify the expansion of IHRL into territory to which it is not suited, not least because—unlike IHRL—IHL binds both parties to an NIAC.[191] This claim, of course, is deprived of some of its urgency (if not force) by the decision of the Supreme Court in relation to detention in NIACs under Security Council resolutions.

The centrepiece of the proposed response to the judicialisation of warfare, however, is to seek to counter the extra-territorial application of the ECHR by derogating from it in respect of future armed conflicts. Such a move has been argued for by those most concerned by the extra-territorial application of the ECHR and its implications for judicial oversight of the conduct of military action,[192] and has become adopted (for now, at least) by Theresa May's government;[193] in many ways it represents a more limited invocation of the same

[188] This is not a new phenomenon: Lord Hailsham is a good example of a thinker on the political right who argued for the limitation of legislative competence in the 1970s and dropped that demand when Margaret Thatcher came to power.

[189] See, most importantly, Ekins, Morgan and Tugendhat (n 141) and House of Commons Defence Committee, *UK Armed Forces Personnel and the Legal Framework for Future Operations* (HC 2013–14, 931).

[190] Crown Proceedings (Armed Forces) Act 1987, s 2.

[191] See Ekins, Morgan and Tugendhat (n 141) 32–3.

[192] ibid, (n 141).

[193] Conservative and Unionist Party, *Forward, Together: Our Plan For A Stronger Britain And A Prosperous Future* (2017), 41: 'Under a Conservative government, British troops will in future be subject to the Law of Armed Conflict, which includes the Geneva Convention and UK Service Law, not the European Court of Human Rights.' Closely related is the commitment, in the context of Northern Ireland, to introducing 'new bodies for addressing the legacy of the past in fair, balanced and proportionate ways which do not unfairly focus on former members of the Armed Forces and the Royal Ulster Constabulary' (34).

impulses which underpinned the (now-dormant) intention to replace the Human Rights Act with a 'British Bill of Rights'.[194] There are, however, a number of reasons for thinking that, though such a move dovetails neatly with the anti-ECHR mood which prevails within the executive and, very often, the country at large, it will not have the effect desired. One of the proposal's most significant lacunae has, however, been effectively filled by events elsewhere: as discussed in Chapter 6, decisions of the High Court and Court of Appeal regarding the doctrine of Crown act of state had opened the stage to private law claims against the Crown arising out of military action abroad of a sort which had until quite recently been untenable. Only with the decision of the Supreme Court in *Serdar Mohammed* was Crown act of state restored to something approaching its traditional breadth and effect. The significance of this fact is that, had the decision of the Court of Appeal stood, a derogation from the Convention as regards military action abroad would have left open the possibility of a claim in private law, which would have required a similar degree of judicial oversight of action upon the battlefield, and may have resulted in greater damages where a claim was successful. This anomaly is no longer possible, and the argument for derogation is stronger as a result; depending, however, on which account of Crown act of state is preferred in future cases, it may be that public law claims in respect of military action abroad remain available. If so, the matter might yet be resolved by means of the classic administrative law fudge: a standard of review so lacking in intensity as to be effectively indistinguishable from a holding that some matter is non-justiciable in the genuine sense.

Nevertheless, several difficulties remain. The first relates to the conditions under which the Convention permits derogation. 'In time of war or other public emergency threatening the life of the nation', it provides, 'any High Contracting Party may take measures derogating from its obligations under this Convention to the extent strictly required by the exigencies of the situation, provided that such measures are not inconsistent with its other obligations under international law.'[195] The Strasbourg Court has never defined 'war'—no derogation having been made on that basis—and the term is deprecated generally in international law, while the UK (as noted above) no longer makes a formal declaration of war in advance of military action. The jurisprudence of the Court of Human Rights demonstrates a hands-off approach to the question of whether or not the initial triggering condition is met, on the basis that '[n]ational authorities are in principle in a better position than the international judge to decide both on the presence of such an emergency and on the nature and scope of the derogations necessary to avert it.'[196] The Court has therefore accepted, for example, in *Lawless v Ireland* that there existed a state of emergency in Ireland as a result of:

> the existence in the territory of the Republic of Ireland of a secret army engaged in unconstitutional activities and using violence to attain its purposes … the fact that this army was also operating outside the territory of the State, thus seriously jeopardising the relations of the Republic of Ireland with its neighbour [and] the steady and alarming increase in terrorist activities from the autumn of 1956 and throughout the first half of 1957.[197]

[194] See, eg, Bill of Rights Commission, *A UK Bill of Rights? The Choice Before Us (Vol 1)* (2012).
[195] European Convention on Human Rights, Art 15.
[196] *Ireland v UK* (1979/80) 2 EHRR 25, [207].
[197] *Lawless v Ireland (No 3)* (1961) 1 EHRR 15, [28].

In *A v UK* the Court of Human Rights accepted that a public emergency existed in the UK post-11 September.[198] It is therefore unlikely that either domestic courts or the Court of Human Rights would gainsay the original judgment upon which a derogation was based.[199] There are, though, particular difficulties associated with fulfilling the requirements of Article 15 in the context of non-defensive military action abroad. It was observed by Lord Bingham in an early case arising out of the Iraq war that, in relation to the totality of the conditions of Article 15, it was:

> hard to think that these conditions could ever be met when a state had chosen to conduct an overseas peacekeeping operation, however dangerous the conditions, from which it could withdraw … It has not been the practice of states to derogate in such situations, and since subsequent practice in the application of a treaty may (under article 31(3)(b) of the Vienna Convention) be taken into account in interpreting the treaty it seems proper to regard article 15 as inapplicable.[200]

The relationship between 'war or other public emergency threatening the life of the nation' has been disputed within academic commentary on Article 15.[201] In particular, it is unclear whether the qualifier 'threatening the life of the nation' applies only to 'other public emergency' or also to 'war'.[202] If it does so apply, then it may be that a war of choice rather than necessity could not meet the requirements of Article 15, unless 'the nation' in question is assumed to be the nation on whose territory the war is being fought.[203] If the 'threatening the life of the nation' requirement does not so apply, then a derogation could be lawfully made notwithstanding that the UK was pursuing a war in a context (such as Iraq and Afghanistan) where it was difficult to claim that the war was one threatening the life of the nation. Lord Bingham's reservations about the possibility of derogation in respect of overseas peacekeeping would not, to this extent, be justified. Either way, the crucial question, as in the *A* case in the House of Lords and in Strasbourg, is likely to be instead that of whether the particular measures taken are necessary and proportionate to the public emergency which is asserted to exist: here, the courts will carry out a review on standard ECHR grounds, albeit possibly with a greater deference (in the domestic courts) or recognising a wider margin of appreciation (in Strasbourg) than might normally be afforded to the relevant decision maker. If the actions taken are held to be disproportionate to the threat, then it is of no consequence that the initial triggering condition has been met. The fact that requirements of necessity and proportionality will be far more difficult to meet in the context of a foreign war of choice reduces the significance of the question of whether

[198] *A v United Kingdom* (2009) 49 EHRR 29.

[199] The only case in which this has happened—*Denmark, Norway, Sweden and the Netherlands v Greece* (applications 3321/67, 3322/67, 3323/67 and 3344/67) ('the Greek case')—was a decision not of the Court but of the Commission, and related to the actions of the Greek regime which came to power in the military coup of 1967.

[200] *R (Al-Jedda) v Secretary of State for Defence* [2007] UKHL 58, [38].

[201] For an articulation of the elements of a 'public emergency', see the Greek case (n 199) [113].

[202] See, eg, the discussion in Admas Habteslasie, 'Derogation in Time of War: The Application of Article 15 of the ECHR in Extraterritorial Armed Conflicts' (2016) 21 *Judicial Review* 302, in which the author argues that the limiting words do not apply to 'war' but only to 'public emergency'.

[203] See, eg, Marko Milanovic, 'Extraterritorial Derogations from Human Rights Treaties in Armed Conflict' in Nehal Bhuta (ed) *The Frontiers of Human Rights: Extraterritoriality and its Challenges*, Oxford University Press (2016).

'threatening the life of the nation' is or is not of general application: what will be necessary in a defensive war at home will differ significantly from what is necessary in an offensive war, or peacekeeping operation, far from the territory of the Contracting Party. What is necessary will also vary as between the phase of a military operation in which activities hostilities are taking place and situations, of the sort at issue in *Al-Skeini* and *Al-Jedda*, in which the UK is an occupying force.

A second difficulty of the plan to derogate from the ECHR in respect of future armed conflict is that the power to derogate does not apply to the entirety of the rights thereunder. Paragraph 2 of Article 15 provides that '[n]o derogation from Article 2, except in respect of deaths resulting from lawful acts of war, or from Articles 3, 4 (paragraph 1) and 7 shall be made under this provision.' Though many of the claims which have been made under the HRA in respect of the wars in Iraq and Afghanistan are made under Article 5 (the right to liberty), a significant proportion are made under Article 3, and the inability to derogate from that provision significantly limits the benefits that might accrue, even if it could be shown that the Article 15 conditions were met. Derogation from Article 5 would be of greatest consequence in the event that the Strasbourg Court disagrees with the Supreme Court as to the existence of a legal basis for detention in a non-international armed conflict; if it does not, then the value of derogation would be restricted to circumstances in which the conditions for the existence of that basis are not met, or they are met and yet—as was the case in *Serdar Mohammed*—there has nevertheless been a breach of the minimum standards which Article 5 establishes. The exception to the exclusion of Article 2 means that a derogation can be made in respect of certain killings; though this may benefit the UK in respect of future armed conflicts abroad, it can have no application where killing takes place outside armed conflict, where the ECHR recognises only a tightly drawn necessity exception to Article 2.

As a matter of domestic law, all of these difficulties could be overcome by a decision not to derogate from the Convention but instead to amend the Human Rights Act so as to create a divergent concept of jurisdiction thereunder (a move which would also neatly evade the difficulties, discussed in Chapter 1, associated with the making of a derogation order under the HRA). Such a move would not, however, allow the armed forces to evade the scrutiny of the Court of Human Rights but rather partially return the UK to the pre-HRA situation of legal accountability for violations of the ECHR being possible only in Strasbourg and not also in the domestic courts, though now in the context in which applications to the Court of Human Rights have become a normal, rather than highly exceptional, aspect of constitutional practice. In reality, however, the derogation from the ECHR in future armed conflicts carried out in combination with measures aimed at the restoration of a form of Crown immunity and/or 'restoration' of Combat immunity would impact most directly not upon those killed or detained on far-off battlefields, but rather on those members of the British armed forces who have benefited from the possibility of seeking compensation under the law of tort alongside the additional oversight mandated by the (non-derogable) investigative obligations under Article 2. If the proposal is to be acted upon, whether in the near future or later, this should happen only in light of a full understanding of its likely effect and numerous limitations. If, alternatively, it is simply a form of political posturing, then those who indulge should be conscious of the fact that they will not always be in power; it will not always be their bêtes noires whose rights are at issue.

V. Drones

A topic of particular, and growing, importance to the combatting of national security threats in recent years has been the use of Unmanned Aerial Vehicles ('drones'), which are now frequently armed (rather than merely carrying out surveillance activities) and which can therefore be used to deploy force in circumstances where conventional military operations would not be practical or politically feasible (or, perhaps, lawful).[204] In August 2015, the Prime Minister announced in Parliament that two British citizens, Reyaad Khan (the primary target) and Ruhul Amin, who had been fighting on behalf of the Islamic State in Syria had been killed in a drone strike conducted by the RAF. These strikes were the first occasion on which Britain had employed drone strikes to kill individuals in a country with which it was not at war at the relevant point in time. In carrying out the attack, however, the UK was mimicking the long-standing practice of the US, which has for many years carried out drone strikes,[205] including on its own citizens, in Pakistan, Yemen and Somalia and in which the UK's intelligence services have occasionally been accused of complicity. This section considers some of the issues which such strikes raise in domestic constitutional law, arguing that the way in which political accountability operates as regards drone strikes as compared to conventional military action, involving either the deployment of troops or, at least, the carrying out of air strikes, exacerbates some of the difficulties of accountability for the use of military force considered in previous sections of the chapter.

A. The International Framework

The basic international legal framework for the lawful use of force via drones (the '*jus ad bellum*') is that outlined above.[206] The UN Charter (like customary international law) prohibits the use of force,[207] though there exists an exception in cases where the state on whose territory force is used consents to its use.[208] Otherwise, force can be lawful (to this extent) only where authorised by the UN Security Council under Chapter VII of the Charter or where it is lawfully taken in self-defence in accordance with Article 51. That provision preserves 'the inherent right of individual or collective self-defence if an armed attack occurs against a Member of the United Nations, until the Security Council has taken measures

[204] For background to the use of drones by the UK armed forces, including issues of terminology, see House of Commons Defence Committee, *Remote Control: Remotely Piloted Air Systems—current and future UK use* (HC 2013–14, 772).

[205] The US, for all the flaws of its drone programmes, eventually made available the 'Presidential Policy Guidance' governing its use of drones: *Procedures For Approving Direct Action Against Terrorist Targets Located Outside The United States And Areas Of Active Hostilities* (22 May 2013). For a consideration of the (many) remaining problems of accountability, see Columbia Law School Human Rights Clinic and Sana'a Center for Strategic Studies, *Out of the Shadows: Recommendations to Advance Transparency in the Use of Lethal Force* (2017).

[206] See Christof Heyns, Dapo Akande, Lawrence Hill-Cawthorne and Thompson Chengeta, 'The International Law Framework Regulating The Use Of Armed Drones' (2016) 65 *International and Comparative Law Quarterly* 791.

[207] Charter of the UN, Art 2(4). The prohibition on the use of force is the basis of the international law crime of aggression—it has been held, however, by the House of Lords that the crime forms no part of domestic law: *R v Jones (Margaret)* [2006] UKHL 16.

[208] Some of the difficulties of such consent are discussed in the context of drone strikes by Heyns et al (n 206) 797–800.

necessary to maintain international peace and security.'[209] This is subject to customary international law requirements of necessity and proportionality,[210] and the right to use force in self-defence does not apply to all armed attacks against the state, but only those of a certain gravity.[211] In the post 11 September period it has come to be widely believed that self-defence as a justification for the use of force may be invoked in relation to non-state actors.[212] Regardless of whether the attacking party is a state or non-state actor, the attack in question need not necessarily be in progress for the right of self-defence to become active: like many other states, the UK maintains that the right of self-defence includes the right to defend oneself against an armed attack which is imminent,[213] though the UK has rejected the existence of a doctrine whereby resort to force is lawful simply in order to 'pre-empt' a future attack.[214] It is this 'anticipatory' self-defence which was invoked in relation to the drone strikes carried out by the UK in Syria, though accounts differed as to which state was being defended. The statement made to the House of Commons following the strikes explained their legal basis as follows:

> We were exercising the UK's inherent right to self-defence. There was clear evidence of these individuals planning and directing armed attacks against the UK. These were part of a series of actual and foiled attempts to attack the UK and our allies, and given the prevailing circumstances in Syria, the airstrike was the only feasible means of effectively disrupting the attacks that had been planned and directed. It was therefore necessary and proportionate for the individual self-defence of the United Kingdom.[215]

The communication subsequently sent to the UN in accordance with Article 51 made reference—where the Prime Minister had not—to the collective self-defence of Iraq.[216] In a memorandum to the JCHR, the government specified that:

> Individual terrorist attacks, or an ongoing series of terrorist attacks, may rise to the level of an "armed attack" for these purposes if they are of sufficient gravity. This is demonstrated by UN Security Council resolutions 1368 (2001) and 1373 (2001) following the attacks on New York and

[209] Charter of the United Nations, Art 51.

[210] See, eg, *Case Concerning Military and Paramilitary Activities In and Against Nicaragua (Nicaragua v United States)* [1986] ICJR 14, [194]. For discussion, see Judith Gardam, *Necessity, Proportionality and the Use of Force by States*, Cambridge University Press (2004) and Dapo Akande and Thomas Liefländer, 'Clarifying Necessity, Imminence, and Proportionality in the Law of Self-Defense' (2013) 107 *AJIL* 563.

[211] [1986] ICJR 14, [191].

[212] See the discussion in Christian J Tams, 'The Use of Force against Terrorists' (2009) *EJIL* 359.

[213] The use of force must be necessary (in that there is no other means of averting the attack) and the force used must be proportionate: see, eg, Attorney General (Lord Goldsmith), 'Attorney-General's Advice on the Iraq War, Iraq: Resolution 1441' (2005) 54 *ICLQ* 767, 768. On the UK position as to imminence, see now Rt Hon Jeremy Wright QC MP, 'The modern law of self-defence', Speech at International Institute for Strategic Studies (11 January 2017).

[214] See Goldsmith (n 213) 768: 'I am aware that the USA has been arguing for recognition of a broad doctrine of a right to use force to pre-empt danger in the future. If this means more than a right to respond proportionately to an imminent attack (and I understand that the doctrine is intended to carry that connotation) this is not a doctrine which, in my opinion, exists or is recognised in international law.' Evolving understandings of 'imminence' may of course close the (legal and conceptual) gap as between anticipatory self-defence and pre-emption proper.

[215] HC Deb 7 Sep 2015, vol 599 col 26.

[216] UK Permanent Representative to the UN, Letter to the UN Security Council (7 September 2015), quoted in Joint Committee on Human Rights, *The Government's policy on the use of drones for targeted killing* (2015–16, HL 141, HC 574), [2.10]: 'the UK has undertaken military action in Syria against the so-called Islamic State in Iraq and the Levant (ISIL) in exercise of the inherent right of individual and collective self-defence. [...] ISIL is engaged in an ongoing armed attack against Iraq, and therefore action against ISIL in Syria is lawful in the collective self-defence of Iraq.'

> Washington of 11 September 2001. Whether the gravity of an attack is sufficient to give rise to the exercise of the inherent right of self-defence must be determined by reference to all of the facts in any given case. The scale and effects of ISIL's campaign are judged to reach the level of an armed attack against the UK that justifies the use of force to counter it in accordance with Article 51.[217]

The classic statement of the requirements that an attack must meet in order to be considered imminent refers to the attack being 'instant, overwhelming, leaving no choice of means, and no moment of deliberation'.[218] Subsequent to the drone strikes in question—and at least in part at the prompting of the Joint Committee on Human Rights[219]—the government has sought to clarify the understanding of imminence it employs by endorsing a series of principles identified by Sir Daniel Bethlehem as relevant to the question of imminence:

> (a) The nature and immediacy of the threat; (b) The probability of an attack; (c) Whether the anticipated attack is part of a concerted pattern of continuing armed activity; (d) The likely scale of the attack and the injury, loss or damage likely to result therefrom in the absence of mitigating action; and (e) The likelihood that there will be other opportunities to undertake effective action in self-defense that may be expected to cause less serious collateral injury, loss or damage.[220]

Also endorsed by the Attorney General on behalf of the government was the observation that '[t]he absence of specific evidence of where an attack will take place or of the precise nature of an attack does not preclude a conclusion that an armed attack is imminent for purposes of the exercise of a right of self-defense, provided that there is a reasonable and objective basis for concluding that an armed attack is imminent.'[221] The memo to the JCHR also explained why the test of imminence was met in the context of the drone strikes in Syria:

> There was clear evidence of Khan's involvement in planning and directing a series of attacks against the UK and our allies, including a number which were foiled. That evidence showed that the threat was genuine, demonstrating both his intent and his capability of delivering the attacks. The threat of attack was current; and an attack could have become a reality at any moment and without warning. In the prevailing circumstances in Syria, this airstrike was the only feasible means of effectively disrupting the attacks planned and directed by this individual. There was no realistic prospect that Khan would travel outside Syria so that other means of disruption could be attempted. The legal test of an imminent armed attack was therefore satisfied.[222]

A later report by the Intelligence and Security Committee cast doubt on this, noting that the issue of imminence in relation to Khan appeared 'to centre not on one specific attack about to take place but on a broader concern that—due to gaps in coverage—a plot might

[217] Government Memorandum to the JCHR.

[218] Letter from US Secretary of State Daniel Webster to Lord Ashburton (6 August 1842) in Caroline Case, (1841) 29 *British and Foreign State Papers* 1129, 1137–8.

[219] JCHR (n 216) [3.41].

[220] Wright (n 213). The original source is Daniel Bethlehem, 'Principles Relevant to the Scope of a State's Right of Self-Defense Against an Imminent or Actual Armed Attack by Nonstate Actors' (2012) 106 *American Journal of International Law* 769.

[221] Wright (n 213).

[222] Government Memorandum to the JCHR.

go undetected'.[223] It is important to note, however, that the ISC did not have access to the entirety of the relevant material. As explained in a footnote to its report:

> The National Security Secretariat has made clear that the Committee has not been provided with all the intelligence, but only the "main primary intelligence reports specifically drawn upon in compiling the contemporaneous assessments and a selection of supplementary reports". We requested sight of any further intelligence reports which would disprove our statement, but the National Security Secretariat declined to provide any such material.[224]

The ISC also encountered difficulty in establishing that the requirements of necessity and proportionality were met.[225] That it is therefore unclear the conditions for the lawful recourse to force in international law were met in relation to the strikes in question calls into question the ability of the UK's political organs—including its organs specialist in both human rights and intelligence matters—to exercise oversight of these matters: while a fuller account of the government's understanding of the legal position has been elicited, the necessary factual material has not been made available. If the government would not make it available to the ISC, it will make it available to no one: Parliament and, through it, the public at large, are left to take the matter on trust.

This leaves to be considered the question of lawfulness under both IHL (the '*jus in bello*') and IHRL. The government argued that IHL applied to the carrying out of drone strikes and there seems to be no dispute that the drone strikes in Syria formed part of the ongoing armed conflict against ISIL in which the UK was involved in Iraq.[226] Where the original reference to the killing in Syria as representing a 'new departure' was understood by many to indicate that the killing had taken place outside of an established armed conflict, it was later conceptualised as relating instead to the domestic constitutional requirements (discussed further below).[227] Had the Syria drone strikes not been part of the Iraq conflict (as the original statement had seemed to imply) then it seems unlikely that the 'conflict' in question—between the UK and the two targets—would have reached the threshold of intensity to constitute an NIAC, and so would not have been governed by IHL at all. The government argued that IHL did, however, apply, and it appears, further, to have taken the view that compliance with IHL was sufficient to fulfil its obligations under IHRL.[228] It is not at all clear that that view is correct. The first question as regards IHRL is whether or not the ECHR applies at all to drone strikes which take place overseas. The question is answered by reference to the same evolving and contested jurisprudence as was considered above in the context of the ECHR's application to acts of the armed forces. Assuming, however, that the point of using drones is specifically that there need be no prior engagement with those against whom force is used, it is possible to skip straight to the outer boundary of the Article 1 jurisdiction question, as disagreed upon by the High Court and the Court of Appeal in *Al-Saddoon*. It was noted above that the latter, allowing an appeal against the

[223] Intelligence and Security Committee, *UK Lethal Drone Strikes in Syria* (HC 2016–17, 1152), [40].
[224] ISC (n 223) 14n.
[225] ISC (n 223) [41]–[47] and [48]–[55].
[226] JCHR (n 216) [2.29]. A number of aspects of the JCHR's report were considered in short pieces published in (2016) 3 *Journal on the Use of Force and International Law*.
[227] See the discussion in JCHR (n 216) Ch 2.
[228] JCHR (n 216) [3.19].

High Court's finding on this point, held that 'in laying down this basis of extra-territorial jurisdiction the Grand Chamber required a greater degree of power and control than that represented by the use of lethal or potentially lethal force alone.'[229]

Though they were not at issue in that particular case, the implications of this divergence of interpretation of *Al-Skeini* for the carrying out of drone strikes is obvious: if the Supreme Court (or the Court of Human Rights) eventually holds either that the High Court's interpretation was the correct one—or simply expands the concept of jurisdiction to similar effect in a later case—then any person who is the target of a drone strike will be considered to be within the jurisdiction of the UK, and the ECHR will apply. The implications of that would be—at a minimum—to open up to review the necessity and proportionality of any given strike. The most relevant substantive provision of the ECHR—Article 2, protecting the right to life—contains within it an ostensibly exhaustive list of bases upon which it is permissible to deprive a person of his or her life, one of which is where it results from the use of force 'in defence of any person from unlawful violence'. It is possible that this is broad enough to encompass the killing of Khan.[230] If it does not, it is similarly possible that, by analogy with the *Hassan* case—relating to Article 5 rather than Article 2—the Strasbourg Court would recognise additional exceptions to Article 2 reflecting those which exist within IHL. The Supreme Court's judgment in *Al-Waheed* would seem to open the further possibility of Article 2 being read in light of the IHL as it relates also to an NIAC, as is the case here. What will matter, then, by analogy with *Al-Jedda*, is whether or not the legal authority under which the strikes took place was suitably explicit as to trump the protection of the ECHR under Article 103 of the UN Charter. Here, we are dealing with the inherent right of self-defence (both individual and, it transpires, collective) rather than the authority of a Security Council Resolution and so the question cannot be answered with reference to the terms of that Resolution, as was true both in *Al-Jedda* and *Al-Waheed*. The effect is that the strike might be held—if the Convention were to apply to the facts in the first place—to be compatible with Article 2 by virtue of being lawful under IHL. Notable here is that derogation from Article 2 is possible in respect of 'deaths resulting from lawful acts of war'; if, however, the death results from a lawful act of war it has been suggested that there is no need, in respect of the killing itself, to derogate at all.[231]

This analysis—though based upon a series of more or less plausible assumptions—holds only to the extent that IHL applies, as it does in both IACs and NIACs. The government has claimed, however, that IHL applies also to the use of lethal force outside of armed conflict altogether, and that a drone killing will be lawful in such circumstances as long as carried out in accordance with IHL.[232] This is self-serving and unconvincing and, pushed on the point by the JCHR, the government refused to commit itself or explain the basis of its view as to the application of IHL in such circumstances. The JCHR responded in strong terms:

> In our view, the response comes close to asserting that the applicable law follows the choice of means by the State to deal with a particular threat to its security: that if the State chooses to deal

[229] *Al-Saadoon v Secretary Of State For Defence* [2016] EWCA Civ 811, [69].

[230] See the discussions in Heyns et al (n 206) and JCHR (n 216), Ch 3, as to the relevant ECHR jurisprudence.

[231] Michael Ramsden, 'British Airstrikes Against ISIS in Syria: Legal Issues Under the European Convention on Human Rights' (2016) *EHRLR* 151, 157.

[232] JCHR (n 216) [2.38].

> with it by military means, the relevant principles and standards are the Law of War, even if the military operation is carried out in an area which is outside armed conflict.[233]

The most important implication of the dispute relates to the use of force in counter-terrorism operations, where there is no armed conflict (neither an IAC or a NIAC) and so, on the traditional understanding, no possibility of a killing being justified according to the principles of IHL and being, by virtue of that fact, compatible with the ECHR (where it applies). This appears an issue ripe for future disagreement if the use of drones is expanded beyond the boundaries of established armed conflicts. Previously, the government had accepted that IHRL applied to the use of drones outside of armed conflict;[234] it now appears to take the view—supported by the Court of Appeal's *Al-Sadoon* judgment discussed above—that it does not apply to the use of drones either within or outside armed conflict.[235]

B. Domestic Legal and Constitutional Issues

The carrying out of drone strikes in Syria in August 2015 illustrates several points regarding the convention, discussed above, whereby Parliament will be consulted prior to military action being commenced. The strikes in question took place in the context of a situation in which the use of force in Iraq had been given by Parliament in 2014, approval for its use in Syria having been withheld the previous year. The Iraq resolution specifically noted that 'this motion does not endorse UK air strikes in Syria as part of this campaign and any proposal to do so would be subject to a separate vote in Parliament'[236] (though the House of Commons in December 2015 voted to extend authorisation to use military force to Syria).[237] The JCHR suggested that this background was the explanation for the government's original insistence that the strike was not in fact part of the same armed conflict:

> it is testament to the remarkable normative strength already acquired by the recently established constitutional convention. Because of the importance attached to that convention, he was keen to establish that the Government had not ignored the will of the Commons, but rather had acted in accordance with the convention, by taking urgent military action and then coming to the Commons at the earliest opportunity to explain the justification for that action. His remarks about the strike not being part of armed conflict were part of his explanation as to why the Government had in fact acted in accordance with the domestic constitutional convention rather than ignored it.[238]

As we have seen above, however, the government's legal position was that the strikes were part of *an* armed conflict to which the law of war applied, and the official notification to the UN justified its legality by reference to the collective self-defence of Iraq (as well as the UK's individual self-defence). It is not easy to square these positions, suggesting that the

[233] Joint Committee on Human Rights, *The Government's policy on the use of drones for targeted killing: Government Response to the Committee's Second Report of Session 2015–16* (2016–17, HL 49, HC 747), [18].
[234] JCHR (n 233) [28]–[29].
[235] ibid, [22].
[236] HC Deb 26 September 2014, vol 585 cols 1365–6.
[237] HC Deb 2 December 2015, vol 603 col 499.
[238] JCHR (n 216) [2.25].

emerging constitutional convention is in tension with the international law position—to abide by one's constitutional duties may involve fudging the issues of international law and vice versa—further emphasising the tension between domestic and international propriety discussed above. Nevertheless, the JCHR forced the government to clarify its position that, though the Syria strikes took place as a matter of law in the context of an armed conflict, it would be equally willing to use force against terrorists outside of armed conflict if necessary, and that it understood the threshold of intensity that a terrorist attack would have to reach to entitle the UK to use self-defence was 'where terrorist violence reaches a level of gravity such that were it to be perpetrated by a State it would amount to an armed attack'.[239] The second element of the convention implicated here is the absence of prior notification of Parliament and the giving by it of consent to the use of force. As discussed above, however, the convention is accepted to admit of exceptions: as was always intended,[240] it does not apply in circumstances of urgency.[241] There seems to have been no serious suggestion that the convention had been breached here, notwithstanding that force was being used precisely where Parliament had previously denied authority for its use. The political constitution appears to have functioned as well as it might have been expected to as regards the strikes and yet still fallen short of meaningful Parliamentary involvement. Elsewhere it will struggle to do even this: the drone strikes at issue were announced to Parliament only because they were not covered by a parliamentary authorisation for the deployment of armed force; drone strikes which are so covered occur routinely, with no notice given to Parliament, and the government refusing to release even details of the location of its UAVs. By the end of 2016, however, it was known that UK Reaper drones had undertaken around 1,700 missions in Iraq and Syria as part of Operation Shader. This leaves only the legal element to consider, where again certain special issues are raised by the strikes in question.

There have been two strands to domestic legal challenges to the involvement of the British military and intelligence services in drone strikes, both of which have been stymied by considerations of justiciability. One strand is to alleged British involvement, in the form of the provision of 'locational intelligence', in US drone strikes in North Waziristan: the relevant case law, involving the doctrine of foreign act of state, is considered in Chapter 6. The second strand was a threatened challenge—never, in the event, brought—to the failure of the government to formulate and to publish a 'targeted killing policy'.[242] This was met by a response asserting that the matter was a 'paradigm example of a case to which these well-established rules of non-justiciability apply.'[243] Assuming this was correct as a matter of law—and at least part of the explanation for the fact that no application for judicial

[239] JCHR (n 233) [11]. The government failed to offer, however, a full account of its views as to the applicable law: 'while high level answers have been given to the Committee's questions, many of the questions are hypothetical (for example, seeking clarification of the Government's position in relation to the use of force outside of armed conflicts) and the answers should not be taken as representing the Government's detailed and developed thinking on these complex issues. The need to take any future action would be considered according to the circumstances of each operation' ([8]).

[240] Ministry of Justice (n 47) [38] and [52]–[55]; Ministry of Justice (n 48) [28].

[241] HC Deb 10 March 2011, vol 524 col 1066: 'We propose to observe that convention except when there is an emergency and such action would not be appropriate'.

[242] Correspondence between Leigh Day and the Secretary of State for Defence (23 September 2015). The claimants were to be Caroline Lucas MP and Baroness Jones of Moulsecoomb.

[243] Correspondence between the government Legal Department and Leigh Day (23 October 2015).

review was ultimately brought—this indicates the very considerable difficulty of challenging the use of drones in the courts: any challenge will be based upon rules of international law which are not incorporated in domestic law and/or will amount to asking the courts to adjudicate upon the sovereign acts of those foreign states with whom the UK acts in conjunction: in the first case, we are dealing with one form of non-justiciability, in the latter case the other type. If it does neither—if, that is, it manages to identify some domestic legal hook upon which to hang a challenge to the use of drones,[244] but without implicating the sovereign acts of foreign states—it will still fall within the understanding of Crown act of state to which the Supreme Court gave effect in *Serdar Mohammed v Ministry of Defence*,[245] which—like the foreign act of state doctrine—is an example of 'true' non-justiciability and which excludes both private and (probably) public law claims in respect of drone strikes. The overall effect is that, whichever factor or combination of factors is dispositive of the issue in any given case, the domestic courts are very unlikely to prove a productive avenue for accountability unless the question of non-justiciability can be overcome. The primary method of overcoming considerations of non-justiciability is—the jurisprudence of the courts makes clear—to identify some statutory requirement that the courts determine the particular issue before them, such as is represented by the rule in section 6 of the Human Rights Act which makes it unlawful for a public authority to act incompatibly with the Convention rights.[246] The question of the Convention's application to situations in which there is an extra-territorial use with no prior control is therefore crucial: any other avenue of challenge is likely to be blocked of by a variety of considerations clustered together under the heading of justiciability.

Another form of legal accountability for the use of drones by the UK is also relevant, however: that provided by the criminal law. It has been argued that the carrying out of drone strikes abroad meets (or at least potentially meets) the criteria of murder in English law:

> There is no reason to doubt that those affected were "reasonable creatures *in rerum natura*", nor that they suffered death, nor that the strike caused their deaths, nor that those involved in the operation were responsible for the strike. The mental element appears straightforward too: according to the report, the very aim of the strike was to kill one of the three men, and, even if the other two deaths were an unwanted side-effect, it must surely have been appreciated that they were virtually certain.[247]

The same account assumes that there would not be available any defence based on the need to prevent an attack, for there is no evidence that an attack on the UK by those killed in Syria was in any way 'imminent', as the law of self-defence requires.[248] The analysis offered is predicated, however, upon the belief that the killing took place—as killing must in order

[244] In the pre-action letter, the grounds identified were the failure to formulate a 'Targeted Killing Policy' (or, if such a policy had been formulated, to publish it).

[245] *Serdar Mohammed v Ministry of Defence* [2017] UKSC 1.

[246] As discussed in Ch 6, one question which this raises is why the statutory basis of the claim in *Noor Khan* was not sufficient to overcome the considerations of justiciability raised by the fact of calling into question the sovereign acts of a foreign state.

[247] Simon Gardner, 'The Domestic Criminal Legality of the RAF Drone Strike in Syria in August 2015' (2016) *Crim LR* 35, 36.

[248] Gardner (n 247) 36–7.

to amount to murder—'under the Queen's peace'.[249] Though that is in accordance with the government's original statements, the position ultimately taken was that the killing took place as part of an NIAC ('in the heat of war, and in the actual exercise thereof')[250] and so not 'under the Queen's peace'.[251] This alone would seem sufficient to prevent criminal responsibility arising. If it does not, there is always the judgment of the DPP as to whether a prosecution is in the public interest to fall back upon but, as it was put by the Joint Committee on Human Rights, 'front-line personnel ... should be entitled to more legal certainty than is offered by the mere expectation that the Director of Public Prosecutions would be unlikely to consider prosecution to be in the public interest.'[252] If the use of drones is extended to situations outside of existing armed conflicts, these questions—like those of compatibility with the ECHR—will become significantly more urgent; better, therefore, to deal with them in advance.

The most important constitutional element of drone warfare, however—even that which involves targeted killing of British citizens—may be neither the procedural questions discussed so far in relation to legal and (ex ante) political accountability within the constitution, but rather the fact that, compared to forms of warfare which put at risk the lives of British forces drone strikes appear to be popular, potentially achieving what the public takes to be an important strategic end without the risk to the armed forces. Though some of that popularity may derive from the impression, given by the language of 'targeting' and 'precision', that the strikes are more limited in their effect than is the case (the strike which killed Reyaad Khan and Ruhul Amin was, strictly speaking, targeting the former, while Abu Ayman al-Belgiki, a Belgian national, was also killed), it cannot all be so. Drone strikes therefore demonstrate an important limit upon the ability of the political process to provide meaningful accountability (however that concept is understood): that outcome relies on there being some opposition to what has happened, either within the formal political process (meaning, most obviously, amongst the Opposition or Members of Parliament generally) or in the broader, all-encompassing domain of informal politics (amongst the press, or public, or some section thereof). Where no meaningful opposition exists, political accountability can be worth very little.

It is unsurprising, against this background, that the formal political response to the carrying out the specific drones strikes in question—reports by the JCHR and the ISC—has focused upon the procedure by which the decision was taken, and the international law compatibility of that decision: there is little evidence of, and little prospect of, substantive opposition to the targeted killing of those considered to pose a threat to the UK and its citizens, but merely a desire to regularise the endeavour. This exemplifies one of the pervasive difficulties of the debate between legal and political constitutionalist approaches which has characterised British public law for several decades: it is difficult—perhaps impossible—to distinguish between a failed process or mechanism of political accountability and one

[249] ibid, 36, quoting Coke.
[250] ibid, quoting Hale.
[251] For discussion of the requirement, and endorsement of a vintage Law Commission proposal that a statutory defence be provided in respect of acts which are 'authorised by the lawful conduct of war', see Peter Rowe, 'The criminal liability of a British soldier merely for participating in the Iraq war 2003: a response to Chilcot evidence' (2010) *Crim LR* 752. *cf* Michael Hirst, 'Murder under the Queen's Peace' (2008) *Crim LR* 541.
[252] JCHR (n 216) [1.50].

which has operated as it should, but in relation to which the background political sentiment is such as to allow something to happen unopposed, or to go 'unpunished'. This is the reason both that everything is ultimately political—in a democratic constitutional order, what happens and what does not happen is ultimately a question of formal and informal politics, with the political consensus of the electorate only ever departed from in the short to medium term—and also that the truth of that first proposition should never be allowed to obscure legal mechanisms of accountability: there are too many things which the social body as a whole would readily tolerate that should not be tolerated, and it is only law—the prior formal commitment to certain substantive and procedural norms, whether or not enforceable in a domestic courts—which prevents the exercise of public power, here the use of force, from lapsing into bare arbitrariness.

VI. Conclusion

A constitutional consideration of the military results in a very different picture than would have been the case even a decade or two ago. Accountability would appear to be increasing on all fronts. While the fundamental democratic objections to the prerogative still hold, they are blunted significantly by the emergence of a convention whereby Parliament's approval is required before the war power is exercised. In large part, then, what was probably always the case is now made manifest: what determines whether the UK goes to war is an undeniably political question, and there is a new method by which the relevant political sentiment may be brought to bear upon the decision-making process. Where British society gets wars it does not want—or claims not to want—it may now be forced to consider more directly its own responsibility for that fact. More concerning, however, is that the convention leaves room for the deployment of Special Forces. In itself this in unobjectionable; coupled, however, with the incentive it creates (and to which the government appears to have responded) to make greater use of Special Forces in circumstances in which regular forces would have previously been deployed, this means that there may result in less rather than more political oversight of the use of the war prerogative. Even this is not true, there is much reason to believe that the interaction between the domestic and international legal considerations muddies both sets of waters, and that decisions to go to war may be more democratic without being in any useful sense 'better' than those of the past.

Common law legal oversight is likely—for reasons elaborated upon in Chapter 6—to remain minimal. Where legal oversight takes place, it is likely to result instead from the extra-territorial application of the ECHR, which is far greater now than was previously the case, and such scrutiny is not as easily evaded as is most political oversight. The decision of the Supreme Court in *Mohammed/Al-Waheed* represents a major victory, demonstrating that the domestic courts will in many circumstances recognise the existence of a legal basis for detention not only in IAC but also in NIAC, meaning that—where the ECHR applies—there nevertheless exists the possibility of detaining compatibly with Article 5. Coupled with the decision of the Supreme Court on Crown act of state considered in Chapter 6, it is clear that as the dust settles—for now—on the military constitution, the extent to which the armed forces will find themselves subject to detailed oversight by the courts is less than might have been the case, and such oversight is less likely than it might have been to result in adverse findings. This oversight is not, however, nothing, and the desire to find some way of excluding the acts of the armed forces abroad from the scope of the Convention altogether may yet lead to a practice of derogating from the Convention, notwithstanding that that process cannot give the executive what it wants: a situation in which the (weak) political limits which apply are the sole practical limits upon the conduct of British troops abroad. The facts discussed in this chapter and elsewhere in this book offer much reason to be suspicious of that desire, and to be grateful that it would appear unachievable.

4

Citizenship

I. Introduction

The first of the themes of the national security constitution which I consider in this Part 2 of the book is that of citizenship. I use that term loosely, to indicate not just the question of citizenship itself, but alongside it also a variety of issues which have in common their reliance upon the fundamental distinction within the UK's law and constitution—a distinction which is similarly central to all legal orders—between those who are citizens and those who are not. The distinction was deemed fundamental by Blackstone, who said that the 'first and most obvious division of the people is into aliens and naturalborn subjects'. Naturalborn subjects are 'such as are born within the dominions of the crown of England that is, within the ligeance, or, as it is generally called, the allegiance of the king'; aliens are 'such as are born out of it.'[1] The first section of the chapter outlines the basic position of the citizen as regards the right of abode, possession of which grants him or her the ability to enter and exit the UK (what I call here the right to travel), and the manner in which the distinction between that position and those of non-nationals allows immigration to be used, as regards the latter, as a tool of national security. Immigration controls can be employed to that end only as regards individuals who are not British citizens or otherwise in possession of the right of abode. The second section therefore considers the circumstances in which citizenship can be deprived from those who hold it on grounds including those pertaining to national security. Not only has the scope for deprivation expanded in the context of the modern intensification of national security objectives: so too has the use of the relevant powers. The third section of the chapter considers the use of passports as a tool of national security in the UK. Here, I am not concerned with citizenship strictly understood: the grant of citizenship does not bring with it an absolute right to a passport and a passport can be withdrawn without citizenship being affected. For that reason, passport measures are often taken in relation to those from whom the citizenship cannot be withdrawn. Nevertheless, the close connection between the possession of a passport and the practical exercise of the right of abode and the right to travel makes

[1] Allegiance, Blackstone continues, is 'the tie, or ligamen, which binds the subject to the king, in return for that protection which the king affords the subject': Blackstone, Commentaries on the Law of England, vol I, 354. See also *Calvin's Case* (1608) 7 Co Rep 1a and, on the correlation of allegiance and protection to which Blackstone refers, Glanville Williams, 'The Correlation of Allegiance and Protection', (1948) 10 *CLJ* 5 and, more recently, Colin RG Murray, 'In the shadow of Lord Haw Haw: Guantanamo Bay, diplomatic protection and allegiance' [2011] *PL* 115.

certain procedural questions just as urgent in the context of passports as in that of citizenship itself. Finally, I consider recent statutory measures which, without removing a person's citizenship, or depriving them of the means of evidencing it, nevertheless work alongside such measures to inhibit the exercise of the right of travel. A consideration of these issues demonstrates how the logic of national security works relentlessly upon the constitutional order, bringing ever more within its grasp.

II. Citizenship and the Right to Travel

Citizenship carries with it the right to travel; that is, the right to enter and exit the UK.[2] To some extent, this has always been true, but older accounts of the right to travel disagree as to the extent to which the right was or might be limited.[3] Blackstone said that the law of England 'regards, asserts, and preserves the personal liberty of individuals' which 'consists in the power of locomotion, of changing situation, or removing one's person to whatsoever place one's own inclination may direct'.[4] One adjunct of that was that 'every Englishman may claim a right to abide in his own country so long as he pleases; and not to be driven from it unless by the sentence of the law.'[5] More contentious was the question of whether the individual had a common law right to leave the realm. Blackstone asserted the existence of such right—'by the common law, every man may go out of the realm for whatever cause he pleaseth, without obtaining the King's leave'[6]—identifying as an exception to that rule only the King's ability to issue the prerogative writ known as *ne exeat regno* which prohibited a subject from travelling abroad without permission.[7] Hale seems to agree: 'At common law any man might pass the seas without licence, unless he were prohibited.'[8] Others suggested, however, that the basic common law position was

[2] It did not always do so. With certain Commonwealth states legislating in the late 1940s for their own citizenship, the British Nationality Act 1948 created a number of sub-categories under the catch-all heading of 'British subject', most importantly that of 'Citizen of the United Kingdom and Colonies', which was not possessed by subjects who were citizens of one of the Dominions. In the 1960s two statutes—the Commonwealth Immigrants Acts 1962 and 1968—introduced a distinction between CUKC's who were and were not subject to immigration control. By design, the distinction operated in practice on essentially racist grounds: for explanation and context, see A Dummett and A Nicol, *Subjects, Citizens, Aliens and Others* (London, Weidenfeld and Nicolson, 1990), Chs 10 and 11.

[3] See W S Holdsworth, A *History of English Law* (London, Methuen & Co, 1937), vol X, 390–3.

[4] Blackstone, *Commentaries*, I, 130.

[5] ibid 133.

[6] ibid 256. See also Lord Diplock in *DPP v Bhagwan* [1972] AC 60, 74, asserting that 'Prior to 1962 [and the enactment of the Commonwealth Immigration Act 1962] the respondent as a British subject had a right at common law to enter the United Kingdom without let or hindrance when and where he pleased and to remain there as long as he liked.' Williams notes that Blackstone's claim is more ambiguous than at times assumed: 'he retracts from this by reciting categories of people under restraint even under the commonly, and then concludes, rather less certainly, that 'at present every body has, or *at least assumes*, the liberty of going abroad when he pleases."' David W Williams, 'British Passports and the Right to Travel' (1974) *ICLQ* 642, 646.

[7] ibid: the King might also, Blackstone says, issue a write commanding a subject who is abroad to return. If either such writ, or that of *ne exeat regno* (or *regnum*) is disobeyed, then 'it is a high contempt of the king's prerogative, for which the offender's lands shall be seized till he return; and then he is liable to fine and imprisonment'.

[8] Sir Matthew Hale, *A Treatise in Three Parts, Part 2, De Portibus Maris*, cited in Daniel Turack, 'Early English Restrictions to Travel' in CH Alexandrowicz (ed) *Grotian Society Papers 1968: Studies in the History of the Law of Nations* (The Hague, Martinus Nijhoff, 1970) 136. See also Hale, *The Prerogatives of the Crown* (London, Selden

that citizens could not travel abroad without permission:[9] Chitty, for instance, spoke of the King's right 'to keep his subjects within the realm, which exists at common law.'[10] If this latter view was true (and referred to a broader limitation than the exception identified by Hale) then it must have been the case that where a general liberty to leave the realm was enjoyed, it was because statute created it. Certainly, a number of statutes over the centuries have purported to create or to limit rights to leave the realm, applying variously either to clergy, to merchants, or to subjects generally.[11] Most notably, Clause 42 of Magna Carta declared it lawful 'for any man to leave and return to our kingdom unharmed and without fear, by land or water, preserving his allegiance to us, except in time of war, for some short period, for the common benefit of the realm.' That clause was, though, excluded from the later reissue of the Charter which was treated as legislation. One commentator identifies as causes of the shift from prohibition to liberty reflected in Blackstone's writings (if indeed such a thing had happened) 'the concurrent conflict of the limitation of royal power' and 'the surge of populations to the colonies' but notes that '[w]here the authority lay for this change in attitude is none too clear.'[12] The writ *ne exeat regno* appears—at least in its public law form—to be obsolete.[13]

Whatever was the position at common law, matters of entry and exit to the UK are now regulated by statute. The Immigration Act 1971 grants all British citizens a right of abode, providing that those having such right 'shall be free to live in, and to come and go into and from, the United Kingdom without let or hindrance'.[14] This basic right is, however, subject to such limits as 'may be required under and in accordance with this Act to enable their right to be established or as may be otherwise lawfully imposed on any person'[15] and to a series of further statutory limitations of both the rights to enter and to exit the country which exist to serve the needs of national security, which themselves exist alongside far broader limitations applicable solely to non-citizens. Though the primary category of persons to whom the 1971 Act affords the right of abode is British citizens, certain Commonwealth citizens also enjoy that right.[16] The latter, but not the former, can be deprived of the right of abode if the Secretary of State thinks that 'it would be conducive to the public good for

Society, 1976) 296, stating that 'By the common law all subjects had free liberty to go and return' while identifying two sorts of inhibitions on that right: *ne exeat regnum* and statutory prohibitions of varying breadth.

[9] On this point see, generally, Turack (n 8). See also NW Sibley, 'The Passport System' (1906) 7 *Journal of the Society of Comparative Legislation*, 32–3.

[10] Chitty, *A Treatise on the Law of the Prerogatives of the Crown*, cited in Turack (n 8) 137 Diplock explains the point by noting that to leave the realm without permission from the Crown would 'deprive the King of the subject's military or other feudal services.' Kenneth Diplock, 'Passports and Protection in International Law' (1946) 32 *Transactions of the Grotius Society* 42, 44.

[11] See, generally, Daniel Turack, 'Freedom of Movement: The Right of a United Kingdom Citizen to Leave His Country' (1970) 31 *Ohio State Law Journal* 247, and Williams (n 6) 644–6.

[12] Williams (n 6) 646.

[13] See the discussion in *Parsons v Burk* [1971] NZLR 244, where an attempt was made to use the writ to prevent the New Zealand rugby team from touring apartheid South Africa, and JW Bridge, 'The Case of the Rugby Football Team and the High Prerogative Writ' (1972) 88 *LQR* 83. For a discussion of the writ in civil context, see *Felton v Callis* [1969] 1 QB 200. Diplock (n 10) 44 had much earlier suggested the prerogative power of *ne exeat regno* had 'lapsed through desuetude'.

[14] Immigration Act 1971, s 1(1).

[15] ibid.

[16] IA 1971, s 2(1)(b).

the person to be excluded or removed from the United Kingdom.'[17] That the right of abode derives from statute has implications for attempts to restrict or limit that right. If we accept the view—first articulated by Laws LJ in *Thoburn*,[18] but now seemingly accepted widely if not unanimously within the judiciary and the academy—that there exists at common law a distinction between 'ordinary' and 'constitutional' statutes (the latter being one 'which (a) conditions the legal relationship between citizen and State in some general, overarching manner, or (b) enlarges or diminishes the scope of what we would now regard as fundamental constitutional rights')[19] then the 1971 Act would appear to be such a statute. If so, it cannot be impliedly repealed; though the doctrine of parliamentary sovereignty would not permit any absolute limitation on their repeal, the jurisprudence of constitutional statutes asserts that—unlike 'ordinary' statutes, which can be repealed by mere implication—such can be repealed only explicitly.[20] And even if we do not accept the *Thoburn* dicta—which the Supreme Court has always been hesitant to explicitly endorse[21]—it is nevertheless the case that the statutory form which the right of abode takes has, I will argue, implications for the ability of the government to limit the possession or exercise of that right via the prerogative, as it does—despite formalist protestations to the contrary—where a British national has his or her passport withdrawn.

First, however, it is useful to consider briefly the various statutory mechanisms by which the right to travel might be limited without a passport being withdrawn. First, the Counter-Terrorism Act 2008 imposes 'notification requirements' on persons convicted of certain terrorist offences;[22] where these apply, a 'foreign travel restriction order' (FRTO) can be imposed on such persons where the 'person's behaviour since the person was dealt with for the offence by virtue of which those requirements apply makes it necessary for a foreign travel restriction order to be made to prevent the person from taking part in terrorism activity outside the United Kingdom'.[23] An FRTO may prevent the person in question travelling outside the UK, travelling to specified countries, or travelling to any countries other than those specified.[24] Second, terrorist prevention and investigation measures (TPIMs) can be imposed under certain conditions on both nationals and non-nationals.[25] The conditions in question include that the Secretary of State reasonably believes the individual to be—or to have been—involved in 'terrorism-related activity'.[26] Amongst the specific

[17] ibid, s 2A.

[18] *Thoburn v Sunderland City Council* [2002] EWHC 195 (Admin).

[19] [2002] EWHC 195 (Admin), [62].

[20] 'For the repeal of a constitutional Act or the abrogation of a fundamental right to be effected by statute, the court would apply this test: is it shown that the legislature's actual—not imputed, constructive or presumed—intention was to effect the repeal or abrogation? I think the test could only be met by express words in the later statute, or by words so specific that the inference of an actual determination to effect the result contended for was irresistible.' [2002] EWHC 195 (Admin), [63].

[21] See, eg, *R (HS2 Action Alliance Limited) v The Secretary of State for Transport* [2014] UKSC 3, [208] and *R (Miller) v Secretary of State for Exiting the European Union* [2017] UKSC 5, [66]–[67]. The judgment of Lord Hope in *H v Lord Advocate* [2012] UKSC 24, [57] accepts—without reference to *Thoburn*—that the Scotland Act 1998 implements a settlement of a 'fundamental constitutional nature' and there is 'incapable of being altered otherwise than by an express enactment.'

[22] Counter-Terrorism Act 2008, Pt 4.

[23] CTA 2008, Sch 5, para 2(3).

[24] ibid, para 1.

[25] Terrorism Prevention and Investigation Measures Act 2011, ss 1–4.

[26] ibid, s 3(1).

measures which might be imposed under a TPIM notice are 'travel measures', by which restrictions can be imposed on a person leaving a specified area, which must be one of the UK, or Great Britain or Northern Ireland (the latter two depending upon the person's place of residence).[27] The specific requirements can include a requirement to not leave that area without the Secretary of State's permission; to give notice before leaving it, or requirements relating to 'travel documents' (including passports) which will be discussed further below. Alongside these—which are capable of limiting the right to exit the country—the Counter-Terrorism and Security Act 2015 (CTSA) introduced a regime by which there might be imposed on individuals a 'temporary exclusion order' (TEO) restricting the right to enter it.[28] Only those who enjoy the right of abode can enter the country without leave, however, and so a TEO can be imposed only upon those who enjoy that right.[29] The only way in which a person can lawfully return to the UK while subject to a TEO is by virtue of a 'permit to return', which may impose conditions and prescribe in detail the method and timing of the return.[30] This allows the state to manage the return to the UK of those, say, who have gone to fight in conflicts in Syria or Libya, but who, because they possess no other nationality, cannot be stripped of their British nationality and the right of abode it entails. When an application is made by a person subject to a TEO, a permit to return must be issued within a 'reasonable time'; the time it prescribes for the return to take place must fall within a 'reasonable period' after the application's making.[31] TEOs link to the question of passports discussed below: when a TEO comes into force, any passport held by the person in question is invalidated, and no passport issued to the person while the TEO is in force and he or she is outside the UK is not valid.[32] In the aftermath of the Manchester Arena bombing of May 2017, however, it emerged that only one TEO had been imposed since the enactment of the CTSA.[33]

III. Immigration Law and National Security

TEOs are necessary to limit the entry into the UK only those who enjoy the right of abode. Those who do not possess that right are subject to immigration restrictions, and one of the ends which such restrictions serve is protecting national security, in that they make it possible to forbid entry to the UK to those considered to represent a threat to it. What the relevant measures are, however, varies depending—for now, at least—on whether one is or is not an EEA national.[34] EEA nationals are governed by the Immigration (European

[27] ibid, Sch 1, para 2.
[28] Counter-Terrorism and Security Act 2015, ss 2–4.
[29] ibid, s 2(6).
[30] ibid, s 2(1) and ss 5–8.
[31] ibid, s 6.
[32] ibid, s (4)–(11).
[33] Peter Walker, 'Rudd admits anti-terror exclusion powers used only once since 2015' *The Guardian* (29 May 2017).
[34] That is, a national of an EU Member State (who is not also a British citizen) or a national of one of either Liechtenstein, Iceland, Norway or Switzerland.

Economic Area) Regulations 2016,[35] which grant them (and, under certain conditions, their non-EEA family members) a right to enter the UK.[36] A person is not, though, entitled to be admitted if his exclusion 'is justified on grounds of public policy, public security or public health',[37] and a person can be removed from the UK on those same grounds.[38] Special conditions apply in certain limited circumstances: a person with a permanent right of residence can be excluded or removed only on 'serious grounds of public policy or public security',[39] while a person under 18 or one who has resided in the UK for a continuous period of 10 years can be taken only on 'imperative grounds of public security'.[40] Generally, however, the requirements imposed by the regulations are that the decision must be proportionate, that it must be based purely on the person's own conduct, and that the conduct in question 'must represent a genuine, present and sufficiently serious threat affecting one of the fundamental interests of society'.[41] Before taking a decision based upon public security, the decision-maker must take account of 'the age, state of health, family and economic situation' of the person, as well as his or her length of residence in the UK, level of 'social and cultural integration' and extent of his or her links with her country of origin.[42]

For non-EEA nationals the Immigration Act 1971 permits a person without the right of abode in the UK to be deported from it where the Secretary of State deems his or her deportation to be 'conducive to the public good.'[43] The same standard is found in the immigration rules as a ground upon which a person can be refused leave to enter the UK (those who are neither UK nationals, Commonwealth nationals with a right of abode nor EEA nationals requiring such leave).[44] An exclusion decision (a non-statutory device) can be made on the same 'conducive to the public good' ground as a deportation order, but only in respect of a person currently outside the UK. An exclusion decision does not attract a statutory right of appeal, but can challenged by way of judicial review. And, alongside the power to deport a non-citizen on public interest grounds, section 8B of the 1971 Act (first inserted into it by the Immigration Act 1999) provides that certain 'excluded persons' must be refused leave to enter or remain in the UK, and that any such leave that a person enjoys is cancelled upon him becoming an excluded person. An excluded person is one who is named in, or of a description which is specified in, either a Security Council Resolution or a measure of the Council of the European Union which requires or recommends that the person not be admitted to the UK.[45]

[35] Made under the authority of the European Communities Act 1972.

[36] Immigration (European Economic Area) Regulations 2016, reg 11.

[37] ibid, reg 23(1).

[38] ibid, reg 23 (6).

[39] ibid, reg 27(3).

[40] ibid, reg 27(4).

[41] ibid, reg 27(5)(c).

[42] ibid, reg 27(6).

[43] Section 3(5) of the 1971 Act provides that a person is liable to deportation if the Secretary of State deems that condition to be met; s 5 permits the Secretary of State to make a deportation order against such a person. A deportation order is 'an order requiring him to leave and prohibiting him from entering the United Kingdom'; such an order 'shall invalidate any leave to enter or remain in the United Kingdom given him before the order is made or while it is in force.'

[44] Immigration Rules, Rule 320(6) ('where the Secretary of State has personally directed that the exclusion of a person from the United Kingdom is conducive to the public good') and (19) (where an immigration officer 'deems the exclusion of the person from the United Kingdom to be conducive to the public good').

[45] IA 1971, s 8B.

A. Statute and Prerogative in Immigration Law and Practice

Before turning to the question of citizenship, it is helpful to address briefly the question of whether the various regimes discussed above exhaust the relevant law. That is, it is clear nowadays that the law on immigration is found, in the first place, within the Immigration Act 1971 and related primary and secondary legislation.[46] The 1971 Act provides, however, that it 'shall not be taken to supersede or impair any power exercisable by Her Majesty in relation to aliens by virtue of Her prerogative.'[47] The question which arises therefore is whether there remains a relevant prerogative power with which the statute might coexist, and—if so—what is the extent of that power. What, that is, might be done in the field of immigration without recourse to the relevant statutory rules and the Immigration Rules which govern the majority of immigration cases?[48] In the past, various dicta asserted the continued existence of the prerogative, which was held to be central to the grant of leave to enter or remain in the UK outside the strictures of the Immigration Rules.[49] More recently, the Court of Appeal has, in *GI v Home Secretary*,[50] held that the Crown retains a prerogative power to exclude an alien from the UK on the basis that there has been no statutory abrogation or modification of that power, without which the prerogative must survive.[51] These claims would seem to be disproven by authoritative Supreme Court jurisprudence as to the role of the prerogative in modern immigration law.[52] In *Munir* it was held that the Immigration Rules were made under the authority of the 1971 Act rather than the prerogative, and that the exercise of a discretion to grant leave to enter or remain in the UK where the Immigration Rules would not have permitted it was similarly a statutory discretion. Lord Dyson, with whom four of his colleagues agreed, held that the saving provision quoted above gave rise to two inferences:

> First, Parliament must have considered that the prerogative power to regulate immigration control did not apply to those who owed their allegiance to the Crown, that is British and Commonwealth

[46] Statutory immigration controls in the UK are perhaps surprisingly recent in origin, having been introduced in modern times only by the Aliens Act 1905 (earlier restrictions, dating from the period of the Napoleonic wars, had been repealed in the middle of the nineteenth century: see the discussion in V Bevan, *The Development of British Immigration Law* (London, Croom Helm, 1986) 58–64). Like later measures, the 1905 Act was a response to a panic over a perceived flood of immigration—in that case, by Russian and Polish Jews fleeing pogroms: see B Gainer, *The Alien Invasion: The Origins of the Aliens Act of 1905* (London, Heinemann, 1972).

[47] Immigration Act 1971, s 33(5). It thus has no application to non-aliens—those who are either Commonwealth (including British) citizens, citizens of the Republic of Ireland, or British protected persons: British Nationality Act 1981, s 50(1).

[48] On the status of those rules—which are not delegated legislation—see the comments of Sedley LJ in *Secretary of State for the Home Department v Pankina* [2010] EWCA Civ 719, [17]: '... the time has come to recognise that, by a combination of legislative recognition and executive practice, the rules made by Home Secretaries for regulating immigration have ceased to be policy and have acquired a status akin to that of law.'

[49] '[I]mmigration was formerly covered by the royal prerogative and it was a matter which lay entirely within the exercise of that prerogative. Much of the prerogative powers vested in the Crown in this field have now been superseded by a statute but there remains ... a residual power in the Crown, through Her Majesty's Secretary of State for Home Affairs, to exercise such residual power as is necessary for the proper control of immigration. In my view, the exercise of discretion in relation to leave to enter outside the rules is an exercise of the remaining part of that prerogative power.' *R v Secretary of State for the Home Department, Ex p Rajinder Kaur* [1987] Imm AR 278, 291 (Glidewell J). See also *R v Secretary of State for the Home Department, Ex p Ounejma* [1989] Imm AR 75 and *Ahmed v Secretary of State for the Home Department* [1999] Imm AR 22.

[50] *GI v Home Secretary* [2012] EWCA Civ 867.

[51] [2012] EWCA Civ 867, [11]–[17].

[52] On which, see Ian MacDonald, 'Rights of settlement and the prerogative in the UK—a historical perspective' (2013) *JIANL* 10.

> citizens, and only applied to aliens. Otherwise, Parliament would surely have made some provision as to how, if at all, the prerogative power was to be exercised in relation to Commonwealth citizens. Secondly, Parliament must have intended that, subject to the saving in section 33(5), all powers of immigration control were to be exercised pursuant to the statute.[53]

The limited position of the prerogative was asserted by the Supreme Court also in a linked case, in which Lord Hope stated that accounts which speak to the continued existence of a prerogative power 'understate' the effect of the 1971 Act, which is 'a constitutional landmark which, for all practical purposes, gave statutory force to all the powers previously exercisable in the field of immigration control under the prerogative.'[54] Though authoritative, this claim would seem to deprive the 1971 Act's saving clause of any effect. To square that circle, it is useful to return to a consideration of the issue which predates the Supreme Court's various attempt to write—as far as possible—the prerogative out of immigration law. Writing long before these judgments, Christopher Vincenzi accepted that the prerogative power in question extended to 'the control of entry, detention and deportation of enemy aliens in time of war, and the recognition, and the control of movement of, foreign diplomats' but queried whether there existed, in relation to aliens, any prerogative beyond that. If there was a further prerogative, he said, it must have taken one of three forms: either it 'include[d] both the exclusion and deportation of friendly aliens', or was 'limited to the exclusion of friendly aliens', or 'include[d] only the deportation of friendly aliens.'[55] And even had such a power once existed, Vincenzi said, one would still be required to determine the extent to which the power in question had been abrogated by the 1971 Act and the immigration scheme created by it, in order to know what was left of it. In light of the dicta quoted above, however, the best view would seem to be that whatever this further prerogative once was, it is fully abrogated by the Immigration Act, and is thus, whether temporarily or permanently, unavailable in law.[56] Only the much more limited prerogative permitting the exclusion and deportation of enemy aliens (as well, perhaps, as the power to detain)[57] survives.

IV. Citizenship and National Security

Citizenship has long been used as a tool of national security, not only via the distinct legal regimes which apply to those who possess it and those who do not (as discussed above),

[53] *R (Munir) v Secretary of State for the Home Department* [2012] UKSC 32, [25].

[54] *R (Alvi) v Secretary of State for the Home Department* [2012] UKSC 33, [31].

[55] Christopher Vincenzi, 'Extra-statutory ministerial discretion in immigration law' [1992] *PL* 300, 310–2.

[56] On the abrogation of the prerogative, see most importantly *Attorney-General v De Keyser's Royal Hotel Limited* [1920] AC 508 and now also the various discussions in *R (Miller) v Secretary of State for Exiting the European Union* [2017] UKSC 5. The issues raised by this element of *Miller* are discussed, albeit before the Supreme Court's judgment, in Robert Craig, 'Casting Aside Clanking Medieval Chains: Prerogative, Statute and Article 50 after the EU Referendum' (2016) 79 *MLR* 1041 and Gavin Phillipson, 'A Dive into Deep Constitutional Waters: Article 50, the Prerogative and Parliament' (2016) 79 *MLR* 1064.

[57] During the Second World War, the prerogative powers available as against enemy aliens were held to include powers to detain: see, eg, *R. v Vine Street Police Station Superintendent, ex parte Liebmann* [1916] 1 KB 268 and, later, *R v Bottrill, ex parte Kuechenmeister* [1947] KB 41.

but also via the possibility of moving individuals from the former category to the latter on the basis of public interest considerations,[58] a power which supplements others permitting deprivation where the Secretary of State is satisfied that a naturalised citizen has acquired citizenship on the basis of fraud, false representation, or concealment of material fact.[59] These latter powers, unlike those of deprivation in the public interest (with an exception we will discuss below) are available even where it would result in that person becoming stateless, reflecting an exception—'where nationality has been obtained by misrepresentation or fraud'—which exists in the Convention on the Reduction of Statelessness to the general rule whereby a Contracting State is not to 'deprive a person of his nationality if such deprivation would render him stateless.'[60] A second potentially relevant international instrument, the Council of Europe's European Convention on Nationality, has never been ratified by the UK and therefore has no application, in either domestic or international law, to the deprivation of citizenship by the UK.

A. Deprivation of Citizenship on Public Interest Grounds

The Convention's position on statelessness as a result of deprivation on (broad) public interest grounds is as follows: states are permitted to retain the right to render a person stateless on certain grounds if the right to do so existed in law at the time of signature, ratification or accession, and the retention was specified at that time. The major overhaul of British nationality law carried out by the British Nationality Act 1981 retained, in very similar form to that found in its 1948 equivalent,[61] a power to deprive individuals of their citizenship[62] where the Secretary of State was satisfied that the person had 'shown himself by act or speech to be disloyal or disaffected towards Her Majesty'; unlawfully traded with, communicated with, or assisted Her Majesty's enemies during time of war; or been sentenced to imprisonment of 12 months or more within five years of naturalisation.[63] The power was subject to two provisos. The first, which applied to all three grounds, was that deprivation could take place only if the Secretary of State was 'satisfied that it is not conducive to the public good that that person should continue to be a British citizen'; the second, which, applied only to the third ground for deprivation, stated that the power in question could not be exercised if it appeared to the Secretary of State 'that that person would thereupon become stateless.'[64] No equivalent of this second limitation had been contained in the 1948 Act as enacted; it was introduced into it by the British Nationality (No 2) Act 1964, at which point the UK made a notification of the retention of a deprivation power of the sort referred to by the Convention.[65] Moreover, the power under the 1981 Act, like that in the

[58] See Matthew J Gibney, 'The Deprivation of Citizenship in the United Kingdom: A Brief History' (2014) 28 *JIANL* 326.

[59] BNA 1981, s 40(3)

[60] Convention on the Reduction of Statelessness, Art 8.

[61] For the evolution of the law before 1948, see Gibney (n 58) 327–8.

[62] Here, 'citizenship' is used to refer to one of a number of legal statuses: BNA 1981, s 40(1).

[63] BNA 1981, s 40(5).

[64] ibid.

[65] Between 1949 and 1973, there were 10 cases in which the deprivation of British citizenship rendered a person stateless: see David Anderson QC, *Citizenship Removal Resulting in Statelessness* (2016), [2.8].

1948 Act before it, could be exercised only in relation to those who had acquired citizenship by naturalisation or registration.[66]

The power contained in the 1981 Act was nevertheless broader in one sense than that which it replaced, in that all of the powers now applied to those citizens who had acquired the status by registration, a possibility introduced by the 1948 Act when it introduced the distinction between Citizens of the United Kingdom and Colonies and other British subjects. The latter could, after a year's residence in Britain, acquire citizenship by registration;[67] now they could be deprived of it on the same basis as those who had acquired it via naturalisation. Though the power of deprivation was transferred over into the new statutory regime, it was not at that point in history exercised with any great frequency: at the point at which the 1981 Act was enacted, it had not been used for eight years.[68] The powers remained largely moribund even after they were transposed into the new statutory regime, and in 2002 'not a single individual had lost his or her citizenship (other than under fraud provisions) for thirty years.'[69] Alongside the obvious national security factors prompting for the changes which subsequently took place, Gibney identifies also one which is less obvious, and more particular to Britain: the riots which took place in parts of England in 2001, ascribed in large part to the existence of racial tensions, 'impressed upon the government the need for greater integration of citizens into a more clearly defined set of British values.'[70]

Whatever the balance of security and other factors, the enactment of the Nationality, Immigration and Asylum Act 2002 saw the law altered in several ways, including via the replacement of the multiple grounds of deprivation with a single standard justifying deprivation: where the Secretary of State was satisfied that 'the person has done anything seriously prejudicial to the vital interests of' either the United Kingdom or a British overseas territory.[71] Even more significantly, the 2002 Act permitted a natural born citizen to be deprived of his or her British citizenship. The new standard was considered in litigation relating to David Hicks, an Australian who sought to acquire British citizenship through registration (as he was entitled to do by virtue of his mother's circumstances) while detained in Guantanamo Bay, with a view to benefiting from an agreement whereby British citizens detained there would be released and returned to the UK. The Secretary of State desired either to refuse the registration, or to grant it and simultaneously deprive Mr Hicks of his citizenship on the grounds of 'disloyalty and disaffection' (terms used in the 1981 Act before it was amended in 2002). The Court of Appeal held that Hicks was entitled to register as a citizen and also that a deprivation on these grounds could not be based—as was the case here—on the conduct of a person at a time when 'he was neither a British citizen nor owed in any other way any allegiance to Her Majesty.'[72] The single standard for deprivation

[66] BNA 1981, s 40(4).

[67] BNA 1948, ss 6–9.

[68] Gibney (n 58) 329.

[69] Gibney (n 58) 330. In 1998 Fransman described it as having 'de facto lapsed through disuse': L Fransman, *Fransman's British Nationality Law*, 2nd edn (London, Butterworth's, 1998) [17.1.2].

[70] Gibney (n 58) 330.

[71] BNA 1981, s 40(2) (as inserted by the Nationality, Immigration and Asylum Act 2002).

[72] *Secretary of State for the Home Department v Hicks* [2006] EWCA Civ 400, [55].

introduced by the 2002 Act was in turn replaced, by the Immigration, Asylum and Nationality Act 2006, with a power to deprive a person of citizenship (again, including those who held citizenship from birth) where the Secretary of State was 'satisfied that deprivation is conducive to the public good.'[73] This expanded power was quickly used to deprive Hicks of his citizenship. In both forms, however, the power to deprive of citizenship was limited by the rule that no deprivation order could be made if the Secretary of State was satisfied that it would make a person stateless.[74] The relevant definition of a stateless person, here as elsewhere, is that found in the Convention relating to the Status of Stateless Persons: it is a 'person who is not considered as a national by any State under the operation of its law'.[75] The limit does not apply to the other grounds of deprivation (fraud, false representation and concealment of a material fact), which continue to be available only in relation to those who acquire citizenship via naturalisation or registration.

This rule that a person might not be deprived of his citizenship where to do so would leave him stateless is therefore the sole substantive limit on the use of the broad 'conducive to the public good' grounds.[76] There are, as in previous incarnations of the power no statutory requirements of reasonableness, necessity, or proportionality, nor for judicial involvement in (or approval of) the making of a deprivation order. The significance of the statelessness limit was explored by the Supreme Court in the context of a challenge to the decision to deprive of his British citizenship, Hilal Al-Jedda, a refugee of Iraqi origin who had been naturalised in the UK and as a result (it seemed) lost his Iraqi citizenship, only to be captured and detained by British troops in Iraq.[77] Shortly after his release, the Secretary of State made an order depriving him of his UK citizenship on the grounds that to do so was 'conducive to the public good'. At first, debate focussed on whether or not Al-Jedda had in fact lost his Iraqi citizenship.[78] Later, however, the Secretary of State argued was that it was possible to deprive a person of his citizenship even where the result was to make that person stateless, so long as the person enjoyed the possibility of regaining a former nationality by means of a formal application only. This interpretation of the deprivation power was rejected by the Supreme Court.[79] So too was the argument that it was necessary to give the provision a purposive construction and so to look to the 'real' or 'active' cause of statelessness, which in the present case would be the failure of Al-Jedda to take steps to restore his Iraqi citizenship, rather than the steps taken by the Secretary of State to deprive him of his UK nationality: why, it was asked, should the provision be understood so as to 'disable the Secretary of State from making it in circumstances in which it remains open to

[73] BNA 1981, s 40(2) (as inserted by the Immigration, Asylum and Nationality Act 2006). Writing of the changes made by the 2006 Act, Caroline Sawyer noted that '[t]here is a broad lack of understanding of the near-arbitrary nature of the provisions and their administrative simplicity, and especially a lack of appreciation that the provisions apply to anyone, including the British-born.' 'Civis Britannicus Sum' No Longer?—Deprivation of British Nationality' (2013) 27 *JIANL* 23, 32.

[74] BNA 1981, s 40(4) (as amended).

[75] Article 1(1).

[76] The Home Office's *Nationality Instructions* (Ch 55, last updated 10 September 2015) state, unhelpfully, that the conduciveness standard means 'depriving in the public interest on the grounds of involvement in terrorism, espionage, serious organised crime, war crimes or unacceptable behaviours' [55.4.4].

[77] For discussions of other elements of Mr Al-Jedda's various dealings with the English courts, see Chs 3 and 6.

[78] See, in the Court of Appeal, *Al-Jedda v Secretary of State for the Home Department* [2010] EWCA Civ 212.

[79] *Secretary of State for the Home Department v Al-Jedda* [2013] UKSC 62, [30].

the person so easily and so immediately to avoid becoming stateless?'[80] The Supreme Court responded that '[s]ection 40(4) does not permit, still less require, analysis of the relative potency of causative factors'. To interpret it as permitting the Secretary of State to claim that 'albeit not holding another nationality at the date of the order, the person could, with whatever degree of ease and speed, re-acquire another nationality' would, it said, 'mire the application of the subsection in deeper complexity'.[81]

The decision of the Supreme Court in *Al-Jedda* prompted an immediate change in the law, in the form of an amendment inserted into the Immigration Act 2014 during its passage through Parliament which added to the 1981 Act a new provision empowering deprivation where it would render the person whose citizenship was thereby deprived stateless. The power can only be exercised under strict and unusual circumstances; circumstances which resemble very closely those of Hilal Al-Jedda. First, the citizenship being removed must result from naturalisation: the new power reintroduces the differential treatment of natural-born and naturalised citizens.[82] Second, the Secretary of State must be satisfied 'that the deprivation is conducive to the public good because the person, while having that citizenship status, has conducted him or herself in a manner which is seriously prejudicial to the vital interests of the United Kingdom, any of the Islands, or any British overseas territory'.[83] Third, and crucially, the Secretary of State must have reasonable grounds for believing that the person, though not the citizen of another country (in which case there would be no need to take advantage of an exception to the rule which prevents deprivation where it would result in statelessness), is 'able, under the law of a country or territory outside the United Kingdom, to become a national of such a country or territory.'[84] The effect of this new provision is to allow deprivation which results in statelessness as long as the statelessness is not *necessarily* permanent; that it may be so in practice is no bar.

Though the conduct of threshold is higher than is that for 'ordinary' deprivation (to which the statelessness limit continues to apply), there are several aspects of this change which are more than a little distasteful. One is that the limitations on its use will not necessarily (or even probably) prevent individuals from being rendered stateless. Indeed, anyone against whom the power is used will by definition be so rendered, and the question will then become whether and how they will manage to acquire a new legal nationality: the Secretary of State need only have reasonable grounds for believing that the person will manage to do so, but this is—of course—no guarantee of success. The temporary statelessness may, on that basis, become permanent, even where the new power is used lawfully and properly. Moreover, the new power matches the situation of *Al-Jedda* so closely as to verge upon being a personalised legal regime for him, almost a modern-day Act of Attainder. It is therefore ironic that the power has not yet been used, in relation either to Al-Jedda or any other person: though a fresh deprivation order was made against him in November 2013, it was made on the basis that Al-Jedda was regarded as a citizen by the government of

[80] [2013] UKSC 62, [31].
[81] ibid, [32].
[82] BNA 1981, s 40(4A)(a).
[83] ibid, s 40(4A)(b).
[84] ibid, s 40(4A)(c).

Iraq and thus the deprivation order would not in fact make him stateless.[85] In recognition of the gravity of this new power introduced, there was inserted into the 1981 Act alongside the new section 40(4A) a requirement to periodically review the power's operation—one year after its introduction, and at three year intervals thereafter.[86] The first report, issued in April 2016, noted that—compared to its international equivalents[87]—the new power was 'an unusually strong one', with the relatively little controversy attracted by it perhaps 'a reflection of underlying attitudes to citizenship'.[88] Given, however, that the power had not yet been used, no specific recommendations were made as to the power's operation.[89] As the most recent deprivation of Al-Jedda's citizenship took place on a distinct basis, the power seems to have undermined the fundamentals of the law's suspicion of statelessness for no gain at all.

Some sense of the law and practice in this area is given by the other case in which the Supreme Court has had the opportunity to consider the law in this area in recent years: that of *Pham*.[90] The claimant was born in Vietnam, and had acquired British citizenship in 1995, before being deprived of it in late 2011 on the basis that in the previous year he had spent time in a terrorist training camp in Yemen. His challenge was based in part on the fact that at the relevant time he was not a Vietnamese citizen; the effect of the order was therefore to make him stateless, being—if the order was upheld—'not considered as a national by any state under the operation of its law'.[91] It had been accepted by the Special Immigration Appeals Commission, which had heard evidence from one of the drafters of the relevant Vietnamese law, that the legislation in question 'was deliberately ambiguous so as to permit the executive to make whatever decisions it wished' and that the executive possesses 'the ability, as a matter of Vietnamese law and/or state practice, to decline to acknowledge, as Vietnamese citizens, individuals of Vietnamese origin whose return it wishes to avoid.'[92] The Supreme Court accepted that the 'operation of its law' standard was to be interpreted broadly, so as to encompass executive practices rather than only legislative instruments, with the effect that '[f]amiliar principles of the rule of law, as it would be understood in this country, are not the governing consideration.'[93] Even on that basis, however, the claim that Pham's deprivation rendered him stateless was false; at the date at which the deprivation order was made, the Vietnamese government had taken no view as to Pham's citizenship and taken no steps to deprive him of it. That it later took the view that he was not a Vietnamese citizen was irrelevant, for that view post-dated the making of the deprivation order by the UK and did not operate retrospectively.

[85] Challenged, unsuccessfully, in *Al-Jedda v Secretary of State for the Home Department* SC/66/2008, (18 July 2014).

[86] British Nationality Act 1981, s 40B.

[87] On which see Sangeetha Pillai and George Williams, 'Twenty-First Century Banishment: Citizenship Stripping in Common Law Nations' (2017) 66 *ICLQ* 521.

[88] Anderson (n 65) [4.1].

[89] ibid, [4.2].

[90] *Pham v Secretary of State for the Home Department* [2015] UKSC 19. In earlier litigation, Pham had been anonymised as 'B2'.

[91] The language used in Art 1 of the Convention relating to the Status of Stateless Persons.

[92] *B2 v Secretary of State for the Home Department*, SC/114/2012 (29 June 2012), [18]–[19].

[93] [2015] UKSC 19, [34].

The point is significant: though there had been discussions between the two governments prior to the deprivation order, none of Pham's details were communicated by the UK to Vietnam until the deprivation order had been made.[94] This would appear to reflect an understanding that, had Vietnam been informed of the details of Pham's activities in advance, it would have immediately stated that he was not a Vietnamese citizen, and the UK would have been unable to make the deprivation order. The statelessness limitation in this way seems to have shaped the UK's dealings the Vietnamese government. Not only is that a somewhat cynical approach, but it would appear to create (at least in theory) incentives to act in a way which is potentially harmful to the security of the UK or other states, with information shared only belatedly, so as not to jeopardise the UK's presumed aim of carrying out the deprivation. *Pham* is, however, of broader significance in confirming that, regardless of the position under the ECHR and EU law, the common law imposes a requirement of proportionality upon the deprivation of citizenship, given the importance of the status. Lord Mance, for example, stated that removal of citizenship 'is, on any view, a radical step, particularly if the person affected has little real attachment to the country of any other nationality that he possesses and is unlikely to be able to return there' and so 'a correspondingly strict standard of judicial review must apply to any exercise of the power contained in section 40(2), and the tool of proportionality is one which would, in my view … be both available and valuable for the purposes of such a review.'[95] The thrust of these remarks was shared by a number of other dicta in the Supreme Court's judgment, and proportionality review of deprivation decisions has taken place in subsequent case law.[96]

B. Procedure and Deprivation

More than in most areas of law, the procedural facet of the deprivation power are crucial, over and above the sense in which the simplicity of the associated administrative procedure renders it 'vulnerable to individual or political opportunism or human error'.[97] The 1981 Act originally provided that before a deprivation order was made, notice was to be given to the potential deprivee of his right to an inquiry, carried out by a Committee of inquiry headed by a person with judicial experience, and including 'such other members appointed by the Secretary of State as he thinks proper.'[98] The changes introduced by the Nationality, Immigration and Asylum Act 2002 included the creation of a two-track mechanism for challenging a deprivation order: in normal cases, to an adjudicator (a jurisdiction later handed over to the Asylum and Immigration Tribunal and then, on its abolition, to the First-tier Tribunal)[99] or to the Special Immigration Appeals Commission (SIAC) if the Secretary of State had certified that the decision was taken wholly or in part on the basis of information which should not be made public on public interest grounds (including in

[94] 'No information about the identity, date and place of birth or alleged activities of the appellant was communicated by the British government to the Vietnamese government until 22nd December 2011' (the date on which the decision notice was served on Pham, the decision having been taken by the Secretary of State two days earlier): SC/114/2012, [7].

[95] [2015] UKSC 19, [98].

[96] See, eg, *S1 v Secretary of State for the Home Department* [2016] EWCA Civ 560.

[97] Sawyer (n 73) 39.

[98] BNA 1981, s 40(7) (as enacted).

[99] The first of these changes was made by the Asylum and Immigration (Treatment of Claimants, etc.) Act 2004.

particular on national security grounds), or in the interests of 'the relationship between the United Kingdom and another country'.[100] This change formalised a legal right of appeal, but made it subject—in the context which is of present interest—to closed material procedures and all of the obstacles which such a procedure creates for those seeking to challenge the relevant decision. These issues are discussed in detail in Chapter 5 and need not be discussed further here. In practice, however, it seems that most, if not all, appeals against deprivation orders made on conducive grounds will be heard in SIAC rather than the Asylum and Immigration Tribunal. Secret justice is in theory an exception; it is in practice the rule. Perhaps unsurprisingly, therefore, there appears never to have been a successful appeal on the merits of the decision to deprive. Though there have been successful appeals against deprivation orders, these have always related to the issue of statelessness.[101]

Other procedural problems, however, exist within the contemporary regime for deprivation of nationality. The making of an order in respect of a person must be preceded by the giving of written notice of the reasons for the deprivation to that person, and communicating that person's right of appeal.[102] The first difficulty is the short time limits which exist: a person given notice of the making of the deprivation order who is outside the UK has only 28 days to lodge an appeal against it.[103] This is compounded by the rules which govern the serving of notice. These provide, amongst other things, that where a person's whereabouts are known, the necessary notice may be given 'by causing the notice to be delivered to him personally or by sending it to him by post'; where those whereabouts are not known, however, it may be given 'by sending it by post in a letter addressed to him at his last known address.'[104] Where the notice is given by post, it is deemed (unless the contrary can be proven, which is likely to prove impossible in practice) either two days after posting (if sent within the UK) or 28 days after posting (if sent from or to a place outside of the UK).[105] Finally, notice is deemed to be given to the relevant person where it is in fact given to a person 'appearing to the Secretary of State … to represent' that person.[106] In and of themselves, these provisions are not necessarily objectionable, though their overall effect is that the notice which is mandated by the statutory scheme will often be constructive rather than actual. In practice, however, the provisions often cause insurmountable difficulties to those who are thus deprived of citizenship, because they are combined with a tendency to make a deprivation order specifically at the point in time when the individual in question is outside of the country and so may not receive the notice in question.[107] Though the

[100] BNA, s 40A(2) and Special Immigration Appeals Commission Act 1997, s 2B.

[101] One example is the *Al-Jedda* case. Another is *Abu Hamza v Secretary of State for the Home Department* SC/23/2003 (5 November 2010).

[102] BNA, s 40(5).

[103] Special Immigration Appeals Commission (Procedure) Rules 2003 (SI 2003/1034) (as amended), r 8 (1). Where the appellant is in the UK, the relevant period is only 10 days. By r 8(5) SIAC 'may extend the time limits in this rule if satisfied that by reason of special circumstances it would be unjust not to do so.'

[104] British Nationality (General) Regulations 2003 (SI 2003/548), reg 10(1).

[105] ibid, reg 10(3).

[106] ibid, reg 10(2).

[107] Alice Ross quotes James Brokenshire, the Minister responsible at the relevant point in time, as denying that this reflects a deliberate strategy: 'It is true that people have been deprived while outside the UK, but I do not accept that it is a particular tactic. It is simply an operational reality that in some cases the information comes to light when the person is outside the UK or that it is the final piece of the picture, confirming what has been suspected'. HC Deb 11 February 2014, col 261WH, quoted in Alice Ross, *Deprivation of Citizenship: What Do We Know?* (2014) 28 *JIANL* 316, 319.

government refuses, on national security grounds to say how many deportation orders are made in respect of persons abroad at the time,[108] Alice Ross of the Bureau of Investigative Journalism (BIJ) has described the cases which the BIJ has investigated as evidencing 'if not a policy, then a strong preference for acting in this way'.[109] Ross describes, for example, the case of an individual who was deprived of citizenship while abroad visiting family in Pakistan and Afghanistan, with notification sent to his address in London:

> Home Secretary revoked his citizenship, again sending the notification to E2's London address. E2 claimed that he only learned of the loss of his citizenship when he was stopped at Dubai airport on his way back to the UK and his passport was confiscated. However SIAC ruled that as he ran a business from his London address, he would surely have had someone checking the post and it was "inconceivable" that they would not have let him know about the notification, and struck out his initial appeal.[110]

Compounding this difficulty is the fact that appeals against deprivation are 'non-suspensive'. When the 2002 Act replaced the possibility of referral to a committee of inquiry with a statutory right of appeal, it provided that a deprivation order could not be made while an appeal against the order was in progress, or could yet be brought.[111] A person notified of a decision to make such an order could therefore appeal against it and, if the appeal was successful, the order would never in fact be made. This provision was, however, repealed by the Asylum and Immigration (Treatment of Claimants, etc) Act 2004, effectively allowing the executive to deprive an individual of his or her citizenship and then remove that person from the country. The right to appeal remains in place, but any appeal must usually now be launched from abroad. Alternatively, where the deprivation order is made when the person is and is known to be out of the country (as is very often the case) the deprivation of citizenship carries with it the loss of the right of abode, including the right to enter the UK. The effect is that the person in question will be unable to return to the UK unless successful in appealing against it.[112] And, being abroad, a deprivee may be unable to meet residence requirements associated with the provision of legal aid. The combination of law and practice in this area—the notice provisions, the non-suspensive nature of the right of appeal and the likelihood of having to exercise it in a closed tribunal, as well as the tendency to make deprivation orders when individuals are outside of the UK—places significant and probably in effect often insurmountable hurdles in the path of those who might wish to contest the deprivation. That the law of the land permits what is effectively exile means we are not here confronted with some outright violation of the principle articulated in Magna Carta, but there is an obvious and disconcerting attempt to whittle down the procedural protections associated with that law to the minimum which can be legally tolerated—often so little as to leave room for interferences with individuals rights and liberties which are,

[108] Anderson (n 65) [2.16].
[109] Ross (n 107) 320.
[110] ibid, 323.
[111] BNA 1981, s 40A (6) (as inserted by the Nationality, Immigration and Asylum Act 2002).
[112] This is not the case in respect of an alien with leave to remain who is made subject of an exclusion order. Of this discrepancy, Rix LJ said in *G1*: 'The difference between the alien with leave to enter or remain and the citizen is surprising and counter-intuitive … and may not have been intended. However, since the statutory amendments referred to above, it is plainly there … [T]he appellant has no one to blame but himself if he is not in a position either to conduct his appeal in country, or to argue by way of judicial review that it would be unlawful to remove him from this country pending his appeal.' [2012] EWCA Civ 867, [59].

or might as well be, arbitrary. And as is often the case in the realm of national security, the political cost of treating (former) British citizens in this fashion is not high.

One final point must be made about the practical implications of these procedural provisions. In several cases, those deprived of citizenship under the powers described above have been shortly afterwards captured by American forces or killed by American drone strikes.[113] The government has—as one would hope—denied any connection between the deprivation of citizenship and that fate of those who are left far from home and without the right to return to the UK, nor any meaningful prospect of challenging the order.[114] It is nevertheless obvious that such strikes could not take place while the target was in Britain; the practice of depriving individuals while they are abroad, as well as the non-suspensive nature of the power to deprive a person of citizenship thus contributes in no small measure to creating the conditions necessary for the extra-judicial killing of persons who were, only shortly before, British citizens. Politically too, the killing of a former British citizen by our American allies is likely to be far less problematic, both domestically and on the international plane, than is the killing of a 'current' citizen, particularly where the loss of citizenship was effected on national security grounds or similar. Finally, but perhaps most alarmingly, it has been suggested that those in respect of whom deprivation orders have been made have been reluctant to make use of their right of appeal because to do so requires making contact with their families or solicitors in the UK and they fear that such contact will potentially assist in targeting them with a drone strike.[115] Given that it has also been alleged that GCHQ has provided 'locational intelligence' to the CIA for use in its drone programme—though attempts to seek even a minimum of legal redress for whatever British involvement there might be in the American activities have been unsuccessful[116]—it is not unthinkable that they may be justified in their fears. There is little prospect whatsoever of ever being in a position to assess the truth of these claims, and if the government denies that it deliberately deprives individuals of their citizenship while they are abroad so as to frustrate their efforts to appeal against it, it is hardly likely to admit that it does so with a view to then handing over details of those persons' whereabouts to the CIA in order that it might kill them. The allegations nevertheless fit with what is known about the law and practice of citizenship deprivation. If they are true, the deprivation can be understood as being intended not merely to deprive persons of their right of abode, but to cut them loose more generally from the system of legal rights and obligations within which, as a UK national, they would otherwise be enmeshed even when abroad.

C. The ECHR and EU Law

The deprivation of a person's citizenship implicates both the Convention on Human Rights and EU law, both of which we need discuss only briefly.[117] In the first case, decisions as

[113] Ross (n 107) 319.

[114] ibid.

[115] ibid 324.

[116] *R (Noor Khan) v Secretary of State for Foreign and Commonwealth Affairs* [2014] EWCA Civ 24, discussed (in relation to the doctrine of foreign act of state) in Ch 6.

[117] Some of the other international regimes which speak to the question of deprivation—mostly not enforceable in domestic law—are considered in Eric Fripp, 'Deprivation of nationality and public international law—an outline' (2014) 28 *JIANL* 367.

to citizenship are liable to—and in the case of the deprivation of citizenship, highly likely to—engage the Article 8 right to a private and family life, 'private life' being a concept which 'covers the physical and psychological integrity of a person' and which 'can therefore embrace multiple aspects of the person's physical and social identity'.[118] The UK is under no obligation to secure the Article 8 rights of those not within its jurisdiction, and it was implied by a Home Office memo on the Immigration Bill 2014 that citizens physically outside the UK are outside its jurisdiction.[119] In evidence to the JCHR, this was (rightly) rubbished by Guy Goodwin-Gill:

> It is certainly wishful legal thinking to suppose that a person's ECHR rights can be annihilated simply by depriving that person of citizenship while he or she is abroad. Even a little logic suffices to show that the act of deprivation only has meaning if it is directed at someone who is within the jurisdiction of the State. A citizen is manifestly someone subject to and within the jurisdiction of the State, and the purported act of deprivation is intended precisely to affect his or rights.[120]

And even if it is correct, as the Home Office has argued, that those who are deprived of citizenship while abroad are not therefore able to argue that a breach of the Convention has taken place, family members in the UK who are affected by the decision to deprive may nevertheless be able to do so. Regardless of how the Convention comes to be engaged, the question to be answered will be that of justification: whether the deprivation is an interference which takes place in pursuit of a legitimate aim and which is proportionate to the advantages—in terms of that aim—which accrue as a result of the interference. Where the decision to deprive is based upon national security considerations, the answer will usually, one can predict, be that deprivation is compatible with Article 8. A second question is whether powers of deprivation which relate only to naturalised citizens (such as that power introduced by the Immigration Act 2014 with a view to depriving Al-Jedda of his citizenship) might be considered to constitute discrimination in the enjoyment of Article 8 rights, contrary to Article 14 of the Convention. The Home Office, at the time of the 2014 Act's passage through Parliament, declared itself 'satisfied that there is an objective and reasonable justification for treating naturalised citizens differently from others.'[121] The ECHR implications of the matter are therefore relatively few and the system of deprivation of citizenship quite capable of being operated compatibly with it, as demonstrated by the Chamber decision in *K2* (the applicant being the same individual designated *GI* in the domestic courts), where it was held that there was sufficient procedural safeguards within the British law on deprivation of citizenship to meet the requirements of the Convention. More importantly, it was held that while an out-of-country appeal may be incompatible with Article 8 'where there exists clear and objective evidence that the person was unable to instruct lawyers or give evidence while outside the jurisdiction', that provision does not 'impose a positive obligation on Contracting States to facilitate the return of every person deprived of citizenship while outside the jurisdiction in

[118] *Genovese v Malta*, application 53124/09 (11 November 2011).

[119] Home Office, *Immigration Bill: European Convention on Human Rights Supplementary Memorandum* (29 January 2014) [13].

[120] Guy Goodwin-Gill, 'Mr Al-Jedda, Deprivation of Citizenship and International Law', Memorandum to the Joint Committee on Human Rights (2014).

[121] Home Office (n 119) [15].

order to pursue an appeal against that decision.'[122] The Chamber nevertheless reaffirmed that a deprivation of citizenship may be incompatible with Article 8 where it is 'arbitrary' (as was not the case here) or as a function of the consequences of the deprivation. In the case of K2, however, the consequences were comparatively slight: 'the applicant had left the United Kingdom voluntarily prior to the decision to deprive him of his citizenship; his wife and child were no longer living in the United Kingdom and could freely visit Sudan and even live there if they wished; and the applicant's own natal family could—and did—visit him "reasonably often"'.[123]

Not all deprivations of citizenship will implicate EU law, though they may do in certain circumstances. In *GI*,[124] the Court of Appeal resisted the claim, made in reliance on the judgment of the Court of Justice in *Rottmann*,[125] that deprivation of citizenship engages EU law even where there is no 'cross-border element'; where the applicant had not exercised, or attempted to exercise, any EU law right. Laws LJ emphasised that such an interpretation would have given rise to certain constitutional difficulties:

> The conditions on which national citizenship is conferred, withheld or revoked are integral to the identity of the nation State. They touch the constitution; for they identify the constitution's participants. If it appeared that the Court of Justice had sought to be the judge of any procedural conditions governing such matters, so that its ruling was to apply in a case with no cross-border element, then in my judgment a question would arise whether the European Communities Act 1972 or any successor statute had conferred any authority on the Court of Justice to exercise such a jurisdiction.[126]

The case law leaves open the possibility that EU law will apply in cases where the exercise of free movement rights has brought an individual within EU law. The principle attraction of showing that EU law is engaged is that the decision-making procedure becomes as a result subject to the protection offered by the Charter of Fundamental Rights—in particular Article 47 of the Charter, which provides that 'everyone whose rights and freedoms guaranteed by the law of the Union are violated has the right to an effective remedy before a tribunal in compliance with the conditions laid down in this Article ...'[127] The Charter has over the ECHR the advantage that a statute which cannot be read compatibly with it is to be 'disapplied',[128] rather than to be made the subject of a declaration of incompatibility.[129] Nevertheless, the jurisprudence of the Court of Justice has so far hewn closely to that of the Court of Human Rights as regards the degree of disclosure which must take place in order for a person to be able to effectively challenge the case against him or her.[130]

[122] *K2 v United Kingdom (Admissibility)* (2017) 64 EHRR SE18, [57].

[123] (2017) 64 EHRR SE18, [62].

[124] *GI v Secretary of State for the Home Department* [2012] EWCA Civ 867.

[125] *Rottmann v Bayern* [2010] ECR 1–1449. See Adrian Berry, 'Deprivation of nationality and citizenship—the role of EU law' (2014) 28 *JIANL* 355.

[126] [2012] EWCA Civ 867, [43].

[127] Charter of Fundamental Rights of the European Union, Art 47.

[128] In accordance with *R v Secretary of State for Transport, ex parte Factortame (No 2)* [1991] 1 AC 60.

[129] See, eg, *Benkharbouche v Embassy of the Republic of Sudan* [2017] UKSC 62 in which both regimes were at issue.

[130] See *ZZ v Secretary of State for the Home Department* [2014] EWCA Civ 7 and *Kiani v Secretary of State for the Home Department* [2015] EWCA Civ 776.

D. The Use of the Power to Deprive

The changed legal position—both substantive and procedural—over time is, however, in many respects less important than is the changed pattern of the powers' use. When the 2002 Act was proposed, the government stated that the 'last time someone was deprived of British citizenship was in 1973 using a similar power in the [1948 Act].'[131] In the new national security context, the use of the powers has expanded significantly and in 2014, a Home Office Minister stated that between 2006 and then, there had been 27 deprivations on conducive grounds.[132] More recently, the annual transparency reports which have emerged as a key source of information in this area shows that four such deprivations took place in 2014,[133] and five in 2015.[134] Citizenship has therefore, for that proportion of the population that has or could obtain a second nationality, come to be in practice contingent upon the individual's conduct, with the relevant legal instruments often doing too little to guide or circumscribe the use of the powers in question.[135] Though distasteful, this change appears to be in large part a modern equivalent to the old idea that the protection of the individual by the Crown is reciprocal to the individual's allegiance to it.[136] It is therefore tempting to conclude that the issue of citizenship has come, as it were, 'full circle', with the liberalising trends of the twentieth century undone by the heightened exigencies of national security and so on. In his consideration of the power, however, Gibney contests that conclusion, suggesting instead that the apparent liberalisation—evidenced by the increasing subjection of deprivation to legal review, the reduction of the range of grounds upon which it might happen, and the willingness to allow deprivation to be limited by considerations of statelessness—was misleading; that, instead, 'British governments … have, at certain historical moments, simply "cherry-picked" different liberal principles to suit their own predetermined ends'.[137] If so, what has happened in the last 15 years is not so much some variation of principle, but rather a simple change of the ends which the government chooses to pursue and the determination with which it is willing to pursue them. And yet it remains the case that these altered priorities are subject to inter-linked legal and practical limitations, which the UK has not (yet) sought to overcome: international law limits significantly, as we have seen, the deprivation of citizenship where it would result in statelessness. Even if the UK was willing—as it has occasionally done and threatened to do elsewhere—to push against those boundaries, the practical problem would remain: there is no state to which

[131] Home Office, *Secure Borders, Safe Haven: Integration with Diversity in Modern Britain*, Cm 5387 (2002), [2.22]. The individual in question, Nicholas Prager, was an RAF sergeant who had been convicted of spying for Czechoslovakia: see *R v Prager* [1972] 1 WLR 260.

[132] HC Deb 7 May 2014, vol 580 col 191.

[133] HM government, *Transparency Report 2015: Disruptive and Investigatory Powers*, Cm 9151 (2015), [5.9].

[134] HM government, *Transparency Report 2017: Disruptive and Investigatory Powers*, Cm 9420 (2017), [5.9].

[135] See Eric Fripp, 'Conducive Deprivation of British Citizenship Status and Statelessness: Further Problems' (2013) 27 *JIANL* 315, 316–8: 'The absence of definite limitations in the statute or the jurisprudence means that the potential scope of conducive denationalisation is not susceptible to close delineation.'

[136] See, eg, Glanville Williams, 'The Correlation of Allegiance and Protection' (1948) 10 *CLJ* 5. For a discussion of the rhetoric of contract in the context of the deprivation of citizenship, see Gibney (n 58).

[137] Matthew J Gibney, '"A Very Transcendental Power": Denaturalisation and the Liberalisation of Citizenship in the United Kingdom' (2013) 61 *Political Studies* 637, 653.

a stateless person can be returned. And so, though the law and practice of the deprivation of citizenship has been expanded greatly in recent years, there are hard-coded limits to its utility. At those limits other mechanisms exist instead, the most important of which relate to passports.

V. Citizenship, Passports and the Right to Travel

There is no absolute link between the issues of citizenship and passports: one can possess citizenship without possessing a passport, and one can have one's passport withdrawn without being deprived of one's nationality. Nevertheless, there is a close and obvious connection between the legal status of British citizenship and the possession of a British passport: only those holding British nationality can obtain a British passport, and a passport is the primary mode by which citizenship (and identity) is evidenced in the modern world. Moreover, when deciding to permit UK nationals to enter, foreign states will take their possession of a British passport as evidence of their 'returnability'; of the willingness of the UK to allow them entry upon departing that foreign state.[138] If that returnability could not be guaranteed, a UK passport would be unable to serve the ends for which people desire to have it. This section considers the law which is the background to and which underpins the use of passports as a tool of national security, starting from a consideration of the legal effect of passports in the context of the citizen's right to come and go from the jurisdiction. Though the consideration of the powers to make a deprivation order sought mostly to understand the law as it has developed, my approach here is more ambitious. I argue, contrary to what has always been taken to be the correct approach, that the withdrawal of passports in exercise of the prerogative is unlawful. Going further than those who have argued that it would be preferable for the citizen to enjoy a statutory right to the enjoyment of a British passport, I argue that if passports are to be used for the national security purposes which have become so prominent, then powers relating to them must be put on a statutory footing.

A. Passports and the Prerogative

In the UK, passports are regulated under the royal prerogative. Chitty says little about them, connecting that which he does say to the King's war powers, which entitle the King to 'adopt measure to prevent the egress or ingress of his enemies out of or into his

[138] 'The great majority of states do not seem to care about the nationality of the person seeking entry to its territory as long as he produces a valid legal passport so that he can be repatriated in case his presence should become undesirable in the country of sojourn …' Daniel Turack, *The Passport in International Law*, Lexington Books (1972), 20. The JUSTICE report discussed below argued, in a period in which possession of a British passport had become detached from a right of abode in the United Kingdom, that passports held by non-patrials (who did not enjoy such right) should indicate the place to which the holder could be returned.

Majesty's dominions.'[139] As a converse of this power, the King may in exercise of his prerogative permit his enemies 'to come into the country without molestation, by granting to him letters of safe-conduct.'[140] Various statutes, Chitty notes, require that letters of safe-conduct ought to be under the Great Seal and enrolled in Chancery,[141] but letters of safe conduct had begun at the time of his writing to give way to 'passports under the King's sign manual or licenses from his ambassador.'[142] This last claim is referenced to Blackstone, who for his part emphasised the 'great tenderness' of English law, which gives friendly aliens the King's protection while their nation is at peace with his and they behave peaceably (though even these might be expelled via exercise of the prerogative).[143] Such individuals, *Calvin's case* had confirmed, could enter the kingdom without any need for a safe conduct.[144] For those from states with whom the country is at war, however, Blackstone claimed that the rule was different: 'no subject of a nation at war with us can, by the law of nations, come into this realm, nor can travel himself upon the high seas, or send his goods and merchandize from one place to another, without danger of being seized by our subjects, unless he has letters of safe-conduct.'[145] These distinctions were carried over into the distinction between passports and safe conducts: the former were given to friends, the latter to enemies.[146]

Until the 1840s, British passports were written in French and contained no description of the bearer, nor his signature.[147] No written regulations seem to have existed to limit or define the circumstances in which they were granted; instead, it was understood that 'applicants for passports should obtain a letter of recommendation from some respectable person known to Government, or from some banker or other responsible person who would vouch from their respectability.'[148] In 1846 the Foreign Office under Palmerston issued a set of 'Regulations respecting Passports' which reformed the matter in various ways. Not only would passports now state the nationality of the bearer for the first time, but they were to be limited to British subjects.[149] Thus began the transformation of the passport into its modern form, a process accelerated by the outbreak of the First World War, with the residual possibility of passport-less travel significantly curtailed and states concerned to assume control over both entry to and exit from their jurisdiction.[150] For most

[139] J Chitty, *A Treatise on the Law of the Prerogatives of the Crown: And the Relative Duties and Rights of the Subject* (London, J Butterworth & Son, 1820) 48.

[140] Chitty (n 139) 48.

[141] By three statutes of Henry VI: 15 Hen 6 c 3; 18 Hen 6 c 8; 20 Hen 6 c 1.

[142] Chitty (n 139) 48–9.

[143] Blackstone, *Commentaries*, I, 251–2.

[144] *Calvin's case* 7 Co Rep 1a, 77 ER 377. For a detailed consideration, see Polly J Price, 'Natural Law and Birthright Citizenship in Calvin' s Case (1608)' (1997) 9 *Yale Journal of Law and the Humanities* 73.

[145] Blackstone, *Commentaries*, I, 251.

[146] Wyndham Beawes, *Lex Mercatoria Rediviva OR, THE MERCHANT'S DIRECTORY*, (Dublin, Peter Wilson, 1754) 209.

[147] Martin Anderson, 'Tourism and the Development of the Modern British Passport, 1814–1858' (2010) 49 *The Journal of British Studies* 258, 262.

[148] *Correspondence respecting passports*, 2356 (1857–58), 1.

[149] 'Passports are granted only to British subjects, or to such foreigners as may have been naturalized by Act of Parliament or received Letters of Denization: in this latter case, the party will be described in the Passport as being either a naturalized British subject, or a denizen, as the case may be.' Cited in *Correspondence respecting passports* (n 148) 2.

[150] For further accounts of the history see Diplock (n 10), Sibley (n 9) and Williams (n 6).

international travellers, passports would now be a sine qua non of exercising their rights,[151] and in the UK the Aliens Order 1920 introduced a requirement that an alien produce a passport or other document proving his identity and nationality. In 1905, the King's Bench Division, considering the soundness of an indictment for conspiracy to obtain a passport by false representations, had defined a passport as:

> a document issued in the name of the Sovereign on the responsibility of a Minister of the Crown to a named individual, intended to be presented to the Governments of foreign nations and to be used for that individual's protection as a British subject in foreign countries, and it depends for its validity upon the fact that the Foreign Office in an official document vouches the respectability of the person named.[152]

The legal form of passports has not, though, evolved along with its legal and practical significance. Notwithstanding a number of recommendations to that effect, the regulation of passports has never been placed upon a statutory footing, and the individual enjoys no legal right to a passport. In 1976, JUSTICE, the British Section of the International Commission of Jurists, issued a report examining some of the legal questions around passports, and recommended 'as a basic constitutional necessity, the early enactment of a brief statute conferring upon all citizens the legal right to a passport.'[153] Without denying that the executive might legitimately wish to prevent citizens from leaving the country, it argued that it should do so only 'by open and judicially-acknowledged means', potentially by seeking to persuade a court to grant a writ of *ne exeat regno*, the persistence of which was at that point in time uncertain.[154] Though it was initially cautious,[155] the government decided to make no move towards the statutory regulation of passports, and subsequent governments repeatedly maintained that position over the intervening decades. Later, a variety of bills were introduced into Parliament which would have created a statutory right to a passport, or at least a statutory right of appeal against its refusal:[156] none made any meaningful progress. For this reason we are, as regards the core legal regulation of passports, in much the same places as we have been since the original historical emergence of passports (subject to the important changes which have taken place in terms of the reviewability of the prerogative powers). The government in its most recent statement of policy on the refusal or withdrawing of passports, articulated the legal position in typically stark terms:

> There is no entitlement to a passport and no statutory right to have access to a passport. The decision to issue, withdraw, or refuse a British passport is at the discretion of the Secretary of State for the Home Department (the Home Secretary) under the Royal Prerogative.[157]

[151] The implication of this process for the citizen-state relationship are considered by John Torpey in his *The Invention of the Passport: Surveillance, Citizenship and the State* (Cambridge, Cambridge University Press, 2010).

[152] *R v Brailsford* [1905] 2 KB 730, 745. For discussion, see Sibley (n 9).

[153] JUSTICE, *Going Abroad—A Report on Passports*, Barry Rose Publishers (1974) [48].

[154] JUSTICE (n 153) [55].

[155] See, eg, the answer given by Lord Goronwy-Roberts to a question by Lord Orr-Ewing at HL Deb 6 May 1976, vol 370 cols 697–720.

[156] One such bill had been entitled the 'Outlawries (No. 2)' bill, with reference to the Outlawries Bill which prevents individuals being designated outlaws without notice and is by tradition is the first item on Parliament's agenda at the beginning of each session. The Outlawries (No. 2) bill, introduced by Nigel Birch, was aimed at the secret removal of passports, and the secret refusal to issue them.

[157] Theresa May, 'The issuing, withdrawal or refusal of passports', HC Deb 25 April 2013 vol 561 col 68WS.

This state of affairs, though not as clear-cut as the executive may wish to make it appear, has important consequences for the use of passports as a tool of national security, and for the individual's ability to challenge that use.

B. Passports and the Right to Travel

It was noted above that the Immigration Act 1971 states the right of abode possessed by all UK citizens subject to procedures 'as may be required under and in accordance with this Act to enable their right to be established or as may be otherwise lawfully imposed on any person.'[158] It therefore grants immigration officers the right to examine, in order to determine whether they are British citizens (and so enjoy the stated right of abode), those who are either entering the country or embarking in it. A person being examined for this purpose can be required to 'produce either a valid passport with photograph or some other document satisfactorily establishing his identity and nationality or citizenship'.[159] The statute, and thus domestic law in its current form, does not therefore make the possession of a passport an explicit precondition of either leaving or entering the jurisdiction, but identifies it as the primary method by which one demonstrates one's right to do so, leaving open the question of what identification other than a passport might be considered to be satisfactory for the purpose. Equivalent provisions were at issue in the incident in 1968 in which journalist Ian Colvin attempted, as a test case, to board a plane at London Airport without a passport. Colvin was refused permission to do so on the basis that none of the alternative documentation he offered convinced the immigration officer of his status as a British citizen or that he otherwise enjoyed the right to embark under the relevant legislation.[160] If that is the case where a person wishes to leave the country, how much more difficult must it be to enter the country without a passport, where one might (if not a citizen) have no legal right to do so? And of course, UK domestic law and practice is not the only relevant consideration: notwithstanding that, as a matter of strict law, one might enter or leave the UK without a valid passport, it is likely that many other states will not permit an individual to enter or leave their territory without such a document and that the private organisations upon whom most of us depend for international travel will often, as would seem to be their right, refuse to carry passengers who cannot produce a valid passport. It is therefore probable that even if a person were capable of satisfying a British immigration officer of the requisite facts about his identity and nationality without a passport, that

[158] Immigration Act 1971, s 1.

[159] ibid, Sch 2, para 4(2)(a).

[160] Writing contemporaneously, William Wade said of the Colvin case that: '… the Aliens Restriction Act ought not to be invoked unless there are genuine grounds for suspecting alien nationality. To turn the law for control of aliens into a law for the control of British subjects, by applying an arbitrarily strict standard of proof, would be an abuse of power for which a British subject would have the usual legal remedies.' HWR Wade, 'Passports and the Individual's Right to Travel' *The Times* (7 August 1968) cited in JUSTICE (n 153) 3. Elsewhere, Wade (writing with Bernard Schwartz) called the power to refuse or cancel passports 'perhaps the only really objectionable arbitrary power which the Crown still claims' and said that its legal justification 'is highly doubtful': B Schwartz and HWR Wade, *Legal Control of Government: Administrative Law in Britain and the United States* (Oxford, Oxford University Press, 1972) 63.

person would nevertheless be unable to travel into or out of the UK. The power to withhold or withdraw passports can therefore be seen to create a dual obstacle to the enjoyment of one's legal rights, the second being all the more important because the executive can fairly claim to have no role in its imposition.

C. Refusing and Withdrawing Passports on National Security Grounds

In 1958 a Foreign Office Minister outlined in Parliament—in response to a question put by the Viscount Stansgate—four sets of circumstances in which the government of the day considered itself justified in refusing a passport to an individual who was otherwise entitled to it. The first was the case of minors being taken from the jurisdiction illegally; the second, those 'believed on good evidence to be fleeing the country to avoid prosecution for a criminal offence'; the fourth, those who had previously been repatriated at public expense and failed to repay the costs incurred. The third category captures neatly both the substance and the rhetoric of what we would now call national security claims, encompassing 'persons whose activities are so notoriously undesirable or dangerous that Parliament would be expected to support the action of the Foreign Secretary in refusing them a passport or withdrawing a passport already issued in order to prevent their leaving the United Kingdom.'[161] Of interest here are, at least, the nod to parliamentary accountability (which in respect of the use of the prerogative is of course by definition post-hoc and often underwhelming) in terms of the self-imposed requirement to exercise the power in a manner to which Parliament can be 'expected' to assent,[162] and the fact that nature of the activities which might fall within this description is left unspecified. Regardless, the number of passports refused or withdrawn in accordance with this policy seems, for most of the twentieth century, to have been very low.

The matter was discussed again in Parliament in 1976 in response to the withdrawal of passports from Britains who had fought as mercenaries in Angola's civil war. The phenomenon was familiar to parliamentarians, numerous passports having been in the preceding years withdrawn from individuals—many former members of the British armed forces—who had fought in conflicts in Africa. The situation which attracted most attention was the withdrawal of passports from persons who had fought for Ian Smith's government in Rhodesia, with an advisory committee set up to report on related cases.[163] The most notable withdrawal of a passport was that of Sir Frederick Crawford (a former colonial administrator who had been Governor of Uganda between 1957 and 1961 and had become a director of the Anglo-American Corporation) for having—after Rhodesia's unilateral

[161] HL Deb 16 June 1958, vol 209 cols 860–861.

[162] A question from Lord Wilmot of Selmeston elicited the admission that the respondent was unaware of any example of the Foreign Secretary taking steps to confirm that the view Parliament was expected to hold was in fact the view it held, though it was suggested that if the Foreign Secretary became aware that Parliament was not in agreement with his assessment of its likely view, he might choose to re-exercise his prerogative 'on the ground that he had made a personal misjudgement'. Lord Wilmot of Selmeston asked whether the Government's position implied that 'the only action open to one aggrieved would be in fact to defeat the Government?' HL Deb 16 June 1958, vol 209 cols 861–862.

[163] HC Deb 17 June 1968, vol 766 cols 723–4.

declaration of independence—pursued 'a course of behaviour which certainly gave every appearance of lending full support to the claims of the régime to have achieved legality and independence.'[164] The questioner in 1976, Lord Orr-Ewing, noted that in a written answer two years earlier a different form of words had been used to describe the phenomenon than had been used in the past: now, it seemed, passports might be withdrawn from those whose 'past or proposed activities are so demonstrably undesirable that the grant or continued enjoyment of passport facilities would be contrary to the public interest.'[165] As Lord Orr-Ewing observed, the wording had 'softened' so as to encompass a broader range of activities, while the reference to Parliament and the view it might be expected to take had been removed.[166] One notable element of the Angola affair was that the government had adopted the practice of returning withdrawn passports to the bearer if he was willing to give undertakings about his future behaviour—primarily, it would appear, that the passport would not be used to travel to Angola. Questioned on another occasion as to the legal effect of the practice, Lord Goronwy-Roberts claimed that 'if, in contravention of an undertaking signed, a person were in fact to leave the country, he would be breaking the law—that is, the 1925 statute—which makes it an offence to obtain a passport (and, in this case, to re-obtain a passport) by signing a false declaration or by not conforming with a signed declaration.'[167] Depending on the specific terms of the undertakings, however, it seems unlikely that an individual who had given those undertakings and later reneged upon them could be said to have made a false declaration for the purposes of the criminal law.

The recruitment of British mercenaries was also the subject of an inquiry by a committee of Privy Councillors chaired by Lord Diplock.[168] Lord Diplock's report asserts, without reference, the citizen's common law right to enter or leave the country as asserted by Blackstone and so the strict legal meaninglessness of the passport: an individual capable of establishing his identity in some other manner would not, it was claimed, be prevented by his lack of passport from leaving the country.[169] Referring to the recent history of withdrawing passports from those acting as mercenaries, the report suggests that on each occasion 'the stable door was shut after the horse had gone'—passports were withdrawn from those had already fought abroad—and in the case of an individual not already known to the Passport Office, there would be no way of knowing of a malign intent which might justify the withdrawal of a passport.[170] The method described above, whereby passports were returned in exchange for a declaration about an individual's future behaviour, was

[164] HC Deb 14 May 1968, vol 764 col 1050. Of particular concern was that the government had offered to return Crawford's passport if he declared his loyalty to the Queen's representative in Rhodesia: HC Deb 14 May 1968, vol 764 cols 1041–1116.

[165] HC Deb 24 June 1974, vol 875 col 357W. Wade described this as 'a polysyllabic way of describing any one whose activities are disapproved of by the government.' HWR Wade, *Constitutional Fundamentals*, rev ed (London, Stevens & Sons, 1989) 63.

[166] HL Deb 6 May 1976, vol 370 cols 699–700.

[167] HL Deb March 9 1976, vol 368 col 1203. The reference is presumably to the Criminal Justice Act 1925, s 26 of which criminalised 'the making by any person of a statement which is to his knowledge untrue for the purpose of procuring a passport.'

[168] Lord Diplock, *Report of the Committee of Privy Counsellors appointed to inquire into the recruitment of mercenaries*, Cmnd 6569 (1976).

[169] Diplock (n 168) [17].

[170] ibid [20].

considered ineffective for the additional reason that a passport could be taken from an individual against his will only via a civil action in detinue[171]—no powers of search or seizure were available—while there was no effective way to sanction (either criminally or civilly) a breach of the relevant undertaking.[172] The withdrawal of a passport being essentially based upon a bluff—the false impression that without a passport, an individual was not permitted to travel abroad—the committee concluded that 'neither the refusal of a passport nor its withdrawal can provide an effective administrative means of preventing or delaying the departure from a country of a would-be mercenary who has been informed about his legal rights.'[173]

Whether or not for those reason, the practice of refusing or withdrawing passports seems to have withered following the end of the various conflicts on the African continent which had seen it flourish in the 1960s and 70s. In December 1984, it was stated in Parliament that no passports had been refused on the grounds of undesirable activities in that or any of the three previous years.[174] Nor were there any withdrawals on those grounds in the five years leading up to December 1989.[175] With the dawn of a global terror threat to which British nationals made a significant contribution, however, passports re-emerged as a tool of national security, alongside a more expansive use of powers—to which passports are always secondary—to deprive individuals of British citizenship. A written statement to Parliament on 25 April 2013 provided an updated account of the government's position on the issuance, refusal and withdrawal of passports, starting from a reassertion of the position that there is no right to a passport, the issuance of which is at the discretion of the Home Secretary, exercising the Royal Prerogative. The statement was more expansive than have been previous accounts of the circumstances in which passport facilities might be refused, making explicit reference for the first time to those who 'may seek to harm the UK or its allies by travelling on a British passport to, for example, engage in terrorism-related activity or other serious or organised criminal activity' and redefining the public interest criteria employed in making decisions about passports.[176] For present purposes, the relevant circumstances in which a passport might be refused or withdrawn are when an individual is subject to (i) an order made by a court or under statute which places restrictions on travel or the possession of a passport; (ii) bail conditions which impose such restrictions; or (iii) 'an order issued by the European Union or the United Nations which prevents a person travelling or entering a country other than the country in which they hold citizenship'.[177] Similarly, a person 'may be prevented from benefitting from the possession of a passport if the Home Secretary is satisfied that it is in the public interest to do so.' This, the statement tells us, 'may be the case' where 'a person whose past, present or proposed activities, actual or suspected, are believed by the Home Secretary to be so undesirable that the grant or continued enjoyment of passport facilities is contrary to the public interest.'[178]

[171] ibid [22].
[172] ibid [22].
[173] ibid [23].
[174] HC Deb 17 December 1984, vol 70 col 8W.
[175] HC Deb 6 December 1989, vol 163 cols 258-9W.
[176] May (n 157).
[177] ibid.
[178] ibid.

Several observations can be made. The first is a trite yet crucial one: this statement amounts to a unilateral redefinition of the public interest by the government of the day of a sort that is only possible because of the absence of statutory regulation in this area. While the prerogative continues to underpin the passport regime, the executive will always dominate in this way the administration of the passport system and the understanding of the public interest which it reflects. Second, the prerogative power not only co-exists with statutory powers such as those, described below, to impose TPIMs including travel measures: such powers will be used in tandem, with the imposition of such an order sufficing to justify the withdrawal of a person's passport. Third, the 'undesirable activities' formulation seems no longer to reflect a distinct and exhaustive ground (as it did in previous statements of policy) but instead merely illustrates one set of circumstances in which the broader public interest will see passport facilities refused. To broaden the power in this way is itself problematic, though not, as we have seen, unprecedented. To illustrate the new and broader approach with the same narrower phrasing previously employed is, however, unacceptable, in that it denies the observer any opportunity to understand what circumstances might now be caught which previously were not. Fourth, the statement bears the marks of the supra-national regimes which now form part of domestic law (as well, perhaps, as the manner in which those regimes have influenced the development of domestic law) in the new reference to the requirement that any withdrawal of a passport be 'necessary and proportionate'. The key point, however, is that while this statement of policy makes possible the use of passports as a tool of national security, national security is just one of a range of factors which might justify the conclusion that it is in the public interest for a person to be deprived of passport facilities. As well as being subject to unilateral redefinition by the executive, the grounds on which passports might be refused or withdrawn have been and continue to be widened significantly. The power was used with increasing frequency by the Labour governments in power between the dawn of the new era of terror in 2001 and 2010, but much more so after the return to power of the Conservative party, at first in coalition with the Liberal Democrats and then as the lone party of government.[179] Since the reformulation of the policy governing the refusal and withdrawal of passports, the number of uses of the prerogative (either in withdrawing or refusing a passport) on national security grounds is as follows: six times in 2013, 24 times in 2014, and 23 times in 2015.[180]

D. Passports and Property

Passports remain useful to terrorists even when they have been 'withdrawn' (and so deprived of the legal effect which the government claims they do not have). They can be altered, or sold for use at home or abroad. More generally, the state which issues a passport has an interest in maintaining the integrity of the passport system and desires, reasonably, to prevent passports being used (even after cancellation) for nefarious purposes.

[179] Between April 2013 and March 2014, the power to withdraw passports was, according to the Immigration and Security Minister, used 14 times: House of Commons Home Affairs Committee, *Counter-terrorism* (HC 2013–14, 231) [95].

[180] HM Government, *Transparency Report 2017: Disruptive and Investigatory Powers*, Cm 9420 (2017), [5.5].

For these reasons, it is necessary not merely to cancel a person's passport, but for the state to take possession of the document itself, so as to prevent its use in a way which is, directly or indirectly, contrary to the interests of national security. In *Ghaini v Jones*,[181] the Court of Appeal held that the police had no power to retain passports which had been taken in the warrantless search of a home where they were not material evidence to prove the commission of a murder: the desire to prevent the bearers from leaving the country was not a legitimate basis for their retention. If a warrant for a person's arrest has been issued, then the passport might—consistently with the current guidance—be withdrawn.[182] But how to retake possession of a passport which has been withdrawn and yet is still physically in the possession of the person in whose name it was issued? Lord Diplock's report on the recruitment of British mercenaries suggested that an action in detinue would be the only way to recover a passport which remained in the possession of the bearer after passport facilities had been withdrawn.[183] Detinue was abolished by the Torts (Interference with Goods) Act 1977, but the refusal to return a passport to its rightful legal owner may constitute a wrongful interference with property in response to which the courts would make an order for its delivery.[184] Additionally, Tom Hickman has suggested that a person who refuses to return a passport is 'presumably guilty of theft.'[185] Another issue which has become evident as the phenomenon of foreign fighters has evolved: the process by which passports are cancelled happens sufficiently slowly that the possibility of cancelling it has proven unsuited to dealing with those whose motives come to the awareness of the authority only at the point when they seek to depart from the country. Though Schedule 7 to the Terrorism Act 2000 permits the temporary seizure of property when a person is stopped at a port in order to determine whether he or she is 'concerned in the commission, preparation or instigation of acts of terrorism,'[186] and though statutory powers have existed in relation to the passports of, for example, football 'hooligans' for many years,[187] until recently no relevant powers existed to seize passports on general national security grounds.

This matter has been addressed by statute. First, it was noted above that one type of 'measure' which may be made under the Terrorist Prevention and Investigation Measures Act 2011,[188] is a 'travel measure' by which the Secretary of State imposes restrictions on an individual from leaving either the UK (or Great Britain or Northern Ireland, depending on where a person lives) or requiring the giving of notice to the Secretary of State before leaving the specified area.[189] But travel measures extend beyond the direct regulation of travel and may include, alongside or instead of such restrictions on travel, a requirement 'not to possess or otherwise control, or seek to obtain, any travel document without the permission of the Secretary of State' and/or 'to surrender any travel document that is

[181] *Ghaini v Jones* [1970] 1 QB 693.
[182] May (n 157).
[183] Diplock (n 168) 22.
[184] Torts (Interference with Goods) Act 1977, ss 1 and 3.
[185] Tom Hickman, 'ISIS, passports and Magna Carta: New national security powers raise complex issues' *UK Constitutional Law Blog* (9 October 2014).
[186] Terrorism Act 2000, Sch 7, para 11.
[187] Under the Football Spectators Act 1989.
[188] Discussed in Ch 2.
[189] Terrorist Prevention and Investigation Measures Act 2011.

in the possession or control of the individual,'[190] where a 'travel document' includes that person's passport,[191] whether issued by the UK or another country or territory.[192] Second, the Anti-social Behaviour, Crime and Policing Act 2014 creates powers to seize 'invalid' travel documents, a category which includes passports which have been cancelled.[193] The power may be exercised by a constable or immigration officer at airports and other 'ports', in which case the passport may be one issued by the UK or a foreign state.[194] Or it may be exercised by a constable at any other place, in which case, only UK passports are included in the power, and only where the passport has been cancelled on 'undesirable activities' grounds and made subject to an authorisation by the Secretary of State.[195] The power under the 2014 Act does not of course apply where the bearer's involvement (or possible future involvement) in undesirable activities is as yet unknown to the authorities, or has not yet been acted upon, and so the passport in question remains valid. For that reason, the Counter-Terrorism Act 2015[196] permits the police to require that 'travel documents' (a passport or a ticket permitting travel) be handed over, as well as to search for,[197] inspect, and retain such documents.[198] These powers are activated where, in relation to a person at a port in the UK, a constable has 'reasonable grounds' to suspect that the person '(a) is there with the intention of leaving Great Britain for the purpose of involvement in terrorism-related activity outside the United Kingdom, or (b) has arrived in Great Britain with the intention of leaving it soon for that purpose.'[199] Where a constable comes into possession of a passport via the exercise of these powers, he must as soon as possible seek authorisation from a 'senior police office' to retain it or return it to the person whose passport it is.[200] If the travel documents are still being held 72 hours later, the retention must be reviewed by a police officer of a suitably high rank, and an application can be granted only if the senior police office is satisfied that there are reasonable grounds for the suspicion in question.[201] Where it is, the passport may be retained while it is being decided whether to make in relation to the individual an order (such as a TPIM 2011) 'for purposes connected with protecting members of the public from a risk of terrorism', whether to charge that person which an offence, or whether to cancel that person's passport.[202] Collectively, these powers neutralise—perhaps entirely—the dangers associated with the ongoing possession of a withdrawn passport.

[190] TPIM Act 2011, Sch 1, para 2(3)(c) and (d).
[191] Ibid, Sch 2, para 2(4).
[192] Ibid, para 2(5).
[193] Anti-social Behaviour, Crime and Policing Act 2014, s 147 and Sch 8.
[194] ABCPA 2014, Sch 8, para 2.
[195] ibid, Sch 8, para 3.
[196] Counter-Terrorism and Security Act 2015, s 1 and Sch 1.
[197] '[O]n an individual's person, in anything that individual has with them, and in 'any vehicle in which the officer believes the person to have been travelling or to be about to travel':
[198] CTSA 2015, Sch 1, paras 1 and 2.
[199] ibid, para 2(1)(a).
[200] ibid, para 4.
[201] ibid, para 6.
[202] ibid, para 5. This retention can last a maximum of 14 days, unless extended (up to 30 days) by a judicial authority on application by a senior police officer: CTSA 2015, Sch 1, paras 8 and 9.

E. Challenging the Withdrawal or Withholding of a Passport

Because passports are regulated by prerogative rather than statute, the extent to which courts will involve themselves in decisions about their grant or withdrawal is a function, in part, of their willingness to review exercises of the prerogative powers.[203] When it was decided in the *GCHQ* case that reviewability was to be a function of a power's subject matter rather than its source,[204] no mention was made of the powers relating to passports and so the question of whether or not their subject matter was such as to render them 'amenable to the judicial process' was left for the while unresolved. Whatever uncertainty was created by *GCHQ* in relation to passports did not persist for long. In *Everett*,[205] the applicant—a British citizen living in Spain—had been refused renewal of his passport because a warrant for his arrest was outstanding in the UK and it was the policy of the Secretary of State not to issue a passport in those circumstances (it is unclear from the report whether there was any causal relationship between the existence of the warrant and his choice to live abroad). In the Court of Appeal, it was accepted that the judge at first instance had been correct to distinguish decisions about passports from the sorts of issues—the making of treaties, foreign policy etc—which had been identified in *GCHQ* as remaining beyond the competence of the courts. O'Connor LJ stated that Mann J's decision that the issue of passport fell into a wholly separate category than do these matters 'seems common sense':

> [A passport] is a familiar document to all citizens who travel in the world and it would seem obvious to me that the exercise of the prerogative ... is in an area where common sense tells one that, if for some reason a passport is wrongly refused for a bad reason, the court should be able to inquire into it.[206]

Though the conclusion is a welcome one, there is little here which sheds any light on the exact scope of the power in question, nor the particular reasons for which it is reviewable. The suggestion is often made that passports have no legal effect, being merely administrative documents which attest to one's identity and nationality. If that is correct, then it is not obvious that the issuance of a passport can represent a prerogative power, for on Wade's account, the prerogative 'consists of legal power—that is to say, the ability to alter people's rights, duties or status under the laws of this country which the courts of this country enforce'.[207] An act which does not alter such rights,

[203] In terms of extra-curial remedies, it may be noted that para 5 of Sch 3 to the Parliamentary Commissioner Act 1967 includes amongst those matters which the Commissioner may not investigate action 'taken by or with the authority of the Secretary of State for the purposes of investigating crime or of protecting the security of the State, including action so taken with respect to passports.' The recommendation of the Independent Reviewer of Terrorism Legislation that the exercise of the passport prerogative should be reviewable by him to the extent it was used in relation to terrorism was rejected by the Government in 2017: Home Secretary, *The Government Response to the Annual Report on the Operation of the Terrorism Acts in 2015 by the Independent Reviewer of Terrorism Legislation*, Cm 9489 (2017), 4–5.

[204] *Council of Civil Service Unions v Minister for the Civil Service* [1985] AC 374, 417.

[205] *R v Secretary of State for Foreign and Commonwealth Affairs, ex parte Everett* [1989] QB 811. See Robert McCorquodale, 'Prerogatives, Passports and Common Sense' (1989) 48 *CLJ* 163, 165.

[206] [1989] QB 811, 817.

[207] Wade (n 165) 58.

duties or status cannot, strictly speaking, be said to be done under the prerogative and Wade therefore suggests that this is true of passports, which have 'no status or legal effect at common law whatever'; a passport is 'simply an administrative document' which 'does not have the slightest effect upon a person's legal rights, whatever they may be, to go abroad and return.'[208] If this is correct, the Crown does not (at common law) require any legal basis for the issue or withdrawal of passports.[209] The better understanding, however, is that whether or not Wade is correct that a thing done by the executive without statutory authority is only an aspect of the prerogative if it affects legal rights, duties etc, he is wrong to think that a passport does not affect those rights and that it therefore cannot be part of the prerogative narrowly defined. We will return to this point below.

The Court of Appeal's position on the legal effect of passports in *Everett* is unclear. Taylor LJ suggests that the effect of the decision in *GCHQ* had been to create a hierarchy with, at its summit, the various non-reviewable powers, but that 'the grant or refusal of a passport is in a quite different category. It is a matter of administrative decision, affecting the rights of individuals and their freedom of travel.'[210] It had been submitted on behalf of the Secretary of State that because 'the grant of a passport involves a request in the name of the Queen to a foreign power to afford the holder free passage and protection ... [and] extends the protection and assistance of the Crown to the holder whilst he is abroad'[211] that it counted as an aspect of the foreign affairs power and so was amongst the unreviewable powers. This was rejected on the basis that the 'ready issue of a passport is a normal expectation of every citizen, unless there is good reason for making him an exception' and that the issues arising from the grant or refusal of passports 'are no more likely to have foreign policy repercussions than those arising, to take the same analogy as before, in immigration cases.'[212] Given the distinction drawn above between the portrayal of a passport as a merely administrative document and that according to which the possession of a passport directly affects the rights of the individual (rather than the ease with which those rights might be exercised), there is a significant tension evident in the description of the grant of a passport as being 'a matter of administrative decision, affecting the rights of individuals and their freedom of travel.' And while the analogy with immigration cases is a fair one—indeed, immigration decisions would seem significantly more likely to implicate foreign policy than do those about the grant of passports—the claim that the 'the ready issue of a passport is a normal expectation of every citizen' must be contrasted with the underlying legal reality that there is (as the government never misses an opportunity to reaffirm) no basis to that expectation and that there is in fact a growing number of categories of person who have can have no such expectation. *Everett* confirms, however, that decisions regarding passports are subject to judicial review. For the most part, the grounds upon which review might be sought are

[208] ibid, 63–4. See also the discussion of the prerogative in HWR Wade, 'Procedure and Prerogative in Public Law' (1985) 101 *LQR* 180. Perry agrees with Wade on this point but uses the example of passports to contest Wade's understanding of a 'legal power': Adam Perry, 'The Crown's Administrative Powers' (2015) 131 *LQR* 652, 662–3.

[209] I take this to be the correct interpretation of *Entick v Carrington* (1765) 19 St Tr 1029 and *Malone v Commissioner for the Metropolitan Police (no.2)* [1979] Ch 344. For discussion, see Ch 2.

[210] [1989] QB 811, 820.

[211] ibid.

[212] ibid.

identical to those which apply generally to the decisions of public law decision-makers.[213] Those deprived of passport facilities will therefore be able to challenge the rationality of the decision, its procedural propriety and, if the decision is considered to constitute an interference with a fundamental common law right, also its proportionality—with the extent of the interference with the protected interest measured against the benefit which results in terms of the legitimate interest which justifies that interest (here, the needs of national security). Figuring in this calculation, however, will be the 'deference' which courts show to political decision-makers in the field of national security, where great weight is given to the original assessment, which will be impugned only in the most exceptional of circumstances.[214]

There is, however, a more ambitious basis upon which the withdrawal of passports might be challenged, based upon the co-existence of the prerogative power and statute. In *XH*,[215] the claimants—both British nationals—had seen their passports cancelled on public interest grounds, and challenged the cancellation inter alia on the grounds that the TPIM Act was intended to be a comprehensive code for the regulation of the holding of passports by alleged terrorists, and so the use made of the prerogative here was unlawful in that it represented an attempt to circumvent the relative provisions of that Act (most obviously, the procedural requirements of, and limitations placed upon the use of, the power to impose a TPIM). They relied upon the well-known line of cases which establish the requirement to make use of statutory powers in preference to parallel prerogative powers,[216] and the impossibility of using the prerogative to frustrate the will of Parliament as expressed in statute,[217] or to undermine a statutory scheme.[218] There is, within the TPIM Act, no express abrogation of the prerogative as it relates to passports. Nor, however, is the prerogative expressly reserved by it, and it was argued here instead that the terms of the 2011 Act necessarily implied such abrogation. In rejecting that claim, the High Court emphasised the differing breadth of the two powers at issue: the prerogative power is available in a far greater range of circumstances than is the power to impose a TPIM, but does not include the power to withdraw a passport (only to require its surrender, in which circumstances it remains valid); TPIMs (unlike the prerogative) are subject to strict time limits, but can impose on an individual a range of measures far more draconian than are the results of the withdrawal of a passport.[219] There are, it concluded, 'major differences between the intended and actual sphere of operation of the Royal Prerogative and the TPIM Act' and that fact 'strongly militates against the suggested implication'.[220]

[213] One exception is demonstrated by the decision of the Supreme Court in *R (Sandiford) v Foreign Secretary* [2014] UKSC 44, where that court confirmed (in obiter) that the ordinary public law approach to the fettering of discretion—whereby a public law decision maker may not fetter the discretion granted by statute—does not apply to the prerogative or common law powers of the Crown.

[214] That the deference shown by the judiciary nevertheless represents an evolution of (and improvement on) the historic position is argued by Aileen Kavanagh, 'Constitutionalism, counterterrorism, and the courts: Changes in the British constitutional landscape' (2011) 9 *ICON* 172.

[215] *R (XH and AI) v Secretary of State for the Home Department* [2016] EWHC 1898 (Admin) and, on appeal, [2017] EWCA Civ 41.

[216] *Attorney-General v De Keyser's Royal Hotel* [1920] AC 508.

[217] *R v Secretary of State for the Home Department, ex p Fire Brigades Union* [1995] 2 AC 513.

[218] *Laker Airways v Department of Trade* [1977] QB 643.

[219] [2016] EWHC 1898 (Admin), [43]–[66].

[220] ibid, [65].

The claim that the prerogative had been impliedly abrogated therefore failed, as it should have: it was clearly not the intention of Parliament, in enacting the 2011 Act, to detract in any way from the Crown's prerogative powers as regards passports, and there is ample space for the two regimes to coexist. *XH* nevertheless brings home the extent to which the existence of multiple statutory regimes relevant to the possession (broadly understood) of passports unacceptably complicates the legal regulation thereof. There are many good arguments in favour of putting in place a statutory framework for the grant of passports. Nor is there any reason to believe that such a statute would not be able to replicate the grounds upon which passports currently might be withdrawn or refused in the public interest—albeit that placing these rules on a statutory basis would deprive the executive of the ability to unilaterally and without notice alter those grounds—nor, in and of itself, increase the opportunities for challenge to grant and refusal of passports which, after all, is already challengeable on ECHR and EU law grounds, as well as on normal common law principles of review. The arguments against such a course of action would seem to rely heavily upon executive convenience (which does not weigh strongly against giving to such an important area of law a clear and coherent framework) and, perhaps, upon the fact that to transpose the legal regime into statute would involve either instituting a legal right to a passport or making clear to the public that they have no such right and justifying that state of affairs; making explicit, that is, that the 'normal expectation of every citizen' referred to in *Everett* has no basis in law. Considered from the executive's point of view, it is easy to see why the flexibility and obscurity of the prerogative is preferred.

There is, however, a further reason for which it may be not merely desirable but rather necessary to place the passports regime on a statutory footing. The argument in *XH* regarding the abrogation of the prerogative power was a limited and well-focussed one, and yet failed. For that reason (amongst others) it may seem futile to propose a more far-reaching challenge to the withdrawal of passports on the basis of the interaction of statute and prerogative, and yet such an argument deserves to be made. It begins from the observations made above regarding the artificiality of the claim that passports have no legal effect (being merely an administrative document with which one proves one's nationality) and therefore that their withdrawal does not interfere with one's rights, but merely renders more difficult their exercise. A better view is that the withdrawal of a person's passport so disrupts his or her ability to exercise certain rights that to claim that he or she continues nevertheless to possess them is not much more than verbal trickery. We noted above the claim in *Everett* that the grant of a passport is a matter 'affecting the rights of individuals and their freedom of travel.' More recently, it has been recognised that the withdrawal of a passport engages free movement rights under EU law. In *MR*,[221] for example, the government had originally sought to argue that the cancellation of a passport did not engage free movement rights under the Citizens Directive but ultimately did not do so. This was the correct approach, said Ouseley J, for '[i]t is obvious that they do':

> After all, the avowed aim of the cancellation was to make it very difficult for MR to travel abroad, and it is clear that it would have that effect. Although an identity card or other means of proving

[221] *R (MR) v Secretary of State for the Home Department* [2016] EWHC 1622 (Admin).

> nationality can be used, the UK does not issue identity cards for the purpose of proving nationality; and a UK citizen relying on other means of proving nationality than a passport will encounter difficulties in air and Eurostar travel …[222]

It seems equally true, however, that the withdrawal of a passport restricts the right to travel—to enter and exit the UK—which is the key adjunct of the statutory right of abode which a British passport holder (who must be a British citizen) by definition enjoys. Where a passport is withdrawn, therefore, the prerogative is being used to disrupt, if not entirely to negate, a statutory right as well as an EU law right, and it is well-established law that to use the prerogative in that manner is not permitted.[223] Though the courts would, I recognise, be very slow to endorse this claim, the 1971 Act should therefore be taken to abrogate the prerogative to the extent that the prerogative might otherwise be used in order to limit one's ability to enter and exit the UK. That is, a statutory passport regime is not merely desirable from a point of view of principle (all citizens should have an enforceable right to a passport) and procedure (the redefinition of the criteria for the grant and refusal of a passport should not be subject to unilateral redefinition by the executive of the day) but also, on this view, necessary as a matter of law, at least to the extent that the executive wishes to refuse or withdraw passports: to do so constitutes an interference with a statutory right of abode for which statutory authority is (or should be) required and for which the prerogative does not, it is submitted, suffice. This answers too Wade's claim as to passports and the prerogative: the better view is that the issuance and withdrawal of passports *does* affect legal rights, and so is a genuine example of a prerogative power even on Wade's restrictive understanding.

Even if such a claim is not accepted, the common law grounds of judicial review do not exhaust the possible bases of challenge to executive acts such as one by which a passport is refused or withdrawn: the European Convention Human Rights is also relevant to the domestic regulation of passports. Article 2 of Protocol 4 to the Convention provides that 'Everyone shall be free to leave any country, including his own' and that 'No restrictions shall be placed on the exercise of these rights other than such as are in accordance with law and are necessary in a democratic society in the interests of national security or public safety, for the maintenance of public order, for the prevention of crime, for the protection of health or morals, or for the protection of the rights and freedoms of others.' In *Kerimli v Azerbaijan*,[224] the Strasbourg Court held that it was this rather than Article 8 which was the proper basis of an applicant's challenge to Azerbaijan's refusal to issue him a new passport where there was a criminal prosecution pending against him. The Court accepted that the refusal 'amounted to a measure restricting his right to leave the country'[225] and held that, because there was no opportunity for re-examination of the justification for refusing the applicant passport facilities, the 'de facto travel ban imposed on the applicant by

[222] [2016] EWHC 1622 (Admin), [15]–[16]. See also *R (XH and AI) v Secretary of State for the Home Department* [2017] EWCA Civ 41, [108]: 'the cancellation of his passport is undoubtedly, and is intended to be, a substantial interference with XH's freedom of movement.'

[223] Though, as noted above, the 1971 Act preserves the prerogative, it does so only insofar as it relates to aliens, and so the saving provision cannot be used to counter the argument made here.

[224] (2016) 62 EHRR 15.

[225] ibid, [47].

way of refusing him a new passport constituted, in reality, an automatic, blanket measure of indefinite duration.'[226] It was therefore disproportionate and for that reason breached Article 2(2).[227] This follows from the Court's earlier assertion that 'any measure on the basis of which an individual is deprived of an identity document such as, for example, a passport, can be seen, without a doubt, as interference in the exercise of one's liberty of movement.'[228] The UK, however, has not ratified Protocol 4—on the basis that Articles 2 and 3 'could be taken, respectively, to confer rights in relation to passports and a right of abode on categories of British nationals who do not currently have that right'[229]—and so nor are the rights in it incorporated into domestic law via the Human Rights Act.[230]

This does not, however, end the question. In *Iletmis v Turkey*,[231] the applicant—a Turk living in Germany—had, while on a trip back to Turkey, his passport confiscated by national authorities, who did not return it until the conclusion of the trial many years later. The Court here was heavily influenced, it seems, by the close personal ties between the applicant and Turkey (which had not ratified Protocol 4), holding that 'the confiscation by the administrative authorities of the applicant's passport and their failure to return it to him for a number of years amount to an interference with the applicant's exercise of his right to respect for his private life.'[232] Because of the ongoing failure of the Turkish authorities to offer evidence of a threat to national security, it became clear that the effective prohibition on leaving the country no longer constituted a 'pressing social need' and so was a disproportionate and hence unjustified interference with the applicant's Article 8 rights.[233] Alongside the particular factual circumstances of the applicant (whose personal and family situation meant that the confiscation of his passport cause him particular difficulty) the Court emphasised that because 'freedom of movement, particularly across borders, is considered essential to the full development of a person's private life ... family, professional and economic ties in several countries, for a state to deprive a person under its jurisdiction of that freedom for no reason is a serious breach of its obligations.'[234] The effect of this is that at least in some cases the decision to withdraw or refuse a passport can be challenged on ECHR grounds in domestic courts via section 6 of the Human Rights Act 1998 and in the Strasbourg Court itself. Whether or not the challenge is likely to succeed will turn on questions of necessity and, particularly, proportionality. On this point, there is a limit to the utility of an analogy between deprivation on national security grounds and those aimed at ensuring an individual does not flee to avoid a criminal trial—in the former case, there is no particular reason to believe that the danger will pass and so the withdrawal or refusal of a passport might result in an individual being deprived of passport facilities indefinitely and yet nevertheless be considered a proportionate interference. The range of cases in which

[226] ibid, [56].

[227] ibid, [57]. See also *Földes and Földesné Hajlik v Hungary* (2008) 47 EHRR 11.

[228] *Baumann v France* (2002) 34 EHRR 44, [62].

[229] Department for Constitutional Affairs, *Report on the UK Government's Inter-Departmental Review of the UK's Position under various International Human Rights Instruments*, July 2004, cited in Joint Committee on Human Rights, *Review of International Human Rights Instruments* (2004–05, HL 99, HC 264) [37].

[230] Human Rights Act 1998, s 1.

[231] (2011) 52 EHRR 35.

[232] ibid, [42].

[233] ibid, [46]–[50].

[234] ibid, [50].

this analysis would even be required, however, depends on how the Court of Human Rights in future cases weighs up the different factors to which it made reference when holding that Article 8 was engaged in the Turkish case. If the emphasis is placed on the possession of personal individual ties to a foreign state, there may be many cases in which an individual is deprived of a passport without Article 8 being engaged; if, instead, its more general remarks about the centrality of international travel are given priority, most if not all withdrawals of passport facilities will be required to satisfy a proportionality analysis. Finally, and as has been noted above, it is now clear that the cancellation or withdrawal of a passport engages EU law and so must meet the substantive and procedural safeguards which it imposes.[235]

F. 'Authority to Carry'

The argument offered above as regards the need to have statutory authority for any interference with the right of abode—with all the consequences that would entail for the legality of the passport regime as it currently is operated—is supported by a consideration of what are known in the UK as 'authority to carry' (ATC) schemes but which are elsewhere called, more helpfully, 'no fly lists'.[236] ATC schemes augment schemes which make 'carriers' (those who transport persons into the UK) liable for certain activities in the sphere of immigration generally, including two schemes found within the Immigration and Asylum Act 1999. The first provides for the imposition of penalties[237] upon the owner of a ship or aircraft which brings to the UK a person who requires leave to enter it but who fails, upon arrival, to produce either an immigration document (which will usually be a passport)[238] 'which is in force and which satisfactorily establishes his identity and his nationality or citizenship' or any visa which is required.[239] The effect is that such people will not normally be able to arrive in the UK through legal means at all.[240] The second scheme attempts, conversely, to deal with illegal means of entry, by imposing penalties upon those found to have transported to the UK 'clandestine entrants'.[241] These powers nevertheless leave a gap which the ATC schemes seek to fill: 'despite the existence of an order excluding or deporting a person from the UK or the existence of an UN or EU travel ban, an individual who does not require a visa for the UK and who poses a terrorist threat may still be able to travel' because the carrier who transports them to the UK 'will not

[235] See, most fully, *R (XH and AI) v Secretary of State for the Home Department* [2017] EWCA Civ 41, [107]–[155].

[236] For a fuller consideration of which, see Paul F Scott, 'Authority to carry in the United Kingdom: the right to travel, the privatisation of security and the rule of law' (2017) *European Public Law* 787.

[237] Immigration and Asylum Act 1999, s 40(2).

[238] ibid, s 40(9).

[239] ibid, s 40(1). There exists a statutory defence in circumstances can be shown by the owner to 'have produced the required document or documents … when embarking on the ship or aircraft for the voyage or flight to the United Kingdom' but the defence will fail where either the document's falsity or the fact that it does not relate to the person who produces it, is 'reasonably apparent': s 40(4) and (5).

[240] This has particular stark effect on those who may, if they are able to arrive in the UK, have a valid claim to asylum: see, in relation to a previous regime, Anne Ruff, 'The Immigration (Carriers' Liability) Act 1987', [1989] *PL* 222 and Frances Nicholson, 'Implementation of the Immigration (Carriers' Liability) Act 1987: privatising immigration functions at the expense of international obligations?' (1987) *ICLQ* 586.

[241] Immigration and Asylum Act 1999, ss 32–39.

always be aware of an exclusion or deportation order or travel ban and so would not be in a position to deny boarding.'[242]

ATC schemes were originally legislated for within the Nationality, Immigration and Asylum Act 2002,[243] on the authority of which there were made—a decade later—regulations for the enforcement of the scheme.[244] Crucially, however, though the 2002 Act recognised the potential existence of such a scheme ('An "authority-to-carry scheme" is a scheme operated by the Secretary of State which requires carriers to seek authority to bring passengers to the United Kingdom'),[245] regulated its contents (both mandatorily and discretionarily),[246] and required that the scheme was laid before Parliament,[247] it did not in the first place empower the creation of the scheme, raising rule of law issues of the sort we considered in Chapter 3 in relation to investigatory powers. The scheme itself, therefore, was made by virtue of what implicitly purported to be a purely administrative act, the publication of 'The Security and Travel Bans Authority to Carry Scheme 2012', laid before Parliament in 2012.[248] It applied to third-country nationals, EEA nationals (and accompanying third country nationals) who were subject to exclusion or deportation orders on public security grounds, and '[i]ndividuals listed by the United Nations or European Union as being subject to travel restrictions due to their association with Al Qaeda or the Taliban.'[249] The scheme identified also those in respect of whom authority to carry would be refused, the common thread running through the categories being the needs of national security.[250] Crucially, however, other EEA nationals were not covered; nor were British nationals. This was not a coincidence: to make British nationals subject to the scheme would potentially result in interferences with their right of abode, of a sort which requires clear (statutory) authority. The 2002 Act did not provide such authority and so could not be used to subvert the right of abode: indeed, it affirmed that '[t]he grant or refusal of authority under an authority-to-carry scheme shall not be taken to determine whether a person is entitled or permitted to enter the United Kingdom'.[251] If this interpretation of the reasons for which the 2012 scheme took the form that it did, it provides further support for believing that to withdraw passports on the basis of the prerogative is impermissible as a matter of law: the withdrawal of a passport represents at least as much of an interference with the (exercise of) the right of abode as does the refusal of authority to carry in respect of a given person, yet as was previously the case with ATC schemes, there exists no statutory authority for that withdrawal. For the imposition of financial penalties upon carriers—which also constitutes an interference with legal rights—clear authority was found in the 2002 Act.[252]

[242] Home Office, *Authority to Carry Scheme 2015* (March 2015), [4].
[243] Nationality, Immigration and Asylum Act 2002, s 124.
[244] The Nationality, Immigration and Asylum Act 2002 (Authority to Carry) Regulations 2012 (SI 2012/2894).
[245] NIAA 2002, s 124(2).
[246] ibid, s 124(3).
[247] ibid, s 124(5).
[248] Home Office, *The Security and Travel Bans Authority to Carry Scheme 2012* (November 2012).
[249] Home Office (n 248) [12].
[250] ibid [15].
[251] NIAA 2002, s 124(8).
[252] ibid, s 124(1).

This claim is strengthened further by the changes which have occurred since the introduction of the original 2012 scheme. The statutory framework is now provided by the Counter-Terrorism and Security Act 2015, which explicitly permits the Secretary of State to make 'authority to carry' schemes, and permits such schemes to be made in relation to carriers both arriving in and departing from the UK.[253] Such a scheme may apply to specified forms of transport or to all carriers, and must give details of those in respect of whom authority must be sought—which may be all persons or 'or may be defined by reference to nationality, the possession of specified documents or otherwise'—and details of those in respect of whom authority to carry may be refused.[254] A person or class of persons may be specified within a given scheme only if to do so 'is necessary in the public interest.'[255] Though this is not how the scheme has in fact been used, the formulation of the provision is such that on its face it could be used in order to implement a scheme which identified only certain nationalities (or worse—there is nothing in the act itself which would prevent the scheme's application to be defined by race or religion), and so constitute an interference with Article 8 of the ECHR (as read together with Article 14), the proportionality of which the courts might be required to determine. The scheme must also set out details of its own procedure, which may include: requirements for: carriers to provide information in advance of travel and in a specified manner and form; and 'for carriers to be able to receive, in a specified manner and form, communications from the Secretary of State relating to the information provided or granting or refusing authority to carry.'[256] Schemes are brought into force by regulations made via the affirmative resolution procedure.[257] Regulations providing for the penalties which apply to breach of authority to carry schemes may also be made under the authority of the Act,[258] and such regulations have in fact been made.[259] They permit the imposition of fines of up to £50,000 for breach of the requirements of an ATC scheme made under the Act—not only the carrying of those in respect of whom authority has been refused, but also the failure to seek such authority and to provide passenger details by a specified time before travel, and in a specified manner and form.[260] The mere prospect of incurring such a penalty will of course be sufficient to motivate compliance with the requirements, and to err—in any marginal cases—upon the side of caution. This coercive apparatus effectively enlists carriers as agents of the state's national security apparatus.

Because the 2015 Act provides the sort of clear statutory authority which the 2002 Act did not, it appears to be lawful to use it to limit the right of British citizens to enter or exit the country: something which if done under the 2002 Act would probably have been unlawful and so was in fact not done. Nevertheless, there remains a question as to whether or not the 2015 Act suffices to meet the requirements of the rule in *Thoburn* for

[253] Counter-Terrorism and Security Act 2015, s 22(1).
[254] ibid, s 22(2).
[255] ibid, s 22(3).
[256] ibid, s 22(5).
[257] ibid, s 23.
[258] ibid, s 24.
[259] The Authority to Carry Scheme (Civil Penalties) Regulations 2015 (SI 2015/957).
[260] ibid.

the repeal (which cannot be implied but only ever explicit) of 'constitutional statutes'.[261] The particular difficulty which arises is that, notwithstanding the clear statutory authority for the making of an ATC scheme, the 2015 Act follows its predecessor in denying that ATC impacts upon the legal rights of individuals, providing that the 'grant or refusal of authority under an authority-to-carry scheme does not determine whether a person is entitled or permitted to enter the United Kingdom.'[262] If the 2015 Act is intended to provide suitably explicit authority for the making of a scheme that in effect limits the right of abode, this provision would seem to prevent it from fulfilling that aim. More than that, however, it is simply unrealistic, making use of a distinction between the strict legal rights of the individual (which may well be unaffected) and the practical reality in which a person in respect of whom authority to carry is refused will only be able to enter the UK if he or she can do so without the involvement of carriers to whom the scheme applies. A person who is entitled to enter the UK but who cannot do so is (for however short the relevant period) in a situation little better than is a person who is not entitled to enter it. This is consistent with the fact that—notwithstanding that the 2015 Act, like the 2002 Act before it, denies that ATC schemes made under it alter the legal right of individuals—the content of the specific scheme which has in fact been implemented under the 2015 Act clearly reflect the more solid legal base that statute gives it.

In March 2015, under the authority of the newly enacted statute, regulations were made,[263] (which expire after seven years)[264] bringing into force a new ATC scheme ('the 2015 scheme') which was laid before Parliament on 2 March 2015, and which came into force alongside the regulations at the end of that month. As such, though Parliament approved the regulations bringing the scheme into force rather than the scheme, it was in a position (at least as a matter of theory) to scrutinise the scheme before doing so. Where that which it replaced was limited in those passengers to whom it applied, the 2015 scheme applies to 'all passengers and crew travelling, or expected to travel, to or from the UK on a class of carrier to which this scheme applies, except for carriers providing information voluntarily [in which case] this Scheme applies to all passengers and crew in respect of whom information is provided.'[265] In practice, it appears that essentially all carriers will be required to provide information, making the application of the new scheme more or less universal both as regards carriers and as regards their passengers.[266] No longer are British

[261] Again, on the assumption that the Immigration Act 1971 meets Laws LJ's criteria of either 'condition[ing] the legal relationship between citizen and state in some general, overarching, manner' or 'enlarge[ing] or diminish[ing] the scope of what we would now regard as fundamental constitutional rights': *Thoburn v Sunderland City Council* [2002] EWHC 195 (Admin), [62].

[262] Counter-Terrorism and Security Act 2015, s 22(7). Though the scheme now also applies to passengers departing the UK, the right to do which is similarly an aspect of the right of abode, the Count-terrorism and Security Act 2015 offers no such disclaimer in relation thereto.

[263] The Counter-Terrorism and Security Act 2015 (Authority to Carry Scheme) Regulations 2015 (SI 2015/997).

[264] ibid, reg 1(3).

[265] *Authority to Carry Scheme 2015* (n 242), [13].

[266] The carriers mandated to supply information (those who must supply information about all passengers and crew rather than some portion thereof) are 'all carriers operating to and from the UK that have been required by the Secretary of State or an immigration officer under paragraph 27 and 27B of Schedule 2 to the Immigration Act 1971 or by a police officer under section 32 of the Immigration, Asylum and Nationality Act 2006, to submit information comprising passenger or crew information.' *Authority to Carry Scheme 2015* (n 242), [10].

(and EEA) nationals excluded, suggesting—rightly or wrongly, and despite the protestations of the 2015 Act—a belief that the 2015 Act is capable of doing something that the 2002 Act was not: carrying out an interference with the rights of abode of those who possess it by virtue of the Immigration Act 1971. Refusal of authority to carry may not 'determine whether a person is entitled or permitted to enter the United Kingdom' but it will stop them in fact entering the UK, and for that clear statutory authority is required. Given this context, I submit once more that the withdrawal of a passport (which will have similar effect) requires statutory authority of a sort which does not currently exist.[267]

VI. Conclusion

The manner in which the state seeks to counteract threats to national security reflects at a very fundamental level the distinction between those who 'belong' to it and those who do not. What we have seen in this chapter is, first of all, the way in which that distinction is made operational in the use of the law of immigration as a tool of national security. Here, the bare existence of the power in question is not contested: nevertheless, the broad terms in which the statutory power of deportation (and corresponding non-statutory power of exclusion) are couched are one possible source of concern, with the executive having made full use of the resulting flexibility in recent years. From the point of view of substance, more concerning is the body of law which permits individuals to be moved from one of the categories Blackstone identified into the other; to be stripped of citizenship and with it their right of abode, so as to become subject to immigration controls, deportation and exclusion and so on. Here, the law has evolved rapidly in the post-11 September period, with the scope for deprivation expanded and certain procedural changes made which significantly limit the possibility of successfully challenging the decision to denaturalise an individual. Even the evolving substance of the law, however, is less significant than are the changes in the practice associated with it, both in terms of the much greater use of the power which has been made (particularly since 2010) and the tendency to deprive of citizenship individuals who are outside the country and for whom the procedural elements of an appeal become an even greater impediment. This expansion in the use of the relevant powers is evident also in the context of the refusal or withdrawal of passports, acts which—despite the growing range of statutory powers available in relation to passports—continue to take place, it is

[267] Indeed, the 2015 scheme provides that one of the categories of person in relation to whom authority to carry *from* the UK may be refused is those 'in respect of whom the Secretary of State has cancelled a passport issued to the person or has not issued a passport on the basis that the person to whom the passport was issued or who applied for the passport has or may have been, or will or may become, involved in activities so undesirable that it is contrary to the public interest for the person to have access to passport facilities.' The existence of this category further undermines the claim that the withdrawal of a passport does not affect one's rights—though the 1971 Act leaves open the possibility that a person whose passport has been withdrawn might meet offer other documentation to satisfy the requirements of an inspection by an immigration officer, that person's formal legal right to exit the country will be of even less value if carriers are liable to be refused authority to take him or her out of the country (and face a significant fine for doing so without authority).

claimed, under the prerogative. The argument made above is that withdrawal of passports under the prerogative, pace William Wade, does in fact alter the rights of individuals, for a passport is in effect a *sine qua non* of the exercise of the rights to enter and exit the UK which are key elements of the right of abode granted to citizens by statute. For that reason, the withdrawal of a passport should not be possible under the prerogative: the Immigration Act 1971 should be taken to have abrogated the prerogative to the extent it may historically have permitted acts incompatible with the right of abode.

5

Secrecy

I. Secrecy in the National Security Constitution

National security relies upon secrecy: secrecy as to those things which might be the target of terrorist activities, at home and abroad, secrecy as to the methods and the strategy of the executive in combatting the various threats, secrecy—sometimes—as to the very content of legal rules themselves.[1] Alongside the older mechanisms of secrecy already established in the UK's constitutional order—many of which have played only small roles in the modern national security constitution—recent decades have seen national security concerns encourage the development of a new body of law which balances the constitutional principle of open justice against the need to ensure that certain information is not disclosed as part of the functioning of the legal process. That body of law—involving the introduction of the closed material procedure (CMP),[2] its spread to a number of other contexts,[3] and its becoming available in civil proceedings generally[4]—augments the older law of public interest immunity (PII). The employment of administrative processes (deportation, indefinite detention without trial, Control Orders, Terrorist Prevention and Investigation Measures) in addressing terrorism, at least in respect of those whose prosecution is rendered difficult or impossible by the effective inadmissibility of intercept evidence,[5] has meant that questions of open justice arise less frequently in the criminal than the civil context, though—as we shall see below—they do indeed sometimes arise there.

This chapter in its first part maps the mechanisms used in order to preserve secrecy within the legal process in relation to the constitutional principles which apply to, and are applied by, the courts: primarily those of open and natural justice. Its argument is, in the first place, that the growth of secrecy in the constitutional order has been substantial—the forms of secrecy, the circumstances to which they apply, and the frequency with which

[1] In the American context, see Dakota S Rudesill, 'Coming to Terms with Secret Law' (2015) *Harvard National Security Journal* 241. Though the nature of 'secret law' is such that one cannot be sure it does not exist, the phenomenon of legal rules which 'require compliance that are classified or otherwise withheld from the public' (249) does not seem to have a direct analogue in the UK, where instead the closest equivalent is, it would seem, the substantial use of made of broad and relatively obscure provisions of statute—see, ie, the discussion of s 94 of the Telecommunications Act 1984, discussed in Ch 2—and the strained and potentially unpredictable interpretations given to openly accessible and well-known provisions: see, eg, the use of s 5 of the Intelligence Services Act 1994 to ground 'thematic' warrants.

[2] Special Immigration Appeals Commission Act 1997.

[3] Anti-terrorism, Crime and Security Act 2001; Prevention of Terrorism Act 2005.

[4] Justice and Security Act 2013.

[5] Regulation of Investigatory Powers Act 2000, ss 17 and 18.

they are invoked, all suggest that the secrecy of justice is perhaps the defining feature of the national security constitution. Moreover, the new and renewed mechanisms of secrecy have repeatedly spread beyond the context which first justified (or was used to justify) their introduction, with the general availability of closed material procedures under the Justice and Security Act 2013 simply accelerating that process. Nevertheless, the growth of secrecy is not a wholly malign change: where mechanisms of secrecy are employed in courts, they are often employed not in relation to judicial processes which would otherwise have taken place openly, but rather processes which in the past were either carried out non-judicially, or not at all. The increased level of secrecy within the legal process is in part, therefore, a function of the constitutionalisation of national security; the work which has been done in subjecting otherwise extra-legal or extra-judicial processes to the dictates of legal rules, in a manner which reflects basic requirements of legality, and thus the oversight of the courts. This does not of course justify complacency: the growth of secrecy is, or will soon be, far beyond what has yet been shown to be necessary, and has too often become something resembling the default approach of both the courts and Parliament. Nevertheless, we must take care, as far as it is practical to do so, to distinguish forms of secrecy which—however unattractive—are preferable to the alternative, from those which are unnecessary, or which come at too high a constitutional price. The second part considers (some of) the mechanisms which exist in order to ensure secrecy within the operation of the executive branch, and the reasons for which these have largely been less prominent within the modern national security constitution.

II. Secrecy in the Courts

The mechanisms under discussion in this chapter often—though not, as we shall see below, inevitably—involve a departure from the constitutional principle of open justice. The classic statement of that principle is found in *Scott v Scott*,[6] in which the House of Lords held that the Divorce Court had no power to hear the case in private, describing its decision to do so as 'a violation of that publicity in the administration of justice which is one of the surest guarantees of our liberties, and an attack upon the very foundations of public and private security.'[7] The general rule, 'since 1857, unquestioned by anything I recognise as an authority' was, according to Lord Halsbury, that 'every Court of justice is open to every subject of the King.'[8] And though the Lord Chancellor, Viscount Haldane, was willing to countenance departures from open justice where necessary, he emphasised that to do so would be permissible only where necessary to do justice; the matter was 'by no means one which, consistently with the spirit of our jurisprudence, can be dealt with by the judge as resting in his mere discretion as to what is expedient.'[9] Lord Halsbury doubted even that, wanting an appropriate case brought before him before he was willing to endorse the possibility.[10]

[6] [1913] AC 417.
[7] ibid, 476.
[8] ibid, 440.
[9] ibid, 438.
[10] ibid, 442

Time has furnished numerous examples of the sort Lord Halsbury sought, and Viscount Haldane's less sceptical but nonetheless firm approach has been that which has stuck. Case after case confirms a tripartite position: the importance of the principle of open justice, the possibility of departing from it where doing justice demands, and the need to limit any departure to the minimum necessary to do justice.[11] The somewhat perverse effect is that often no sooner is judicial homage paid to open justice than some action inconsistent with it is taken.

The reasons for and nature of the various departures evidenced in the law reports are multifarious. In *Attorney General v Leveller Magazine*,[12] the House of Lords by a majority upheld an order made by magistrates in the course of a trial under the Official Secrets Acts which permitted a witness to be described as 'Colonel B' and for his real name to be made known only to the court, the defendants and their counsel. Magazines which had published his name were not, however, guilty of contempt of court in interfering with the due administration of justice because they had deduced the Colonel's name from information he had provided in open court and which had not been protested by either the court or the prosecution. Though Lord Edmund-Davies, dissenting, doubted that the court had the power to make an order to the public at large prohibiting publication of information and the violation of which would automatically constitute a contempt,[13] even he had no difficulty with the making of the original order, claiming that '[i]t is beyond doubt that a court has a wide inherent jurisdiction to control its own procedure. In certain circumstances it may decide to sit wholly or in part in camera.'[14] This line of authority extends to the present day. In *Bank Mellat (No. 1)*,[15] Lord Neuberger reasserted that courts possess an 'inherent power to receive evidence and argument in a hearing from which the public and the press are excluded' and can 'even give a judgment which is only available to the parties'. There are, however, tightly drawn limits:

> Such a course may only be taken (i) if it is strictly necessary to have a private hearing in order to achieve justice between the parties, and, (ii) if the degree of privacy is kept to an absolute minimum.[16]

One important example is the 'trial within a trial' in which the admissibility of evidence is determined. Victims of blackmail are anonymised so as to encourage their coming forward in aid of legal proceedings.[17] Other potentially relevant cases include those 'where children are involved, where threatened breaches of privacy are being alleged, and where commercially valuable secret information is in issue.'[18] Where the test is met, the derogation from open justice is not in the court's discretion but mandatory.[19]

[11] See, eg, *re K (infants)* [1965] AC 201 and *Attorney General v Leveller Magazine Ltd* [1979] AC 440.
[12] [1979] AC 440.
[13] [1979] AC 440, 464.
[14] ibid.
[15] *Bank Mellat v Her Majesty's Treasury (No. 1)* [2013] UKSC 38.
[16] [2013] UKSC 38, [2] citing *A v Independent News & Media Ltd* [2010] EWCA Civ 343 and *JIH v News Group Newspapers Ltd* [2011] EWCA Civ 42,
[17] See, eg, *R v Socialist Worker Printers and Publishers Ltd, ex parte Attorney-General* [1975] QB 637.
[18] *Bank Mellat v Her Majesty's Treasury (no. 1)* [2013] UKSC 38, [2] per Lord Neuberger. See also *A v BBC* [2014] UKSC 25, [29].
[19] *AMM v HXW* [2010] EWHC 2457 (QB), [34].

As we shall see below, the possibility of departures from open justice is bounded, most importantly, by the requirement to act consistently with the rules of natural justice. The constitutional order thus represents a clear hierarchical relationship between the two; natural justice is valued more highly than open justice, with the ability to violate the latter limited precisely by the impossibility of violating the latter. Three points might be made about this position. The first is that to state it thus risks misrepresenting the relationship between the doing of justice and the rules of natural justice: better to consider the rules of natural justice as representing an element of justice itself (rather than, as with the principle of open justice, some derivative thereof). What is really being said, therefore, is that justice cannot require the doing of injustice. The second is that this position is of course limited to situations in which there is no statutory authority for the doing of injustice: leaving aside the position under the European Convention on Human Rights, it is clear that if Parliament is sovereign—if it can make any law whatsoever—then it can legislate to permit, or even require, the doing of injustice. If it has done so only in limited circumstances, that is not because of any legal obstacle, but because to do so will usually be politically intolerable. The third point is substantive. To make a claim about the constitutional significance of the principle of natural justice requires some certainty about what that principle entails. We shall encounter below a variety of acts or mechanisms which the courts have held to be incompatible with natural justice. The only point that requires to be made here—which structures much of the discussion—is that it is tempting, but wrong, to take a formalistic approach to natural justice; to say that justice is done when an equality of arms is maintained as between the parties, but not done when that equality of arms is subverted. My claim here is that such formalism is misleading; that injustice can be done without there existing any inequality of arms as between the parties.

A. Public Interest Immunity

Before the changes described below, the most prominent mechanism for ensuring secrecy in the courts was the law of public interest immunity (PII)—what was previously called 'Crown privilege'—whereby sensitive material is not disclosed within the judicial process and no party is permitted to rely upon it. The most significant feature of PII in the contemporary national security constitution, however, has been its inability to cope with the demands placed upon courts by the litigation arising out of the UK's misadventures abroad.

i. PII and its Development Over Time

When the Crown Proceedings Act 1947 put in place for the first time the rule that 'the Crown may be required by the court to make discovery of documents and produce documents for inspection' that provision was subject to 'any rule of law which authorises or requires the withholding of any document or the refusal to answer any question on the ground that the disclosure of the document or the answering of the question would be injurious to the public interest.'[20] In the period before 1947, the law on Crown privilege

[20] Crown Proceedings Act 1947, s 28.

had demonstrated a tendency to expand beyond what was justifiable by reference even to a generous reading of the public interest.[21] This was true both in terms of those things for which the privilege came to be routinely claimed, but also in terms of specific uses. In the former category, Harry Street identified the claiming of privilege for official reports which formed the basis of libel claims and in relation to the medical reports of soldiers in divorce cases;[22] in the latter, he cites the example of *West v West*,[23] 'an action against a father-in-law whose allegedly slanderous conversations with the Lord Chamberlain about the plaintiff had caused her no longer to be invited to court balls'[24] in which the claim of privilege was upheld by the court. The high-point of Crown privilege came in *Duncan v Cammell Laird*, arising out of the sinking in 1939 of HMS Thetis during submergence tests in Liverpool Bay, with the loss of 99 lives.[25] When a civil claim was brought against the contractors who had constructed the submarine, the claimants sought production of a number of documents, including the plans for its construction, only to be met with an affidavit signed by the First Lord of the Admiralty opining that 'it would be injurious to the public interest that any of the said documents should be disclosed to any person'.[26] When this claim of privilege was challenged to the House of Lords, the Law Lords resolved conflicting dicta as to the correct approach of the courts when faced with a claim of privilege by unanimously holding that a Ministerial certificate asserting, in relation to certain material or documents, that the balance of the public interest lay in their non-disclosure, was dispositive of the issue.[27] The Lord Chancellor, Lord Simon, held that 'the rule that the interest of the State must not be put in jeopardy by producing documents which would injure it is a principle to be observed in administering justice' and was, in fact 'a rule on which the judge should, if necessary, insist, even though no objection is taken at all.[28] He gave as examples of possible such circumstances 'where disclosure would be injurious to national defence, or to good diplomatic relations or where the practice of keeping a class of documents secret is necessary for the proper functioning of the public service'.[29] This recognises the possibility both of 'contents claims'—where the content of a specific document renders its non-disclosure necessary—and that of 'class claims'—where the document belongs to a class which must, as a whole, not be disclosed, regardless of whether the specific contents of any document within the class are in fact sensitive.

The correctness of the *Duncan* judgment has been (very strongly) contested on a number of bases, including the alleged misuse of both Scottish and English precedent,[30] and the

[21] See, for context, Joseph M Jacob, 'From Privileged Crown to Interested Public' [1993] *PL* 121.

[22] Harry Street, 'State Secrets: A Comparative Study' (1951) 14 *MLR* 121, 128–9.

[23] *West v West* (1911) 27 TLR 476.

[24] Street (n 22) 128. The case is discussed by David Williams an example of a failed attempt to evade Crown privilege by 'calling some official as a witness and seeking to elicit in oral examination what could not be obtained by the disclosure of documents': *Not in the Public Interest: The Problem of Security in Democracy* (London, Hutchinson and Co, 1965) 202.

[25] *Duncan v Cammell Laird* [1942] AC 624. For the decision on the substance of the claim, see *Woods v Duncan* [1946] AC 401.

[26] [1942] AC 624, 626–7.

[27] ibid, 638–43.

[28] ibid, 642.

[29] ibid. Williams (n 24) 194 notes that these final words 'must rank among the more imprecise utterances of English judges'.

[30] D H Clark, 'Administrative Control of Judicial Action: The Authority of Duncan v Cammell Laird' (1967) 30 *MLR* 289.

mismatch between the invocation of national security in the case and what the historical record suggests was the reality of the situation.[31] In any event, the rule it established, forged in a time of national peril, did not long persist. In *Conway v Rimmer* it was held—contrary to what had been said in *Duncan*—that the courts in fact were to decide for themselves whether or not the balance of the public interest is as the Ministerial certificate which underlies a claim of public interest immunity claims it to be.[32] In this period, the name of Crown privilege was mostly abandoned, to be replaced by the modern language of PII,[33] on the basis that 'it is not a matter of privilege and it is not confined to the Crown.'[34] Subsequent case law confirms both that the PII need not be made by an organ of the state[35]—indeed, 'it must always be open to any person interested to raise the question and there may be cases where the trial judge should himself raise the question if no one else has done so'[36]—and that, though the usual practice is for PII claims to be made in the form of a Ministerial certificate (accompanied, if necessary, by a closed annex), such a claim might be upheld where no such certificate exists.[37]

Following the acceptance of executive supremacy in *Duncan* and its subsequent rejection in *Conway v Rimmer*,[38] the most important event in the modern history of PII was the abortive Matrix Churchill ('Arms to Iraq') trial of the early 1990s, which collapsed when it transpired that the sale of 'dual use' goods to Iraq in apparent breach of export sanctions had been done with the approval of members of the government (who had failed to give a full account to Parliament of changes in its policy regarding the export of such goods) and that one of the key individuals was in fact working for MI6. A number of PII certificates had been signed by various Ministers, relating to documentation alleged to be vital to the defence case.[39] Two questions caused particular difficulty: was PII available in the context of criminal law and, if so, was it available on the same terms as in the civil context? This latter question was particularly important in relation to the making of so-called 'class' claims for PII, which related not to the specific contents of the documents at issue, but the alleged sensitivity of the class of documents to which they belonged. Following criticism of the practice

[31] Maureen Spencer, 'National Security, Bureaucracy and Access to Justice: New Light on Duncan v Cammell Laird' (2004) 55 *NILQ* 3.

[32] *Conway v Rimmer* [1968] AC 910. In Scots law the same reversal (probably better understood as a reversion back to the prior rule of Scots law, on which the wrongness of Duncan was particularly galling) was effected earlier: *Glasgow Corporation v Central Land Board* 1956 SC (HL) 1.

[33] See, on the history of PII, Simon Brown, 'Public Interest Immunity' [1994] *PL* 579. The deeper historical roots of Crown privilege remain largely unexplored. For a flavour, however, see HG Hanbury, 'Equality and Privilege in English Law' (1952) 68 *LQR* 173.

[34] *Buttes Gas and Oil Co v Hammer (No 3)* [1981] QB 223, 262 per Brightman J.

[35] See, eg, *D v National Society for the Prevention of Cruelty to Children* [1978] AC 171.

[36] *R v Lewes Justices, ex parte Secretary of State for the Home Department* [1973] AC 388, 400.

[37] *R (FI) v Secretary of State for the Home Department* [2014] EWCA Civ 1272.

[38] The effect of *Conway* was not, however immediate, and the new regime was subject to what Spencer and Spencer describe as 'determined resistance' by officials: see Maureen Spencer and John Spencer, 'Coping with *Conway v Rimmer* [1968] AC 910: How Civil Servants Control Access to Justice' (2010) 37 *Journal of Law and Society* 387, 409.

[39] These issues were considered by the Scott Report: see, most importantly, The Right Honourable Sir Richard Scott, *Report of the Inquiry into the Export of Defence Equipment and Dual-Use Goods to Iraq and Related Prosecutions*, (HC 1995–96, 115), G18.43–106. The constitutional implications of the Scott report (including for PII) were considered most fully in Adam Tomkins, *The Constitution After Scott: Government Unwrapped* (Oxford, Oxford University Press, 1998).

of making class claims within the Scott report this practice was later abandoned (generally, rather than simply in relation to the criminal law)[40] and even before Scott reported, the *Wiley* case had confirmed the modern practice of balancing the public interest in disclosure against that in non-disclosure.[41] Though the original assessment is made by the relevant Minister, and usually communicated to the court in a PII certificate, the court is entitled to examine the relevant documents and reject the Minster's assessment as to where the balance lies. In keeping with general principles of public law, however, courts will be very slow to disagree with the executive's assessment as to what national security in particular requires by way of non-disclosure.[42]

One more point can be made about PII, before turning to its use in specific contexts. There are a number of statutes which acknowledge or reference the existence of PII (though not always directly, and not always by that name). I have noted the 1947 Act; reference will be made below to, amongst others, the Criminal Procedure and Investigations Act 1996. Nevertheless, it is important to underline that the law of PII is not itself a creature of statute. Rather, in developing the rules of PII, the Supreme Court has said, the courts were exercising 'inherent power in controlling [their] own procedures by deciding the scope of disclosure in cases involving confidential material.'[43] Leading accounts of the inherent jurisdiction emphasise that it belongs neither to statute nor to the common law, but instead derives 'from the very nature of the court as a court of law'.[44] Its most important feature is that it 'is exercisable as part of the administration of justice': 'It is part of procedural law, both civil and criminal, and not of substantive law; it is invoked in relation to the process of litigation.'[45] The nature of the law of PII has implications for the use which might be made of it: the inherent jurisdiction cannot be exercised incompatibly with statute, nor with the rules of court.[46] PII continues to play a significant role in the modern national security constitution. It is difficult, however, if not impossible to know exactly how frequently such claims are made: no figures are kept.[47]

[40] 'Under the new approach, Ministers will focus directly on the damage that disclosure would cause. The former division into class and contents claims will no longer be applied. Ministers will claim public interest immunity only when it is believed that disclosure of a document would cause real damage or harm to the public interest': The Attorney General (Sir Nicholas Lyell) HC Deb 18 December 1996, vol 287 col 949ff.

[41] *R v Chief Constable of West Midlands Police, ex parte Wiley* [1995] 1 AC 274.

[42] See, eg, *The Secretary of State for Foreign and Commonwealth Affairs v Assistant Deputy Coroner for Inner North London* [2013] EWHC 3724 (Admin), [28]–[36]. Brown (n 33) 589 notes that the 'mere incantation of the phrase of itself instantly discourages the court from satisfactorily fulfilling its normal role of deciding where the balance of the public interest lies.'

[43] *Al Rawi v Security Services* [2011] UKSC 34, [20].

[44] Sir Jack IH Jacob, *The Fabric of English Civil Justice* (London, Sweet & Maxwell, 1987) 60. Jacob calls the inherent jurisdiction the 'most extraordinary source of law in the English legal system' and identifies as the underlying principle that 'the essential character of a court of law necessarily involves that it should be invested with the power to maintain its authority, to control and regulate its process and to prevent its process from being abused or obstructed.' For a more sceptical take, see MS Dockray, 'The Inherent Jurisdiction to Regulate Civil Proceedings' (1997) 113 *LQR* 120.

[45] IH Jacob, 'The Inherent Jurisdiction of the Court' (1970) 23 *Current Legal Problems* 23, 25.

[46] Dockray (n 44) 128 suggests that 'the inherent jurisdiction may supplement but cannot be used to lay down procedure which is contrary to or inconsistent with a valid rule of the Supreme Court'. This claim was approved by the Court of Appeal in *Raja v Van Hoogstraaten* (No 9) [2008] EWCA Civ 1444; [2009] 1 WLR 1143, [74]–[78]: the rule 'pre-CPR ... was that the inherent powers of the court could not be invoked to do something which was inconsistent with a rule' and '[t]he same position has obtained since the introduction of the CPR'.

[47] Adam Tomkins, 'Justice and Security in the United Kingdom' (2014) 47 *Israel Law Review* 305, 308.

ii. PII in Criminal Contexts

PII has also long been available in the criminal context. Though the practice can be traced back at least as far as the treason trials of 1794,[48] the first modern authority is *Marks v Beyfus*,[49] in which the Court of Appeal upheld the decision of the judge to refuse to order the Director of Public Prosecutions to answer questions regarding the source of information received by him from informants. The Court, however, noted that the rule—what we would now recognise as a form of PII—could not be applied without exceptions; that:

> if upon the trial of a prisoner the judge should be of opinion that the disclosure of the name of the informant is necessary or right in order to shew the prisoner's innocence, then one public policy is in conflict with another public policy, and that which says that an innocent man is not to be condemned when his innocence can be proved is the policy that must prevail.[50]

In practice, however, the question of PII in criminal contexts did not normally arise until recent decades, because 'disclosure [in criminal cases] was left largely to the judgment of the prosecuting authorities and the prosecution, and only exceptionally did the court make any ruling.'[51] Where courts developed principles of PII in civil proceedings, they often asserted the limited reach of their remarks: as Viscount Simon stated in *Duncan v Cammell Laird*, '[t]he judgment of the house in the present case is limited to civil actions and the practice, as applied in criminal trials where an individual's life or liberty may be at stake, is not necessarily the same.'[52] Lord Scott, in relation to the specific question of whether PII class claims were permitted in criminal trials (a central question in the Matrix Churchill affair), said that 'it cannot possibly be supposed that the dicta regarding PII class claims to be found in *Duncan v Cammell Laird*, in *Conway v Rimmer*, in the *Burmah Oil* case, in *Air Canada v Secretary of State for Trade*, were intended to have any application to criminal trials.'[53]

As law diverged so might practice: at times the same material would be disclosed in a criminal case but made subject of a PII claim in a later civil case,[54] reflecting, perhaps, the same considerations that saw Viscount Kilmuir, then Lord Chancellor, make a statement to the House of Commons outlining the underlying basis for Crown Privilege and the manner in which it would be exercised, in which he proposed that 'if medical documents, or indeed other documents, are relevant to the defence in criminal proceedings, Crown privilege should not be claimed.'[55] The clear implication is that it was well understood,

[48] *R v Hardy* (1794) 24 St Tr 199. On the trials—of Thomas Hardy, John Horne Tooke and John Thelwall, members of the London Corresponding Society—see A Wharam, *The Treason Trials of 1794*, (Leicester, Leicester University Press, 1992).

[49] (1890) 25 QBD 494.

[50] (1890) 25 QBD 494, 498.

[51] *R v H* [2004] UKHL 3, [19]. See also John Andrews, 'Public interest and criminal proceedings' (1988) *LQR* 410, 412 noting that 'the principles in respect of the exclusion of evidence on grounds of public interest in criminal cases are vague almost to a point of nonexistence'.

[52] [1942] AC 624, 633–4.

[53] Scott (n 39) [G18.83], quoted in Tomkins (n 39) 189n.

[54] See the remarks of Lord Reid in *Conway v Rimmer* [1968] AC 910, 942–3: 'The Attorney-General did not deny that, even where the full contents of a report have already been made public in a criminal case, Crown privilege is still claimed for that report in a later civil case. And he was quite candid about the reason for that. Crown privilege is claimed in the civil case not to protect the document—its contents are already public property—but to protect the writer from civil liability should he be sued for libel or other tort.'

[55] HL Deb 6 June 1956, vol 197 col 745.

by both government and courts, that PII in the criminal context raises issues over and above those raised by its invocation in the civil sphere, with much of the background to the Scott report relating to the question of whether 'class' claims for PII were available also in criminal proceedings.[56] This particularity is reflected more directly in the impossibility of claiming PII in respect of material which might demonstrate the defendant's innocence, an exclusion which implies that the conclusory nature of Ministerial PII certificates, established by *Duncan v Cammell Laird*[57] and ended by *Conway v Rimmer*,[58] 'never applied to criminal trials,'[59] at least in respect of such material. That it reflected also modern practice was made clear by Lord Scott with reference to a series of cases,[60] including *R v Agar*, in which Mustill LJ remarked that there was a 'strong, and absent any contrary indication, overwhelming public interest, in keeping secret the source of information: but, as the authorities show, there was an even stronger public interest in allowing a defendant to put forward a tenable case in its best light'.[61] The best understanding of the issue, Scott suggested, was therefore that PII could never be successfully claimed in respect of material which may prove the defendant's innocence or non-disclosure of which may lead to a miscarriage of justice—the possibility that 'the public interest that a defendant in a criminal trial should have a fair trial and that an innocent man should not be convicted' would have to give way to the public interest in disclosure was 'a grotesque one'.[62] Instead, as it was put in the Scott report itself, 'in criminal cases the only question should be whether the documents might be of assistance to the defendant.'[63] In respect of evidence providing such assistance, there is no place for a *Wiley*-style balancing exercise:[64] such material cannot be withheld.

At the same time as the Scott report was considering the availability of (and limits to) PII, however, a series of cases raised issues of PII in the criminal context. In *R v Ward*,[65] it was held that where the prosecution was seeking to claim PII for documents helpful to the defence, it was under a duty to disclose that fact to the defence in order that the court could be asked to rule on the claim: 'If, in a wholly exceptional case, the prosecution are not prepared to have the issue of public interest immunity determined by a court, the result must inevitably be that the prosecution will have to be abandoned.'[66] This broad rule was hollowed out somewhat by the Court of Appeal in *R v Davis*,[67] where it was accepted that in some cases, it would be permissible for the prosecution to withhold details of the category into which the relevant material fell and for the hearing to take place *ex parte*.

[56] A dispute which turned in large part on the interpretation of *R v Governor of Brixton Prison, ex parte Osman* [1991] 1 WLR 281 which was, however, not a criminal case but related to Mr Osman's extradition to Hong Kong: for discussion, see Tomkins (n 39) 185–9.

[57] [1942] AC 624.

[58] [1968] AC 910.

[59] Richard Scott, 'The Use of Public Interest Immunity Claims in Criminal Cases' [1996] 2 *WebJCLI*.

[60] *R v Hallett* [1986] Crim LR 462; *R v Clowes* [1992] 3 All ER 440.

[61] *R v Agar* [1990] 2 All ER 442, 448.

[62] Scott (n 59). See also Andrews (n 51) 415–6. In *Neilson v Laugharne* [1981] 1 QB 736, 753 Oliver LJ said that '[i]f public policy prevents disclosure, it prevents it, in my judgment, in all circumstances except to establish innocence in criminal proceedings.'

[63] Scott (n 39) [G18.79], quoted in Tomkins (n 39) 191n. See also Richard Scott, 'The Acceptable and Unacceptable use of Public Interest Immunity' [1996] *PL* 427.

[64] *R v Chief Constable of the West Midlands ex parte Wiley* [1995] 1 AC 274.

[65] *R v Ward* [1993] 1 WLR 619.

[66] [1993] 1 WLR 619, 681B.

[67] [1993] 1 WLR 613.

In certain highly exceptional cases, the application might lawfully be made without notice to the defence.[68] Such eventuality was accepted as an abstract possibility because '[t]he only way of avoiding ex parte applications in that rare class of case would be to say that the prosecution must choose between following the normal inter partes procedure or declining to prosecute. Rare though these highly sensitive cases will be, they are likely to be serious cases which it would be in the public interest to prosecute.'[69] The categories outlined in *Davis* were discussed further in *R v Keane*, where it was said that 'ex parte applications are contrary to the general principle of open justice in criminal trials' which 'were sanctioned in R v Davis … solely to enable the court to discharge its function in testing a claim that public interest immunity or sensitivity justifies non-disclosure of material in the possession of the Crown.'[70] They should therefore be limited to cases meeting that description: it, unlike the use of PII itself, involves a departure from open justice, which is incompatible even with a narrow formalist conception of natural justice. This meta-level departure is justified in the name of the public interest, reflecting the concern that 'to disclose even the category of the material in question would in effect be to reveal that which the Crown contends should not in the public interest be revealed.'[71] Because this breach of constitutional principle, which takes place at the stage at which the question of disclosure (rather than that of criminal liability) is determined, does not ultimately threaten the fairness of the proceedings—it cannot, because it is bounded by the rule that if the material's non-disclosure will prevent a fair trial it must be disclosed—then the claim that the public interest requires an ex parte hearing can be allowed to triumph. The absolute requirements of fairness which prevail at the first order allow us to tolerate a less stringent second-order requirement.

In the meantime, however, Parliament had addressed the point by enacting the Criminal Procedure and Investigations Act 1996, one of a number of measures which 'in effect sanctioned' the regime which had developed.[72] The 1996 Act imposes upon the prosecution a general duty of disclosure of any material 'which might reasonably be considered capable of undermining the case for the prosecution against the accused or of assisting the case for the accused.'[73] This duty is subject to the rule that '[m]aterial must not be disclosed under this section to the extent that the court, on an application by the prosecutor, concludes it is not in the public interest to disclose it and orders accordingly.'[74] In the leading case on PII in the criminal context, the House of Lords confirmed that the same basic principle asserted by the decision in *Marks v Beyfus* continues to apply, so that while material might—in accordance with the 1996 Act—lawfully be withheld notwithstanding that it 'may weaken the prosecution case or strengthen that of the defence', non-disclosure could not take place where its effect may be 'to render the trial process, viewed as a whole, unfair to the defendant'.

68 [1993] 1 WLR 613, 617.

69 ibid.

70 *R v Keane* [1994] 1 WLR 746, 750.

71 [1993] 1 WLR 613, 617.

72 *R v H* [2004] UKHL 3, [20].

73 Criminal Procedure and Investigations Act 1996, s 3. The CPIA regime is supplemented by the *Attorney General's Guidelines on Disclosure: For investigators, prosecutors and defence practitioners* (December 2013). The place of PII within the broader disclosure regime is considered by Mike Redmayne, 'Criminal Justice Act 2003: (1) Disclosure and its discontents' (2004) *Crim LR* 441, 454–459.

74 ibid, s 3(6).

In such a case, 'then fuller disclosure should be ordered even if this leads or may lead the prosecution to discontinue the proceedings so as to avoid having to make disclosure.'[75] The effect is to give the highest possible priority to the value of fairness: notwithstanding that PII is not per se a departure from open justice, in some circumstances it can operate so as to violate the principle of natural justice. This, the House of Lords made clear, is not permitted. If Parliament was to desire to authorise such unfairness, we can assume that the courts would require it to employ the most explicit possible statutory language (which would not, alone, resolve the problem of compatibility with the European Convention on Human Rights).

Where necessary in order to secure the defendant's right to a fair trial, particularly in ex parte hearings of the sort which it was accepted in *Davis* (and later in *R v Keane*)[76] would take place in exceptional circumstances, the House of Lords was willing to countenance the appointment of a security-cleared special advocate in PII proceedings, again on the basis that to do so was necessary for fairness to be done to the defendant.[77] The requirement of fairness emerges once again as a backstop to the PII process: not this time negatively, as when it prevents material helpful to the defence from being withheld, but rather positively, in permitting the courts, albeit as a last resort, to take steps to mitigate the unfairness which would otherwise result from the PII process. As with the actual use of PII discussed above, this case law demonstrates again that in the criminal context the bright line formalist divide between open justice and natural justice is unsustainable. PII continues to be employed in the criminal context, and the Court of Human Rights accepts the possibility that its use will be Article 6 compliant,[78] even if in certain circumstances (mostly relating to facts prior to the 1996 Act) the procedures adopted have been found to have infringed on the right to a fair trial.[79] In the same case in which the possibility of appointing a Special Advocate in ex parte hearings was established, the House of Lords held that there was 'no dissonance between the principles of domestic law and those recognised in the convention jurisprudence'[80] and provided detailed guidance aimed at ensuring that PII claims can be made and disclosure take place in a fashion compatible with Article 6 even where the PII claim is determined in the absence of the defendant.[81]

B. In Camera Trials

Many of the points made about the use of PII in criminal contexts apply also to the related phenomenon of the 'in camera trial' which has emerged in recent years.[82] An in camera

[75] *R v H* [2004] UKHL 3, [36].

[76] [1994] 1 WLR 746.

[77] *R v H* [2004] 2 AC 134 (HL), [22]. This point is now subject to the decision in *Al-Rawi*, discussed below.

[78] See *R (Director of Public Prosecutions) v Acton Youth Court* [2001] EWHC Admin 402, [34] and the Strasbourg case law cited there.

[79] Eg, *Edwards and Lewis v United Kingdom* (2005) 40 EHRR 24.

[80] [2004] 2 AC 134 (HL), [33].

[81] ibid.

[82] On the phenomenon, see more fully Paul Scott 'An inherent jurisdiction to protect the public interest: from PII to 'secret trials'' (2016) *King's Law Journal* 259. These points are not wholly new however: see, eg, *Norman v Matthews* (1916) 85 LJ (KB) 857 and *R v Governor of Lewes Prison, ex parte Doyle* [1917] 2 KB 254.

trial is one which takes place wholly or partially behind closed doors, with the press and/or public excluded, but with the defendant and his or her representatives present. A first point to make is that there exists statutory authority for holding an in camera trial: the Official Secrets Act 1920, for instance, permits a court hearing proceedings under the Official Secrets Acts to exclude some or all of the public from the court where 'the publication of any evidence to be given or of any statement to be made in the course of the proceedings would be prejudicial to the national safety',[83] though sentencing must take place in public.[84] Elsewhere, a power to hold in camera trials is acknowledged by the Administration of Justice Act 1960, which provides that it is not a contempt of court to publish information about proceedings which have taken place in camera, but exempts from that rule situations in which 'the court sits in private for reasons of national security during that part of the proceedings about which the information in question is published'.[85] Such power is also acknowledged by the Criminal Procedure Rules.[86] Nevertheless, the modern law of in camera trials is an instantiation of the same inherent jurisdiction which was identified above as the basis of PII. This was confirmed by the Lord Chief Justice in *Wang Yam*, where he said that the order made in relation to the defendant's trial was not made under either the Criminal Procedure Rules or the Official Secrets Act, but instead that the trial judge, Mr Justice Ouseley, had 'rightly held in his public judgment that he had an inherent power to exclude the press and the public where the interests of justice required it'.[87] Later, in the context of an application to have the terms of the order varied so as to permit Wang Yam (who had been convicted after retrial)[88] to make an application to the Court of Human Rights, it was said that 'the Court which makes an "in camera" order pursuant to its inherent jurisdiction must have the inherent power to make an order which makes that exclusionary order effective.'[89] Ouseley J refused the application to vary the order and when judicial review of this refusal was sought, the Divisional Court held that 'the court must have an inherent power to issue an ancillary order or direction whose express object is to secure the purpose of the order made in court.'[90] The Supreme Court later dismissed an appeal against this decision.[91] The implications of an in camera order do not, this shows, end with the conclusion of the criminal trial in respect of which it is made. In *Wang Yam*, the alleged effect of the order has been to prevent him from seeking to vindicate his rights

[83] Official Secrets Act 1920, s 8(4).

[84] The Law Commission's consultation on the reform of the law of official secrets (discussed below) proposed making this statutory power subject to a necessity test of the sort which applies where the inherent jurisdiction is used instead: Law Commission, *Protection of Official Data: A Consultation Paper*, Consultation Paper No 230 (2017), [5.41].

[85] Administration of Justice Act 1960, s 12(1)(c).

[86] Criminal Procedure Rules, 6.1 and 6.6.

[87] *R v Wang Yam* [2008] EWCA Crim 269, [5]–[6].

[88] A possible explanation for the desire to hold the trial—for the murder of the writer Allan Chappelow—in camera is found in a contribution to the *London Review of Books* by Nicholas Phillips, formerly Lord President of the Supreme Court, who wrote that 'apparently Wang Yam had some link to the Security Services, which he wished to rely on by way of defence.' Nicholas Phillips, 'Closed Material' (2014) 36 *LRB* 29. A book on the trial is forthcoming: T Harding, *Blood on the Page* (London, Heinemann, 2018).

[89] [2014] EW Misc 10 (CCrimC), [79].

[90] [2014] EWHC 3558 (Admin), [55].

[91] The conviction was referred to the Court of Appeal by the Criminal Cases Review Commission when new evidence emerged, but the conviction was upheld but it in September 2017.

under the ECHR; elsewhere, the effect of the original in camera order has included the redaction of subsequent civil and criminal judgments arising out of the same set of facts.[92]

Subject to what will be said below about the constitutional implications of the power, the conclusion that the power to make an in camera order is an aspect of the inherent jurisdiction is not necessarily problematic. Nevertheless, it is striking that the courts are at times inconsistent on this point—see, for instance, *Incedal*,[93] in which the court spoke instead of 'common law' power to order an in camera trial[94]—and that they are uncurious as to what, if anything, might be at stake in the distinction between in camera trials as a common law phenomenon and in camera trials as an example of the use of the inherent jurisdiction. Where *Wang Yam* involved a murder trial partly in camera, in *Incedal*, the original order not only required the trial to take place wholly in camera (with it being prohibited to publish reports of the trial) but also prohibited the publication of the identities of the defendants. The Court of Appeal subsequently varied the order to have elements of the trial held in open court, and to permit the naming of the defendants.

It is also notable that the power's existence is usually asserted rather than evidenced, with no legal authority cited. To take *Incedal* as an example of this phenomenon: reference is made therein to both *Wang Yam* (and a subsequent case, *ex parte A*)[95] and, as well as to *Bank Mellatt v HM Treasury (No.2)*. While it cannot be disputed that both of the earlier criminal cases *exemplify* the power in question, neither *establishes* it. Nor does either case speak to its source beyond the bare claim by the Lord Chief Justice already cited. That holding is a weak foundation for a power as broad as that of holding an entire trial in camera. The reference to *Bank Mellatt* is also of interest. Not only would it appear that the wrong case was cited (the relevant paragraph is presumably that of *Bank Mellatt (No. 1)*[96] rather than *(No. 2)*,[97] which was handed down by the Supreme Court simultaneously), but (a) that case was a civil proceeding (an application to set aside an order made under the Counter-Terrorism Act 2008) and (b) the departure from open justice at issue was one which had a basis, albeit

[92] See, eg, *R v Khyam* [2008] EWCA Crim 1612 and *Amin v Director General of the Security Service* [2013] EWHC 1579 (QB). The connection between the redaction and the original in camera order is stated in *Amin v Director General of the Security Service* [2014] EWCA Civ 598, [10].

[93] *Guardian News and Media Ltd v Incedal* [2014] EWCA Crim 1861. The case involved the trial of Erol Incedal and Mounir Rarmoul-Bouhadjar for a variety of terror offences. The reason for which an in camera trial was required was never disclosed, though the Court of Appeal judgment, at [4], suggests the involvement of the Security and Intelligence Agencies. Given the domestic nature of the offences, the relevant body would presumably be MI5. In a later (unsuccessful) challenge to the associated reporting restrictions, the Lord Chief Justice noted that:

> It is a significant, important and proper part of the duties of the Security Services of the United Kingdom that they act in accordance with the law ... Thus, when the decision is made by the court, subject to any appeal, they must abide by that decision even if they disagree with it. If a decision is made by the prosecutor to proceed, then the Security Services and the police must provide to the prosecutor all the assistance the prosecutor requires. It is part of their duty to abide by the rule of law and the constitutional principles we have set out.

[2016] EWCA Crim 11, [62].

[94] '[A]s rightly accepted by Mr. Hudson (for the media), the Court has a common law power to hear a trial (or part of a trial) in private ('in camera')': [2014] EWCA Crim 1861, [11].

[95] *R v The Crown Court at the Central Criminal Court, ex parte A* [2006] EWCA Crim 4.

[96] *Bank Mellat v HM Treasury (No 1)* [2013] UKSC 38.

[97] *Bank Mellat v HM Treasury (No 2)* [2013] UKSC 39.

weak, in statute.[98] Though the dicta in *Bank Mellatt* support the Court of Appeal's decision ('it has long been accepted that, in rare cases, a court has inherent power to receive evidence and argument in a hearing from which the public and the press are excluded, and that it can even give a judgment which is only available to the parties')[99] reliance on a civil case in order to support the existence of a power to hold (part of) a criminal trial in camera might be thought complacent: as was pointed out in relation to PII by Viscount Simon long ago, criminal trials are a different beast for the simple reason that 'an individual's … liberty may be at stake.'[100] The dicta from *Bank Mellat* are not here relied upon either primarily or exclusively, but it might be preferable if they were not relied upon at all. Nevertheless, the effect of the decisions in *Wang Yam* and *Incedal* is that though multiple decisions of the Court of Appeal (and one of the Supreme Court)[101] now attest to the existence of the competence to hold a criminal trial entirely in camera, none contains a full discussion of its origin.

Moving on from this basic question, the next issue to address is the relationship between in camera trials and the constitutional principles from which we began: open justice and natural justice. PII is held not to represent a departure from the principle of open justice, as the parties, press and public are permitted to observe proceedings, and no closed judgment is published (at least in the primary proceedings). This is not true of an in camera trial, which by definition sees press and public excluded from at least part of the trial. An in camera trial is not, however, simply an evolution of PII. First, an in camera trial is—from the point of view of both prosecution and defence—in certain ways superior to PII: the defence is allowed to know the content of all of the relevant material, while the prosecution is able to rely upon that material, not being forced to choose between the public interest in keeping it secret and the public interest in being able to rely upon it within the trial process. This suggests a second point: in camera trials are in many ways a parallel mechanism, applicable to different types of material. That is, one of the reasons for which it will be possible to permit the defendant and his or her counsel to become aware of the content of the material without harming the public interest is that they are already aware of it; often, as has been true of several of the in camera cases, the sensitive material will form part of the defence case. The effect will, it seems, often be that the two mechanisms are employed alongside another, with some material subject to PII (and not admitted in evidence at all) and other material disclosed only in camera.

Nevertheless, the prosecuting authorities do not simply get to choose between the two, as the greater challenge which in camera trials pose to fundamental constitutional principles is reflected in a higher hurdle which must be overcome if the court is to order an in camera trial. Where PII can be claimed wherever the executive (or the court itself) takes the view that disclosure poses a 'real risk of serious prejudice to an important public interest',[102] the needs of national security are not in and of themselves capable of justifying a departure

[98] Constitutional Reform Act 2005, s 40(2) and (5). For discussion of the decision, see Paul Scott, 'Crossing the Rubicon: closed hearings in the Supreme Court' (2014) 18 *Edinburgh Law Review* 88.
[99] *Bank Mellatt (No. 1)* [2013] UKSC 38, [2].
[100] *Duncan v Cammell Laird* [1942] A.C. 624, 633–4.
[101] *R (Wang Yam) v Central Criminal Court* [2015] UKSC 76.
[102] *R v H* [2004] UKHL 3, [36].

from the principle of natural justice. Instead, open justice can be departed from only where a superior constitutional principle is in play: the example given in the case law is where to refuse to order an in camera trial would threaten the administration of justice by 'deterring the Crown from prosecuting a case where it otherwise should do so'.[103] This position, which reflects that 'the paramount object of the Court is to do justice',[104] mirrors Lord Devlin's observation, long ago, that 'a principle of judicial inquiry, whether fundamental or not, is only a means to an end' and so '[i]f it can be shown in any particular class of case that the observance of a principle of this sort does not serve the ends of justice, it must be dismissed; otherwise it would become the master instead of the service of justice.'[105] In *Incedal* it was emphasised that it is not enough that there is some possibility that the prosecution might be dropped: instead, there must be a 'serious possibility' that the administration of justice will be frustrated. The Court of Appeal offered three reasons for setting the bar at that relatively high point:

> (1) the inherent uncertainty at the stage when an in camera hearing is sought, emphasised by constitutional authority as to the power to discontinue a prosecution resting with the Attorney General and Director of Public Prosecutions while the concerns may very likely emanate from the Agencies; (2) the desirability of avoiding even the appearance of a "threat" or "blackmail" on the part of the Crown as to the discontinuance of the proceedings; (3) the fact that satisfaction of the test does not deprive the Court of decision-making power; the risk that the Crown might be deterred from prosecuting means the Court may (not must) permit a departure from the principle of open justice.[106]

The second point relates to natural justice: the case law is unambiguous that the ordering of an in camera trial does not, by itself, represent a violation of that principle. The Court of Appeal in *Incedal* emphasised that 'a hearing in camera involves a departure from the principle of open justice, not from natural justice' and that unlike in a closed material procedure, the 'defendant in an in camera hearing has the right to know the full case against him and to test and challenge that case fully'.[107] This conclusion is buttressed by a quotation from the judgment of Lord Dyson in *Al Rawi*,[108] in turn referencing Lord Bingham in *Davis*: 'the rights of a litigating party are the same whether a trial is conducted in in camera or in open court and whether or not the course of the proceedings may be reported in the media …'[109] Lord Bingham was in *Davis* acknowledging the *Scott v Scott* testament to open justice and simultaneous recognition of the need in exceptional circumstances to depart from it, and contrasting such departures (which do not diminish the rights of a litigating party) with the use of anonymous witnesses in *Davis*, which did. In citing back to him, Lord Dyson in *Al Rawi* was similarly distinguishing the use of closed material procedure

[103] *Incedal* [2014] EWCA Crim 1861, [17].

[104] ibid. See on this priority of the administration of justice, G Nettheim, 'Open Justice and State Secrets' (1985–86) 10 *Adelaide Law Review* 281.

[105] *In re K* [1965] AC 201, 238.

[106] [2014] EWCA Crim 1861, [18]. See also the discussion of the Court of Appeal of these issues when refusing an application to bring an end to the reporting restrictions imposed at the time of the trial: [2016] EWCA Crim 11, [51]–[62].Though the Court of Appeal claims to 'take' the serious possibility test from *A and ors* and *Wang Yam*, in neither of those cases is it spelt out explicitly.

[107] [2014] EWCA Crim 1861, [36].

[108] *Al Rawi v Security Service* [2011] UKSC 34, [27].

[109] *R v Davis* [2008] UKHL 36, [28].

from the mere departure from open justice: *Scott v Scott* can justify the latter but is not authority for the proposition that 'the court may sanction a departure from the natural justice principle (including the right to be present at and participate in the whole or part of a trial).'[110]

Gross LJ's judgment in the Court of Appeal therefore seeks to yoke *Incedal* to that line of authority which deals with departures from open justice, distancing it from anything that has been said—in *Davis*, *Al Rawi* etc—about breaches of natural justice, for which those cases, amongst others, would seem to make clear that statutory authority will always be necessary. In doing so he gives effect to the formalist conception of natural justice, which considers in the first place the question of whether an equality of arms is maintained as between the parties. But, we have noted in the context of PII, the formalist conception breaks down in practice: notwithstanding that the PII process is not inherently unfair, it might be implemented in such a way as to render a trial unfair. It is that possibility, we have said, which defines the outer limit of the courts' ability to accept a claim of PII. The point is equally true in the context of in camera trials: even allowing that such a trial is not in and of itself unfair (or, rather, contrary to the principle of natural justice) it is no less conceivable to it might end up being so in practice. The Court of Appeal in *Wang Yam* noted that the judge who had made the original in camera order had been clear in holding that 'the interests of justice could never justify excluding the press and the public if the consequence would be that the trial would not be fair'.[111] Though a similar reference to natural justice as an outer limit on the use of the inherent jurisdiction is absent from the judgment in *Incedal*, it is submitted that it represents a correct statement of the law. Thus, as with PII, the inherent jurisdiction cannot be used in a manner which is contrary to the overarching requirement to do justice; though the needs of justice can justify a violation of the principle of open justice, the need to do justice cannot require the court to do an injustice.

While the Court of Appeal therefore gave a judgment in *Incedal* more in line with constitutional principle than the original order of the trial judge, it is important to be clear that it did so not because of a disagreement as to the role of constitutional principle in the ordering of an in camera trial, but as a result of a disagreement with the extent to which the departure from constitutional principle was necessary on the particular facts of the case.[112] Even in relation to the anonymisation of the defendants (a departure from open justice whose possibility is, it must be noted, well-established)[113] the Court of Appeal's stance was less firm than would have been desirable. It expressed its 'grave concern as to the cumulative effects of (1) holding a criminal trial in camera and (2) anonymising the Defendants' and found it 'difficult to conceive of a situation where both departures from open justice will be justified'.[114] It would have been preferable to make the point in terms of principle; to say, that is, that the combination of the in camera order and the anonymity of the defendants was sufficient to render the trial inherently unfair, such that the court had no power to make this combination of orders. To do so would have been particularly desirable to the extent

[110] *Al Rawi v Security Service* [2011] UKSC 34, [27].
[111] *R v Wang Yam* [2008] EWCA Crim 269, [6].
[112] [2014] EWCA Crim 1861, [37].
[113] See, eg, *Marines A & Ors v Guardian News and Media & Other* Media [2013] EWCA Crim 2367.
[114] [2014] EWCA Crim 1861, [47].

that it would represent the abandonment of the formal conception of natural justice which prevails in the case law, whereby unfairness can only ever be contingent unless an inequality of arms has been created as between the parties. In an interview given shortly after the publication of the judgment in *Incedal*, the Lord Chief Justice expressed the opinion that '[t]here ought to be clear guidelines and rules so the prospect of an anonymous defendant is one I would hope we never see again in our courts.'[115] This comment ignores that it was open to the Court of Appeal to take a clearer stand on the issue than it in fact did; to use the language of natural justice as well as, or instead of, that of justification. If the constitutional principles of open and natural justice appear to have been compromised by recent developments, the courts—quick to find in their inherent jurisdiction the power to hold trials in camera, and quick, too, to make use of that power—must shoulder much of the blame.

C. Closed Material Procedures

The previous sections discussed first the phenomenon of public interest immunity and then that of the in camera trial. In both cases, it was noted that no statutory authority exists—or is required—for the use of the procedure; because they are only contingently incompatible with the principle of natural justice, they can take place without such authority. In this section, we turn to consider another mechanism by which the public interest is protected against disclosure of sensitive information: the closed material procedure (CMP). A CMP differs from PII and an in camera trial in that material subject to such a procedure can be relied upon by the court (unlike in PII) but cannot be made known to the relevant (usually non-state) party (unlike in an in camera trial). The result is that proceedings in which a CMP is employed are split into open and closed phases. In the open phase, the relevant party and his legal representative may be present but the sensitive material cannot be disclosed. In the closed phase, the material can be disclosed to the court, but the relevant party and his representative are, like the press and public, excluded. The closed material can be shown only to a 'special advocate', a security-cleared barrister who is permitted to communicate with his or her 'client' beforehand but who, after viewing the material, can communicate with that person only—in the usual case—with the permission of the court. Though sensitive material cannot be disclosed in full, it may be that a summary of the material (in the usual parlance, a 'gist') may be made available. A CMP, it goes almost without saying, presents a very significant obstacle to those whose attempt to challenge a decision taken by the executive is subject to such a procedure, which the presence of a special advocate can only do so much to counteract.[116]

[115] John Hyde, 'Lord chief justice attacks court secrecy' *Law Society Gazette* (12 November 2014) available at www.lawgazette.co.uk/news/lord-chief-justice-attacks-court-secrecy/5045032.fullarticle.

[116] See the comments of practitioners who have acted as special advocates on the ability of such advocates to counter the inherent unfairness of CMPs: Martin Chamberlain, 'Special Advocates and Procedural Fairness in Closed Proceedings' (2009) 28 *Civil Justice Quarterly* 314 and 'Update on Procedural Fairness in Closed Proceedings' (2009) 28 *Civil Justice Quarterly* 448, and Tim Otty, 'The Slow Creep of Complacency and the Soul of Justice' [2012] *EHRLR* 267.

i. The Introduction and Spread of CMP

The original impetus for the introduction of CMP in the UK was the decision of the European Court of Human Rights in *Chahal*.[117] The applicant, a Sikh separatist, challenged the intention to deport him, as well as the mechanism which existed to permit him to challenge a deportation order. At the relevant time a person being deported on national security grounds enjoyed no right of appeal,[118] but was permitted to make representations to an 'advisory panel' (the 'three wise men'). The Court of Human Rights explained the procedure:

> The person concerned is given an opportunity to make written and/or oral representations to an advisory panel, to call witnesses on his behalf, and to be assisted by a friend, but he is not permitted to have legal representation before the panel. The Home Secretary decides how much information about the case against him may be communicated to the person concerned. The panel's advice to the Home Secretary is not disclosed, and the latter is not obliged to follow it.[119]

Though there existed also the possibility of seeking judicial review of the decision, that procedure did not allow for a consideration of the factual basis of the decision and would likely see the Secretary of State's decision subjected to only a very weak review. In the event, the Court of Human Rights found that, contrary to Article 13 of the Convention, Chahal did not have an 'effective remedy' for the violation of his rights.[120] While acknowledging that national security might require the taking of decisions in reliance upon confidential information, the national security context could not be invoked to justify the absence of effective control by the domestic courts. Here, the Court gave weight to the fact that 'in Canada a more effective form of judicial control has been developed in cases of this type', which it took to illustrate that 'there are techniques which can be employed which both accommodate legitimate security concerns about the nature and sources of intelligence information and yet accord the individual a substantial measure of procedural justice.'[121] Though later research has called into question the Court's understanding of the relevant Canadian processes and its comparative method,[122] the UK responded by enacting the Special Immigration Appeals Commission Act 1997, which created the eponymous body, SIAC. Those being deported on national security or related grounds could challenge the decision to deport them in SIAC, which would adopt a CMP in considering their challenge. Over time, the use of CMP expanded in two ways.[123] First, the jurisdiction of SIAC itself expanded: alongside

[117] *Chahal v United Kingdom* (1997) 23 EHRR 413.

[118] Asylum and Immigration Appeals Act 1993, Sch 2, para 6, which provided that s 15(3) of the Immigration Act 1971 was to apply (with modifications) to certain rights of appeal under the 1993 Act.

[119] (1997) 23 EHRR 413, [60].

[120] ibid, [155].

[121] ibid, [131].

[122] See, eg, David Jenkins, 'There and Back Again: The Strange Journey of Special Advocates and Comparative Law Methodology' (2010–11) 42 *Columbia Human Rights Law Review* 279, 351 in which Jenkins observes that the relevant dicta 'displayed critical methodological flaws that would have serious and unanticipated consequences not only in the United Kingdom, but also back in Canada.'

[123] See John IP, 'The Rise and Spread of the Special Advocate' [2008] *PL* 717 and, for a theoretical consideration of the matter, which explores the possibility that human rights law is not the limit to the spread of, but rather a (the?) source of the CMP, see Eva Nanopoulos, 'European Human Rights law and the Normalisation of the 'Closed Material Procedure': Limit or Source? (2015) 78 *MLR* 913.

appeals against deportation and other immigration decisions where taken on the ground that the exclusion or deportation etc was conducive to the public good, SIAC now enjoys jurisdiction over certain naturalisation and citizenship decisions, including those to deprive a person of his citizenship where it has been taken wholly or partly in reliance upon information which cannot be made public on, eg, national security grounds.[124] Second, a number of other bodies were given by statute the authority to employ a CMP in specified types of proceeding.[125] These include the Proscribed Organisations Appeal Commission;[126] the Employment Tribunal when hearing racial discrimination claims where issues of national security arise;[127] and the High Court itself in cases relating to the freezing of assets in order to disrupt the financing of terrorism,[128] or challenges to the imposition of a Terrorist Prevention and Investigation Measure.[129]

The use of CMP in SIAC is not necessarily incompatible with the ECHR, for the Court of Human Rights has held that the decisions regarding, for example, expulsion are not within the ambit of Article 6(1) of the Convention, in that they do not constitute a determination of one's civil rights and obligations.[130] The Strasbourg Court did eventually hold, however, in *A v United Kingdom*, that in cases involving liberty the Convention imposes essentially the same standard as is imposed by Article 6 of the Convention in its criminal aspect, and so a person challenging the imposition of a measure which represents a deprivation of liberty is required by Article 5(4) to be made aware of a core irreducible minimum of the case against him, so as to enable him or her to 'give effective instructions to the special advocate'.[131] If the open evidence against a person consists 'purely of general assertions' and an adverse judgment is based 'solely or to a decisive degree' upon secret evidence, then there will be a breach of Article 5.[132] Soon afterwards the House of Lords, in *AF (No. 3)*, applied this decision in a case relating to control orders, holding that none of the defendants had been given sufficient information to meet the standard identified by the Strasbourg Court.[133] On the other hand, the *AF (No. 3)* disclosure requirements are not of universal application: in *Home Office v Tariq*,[134] the Supreme Court held that in the context of proceedings brought in the Employment Tribunal by an immigration officer whose security clearance had been withdrawn, alleging discrimination on racial or religious grounds, there was no requirement that a gist of the material be provided if to do so was harmful to the interests of national security. A similar body of case law exists upon the relationship between CMP and EU law, and in particular the Charter of Fundamental Rights. In *ZZ*, the CJEU, on a preliminary

[124] See, eg, Special Immigration Appeals Commission Act 1997, s 2B (relating to deprivation of citizenship, inserted by the Nationality, Immigration and Asylum Act 2002) and s 2D (relating to certain nationalisation and citizenship decisions, inserted by the Justice and Security Act 2013).

[125] See Eric Metcalfe, *Secret Justice: a JUSTICE report*, JUSTICE (2009), [79].

[126] Under the Terrorism Act 2000, Sch 3.

[127] See, now, Equality Act 2010, s 117.

[128] Counter-Terrorism Act 2008, Pt 6.

[129] Terrorism Prevention and Investigation Measures Act 2011, Sch 4.

[130] *Maaouia v France* (2001) 33 EHRR 42.

[131] *A v United Kingdom* (2009) 49 EHRR 29, [220].

[132] ibid.

[133] *Secretary of State for the Home Department v AF (No 3)* [2009] UKHL 28. See Aileen Kavanagh, 'Special Advocates, Control Orders and the Right to a Fair Trial' (2010) 73 *MLR* 824.

[134] *Home Office v Tariq* [2011] UKSC 35.

reference from the Court of Appeal, held that the relevant Directive, when interpreted in light of Article 47 of the CFR, required the domestic courts to ensure that 'failure by the competent national authority to disclose to the person concerned, precisely and in full, the grounds on which a decision taken under article 27 of that Directive is based and to disclose the related evidence to him is limited to that which is strictly necessary' and that, in any event, such a person is informed of 'the essence of those grounds in a manner which takes due account of the necessary confidentiality of the evidence.'[135] As interpreted by the Court of Appeal on the return of the reference, this judgment has the effect of introducing a requirement of disclosure that is analogous to, though independent of, the *AF (No. 3)* regime, and which will apply in that subset of substantive SIAC appeals to which EU law applies.[136] Later case law, however, has held that EU law similarly recognises that an irreducible minimum of disclosure is not required in all cases where rights protected by EU law are at issue.[137] As such, the ability of the two external legal regimes to overcome the inherent unfairness of the closed material procedure is limited by an implicit—and contestable—hierarchy of rights.

Though CMPs destroy the equality of arms as between the parties and so are contrary to the principle of natural justice, that principle is subject to statutory authority, which usually exists. One exception is worth considering.[138] In *Bank Mellat*,[139] the applicants challenged the imposition of an order under the Counter-Terrorism Act 2008, with the High Court (authorised by statute to do so)[140] holding a closed hearing and producing a closed judgment. On appeal, eventually, to the Supreme Court, the Treasury argued that the Supreme Court should itself hold a closed hearing in order to examine that closed judgment. First, however, it was necessary to determine whether it was possible for the Supreme Court to do so. Unlike the Civil Procedure Rules, the Supreme Court Rules at that point in time made no provision for CMP, stating instead that appeals were to be heard in open court except where it was 'necessary in the interests of justice or in the public interest' for them to take place in private.[141] The relevant statute, the Constitutional Reform Act 2005, gave the Supreme Court the power to 'determine any question necessary … for the purposes of doing justice'[142] but made no explicit provision for CMP. Notwithstanding the thinness of this authority, the Court held that it did indeed have the power to employ a CMP, essentially on the pragmatic basis that if it could not unacceptable consequences would follow: the Supreme Court would be compelled either allow the appeal (or dismiss it) or to decide it without seeing all of the relevant material. None of the principles cited in opposition—including the idea that

[135] *ZZ (France) v Secretary of State for the Home Department (C-300/11)* [2013] QB 1136.

[136] *ZZ (France) v Secretary of State for the Home Department (No 2)* [2014] EWCA Civ 7.

[137] *R (Kiani) v Secretary of State for the Home Department* [2015] EWCA Civ 776.

[138] See also *Roberts v Parole Board* [2005] UKHL 45, in which the appointment of a special advocate without statutory authority was permitted in order to ameliorate the unfairness of process of non-disclosure which was itself clearly authorised.

[139] *Bank Mellat v Her Majesty's Treasury (No. 1)* [2013] UKSC 38.

[140] Counter-Terrorism Act 2008, s 66 and 73. In the latter, 'rules of court' are defined as 'rules for regulating the practice and procedure to be followed in the High Court or the Court of Appeal or in the Court of Session'. No mention is made of the Supreme Court, which had been created by the Constitutional Reform Act 2005, but had not begun operation by the time at which the 2008 Act was enacted.

[141] Supreme Court Rules 2009 (SI 2009/1603) (L. 17), r 27(1).

[142] Constitutional Reform Act 2005, s 40(5).

there is something especially offensive to constitutional principle in the highest court holding a closed hearing—sufficed to overcome this basic consequentialism.

Though there is an undeniable logic in this position, the fact of beginning from pragmatic rather than principled considerations resulted in a decision in clear tension with the courts' approach elsewhere. Though somewhat drastic in its consequences, taking seriously the principles of open and natural justice would have meant insisting that clear statutory authority was required; Parliament, having failed to provide it, should take responsibility for any injustice which might result. What grates about the decision in *Bank Mellat*, however, is not the abstract point—that the Supreme Court has the power to hold a closed hearing if necessary to do justice—but its application to the specific circumstances of the case before it: the decision that it was necessary here for the Supreme Court to hold a closed hearing. Having seen the material in question, it is very clear that the Justices, including those in the majority on the general point, considered that they had been manoeuvred—perhaps even misled—into holding a closed hearing in order to view material that did not assist them: there was 'nothing in it which could have affected [their] reasoning in relation to the substantive appeal, let alone which could have influenced the outcome of the appeal.'[143] This is another danger of secret justice: a court willing to hold a closed hearing without clear statutory authority because the alternative to doing so is unpalatable, and a government which refuses to answer basic questions about the relevance of the closed material in order to give that same court no choice but to hold a closed hearing (despite 'real misgivings')[144] in order to see what light, if any, that material shed on the substantive point. None of the relevant parties are put in a good light by the *Bank Mellat* affair. Nevertheless, the spread of this type of secret justice in the UK is in the main a function not of judicial acquiescence but of legislative determination, most strikingly in the form of the Justice and Security Act 2013.

ii. PII, CMP, and the Justice and Security Act 2013

Notwithstanding the constitutionally obnoxious nature of CMP—which trades one injustice for another—the combination of explicit statutory authority for its use and the relatively limited (if ever-expanding) scope of that authority might nevertheless be thought sufficient to render it a tolerable, if regrettable, addition to the constitutional landscape. Both of these facets were, however, challenged by the *Al-Rawi* litigation,[145] in which the Supreme Court was faced with the question of whether the courts had the power to order a closed material procedure in an ordinary civil claim. The Supreme Court's robust rejection of the possibility was offered in terms of the dual principles of open justice, on one hand, and natural justice, on the other. Lord Dyson, for example, stated both that '[t]he open justice principle is not a mere procedural rule' but rather a 'fundamental common law principle' and that, simply, barely, 'trials are conducted on the basis of natural justice.' These principles were held to constitute limitations upon the broad inherent power of the courts to regulate their own procedure:

> The basic rule is that (subject to certain established and limited exceptions) the court cannot exercise its power to regulate its own procedures in such a way as will deny parties their fundamental

[143] [2013] UKSC 38, [66].
[144] ibid, [64].
[145] Culminating in the decision of the Supreme Court in *Al Rawi v The Security Service* [2011] UKSC 34.

> common law right to participate in the proceedings in accordance with the common law principles of natural justice and open justice.[146]

Emphasising these principles serves to distinguish CMP, the introduction of which was here held to be beyond the scope of the court's inherent jurisdiction, from the use of the PII process, for which statutory authority is neither asked nor offered.[147] Lord Dyson in *Al Rawi* notes that the PII process 'fully respects the principles of open justice and natural justice':[148] the former, presumably, because it does not result in a closed judgment and thereby prevent the parties from knowing why they have won and lost respectively; the latter because it does not result in an inequality of arms as between the parties—both are able to know and rely upon the full range of material upon which the court will base its judgment.

Whether or not that is correct, the related phenomenon of the in camera trial—discussed above—demonstrates that the inherent jurisdiction can be employed in a manner which is unambiguously incompatible with the principle of open justice, as long as the administration of justice requires it. It is the principle of natural justice which represents there the outer limit of procedural innovation. Here too, it is CMP's incompatibility with *natural* justice which leads to a statutory basis for its use being demanded. And, dicta in *Al Rawi* make clear, that incompatibility with natural justice consists in the facts that CMP creates an inequality of the parties' arms: parties must know the case against them and the material on which it is based, and have the opportunity to call their own witnesses and to cross-examine opposing witnesses.[149] They should, in short, be permitted access to the same range of legal tools as is available to their opponents. This is the same formalism we have encountered at work in relation both to PII and to in camera trials. In both cases, however, the law ultimately (perhaps grudgingly) reflects the limits of such formalism, with the courts accepting that both regimes might result in a breach of natural justice notwithstanding that they are, in the abstract, compatible with it. Were the principle of natural justice conceived of more generously, therefore, one could certainly envisage circumstances in which the application of the law of PII in a civil case would lead to a breach of natural justice notwithstanding that equality of arms was maintained. It may be, for example, that where the material in respect of which immunity is claimed is so central to the claim being advanced that the court, by accepting the claim and rendering that material inadmissible, is effectively allowing the public interest in non-disclosure to outweigh the public interest in the administration of justice and will have no choice but to strike out the claim. The court in such a case has effectively decided that 'the public interest in maintaining confidential information trumps the public interest in the administration of justice to the extent that on that ground a trial has been denied altogether.'[150]

It was this possibility—that a successful PII claim would render a case untriable—that had originally led the government to seek a CMP in *Al Rawi*: if a CMP was not ordered,

[146] [2011] UKSC 34, [22].

[147] See *Duncan v Cammell Laird & Co Ltd* [1942] A.C. 624; *Conway v Rimmer* [1968] A.C. 910; *R v Chief Constable of the West Midlands ex parte Wiley* [1995] 1 AC 274.

[148] [2011] UKSC 34, [48].

[149] [2011] UKSC 34, [12]–[13].

[150] [2011] UKSC 34, [16].

and the court refused to strike out the claim for damages against the Security Services, the government would have no choice but to pay unmerited compensation, for to prove the claim's alleged lack of merit would involve disclosing material that was too sensitive to be disclosed. The question of whether *Al Rawi* was indeed untriable on the ordinary law of PII was never answered, for the mammoth PII process which would have been required did not take place, the case having been settled before the Supreme Court gave judgment.[151] The general question as to whether such a case could ever exist was more problematic. The government relied heavily upon a single example, *Carnduff v Rock*,[152] arising out a contractual claim by a police informer against a police inspector and his chief constable and the argument that to try the case would require disclosure of material in respect of which the police would claim PII. Without having first gone through the PII process, however, the defendant applied to have the claim struck out. The Court of Appeal did so, on the basis that the only way it could be tried was if the Court required the police to disclose material in respect of which they were likely to claim PII and which claim would inevitably be accepted. As it was put by Laws LJ, 'such a position could only be avoided if the police made comprehensive admissions which absolved the court from the duty to enter into any of these issues. But a case which can only be justly tried if one side holds up its hands cannot, in truth, be justly tried at all.'[153]

It has been pointed out, however, that this views the matter only from the point of view of the police; seen from the claimant's point of view, the striking out is potentially just as unfair as would be to the police the effective compulsion to concede the claim—an arguable claim has not been determined by the court and the plaintiff, having been unable to vindicate and enforce his legal rights, has lost out as a result. As such, Laws LJ's position in *Carnduff* 'amounts to saying that a claim brought in good faith and which on the face of it was arguable nevertheless amounted to abuse of process; and for no better reason than that the police were going to make a PII claim.'[154] Johnathan Parker LJ put the matter even more starkly than his colleague, saying (in dicta that seem to be in at least prima facie in tension with the courts' alleged duty to do justice) that 'if a fair trial of the issues in the case would necessarily involve the disclosure by the authorities of information or material which is sensitive or confidential and the disclosure of which is not in the public interest, and if that in turn means that it would be contrary to the public interest that the trial should take place, then the case should not be allowed to proceed.'[155] This reads as though the court has shied away from its duty to do justice; a position that is untenable even in the context of a unsympathetic plaintiff making an unattractive claim (as in *Carnduff*) but which elsewhere would be clearly recognised for what it is—a renunciation of the very raison d'etre of the court. The conclusion was arrived at without acknowledgement of the competing interests implicitly being weighed one against the other, and without reference to the deep injustice

[151] Tomkins (n 47) 317.
[152] *Carnduff v Rock* [2001] EWCA Civ 680.
[153] [2001] EWCA Civ 680, [36].
[154] Adrian Zuckerman, 'Closed material procedure—denial of natural justice: Al Rawi v The Security Service [2011] UKSC 34' (2011) *Civil Justice Quarterly* 345, 353.
[155] [2001] EWCA Civ 680, [36].

done where a good faith claim is struck out.[156] Though there is no inequality of arms here, there is nevertheless an unfairness.

Adam Tomkins describes *Carnduff* as 'almost certainly wrongly decided' and suggests that '[t]he great problem with [the case] is that none of the leading case law on PII was cited by the court.'[157] Nevertheless, *Carnduff* became emblematic of a supposed category of cases in which national security required the non-disclosure of relevant material and which therefore, under the law of PII, could have only been tried without that material being presented in evidence.[158] The principal claim was that this would permit cases without merit to succeed (as would happen, it was argued, in *Al Rawi*, in relation to which no liability was ever admitted). Such outcome would constitute an injustice and, it was argued, the only way to mitigate that injustice was via the lesser injustice of a CMP. Though the Justice and Security Act 2013 (JSA), enacted specifically so as to permit what the Supreme Court in *Al Rawi* prohibited, does not make the ordering of a CMP contingent upon the case being otherwise untriable, it is clear that several of the cases in which a CMP has been ordered on the authority of the JSA in the early period of that statute's operation do fall into that category: they were untriable even on a proper understanding of the law of PII, and so exemplify unambiguously the possibility which previously was sought to be established with reference to the dubious evidence of *Carnduff v Rock*.[159] It seems at least plausible, therefore, that the possibility of ordering a CMP under the JSA contributes to the overarching requirement that the courts do justice: though it provides for interference with the principles of both open and natural justice, it operates according to the logic of the lesser evil—were CMP not available, a greater injustice might be done. This balancing of injustice, however, was not

[156] See also *Home Office v Tariq* [2011] UKSC 35, [38]–[40], in which Lord Mance states in relation to the paying of potentially unmeritorious claims or the striking out of meritorious claims that '[n]either of these possibilities is one which the law should readily contemplate ... The rule of law must, so far as possible, stand for the objective resolution of civil disputes on their merits by a tribunal or court which has before it material enabling it to do this.' In *Ellis v Home Office* [1953] 2 QB 135, the defendant claimed privilege in relation to certain reports which may have been of assistance to the plaintiff (a prisoner) in claiming damages for injuries suffered in an assault allegedly caused by the negligence of Home Office employees, in breach of the duty of care owed to him under prison rules. At first instance, Devlin J dismissed the action but expressed his 'uneasy feeling that justice may not have been done because the material before [him] was not complete' The case was effectively untriable, albeit not in the *Carnduff* sense where the Court felt compelled to strike it out. Though, like Devlin J, the Court of Appeal was bound by the authority of *Duncan v Cammell Laird*, several remarks were made which urged the government not to rely, as here, on broad class claims to privilege. David Williams notes that the disquiet aroused by Ellis 'was expressed strongly enough to penetrate even the well-insulated corridors of Whitehall' and resulted in an announcement by the Lord Chancellor of certain categories of cases in which the Crown would not insist upon non-disclosure: Williams (n 24) 192–3. The facts of *Ellis*—as well as certain alterations of procedure which would limit the possibility of a recurrence—were discussed by Lord Kilmuir in a statement to the House of Lords: HL Deb 6 June 1956, vol 197 cols 741–748. *Ellis* of course pre-dates *Conway v Rimmer*, which overrides *Duncan v Cammell Laird* and confirms the court as the body which determines whether material should be disclosed. A body of case law analogous to *Ellis* is discussed in David Heaton, 'Carnduff, Al Rawi, the 'unfairness' of public interest immunity and sharp procedure' (2015) *Civil Justice Quarterly* 191, who uses it to argue that the *Canrduff* was wrongly decided and that PII cannot render a trial unfair. The better view, however, is that PII can and does render trials unfair at times, and where it has been allowed to do so in the past an injustice has been done without Parliamentary authorisation.

[157] Tomkins (n 47) 320.

[158] Secretary of State for Justice, *Justice and Security Green Paper*, Cm 8194 (2011), [1.33]–[1.36].

[159] *cf v Security Service; Mohamed v Foreign and Commonwealth Office* [2013] EWHC 3402 (QB), [43]; *R (Sarkandi and others) v Secretary of State for Foreign and Commonwealth Affairs* [2014] EWHC 2359 (Admin), [40]; *McGartland v Attorney General* [2014] EWHC 2248 (QB), [5].

within the scope of the courts' inherent jurisdiction—only Parliament could authorise the doing of the injustice which was necessary to do eventual, partial, justice. To reaffirm: no court has, in the era of the modern law of PII, ever squarely confronted the injustice which comes from either trying such a case without material relevant to its disposal or simply striking out the claim; nor the question of how such injustice can be compatible with the overriding duty of the courts to do justice. In such event, it seems impossible to sustain the dichotomy which has emerged, and to which *Al Rawi* contributes, between open justice and natural justice—between a constitutional principle which can, where necessary in the interest of justice, be violated by in exercise of the court's inherent jurisdiction and one which cannot. A departure from open justice—or even the application of the law of PII, which, if Lord Dyson is to be believed, involves no such departure—may lapse into a violation of natural justice, and yet we have no clear sense of how the courts will deal with that eventuality, at least in the civil context. The enactment of the Justice and Security Act 2013 renders it unlikely that this failing will be remedied in the near term.

iii. The Justice and Security Act 2013

Part 2 of the 2013 Act permits a court which is 'seised of relevant civil proceedings' to declare that the proceedings are 'proceedings in which a closed material application may be made to the court' whether on the application of any party to the case or the Secretary of State, or on its own initiative.[160] Two conditions are to be met if such a declaration is to be made.[161] The first is that, in the course of the proceedings, a party to them would be required to disclose 'sensitive material' to some other party, whether or not itself a party to the proceedings, or that such disclosure would be required except for one of several supervening methods by which that necessity might be avoided. These are, in turn: first, that PII might be claimed in relation to the material (in which case the material might be unavailable for any party to proceedings to rely upon); second, the possibility of choosing not to rely on the material in question (which may, of course, mean in practice simply conceding the point to which that material relates and causing in that way an injustice to be done); third, the rule, contained in the Regulation of Investigatory Powers Act 2000, which excludes from legal proceedings (and so disclosure) the content of intercepted communications, or which 'tends … to suggest' that one of a variety of things, including the interception of communications, have taken place; finally, 'any other enactment that would prevent the party from disclosing the material but would not do so if the proceedings were proceedings in relation to which there was a declaration under this section.'[162] 'Sensitive material' is 'material the disclosure of which would be damaging to the interests of national security'.[163]

[160] Justice and Security Act 2013, s 6(1). The ability of the court to make a declaration either on its own accord or on the application of either party was introduced only belatedly, and argued for—including by the JCHR—on the basis that such a scenario was necessary in order to ensure an equality of arms: Joint Committee on Human Rights, *Legislative Scrutiny: Justice and Security Bill* (2012–13, HL 59, HC 37), [46]–[52].

[161] JSA 2013, s 6(3). Even where the conditions are met, the statute leaves open a discretion to decline to make a declaration, though it will be a 'rare and exceptional case' in which that discretion is exercised: *Belhaj v Straw* [2017] EWHC 1861 (QB), [32].

[162] JSA 2013, s 6(4).

[163] ibid, s 6(11). As foreseen by the Green Paper, the category of material to which the power to make a CMP declaration was to have applied was far broader than is provided for by the 2013 Act: see Joint Committee on Human Rights, *The Justice and Security Green Paper* (2010–12, HL 286, HC 1777), [36]–[47].

The second condition is that 'it is in the interests of the fair and effective administration of justice in the proceedings to make a declaration.'[164] It was this requirement which was the subject of most attention prior to the enactment of the Justice and Security Act: in his analysis of the statute, Adam Tomkins described it as the 'lynchpin' of the JSA regime and as a response to two amendments which the House of Lords sought to make to the bill during the legislative process: first, one which would have introduced into the process for ordering a CMP under the Act a balancing test equivalent to that used in PII. Second, a 'last resort' rule, whereby a CMP could be ordered only if the court considered that 'a fair determination of the proceedings is not possible by any other means'.[165] Tomkins suggested that, in light of certain constitutional tools possessed by, and duties imposed upon, the courts—the principle of legality; the interpretive obligation in section 3 of the Human Rights Act 1998—and, in particular, certain dicta in *Bank Mellat* aimed at avoiding a repeat of the situation which saw the Supreme Court employ a closed procedure unnecessarily,[166] the effect of the 2013 Act 'ought to be that no trial will be permitted to adopt CMP unless the court is satisfied that there are no alternative means by which litigation can proceed.'[167] That is, a 'last resort' rule is effectively implemented, notwithstanding that it is no such explicit requirement is found on the face of the Act.

Reflecting the basic truth that CMP is a greater constitutional evil than is PII, a court may not consider any application for a CMP made by the Secretary of State unless it is satisfied that the Secretary of State 'has, before making the application, considered whether to make, or advise another person to make, a claim for public interest immunity in relation to the material on which the application is based.'[168] Where the court declares that proceedings are proceedings in which a closed material application can be made, it must keep that declaration under review and revoke it if it considers that it is 'no longer in the interests of the fair and effective administration of justice in the proceedings.'[169] The parties are to be permitted by rules of court to apply to the court to not disclose certain material, to which—if the application is accepted—the usual CMP process applies: the material is disclosed to the court and to any special advocate who has been appointed, but not to the other party or his or her representative.[170] The practice of gisting—required, we have noted, by the ECHR and EU law in certain circumstances—is reflected in a duty placed on the court to consider requiring a party permitted not to disclose material to provide a summary of that material.[171] Where a party either decides not to disclose material it has not been given

[164] JSA 2013, s 6(5).

[165] Discussed by Tomkins (n 47) 325. For a prior discussion of the 'last resort' issue, see JCHR (n 163) [63]–[67].

[166] [2013] UKSC 38, [68]–[74].

[167] Tomkins (n 47) 328.

[168] JSA 2013, s 6(7). This precondition is, however, of limited effect: the claim for PII not be made, nor need it appear to the court that the claim would succeed: *Belhaj v Straw* [2017] EWHC 1861 (QB), [52], and the authorities cited there. It has been, however, suggested that the pre-condition is 'not formulaic' and so requires the Secretary of State to 'consider, in essence, whether, having regard to the sensitive material, PII rather than an application for a declaration is the more appropriate course in the relevant civil proceedings': *McCafferty v Secretary of State for Northern Ireland* [2016] NIQB 47, [26].

[169] JSA 2013, s 7.

[170] ibid, s 8(1)(a).

[171] ibid, s 8(1)(d).

permission to withhold or declines to provide, in respect of material it has been permitted to withhold, a summary it has been required by the court to provide, the Act requires that the court have the power to prevent the party from relying upon it or to force that party to make relevant concessions.[172] The disclosing party—often, though not necessarily, the state—therefore retains the ultimate power to decide not to disclose the material whose sensitivity it asserts, though to so refuse may leave it in the position in which it found itself as a result of *Al-Rawi*: paying out compensation in order to settle claims which it holds to be meritless. Alongside these provisions, the 2013 Act transferred the jurisdiction over judicial review of certain immigration decisions (relating to exclusion or the refusal to naturalise or register a citizen) away from the High Court and to SIAC, where a CMP will take place as standard, without the conditions laid down for a CMP in the civil courts having to be met.[173]

The use of the power to order a closed material procedure under the Justice and Security Act 2013 in the time since its enactment suggests that Tomkins' understanding of the relevant law was complacent. At the time of writing, a number of cases under the JSA have been decided by the High Court, several of which have been the subject of decisions by the Court of Appeal.[174] One of these cases offers the most authoritative account of how the relevant provisions—and in particular the two conditions—are to be interpreted. In *Sarkandi* it was argued—with reference to the criticisms made of CMP in both *Al-Rawi* and *Bank Mellat*—that a CMP should be a measure of last resort and that, as it was paraphrased by the judge, 'an inherently unfair closed material procedure should be adopted only if everything else is even more unfair.'[175] Rejecting this argument, the Court of Appeal noted that the ordering of a CMP was clearly authorised by the 2013 Act, and the power to order it subject to clear conditions. For those reasons, the only limit on the interpretation of the relevant provisions was that the statute must be interpreted compatibly with Article 6 of the Convention. There was 'no reason to give the statutory provisions a narrow or restrictive construction' and its provisions 'should be given their natural meaning and applied accordingly'.[176] It was accepted, however, that the judge at first instance had been correct in holding that 'it cannot be in the interests of the fair and effective administration of justice in the proceedings to make a section 6 declaration … unless it is necessary to do so, and that it will not be necessary to make a declaration if there are satisfactory alternatives.'[177] In the specific context of that case, the Court of Appeal upheld the judge's decision that there were no satisfactory alternatives here, holding that 'a PII claim would be bound to lead to the withholding, and thus to the exclusion from consideration, of important detail in the material taken into account by the Secretary of State in reaching his decision, and that the judge was right to say that such detail was essential to an evaluation of the substantive [issue].'[178] We would want, however, to be careful in our use of the term 'essential' here, particularly when the

[172] ibid, s 8(3)(a).
[173] ibid, s 15.
[174] There has so far been no decision of the Supreme Court on these questions: on several occasions that Court has refused permission to appeal against relevant judgments of the Court of Appeal.
[175] *R (Sarkandi) v Secretary of State for Foreign and Commonwealth Affairs* [2015] EWCA Civ 687, [54].
[176] [2015] EWCA Civ 687, [58].
[177] ibid, [61].
[178] ibid, [63].

detail itself has been described, more weakly, as 'important' only moments previously. If the material is truly such that to resolve the dispute without reference to it would be unfair to one party or the other, then it is fair to fall back on a CMP. If, however, it is not, then CMP is not the 'last resort' that Tomkins predicted it to be.

Similarly, the courts have consistently rejected any attempt to induce further disclosure than the terms of the Act require—specifically, a core minimum of the sort that *AF (No 3)* requires in certain circumstances implicating particular individual rights—by reference to common law duties.[179] The one means by which those challenging applications for section 6 declarations have had some success derives from the provision in the Act whereby nothing in the relevant sections 'is to be read as requiring a court or tribunal to act in a manner inconsistent with Article 6 of the Human Rights Convention',[180] but here again the relatively limited scope of *AF (No 3)*, as well as the much weaker requirements of disclosure attested to by *Tariq* have ensured that section 6 has been able to operate compatibly with Article 6 without great difficulty.[181] Few if any claims in respect of which a CMP application under the 2013 Act is made will implicate the fullest requirements of disclosure associated with interferences with liberty.

The constitutional issues raised by the JSA were reflected also in two post-legislative review requirements which it imposed. The first is the duty on the Secretary of State to prepare and lay before Parliament an annual report on applications for CMPs made under the 2013 Act, the number of CMP declarations made, and the number of final (substantive) judgments given in such proceedings, as well as whether those judgements are or are not closed.[182] There is available, therefore, a summary of the extent to which the JSA is made use of in practice. Nevertheless, the annual reports have limitations, not least because they originally adhered to the bare statutory requirements, giving quantitative data but not directing the reader to the cases to which the figures related.[183] As one response to that first report noted, the effect was to demonstrate that 'the section 12 reporting requirements do not ensure that enough information will be provided so that the public can be adequately informed about the occasions when CMPs are sought and why declarations are made or not made.'[184] The necessary detail is now mostly provided, though without statutory compulsion.[185] If the reporting requirement is to do useful work in counteracting the damage done to open justice by the use of CMP and the routine production of closed judgments, then the provision of key detail should not be a matter of contingent practice, but should be mandated by the statute which permits that use. On the basis of these reports, as well as a consideration of the cases which have not yet made it into one of the annual reports, several observations might be made about the use of the JSA in the years since its enactment. The first is the quantitative one: the number of applications made has risen from five in the first

[179] *Khaled v Secretary of State for Foreign and Commonwealth Affairs* [2017] EWHC 1422 (Admin), [24]–[42].

[180] JSA 2013, s 14(2)(c).

[181] See, eg, *K, A and B v Secretary of State for Defence* [2017] EWHC 830 (Admin).

[182] JSA 2013, s 12.

[183] The first report was: Ministry of Justice, *Report on use of closed material procedure (from 25 June 2013 to 24 June 2014)* (July 2014).

[184] Lawrence McNamara and Daniella Lock, *Closed Material Procedures Under the Justice And Security Act 2013: A Review of the First Report by the Secretary of State*, Bingham Centre Working Paper 2014/03 (August 2014), 7.

[185] *cf* Ministry of Justice, *Report on use of closed material procedure (from 25 June 2015 to 24 June 2016)* (November 2016).

year of operation,[186] to 11 in the second,[187] and 12 in the third.[188] All of those not made by the Secretary of State were made by the Chief Constable of the PSNI. The number of declarations that a CMP application may be made has risen from two to five to seven within the period for which figures are available. Though this is not yet drastic, it does suggest that the JSA will be put to work on an increasingly frequent basis, probably in the context of cases which were not and could not have been anticipated at the time of its enactment. Perhaps the most striking aspect, however, is that observed in the Bingham Centre's response to the first annual report, which notes the range of cases in which a section 6 application had been made in the first year of the statute being in force. It seemed, the authors said, that 'nothing is off the table and, importantly, we are a long way from the archetypal case that was the impetus for the legislation, which was an action against the government by returning Guantanamo detainees.'[189] This is true, and most true of the manner in which CMPs have become a common feature of case law relating to the Northern Irish Troubles, in which attempts to seek redress for apprehended injustice have been stymied by applications for a closed material procedure. The consequences of the growth of secrecy stretch, then, rather further back in time than the origins of the modern national security constitution, and work to prevent a reckoning with a past which is perhaps uglier, even less edifying, than are certain elements of the UK's response to the modern national security context. It is not clear how, if this is—as it seems to be—the new norm, the UK will ever deal fully with its past. Certainly, the JSA seems to rule out the use of the courts as the venue for such an endeavour, and there seems little appetite to employ the political institutions to that end in a general, rather than context-specific, way.

The second form of post-legislative review mandated by the 2013 Act is that a person—in practice, the Independent Reviewer on Terrorism Legislation—must carry out a review of the operation of the CMP regime that Act introduced in the five years following its coming into force. The report must be laid before Parliament by the Secretary of State to whom it is submitted, subject to the possibility of excluding from the version laid before Parliament any part of the report which 'would, in the opinion of the Secretary of State, be damaging to the interests of national security if it were included in the copy laid before Parliament.'[190] By that point, it may be that we have a consideration by the Supreme Court of the proper interpretation of the two criteria for the making of a CMP declaration. Five years is, however, long enough for the exceptional to become, if not prosaic, then certainly routine. The review, when it happens, may assist in softening some of the sharp edges of the JSA regime, but it seems unthinkable that it will do anything to reverse the growth in both the availability and the use of CMP: certainly, since the decision of the Strasbourg Court in *Chahal*, the story has been one of almost uninterrupted expansion. Secrecy and the abandonment of equality of arms—and with them the violation of the principles of open and natural justice—are central to the modern national security constitution; the more widespread these phenomena become, the more difficult it becomes to identify some aspect of the constitutional order not shaped by the exigencies of national security.

[186] Ministry of Justice (n 183) 3.

[187] Ministry of Justice, *Report on use of closed material procedure (from 25 June 2014 to 24 June 2015)* (October 2015).

[188] Ministry of Justice (n 185) 4.

[189] McNamara and Lock (n 184) 8.

[190] JSA 2013, s 13.

III. Executive Secrecy

In this final part of the chapter I consider a series of other mechanisms which exist within the constitutional order in order to prevent harm to the public interest generally, and national security in particular, against the harm caused by the disclosure of sensitive information.[191] This section is not, of course, exhaustive, but nevertheless gives a sense of the ways in which certain legal (and non-legal) regimes have (and have not) been relevant to the protection of secrecy within the modern national security constitution. It should be noted here that the key conventions have little to say on the point: the Ministerial Code provides only that 'Ministers should be as open as possible with Parliament and the public, refusing to provide information only when disclosure would not be in the public interest' and that the question 'should be decided in accordance with the relevant statutes and the Freedom of Information Act 2000.'[192] The Civil Service Code, on the other hand, provides that those to whom it applies must not 'disclose official information without authority' and that 'this duty continues to apply after you leave the Civil Service'.[193]

A. Defence and Security Media Advisory Notices

It is useful to remember, for the point at times gets lost, that not all of what sounds in the constitutional order is law. Though not as significant as it once was, a key mechanism by which secrecy as regards certain themes of the constitution—originally defence, but now national security generally—is ensured is the system of Defence and Security Media Advisory Notices (previously 'DA-notices' and, before that, 'D-Notices'), by which the media is requested not to publish certain material on national security grounds.[194] Here, there is no law—no statutory or other basis of the system—and no sanctions: adherence to DSMA Notices is voluntary and though in some cases the failure to abide by the notices will leave individuals open to prosecution under the Official Secrets Act, there is no direct legal sanction associated with breach thereof.[195] The system, introduced in 1912 and reinstituted in 1945 in place of the wartime regime of censorship, first came to public attention when Harold McMillan acknowledged the existence of the Committee in response to a question in the House of Commons. Though the history of what is now the DMSA regimes appears, from the various parliamentary reports which have discussed it, to have operated to the

[191] Particularly important work on this topic includes Williams (n 4124), D Vincent, *The Culture of Secrecy: Britain, 1832–1998* (Oxford, Oxford University Press, 1999) and C Moran, *Classified: Secrecy and the State in Modern Britain* (Cambridge, Cambridge University Press, 2012).

[192] Cabinet Office, *Ministerial Code* (December 2016), [1.2(d)].

[193] The Civil Service Code (March 2015).

[194] The fullest treatment of the topic is found in N Wilkinson, *Secrecy and the Media: The Official History of the United Kingdom's D-Notice System* (London, Routledge, 2009). An earlier history of the Committee which administers the system is given by Alasdair Palmer, 'The History of the D Notice Committee' in C Andrew and D Dilks (eds), *The Missing Dimension: Governments and Intelligence Communities in the Twentieth Century* (London, Macmillan, 1984).

[195] For a consideration of the relationship between the two, see Douglas Fairley, 'D Notices, Official Secrets and the Law' (1990) 10 *OJLS* 431.

satisfaction of both government and press, a number of incidents in the years following its avowal cast the system in a negative light. In the first, the journalist Chapman Pincher had published in the *Daily Express* details of 'cable-vetting' carried out by the government under the authority of section 4 of the Official Secrets Act 1920.[196] Where Chapman believed the Secretary of the Committee to have cleared the story for publication, the Secretary of the Committee believed otherwise. Judging a deliberate breach of the D notices to have taken place, Harold Wilson set up an enquiry by a Committee of Privy Councillors headed by Lord Radcliffe, which concluded that there had been no such breach.[197]

In the second, Johnathan Aitken (who would later crusade against 'the cancer of bent and twisted journalism' in the UK, armed only 'with the simple sword of truth and the trusty shield of British fair play') was—along with other journalists, and the alleged source—prosecuted under the Official Secrets Act 1911 in relation to a story published in the *Sunday Telegraph* regarding the Biafran war, and based upon a confidential report produced by the Defence Adviser to the High Commission in Lagos.[198] Though the jury eventually acquitted all of the accused, the bringing of the prosecution degraded trust in the D-notice system: the paper which published the article had sought and received clearance in the prescribed fashion, and the press had generally believed (though without a clear basis) that no prosecutions could be brought in relation to its publication of material cleared by the Committee.[199] Apart from these particular difficulties, the system had grown unwieldy, with the frequent publication of new notices resulting in a large number of overlapping instructions. In 1971, all notices which existed were withdrawn and replaced by 12 standing notices, reduced to 5 in the year 2000 which, with slight modification to reflect later developments, remain in force at present. These are: DSMA-Notice 01 (Military operations, plans and capabilities); DSMA-Notice 02 (Nuclear and non-nuclear weapons and equipment); DSMA-Notice 03 (Military counter-terrorist forces etc operations, activities and communications methods); DSMA-Notice 04 (Physical property and assets); DSMA-Notice 05 (Personnel and their families). The system is currently overseen by a Defence and Security Media Advisory Committee, whose secretary writes, with reasonable frequency, to editors judged to have breached the notice system in order to remind them of the content of the notices which are in place, and of the willingness of the Committee to provide advice on publication.

The system has only occasionally attracted public attention in recent decades. Between 2004 and 2006 several general letters were sent by the Committee secretary to newspaper editors in order to advise as to the possible consequences of providing excessive detail of the countermeasures being taken by British troops in Iraq against the use of roadside

[196] The story is told in P Hedley and C Aynsley, *The D-Notice Affair* (London, Michael Joseph, 1967). See also Wilkinson (n 194) s 7, and Moran (n 191) Ch 4, where the affair is described as 'Britain's Watergate'. The law related to 'cable-vetting' and its modern equivalents is considered in Ch 2 of the present work.

[197] *Report of the Committee of Privy Councillors Appointed to Inquire into 'D' Notice Matters*, Cmnd. 3309 (1967). Radcliffe's report was rejected out of hand by the government which had commissioned it in a White Paper published on the same day: *The D-Notice System*, Cmnd 3312 (1967). The public and press response to the Wilson government's attempt to deflect blame was extremely negative: see Moran (n 191) 155–164, arguing that 'the great loser of the affair was the secret state' with the D-Notice system discredited and a new zeal for investigative journalism touching on national security issues having emerged.

[198] Aitken's own account is contained of the affair is found in J Aitken, *Officially Secret* (London, Weidenfeld and Nicolson, 1971).

[199] See Wilkinson (n 194) Ch 45, Moran (n 191) and Fairley (n 195).

explosives. Notices were also sent regarding the publication by Wikileaks of US national security information, and later the content of the Snowden revelations.[200] One of the few academic considerations which has been offered in the modern era quotes the then Secretary of the Committee as stating that 'September 11 has changed nothing'; not only did the same notices as before remain in place, but he had 'very consciously ensured that the way in which I interpret them has also remained unchanged.'[201] The author notes, however, that 'the way in which information is becoming available' may be 'a greater catalyst for change than anything hitherto'.[202] This would seem to be obviously correct: the system in large part presupposes a media landscape which belongs to a bygone age and though some of those features of the system which most directly presuppose such a system—the confidentiality of the content of the notices, and the related unwillingness to provide them to publications considered to be in some way subversive—have passed into history, it is unclear that the system can do useful work in the modern media environment. Nevertheless, an independent review of the system, completed in 2015, endorsed its continuation in the face of the challenge posed by, most importantly, the 'impact of new digital media—unregulated, often offshore, fluid and easily accessed'.[203] Without it, it was said, 'the media would be left without a robust system to avoid inadvertent disclosure, with all the potential for them to reveal information that could be both harmful to national or personal security, as well as to their own reputation.'[204] The review also noted, however, 'a lack of direction within the Committee that oversees the system, patchy engagement by government departments (which has contributed to uncertainty within the media about the strength of the government commitment to the system), weak accountability and questions about which government department is best placed to operate the system.'[205] It recommended (most importantly) that a new system of nomenclature be put in place to reflect that the DSMA system encompassed matters other than defence, as well as the restructuring of the Committee. Notwithstanding the review, however, the limitations of the system are demonstrated with increasing frequency. In the context of speculation regarding the relationship between Donald Trump and Russia which circulated prior to the former's inauguration—based in large part upon a dossier compiled by an ex-MI6 agent—the DSMA Secretariat reminded the UK media that one DSMA notice request that editors seek DSMA advice before disclosing 'the identities, whereabouts and tasks of people who are or have been employed by these services or engaged on such work'. The individual in question was named almost immediately by the US media, and then by the UK press. The incident suggests, at the very least, two things: one, that the international nature of the modern media weakens and perhaps destroys the logical basis of the DMSA system and, two, that if the system is to operate as intended, the UK press as a whole must be convinced that the disclosure material covered

[200] One of the emails sent is quoted at length in Ian Cobain, *The History Thieves: Secrets, Lies and the Shaping of a Modern Nation* (London, Portobello Books, 2016) 60.

[201] Pauline Sadler, 'Still keeping secrets? The DA-Notice system post 9/11' (2007) *Communications Law* 205, 210.

[202] Sadler (n 201) 211.

[203] The Defence Advisory Notice System and The Defence Press and Broadcasting Advisory Committee, *Report of the Review* (March 2015). See also the *Government Response to the Review of the Defence Advisory Notice System and the Defence Press and Broadcasting Advisory Committee*, [13].

[204] DA Notice Committee (n 203) [41].

[205] ibid 3.

by it is genuinely potentially harmful to national security. Where it is not so convinced, the balance of incentives upon which the system relies does not apply.

B. The Official Secrets Acts

If DSMA notices rely on the force of persuasion to protect the interests of national security, then the various Official Secrets Acts exemplify the force of law in perhaps its harshest incarnation.[206] The most recent of these, the Official Secrets Act 1989, was passed following a period in which the reputation of the legislation—and in particular the Official Secrets Act 1911,[207] in which the relevant offences were contained—had suffered great damage as a result of a number of prosecutions brought under it, both successful and not.[208] In the 'ABC' trial of 1978, from which resulted the *Leveller* case mentioned above in relation to open justice, three defendants were prosecuted in relation to an article published entitled 'The Eavesdroppers' in *Time Out* regarding the work of GCHQ[209] and discussions which had taken place between them, one of whom was a former GCHQ officer. The most serious of the charges (under section 1 of the 1911 Act) were dropped, and the guilty verdicts in relation to the less serious charges did not result in custodial sentences. In the first half of the 1980s, several other incidents contributed to the impression of an excessively broad, and excessively punitive, statute which the state was too ready to deploy against those who in fact posed no genuine threat to its security. First, Sarah Tisdall pleaded guilty to an offence under section 2 of the 1911 Act—receiving six months in prison—having leaked to *The Guardian* documents detailing the arrival of American cruise missiles in the United Kingdom and the manner in which the Home Secretary would present that information to the House of Commons.[210] A few years later, Clive Ponting, who had leaked to Tam Dalyell documents concerning the sinking of the Belgrano during the Falklands War (and which showed that certain elements of the official narrative relating to that sinking were untrue) was also charged with a Section 2 offence, but pleaded not guilty and was acquitted, despite the judge having declared that 'the public interest is what the government of the day says

[206] On the history of law of official secrets, see D Hooper, *Official Secrets: The Use and Abuse of the Act* (London, Secker & Warburg, 1987) and R Thomas, *Espionage and Secrecy* (London, Routledge, 1991). See also, from a more theoretical perspective, A Rogers, *Secrecy and Power in the British State: History of the Official Secrets Act, 1919–89* (London, Pluto Press, 1997). See also Moran (n 191) and Vincent (n 191).

[207] The 1911 Act, like its 1889 predecessor, was passed through Parliament via a process not deserving of the label perfunctory. For a discussion, see Hooper (n 206) 29–31, who notes that there had been 'no serious discussion in Parliament' of the 'greatly enlarged powers' contained in the 1911 Act. Not discussed here are the Official Secrets Acts 1920 and 1939. The 1939 Act makes only a single amendment to the 1911 Act, substituting a s 6 of considerably reduced scope: for discussion see Hooper (n 206) Ch 5. The 1920 Act—much of which remains on the statute book—contains a number of separate offences, and previously contained (in a now repealed provision) powers for the bulk interception of external telegrams, discussed in Ch 2.

[208] The 1911 Act remains partly in force; the offences therein which are still in force relate to espionage (or spying): see, for a modern prosecution, *R v Daniel James* [2009] EWCA Crim 1261. The key provision, s 2, was however repealed by the 1989 Act, having earlier been criticised by Lord Franks: *Report of the Committee on s 2 of the Official Secrets Act 1911*, Cmnd 5104 (1972).

[209] The article was co-authored by Mark Hosenball, an American journalist whose challenge to his deportation on public interest grounds prefigured many of the themes of the national security constitution discussed in this work: *R v Home Secretary, ex parte Hosenball* [1977] 3 All ER 452.

[210] Hooper (n 206) Ch 11.

it is' and directed the jury to convict.[211] Another significant element of the background to the 1989 Act was the publication by former MI5 officer Peter Wright of his memoir *Spycatcher*[212] and the subsequent battle to suppress the content of the book, which culminated in the decision of the House of Lords in *Attorney General v Observer Ltd*,[213] in which it was held that—due to the widespread publication of the relevant material in other jurisdictions—the allegations it contained were no longer confidential and their publication could no longer be restrained by injunction.

The 1989 Act,[214] which remains (for now) the current law, contains no public interest defence.[215] It creates three offences which are of particular interest from the point of view of secrecy. The first is an offence, capable of being committed either by a person who is or has been 'a member of the security and intelligence services'[216] or 'a person notified that he is subject to the provisions of this subsection' of disclosing, without lawful authority, 'any information, document or other article relating to security or intelligence' which has come into that person's possession by virtue of his membership of those services or while the relevant notification is in place.[217] A second offence, applying to Crown servants and government contractors adds the requirement that the disclosure be a 'damaging' one.[218] This additional requirement does not, however, go far in limiting potential liability. A 'damaging' disclosure is one which 'causes damage to the work of, or of any part of, the security and intelligence services' or which 'is of information or a document or other article which is such that its unauthorised disclosure would be likely to cause such damage or which falls within a class or description of information, documents or articles the unauthorised disclosure of which would be likely to have that effect.'[219] In each case, a defence is available if the individual in question can prove that he did not know and had no reasonable cause to believe either that the document or information related to security or intelligence or, where appropriate, that its disclosure would be damaging.[220] Similar offences to this latter one exist also as regards defence and international relations.[221] Where information to which these provisions apply has come into the possession of a person as a result of disclosure without lawful authority (or disclosure in circumstances that a requirement of confidence exists or could reasonably be expected to exist) that person's disclosure of the information is itself an offence if made without lawful authority and knowing (or having reasonable cause to believe) that it is protected against disclosure by the 1989 Act and that it has come

[211] Ponting's own account of the affair is found in C Ponting, *The Right to Know: The Inside Story of the Belgrano Affair* (London, Sphere Books, 1985). See also R Norton-Taylor, *The Ponting Affair* (London, Cecil Woolf, 1985). See also Hooper (n 206) Ch 12.

[212] *Spycatcher: The Candid Autobiography of a Senior Intelligence Officer* (New York, Viking, 1987).

[213] *Attorney-General Appellants v Observer Ltd* [1990] 1 AC 109.

[214] The Official Secrets Act 1989, the enactment of which was preceded by the publication of the White Paper, *Reform of Section 2 of the Official Secrets Act 1911*, Cm. 408 (1988).

[215] See the discussion of point, including the background to the 1989 Act, in *R v Shayler* [2002] UKHL 11.

[216] Meaning 'the work of, or in support of, the security and intelligence services or any part of them, and references to information relating to security or intelligence include references to information held or transmitted by those services or by persons in support of, or of any part of, them.' OSA 1989, s 1(9).

[217] OSA 1989, s 1(1).

[218] ibid, s 1(3).

[219] ibid, s 1(4).

[220] ibid, s 1(5).

[221] ibid, s 2 and 3.

into his or her possession without lawful authority or in circumstances that a requirement of confidence does or could be reasonably expected to exist.[222] The offence, which covers—most importantly—journalists, applies only where the disclosure is damaging and is made knowing, or having reasonable cause to believe, that it is damaging.[223]

What is interesting, however, about the growth in secrecy within the modern national security constitution, is how little visible role the Official Secrets Acts have played. In the time frame under consideration, the highest profile prosecutions under that Act have related to former MI5 agent David Shayler, who revealed what he alleged were details of certain nefarious activities of the Security Service, and so speak to the theme of the present work only indirectly.[224] *Shayler* confirms that there is no public interest defence (based either upon the objective position of the defendant's subjective belief) to the offences found in the 1989 Act, but left open the question of whether a defence of necessity exists.[225] Katherine Gun, a GCHQ translator, was charged with an offence under section 1 of the 1989 Act when she leaked an email from an agent of the National Security Agency, in which he requested assistance in the bugging of the United Nations offices of certain non-permanent members of the UN Security Council.[226] At trial, however, the prosecution declined to offer evidence—based in part on the difficulty which would be faced in disproving the defence of necessity—and Gun walked free.[227] In 2005 a civil servant and a parliamentary researcher were charged and convicted of offences under the Act relating to the leak of a record of a conversation between Tony Blair and George Bush. The resulting case, *R v Keogh*,[228] saw it clarified by the Court of Appeal that the bulk of the offences created by the Act are not, strictly speaking, strict liability offences:

> In reality the offence will not be committed if the defendant did not know and had no reasonable cause to believe in the existence of the ingredients of the offence as defined in sections 2(3) and 3(4) respectively. In practice therefore the analysis of the defendant's alleged criminality requires attention to be given to his state of mind at the moment when the intentional disclosure took place. In the words of sections 2(3) and 3(4) his knowledge, or whether he has reasonable cause to believe in the features identified in these sections, will almost inevitably, or at least very often, be in issue.[229]

The effect is that the defendant is not required to prove that he did not know the material in question was such as to fall within one of the Official Secrets Act categories, or that he did not know (or have reasonable cause to believe) that its disclosure will be damaging.[230]

Despite these events, the 1989 Act has played a smaller part than might be expected in recent decades, particularly when compared to that role played by its predecessors during the 1970s and 80s. In part, the two things must be causally linked: many of the prosecutions

[222] ibid, s 5.
[223] ibid, s 5(3).
[224] *R v Shayler* [2002] UKHL 11.
[225] [2002] UKHL 11, [17]. See, commenting, Alex Bailin, 'The last Cold War statute' (2008) *Crim LR* 625.
[226] See the discussion in Bailin (n 225) 627.
[227] Bailin (n 225).
[228] *R v Keogh* [2007] EWCA Crim 528. See also the case of Derek Pasquill, charges against whom (relating to the leaking to sensitive information to the press) were dropped in 2008—allegedly because prosecutors realised that material which would have to be disclosed undermined the claim that the leaks were damaging.
[229] [2007] EWCA Crim 528, [19].
[230] See Ben Fitzpatrick, 'Reverse burden and Article 6(2) of the European Convention on Human Rights: official secrets' (2008) 72 *Journal of Criminal Law* 190.

in question were a source of great embarrassment and so it is hardly surprising that the 1989 Act, more draconian than its predecessors, is not routinely invoked. Secondly, as in *Keogh*, the 1989 Act may stand in tension with the human rights framework put in place in 1998 (and if not as interpreted by the domestic courts, then perhaps as interpreted by Strasbourg). There, for example, the section 3 interpretive duty to read and given effect to legislation in a way compatible with the Convention rights (in this case Article 6) influenced the Court of Appeal's decision. Similarly, the existence and scope of any defence of necessity will eventually, it would seem, be determined in part by reference to Article 10 of the Convention. If this is the case, to deploy the Act sparingly avoids giving the courts the opportunity to read down its provisions. Finally, and perhaps most crucially, that the 1989 Act is not deployed does not mean it does not influence behaviour. We can assume that each and every person subject to the specific offences described above is well aware of the Act's continued existence and of the resulting consequences of any unauthorised disclosure of information relating to intelligence and security. The Act underpins the national security constitution whether or not its name is ever spoken and may, in fact, have greater effect specifically because not deployed with the same alacrity that seemed at times to be the case for its predecessors.

The law on official secrets may not, though, exist much longer in its present form: the Law Commission has recently consulted on repealing it and replacing it with a new statute protecting official information against disclosure.[231] Limitations of space prevent a full consideration of these proposals—which may well never make it into law—but it is useful to highlight key elements. One is to address the alleged disincentive to bringing OSA prosecutions which arises from the fact that it is necessary to show that the disclosure was damaging to the relevant specified interest or was of information within a category of information the disclosure of which without authorisation is likely to cause damage to that interest.[232] Proving that fact as part of a prosecution might, it suggested, cause further damage, effectively allowing damaging disclosures to be made with impunity, and so the Law Commission suggested the requirement be removed. Second, and going further than what was decided in *Keogh*, the Law Commission further proposed that 'proof of the defendant's mental fault should be an explicit element of the offence contained in the Official Secrets Act 1989',[233] though the offences should—it suggested—remain strict liability offences in their application to members of the security and intelligence agencies and persons notified of the application to them of the Act.[234] The paper proposed the introduction of a defence of prior publication, but only in relation to the disclosure of information which was 'already lawfully in the public domain and widely disseminated to the public'.[235] It claimed, however, that to introduce a public interest defence 'risks creating legal uncertainty and has the potential to undermine the efficiency of the criminal justice system' and so the disadvantages of doing so outweigh its benefits.[236] Public interest disclosure should

[231] Law Commission, *Protection of Official Data: A Consultation Paper*, Consultation Paper No 230 (2017).
[232] Law Commission (n 231) [3.148].
[233] ibid [3.151].
[234] ibid [3.167].
[235] ibid [3.204].
[236] ibid [7.64].

instead—it suggested—be handled via a Commissioner model, with members of the intelligence services able to bring matters of concern to the Investigatory Powers Commissioner. Perhaps most important, however, is that the proposals are underpinned by an obvious desire to return the law of official secrets to the state's toolbox for dealing with threats to its security: if the Act was to be in some ways watered down in its effects, it was only so that it might be more regularly deployed.

C. Freedom of Information

Since the end of the Cold War and the end of the era in which the Official Secrets Acts were frequently used to increase executive secrecy, the basic scheme of government openness has in many ways been turned on its head by the enactment of the Freedom of Information Act 2000. The general right of access to information held by public authorities which is created by section 1 of that act—the rights to know whether the public authority holds information of a description specified in a request to and, if it does, for the requester to have that information communicated to him or her—is subject to a variety of relevant exceptions, some of them relating only to the latter right (exempting the information from disclosure) and some also to the former (creating a regime whereby the public authority in question is permitted to neither confirm nor deny that it hold the information requested). These exist over and above the exclusion of the security services from the FOI scheme. One exception, that relating to information which was 'directly or indirectly supplied to the public authority by, or [which] relates to' a variety of bodies including the Security Services, the Investigatory Powers Tribunal, and the Intelligence and Security Committee of Parliament, is absolute.[237] This is, in the normal course of events, an absolute exemption—where it applies, there is no need to balance the public interest factors favouring and disfavouring disclosure. Moreover, the duty to confirm or deny if such material is held does not arise where compliance with it 'would involve the disclosure of any information (whether or not already recorded) which was directly or indirectly supplied to the public authority by, or relates to one of the listed bodies.[238] 'Relates to' is interpreted widely (though the ICO considers that a request must be 'in the territory of national security' if the exemption is to apply),[239] and whether information 'relates to' one of the bodies in question is determined according to the civil standard of proof, meaning that it only need be more likely than not that it does.[240] And for the purposes of establishing that information engages either of these rules, a certificate signed by a Minister of the Crown is conclusive (subject to the possibility of an appeal to the Information Tribunal).[241]

A second exemption addresses information which does not fall within the first where its exemption from disclosure is nevertheless 'required for the purpose of safeguarding

[237] FOIA 2000, s 23.

[238] ibid, s 23(5). 'Would' is here interpreted to mean that the eventuality is more likely than not: see *Commissioner of Police of the Metropolis v Information Commissioner*, EA/2010/0008 (23 May 2010).

[239] Information Commissioner's Office, *Freedom of Information Act: Security bodies (section 23)*, version 2.0 (2013), [19]–[21].

[240] *Commissioner of Police of the Metropolis v Information Commissioner*, EA/2010/0008 (23 May 2010).

[241] FOIA 2000, s 23(2).

national security.'[242] The right to neither confirm nor deny whether the information held is available where, and to the extent that, the same criterion applies.[243] Again, a Ministerial certificate certifying that exemption from one or the other of the duties (to confirm or deny, and to disclose) is or was required for the purpose of safeguarding national security is conclusive of the question.[244] Again, such a certificate is subject to a right of appeal to the Information Tribunal. Though there is no statutory definition of 'national security', the Information Tribunal has followed the lead of the House of Lords in *Rehman* in its interpretation of the phrase.[245] 'Required' is taken to mean something more than merely 'useful', being interpreted by the ICO as 'reasonably necessary': 'It is not sufficient for the information sought simply to relate to national security; there must be a clear basis for arguing that disclosure would have an adverse effect on national security before the exemption is engaged.'[246] Unlike the first exemption, this one is not absolute, but rather is subject to a public interest balancing test. And though the NCND elements of the exemptions are not mutually exclusive (and so can be cited together in relation to the same information as long as both are independently engaged)[247] the exemptions from the duty of communication are mutually exclusive (that is, section 24 applies only to information not caught by section 23), and so cannot both apply to the same information. They may, however, be cited 'in the alternative' (even though only one applies) where to cite one or the other exemption specifically would reveal information about the involvement (or non-involvement) of the relevant security bodies.[248] The combined effect of these provisions and their interpretation is that the modern freedom of information regime neatly—and, it seems, fully—accommodates the exigencies of national security. As with the secrecy in the legal process described above, however, even the formalisation of the matter necessitated by the modern freedom of information regime must count as a significant advance, prompting as it does the formalisation of the relevant rules and the creation of clear (if usually futile) avenues of challenge for those to whom disclosure is refused.

D. Public Records

One more point bears mentioning at this stage, even though its relevance for the modern national security constitution remains limited: the law of public records. The relevant law is mostly found in the Public Records Act 1958,[249] which transferred responsibility for such

[242] ibid, s 24(1).
[243] ibid, s 24(2).
[244] ibid, s 24(3).
[245] *Norman Baker v the Information Commissioner and the Cabinet Office*, EA/2006/0045 (4 April 2007).
[246] Decision notice FS50178276 (10 December 2009), and see also *Philip Kalman v Information Commissioner and the Department of Transport*, EA/2009/0111 (8 July 2010).
[247] *The All Party Parliamentary Group on Extraordinary Rendition v Information Commissioner and the Foreign and Commonwealth Office*, EA/2011/0049-0051 (3 May 2012).
[248] Information Commissioner's Office, *Freedom of Information Act: How sections 23 and 24 interact*, version 1.0 (2012), [26]. See *Norman Baker v the Information Commissioner and the Cabinet Office*, EA/2006/0045 (4 April 2007).
[249] For contemporary comment on which, see Theodore Plucknett 'The Public Records Act 1958' (1959) 22 *MLR* 182.

records to the Lord Chancellor,[250] and gave the still-current form to the role of the Keeper of Public Records.[251] The 1958 Act defines the scope of 'public records' and requires the person responsible for such records to select records worthy of preservation and to transfer them (usually) to the National Archive within 20 years (this figure having been reduced from the original term of 30 years).[252] The department which holds the records may seek permission to retain records beyond the 20-year period for administrative purposes or where the records 'ought to be retained for any other special reason', with the approval of the Secretary of State.[253] This allows for the indefinite retention of the relevant records, and is used primarily for national security records, in relation to which there is in place a 'signed instrument' of the Lord Chancellor (the latest in a series of such instruments), which authorises (but does not require) a blanket retention of records falling within broad categories, in respect of each of which the 'special reason' for retention is that 'transfer of the records after that period to the Public Record Office or a place of deposit appointed by the Lord Chancellor under the Act will create a real risk of prejudice to national security'.[254] The Secretary of State is advised on these matters by a statutory non-departmental body known as the 'Advisory Council on Public Records',[255] which—together with the (non-statutory) Forum on Historical Manuscripts and Academic Research—is encompassed by the (also non-statutory) Advisory Committee on National Records and Archives. All three are chaired by the Master of the Rolls, who enjoyed historical responsibility for public records.

The Advisory Council on Public Records also advises on matters arising in the context of freedom of information requests which relate to 'historical records', which public records become twenty years after creation.[256] The FOIA amended the Public Records Act so as to provide that it is the duty 'of the Keeper of Public Records to arrange that reasonable facilities are available to the public for inspecting and obtaining copies of those public records in the Public Record Office which fall to be disclosed in accordance with' the 2000 Act.[257] More such records will be disclosed under this regime than under the normal FOI regime: a number of the exceptions on disclosure contained in the FOIA are disapplied generally in relation to historical records, and others are made unavailable over time, so that few remain available in relation to records that are 60 years old.[258] Amongst those which remain available at that point in time, however, are the exemptions discussed above, regarding to material which was 'directly or indirectly supplied to the public authority by, or relates to' a number of bodies which exist within the national security constitution and information which is required to be exempt 'for the purpose of safeguarding national security'. These exemptions remain available as regards historical records, however much time has elapsed: while the latter is—as noted above—always a qualified exception, however, the former

[250] PRA 1958, s 1.

[251] ibid, s 2.

[252] ibid, s 3(4). The reduction was effected by the Constitutional Reform and Governance Act 2010.

[253] PRA 1958, s 3(4).

[254] The Lord Chancellor's Security and Intelligence Instrument, *Retention of Public Records Under Section 3(4) of the Public Records Act 1958* (19 December 2011), [5].

[255] PRA 1958, s 1(2).

[256] ibid, s 2A. This was reduced from 30 years when the change was made for the purposes of the Public Records Act.

[257] PRA 1958, s 5(3), as amended.

[258] FOIA 2000, s 63.

becomes qualified rather than absolute in its application to historical records.[259] There is therefore scope for the relevant public interest criteria to evolve over time, and with them the question of what historical records are and are not disclosed on this basis. Moreover, the Secretary of State must be consulted before disclosure of historical records is refused on the basis of one of the qualified exemptions which apply to them.[260] Material which has been transferred to the National Archive can be designated 'open'; where it has not been so designated, however, the balance of the public interest is determined by the transferring department rather than the National Archive, subject again to consultation with the Secretary of State.[261] In practice, therefore, both the question of transfer to the National Archives and the eventual question of release under the FOIA will be heavily—perhaps decisively—influenced by the Advisory Committee. Unsurprisingly, perhaps, there is a clear 'establishment' bent to the Committee, with security and defence interests well represented.

The ongoing nature of the national security issues which form the background to the constitutional questions discussed in this book are such that it is hardly surprising, or objectionable, that the law of freedom of information is of little utility in shedding light upon them (while they are simply too recent for the law of public records to yet speak to them).[262] Nevertheless, the law and practice of freedom of information in the national security arena demonstrates certain features which mirror the point made above about the use of closed material procedures in civil proceedings: that is, the law has a reach that is perhaps wider than would have been anticipated, and in practice stretches far beyond what the concept of national security calls immediately to mind at the present time. To take some examples, one recent decision of the First-tier Tribunal upheld (in part) a decision notice upholding the refusal of the National Archives and the Ministry of Defence to reveal records relating to the bombing of McGurks' Bar in Belfast in 1971.[263] Amongst the relevant exemptions were those relating to the security bodies and to national security, both of which are—in the context of historical records—qualified and so subject to a public interest test. Also invoked was the exemption in section 26, which related to material whose disclosure 'would, or would be likely to, prejudice … the defence of the British Islands or of any colony, or … the capability, effectiveness or security of any relevant forces.' The Tribunal made two points about its approach to the public interest. First, that 'engaging the national security and defence exemptions necessarily requires a particularly strong public interest to justify disclosure' and, second, that in considering such matters, it takes an approach which 'acknowledges the relevant institutional competence of the public authority which makes the assessment'.[264] The combined effect is that the decision of the relevant body as to where the public interest lies is, in practice, very unlikely to be departed from by any of the external decision-makers. Even if it is, the freedom of information 'veto' power remains intact, albeit

[259] ibid, s 64(2).

[260] ibid, s 65(1)(a).

[261] ibid, s 66.

[262] Though the shortened, 20-year period which has been instituted means that it will not in fact be long before material relating to the aftermath, say, of the 9/11 attacks has passed the 20-year mark; the framework outlined above, however, means that it is highly unlikely that—even after that point—much of relevance will enter the public domain.

[263] *Ciaran Arthurs v Information Commissioner* [2017] UKFTT 2016_0060 (GRC).

[264] [2017] UKFTT 2016_0060 (GRC), [101].

greatly weakened by the decision of the Supreme Court in *Evans*.[265] In the case of McGurk's Bar, the position that disclosure would be contrary to the public interest is not evidently irrational: as a witness for the Home Office explained to the Tribunal, the threat from terrorism remains 'severe' and the bombing in question is 'still a source of tensions, with a memorial recently being vandalised.'[266] That is, the position of these facts at the start of a process which—notwithstanding the Good Friday Agreement of 1998—remains ongoing makes it plausible that security and defence considerations might justify their continued secrecy.

What the case law shows, however, is that even much older facts can be deemed too sensitive to disclose. In *Keane*,[267] a historian had sought disclosure under the FOIA of a historical file containing records of paid Irish informants working for the Metropolitan Police in the period between 1890 and 1910. The request was made more than a century after the conclusion of the period to which the relevant file referred but was refused on the basis of the national security exemption (particularly in terms of the effect of disclosure upon the state's ability to recruit informants) and that relating to health and safety—the health and safety in question being that of descendants of those named as informants, even in the distant past. When the Information Commissioner's upholding of the refusal to disclose was challenged in the First-Tier Tribunal, the majority upheld it once more, holding that the public interest balancing test favoured the application of the national security exemption; the dissenting member of the Tribunal denied that it the exemption was engaged at all, and so the question of balance did not arise.[268] The majority's decision was upheld by the Upper Tribunal.[269] The decisions of both the First-Tier and Upper Tribunals in *Keane* reflect to a considerable degree the specific context of informants within which the question arose, with there having been repeated consideration of the question of 'how long is long enough' and whether, for example, there is a relevant distinction between informants in late nineteenth-century Ireland and those who operated during the English Civil War. The position which has been taken appears to be that, notwithstanding the theoretical commitment of the police and security services to eternal secrecy, there is indeed a relevant difference:

> Informants in the Irish conflict were operated by agencies still in existence today and still in full operation. Furthermore, there are lingering embers from this conflict, however tangential they may be. Revelations about informants in 17th century affairs cannot be held the responsibility of anyone or any organisation still existing, whereas a revelation about Ireland could easily be linked to the MPS or MI5. As long as the MPS is operating in this way, anything they did in the past retains strong protection because it would be exactly they and no one else that would be responsible for redeeming the promise of perpetual secrecy.[270]

Nevertheless, as with the issue of closed material procedures under the Justice and Security Act, what we see is the implication of the contemporary national security constitution—justified by contemporary conditions—for the possibility of becoming aware of, and then

[265] R (Evans) v Attorney General [2015] UKSC 21.
[266] [2017] UKFTT 2016_0060 (GRC), [88].
[267] *Keane v Information Commissioner* [2016] UKUT 461 (AAC). See also *Metropolitan Police v Information Commissioner* [2008] UKIT EA 78 and *Marriott v Information Commissioner* [2011] UKFTT EA 183.
[268] [2015] UKFTT EA 13 (GRC).
[269] [2016] UKUT 461 (AAC).
[270] [2015] UKFTT EA 13 (GRC), [38].

coming to terms with, Britain's past deeds (and perhaps misdeeds). Though this phenomenon is particularly acute in the Irish context, elsewhere litigation has sought to understand and challenge Britain's roles in, for example, Kenya and the British Indian Ocean Territory.[271] My claim here is not that the past is irrelevant to contemporary national security—nor even that the specific freedom of information decisions discussed are incorrect—but rather that considerations of national security should not be permitted to make a reckoning with the past impossible, and that care should be taken to distinguish between secrecy necessary to protect national security directly, and secrecy which is necessary to prevent, in the first place, embarrassment or anger, and national security only as some derivative thereof.

IV. Conclusion: Secrecy in the National Security Constitution

The tendency towards secrecy in the UK courts in recent decades gives the impression of being something of a juggernaut—progress has taken place in one direction only, and whenever halted by the courts, it has usually been reanimated with some gusto by the legislature. The consideration of the application of the principles of open and natural justice to the civil sphere, however, suggests that the legislative intervention which cut across the development of the law following *Al Rawi* deprived the courts of the opportunity of resolving certain fundamental questions about the interaction of open justice and natural justice with the courts' duty to *do* justice. Is it more obnoxious from the point of view of natural justice to try an issue in the absence of all the relevant material or to strike it out as untriable? An overarching duty to *do* justice provides no solution to that question, but the Justice and Security Act 2013 ensured that the courts were never forced to recognise these duelling injustices and confront their implications. As a result, the unsustainable formalism of the conception of natural justice on which they had relied, in which the maintenance of an equality of arms is sufficient to keep one on the right side of the open/natural justice divide, was never openly acknowledged or addressed. The use to which the JSA has been put since its enactment now continues the expansion of secrecy, but now with little scope for the common law to resist it, and with an ever-wider range of litigation—much of it far removed from the scenarios used to justify the enactment of the JSA—taking place subject to its provisions.

In the criminal context, the respective injustices are different and so the ambiguity absent: the interest of natural justice in ensuring the fairness of convictions are prioritised over the administration of justice in form of the bringing of the prosecution. While the object of doing justice permits the use of PII and the holding of trials in camera (only the latter recognised as a breach of open justice) it does not countenance unfairness, or the breach of natural justice: the criminal context exposes the limitations of the formalist conception of natural justice. It is for this reason disappointing that in *Incedal* the Court of Appeal

[271] See, eg, *Keyu v Secretary of State for Foreign and Commonwealth Affairs* [2015] UKSC 69 and the Bancoult litigation, most importantly *R v Secretary of State for Foreign and Commonwealth Affairs, ex parte Bancoult (No 2)* [2008] UKHL 61.

nevertheless seeks to make use of that conception, framing its disagreement with the trial judge in terms of justification where the concept and language of fairness was better placed to do the relevant work. It is likely that the terms of the judgment in *Incedal* will be pushed to their limits, with the allegedly exceptional circumstances turning out to be more frequent than was claimed therein, and a variety of other circumstances argued to require departures from open justice. The time will come, therefore, for a court to take a stand; to face up to the inadequacy of the conception of the open/natural justice boundary which underlies it and in turn, perhaps, to check this extension of secrecy into and within the criminal realm. Elsewhere in the constitution, a preference for secrecy remains widespread. We have addressed here only some of the relevant mechanisms: even that partial treatment, however, suffices to demonstrate the multiplicity of contexts within which, and methods by which, secrecy is secured. The threatened reform of the Official Secrets Acts will likely constitute the first major push back against executive (rather than curial) transparency which has taken place since New Labour came to power in 1997. If so, however, it can hardly be regarded as anomalous: as this chapter has shown, it would be entirely in keeping with the trend towards ever greater secrecy which has been perhaps the central feature of the modern national security constitution.

6

Justiciability

I. Introduction

The modern national security efforts of the UK have generated a significant quantity of litigation.[1] Given that the acts in question relate to some combination of military action, foreign policy and national security (all topics on which the courts are traditionally reticent to second-guess the executive) and frequently possess a transnational dimension (being, that is, done in co-operation with one or more states, or under the auspices of some international organisation) that litigation has in many cases prompted a reconsideration of the boundaries of justiciability: what the courts will and will not adjudicate upon; what is suitable for their consideration, and what must be recognised in law as the exclusive province of the executive, as well as why. It is those rules, and their implications for the national security constitution, that are considered in this chapter.

The chapter is divided in three sections. The first is the bare question of the justiciability of foreign affairs, in relation to which it is argued that the law is shot through with indeterminacy. I respond to that indeterminacy by providing an account of the non-justiciability of foreign affairs which denies the premise; which explains, that is, that foreign affairs are not, properly understood, generally non-justiciable at all. This argument is tenable only in the context of an account of what is genuinely non-justiciable, which I offer in the second and third sections, via consideration of, first, a rule of justiciability which applies to the sovereign acts of foreign states and, second, a doctrine which applies to the acts not of foreign states but of the UK. In each of the three contexts—the general justiciability of foreign affairs, 'foreign act of state', and 'Crown act of state'—the modern national security context has precipitated considerable doctrinal evolution. Before that, however, it has brought clarification: doctrines developed in previous eras, and which reflect certain assumptions about the proper division of constitutional authority, have been brought into the light of day and, in some ways at least, finessed and rationalised. Unlike as regards certain other of those addressed in Part 2 of this book, the picture which emerges must be judged to be not

[1] One reason for this is that, as noted in Ch 3, modern military endeavours take place without a formal declaration of war and so without enemies being rendered enemy aliens, who have no access to the courts: see *Amin v Brown* [2005] EWHC 1670 (Ch). Another is the availability of legal aid to persons not resident in the UK. The proposed introduction of a residency test (which would have applied in most circumstances) was held by the Supreme Court to be ultra vires the Legal Aid, Sentencing and Punishment of Offenders Act 2012 in *R (Public Law Project) v Lord Chancellor* [2016] UKSC 39. At first instance, Moses LJ had said that it was 'worth drawing attention to the fact that the residence test will exclude from access to legal aid individuals resident abroad who have been subject to serious abuses at the hands of UK forces': [2014] EWHC 2365 (Admin), [31].

as a negative, or even a broadly neutral, one, but in fact as demonstrating a clear, if uneven, improvement upon the status quo ante. This is not, of course, to say that there is not much to be regretted in the courts' approach to these issues: the law of justiciability remains in many way problematic, and the doctrines of foreign and Crown act of state do not cease to be in considerable tension with basic rule of law values simply because they are less extensive than was once the case.

II. Justiciability (and Foreign Affairs) Generally

Here I consider the justiciability of foreign affairs in English law,[2] assuming, in line with the orthodox position, that justiciability cannot depend upon the nature of relevant proceedings:[3] what is and is not justiciable in public law proceedings should be equally justiciable (or not) in private law proceedings. The justiciability of foreign affairs has historically been tied up in the question of the justiciability of the prerogative powers, amongst which that to conduct foreign affairs is usually identified (whether under that name or in the form of a variety of powers which orbit around that topic).[4] Nevertheless, the question of whether the conduct of foreign affairs truly represents an exercise of the prerogative has diminished in importance as the source of the power has been displaced as the determinative factor of whether some act might be reviewed by the courts. The received wisdom is that the exercise of prerogative powers—the residue of the once-great powers exercised by the Monarch in person—was not amenable to review by the courts until the decision of the House of Lords in the *GCHQ* case, relating to a ban on membership of trade unions by employees of the Government Communication Headquarters. Rather than reviewability being determined by the source of a power—that is, the question of whether it derived from statute or was part of the prerogative—the approach of the courts since *GCHQ* has been to determine reviewability by reference to the subject-matter of the power in question. Lord Roskill identified powers which he took to be unsuited to judicial overview:

> Many examples were given during the argument of prerogative powers which as at present advised I do not think could properly be made the subject of judicial review. Prerogative powers such as those relating to the making of treaties, the defence of the realm, the prerogative of mercy, the grant of honours, the dissolution of Parliament and the appointment of ministers as well as others are not, I think susceptible to judicial review because their nature and subject matter are such as not to be amenable to the judicial process.[5]

[2] On this topic see, very usefully, Dominic McGoldrick, 'The Boundaries of Justiciability' (2010) *ICLQ* 981.

[3] See, eg, *Serdar Mohammed v Secretary of State for Defence* [2015] EWCA Civ 843, [324]: 'In our view, whether issues are justiciable cannot depend on the nature of the proceedings. On the contrary, what is suitable for adjudication by a court must be determined by the court on the basis of the subject matter in dispute. Accordingly, what is justiciable in public law proceedings is also justiciable in private law proceedings.'

[4] See, eg, HM Government, *The Governance of Britain*, CM 7170 (2007), 17, listing prerogative powers including those to: 'Deploy and use the Armed Forces overseas; Make and ratify treaties … Acquire and cede territory … Conduct diplomacy; Send and receive ambassadors …'.

[5] [1985] AC 374, 418. Not all of the listed powers survive: see, eg, the Fixed-term Parliaments Act 2011, which effectively abolishes the power to dissolve Parliament.

Lord Fraser for his part distinguished powers such as that at issue in the case before him from those to which the traditional approach to reviewability might apply—this latter category including, crucially, the conduct of foreign policy and the 'control' of the armed forces, which between them encompass much or all of the subject-matter of the cases under consideration here.[6] A point should be made here about the implications of bringing an end to the subject matter/source distinction. If the distinction has truly ceased to be legally determinative then not only should it be possible—post-*GCHQ*—for prerogative powers to be reviewable, but similarly for statutory powers to be non-reviewable: that is, if subject matter rather than source is what matters, it would seem to follow that certain statutory powers might, by virtue of their subject matter, be excluded from the purview of the courts. And yet that does not seem to be true: on the contrary, the existence of a statutory power (we shall see below) works to overcome prima facie non-justiciability. That this issue has not yet caused significant difficulty is a function of the care which has been taken in replacing prerogative powers with statute. It remains the case that the most politically sensitive powers (those most obviously raising issues of high policy) remain part of the prerogative; where powers have been shifted to a statutory form in the decades since *GCHQ*, it has been those which are less sensitive—the management of the civil service,[7] for example, or the dissolution of Parliament.[8] Even there, however, the statutory framing of the powers works to exclude courts: because there is no person or institution entrusted with a statutory power to dissolve Parliament, there is no discretion which might be challenged (and the justiciability of which the courts would require to determine). That this correlative move does not seem to have happened is particularly important given the role of statute in overcoming prima facie non-justiciability. If, that is, the partial reviewability of the prerogative was accompanied by the introduction of non-justiciable statutory powers, then statute could no longer be assumed to play that supervening role; that it in fact does suggests that there may be certain powers which will never be considered suitable for placing upon a statutory footing.

These points aside, we see that to determine the justiciability of foreign affairs it is no longer sufficient to identify the source of the power to conduct such affairs. What instead determines the question, however, is not at all clear, with the modern case law divulging a number of factors which have been invoked by the courts in relation to the question of whether or not some aspect of foreign affairs is justiciable and demonstrating inconsistency on the question of whether there are certain matters which can never be the subject of a determination by the courts—whatever the reason—or whether the matter will always and everywhere be decided in the context of the particular case. In one of the earliest post-11 September cases, *Abbasi*,[9] it was said by Lord Phillips (then the Master of the Rolls) that '[t]he issue of justiciability depends, not on general principle, but on subject matter and suitability in the particular case.'[10] In *Abbasi*, the claimant was a UK national detained in the Guantanamo Bay prison operated by the US in Cuba which—the case law

[6] [1985] AC 374, 398.
[7] Constitutional Reform and Governance Act 2010, Pt 1.
[8] Fixed-term Parliaments Act 2011.
[9] *R (Abbasi) v Secretary of State for Foreign and Commonwealth Affairs* [2002] EWCA Civ 1598.
[10] [2002] EWCA Civ 1598, [85].

at the time suggested—was a 'legal black hole' in which, the Court of Appeal accepted, he was being 'arbitrarily detained'.[11] Though it was ultimately of little value to Abbasi himself, the Court found against the government's argument that the matter was non-justiciable, largely as a result of the decisions as to the reviewability of the prerogative since *GCHQ*. The legitimate expectation Abbasi enjoyed—that the UK government would consider making representations to its US counterpart—had, however, been fulfilled: his request for assistance had been considered and general discussion about the status of British detainees in Guantanamo had taken place,[12] with nothing more required of the UK authorities. It is difficult to escape the conclusion that the Court of Appeal's conclusion here—though falling far short of what would have been necessary to result in the claimant's escape from the 'legal black hole'—was motivated in part by a revulsion at the situation in which a British national found himself: 'subject to indefinite detention in territory over which the United States has exclusive control with no opportunity to challenge the legitimacy of his detention before any court or tribunal.'[13] And so, though the key dictum has been repeatedly invoked in order to argue that the courts should treat as justiciable some question or set of facts which elsewhere would be held non-justiciable, at times exactly the opposite conclusion emerges from cases in which the cause would appear to be considered less vital, or at least more distant from the core concerns of an English court.

At this opposite end of the spectrum is *Al-Haq*,[14] in which a Palestinian NGO sought, inter alia, a mandatory order that the UK government 'use its best endeavours' to meet its obligations under international law as regards an alleged breach of customary international law by Israel. Little sympathy for the claimant's position is evident in the High Court's judgment which held, apart from anything else, that the applicants had no standing to bring their claim. But it is on the question of the justiciability that the attitude of the Court is made manifest and, in particular, in the statement that '[i]t is not the case that in the modern administrative State there are no no-go areas for the Court.'[15] Not only does this suggest that the key dictum from *Abbasi* is false—that there are certain issues upon which the courts will not (or cannot) pronounce[16]—but *Al-Haq* evidences also the sheer range of factors which might be taken as speaking to the question of justiciability and, most problematically, the difficulty of establishing the relation between them. This is clear in particular from the opinion of Cranston J, who notes that the issue is non-justiciable not only by reasons of the courts' institutional unsuitability for deciding the underlying factual questions, but also because there were no 'judicial or manageable standards'; because—unlike in comparable cases—there was no 'domestic foothold'; on the basis of the principle of comity; and, because the case raised issues of 'high policy' which 'under our constitutional settlement … lie within the exclusive purview of the executive.'[17] While all of these points might individually be true, an approach which pulls each factor out of the jurisprudential

[11] ibid, [64].

[12] ibid, [107].

[13] ibid, [66]. See also *Al Rawi v Secretary of State for Foreign and Commonwealth Affairs* [2006] EWCA Civ 1279, [2]–[4].

[14] R *(Al-Haq) v Secretary of State for Foreign and Commonwealth Affairs* [2009] EWHC 1910 (Admin).

[15] [2009] EWHC 1910 (Admin), [53].

[16] Note though the hesitation evidenced by the triple negative formulation.

[17] [2009] EWHC 1910 (Admin), [55]–[60].

hat, one after another, is not easily systematised as a coherent and predictable body of law. And yet too often case law on the justiciability of foreign affairs takes exactly that approach. I propose, therefore, to rethink the question of non-justiciability, both generally and as it applies to foreign affairs.

A. Rethinking (Non-)Justiciability

The best starting point for any contemporary discussion of justiciability is the decision of the Supreme Court in *Shergill v Khaira*.[18] Unlike almost all of the case law discussed elsewhere in this chapter, *Shergill* does not have any an international or security dimension. Instead, it relates to a dispute within a Sikh sect based in England, with the question of justiciability arising because the Supreme Court was required to rule upon the extent to which the courts can and should refuse to determine religious questions. The Court of Appeal had held the entire matter to be non-justiciable, stating that there were questions 'on which a court is not competent to speak with authority, because of the limitations inherent in the nature of the judicial process, and therefore should not speak' and that the matter at the heart of the case was such a question.[19] In the Supreme Court, the judgment of Lords Neuberger, Sumption and Hodge (with which Lords Mance and Clarke agreed) contains a broader discussion of justiciability, which they distinguish from other rules—such as of state immunity or the act of state doctrine[20]—which 'may result in an English court being unable to decide a disputed issue on its merits'.[21] Properly understood, they say, non-justiciability refers to 'an issue is said to be inherently unsuitable for judicial determination by reason only of its subject-matter.'[22] This must be correct: the language of non-justiciability suggests not a mere unwillingness on the part of the judiciary, but rather a legal inability. It must also be distinguished from situations in which, as a result of the area of policy within which a legal question arises for determination, the courts apply a less intensive standard of review to actions of the executive—what is sometimes called 'super Wednesbury' review—or where, in recognition of the democratic credentials (and associated political accountability) of that decision maker, they 'defer' to that person's assessment of whether some interference with a legally protected interest is proportionate to the benefit that results from it as regards whatever aim is identified as justifying it.

Two forms of non-justiciability are identified by the Supreme Court in *Shergill*. The first arises where the issues are entirely beyond the 'constitutional competence assigned to the courts under our conception of the separation of powers' and is distinguished by its absolute nature.[23] Where a question is non-justiciable in this sense, it does not matter that

[18] *Shergill v Khaira* [2014] UKSC 33.

[19] *Khaira v Shergill* [2012] EWCA Civ 983, [69]–[73].

[20] The judgment refers to act of state as conferring 'immunity from liability on certain persons in respect of certain acts.' This would seem to be a reference to Crown act of state rather than foreign act of state (on the distinction between which, see below) as only the former, in its tort defence aspect, can be said to have the effect described. Even here, however, there is a difficulty: as discussed below, Crown act of state was at the time that *Shergill* was decided considered a dualist doctrine, with the 'tort defence' limb existing alongside a 'justiciability' limb.

[21] [2014] UKSC 33, [41].

[22] ibid.

[23] [2014] UKSC 33, [42].

it may be necessary to adjudicate upon it in order to vindicate some legal right a person has; 'even if it is necessary to do so in order to decide some other issue which is itself unquestionably justiciable.'[24] For that reason non-justiciability of this sort, which 'may result in a denial of justice which could only exceptionally be justified either at common law or under article 6 of the Human Rights Convention' is necessarily exceptional.[25] The Supreme Court gives two examples of this form of non-justiciability, which we can call 'type 1'. The first is that of foreign act of state, discussed below. The second is that of parliamentary privilege, exemplified for the Supreme Court by the decision in *Prebble v Television New Zealand Ltd*,[26] in which the Privy Council held that the lower court had been correct to strike out pleadings relating to the statements of a Minster in the New Zealand Parliament which the defendants had wished to rely upon in their defence to a claim of defamation by the Minister against them. That is, though the material in question might well have been relevant to the determination of the issues, the law of parliamentary privilege rendered it non-justiciable in the strictest of senses, and the claim was to be determined without reference to it. This is a useful illustration of the starkness of the effect of a holding that a certain issue is non-justiciable: a legal system distributes rights and obligations, and yet that distribution may be incorrectly ascertained—or not ascertained at all—where courts are unable or unwilling to consider certain topics or questions. It illustrates too the need to limit carefully the range of such topics or questions, for the consequences for individuals may be very severe indeed.

The second category of non-justiciability—'type 2'—is, however, less coherent and its articulation works to undermine the clarity of the Supreme Court's initial account of the concept of justiciability. This second category 'comprises claims or defences which are based neither on private legal rights or obligations, nor on reviewable matters of public law' such as, Lords Neuberger, Sumption and Hodge say, 'domestic disputes; transactions not intended by the participants to affect their legal relations; and issues of international law which engage no private right of the claimant or reviewable question of public law.'[27] The difficulty with these examples is made immediately clear by the description of the consequence which attend them: they 'might well be non-justiciable in this sense if the court were asked to decide them in the abstract' but 'must nevertheless be resolved if their resolution is necessary in order to decide some other issue which is in itself justiciable.'[28] As that account itself suggests, this second category is best understood as not relating to justiciability at all. In cases of non-justiciability, the underlying legal question remains unresolved, for to resolve it—to vindicate the underlying rights—would require the courts to grapple with matters which are, in the words used here, 'inherently unsuitable for judicial determination'. What are instead being included in this second category of non-justiciability are situations in which the court will not answer a legal question, because there is no legal question, no issue of domestic law, for them to do so. As soon as such a question arises—as soon as there is some other issue 'in itself justiciable', in the sense, we see now, of being a legal question

[24] ibid.
[25] ibid.
[26] [1994] 3 NZLR 1.
[27] [2014] UKSC 33, [43].
[28] ibid.

which the courts are capable of answering, and not itself non-justiciable in the true sense—the courts will resolve that question, whether it be a matter of public or private law.

What the Supreme Court identifies here as a category of non-justiciability is therefore better understood as the converse of the fact that the courts will only decide questions as to the actual distribution of rights and liabilities, according to the law which falls to be applied in the domestic courts. Where they refuse to 'adjudicate on the international acts of foreign sovereign states or to review the exercise of the Crown's prerogative in the conduct of foreign affairs'—to take the examples used here—they do so, the Supreme Court correctly states, because 'no legal right of the citizen is engaged whether in public or private law' and not because the determination of the right would require them to engage with matters which are inherently unsuitable and so must go unvindicated. And this reference to public and private law should have its domestic nature foregrounded: often, what is treated as an issue of justiciability, or of the absence within the applicable law of 'judicial or manageable standards', is in fact a direct and natural consequence of the constitution's dualism, which prevents international law from creating rights applicable in domestic courts except to the extent provided for by Parliament.[29] This failure to distinguish these two concepts—which is frequently evidenced by treatments of the issue—would seem to account for many of the difficulties and persistent uncertainties of contemporary justiciability doctrine as it relates to foreign affairs.

The force of the point can be demonstrated with reference to the *CND* case,[30] in which the High Court declined to give an advisory declaration that it would be unlawful for the UK to undertake military action in Iraq. Though the judgment reflects a certain confusion about the status of customary international law in domestic law, the issue is captured in Simon Brown's attempt to distinguish the case before him from others in which the courts had been willing to undertake the interpretation of international instruments (primarily *Adan*).[31] 'Should the court,' he asked 'declare the meaning of an international instrument operating purely on the plane of international law?' No, was his answer: 'All of the cases relied upon by the applicants in which the court has pronounced upon some issue of international law are cases where it has been necessary to do so in order to determine rights and obligations under domestic law.'[32] Here, there was 'no point of reference in domestic law to which the international law issue can be said to go; there is nothing here susceptible of challenge in the way of the determination of rights, interests or duties under domestic law to draw the court into the field of international law.'[33] Rather than demonstrating why the matter is not justiciable, these comments demonstrate that the case is not in fact one in which it was necessary to consider the question of justiciability at all. That is, the Court did not answer the legal question because there was no legal question for it to answer; only had there been some point of domestic law to decide and the Court had declined to do so for some reason—the high policy nature, say, of the decision to go to war—would we have been dealing with justiciability in the type 1 sense. The question of what was decided in *CND*

[29] See now in particular the overview of the issue found in the judgment of the Supreme Court in *R (Miller) v Secretary of State for Exiting the European Union* [2017] UKSC 5, [55]–[57].

[30] *R (Campaign for Nuclear Disarmament) v Prime Minister* [2002] EWHC 2777 (Admin).

[31] *R v Secretary of State for the Home Department, ex parte Adan* [1999] 1 AC 293.

[32] [2002] EWHC 2777 (Admin), [36].

[33] ibid.

(and why) continues to be debated in subsequent case law. In a recent case, Lord Sumption has suggested of the case that 'if domestic law rights, interests or duties had been engaged, the court would not have regarded the issues as non-justiciable.'[34] Whether or not this is true as a counter-factual, it seems to correctly state the legal position: not only was *CND* not a case about non-justiciability properly so called, but had it been such a case, the matters would have been justiciable.[35] We can see also from this that the absence of a 'domestic foothold' in a given case—itself frequently identified as justifying non-justiciability—is simply the correlative of this first point: to say that there is no domestic foothold is to say that the only legal questions are pure questions of international law which the courts have no authority to decide.

In light of this distinction, it is worth noting that the literature has never adequately addressed William Wade's contention that prerogative includes only legal power: 'the ability to alter people's rights, duties or status under the laws of this country which the courts of this country enforce'.[36] On that basis, we must doubt the correctness of the assumption that the conduct of foreign affairs—which in and of itself does not and cannot result in changes to that distribution—takes place under the prerogative. There is much to be said for this account: on the prevailing interpretation of the common law rule of law, the state needs legal authority only for those acts which have legal effects, which conflict with or alter the public law or private law rights of legal persons.[37] For those acts which do not—which are purely administrative—no such authority is required.[38] If an act—to enter into talks about some aspect of international affairs, say, with partners abroad—does not affect legal rights, then it does not seem to require legal authority at all, and so it is difficult to make sense of the claim that there exists a legal power to carry it out.[39] Moreover, the number of those 'powers' traditionally listed as part of the prerogative which would have to be excised from any list reflecting Wade's additional criterion would be smaller than might originally thought given that at least one power traditionally thought not to involve an alteration of rights does (it is argued elsewhere in this book) in fact do so.[40]

Two points might be made about this: the first is that the specific examples given by both Lords Fraser and Lord Roskill in *GCHQ* include a large proportion which are non-justiciable in the type 2 sense: they have no legal effect and so there is nothing which the courts might review even if they were minded to do so. This includes, for example, the making of treaties (which by virtue of our constitutional dualism do not sound in

[34] *Serdar Mohammed v Ministry of Defence* [2017] UKSC 1, [79].

[35] Lord Sumption's reading is disputed by Lord Mance: [2017] UKSC 1, [48]. See also Lord Sumption, 'Foreign Affairs in the English Courts Since 9/11' (14 May 2012).

[36] See HWR Wade, *Constitutional Fundamentals*, rev ed (London, Stevens & Sons, 1989) 58 and 'Procedure and Prerogative in Public Law' (1985) 101 *LQR* 180.

[37] See the discussions in the chapters by Tomkins (disputing this view), Endicott, and Scott (both of whom endorse it) in A Tomkins and P Scott (eds), *Entick v Carrington: 250 Years of the Rule of Law*, (Oxford, Hart Publishing, 2015).

[38] The rule of law implications of this account are considered in Adam Perry, 'The Crown's Administrative Powers' (2015) 131 *LQR* 652.

[39] It would though be necessary to clearly distinguish from the question of foreign affairs generally those situations in which, as the Supreme Court put it in *Miller*, 'the effect of an exercise of prerogative powers is to change the facts to which the law applies', including the declaration of war (as a result of which otherwise lawful actions may become treasonous, and friendly aliens may become enemy aliens): [2017] UKSC 5, [53].

[40] See the discussion of the legal effect of passports in Ch 4.

domestic law) and the conduct of foreign policy. To mention these in the context of the ongoing non-justiciability of the prerogative risks undermining the simultaneous claim that the other powers mentioned (those which do have legal effect) are non-justiciable. That many of those powers have later been found to be in fact justiciable similarly calls into question that account. It is submitted, therefore, that the better (default) view is that all prerogative powers which have legal effect as a matter of domestic law (which, on one view, are all those that are properly regarded as part of the prerogative) should be recognised as justiciable, even if the flexibility of the substantive standard of judicial review may result in only extremely light-touch oversight by the courts.[41] That not everything done by virtue of the prerogative properly so called is justiciable is a function not of rules special to the prerogative but instead, as discussed below, the doctrine of Crown act of state.

B. The Justiciability of Foreign Affairs

This stricter definitional approach helps to simplify our task by showing that many of the cases said to exemplify the courts' approach to justiciability do no such thing. It will, however, only go so far in providing clarity as to how the courts will approach particular cases: this account does not remove areas of uncertainty but simply shifts the relevant uncertainty to a different place within the legal landscape. It often remains, that is, open to a court to find a domestic foothold—to show that there is, contrary to first appearances, some issue of domestic law which the courts will be required to, and will in fact, resolve—through a suitably creative framing of the case brought before it. *Abbasi* would seem to exemplify that possibility: framed as relating to the conduct of foreign relations by the UK, the case raises no issue of domestic law; framed, instead, as relating to the rights of protection owed to the citizen by his government (which turn out to be rather fewer than might be desired), the case raises a matter which the domestic courts are able to rule upon. The same can be said of *Rahmatullah*,[42] relating to the issue (and sufficiency of the return to) a writ of habeas corpus in respect of Yunus Rahmatullah, a Pakistani national detained by the UK in Iraq and handed over to US authorities in accordance with a Memorandum of Understanding between the two. By framing the matter as relating purely to the domestic lawfulness of the relevant acts, the Supreme Court was able to find that the writ did issue, but also that the return was sufficient; had the matter been framed as relating to international relations and the compatibility of the transactions of sovereign states with international law, even this pyrrhic victory would have been impossible. The point can be made once again that there exist—in most if not all cases—paths by which the court called upon to decide a question can arrive at whatever conclusion seems most apt in the circumstances, though of course to identify a suitable 'domestic foothold' does not exclude that the question thus identified will be held to be non-justiciable in the strict sense: the process of determining justiciability, however, starts from (rather than ending at) the identification of the domestic foothold.

[41] See on this point also Lord Sumption (n 35).

[42] *Rahmatullah v Secretary of State for Foreign and Commonwealth Affairs (No. 2)* [2012] UKSC 48. For commentary, see Hayley J Hooper, 'Shining light on the darkness? Rahmatullah v Secretary of State for Foreign and Commonwealth Affairs and Secretary of State for Defence' [2013] *PL* 213.

i. Absolute or Relative?

Another advantage of this account is that it allows us to resolve other, related, uncertainties which exist within the case law. One such uncertainty is whether the presence of one of the offending factors considered above renders a question absolutely non-justiciable (that is, it means that the courts cannot decide the question at all) or whether it simply means that the courts should hesitate to address the question. Both interpretations can be supported based upon material in the case law, in some cases within the very same judgements. We have quoted above the depiction of certain elements of the administrative state as 'no go areas'. At the other end of the spectrum, we might note Lord Bingham's discussion of the question of justiciability in *R v Jones*,[43] in which the House of Lords dismissed a number of criminal appeals based on alleged desire of the defendants (who had trespassed on military bases immediately prior to the invasion of Iraq) to prevent the commission of the (international) crime of aggression. Lord Bingham stated that to recognise such a crime in English law would require the courts to decide upon 'call for a decision on the culpability in going to war either of Her Majesty's Government or a foreign government, or perhaps both if the states had gone to war as allies.'[44] There are, however:

> well-established rules that the courts will be very slow to review the exercise of prerogative powers in relation to the conduct of foreign affairs and the deployment of the armed services, and very slow to adjudicate upon rights arising out of transactions entered into between sovereign states on the plane of international law.[45]

A few years earlier, also in the *CND* case, Kay J in the High Court had stated that though the law had moved on since the *GCHQ* case, '[f]oreign policy and the deployment of armed forces remain non-justiciable',[46] where non-justiciability seems to suggest not a hesitation to adjudicate upon the issue but rather an absolute bar to doing so. One interpretation is that the ambiguity is convenient to the courts: where the allegedly countervailing factors are strong, cases which talk of 'no go areas' and the like permit the courts to ignore them if to do so seems politic. Conversely, where the court sees an injustice which must be remedied, talk of being slow to intervene rather than incapable of doing so permit the courts to step in as long as suitably compelling countervailing factors can be identified. Another is that the answer to the question varies depending on the reason for non-justiciability; that, for example, the fact that it pertains to matters of high policy means that the courts will not normally decide some question but that it may do so exceptionally depending on the gravity of the issues raised, while other bases of non-justiciability are exclusionary, taking no account of any countervailing considerations. The better view, however, must be that any apparent ambiguity reflects a failure to clearly distinguish different forms of justiciability and non-justiciability in the context of foreign affairs. Where a matter is non-justiciable because there is no domestic law question to answer (type 2), then the acquisition of a suitable domestic foothold will nevertheless often see the courts apply a weak standard of

[43] *R v Jones* [2006] UKHL 16.
[44] [2006] UKHL 16, [30].
[45] ibid.
[46] [2002] EWHC 2777 (Admin), [50].

review in any relevant public law proceedings. This should not, however, be confused with their willingness to review the acts in question at all, which is not a matter of choice where there is such a legal question to be answered. Where, however, there is true, type 1, non-justiciability, then it is not a matter of mere hesitation: there can be no review of the issues, and so the question of what standard of review should be applied does not arise.

ii. Overcoming Prima Facie Non-Justiciability?

The other major area of uncertainty within the case law on justiciability relates to a situation of prima facie non-justiciability, and what factors will suffice to overcome that status. This too becomes clearer once the distinction is drawn between the two forms of non-justiciability discussed in *Shergill*. That is, where we are discussing type 2 non-justiciability, we are not—we now see—overcoming some prima facie non-justiciability, but identifying some domestic legal question that the courts might answer and in doing so producing a justiciable issue in the first place. The first part of our answer is therefore reasonably straightforward: when a statute requires the courts to decide a question, they must do so. For that reason, the landscape of justiciability is much altered by the enactment of the Human Rights Act 1998, section 6 of which makes it unlawful for a public authority to act in a way which is incompatible with the Convention rights, and some of the case law that is generally bundled together with non-justiciability is really about the extent to which the ECHR (and so the HRA) reaches matters which would not otherwise give rise to questions of domestic law.[47] The HRA therefore creates questions of law where often none would have otherwise arisen, and so requires the courts to adjudicate in areas of policy where there would previously have been no legal hook on which to hang some consideration of the matter.[48] To the extent that issues remain non-justiciable in the type 2 sense, it is because the Strasbourg Court has, in its interpretation of the relevant provisions of the Convention, denied that certain of those acts which would be considered non-justiciable at common law, implicate the Convention rights. And where we are dealing instead with type 1 non-justiciability, such non-justiciability (being an aspect of the common law) is superseded by a statutory mandate, of which—again—the HRA is likely to be the most important example. The effect is that statute suffices to overcome both type 1 and type 2 non-justiciability, but for different reasons: in the first case, because it supplants the common law rule and the constitutional concerns which it embodies; in the second, because it creates a legal question where one would otherwise not have existed, and which the courts can therefore be called upon to answer.

Greater difficulty is found where the legal issues to be resolved does not derive from statute, for outside of that situation it will often be far less clear whether there is some question to answer or not. Here, we can connect back the question to the discussion above regarding the nature of the prerogative and, in particular, the question of whether the

[47] See, eg, *R (Gentle) v Prime Minister* [2008] UKHL 20.

[48] See also *R (Lord Carlile of Berriew QC) v Secretary of State for the Home Department* [2014] UKSC 60, [30] 'So far, therefore, as the traditional treatment of foreign policy or national security decisions depends on the non-justiciability of the Crown's prerogative to conduct the United Kingdom's foreign relations or of measures taken in the interests of national security, it cannot apply in cases where a scrutiny of such decisions is necessary in order to adjudicate on a complaint that Convention rights have been infringed.'

prerogative power should—as Wade suggests—be tightly defined so as to encompass only those acts which alter the distribution of legal rights and liabilities and (conversely) so as to exclude those acts which have no such effect. Those prerogative powers which do have legal effect cannot, by definition, be non-justiciable in the type 2 sense: they have legal effects upon which the courts are able and willing to rule. If they are non-justiciable, it must be the case that they are type 1 non-justiciable Those which do not—which are part of the prerogative only if the prerogative is broadly defined—would seem to be non-justiciable in the type 2 sense: having no legal effect, they cannot give rise to a legal question which the courts are capable of deciding. It becomes crucial, here, however to distinguish (in a manner which is not always done) between the third source powers of the Crown (those which derive from the Crown's corporate status and are exercised by the Crown's ministers, and which are capable of altering the distribution of legal rights and obligations) and those powers which are purely administrative: which require no legal source because they have no legal effect. Discussion as to whether there exist legal limits upon the latter are hindered by a failure to consistently distinguish them from the former.

C. The Justiciability of Foreign Affairs

The preceding discussion hints at the extent to which the courts, in responding to challenges brought against disparate aspects of the UK's broad response to threats to national security in the twenty-first century, have been required to address questions about their role in relation to foreign affairs. In many ways, the response has been an admirable one—the courts have been more hesitant than had often been the case in the past to conclude that they have no ability to adjudicate upon the sorts of questions raised by modern national security endeavours. Nevertheless, there is so much of the question of justiciability that remains uncertain, or under-explained, that the picture which emerges is of a landscape in which the courts will always be able to find an appropriate dictum to justify their instinct as to what it is or is not advisable for them to do in any particular case; to hold a matter justiciable or non-justiciable almost entirely at their discretion. This indeterminacy appears at times to result in a scenario in which the judge encounters the law as though it were a buffet, with a convenient decision available in order to justify, in any particular case, both holding that a given matter is justiciable and holding that it is not, and useful dicta never far from hand. In an area of law far more likely than most to implicate sensitive political questions of a sort with which judges may wish—regardless of what the law might permit or require them to do—to avoid tangling, it is difficult to avoid the conclusion that the indeterminacy is, if not deliberate, then at least convenient: it is in nobody's interests to bring it to an end. In place of this pervasive ambiguity, I have offered an account of the justiciability of foreign affairs which holds up as its key insight that foreign affairs is not non-justiciable at all. This account, I submit, creates a much clearer picture of the role of the courts in relation to foreign affairs than currently exists in the case law, but is not for that reason inconsistent with that case law. To adopt it would, however, require the courts to renounce much of the constitutional genuflecting in which they participate—the frequent references to their limited expertise and secondary constitutional position—and simply acknowledge that where there is a legal question to answer, they will answer it, saving the institutional considerations for the point at which the appropriate standard of review is identified and applied. It would also require, however, a much clearer sense than has generally existed of what are, in the context of foreign affairs, the bases of true (type 1) non-justiciability: it is to that question which I turn in the second and third parts of this chapter.

III. Foreign Act of State

The doctrine of foreign act of state is invoked in a small number of cases which address the fall-out from some of the UK's most problematic national security interventions. As its name suggests, it applies where the domestic courts are asked to determine an issue which would require them to adjudicate upon the sovereign acts of foreign states, including the 'legality, validity or acceptability of such acts, either under domestic law or international law'.[49] Like the law of justiciability generally, foreign act of state has been forced to mature rapidly in the context of the modern national security case law, and is now the subject of the Supreme Court's leading decision in *Belhaj v Straw*.[50] The doctrine has a complex history, the English jurisprudence having often hewed closely to the evolving approach of the American courts on the same topic, and it is no longer clear that many of the twentieth-century decisions on the doctrine contribute to an understanding of the current law.[51] It is therefore most helpful to focus attention on the line of authority which starts with the decision in *Yukos Capital SARL v OJSC Rosneft Oil Company*.[52] There, the Court of Appeal rejected some of the unduly subtle distinctions which had been constructed within this area of law, and offering the following description of its nature and effect:

> It would seem that, generally speaking, the doctrine is confined to acts of state within the territory of the sovereign... The various formulations of the paradigm principle are apparently wide, and prevent adjudication on the validity, legality, lawfulness, acceptability or motives of state actors ... It has been applied in a wide variety of situations, but often arises by way of defence or riposte: as where a dispossessed owner sues in respect of his property, the defendant relies on a foreign act of state as altering title to that property, and the claimant is prevented from calling into question the effectiveness of that act of state.[53]

The breadth of this formulation is offset against a series of limitations to the doctrine which the Court of Appeal enumerates. The first is the territorial limitation evident in the passage quoted above.[54] The second is the most important, and we return to it

[49] *Kuwait Airways Corporation v Iraqi Airways Co* [2002] UKHL 19, [24].

[50] *Belhaj v Straw* [2017] UKSC 3.

[51] FA Mann observed that the doctrine 'displays in every respect such uncertainty and confusion and rests on so slippery a basis that its applications becomes a matter of speculation.' 'The Foreign Act of State' (1986) 11 *Holdsworth Law Review* 15. How far the situation has improved in the meantime is uncertain. See also, generally, FA Mann, *Foreign Affairs in English Courts* (Oxford, Oxford University Press, 1986). Matthew Nicholson, 'The Political Unconscious of the English Foreign Act of State and Non-Justiciability Doctrine(s)' (2015) 64 *ICLQ* 743 discusses the doctrine's political implications. For modern considerations of the US and Australian doctrine, see John C Harrison, 'The American Act of State Doctrine' (2016) 47 *Georgetown Journal of International Law* 507 and Matthew Alderton, 'The Act of State Doctrine: Questions of Validity and Abstention from Underhill to Habib' (2011) 12 *Melbourne Journal of International Law* 1.

[52] *Yukos Capital S.A.R.L v OJSC Rosneft Oil Company* [2012] EWCA CIV 855.

[53] [2012] EWCA Civ 855, [66].

[54] ibid, [68].

below: it confirms that the doctrine 'will not apply to foreign acts of state which are in breach of clearly established rules of international law, or are contrary to English principles of public policy, as well as where there is a grave infringement of human rights.'[55] A third limitation is that judicial acts will not be treated as acts of state for the purpose of the doctrine; a fourth that it does not apply to the commercial acts of foreign states, regardless—it would appear—of who has carried out the act(s) in question.[56] A fifth limitation—the 'Kirkpatrick exception'[57]—is the logical converse of the doctrine's dominant formulation, whereby what is forbidden (adjudication on the 'validity, legality, lawfulness, acceptability or motives of state actors') does not extend to the mere question of whether some act has occurred.[58] Finally, any challenge to the 'validity' (etc) of an act must, if it is to justify the courts leaving some question unresolved, be central to that question. In the words of the Court of Appeal, 'challenges to foreign acts of state, in order to invoke the act of state doctrine, must ... lie at "the heart" of a case, and not be a matter of merely ancillary or collateral aspersion: and that a test of necessity to a decision may therefore be a useful test.'[59]

Given the significant element of international cooperation within the contemporary Western response to national security threats, it is unsurprising that the foreign act of state doctrine has become a prominent feature of the modern national security constitution. In *Noor Khan* the applicant challenged the provision to the CIA—as had been alleged by media reports to have taken place—of 'locational intelligence' used in targeting drone strikes including that which had killed the applicant's father, in North Waziristan in 2011.[60] The relief sought by the applicant gives a sense, however, of the distance between these facts and the claim in the English court—what was wanted was a declaration that:

> a UK national who kills a person in a drone strike in Pakistan is not entitled to rely on the defence of combatant immunity [and so] a GCHQ officer or other Crown servant in the United Kingdom may commit an offence under ss. 44-46 of the Serious Crime Act 2007 ... when passing locational intelligence to an agent of the US Government for use in drone strikes in Pakistan.[61]

The claimants did not seek to have the court adjudicate directly upon the acts of the US in carrying out drone strikes, and there is no clear discussion as to whether the public policy exception to the foreign act of state doctrine (discussed below) might have applied to those acts (though the exception seems highly unlikely to apply to lawful acts of war). Indeed, the claimant appears—from the judgment of the Court of Appeal—to have argued that the doctrine did not apply at all as they were 'not asking the court to sit in judgment on the acts of CIA officials either by declaring that they are unlawful or by condemning them in any other way'; nor 'inviting the court to adjudicate on the legality or acceptability of the acts of the CIA officials either under our domestic law or under international law.' Reliance was therefore being placed upon *Rahmatullah v Secretary of State for Defence*,[62] in which

55 ibid, [69]–[72].

56 [2012] EWCA Civ 855, [92]–[94].

57 Named for the decision of the US Supreme Court in *Kirkpatrick v Environmental Tectonics Corporation International* 493 US 400 (1990).

58 [2012] EWCA Civ 855, [95]–[104].

59 ibid, [109].

60 See also the discussion in Ch 4 of this book in the context of the killing of those who have recently been deprived of their UK citizenship on public interest grounds.

61 *R (Noor Khan) v. Secretary of State for Foreign and Commonwealth Affairs* [2014] EWCA Civ 24, [6].

62 *Rahmatullah v Secretary of State for Defence* [2012] UKSC 48.

the Supreme Court had been willing to issue a writ of habeas corpus directed to the Secretary of State in relation to an individual detained by British forces in Iraq but who had, by that point in time, been handed over to the US and was being detained in Afghanistan. In doing so, it had emphasised that it was considering only the UK's actions, and so not sitting in judgment on the acts of a foreign state.[63] The analogy was rejected by the Court of Appeal which, holding, like the High Court before it, that the doctrine of foreign act of state applied to these facts, emphasised that the bare reality of what it was being asked to decide and what would be the effect of making the declaration sought—that those providing the intelligence were potentially guilty, under domestic criminal law, of a series of offences secondary to murder. It was, in effect, being asked 'to condemn the acts of the persons who operate the drone bombs'[64] and 'a finding by our court that the notional UK operator of a drone bomb which caused a death was guilty of murder would inevitably be understood (and rightly understood) by the US as a condemnation of the US.'[65]

Though the Master of Rolls emphasised that the he reached this conclusion without regard to the evidence which had been given as to the likely effect of the court making the declaration asked for ('serious harm to the national security and the international relations of the United Kingdom')[66] it is very clear from these remarks as to the effect of the decision that it is the apprehended impact upon the relations of the UK with its allies which motivates the Court of Appeal's decision here. A second reason is, however, offered: that the claimant had not (as the High Court said and with which the Court of Appeal agreed) found 'any foothold other than on the most precarious ground in domestic law.'[67] This observation—as is evident from the description above of the relief sought—is a fair one, but raises the question of how the Court might have disposed of a case in which the domestic foothold was surer but the international context just as sensitive. We will return to that point below. If nothing else, *Noor Khan* makes clear that foreign act of state is a considerable obstacle to attempts to achieve legal redress for acts which the UK does in concert with foreign states; as discussed in Chapter 7, however, such acts are likely now the rule rather than the exception, and so we are dealing here with a doctrine whose significance is potentially far greater than in the at times arcane disputes of the past, and likely only to grow.

A. The Public Policy Exception

Whatever the exact scope of the doctrine, it is not absolute, but subject to the exception mentioned above which applies in the case of foreign acts of state which 'are in breach of clearly established rules of international law or are contrary to English principles of public policy, as well as where there is a grave infringement of human rights.'[68] Where several of

[63] 'This court is not asked to 'sit in judgment on the acts of the government of another, done within its own territory' as in *Underhill v Hernandez* (1897) 168 US 250, 252. The illegality in this case centres on the UK's obligations under the Geneva Conventions. It does not require the court to examine whether the US is in breach of its international obligations ...' [2012] UKSC 48, [53] (Lord Kerr).

[64] [2014] EWCA Civ 24, [36].

[65] ibid, [37].

[66] ibid, [22].

[67] ibid, [34].

[68] *Yukos Capital SARL v OJSC Rosneft Oil Company* [2012] EWCA Civ 855, [69].

the alleged exceptions identified by the Court of Appeal in *Yukos Capital* are in fact merely the boundaries of the rule, the public policy exception is properly so-called: it excludes from the effect of the rule matters which prima facie fall within it. The exception is demonstrated by the decisions in *Oppenheimer v Cattermole*[69] and *Kuwait Airways Corporation v Iraqi Airways Co (Nos 4 and 5)*.[70] In the first of these, the applicant (a German Jew who had fled the Nazi regime in Germany) sought to take advantage of a double taxation treaty which relied upon him being a German national; he was denied the right to do so on the basis of a Nazi decree of 1941 which deprived Jews living abroad of their German nationality. Though the House of Lords held that the applicant had ceased, by the operation of the German Basic Law, to be a German national, several of the Law Lords suggested that the decree in question would not have been recognised by the English courts as having effectively deprived the applicant of his citizenship. Characterising the relevant rule as one which 'takes away without compensation from a section of the citizen body singled out on racial grounds all their property on which the state passing the legislation can lay its hands and, in addition, deprives them of their citizenship,' Lord Cross said that '[t]o my mind a law of this sort constitutes so grave an infringement of human rights that the courts of this country ought to refuse to recognise it as a law at all.'[71] Questioning the claim that for some of those to whom it applied, the 1941 decree had a positive or desirable effect, Lord Salmon doubted 'whether the question as to whether an enactment is so great an offence against human rights that it ought not to be recognised by any civilised system of law can depend upon its impact upon the facts of any particular case.'[72]

The exception was widened out in the *Kuwait Airways* case, which arose from the acts of Iraq after its invasion of Kuwait in 1990. Having annexed Kuwait, the Iraqi government ordered Kuwait Airways to fly ten of its planes to Iraq, before dissolving the company by decree and transferring all of its property to Iraqi Airways. The House of Lords held that domestic courts were entitled to have regard to the international law position when deciding whether or not to recognise a foreign law. Lord Nicholls of Birkenhead said of the legal position that:

> In appropriate circumstances it is legitimate for an English court to have regard to the content of international law in deciding whether to recognise a foreign law … Nor does the "nonjusticiable" principle mean that the judiciary must shut their eyes to a breach of an established principle of international law committed by one state against another when the breach is plain and, indeed, acknowledged. In such a case the adjudication problems confronting the English court in the *Buttes* litigation do not arise. The standard being applied by the court is clear and manageable, and the outcome not in doubt. That is the present case.[73]

Relevant to his conclusion was the changing standards of the time against which measures might be judged and, in particular, the way in which the interdependence of nations had rendered more urgent adherence to the norms of international law. Lord Steyn specifically rejected a submission that the exception to foreign act of state be limited to human rights

[69] *Oppenheimer v Cattermole* [1976] AC 249.
[70] *Kuwait Airways Corporation v Iraqi Airways Co* [2002] UKHL 19.
[71] [1976] AC 249, 278.
[72] ibid, 283.
[73] *Kuwait Airways Corpn v Iraqi Airways Co (Nos 4 and 5)* [2002] UKHL 19, [26].

cases, holding that it might apply equally to flagrant breaches of international law. Though not every such breach would trigger the public policy exception, Iraq's conduct was 'a paradigm' of that which would.[74] Lord Hope nevertheless emphasised the relative narrowness of the exception, and the terms in which he did so are illuminating, emphasising the importance within international law of the principle of comity (which 'requires our courts to recognise the jurisdiction of the foreign state over all assets situated within its own territories') from which a judge should be slow to depart, for he 'may have an inadequate understanding of the circumstances in which the legislation was passed' and declining to recognise it 'may be embarrassing to the executive, whose function is so far as possible to maintain friendly relations with foreign states.'[75] That is, the reason for hesitating to recognise a limitation to the act of state doctrine—that to do so would imperil foreign relations—is the same as that given for recognising the doctrine in the first place. The exception then, is a general public policy exception: though violations of human rights norms or international law (at least those of sufficient gravity) may trigger it, they are instantiations of a broader exception; one which has expanded over time in order to encompass fact patterns other than those originally contemplated in *Oppenheimer v Cattermole* and is logically capable of further expansion.

B. Belhaj

Within the context of the modern national security constitution, the relevance of the public policy exception, like that of the doctrine itself, emerges most clearly in the context of the *Belhaj* litigation, the underlying facts of which represent—amongst at times rather stiff competition—perhaps the most outrageous conduct engaged in by the UK within the modern national security context which has so far come to light. The claimant, Abdul Hakim Belhaj, was a Libyan dissident, the leader of the Libyan Islamic Fighting Group, who had fled Libya in order to escape the reach of Colonel Gaddafi, moving first to Afghanistan and later to China. Shortly before Tony Blair concluded the so-called 'deal in the desert' with Gaddafi, bringing Libya back into the international fold after decades of exclusion, Belhaj and his pregnant wife Fatima Boudchar sought to travel to London in order to seek asylum in the UK. They were instead detained by Chinese border agents and transported to Kuala Lumpur. It is here that the UK appears to have entered the fray, allegedly becoming aware of the pair's location and informing the Libyan intelligence services of it, while American authorities separately schemed to take custody of them and hand them over to Libya. Belhaj and his wife were, under the pretence of being transported eventually to London, taken to Bangkok, where they were detained, mistreated, and transported to Tripoli. Boudchar was released three months later; Belhaj not until 2010. Evidence of British complicity in the treatment of Belhaj and Boudchar emerged only as a result of the Libyan revolution in 2011, in which the Gaddafi regime fell, and the fortuitous early arrival in the office of Moussa Koussa, the head of the Libyan External Security Office, of a researcher from

[74] [2002] UKHL 19, [114].
[75] [2002] UKHL 19, [138].

Human Rights Watch. Amongst the documents found there was a letter from MI6's head of counter-terrorism Sir Mark Allen, which (as quoted in the relevant judgment) read as follows:

> Most importantly, I congratulate you on the safe arrival of [Mr. Belhaj]. This was the least we could do for you and for Libya to demonstrate the remarkable relationship we have built up over recent years. I am so glad … [Mr. Belhaj's] information on the situation in this Country is of urgent importance to us. Amusingly, we got a request from the Americans to channel requests for information from [Mr. Belhaj] through the Americans. I have no intention of doing any such thing. The intelligence about [Mr. Belhaj] was British. I know I did not pay for the air cargo. But I feel I have the right to deal with you direct on this and am very grateful to you for the help you are giving us.[76]

Chapter 5 discussed the claims arising from the detention of UK nationals and residents in Guantanamo bay. Those claims were eventually settled for large sums of money, avoiding the complex and sensitive litigation which would have otherwise followed and allowing the government to bring the matter to an end without admitting, or being found to be at, fault.[77] The same approach was attempted in relation to Belhaj, and a second Libya dissident, Sami al Saadi—who had, along with his family, also been rendered into Libyan custody by, allegedly, the CIA and MI6—accepted more than £2 million in compensation in exchange for dropping his litigation.[78] Belhaj, however, refused such a deal, seeking only nominal compensation and an apology on behalf of those who he claimed were responsible for his treatment—primarily the head of counter-terrorism within MI6, Sir Mark Allen, and Jack Straw, who as foreign secretary between 2001 and 2006 was the responsible Minister. He brought civil claims against those individuals and others on a variety of grounds, and it was in that context that the doctrine of foreign act of state became newly relevant, the defendants arguing that it prevented the courts from hearing the claims against the various UK officials.

In the High Court,[79] Simon J held that 'the Defendants are correct in their submission that the case pleaded against them depends on the Court having to decide that the conduct of US officials acting outside the United States was unlawful, in circumstances where there are no clear and incontrovertible standards for doing so and where there is incontestable evidence that such an enquiry would be damaging to the national interest.'[80] The judge did not, to his credit, shrink away from the implications of this decision: it would mean that 'what appears to be a potentially well-founded claim that the UK authorities were directly implicated in the extra-ordinary rendition of the Claimants, will not be determined in any domestic court; and that Parliamentary oversight and criminal investigations are not adequate substitutes for access to, and a decision by, the Court.'[81] In the Court of Appeal, however, there was painted a picture of the doctrine founded not on issues of judicial competence, but rather 'the principle of the sovereign equality of states and … the principle of

[76] *Belhaj v Straw* [2014] EWCA Civ 1394, [13]. Insertions are as found in the original.

[77] See Adam Tomkins, 'Justice and Security in the United Kingdom' (2014) 47 *Israel Law Review* 305, 317.

[78] For details of the al Saadi case, see the resources collected by Reprieve, who assisted the family in their legal action: www.reprieve.org.uk/case-study/al-saadi-family/.

[79] *Belhaj v Straw* [2013] EWHC 4111 (QB).

[80] [2013] EWHC 4111 (QB), [150].

[81] ibid, [151].

international comity.'[82] That court concluded that though the doctrine was engaged by the various claims brought by Belhaj, those claims fell within an expanded variant of the public policy exception which applied even (as had not been the case in *Kuwait Airways*) where the court 'if it exercised jurisdiction, would be required to conduct a legal and factual investigation into the validity of the conduct of a foreign state.'[83] It gave several reasons for this conclusion, amongst them that the courts would not be entering the sort of 'judicial no-man's land' which sometimes arises in cases involving conduct on the international plane,[84] and the absence of any other forum in which the allegations might be tried:

> the stark reality is that unless the English courts are able to exercise jurisdiction in this case, these very grave allegations against the executive will never be subjected to judicial investigation. The subject matter of these allegations is such that, these respondents, if sued in the courts of another state, are likely to be entitled to plead state immunity. Furthermore, there is, so far as we are aware, no alternative international forum with jurisdiction over these issues. As a result, these very grave allegations would go uninvestigated and the appellants would be left without any legal recourse or remedy.[85]

The final reason offered was that any harm done to the foreign relation interests of the UK did not outweigh the factors in favour of deciding the Belhaj case: 'In this particular context,' the Court of Appeal stated, 'the risk of displeasing our allies or offending other states, and even the risk of the consequences of varying severity which it is said are likely to follow, cannot justify our declining jurisdiction on grounds of act of state over what is a properly justiciable claim.'[86] Though there is much to admire in the Court of Appeal's judgment, there are elements of it which are concerning, not least the claim that the reasons are said to justify the decision it arrives at—that the public policy exception to foreign act of state permits the consideration of the private law claims here—do so when 'considered cumulatively'. First, such a holding creates exactly the sort of the uncertainty we have discussed above in terms of the wider question of justiciability, preventing courts which later address the issue from understanding which of the reasons might themselves have justified the conclusion, and which not; what to do in future cases where only some of them are present, and how that answer might vary depending on which are present and which not. The result is that a court, starting from the decision of the Court of Appeal in *Belhaj*, might justify either conclusion with—if not equal—then at least similar plausibility: the law of foreign act of state is therefore at least as political, and probably much more so, than is the broader question of justiciability. This leads to a second point: by juxtaposing the issues of whether there exist 'judiciable or manageable' standards and the potential damage to international relations, the Court of Appeal muddies the waters as to the basis of foreign act of state, and how (if at all) it is distinct from the question of the justiciability of foreign affairs in general. Moreover, by emphasising the exceptionality of the facts in *Belhaj*, the Court of Appeal creates the possibility that a later court will hold that a later set of alleged facts involves a

[82] [2014] EWCA Civ 1394, [67].
[83] ibid, [114].
[84] ibid, [118].
[85] ibid, [119].
[86] ibid, [120].

relatively minor violation of human rights, and so can safely be allowed to fall into the dark part of a doctrine which the Court of Appeal in *Yukos Capital* described as having the nature of silhouette.[87]

By the time it was heard in the Supreme Court, this element of *Belhaj* had been joined with claims brought by Yunus Rahmatullah (the same individual whose habeas corpus application was discussed above) which similarly implicated foreign act of state.[88] In holding that that neither set of claims were obstructed by the doctrine of foreign act of state (nor by the law of state immunity, not considered here) the Supreme Court managed to avoid some of the difficulties of the Court of Appeal's decision as regards the public policy exception. The majority judgment is that of Lord Neuberger, who offers a classification of the rules which make up the foreign act of state doctrine which includes, first, two variants which are limited to the territory of the state in question: 'the courts of this country will recognise, and will not question, the effect of a foreign state's legislation or other laws in relation to any acts which take place or take effect within the territory of that state'[89] and 'will recognise, and will not question, the effect of an act of a foreign state's executive in relation to any acts which take place or take effect within the territory of that state'.[90] These two rules apply to property rights, with the key uncertainty being whether or not the second applies equally to interferences with property rights which are unlawful according to the law of the state in which they take place. The first, says Lord Neuberger, is a rule of private international law; so too, probably, is the second.[91] Where the position of the first and third rules is less certain, the second rule applies only to acts done to property and not injuries to persons.[92] The third rule encompasses situations involving issues which are 'inappropriate for the courts of the United Kingdom to resolve because they involve a challenge to the lawfulness of the act of a foreign state which is of such a nature that a municipal judge cannot or ought not rule on it'.[93] Such issues, Lord Neuberger suggests, include 'dealings between sovereign states' and 'the legality of acts of a foreign government in the conduct of foreign affairs.'[94] It is with the next entry in this category that the trouble begins: Lord Neuberger identifies as part of the third rule of foreign act of state the fact that 'international treaties and conventions, which have not become incorporated into domestic law by the legislature, cannot be the source of domestic rights or duties and will not be interpreted by our courts.'[95] This must be incorrect, for it conflates the false (type 2) non-justiciability which derives from the constitution's dualism with what I argue below is the true (type 1) non-justiciability of foreign act of state. Nevertheless, this category can be severed from Lord Neuberger's account without damage to the basic classification. It is these second and third rules which make up

[87] [2012] EWCA Civ 855, [115].

[88] See the first instance judgment of Mr Justice Leggatt: *Rahmatullah v Ministry of Defence* [2014] EWHC 3846 (QB)

[89] *Belhaj v Straw* [2017] UKSC 3, [121]. Lord Neuberger suggests that 'there is a strong argument for saying that [this rule] is not part of the Doctrine at all' ([120]). This seems correct: it would appear to be a free-standing, and more general principle, which is not usefully grouped together with those which follow.

[90] [2017] UKSC 3, [122].

[91] ibid, [150].

[92] ibid, [135]–[147].

[93] ibid, [123].

[94] ibid.

[95] ibid.

the doctrine of foreign act of state as traditionally understood: indeed, the case for treating them as separate rules is not compelling, and it may be preferable to understand them as the two (international and domestic) sides of the same doctrinal coin.[96]

Lord Neuberger identifies also a possible fourth rule, by which—in the words of Rix LJ in *Yukos Capital*—'the courts will not investigate acts of a foreign state where such an investigation would embarrass the government of our own country'.[97] Lord Neuberger is rightly sceptical as to the existence of this rule, of which there is, he says, 'little authority to support the notion that the fourth rule is part of the law of this country.'[98] This seems fair: the hypothesised fourth rule is objectionable in principle in a way in which none of the others, which reflect (or can be plausibly claimed to reflect) established constitutional principle, would appear to be. One problem, however, is where this scepticism leaves the decision in *Noor Khan*: as noted above, the second justification offered for the Court of Appeal's decision (the fragility of the claim's foothold in domestic law) implies that a more robust such foothold might have seen the claim succeed. If the first reason offered (the doctrine of foreign act of state in its 'embarrassment' incarnation) transpires to be incapable of obstructing a claim with the subject matter as in *Noor Khan*, then there must exist the possibility that the doctrine of foreign act of state does not create a bar to such claims at all. Where elsewhere the conceptual foundations of foreign act of state have been pondered at length and in detail, Lord Neuberger contents himself with the observation that 'is based on judicial self-restraint, in that it applies to issues which judges decide that they should abstain from resolving' and, unlike the first two rules which make up the doctrine, it is 'purely based on common law, and therefore has no international law basis'.[99] The public policy exception—including where the legislation or act in question represents a 'serious violation of international law'—Lord Neuberger recognises as applying to all three (or four, if appropriate) rules.[100]

Applying this new, authoritative understanding of foreign act of state to the relevant facts, Lord Neuberger suggests, in the first place, that the doctrine does not apply to what was done to Belhaj, there being no 'suggestion that there was some sort of formal or high-level agreement or treaty between any of the states involved which governed the cooperation between the executives of the various countries concerned.'[101] He underlines here that 'the mere fact that officials of more than one country cooperate to carry out an operation does not mean that the third rule can be invoked if that operation is said to give rise to a claim in domestic law' and that it would be 'positively inimical to the rule of law if it were otherwise.'[102] On one hand, this is a heartening conclusion, for—as noted above—the

[96] Separate classifications are offered by Lord Mance [35]–[45] and Lord Sumption [228]–[238]. The former is similar to that of Lord Neuberger; the latter (which is bi-rather than tri-partite) excludes the rule which is the first of three parts in the classifications of Lords Mance and Neuberger and is best understood as being distinct from foreign act of state. In Lord Sumption's categories of 'municipal' and 'international' foreign act of state, the primary distinction between the two is that the former applies only to acts on the state's territory; the latter is not so limited.

[97] [2017] UKSC 3, [124], citing *Yukos Capital SARL v OJSC Rosneft Oil Co (No 2)* [2014] QB 458, [65].

[98] [2017] UKSC 3, [132].

[99] ibid, [146].

[100] ibid, [153]–[157].

[101] ibid, [167].

[102] ibid.

necessity of cooperation with other states in the field of national security means that most (if not, in fact, all) actions taken by the UK will be taken in some degree of cooperation with officials of one or more other country. The requirement that some higher-level agreement exist (perhaps even, Lord Neuberger's language suggests, one which is formalised in writing) means that many of those involved in such actions will not for that reason alone be able to avail themselves of the protection of foreign act of state. On the other hand, this reading of the underlying facts of *Belhaj* is such as to downplay the political acts and political choices which fed into the mistreatment of Belhaj and his family, and to make political accountability more difficult than it should be within a constitutional order worthy of the name. It might even be read as an attempt to suggest, in defiance of constitutional traditions of ministerial responsibility, that the dealings with the Libyan regime were in some sense the work of a rogue actor, for which no member of the British government, and certainly not the government as a whole, should be held responsible. That would be just as disturbing, if for very different reasons, as the conclusion that the international cooperation was carried out at a high-level and with full awareness of its human cost, and there is no a priori reason to consider the former narrative any more plausible than the latter. The second of Lord Neuberger's rules cannot apply because we are dealing here with harm to persons and not property.[103] Nor did it apply to the facts of *Rahmatullah*: the claimant's mistreatment took place in the jurisdiction of Afghanistan rather than that of the US, and included physical and mental harm rather than harm to property.[104] Moreover, though there existed a formal memorandum of understanding between the UK and the US, that document did not bear on the allegations of complicity in unlawful detention and mistreatment, and so the third rule could not apply.[105] In both cases, however, Lord Neuberger held that even if the doctrine applied, the relevant facts would fall within the public policy exception.[106] The result is that while the both the doctrine of foreign act of state and the public policy exception to it enjoy a new certainty, the cases can go to trial, albeit that they will do so behind the veil of a closed material procedure.[107]

C. Foreign Act of State and Justiciability Generally

One unresolved question about the doctrine of foreign act of state is the extent to which it is subject to the same supervening factors as is—and in particular whether it enjoys the same relationship with statute as does—the general issue of justiciability discussed above; whether, that is, foreign act of state non-justiciability belongs to the first or second category of non-justiciability identified by the Supreme Court in *Shergill v Khaira*, as outlined above. In *Noor Khan* one factor emphasised by the High Court in deciding that the doctrine applied was that the claimant had 'not found any foothold other than on the most precarious ground in domestic law'. Based on what has been said above, this does not seem to speak

[103] [2017] UKSC 3, [169].
[104] ibid, [170].
[105] ibid, [171].
[106] ibid, [168] and [172].
[107] *Belhaj v Straw* [2017] EWHC 1861 (QB); *Rahmatullah v Ministry of Defence* [2017] EWHC 547 (QB).

to foreign act of state directly, but instead exemplifies the position in which the courts do not answer a legal question not because they refuse to but because there is no question for them to answer. The same might be said of those cases which seem to associate the foreign act of state rule with the absence of 'judicial or manageable standards'—most notably *Buttes Gas*. In both cases, we need to consider the counter-factual: had there been a sturdier foothold in domestic law, one which would inevitably provide the relevant judicial and manageable standards for the courts to apply, would the courts have answered the relevant question—applied the relevant standards—notwithstanding that to do so might nevertheless have required them to adjudicate upon the sovereign acts of a foreign state? The implication of the stress placed upon the precarity of the relevant 'foothold' in *Noor Khan* is that a sturdier foothold would have seen the matter rendered justiciable; that foreign act of state non-justiciability is no different from the purported non-justiciability of foreign affairs generally. This is an attractive conclusion but, it seems, a false one. Lord Mance in *Belhaj* notes exactly this point, and that it would seem to follow that 'if the claimant [in *Noor Khan*] had had some substantive claim (eg for damages in his father's or his own right), the claim would, in Leggatt J's view, have been justiciable.'[108] Though he does not need to, and does not, decide this point, Lord Mance states that 'that is unlikely to be correct.'[109] Similarly, Lord Sumption notes that 'not all cases in which the foreign act of state doctrine is applied to transactions between states lack "judicial or manageable standards" for their decision' and that '[o]n the facts of *R (Noor Khan) v Secretary of State for Foreign Affairs*, the courts would have been competent to apply English criminal law to the operators of drones over Pakistan.'[110] The point, then, is that where courts decline to do such things 'it is usually not because of any lack of legal standards, but because it would be contrary to principle.'[111] This must be correct: the implication that foreign act of state non-justiciability is, like the question of the justiciability of foreign affairs more generally, an example of type 2 *Shergill* non-justiciability is a false one. This, of course, is in keeping with the original dicta in *Shergill* in which it was noted that paradigmatic of type 1 non-justiciability was the 'non-justiciability of certain transactions of foreign states' (a concept which must now of course be read in light of the Supreme Court's decision in *Belhaj*). And in *Belhaj* Lord Neuberger seems to regard the point as uncontroversial—talking in the context of his third 'rule', he says of the doctrine generally that where it applies 'it serves to defeat what would otherwise be a perfectly valid private law claim'.[112]

This does not, however, close the matter. The applicability of the doctrine of foreign act of state means that the courts cannot address the issue even where to do so is necessary in order to decide upon the distribution of legal rights and obligations. This, it seems, is true (type 1) non-justiciability. We know from discussion above that type 2 non-justiciability can be 'overcome' (or, perhaps better, falsified) by the statutory institution of some legal power or duty to decide questions which the court would not otherwise address because of the absence of a legal question to determine. Can statute similarly render justiciable

[108] [2017] UKSC 3, [94].
[109] ibid.
[110] [2017] UKSC 3, [244].
[111] ibid.
[112] [2017] UKSC 3, [144].

something which is type 1 non-justiciable? No answer can be offered on the basis of an analogy between the two forms of justiciability: as we have already seen, the two are wholly distinct. Nevertheless, it is submitted that the answer is that even true non-justiciability—of which foreign act of state is our first example—might be overcome by statute. I offer several reasons for that conclusion.

The first, and most fundamental, reason is that Parliament is sovereign: it can make or unmake any law whatsoever and, to the extent that exceptions to that have been hypothesised or argued for, none of them would seem to speak to the question of justiciability. If Parliament empowers or requires the courts to decide a question which involves the consideration of otherwise inherently unsuitable issues, they may (must) do so. Secondly, and generally, there appears to be no issue of justiciability under the Human Rights Act 1998: if the courts must address otherwise non-justiciable issues in order to decide whether a public authority has acted unlawfully under section 6 of the Act, they will do so. There is no suggestion in *Belhaj* that the doctrine might apply to HRA claims. If that were not enough, we can identify other statutory regimes which point to the same conclusion. One relates to the particular circumstances of parliamentary privilege which, it will be recalled, was identified by the Supreme Court in *Shergill v Khaira* as one of the key examples of type 1 non-justiciability. The record shows that Parliament has legislated to permit the waiver of privilege, rendering proceedings justiciable in defamation proceedings.[113] Another set of statutes relates to the conduct of foreign policy: various statutes, including the Geneva Conventions Act 1957, the International Criminal Courts Act 2001, the Criminal Justice Act 1988 and the Serious Crimes Act 2007 criminalise conduct contrary to the Geneva Conventions and the Convention Against Torture, and extend the ambit of the criminal law extra-territorially in certain cases.[114] The effect of the relevant provisions would be severely blunted if they were to be subject to a doctrine of foreign act of state.

This conclusion—which can only be provisional—means that statute might be relevant to the question of justiciability in two quite distinct ways: in type 2 non-justiciability, statute can create a domestic legal hook where none exists, permitting courts to adjudicate upon matters which would not, apart from that statute raise issues of domestic law. Second, in relation to type 1 non-justiciability, statute can overcome the inherent unsuitability of some question for judicial determination; the courts must answer a question if Parliament requires them to. This conclusion seems to follow from the material canvassed, but it implies that there might exist anomalies, where a statutory cause of action might be justiciable but a private law claim arising out the same facts yet based upon common law principles would not be. There would seem, therefore, to be some way to go before we can be confident in our understanding of this form of non-justiciability and its implications. In the meantime, it is worth saying something briefly about the possibility of non-curial forms of redress, focusing on the *Belhaj* affair.

113 See s 13 of the Defamation Act 1996 (now repealed by the Deregulation Act 2015).

114 I take these examples from Tom de la Mare, *Foreign Affairs: Forbidden Territory for the Courts*, paper presented to the Administrative Law Bar Association (27 July 2013).

D. *Belhaj* Beyond the Courts

Alongside the civil proceedings in *Belhaj*, there existed for a period the possibility that criminal charges might result from the same facts. Criminal proceedings would have raised new and important points of law, for after the *Noor Khan* case—in which the criminal law was implicated only peripherally—there remain important questions about the ability of foreign act of state to prevent the courts from adjudicating upon questions of criminal responsibility.[115] Unfortunately, those questions will not be answered in the context of the *Belhaj* and *Al Saadi* cases: in June 2016, the Crown Prosecution Service announced that there was insufficient evidence to bring criminal charges against Sir Mark Allen. It noted, however, that there was sufficient evidence to support the conclusions that Allen had:

1. been in communication with individuals from the foreign countries responsible for the detention and transfer of the Belhadj and Al Saadi families;
2. disclosed aspects of what was occurring to others within this country; and
3. sought political authority for some of his actions albeit not within a formal written process nor in detail which covered all his communications and conduct.[116]

This final point excludes the possibility that MI6's involvement with the rendition process might have been authorised under section 7 of the Intelligence Services Act 1994, which would have quashed any criminal liability arising from those acts. Alongside this, an inquiry, headed by Sir Peter Gibson into the UK's possible involvement in mistreatment of detainees by the Security and Intelligence Services (and so excluding those detained in Iraq and Afghanistan, whose litigation is discussed further below) had been announced in 2010, but brought to a premature end in 2012 when the CPS announced an investigation into the *Belhaj* and *Al Saadi* cases, providing only an oversight of its preparatory work and a large number of questions it would have sought to answer if it had run to completion.[117] In the announcement of the inquiry's discontinuation, the Justice Secretary had stated that the government 'fully intend[s] to hold a judge-led inquiry into these issues, once it is possible to do so and all related police investigations have been concluded'.[118] By the time that happened, however, responsibility for the question of detainee treatment had been handed over to the Intelligence and Security Committee, which has not yet reported.[119]

This picture demonstrates some of the significant difficulties of achieving any sort of meaningful accountability within the national security constitution. There are problems of both practicality and politics in attempting to prosecute members of the security services or even the government as regards actions taken in ostensible pursuit of national security ends. And if acts have been carried out which constitute offences under the relevant domestic law, civil remedies are necessarily second-best. But even these cannot be relied

[115] For a discussion of Crown act of state's application to criminal law, see below.

[116] Crown Prosecution Service statement: Operation Lydd, 9 June 2016.

[117] The Detainee Inquiry, *Report of the Detainee Inquiry*, December 2013.

[118] HC Deb 18 January 2012, vol 538 cols 751–2.

[119] The ISC had earlier produced a report into the subject of rendition, reporting in 2007: Intelligence and Security Committee, *Rendition*, Cm 7171 (2007). This predates the coming to light of the facts of the treatment of the Libyan dissidents.

upon: the executive has at its disposal (and in the Libyan cases has deployed in full) a panoply of tools by which the vindication of civil rights might be obstructed or delayed, or rendered so impractical as to amount to a denial of justice. Extra-curial 'remedies' such as are provided by inquiries of the Gibson sort must, if justice is to be done, take a backseat to the criminal and civil processes, so as not to undermine the doing of justice, and are subject to political manipulation at a very fundamental level. The mechanisms of publicity which apply therein are likely in many ways to fall below the standards which apply in the context of civil trials.[120] In relation to the Gibson Inquiry (which was not constituted under the Inquiries Act 2005)[121] the Inquiry was given—in a Protocol agreed between the Inquiry and the government—a commitment that it would receive:

> … the full support of, and cooperation from, HMG and its security and intelligence agencies. This includes access to all relevant government papers, and an expectation that serving government officials will attend as witnesses if the Inquiry so requests.[122]

For its part, the Inquiry made a series of commitments related to the handling and publication of material, including to 'respect the understandings and commitments made or given by HMG, including through its intelligence and security agencies, to the authorities and/or agencies of any foreign government concerning the confidentiality, security and protection against public disclosure of any information to which those understandings and commitments relate'.[123] Procedures were put in place to clear material for publication, with the final decision in the event of a dispute between the Inquiry and the Cabinet being made by the Cabinet Secretary.[124] Much of the evidence was to be given in private.[125] Shifting responsibility for the issue of detention to the ISC may yet increase the degree to which relevant material is considered (if not disclosed to the public) given the changes made to it by the Justice and Security Act 2013. What it will almost certainly do, however, is further undermine public confidence in the conclusions eventually arrived at.

The doctrine of foreign act of state has been forced out of the shadows by developments in the national security constitution. Though much of the clarificatory and limiting work in recent years in fact happened outside of that context, it is often the case that such work is done in relatively innocuous cases with an awareness of its significance elsewhere, in more obviously political and more controversial disputes. The very existence of the doctrine is in considerable tension with ideas of the rule of law, and the broader the scope recognised to it by the courts, the more likely that the domestic executive can attempt to evade the legal consequences of its actions simply by acting in concert with other states. Given the

[120] A statutory inquiry carries with it a duty to take reasonable steps to secure public access (s 18) though this is qualified by s 19, which provides, inter alia, that restrictions may be imposed on attendance at or disclosure of evidence given to or produced by the inquiry in question, where such restrictions are believed by either the responsible Minister or the inquiry's chairman to be necessary in the public interest having regard to 'any risk of harm or damage that could be avoided or reduced by any such restriction' including 'damage to national security or international relations.'

[121] Unlike the *Baha Mousa* and *Al-Sweady* inquiries discussed in Ch 3 and again in Ch 7. A statutory inquiry brings with it powers to compel the giving of evidence of or the provision of material (Inquiries Act 2005, s 21) though this is subject to the same rules of public interest immunity as apply in civil proceedings generally (s 22).

[122] The Detainee Inquiry and HM Government, *Protocol for the Detainee Inquiry*, [4].

[123] Detainee Inquiry (n 123) [9(b)].

[124] ibid [17].

[125] ibid [19]–[27] and [35]–[39].

internationalisation of the processes of national security described in other chapters of this work, this is deeply troubling: the foreign act of state doctrine reveals itself the enemy of legal accountability in the modern national security constitution. Nevertheless, the eventual result of the *Belhaj* litigation suggests that the courts are willing and able to respond robustly to conduct which they regard as outrageous, even if in doing so they reaffirm the foundations of the doctrine. Where there is no international cooperation, there will be no option of invoking the foreign act of state doctrine. There may, however, be the option of invoking a separate, parallel, doctrine known as Crown act of state, to which we now turn.

IV. Crown Act of State

The third issue we must consider under the heading of justiciability is the doctrine known as Crown act of state.[126] Here, however, we must venture beyond that question, for Crown act of state has generally been taken to be not one rule but two. That is, until very recently (when the argument that Crown act of state is a single rule found success before the Supreme Court), the courts have repeatedly affirmed its dualist character, and so where it was usual to talk of a single doctrine, what was in fact being discussed were two rules (or 'limbs') differing along (at least) the following axes: their normative bases, the acts to which they applied, the locations in which they applied, the persons against whom they applied. I consider, in turn, the justiciability limb of Crown act of state and the tort defence limb, offering an account of what is at stake both in the developments which have taken place as regards both limbs in recent years, and—in particular—of the significance of the decision of the Supreme Court in *Serdar Mohammed v Ministry of Defence*, in which much of what we thought we knew about the doctrine was washed away, to be replaced with a doctrine which is worryingly broad but in several ways still uncertain. The prominence of national security concerns within the legal constitution has forced the courts to update and to clarify some of the more problematic elements of the constitutional order. Elsewhere this process has seen the relevant doctrines weakened and the scope for legal accountability increased. Notwithstanding strong indications to the contrary, that has not been the case with Crown act of state.

A. The Justiciability Rule of Crown Act of State

The doctrine of Crown act of state applied—in the most famous formulation of 'act of state'—to acts 'of the Executive as a matter of policy performed in the course of its relations

[126] The general literature on Crown act of state is not large. It includes WH Moore, *Act of State in English Law* (London, John Murray, 1906); ECS Wade, 'Act of State in English Law: Its Relations with International Law' (1934) 15 *BYIL* 98; Lord McNair, *International Law Opinions* (Cambridge, Cambridge University Press, 1956), vol I, 111–117; JG Collier, 'Act of State as a Defence Against a British Subject' (1968) 26 *CLJ* 102; Amanda Perreau-Saussine, 'British Acts of State in English Courts' (2008) 78 *British Yearbook of International Law* 176; Paul Scott, 'The Vanishing Law of Crown Act of State' (2015) 66 *NILQ* 367.

with another state, including its relations with the subjects of that state, unless they are temporarily within the allegiance of the Crown'.[127] In its non-justiciability form, the doctrine was closely linked to the position regarding the justiciability of the prerogative; indeed, on some views, it was no more than an instantiation thereof.[128] This limb was, it seemed, much degraded in recent times, for the same reasons as were noted above in the context of the prerogative generally. The courts in the modern case law have, in keeping with developments elsewhere, focussed not on the source of the power—as would once have been sufficient—but instead on the specific act being challenged. In *Serdar Mohammed*, it was noted by Leggatt J in the High Court that the relevant act—the detention of the claimant (an Afghan national) by British forces in Afghanistan—was 'plainly justiciable':[129]

> The courts have ... continued to exercise considerable restraint when invited to review executive decisions involving matters of foreign policy. Such restraint, however, no longer rests on a rule that certain areas of decision-making by the executive such as foreign policy are "no-go" areas for the courts but on a consideration of whether or to what extent the particular decision of the executive with which the case is concerned is or is not "justiciable".[130]

The Court of Appeal concurred.[131] The effect of this treatment of the matter is that the justiciability limb of Crown act of state would bite far less frequently than might once have been the case: in almost all cases brought before a court, the underlying high policy decision will be severable from the specific, and allegedly tortious, act which is the subject of a claim against the Crown. That is not to say, however, that it might not succeed—one can easily envisage that those whose property was damaged as part of, say, a bombing campaign in foreign lands would be rebuffed by the courts on the basis that it was impossible to separate the high-level decision to conduct the campaign from the act (the bombing) which resulted in the property damage. There are therefore several points which follow from the non-justiciability limb of Crown act of state as understood in the High Court and Court of Appeal. The first is that the name can now be seen to be something of a misnomer. Though an act which meets the standard definition of an 'act of state' will often be non-justiciable, meeting that definition is neither a necessary nor sufficient condition for a successful invocation of the justiciability limb. If the definition is of value, it is only as a (contingent) inference from the sorts of cases where high policy is at issue and into which the courts will not therefore stray. The second is that justiciability appears not to be a function of either the physical location of an act or the identity of the person against whom it is done. Third, it seems to have become settled in the case law that justiciability does not differ as between public law and private law proceedings. The Court of Appeal noted that:

> whether issues are justiciable cannot depend on the nature of the proceedings. On the contrary, what is suitable for adjudication by a court must be determined by the court on the basis of the

[127] Wade (n 126) 103. See also the account of the nature of an act of state offered by Lord Pearson in *Attorney-General v Nissan* [1970] AC 179, 237.

[128] Peter Cane 'Prerogative Acts, Acts of State and Justiciability', (1980) 29 *ICLQ* 680. Gilmour said that 'whereas all acts of State are acts of prerogative, not all prerogative acts are acts of State.' DR Gilmour, 'British Forces Abroad and the Responsibility for their Actions' [1970] *PL* 120, 145.

[129] *Serdar Mohammed v Minstry of Defence* [2014] EWHC 1369 (QB), [381]. 'Determining whether an individual has been unlawfully deprived of their liberty is quintessentially a matter for a court.'

[130] [2014] EWHC 1369 (QB), 376.

[131] *Serdar Mohammed v Secretary of State for Defence* [2015] EWCA Civ 843, [323].

> subject matter in dispute. Accordingly, what is justiciable in public law proceedings is also justiciable in private law proceedings.[132]

The fourth—perhaps most important—is that these decisions appear to assume that the non-justiciability limb of Crown act of state exemplifies non-justiciability of the first type identified in *Shergill*: this is not merely about the existence (or otherwise) of some legal question which the courts might be called upon to answer, but assumes that certain matters are not suitable for consideration by the courts, even if the effect is that legal rights go unenforced. That is, if much of the alleged non-justiciability of the prerogative can—as was argued above—be explained as representing type 2 non-justiciability, Crown act of state non-justiciability is an exception.

New difficulties arise, however, from the Supreme Court's treatment of the non-justiciability limb. There, a majority of the court rejected the dualist understanding of Crown act of state, holding (as discussed further below) that there is no separate tort defence. The rule which was left in place, however, was variously categorised as a rule of justiciability and one of the substantive law of tort. In either case, several of the points made about the implications of the rule no longer hold true. The first is its scope, diminished (the courts below held) as a result of developments in the context of the reviewability of the prerogative. Here, Lord Mance (who treats the non-justiciability rule as the entirety of Crown act of state) rejected the separation of a policy decision from its practical implementation which had underpinned the decisions below, holding instead that 'Crown act of state must be potentially applicable to acts in execution of policy-makers' decisions as it is to the decisions themselves.' For it to apply to given acts, he held (in agreement with Lord Sumption), it is necessary that:

> (i) they must involve an exercise of sovereign power, inherently governmental in nature; (ii) done outside the United Kingdom; (iii) with the prior authority or subsequent ratification of the Crown; and (iv) in the conduct of the Crown's relations with other states or their subjects (possibly excluding persons owning allegiance to the Crown).[133]

Though the judgments of Lord Sumption and Lady Hale disagree as to the nature of the rule (the former treating Crown act of state as an aspect of the substantive law of tort;[134] the latter holding that it must in fact possess two limbs precisely because, if it does not, then the justiciability limb must be as extensive as Lord Mance suggests)[135] both agree as to basic features of an act in respect of which it might be available. As such, the rule is—regardless of its nature—significantly broader than the High Court and Court of Appeal had recognised.

Secondly, however, it no longer seems to be the case that the rule is co-extensive with public law justiciability. This is obviously not problematic for those who regard it to be of some other nature. For Lord Mance, however, who treats the rule as one of non-justiciability, it is unclear how that distinction is justified (or even whether it is appreciated). This sort

[132] [2015] EWCA Civ 843, [324]. See also *R (Maya Evans) v Secretary of State for Defence* [2010] EWHC 1445 (Admin) in which the Divisional Court reviewed, in a public law claim, matters related to those which were here argued to be non-justiciable.

[133] [2017] UKSC 1, [72].

[134] ibid, [80]

[135] ibid, [33]

of unhelpful and under-theorised differentiation is evident also in the third issue, that of overcoming justiciability. Lord Mance clearly takes the view that Crown act of state non-justiciability is an example of the first category identified in *Shergill v Khaira*—what we have discussed above as type 1, or 'true' non-justiciability—whereby a court cannot consider the relevant matter even where 'necessary to do so in order to decide some other issue which is itself unquestionably justiciable'.[136] As noted above, however, even this true, type 1, non-justiciability is not absolute, in the sense of preventing the courts form considering the matter at any time and for any reason. Instead, it might be overcome by statute which empowers or obliges the courts to resolve some relevant legal question. This conclusion ties in with the government's concession that the doctrine of Crown act of state cannot act as a bar to claims brought under the Human Rights Act.[137] It nevertheless creates the potential for anomalies in any case in which the basis of the tort claim is a statutory, as opposed to common law, rule. In sum, the picture which emerges is messy, and only adds to the confusion caused by the Supreme Court's inability to agree upon the nature of the rule which survives its judgment. Nevertheless, the basic implications of the decision is clear—a range of acts which would, on the approach of the High Court and Court of Appeal, be capable of grounding a successful claim in tort, cannot—on the approach of the Supreme Court—do so. That point outranks in importance all the uncertainty regarding the status of the doctrine, and its implications for other areas of law. The decision of the Supreme Court therefore represents a significant victory for the executive within its wider project of resisting the juridification of warfare, though not one which addresses in any way the difficulties caused by the extra-territorial application of the ECHR.[138]

B. The Defence of Crown Act of State

The second limb of the doctrine of Crown act of state takes us away from the question of justiciability into that of defences: we are dealing here with acts upon which the courts are capable of adjudicating upon but in relation to which they accept the existence of a defence—in tort, and perhaps also to criminal proceedings—and which therefore operates on a different plane to the rules we have been considering until now. Like those other rules, however, it re-emerges in the context of the modern national security constitution and has been shaped by some of the same forces which were discussed in Chapter 5. In this section, I explain the background to and development of the rule and consider the implications of it having been written out of law by the judgment of the Supreme Court in *Serdar Mohammed*.

i. Background: The Crown's Immunity in Tort

The tort defence rule of Crown act of state was the residue of a much broader immunity once possessed by the King—encapsulated in the maxim that 'the King can do no wrong'—and

[136] [2014] UKSC 33, [42].
[137] [2017] UKSC 1, [14].
[138] See the discussion in Ch 3.

which, over time, came to be seen as belonging to the Crown in its institutional capacity.[139] It thus became in practice necessary to answer a set of complex questions in order to determine whether or not any particular public authority was or had been an emanation of the Crown and thus might avail itself of the immunity. This had predictable results in terms of the quantity and quality of the anomalies which might be identified within the constitutional landscape.[140] Even in relation to those actors who were emanations of the Crown and so might avail themselves of its (substantive) institutional immunity,[141] however, the picture was not as grave as the simple invocation of the maxim might be taken to suggest: the immunity was undercut to a significant degree by the availability of a remedy known as a petition of right, which was given statutory basis by the Petitions of Right Act 1860 but which was not available in relation to claims in tort.[142] In tort claims too, however, the common law supplied a method by which the legal gap left by Crown immunity might be partially filled, permitting a claim in tort to be brought against the Crown servant responsible for the wrongful act: institutional immunity co-existed with personal liability. Before the institutional immunity was brought to an end, this possibility was often made the basis of a legal fiction whereby the Crown would identify one of its servants to be personally liable for the wrongful act and indemnify that person against any damages that might be awarded against him or her. The courts disapproved of this practice: in *Adams v Naylor*[143] the House of Lords reaffirmed that the Crown was no party to the case, and that to call the defendant 'nominal' was misleading, for it was in relation to him—and not the Crown—that possession of the relevant duties had to be shown.[144] Several of the Law Lords suggested, in turn, that the case demonstrated the urgency of legislating on the matter of the Crown's liability in tort.[145] On the basis of these remarks, the Court of Appeal in *Royston v Cavey*[146] held that it had 'no jurisdiction to continue the hearing of a case where the cause of action alleged against a defendant is in truth not against the real defendant but against a name furnished for the purpose of trying an issue by agreement between the parties.'[147] These decisions precipitated the emergence of draft legislation from the limbo in which it had become stuck and its enactment as the Crown Proceedings Act 1947.[148]

[139] Maitland said that 'I believe … that an habitual and perfectly unambiguous personification of the Crown—in particular, the attribution of acts to the Crown—is much more modern than most people would believe. It seems to me that in fully half the cases in which Sir William Anson writes 'Crown', Blackstone would have written 'King'.' Frederic Maitland, 'The Crown as Corporation' (1901) 17 *LQR* 131, 139.

[140] See, eg, JH Morgan 'Introduction: Remedies Against the Crown' in GE Robinson, *Public Authorities and Legal Liability* (London, University of London Press, 1925), xvii–xxix.

[141] 'Crown immunity' is often used also to denote the presumption that statute does not apply to the Crown (nor the monarch) except by express words or necessary implication: see, eg, *Secretary of State for Justice v Black* [2016] EWCA Civ 125.

[142] *Viscount Canterbury v Attorney-General* (1842) 1 Ph 306. See also *Tobin v R* (1864) 16 CBNS 310 and *Feather v R* (1865) 6 B&S 257.

[143] *Adams v Naylor* [1946] AC 543.

[144] [1946] AC 543, 550.

[145] ibid, 552–3 and 555.

[146] *Royston v Cavey* [1947] KB 204.

[147] [1947] KB 204, 209.

[148] On the background to which see Joseph M Jacob, 'The Debates behind an Act: Crown Proceedings Reform 1920–1947' [1992] *PL* 452 and TT Arvind, 'Restraining the State through Tort? The Crown Proceedings Act in Retrospect' in TT Arvind and J Steele (eds), *Tort Law and the Legislature: Common Law, Statute and the Dynamics of Legal Change* (Oxford, Hart Publishing, 2013).

ii. The Crown Proceedings Act 1947

For present purposes, the key provision of the 1947 Act is section 2, which (subject to the rest of the Act's provisions) renders the Crown 'subject to all those liabilities in tort to which, if it were a private person of full age and capacity, it would be subject … in respect of torts committed by its servants or agents'. This rule is caveated by the provision that no proceedings shall lie against the Crown by virtue thereof 'in respect of any act or omission of a servant or agent of the Crown unless the act or omission would apart from the provisions of this Act have given rise to a cause of action in tort against that servant or agent or his estate.'[149] The meaning of this caveat has been the source of some confusion. Writing contemporaneously, Glanville Williams said of it that:

> It is thought that this proviso was inserted in order to make it plain that the Crown was to participate in the defence of "act of state" that is open to the servant under the rule in Buron v. Denman. But if this was the intention, the proviso used a bludgeon to kill a fly—and the fly was already dead, because where the servant has the defence of "act of state" it cannot be said that he has committed a tort within the words of section 2(1)(a), and thus there is nothing for which the Crown could in any event be liable.[150]

That is, the caveat seems to be designed as a savings clause which prevents the introduction of Crown liability in tort from being used to create liability where none had, as a result of the doctrine of Crown act of state, previously existed. One claim made in recent case law is that the 'savings clause' could not in fact have been intended to have that effect, for if it had, it would have made reference to the liability of the Crown itself rather than that of its agent. In the Supreme Court in *Serdar Mohammed*, Lady Hale (who held, unlike the majority, that there does exist a separate tort defence of Crown act of state) rejected this, noting that because the basic function of the 1947 Act was to make the Crown vicariously liable for the acts of its servants, it was logical that it made clear that it was not making 'any difference to the previous law relating to the liability of that servant or agent, even if the previous law in question is one which applies only to Crown servants or agents.'[151] For that reason, whether or not Williams was correct that it was the proviso's inclusion was unnecessary, 'there is no reason to doubt that the previous law of Crown act of state, whatever it was, was left intact.'[152] None of this tells us, however, about the nature of the tort defence which had been thereby retained, the residue of a once general immunity. For that, it is necessary to return to the case from which it is usually held to arise, *Buron v Denman*.[153]

Buron was a Spanish slave trader from whom slaves had been taken by Denman, a British naval commander, from the Gallinas Islands on which they had been held. Though Denman had not been instructed to carry this out, his actions were the subject of praise by a number of senior figures including the Lord of the Admiralty.[154] Buron brought an

149 Crown Proceedings Act 1947, s 2(1).
150 G Williams, *Crown Proceedings* (London, Stevens and Sons, 1948) 44.
151 [2017] UKSC 1, [41].
152 ibid.
153 *Buron v Denman* (1848) 2 Exch 167, 154 ER 450. The decision in the Supreme Court, in which it was held that *Buron* merely confirmed that subsequent ratification of an act is equivalent to prior authorisation, suggests *The Rolla* (1807) 6 Robinson 364 as an earlier example, to which *Buron* is a mere clarification.
154 An excellent account of the facts of the case is given in Charles Mitchell and Leslie Turano, 'Buron v Denman (1848)' in C Mitchell and P Mitchell (eds), *Landmark Cases in the Law of Tort* (Oxford, Hart Publishing, 2010).

action in trespass against him in the English courts where it was dismissed by the Exchequer Court. The report of the case offers the summary of Parke B, who refers to Denman's actions as being 'justified as an act of state.'[155] The predominant understanding of the case in the twentieth century has been that it established, alongside the non-justiciability rule of Crown act of state, a second limb, whereby a defence to a claim in tort was available in respect of acts of state carried out by the Crown, or with its approval or ratification. That is, the courts were not prevented from adjudicating upon the matter (as the non-justiciability limb would imply) but considered there to exist an affirmative defence where the conduct in question was authorised by, or subsequently ratified by, the Crown. The dualism of the doctrine was recognised by Emelyn Wade[156] and Lord McNair,[157] and it was the tort defence which Glanville Williams took the 1947 Act to be concerned to preserve. There was, however, no reported case after *Buron v Denman* which unambiguously exemplifies the successful pleading of the tort defence.[158] And while in *Nissan v Attorney General*,[159] the doctrine's dualism appeared to be accepted by certain of the Law Lords,[160] that acceptance was necessarily obiter, for in that case it was held that the act at issue was not an act of state. The doctrine was however, recognised by the lower courts in recent case law, albeit in a form, incorporating public policy considerations, far narrower than commentators had assumed. Taken together with the gutting of the justiciability limb, Crown act of state could reasonably be considered to be vanishing from the constitutional landscape.[161]

In its recent consideration of the question, however, the Supreme Court expansion (or, perhaps, restoration) of the non-justiciability limb of Crown act of state was accompanied by the rejection of the existence of the tort defence. Where the prevailing interpretation of *Buron v Denman* has been that it established (or at least evidenced) a second limb of Crown act of state, the view taken by the majority here was that *Buron* is (as was unsuccessfully argued below) simply an instantiation, or a corollary, of the non-justiciability rule, which has the effect that a 'claim which is non-justiciable against the Crown itself cannot be justiciable against the servants or agents who, with the Crown's authority or subsequent ratification, undertook the relevant acts'; such possibility would involve the subversion of Crown act of state.[162] Lord Mance, Lord Sumption and Lord Neuberger each took the effect of *Buron* to be only that subsequent ratification of a particular act was, for the purposes of the non-justiciability rule, equivalent to prior authorisation.[163] And, later authorities, which had appeared to recognise the dualism of Crown act of state, did not in fact do so, or did so only in obiter. Only Lady Hale was willing to preserve the traditional dualism, in large part on the basis that to not do so would imply exactly that extension of the non-justiciability rule which in fact was carried out by the Supreme Court here.[164]

[155] *Buron v Denman* (1848) 2 Exch 167, 154 ER 450, 459.

[156] ECS Wade, 'Act of State in English Law: Its Relations with International Law' (1934) 15 *British Yearbook of International Law* 98, 101.

[157] McNair (n 126).

[158] Some candidates are *Secretary of State for India v Kamachee Boye Sahaba* (1859) 13 Moo PCC 22, (1859) 19 ER 836 and *Walker v Baird* [1892] AC 491.

[159] *Nissan v Attorney-General* [1970] AC 179.

[160] See, eg, [1970] AC 179, 220B–C (Lord Morris) and 231D (Lord Wilberforce).

[161] Scott (n 126).

[162] [2017] UKSC 1, [62].

[163] ibid, [68], [84], and [100].

[164] ibid, [33].

Though the Court of Appeal's approach had 'very real attractions', she said, it had no basis in the jurisprudence,[165] and though the tort defence was not as broad as some commentators had suggested, it nevertheless encompassed a certain class of act: 'acts which are by their nature sovereign acts, acts which are inherently governmental, committed in the conduct of the foreign relations of the Crown.'[166] The effect must be that as far as the law is now concerned, there is no tort defence of Crown act of state; the 1947 Act was not merely moot (as Williams suggested) but doubly moot. *Buron v Denman* is not the source of a rule which is wholly at odds with the rule of law amounting, I previously suggested, to a rule that 'the Crown's say-so is sufficient to give rise to a defence in law to wrongful conduct upon which the courts are otherwise capable of adjudicating.'[167] Instead, it is simply a stark illustration of a rule which is both older than itself and which accords much better, if still imperfectly, with the historical approach to justiciability, not least in encompassing a range of matters which other modern understandings of non-justiciability would have failed to reach. Crown act of state, after *Serdar Mohammed*, is a simpler doctrine, but one which is further-reaching than had previously been understood.

C. Unanswered Questions

Certain basic questions about the scope of Crown act of state remain unanswered, and are in fact complicated by the new uncertainty as to the nature of the surviving rule. Within a dualist conception of Crown act of state, it appeared that the non-justiciability limb applied without reference to either the location of the act or the person against whom the alleged tort was committed. By contrast, the best understanding of the tort defence limb is that at least one, and perhaps both, of those factors is relevant to the question of whether the tort defence is available in any particular circumstances. The easiest permutation is that of an act done to citizen within the UK (or, perhaps, the British Islands, a term used in statute to denote 'United Kingdom, the Channel Islands and the Isle of Man').[168] In that scenario, the defence of Crown act of state is unavailable: the Crown cannot grant its immunity to acts done by its servants and agents. Though that proposition is nowhere called into question, where in law it is established is not always clear. Where authority is offered, the authority is usually that of *Entick v Carrington*.[169] Where Lord Camden was canvassing the possible bases of a power of search and seizure for seditious libel, he considered—alongside the fact that such a power had been employed, without challenge since the Glorious revolution, and the fact that such a power was of evident utility—the claim that 'it is necessary for the ends of government to lodge such a power with a state officer.' To this he replied that 'the common law does not understand that kind of reasoning' and noted that in the previous century 'Serjeant Ashley [had been] committed to the Tower … by the House of Lords only for asserting in argument, that there was a "law of state" different from the common law',

165 ibid, [34].
166 ibid, [36].
167 Scott (n 126) 372.
168 See the discussion in Ch 2.
169 *Entick v Carrington* (1765) 29 St Tr 1029. Wade identifies *Entick* along with the *Parlement Belge* (1879) 4 PD 129 and *Walker v Baird* [1892] AC 491: Wade (n 126) 98. Collier (n 126) 111 agrees, but see Cane (n 128) 686.

while the judges who had decided in the King's favour the case of the Ship Money 'were impeached for holding, first, that state-necessity would justify the raising money without consent of parliament; and secondly, that the king was judge of that necessity.'[170] To retrofit this element of Crown act of state onto *Entick* in this way seems to assimilate the rule with a claim of state necessity: the courts allow a defence to claims arising out of certain acts precisely because what was done was adjudged, by those authorised to speak on behalf of the state, to be necessary in its interests. And so, any successful pleading of the tort defence limb dilutes the grand rhetoric of Lord Camden. Rather than the common law knowing nothing of this sort of reasoning, it does so only as regards certain places, and certain people.

The next question is whether the tort defence might ever be pleaded in relation to acts which take place in the UK. On this point, the leading case is *Johnstone v Pedlar*.[171] That case speaks to the availability of Crown act of state because it had been suggested that the doctrine could be pleaded against the claimant because he was an alien: a naturalised American who had returned to Ireland to take part in the Rising of 1916. The House of Lords dismissed this on the basis that an alien resident in the UK was in temporary allegiance to the Crown, but it left open the possibility that a person who is not in such temporary allegiance to the Crown might find his or her claims in tort met with a successfully plea of Crown Act of state.[172] This account suggests an alternative, though not necessarily incompatible, way of conceptualising the limits to the availability of Crown act of state, based on the correlation between the allegiance that a person owes to the Crown and the protection that he or she is therefore afforded by the Crown and 'its' law.[173] One difficulty with that understanding, however, is that the relevant protection is very weak indeed: there seems no positive duty on the executive of the day to act to assist UK nationals abroad, and so the 'protection' is at best defined negatively, by the inability of the executive to plead the Crown act of state tort defence against its nationals.[174] It may also have the unwelcome implication that a person who is a British national but who by virtue of some treasonous act has violated his allegiance and, in consequence, renounced his protection, can under certain circumstances—though not necessarily within the UK itself—see a claim brought by him successfully repelled by a plea of Crown act of state. If correct, this brings the law on Crown act of state into close communion with the law of treason and the various difficulties associated with it ever since the decision of the House of Lords in *Joyce v DPP*, regarding the conviction of 'Lord Haw Haw' for treason.[175] The decision of the Supreme Court, however, and the insistence there upon the limitation of the foreign act of state rule to acts done outside the UK, would seem to answer the question, albeit that it seems foolish to exclude altogether the possibility of Crown act of state applying to acts done to enemy aliens in the UK in time of war unless and until that question is explicitly determined. What must be remembered also is that the prerogative encompasses substantive powers of detention and

[170] (1765) 29 St Tr 1029, 1073.

[171] *Johnstone v Pedlar* [1921] 2 AC 262.

[172] See, eg, [1921] 2 AC 262, 297–8 (Lord Phillimore).

[173] Glanville Williams, 'The Correlation of Allegiance and Protection' (1948) 10 *CLJ* 5.

[174] See, eg, *R (Abbasi) v Secretary of State for Foreign & Commonwealth Affairs* [2002] EWCA Civ 1598, and CRG Murray, 'In the shadow of Lord Haw Haw: Guantanamo Bay, diplomatic protection and allegiance' [2011] *PL* 115.

[175] *Joyce v DPP* [1946] AC 347.

deportation in respect of such persons: if that power is lawfully exercised, there is no need for any defence of Crown act of state.

The final configuration of nationality and geography—acts done to British subjects outside of the British Islands—also threatens the logic of that improved account. Though on this point there is no clear and authoritative decision of the courts, there is a strong tendency to take the view that the tort defence's availability is not a function of the nationality of those to whom the alleged wrong has been done. In *Nissan v Attorney General*,[176] for instance, though the act in question was ultimately adjudged not to be an act of state, several of the judges in the House of Lords cast doubt on the idea that the defence might be available as against those who held foreign nationality but not those who held British nationality.[177] Lord Morris of Borth-y-Gest[178] and Lord Wilberforce, though not expressing concluded views on the point, noted the potentially anomalous circumstances which would result,[179] while Lord Pearce stated that:

> In this state of authority and doctrine it appears to me to be impossible to accept the broad proposition that in no case can the plea of act of state, in the sense that a particular act by the Crown is not cognisable by a British court, be raised against a British subject. On the contrary, as regards acts committed abroad in the conduct of foreign relations with other states, the preponderance of authority and of practice seems to me to be the other way.[180]

Only Lord Reid was of the opinion that 'a British subject—at least if he is also a citizen of the United Kingdom and Colonies—can never be deprived of his legal right to redress by any assertion by the Crown or decision of the court that the acts of which he complains were acts of state.'[181] Though the matter has not yet been settled, this is also the prevailing view in the case law arising out of the war on terror. In *Al-Jedda v Ministry of Defence*[182] (the claimant being the same person whose British citizenship and, more specifically, the attempt to deprive him of it has been, we saw in Chapter 6, the subject of herculean efforts on the part of the UK), it was said at first instance by Underhill J that '[i]f the true basis of the rule … is that acts done by the Crown abroad in the conduct of foreign relations are of their nature not cognisable in the English court, I can see no reason of principle why the position should be any different where the person injured happens to be a British citizen: the nature of the act is the same.'[183]

This, though, seems to rely upon an unhelpful conflation (or at least failure to adequately distinguish) the two limbs of the doctrine, and so should not be relied upon. And because Underhill J, like a majority of the Court of Appeal after him,[184] took the view that the detention of Al-Jedda was lawful, the consideration of the issue was necessarily obiter. The same view dominates in *Serdar Mohammed* and *Rahmatullah*, though again the point did not need to be determined there either as neither has British nationality. Leggatt J in the

176 *Nissan v Attorney General* [1970] AC 179.
177 See SA de Smith, *Civis Britannicus Sum* (1969) 32 *MLR* 427.
178 [1970] AC 179, 221D.
179 ibid, 240E.
180 ibid, 235E-F.
181 ibid, 213C-D.
182 *Al-Jedda v Ministry of Defence* [2009] EWHC 397 (QB).
183 [2009] EWHC 397 (QB), [80].
184 *Al-Jedda v Ministry of Defence* [2010] EWCA Civ 758.

High Court found it 'difficult to see how the nationality of the claimant can in principle be relevant'.[185] It is submitted that this view is the better one, but though it avoids the anomalies identified in *Nissan*, other difficulties are caused, not least that it would seem to exclude the most plausible normative basis for the rule. Had this view been ultimately endorsed as part of the ratio of some decision on Crown act of state, then the idea of the Crown act of state tort defence's availability against any particular individual as a function of that individual's allegiance (whether general or local) or non-allegiance to the Crown would have failed: the citizen abroad still owes allegiance to the Crown and so should, if that logic is correct, not be susceptible to a plea of Crown act of state. Instead, the defence's availability is (with the possible exception of circumstances in which enemy aliens are the subject of the act in question) would have been solely a function of geography. These problems persists, however, following the decision of the Supreme Court in *Serdar Mohammed*, given the uncertainty which it creates as to the nature of that element of the doctrine which persists. Though the Supreme Court—as it was entitled to do—showed no desire to engage with these difficult questions,[186] it seems unclear what logic would justify a distinction between a citizen and a non-citizen in the context of a rule that is either one of justiciability or simply an aspect of the substantive rule of tort.

i. A Human Rights Exception?

In the High Court in *Serdar Mohammed*, it was argued that the courts should recognise to the tort doctrine of Crown act of state a human rights exception of the sort recognised to the foreign act of state rule, as discussed above, on the basis that 'the courts must hold the Crown to at least the same standards as a foreign state.'[187] In rejecting that submission, Leggatt J emphasised the distinction between the underpinnings of the two: the first was conceived of by him as a rule of the conflict of laws; the latter is based upon 'principles of sovereignty, comity between nations and judicial restraint.'[188] The question was of course of less significance than it might have been given that the reconceptualisation of the tort defence in the judgments of the High Court and Court of Appeal opened the door to a direct consideration of the relevant public policy issues.[189] For that reason, the existence or non-existence of a human rights exception was unlikely to be the material to the resolution of particular cases. The judgment of the Supreme Court, however, reopens the question, with the judges who addressed the question being in agreement that Crown act of state would not apply to claims of torture.

One way of understanding that exception is that the doctrine applies only to acts authorised or ratified by the government, and that the government would never authorise or ratify the conduct of torture. Lady Hale preferred, however, to treat the government's acceptance

[185] [2014] EWHC 1369 (QB), [397].
[186] [2017] UKSC 1, [37], [81].
[187] [2014] EWHC 1369 (QB), [407].
[188] ibid, [408]
[189] [2015] EWCA Civ 843, [375]: 'If, however, we are correct in our conclusion that the limb of act of state which operates as a defence to claims in tort is essentially a principle of public policy, we have difficulty in seeing how it could be successfully invoked if the conduct in issue constituted a grave breach of international law or human rights law.'

that the doctrine does not apply to torture or the mistreatment of detainees as 'an acknowledgement that such acts are not inherently governmental, rather than creating exceptions to a general rule.'[190] Lord Sumption was unwilling to endorse that position, both because there are 'well documented modern instances across the world of the use of torture and other forms of maltreatment as an instrument of state policy authorised at the highest levels' and because, both according to both international and domestic law, 'torture is by definition a governmental act'.[191] He therefore suggested instead that the best understanding of the matter was that, in light of the strength of UK public policy against the use of torture (reflected most clearly in *A v Secretary of State for the Home Department No. 2*)[192] such use could not be a lawful exercise of the prerogative and, therefore, it could not be an act of state; nor 'would there be any inconsistency with the proper functions of the executive in treating it as giving rise to civil liability.'[193] Though the effect of these remarks is of course a welcome one, a more robust assertion of the common law's (present and ongoing) commitment to the unacceptability of torture and other activities contrary to public policy would have been desirable.

ii. Crown Act of State and the Criminal Law

One final question arises. Crown act of state as a defence to wrongful acts has been applied, in all of the relevant case law, to civil wrongs. But not all wrongs are civil wrongs, and much of the literature on Crown act of state suggests, or even assumes, that it may also be available in relation to criminal wrongs.[194] We see this, for example, in the work of Emelyn Wade,[195] Lord McNair,[196] JG Collier,[197] and Peter Cane.[198] In almost every case, the eventual basis of the assertion—whether made confidently or with hesitation—appears to be the same: the discussion of the point by James Fitzjames Stephen in his *History of the Criminal Law of England.*[199] Distinguishing between acts done in time of war (which are of no concern to the criminal law and so to him) and warlike acts done in times of peace, Fitzjames Stephen points out that 'an act of State may involve consequences which, if wilfully brought about by a private person, would or might be criminal.'[200] Though accepting that he knows of no example of the principle being tested in a criminal prosecution, Fitzjames Stephen expresses the view that acts of State—either carried out by, or, as in *Buron v Denman*, subsequently adopted by, a public authority—'fall outside the sphere of the criminal law'.[201]

[190] [2017] UKSC 1, [36].

[191] ibid, [96].

[192] *A v Secretary of State for the Home Department (No 2)* [2005] UKHL 71.

[193] [2017] UKSC 1, [96].

[194] See also *Nissan v Attorney General* [1970] AC 179, 231 (Lord Wilberforce): one limb of Crown act of state provides 'a defence to an act otherwise tortious or criminal, committed abroad, provided that the act was authorised or subsequently ratified by the Crown.'

[195] Wade (n 126) 98. Before Wade, Moore (n 126) 94 also accepted the defence's availability in criminal proceedings.

[196] McNair (n 126) 111.

[197] JG Collier, 'Act of State as A Defence Against a British Subject' (1968) *CLJ* 102, 109–110.

[198] Cane (n 128) 682fn.

[199] James Fitzjames Stephen, *A History of the Criminal Law of England* (London, MacMillan & Co, 1883) vol II, 61–5.

[200] ibid 63.

[201] ibid 63.

In the absence of directly relevant authority he relies upon logical inference from the civil case law in which the principle had been 'repeatedly affirmed' and 'if a man is not even liable civilly for an act of State' he says, 'it would seem to follow *a fortiori* that he cannot be liable criminally.'[202]

Notwithstanding that it was repeatedly relied upon by scholars for around a century after it was made, there exist several reasons for being sceptical of this claim. The first is its antiquity: Fitzjames Stephen was writing before almost all of the relevant case had been decided. The second is that it is under-theorised. Stephen's comments predate the articulation of the distinction between the justiciability limb and the tort defence of Crown act of state and all that follows from it. The third, and most damning, is the absence of relevant case law, with none being available to Stephen at the time he wrote, and none having been decided since. Nevertheless, if we think of the Crown act of state tort defence as the residue of the Crown's immunity in tort, it serves to recall that the Crown's immunity was never solely in tort but extended also to the criminal sphere, and that the criminal immunity has never been statutorily emptied out in the manner in which the tort immunity was by the 1947 Act. How far, exactly, the Crown's criminal immunity traditionally extended is, however, unclear. Maurice Sunkin suggests that 'it is now assumed that government departments and Crown bodies are immune from criminal liability whatever the crime, unless that immunity is removed or diminished by Parliament'[203] but, later, that 'there is no doubt that if prosecuted and found guilty servants of the Crown will incur *personal* criminal liability for their crimes, even when committed during the course of their official actions.'[204] This leaves open the question of 'the imposition of criminal liability on offices of the Crown, government departments and Crown bodies *as such*, in other words the imposition of liability for *official* rather than *personal* actions'.[205] There was therefore some reason to believe that the Crown may have continued to enjoy sufficient criminal immunity as to cover certain acts done abroad, and to prevent any criminal liability arising out of those acts. Though the fact that this conclusion could have been tested only in the unlikely event that a relevant prosecution was brought made the matter—barring unforeseen circumstances—largely hypothetical, it is nevertheless obvious that this possibility was (even) more concerning than is that of the executive successfully pleading the defence in a civil case.

Even if this logic was previously sound, the possibility of a Crown act of state defence to a criminal charge is undermined by the decision of the Supreme Court in *Serdar Mohammed* in which, as we have seen, the tort defence is written out of the picture, with only the other limb of the doctrine—variously conceptualised as a rule of the substantive law of tort, or one of justiciability—left intact. The uncertainty as to the nature of the remaining rule makes it difficult to consider the implications for its application to the criminal law. If it is an aspect of the substantive law of tort, it cannot for that reason alone be part of the

[202] ibid 63–4.

[203] Maurice Sunkin, 'Crown immunity from criminal liability in English law' [2003] *PL* 716. See also Halsbury's Laws of England, *Constitutional and Administrative Law*, vol 20 (2014), [606] which suggest that at common law servants of the Crown cannot have criminal proceedings brought against them in relation to crimes alleged to have been committed by them in their capacity as representatives of the Crown. The authority offered for that proposition is that of *Macbeath v Haldimand* (1786) 1 Term Rep 172 and *Dunn v MacDonald* [1897] 1 QB 555, CA. Both cases relate to the context of contract and no specific authority is offered for the context of the criminal law.

[204] Sunkin (n 203) 723.

[205] ibid.

substantive criminal law, and there is no reason to believe that the criminal law separately contains some equivalent rule. If it is a rule of justiciability, the application of the doctrine to the criminal context becomes very complex. First, many acts done which fall within the non-justiciability rule as defined by the Supreme Court would not attract criminal liability in the first place. Second, the fact that statute suffices to overcome non-justiciability creates the possibility that the availability of Crown act of state as a defence to criminal law will depend on whether the relevant offence derives from common law or statute: in the latter case, but not the former, the non-justiciability would be overcome. Such a result contains more than a little absurdity, though mitigated in part by the fact that very often the sort of acts to which the doctrine might become relevant will only constitute criminal offences because the relevant offence has been extended to certain places or persons by statute.[206] We should therefore hesitate before accepting that Crown act of state applies also to the criminal sphere, though the possibility cannot be entirely discounted. This conclusion makes even more concerning the casual and unjustified reliance placed upon Stephen's work by Lady Hale in her opinion in *Serdar Mohammed*. She states that 'if act of state is a defence to the use of lethal force in the conduct of military operations abroad, it must also be a defence to the capture and detention of persons on imperative grounds of security in the conduct of such operations. It makes no sense to permit killing but not capture and detention, the military then being left with the invidious choice between killing the enemy or letting him go.'[207] The logic is based upon a false premise: an act done under in the circumstances described would not in fact attract criminal liability in the first place.[208] Nevertheless, if Lady Hale wishes there to exist a rule which unambiguously excludes the possibility of such liability arising, then the appropriate course of action would be for Parliament to legislate for such a rule.

V. Conclusion: The Courts and the Executive in the National Security Constitution

Because of its non-statutory form, the many and major developments which have taken place in the field of justiciability have been far less prominent than have those areas

206 By, eg, the Criminal Justice Act 1948. In the case of the law of murder, s 9 of the Offences Against the Person Act 1861 provides, as amended, that 'Where any murder or manslaughter shall be committed on land out of the United Kingdom, whether within the Queen's dominions or without, and whether the person killed were a subject of Her Majesty or not, every offence committed by any subject of Her Majesty in respect of any such case, whether the same shall amount to the offence of murder or of manslaughter … may be dealt with, inquired of, tried, determined, and punished … in England or Ireland.'

207 [2017] UKSC 1, [32].

208 The actus reus of the crime of murder in English law requires that the victim be 'under the Queen's peace', and so where the killing takes place outwith that situation, there can be no murder: 3 *Co Inst* 47. See though Michael Hirst, 'Murder under the Queen's Peace' (2008) *Crim LR* 541, 542 arriving at the same conclusion though on the basis that 'killing in the heat of combat is not "unlawful" in the first place' and so there is no need to 'invoke the Queen's peace in order to exclude such acts from the ambit of the offence.' *cf* also Peter Rowe, 'The criminal liability of a British soldier merely for participating in the Iraq war 2003: a response to Chilcot evidence' (2010) *Crim LR* 752. A recent (though inconclusive) judicial consideration of the requirement can be found in *R v Adebolajo* [2014] EWCA Crim 2779.

of law—investigatory powers, restriction of travel, secrecy—which rely in whole or in part on the introduction and amendment of statutory authority, with all of the attendant prior debate, parliamentary scrutiny and, at the end of the process, a clear form of words whose meaning can be debated and whose merits disputed. Against this, this chapter has argued that the only way to bring coherence to the general law on the justiciability of foreign affairs is to erase from the picture many of the concepts generally considered in relation to it: a matter is properly regarded as non-justiciable, I have argued, when (and only when) the need to avoid addressing it will cause the courts to allow otherwise enforceable legal rights to be unvindicated. Where, instead, the courts do not answer a legal question because there is no legal question to answer, but only—say—an issue of unincorporated international law which our dualist constitution forbids the courts from applying, or an abstract matter without some legal foothold on which the courts might hang their judgment, we are not dealing with issues of justiciability at all. And both of these issues are distinct from the question of the appropriate standard of review. Even with that clarification, however, it has been argued that the law of non-justiciability remains imprecise: there is an open texture to all of the relevant elements of the law, and to turn the question (as this account in part does) into one of the appropriate standard of review hardly eliminates indeterminacy. The common law method in this way seems to collapse at the margins, and the justiciability of foreign relations is revealed—perhaps inevitably—as the most political of all areas of law, in which the courts run up against the conflicting impulses of, on one hand, legal principle and, on the other, the practicalities of international relations and its impact upon the pursuit of national security. The same might be said of the doctrines of foreign act of state and Crown act of state. The former has shifted perceptibly towards a more limited non-justiciability without arriving at a place where one can be confident of how the courts will apply the doctrine in question to any particular set of facts. Or, rather, where one can be confident that what will determine their application to any particular set of facts will be what has been said in previous case law, rather than—say—a holistic and impressionistic assessment of the political implications of the issue; how sensitive it is, as regards the UK and its allies, and how far it strays beyond the bounds of what the judiciary can reasonably (if tacitly) overlook. The latter reveals itself as the most consequential of the justiciability rules, excluding many private law claims which would otherwise be possible and serving—belatedly but unambiguously—as a major victory for the executive in its attempts to exclude large chunks of its national security endeavours from the scope of legal accountability.

7

Sovereignty

I. Introduction

The present work is a contribution to the literature on the domestic constitutional order of the UK, and focuses upon the law and practices which constitute that order as they apply to threats to national security. At several points, however, we have considered the law as it applies to acts done outside of the UK because of the manner in which security at home necessitates action abroad, and because, for example, such action might have consequences in domestic law, under—for example—the criminal law, or the ECHR as implemented by the HRA. We have also, however, strayed beyond the domestic legal regime, to consider the way in which certain acts of the UK are influenced by, and resonate within, a body of international law which is only exceptionally given effect in domestic law. This chapter, which acts as a conclusion to the book as a whole, develops the broader theme which both these examples instantiate: the way in which national security, perhaps to a greater extent than all other policy aims, takes place in a context which is international—the threat itself, the law and policy by which the UK responds to that threat, the institutions that make or determine or otherwise influence that law—and so works to call into question the sovereignty of the UK (as it will that of all, or almost all, individual states).

Here, then, we mean sovereignty not as a legal attribute of the Crown-in-Parliament but rather the sense in which the state (and not solely its legislature) can (or, more frequently here, cannot) look to achieve its aims acting alone, without reference to the needs and interests of those other states with which it coexists on the international plane. It is not any part of my argument that sovereignty is *uniquely* threatened in the national security context, nor that it is *newly* threatened in that context. It is, however, the case—I argue—that the extent to which both the perceived threats to national security and the legal responses to them are international in nature is a distinctive feature of the modern national security constitution, which to that extent is in fact an inter-national security constitution. This chapter's argument is a simple one: the internationalisation of national security logically and necessarily complicates, and often undermines, the processes of accountability which have developed (or been imposed) in order to hold the executive to account for its actions in the domain of national security. In a category of such cases, the effect of such internationalisation is to render meaningful accountability impossible. If much of what has been discussed in this book exemplifies the constitutionalisation of national security—with new (and sometimes stronger) forms of (often legal) accountability developed and implemented in the period under discussion—this final chapter suggests that the internationalisation of national security works to counteract, and in some contexts nullify, the effect of those developments.

II. From National Security to International Security

In this first section, I consider the ways in which the concept of national security has evolved—in law and in practice—into something which resembles instead international security. That is, quite separately from the issues addressed in Chapter 3 regarding the regulation by international law of the use of military force abroad, the 'domestic' element of national security has over time shed its domestic skin, and come to reflect—again, in both legal doctrine and in practice—something that seems to be a truly international security and, even when it is not quite that, is certainly an internationalised national security.

A. The Internationalisation of Terrorism in Domestic Law

In Chapter 1, certain aspects of the legal definition of terrorism in UK law were discussed, as was its evolution over time. There, in particular, it was shown that the definition has become overbroad; that many of those activities which do or might count as terrorism in domestic law should not do so. Here, however, we can focus upon another element of the evolution of the legal approach to terrorism: its geographic scope. Before 2000, the law focused almost exclusively on acts relating to Northern Ireland: the Prevention of Terrorism Act 1974 (PTA) proscribed certain listed organisations and permitted the Secretary of State to add to the list 'any organisation that appears to him to be concerned in terrorism occurring in the United Kingdom and connected with Northern Irish affairs, or in promoting or encouraging it.'[1] Similarly, the power to make exclusion orders introduced by that Act could be exercised by the Secretary of State 'in such way as appears to him expedient to prevent acts of terrorism (whether in Great Britain or elsewhere) designed to influence public opinion or Government policy with respect to affairs in Northern Ireland.'[2] The effect was that although terrorism was defined generally, the more intrusive of the powers by which it was to be addressed were available only in relation to a specific category of terrorism: that concerned with Northern Ireland either because—before 1974—they were found in statutes which extended only to that province,[3] or because—from 1974 onwards—the (UK-wide) statutes explicitly limited their application in various ways. Later incarnations of the PTAs extended the scope of terrorism with which they were concerned, though without renouncing the distinction between Northern Irish and other terrorism. For example, though the 1989 Act included the same general definition of terrorism, certain of the powers were concerned both with acts of terrorism 'connected with the affairs of Northern Ireland'[4] and acts of terrorism 'of any other description except acts connected solely with the affairs of the United Kingdom or any part of the United Kingdom other than Northern Ireland.'[5] The internationalisation of national security within the context of counter-terrorism therefore in its initial phase distinguished the target of the terrorist action, and so placed

[1] Prevention of Terrorism (Temporary Provisions) Act 1974, s 1(3).
[2] PTA 1974, s 3(1).
[3] Such as the Northern Ireland (Emergency Provisions) Act 1973.
[4] Prevention of Terrorism (Temporary Provisions) Act 1989, s 4(2).
[5] PTA 1989, s 9(3)(b).

international terrorism in a separate legal box to the terrorism with which it had previously concerned itself.

The Terrorism Act 2000 demonstrates explicitly the increasingly international understanding of national security which prevails. The definition of terrorism found there involves three elements: the use or threat of action where the action falls within one of a number of categories,[6] and where it is 'is designed to influence the government or an international governmental organisation or to intimidate the public or a section of the public',[7] and where 'the use or threat is made for the purpose of advancing a political, religious, racial or ideological cause.'[8] Leaving aside the specified acts the use or threat of which might constitute terrorism, there are several aspects of this definition which stand out. The 'action' in question need not be taken within the UK in order to count as terrorism,[9] while a reference to any person or property is a reference 'to any person, or to property, wherever situated';[10] any reference to the public 'includes a reference to the public of a country other than the United Kingdom';[11] and 'the government' means 'the government of the United Kingdom, of a Part of the United Kingdom or of a country other than the United Kingdom.'[12] The effect of this definition is to bring within the definition of terrorism any relevant act, done anywhere, for the purpose of influencing any government or intimidating (a section of) the public of any country, where the act is done (or the threat is made) for the purpose of 'advancing a political, religious, racial or ideological cause.' One consequence of this expansion was noted in Chapter 1 in the context of the law on proscription: the expanded definition of terrorism permits the proscription of organisations which do not operate in, and pose no threat to, the UK as a cheap tool of foreign policy. More generally, we see that though this concept of terrorism exists in one particular (set of) legal system(s) it reaches far beyond, constrained by considerations of geography neither in terms of where an act is done or the public or government at whom the relevant acts are directed. It is in this way more than merely international: it is now almost possible to have terrorism without nations. Only the fundamental ideological precept that terrorism is something which necessarily represents an illegitimate intervention into the political process (formal or informal) by a non-state actor prevents that link from being broken once and for all. No matter how terrorism evolves, it remains central to the dominant conception thereof—and implicit in its legal incarnation in the United Kingdom—that it cannot be done by states, but only to them.

B. The Internationalisation of National Security

In the introduction to this book, I defined one component of its title ('national security') in accordance with the pragmatic definition offered by Lord Hoffmann in *Rehman*.

[6] Terrorism Act 2000, s 1(a).
[7] ibid, s 1(b) as amended by the Terrorism Act 2006.
[8] ibid, s 1(c) as amended by the Counter-Terrorism Act 2008.
[9] ibid, s 4(a).
[10] ibid, s 4(b).
[11] ibid, s 4(c).
[12] ibid, s 4(d).

'[T]here is no difficulty about what 'national security' means,' he said there: it means 'the security of the United Kingdom and its people.'[13] In *Rehman*, however, the specific question upon which the House of Lords was called upon to answer was how widely that term should be interpreted. The appellant was a Pakistani national, made the subject of a deportation order on public interest grounds because of his involvement with Islamic terrorist groups and notwithstanding that the Secretary of State had recognised that 'Ur Rehman and his United Kingdom-based followers are unlikely to carry out any acts of violence in this country'.[14] Hearing an appeal against the order,[15] SIAC made two findings of relevance to us. The first was that the statutory categories—'national security', 'international relations', and 'other political reasons'[16]—were to be read disjunctively, meaning that in Rehman's case the Secretary of State having relied originally upon national security, he could not 'broaden his grounds to avoid difficulties which he may encounter in proving his case'.[17] As regards the definition of 'national security', SIAC noted the absence of both statutory definition of the term and of prior authority on the point, holding eventually that:

> [i]n the circumstances, and for the purposes of this case, we adopt the position that a person may be said to offend against national security if he engages in, promotes, or encourages violent activity which is targeted at the United Kingdom, its system of government or its people. This includes activities directed against the overthrow or destabilisation of a foreign government if that foreign government is likely to take reprisals against the United Kingdom which affect the security of the United Kingdom or of its nationals. National security extends also to situations where United Kingdom citizens are targeted, wherever they may be.[18]

Though the language of 'reprisals' is unhelpfully vague, it is clear that this definition makes room for what we might call 'international national security' only in an attenuated form. That is, national security refers in the first place to the security of the UK and its citizens (as Lord Hoffmann would later declare);[19] the security of other states is a distinct issue,

[13] *Secretary of State for the Home Department v Rehman* [2001] UKHL 47, [50]. In *Esbester v United Kingdom* [1993] ECHR 64, the Security Service Act 1989 was challenged on the basis that it lacked the accessibility and foreseeability required by the Convention, including on the basis that 'the interests of national security' was only partly defined. The Commission held, however, that the principles developed on this point 'do not necessarily require a comprehensive definition of the notion of "the interests of national security"': 'Many laws, which by their subject-matter require to be flexible, are inevitably couched in terms which are to a greater or lesser extent vague and whose interpretation and application are questions of practice.'

[14] [2001] UKHL 47, [1].

[15] *Secretary of State for the Home Department v Rehman* [1999] INLR 517.

[16] The statutory power relied upon referred only to deportation being 'conducive to the public good', but the regime for challenging the decision to deport (the first stage of the making of a deportation order) excluded the usual right of appeal on more limited grounds: where the decision to make an order was that the person's deportation was conducive to the public good 'as being in the interests of national security or of the relations between the United Kingdom and any other country or for other reasons of a political nature': Immigration Act 1971, s 15(3).

[17] [1999] INLR 517, 528.

[18] ibid.

[19] There is nothing made here of the nation/state distinction, but it is helpful to note that when we talk of 'national security' we are in speaking in fact of the security of the state: that the UK is a multi-national state seems no longer to be contested by any significant academic or political faction (albeit that the abstract recognition of that fact is, in light of the question of Northern Ireland, not easy to map onto the UK as we find it). And yet the individual nations of England, Scotland and Wales are not—for the present time—recognised as having security needs distinct from those of UK as a whole (here too, and for many of the same reasons, Northern Ireland is a special case). The 'national security' which is reserved to Westminster by the various devolution settlements is reserved specifically because national security is really state security. For a consideration of the question of security as applied to Scotland (and in particular in relation to the possibility of an independent Scotland), see Andrew W Neal (ed), *Security in a Small Nation: Scotland, Democracy, Politics*, Open Book Publishers (2017).

which becomes relevant only indirectly, via the harm that reprisals of those other states may cause to the security of the UK and, again, its citizens. This can be distinguished from a definition of national security which includes directly the security of other states (or at least some subset thereof) on the basis, perhaps, that the stability of the international system as a whole promotes the security of each of the individual states which makes it up, or because the security of the UK is so closely tied to that of particular other states that an attack on them can reasonably be interpreted as an attack on it. How far the practical consequences of this indirect internationalisation of national security would stretch is determined in the first place by the concept of 'reprisals'. The judgment of SIAC suggests that counsel for Rehman had referred to the taking of reprisals by a foreign state alongside the possibility of such a state 'permit[ting] terrorism against the UK'.[20] This differentiation suggests that the concept of a 'reprisal' is a limited one and seems in context to refer not even to situations in which there is some omission or passivity by a foreign state which allows a third party to carry out attacks upon the UK (to which the language of 'permitting' must be taken to refer), but rather to its active involvement in such attacks. It seems unlikely to include purely diplomatic responses and it is unlikely, if it does not, that it includes other changes to the regimes by which states cooperate or collaborate with each other. Nevertheless—as we shall see below—it is in that realm in which the international dimension of national security is most likely to impact upon the security of the UK.

Both these elements of SIAC's decision, however, were overtaken by the decision of the House of Lords, where it was held, first, that the three grounds did not have to be considered disjunctively, but that the Secretary of State might instead take an overall view of whether the deportation of a particular individual was conducive to the public good. On the second point, regarding the ability of 'national security' to encompass actions taken against states other than the UK itself, Lord Slynn of Hadley argued that 'in contemporary world conditions, action against a foreign state may be capable indirectly of affecting the security of the United Kingdom.'[21] He continued:

> The means open to terrorists both in attacking another state and in attacking international or global activity by the community of nations, whatever the objectives of the terrorist, may well be capable of reflecting on the safety and well-being of the United Kingdom or its citizens. The sophistication of means available, the speed of movement of persons and goods, the speed of modern communication, are all factors which may have to be taken into account in deciding whether there is a real possibility that the national security of the United Kingdom may immediately or subsequently be put at risk by the actions of others. To require the matters in question to be capable of resulting "directly" in a threat to national security limits too tightly the discretion of the executive in deciding how the interests of the state, including not merely military defence but democracy, the legal and constitutional systems of the state, need to be protected.[22]

[20] [1999] INLR 517, 527.

[21] [2001] UKHL 47, [16]. See also the remarks of Lord Woolfe MR in the Court of Appeal: 'Whatever may have been the position in the past, increasingly the security of one country is dependent upon the security of other countries. That is why this country has entered into numerous alliances. They acknowledge the extent to which this country's security is dependent upon the security of other countries … An attack on an ally can undermine the security of this country.' *Secretary of State for the Home Department v Rehman* [2000] 3 WLR 1240, [34].

[22] [2001] UKHL 47, [16].

Though he accepted that 'there must be a real possibility of an adverse affect on the United Kingdom' arising from the actions of the person alleged to pose a threat to national security, he rejected the claim that the adverse effect had to be 'direct or immediate.'[23] This was echoed by Lord Steyn, who said that '[e]ven democracies are entitled to protect themselves, and the executive is the best judge of the need for international co-operation to combat terrorism and counter-terrorist strategies. This broader context is the backcloth of the Secretary of State's statutory power of deportation in the interests of national security.'[24] The decision of the House of Lords—which remains amongst the leading considerations of the question by the highest court—therefore endorses an understanding of the term at issue whose implications differ in important ways from those of the understanding which prevailed in SIAC. That is, an attack on a foreign state may cause (actually or potentially) harm to the UK because of—in Lord Steyn's telling—the need for international cooperation in addressing the threat of terrorism. This again incorporates the security of a foreign state into the domestic concept of national security only indirectly but, compared to the understanding of the term which prevailed in SIAC, the incorporation is far broader, encompassing—it would seem—any act or threatened act which puts at risk that cooperation, rather than only those liable to result in 'reprisals' against the UK.

The problem with this view—and the danger lurking within the logic to which Lords Slynn and Steyn subscribe—is that cooperation in matters of counter-terrorism may be influenced by any number of factors beyond, and almost by definition less compelling that, those of security (whether that of the UK or any other state). That is, it would not require one to go much further than the House of Lords explicitly did to include within the concept acts which harm the international cooperation upon which the security of the UK relies but which are not themselves harmful to the security of some other state or the broader community of nations; acts which are harmful in the first place only to international relations, and through it to the security of the UK and its people. We will have reason to consider that point further below. For now, it suffices to note that the language of 'national security'—whose interpretation by the House of Lords has never been overtaken—operates throughout the constitutional order we have been considering. The work of the security and intelligence agencies is bounded by the functions given to them by statute, which in each case includes 'national security'.[25] 'National security' is one of the very few grounds upon which the most intrusive of investigatory powers are available, and one of the others (the interests of the UK's economic well-being) can justify the use of those powers only 'so far as those interests are also relevant to the interests of national security.'[26] The possibility of making a declaration under section 6 of the Justice and Security Act 2013 is contingent upon—inter alia—the proceedings being those in which 'sensitive material' would have to be disclosed; that is, 'material the disclosure of which would be damaging to the interests

[23] ibid.

[24] [2001] UKHL 47, [28].

[25] See, eg, Security Service Act 1989, s 1(2) (which continues 'and, in particular, its protection against threats from espionage, terrorism and sabotage, from the activities of agents of foreign powers and from actions intended to overthrow or undermine parliamentary democracy by political, industrial or violent means.').

[26] See, eg, Investigatory Powers Act 2016, s 20(2)(a) and (4).

of national security.'[27] Reading the relevant passages of *Rehman*, we see how the House of Lords' approach to the definition of that term works to expand—to a considerable if necessarily indeterminate degree—the range of material which that formulation covers. What exactly it would cover would appear to be tied up in the concepts of 'actions' and 'adverse'. Though the most important fact about such a phrase as it exists in law is usually suggested to be the absence of an authoritative definition, it seems that the most important question about its meaning has in fact been answered: though 'there must be a real possibility of an adverse effect on the United Kingdom', 'national security' is capable of being harmed by acts done to other states which threaten the international cooperation upon which modern national security endeavours rely. To this extent, it is in line with the expansive definition given to terrorism by the 2000 Act, which includes acts done in relation to other public and other governments, and without even the requirement that the act reflect back in some way upon the interests of the UK.

Even this expanded definition, however, falls short of one which renders international relations per se an element of national security and, indeed, the fact that some of the specific statutory definitions encountered throughout this book place international relations (or some facet thereof) on a footing similar or wholly equivalent to that of national security, or are otherwise broad enough to encompass it, demonstrates that there remains a legal, as well as conceptual, gap between the two. The 'conducive to the public good' standard, for example, which frames the power to deprive persons of their citizenship includes the question of 'the relations between the United Kingdom and any other country', deprivation on which basis is appealed to SIAC rather than in the normal way. The Official Secrets Act 1989 creates offences regarding the damaging disclosure of material relating to international relations analogous to those relating to damaging disclosures of material related to intelligence and defence.[28] Most strikingly, the Telecommunications Act 1984 included a power (to be repealed by the Investigatory Powers Act 2016) which could be used in pursuit of one of two (sets of) interests: 'national security or relations with the government of a country or territory outside the United Kingdom'.[29] Though that statute predates the giving of an expansive definition to 'national security', it nevertheless demonstrates that the former does

[27] Justice and Security Act 2013, s 6(11). For an example, see *Belhaj v Straw* [2017] EWHC 1861 (QB), [59], where Mr Justice Popplewell identified a series of ways in which the disclosure of material which would have to be disclosed within the litigation process would damage the interests of national security: 'It would be contrary to the policy behind NCND in a way which would damage national security. It would reveal operational details of the activities of the security services in relation to intelligence of importance to national security. Such disclosure is itself damaging to national security irrespective of whether the particular intelligence itself remains sensitive, in the same way as disclosure of intelligence communications received from foreign services can itself damage liaison relationships so as to damage national security, irrespective of the current sensitivity of the intelligence itself. How the security services go about their functions in the way revealed by the disclosable s.6 material is a matter which the interests of national security require should be kept secret both from those involved in the subject matter of this material and, equally importantly, all others whose intentions may be hostile to the security of the country and its nationals. Disclosure of the disclosable s.6 material would also risk identification of security services staff and would involve disclosure of information likely to be of benefit to terrorists and other criminals, both of which would damage national security.' *cf R (Maya Evans) v Secretary of State for Defence [2013] EWHC 3068* (Admin), [31], in the PII context.

[28] Official Secrets Act 1989, s 3.

[29] Telecommunications Act 1984, s 94.

not entirely subsume the latter. Even though, that is, an act damaging to international relations can implicate—indirectly, but no less clearly—the interests of national security, not all such acts do so.

III. The International Pursuit of National Security and its Consequences

We have discussed elsewhere the fact that military action abroad is largely circumscribed by international law, which determines—with varying degrees of clarity and certainty—both the circumstances in which resort to force will be lawful and the limitations which exist upon the use of that force, whether found in international humanitarian law, international human rights law, or some combination of the two. In this section I consider other ways in which the international element of the national security constitution works to complicate processes of constitutional accountability. It is useful to start, however, with reference to the UK's National Security Strategy (NSS)—published in 2015—which reaffirms the point that in 'almost every aspect of our national security and prosperity, we must work with others, not because we cannot work alone, but because the threats and opportunities are global'[30] and so commits the UK to its partnerships in the 'Euro-Atlantic area' (including NATO) but also far beyond.[31] In particular, it notes that the Middle East and North Africa are 'a significant source of both threat and opportunity, and will remain vital to our national security and prosperity.'[32] The UK would therefore 'continue to devote significant resources to building the relationships we need in this region, and to tackling the threats from it.'[33] The practical significance of much of the content of the Strategy is difficult to assess: as we have seen, the proximate causes of much legal change in (and probably also outside of) the national security context are issues and events far more urgent, farless rational than an overarching and detailed strategy revisited at five-year intervals. Nevertheless, the NSS testifies to the international dimension of the national security endeavour; what follows here is an attempt to understand the consequences of that fact for the constitutional landscape.

The international dimension of national security is equally apparent in counter-terrorism, as made evident by the UK's counter-terrorism strategy,[34] the implementation of which is, as the terrorist threat itself is repeatedly emphasised to be, a necessarily international endeavour, incorporating both bilateral and multilateral cooperation. On the first point, the CONTEST strategy emphasises that the US 'remains our closest ally on counter-terrorism', with intelligence sharing and law enforcement collaboration ensuring

[30] HM Government, *National Security Strategy and Strategic Defence and Security Review 2015 A Secure and Prosperous United Kingdom* (2015), [5.18]. This document's predecessor—HM government, *A Strong Britain in an Age of Uncertainty: The National Security Strategy*, Cm 7953 (2010)—also emphasises the international dimension of both threats and responses to national security, though on a smaller scale.

[31] HM Govt (n 30) Ch 5.

[32] ibid [5.55].

[33] ibid.

[34] HM Government, *CONTEST: The United Kingdom's Strategy for Countering Terrorism* (July 2011).

that 'we are able to make best use of one another's resources to deliver a coordinated response to the threat.'[35] International cooperation, however, again stretches far beyond the US: 'reflecting the shared threat from terrorism, we continue to work very closely with European partners and with many states across Africa, the Middle East and Asia.'[36] On the second point, the strategy identifies certain reasons for which the importance of multilateral organisations to counter-terrorism work is increasing over time:

> They can set frameworks which enable specific counter-terrorism measures (for example in connection with terrorist finance or aviation security). They provide security assistance and advice to third countries. They can govern the exchange of some data between Member States.[37]

Some of these multilateral dimensions we have considered elsewhere in the present work: the UN and EU involvement in asset-freezing and their contribution to the 'authority to carry' schemes by which travel into and out of the UK is restricted.[38] In these cases, the effect is to deprive the UK of much (sometimes all) of its discretion in the combatting of terrorism: the decision to include some person's name on the relevant sanctions list or equivalent is taken at the supranational level, and more or less automatically given effect in domestic law. Though it would be possible to analyse these regimes in terms of the UK's sovereignty (and indeed, the Sanctions Bill which will give effect to the relevant UN regime post-Brexit has been advertised as being intended to establish 'a new sovereign UK framework to implement international sanctions on a multilateral or unilateral basis')[39] there is a certain futility in doing so: once it is recognised that such cooperation is desirable (and in areas such as finance and travel, that judgement seems entirely reasonable) then it logically follows both that there should be a central coordination mechanism and that individual states should have limited (if any) discretion as to whether they implement those measures. If the UK so desires, it is welcome—as the EU example shows all too well—not to participate in the relevant supra-national regime. Where there may appear to be a loss of (a form of) sovereignty is not as a direct and simple consequence of the supra-national element of national security, but instead in the ability of any individual state to choose the values which govern the national security effort: how the 'balance' between security and liberty (or whatever other good we see ourselves as limiting in its name) is struck.

More revealing, therefore, is the sort of bilateral cooperation which takes place between the UK and its count-terrorism partners, in which there is no obvious loss of sovereignty because the UK's participation is deliberate and not subsumed—politically and practically—within supranational organisations and the wider international context.[40] Leaving aside purely military cooperation,[41] these partnerships manifest themselves in a

[35] HM Govt (n 34) [11.13].

[36] ibid.

[37] HM Govt (n 34) [11.14].

[38] See Chs 1 and 4.

[39] HL Deb 28 June 2017, vol 783 col 438.

[40] For an excellent analysis of some of the matters raised by counter-terrorism cooperation (discussed in their historical context) see CRG Murray, 'Out of the Shadows: The Courts and the United Kingdom's Malfunctioning International Counter-Terrorism Partnerships' (2013) *Journal of Conflict & Security Law* 193.

[41] In the military context, the question of mistreatment was addressed by the High Court in *R (Maya Evans) v Secretary of State for Defence* [2010] EWHC 1445 (Admin) in relation to the transfer of prisoners detained by UK armed forces to the Afghan National Directorate of Security in accordance with a memorandum of Understanding concluded by the governments of the UK and Afghanistan in 2006. The UK's policy was that detainees

number of ways which are—or may become—relevant to the domestic constitutional order, and in particular to the question of whether or not the UK's opposition to the conduct of torture and related practices is undermined by this cooperation. The relevant context has two dimensions. One is the UK's own position: torture (the intentional infliction of 'severe pain or suffering on another') is prohibited by the domestic law, whether carried out in the UK or elsewhere.[42] This prohibition is buttressed by Article 3 of the ECHR ('No one shall be subjected to torture or to inhuman or degrading treatment or punishment')—which is transposed into domestic law by the HRA 1998, is absolute, and cannot be derogated from—and the UK's ratification of the UN Convention Against Torture and Other Cruel Inhuman or Degrading Punishment. This latter defines torture as the doing of any act by which 'severe pain or suffering, whether physical or mental, is intentionally inflicted on a person' for a number of purposes and where the pain or suffering 'is inflicted by or at the instigation of or with the consent or acquiescence of a public official or other person acting in an official capacity.'[43]

There are several reasons for which this disavowal of torture might be taken with the proverbial pinch of salt: torture (or actions equivalent to it) was a mainstay of the British Empire (including in its twilight years);[44] there are documented examples of treatment approaching torture in the context of modern military endeavours;[45] the 'five techniques' (wall-standing, hooding, subjection to noise, deprivation of sleep, and deprivation of food) were an aspect of the UK's response in the early years of the Northern Irish Troubles and, though the Court of Human Rights (as opposed to its Chamber) eventually held that those techniques were merely 'inhuman and degrading treatment' rather than torture strictly understood,[46] the historical record would seem to justify the stronger charge.[47] Nevertheless, the rhetorical opposition to torture is now more robust than ever, and is buttressed by the opposition of the courts to the use of evidence obtained by torture. It is clear, for example, that domestic courts cannot receive evidence obtained by torture carried out by, or with the complicity of, British officials;[48] called upon to determine whether they may

were not to be so transferred where there was a real risk that they would be subjected to torture or other serious mistreatment. The High Court held that transfers to one NDS facility were unlawful, while those to two other facilities could take place lawfully only if certain additional safeguards against torture or serious mistreatment were implemented. See also the case of Yunus Rahmatullah, discussed in various contexts in Ch 6.

[42] Criminal Justice Act 1988, s 134. See also the Bill of Rights 1689, Art 10: 'excessive Baile ought not to be required nor excessive Fines imposed nor cruell and unusuall Punishments inflicted'.

[43] UN Convention Against Torture and Other Cruel Inhuman or Degrading Punishment, Art 1.

[44] See, eg, *Mutua v The Foreign and Commonwealth Office* [2011] EWHC 1913 (QB), [125], relating to British response to the Mau Mau Uprising, where Mr Justice McCombe said that '[t]here is ample evidence even in the few papers that I have seen suggesting that there may have been systematic torture of detainees during the Emergency.' After the government unsuccessfully argued that the claims were time-barred, they were settled for approximately £20 million in 2013. Though legal liability was not admitted, the government accepted that 'Kenyans were subject to torture and other forms of ill treatment at the hands of the colonial administration.' As part of the settlement, the United Kingdom funded a memorial to the victims of colonial abuses in Nairobi.

[45] See most notably the Rt Hon Sir William Gage, *The Report of the Baha Mousa Inquiry* (HC 2011–12, 1452-I).

[46] *Ireland v United Kingdom* (5310/71) [1978] ECHR 1.

[47] In 2014, the Irish government requested that the Court of Human Rights revisit the 1978 judgment in accordance with Rule 80 of its rules, which permits a party to request the Court to revise a judgment within six months of 'the discovery of a fact which might by its nature have a decisive influence and which, when a judgment was delivered, was unknown to the Court and could not reasonably have been known to that party'.

[48] *A v Secretary of State for the Home Department* [2005] UKHL 71, [1].

receive evidence which was or may have been obtained by torture carried out without the involvement of British officials, the House of Lords took a superficially robust view on the matter. Lord Bingham characterised the question not as an aspect of the law of evidence but rather as a matter of constitutional principle; that of 'whether evidence obtained by torturing another human being may lawfully be admitted against a party to proceedings in a British court, irrespective of where, or by whom, or on whose authority the torture was inflicted.'[49] To that constitutional question he—along with the other Law Lords—gave 'a very clear negative answer.'[50] Only suitably explicit statutory authority would overcome this common law principle, and none was available. Where Lord Bingham, however, had (along with Lord Nicholls of Birkenhead and Lord Hoffmann) concluded that the court in question (here, SIAC) should admit evidence in relation to which some plausible reason was advanced for believing that it was obtained by torture only if it could be satisfied on the balance of probabilities that the evidence was not so obtained, a majority in the House of Lords held that the correct approach was the opposite one: that of determining on the balance of probabilities whether the evidence was obtained by torture and admitting it unless satisfied that it was so obtained.[51] Lord Bingham suggested that in so deciding, the House of Lords was lending 'its authority to a test which will undermine the practical efficacy of the Torture Convention and deny detainees the standard of fairness to which they are entitled' under the ECHR.[52] Though the headline effect of the decision was therefore to insulate the domestic legal system (and the UK more generally) from the practice of torture, we see clearly that the degree of international cooperation in the field of national security provides a mechanism by which the consequences of torture (if not its practice) can enter the domestic system and begin to erode those values which the system professes.

A. 'Deportation with Assurances'

As we canvass the counter-terrorism landscape, this phenomenon—whereby the values professed by the single sovereign state are at odds with the practices in which it becomes involved as part of the international dimension of counter-terrorism—recurs frequently. One example is that of extradition, the issues raised by which have been frequently been pronounced upon by the Strasbourg Court. In *Ahmad v United Kingdom*,[53] the Court held—in relation to a number of applicants, including the infamous Egyptian cleric Abu Hamza—that, in the event the applicants were extradited to the United States, there would be no violation of Article 3 as a result either of the conditions in which they would be held in ADX Florence (the maximum-security prison) or the length of the sentences they might be expected to serve. In relation to each, however, assurances had been given that prosecutors would not seek the death penalty against them, as permitted by the treaty

[49] [2005] UKHL 71, [10].
[50] ibid, [51].
[51] See, eg, [2005] UKHL 71, [154].
[52] [2005] UKHL 71, [62].
[53] *Ahmad v United Kingdom* (2013) 56 EHRR 1. The decision is subject to strong criticism in Natasa Mavronicola and Francesco Messineo, 'Relatively absolute? The undermining of article 3 ECHR in Ahmad v UK' (2013) 76 *MLR* 589.

governing extradition to the US. Also relevant was that the US had committed to not designating the individuals being extradited as 'enemy combatants' and to not trying them before a military commission.[54] These issues aside, however, it is not clear that the question of extradition in the counter-terrorism context raises questions of constitutional law over and above those of extradition generally. More salient is the practice—noted in Chapter 1—of 'deportation with assurances' (DWA). It was shown in the context of the discussion of the UK's counter-terrorism constitution that much of the modern legal response to the threat of terrorism is a function of the decision of the Court of Human Rights in *Chahal v United Kingdom*, in which it was held that there was a 'real risk' that the deportation of the applicant to India would result in treatment contrary to Article 3 of the Convention; to deport him in such circumstances would therefore itself be a breach of Article 3. Combined with the unavailability of intercept evidence in criminal proceedings, the effect of the decision in *Chahal* was to incentivise the introduction of a series of civil mechanisms restricting to a greater or lesser degree the liberty of those on whom they were imposed. Alongside these mechanisms, efforts were made to reach agreement with the states which would receive any deportees that they would not be tortured on return.

The reliance on the relevant Memoranda of Understanding (MoU) was challenged by Abu Qatada (sometimes 'Othman'), a Muslim cleric who was granted the status of refugee in the UK in the mid-1990s but later detained under the system of detention pending deportation found in the ATCSA 2001 and—on its demise—made subject to a control order under the PTA 2005. With a view to deporting him, the UK had concluded an MoU with Jordan, which provided that '[i]f arrested, detained or imprisoned following his return, a returned person will be afforded adequate accommodation, nourishment, and medical treatment, and will be treated in a humane and proper manner, in accordance with internationally accepted standards.'[55] During the period of his residence in the UK, Qatada had been convicted in absentia in a Jordanian court of terrorism related offences. The convictions were alleged by Abu Qatada to be founded in large part upon evidence obtained by torture. The use of evidence obtained via torture had not been explicitly addressed in the MoU, which nevertheless provided that '[a] returned person who is charged with an offence following his return will receive a fair and public hearing without undue delay by a competent, independent and impartial tribunal established by law'.[56] When Qatada challenged his pending deportation on the basis that it would result in breaches of, inter alia, Articles 3 and 6 of the Convention, the House of Lords accepted that SIAC was entitled to consider closed material—not disclosed to the deportee—when considering the question of safety on return, and that SIAC's decision in the circumstances of the case (including the existence of the MoU) made it unlikely his Article 3 rights would be violated was not irrational.[57] On the Article 6 point, Lord Philips held that:

> Before the deportation of an alien will be capable of violating article 6 there must be substantial grounds for believing that there is a real risk (i) that there will be a fundamental breach of the

[54] As originally provided for by the presidential order 'Detention, Treatment, and Trial of Certain Non-Citizens in the War Against Terrorism' (13 November 2001) and, following the decision in *Hamdan v Rumsfeld* 548 US 557 (2006), the Military Commissions Act of 2006 and then the Military Commissions Act of 2009.

[55] *Memorandum of Understanding between the Government of the United Kingdom of Great Britain and Northern Ireland and the Government of the Hashemite Kingdom of Jordan regulating the provision of undertakings in respect of specified persons prior to deportation* (10 August 2005), [1].

[56] MoU (n 55) [6].

[57] *RB (Algeria) v Secretary of State for the Home Department* [2009] UKHL 10.

principles of a fair trial guaranteed by article 6 and (ii) that this failure will lead to a miscarriage of justice that itself constitutes a flagrant violation of the victim's fundamental rights.[58]

Abu Qatada's future trial in Jordan, the Law Lords therefore said, would not fall foul of the first limb of this test notwithstanding that it would, if it took place in a state which was party to the Convention, be incompatible with Article 6.

The Court of Human Rights, considering the Article 3 question, noted that 'the United Kingdom and Jordanian Governments have made genuine efforts to obtain and provide transparent and detailed assurances to ensure that the applicant will not be ill-treated upon return to Jordan' and that the resulting MoU is 'superior in both its detail and its formality to any assurances which the Court has previously examined'.[59] While expressing significant concern about certain elements of the MoU regime, the Court nevertheless held that Abu Qatada's deportation to Jordan in accordance with it would not result in a violation of Article 3.[60] The Strasbourg Court held, however, that the admission of material obtained by torture is 'manifestly contrary, not just to the provisions of Article 6, but to the most basic international standards of a fair trial' and that it would 'make the whole trial not only immoral and illegal, but also entirely unreliable in its outcome' and so lead to a 'flagrant denial of justice if such evidence were admitted in a criminal trial.'[61] Abu Qatada having demonstrated that there was a real risk that the evidence adduced against him would have been obtained by torture (the highest burden which could, the Court held, fairly be imposed upon him) the Strasbourg Court held—in line with the decision of the Court of Appeal but contrary to the House of Lords' conclusion—that 'there is a real risk that the applicant's retrial would amount to a flagrant denial of justice' and so his deportation to Jordan would be a violation of Article 6 of the Convention. Qatada was eventually deported following the conclusion of an agreement between the UK and Jordan which ensured that torture evidence would not be used against him;[62] both of the criminal trials he faced in Jordan resulted in his acquittal.

Along with the MoU completed with Jordan, the UK has completed similar agreements with Lebanon, Ethiopia and Morocco, and has completed an exchange of letters on the matter with Algeria. An MoU completed with Libya in 2005 is no longer in force following the Libyan revolution. Where the assurances received from Algeria were, like those received from Jordan,[63] originally held to be adequate,[64] SIAC had rejected as inadequate those received from Libya, concluding that it could not 'have the confidence which we need to have, for the return of the Appellants not to breach the UK's international obligations' because there was 'too much scope for something to go wrong, and too little in place to

[58] [2009] UKHL 10, [141].

[59] *Othman (Abu Qatada) v United Kingdom* (2012) 55 EHRR 1, [194].

[60] (2012) 55 EHRR 1, [207].

[61] ibid, [267].

[62] *Treaty on Mutual Legal Assistance in Criminal Matters between the United Kingdom of Great Britain and Northern Ireland and the Hashemite Kingdom of Jordan*, Cm 8612 (2013).

[63] *Othman v Secretary of State for the Home Department* SC/15/2005 (26 February 2007) and see *RB (Algeria) and OO (Jordan)* [2009] UKHL 10.

[64] *Y v Secretary of State for the Home Department* SC/36/2005 (24 August 2006). Later, however, SIAC held that the assurances of Algeria were no longer adequate in light of the limitations in regime by which the condition of those deported there were monitored: see *BB, PP, W. U, Y and Z v Secretary of State for the Home Department* SC/39/2005 (18 April 2016).

deter ill-treatment or to bring breaches of the MOU to the UK's attention'.[65] SIACs general approach has seen it deny attempts to argue that assurances received from countries in which systemic violations of human rights take place are inherently unreliable. Instead, it will make a judgment which involves a consideration of the evidence available regarding the MoUs, 'an evidenced based judgment' which takes account of what SIAC has been told about 'their strength, the intent behind them and the incentive to adhere and penalties for breach in the political circumstances prevailing'.[66] It has identified the following four matters to be addressed when considering whether assurances can be relied upon:

(i) the terms of the assurances must be such that, if they are fulfilled, the person returning will not be subject to treatment contrary to article 3;
(ii) the assurances must be given in good faith;
(iii) there must be a sound objective basis for believing that the assurances will be fulfilled; and
(iv) fulfilment of the assurances must be capable of being verified.[67]

The effect, it has been argued, is that the 'Secretary of State's assessment that assurances can be relied upon are subject to the very closest of scrutiny'.[68] Even if this is true, however, SIAC can and does employ a closed process in many of the relevant cases, meaning that much of—and perhaps the crucial element of—the scrutiny which is carried out is carried out behind closed doors and kept from the view of both the deportee and the public at large. In light of the considerable effort gone to in order to conclude the various MoUs and then to scrutinise their application in particular cases, a notable feature of the DWA regime is the small number of persons to whom it has been applied. Abu Qatada was ultimately deported outside of it and the most recent figures available suggest only 12 persons have ever been deported in upwards of a decade of its 'operation'.[69] A review of the regime, initiated in 2013, was published only in 2017, and concluded that though 'DWA is capable of playing a significant role in counter-terrorism, especially in prominent and otherwise intractable cases which are worth the cost and effort' the UK's experience 'amply demonstrates' that 'it can be delivered effectively and legitimately only if laborious care is taken.'[70] Even the most careful approach, however, will not—the Libyan example shows—suffice in the absence of a willing partner.

The effect of the DWA regime—given only a partial and somewhat hesitant endorsement by the Court of Human Rights—is to prevent the outsourcing of mistreatment to foreign partners: where there is a real risk of torture on return deportation will be a violation of Article 3 and, where there is a real risk of torture evidence being admitted in subsequent criminal proceedings, so too may there be a violation of Article 6 of the Convention. And though there remains the obvious possibility that assurances that are given and relied upon

[65] *DD and AS v Secretary of State for the Home Department* SC/42/2005 and SC/50/2005 (27 April 2007), [371].
[66] SC/36/2005, [394].
[67] *BB v Secretary of State for the Home Department* SC/39/2005 (5 December 2006), [55].
[68] Jennifer Tooze, 'Deportation with assurances: the approach of the UK courts' [2010] *PL* 362. See also Kate Jones, 'Deportations with assurances: addressing key criticisms' (2008) 57 *ICLQ* 183. One interesting element of the literature in this area is that it contains numerous contributions produced by individuals working within the relevant government departments.
[69] HM Government, *Transparency Report 2017: Disruptive and Investigatory Powers*, Cm 9420 (2017), [5.10].
[70] David Anderson QC (with Clive Walker QC), *Deportation with Assurances*, Cm 9462 (2017).

will simply not be adhered to—as in the *Agiza* and *Alzery* cases[71]—the truth is that even where it operates to the highest possible standards, with clear and reliable assurances given and independent monitoring made available, DWA has a corrosive effect upon the broader community of nations and the values which the UK purports to uphold, tacitly sanctioning their misdeeds as long as daylight is maintained between the ordinary operation of the relevant judicial system (if that is not too positive a term for a regime in which a real risk of torture exists) and its application to those deported by the UK. It was noted above that SIAC (along with higher courts) has taken the view that assurances might be deemed reliable notwithstanding that they are given by a country which has a record of mistreating detainees etc: in reality, no other position is compatible with the very notion of DWA, for to reject the assurances of such states would leave the courts in the catch-22 identified by Lord Phillips, whereby the very fact that assurances were necessary rendered them unreliable.[72] Nor is it clear what the various states which have concluded MoUs with the UK have been promised, or indeed received, in return. Below, I discuss some of the ways in which the internationalisation of national security feeds back into the domestic legal system and works—at times—almost to poison it. Here, however, we see a first implication of the international dimension: the desire to make suspected terrorists somebody else's problem requires that deals are done, if not with the devil, then certainly with regimes which do not even pretend to uphold the standards the UK sets for itself.

B. International Cooperation and the Possibility of (Political) Accountability

A second point under this heading relates to the indirect effect upon the domestic constitutional order of the fact that all or almost all national security endeavours now have an international dimension. This has (at least) three relevant aspects. The first is those additional legal obstacles—primarily the doctrine of 'foreign act of state'—which apply in contexts in which there is an international dimension to national security endeavours. That question was considered in Chapter 6 and is not addressed further here. The second, like the issues considered in the previous section, emerges out of the fact that contemporary national security endeavours do not merely involve international co-operation but rely in particular upon cooperation between, and close collaboration with, the agents of states who have—to put the point in its weakest form—dubious records on respecting fundamental rights. This cooperation influences the methods by which the UK's constitutional order seeks to secure (or not) accountability for such misdeeds. It was noted briefly in Chapter 3 that there have been two public inquiries into the actions of British troops as part of the wars in Iraq and Afghanistan: the Baha Mousa Inquiry[73] and the Al-Sweady Inquiry,[74]

[71] Ahmed Agiza and Mohammed Alzery were deported from Sweden to Egypt by CIA officers working with Swedish officials and tortured there in violation of assurances given prior to their deportation. See *Agiza v Sweden* CAT/C/34/D/233/2003 (24 May 2005); *Alzery v Sweden* CCPR/C/88/D/1416/2005 (10 November 2006).

[72] [2009] UKHL 10, [115].

[73] Rt Hon Sir William Gage, *The Report of the Baha Mousa Inquiry* (HC 2011–12, 1452-I).

[74] Sir Thayne Forbes, *The Report of the Al Sweady Inquiry: Executive Summary* (HC 2014–15, 819).

both of which were constituted under the Inquiries Act 2005. The Baha Mousa Inquiry took place in order to consider facts whose compatibility with the ECHR had been considered by the domestic courts and the Strasbourg Court under the umbrella of the *Al-Skeini* case.[75] Mousa had died in British custody in Basra, Iraq, in 2003 and one British Army Officer had admitted inhumane treatment before a Court Martial in 2007 (with six others acquitted). Significant compensation had been paid to his family and others who had been mistreated in Basra. The inquiry, conducted by Sir William Gage, reported in 2011, concluding that—in the Chairman's summation—the events in question 'constituted an appalling episode of serious, gratuitous violence on civilians which resulted in the death of one man and injuries to others'.[76] The Al-Sweady Inquiry, led by Sir Thayne Forbes, commenced in 2009, charged with considering allegations that a number of Iraqis taken into custody following 'the Battle of Danny Boy' in Southern Iraq in 2004 had been tortured or murdered. Following an ugly lapse in the public interest immunity process—whereby PII was claimed by the government in respect of information which had in fact already been disclosed by it elsewhere[77]—the inquiry concluded in 2014 that though some mistreatment had taken place, 'the most serious allegations, made against the British soldiers in the Battle of Danny Boy and its aftermath … have been found to be wholly without foundation and entirely the product of deliberate lies, reckless speculation and ingrained hostility.'[78] Though in both cases the inquiry which ultimately took place was in part carried out because it was required by the ECHR and the HRA, it is striking that in each—which, despite their very different outcomes, were examples of unusual detailed and thorough scrutiny in the field of national security, broadly understood, carried out by senior judges—the acts at issue were acts of British armed forces, carried out alone. Where there has been cooperation with foreign partners (whether in a strictly military context or in a counter-terrorism capacity) accountability has proven much more difficult to secure, and the chosen methods of accountability are consistently weaker than public inquiries.

The point can be made with reference to two reports carried out by the Intelligence and Security Committee of Parliament (ISC): one on the handling of detainees by UK intelligence personnel in Afghanistan, Guantanamo Bay and Iraq,[79] and another on rendition.[80] The ISC was entitled at the relevant time to request (subject to certain limits) material from the heads of the SIAs,[81] but there was no obligation to lay its ad hoc reports before Parliament,[82] and even if such reports were so laid, material could be excluded from them (as from the Committee's annual reports) where it appeared to the Prime Minister (following consultation with the Committee) that its inclusion would 'would be prejudicial to the continued discharge of the functions' of the SIAs.[83] This final formulation would undoubtedly encompass a situation in which the publication of information harmed the

[75] Discussed in Ch 3.

[76] Sir William Gage, Statement introducing the report of the Baha Mousa Inquiry (8 September 2011).

[77] See *Al-Sweady v Secretary of State for Defence* [2009] EWHC 1687 (Admin) and the discussion in Adam Tomkins, 'National security and the due process of law' (2011) 64 *Current Legal Problems* 215.

[78] Forbes (n 75) [740].

[79] Intelligence and Security Committee, *The Handling of Detaineees by UK Intelligence Personnel in Afghanistan, Guantanamo Bay and Iraq*, Cm 6469 (2005).

[80] Intelligence and Security Committee, *Rendition*, Cm 7171 (2007).

[81] Intelligence Services Act 1994, Sch 3, para 3.

[82] ISA 1994, s 10(6), which applies only to reports of the ISC under s 10(5).

[83] ibid, s 10(7). These provisions have since been supplanted by the Justice and Security Act 2013.

intelligence sharing relationships upon which the work of the SIAs (particularly MI6 and GCHQ) very heavily depends. Though the effect is to create a fuller form of accountability than was traditionally possible on the political side of the national security constitution—and in relation to which the position is improved by reforms in the Justice and Security Act 2013—it is still one which is heavily compromised by the needs of national security, and falls far short of the judge-led public inquiries described above. It seems not at all coincidental that this lesser form of scrutiny was chosen where the acts at issue were carried out by, or in conjunction with, foreign allies (and, most importantly, the United States), information supplied by which can be treated as 'sensitive' (and so able to be withheld from the ISC) under both the old and new regimes.

The first of the reports dealt in particular with those detained in US custody, and therefore not—due to the US' interpretation of the relevant international legal framework—subject to the Geneva Conventions. The report identified only 'limited and specific' breaches of the relevant frameworks by UK officials,[84] but recommended a number of changes of practice: informing ministers before deploying staff to interview detainees held by another country,[85] and where 'any UK official has concerns about the treatment of detainees'; clear instruction to UK intelligence personnel 'as to their duties and responsibilities in respect of the treatment of detainees and of the reporting procedures in the event of concerns';[86] the investigation and following up of concerns reported to foreign partners.[87] Finally, the ISC recommended that 'the UK authorities should seek agreement with allies on the methods and standards for the detention, interviewing or interrogation of people detained in future operations'.[88] The second ISC report found no evidence of any UK complicity in what it called 'extraordinary rendition' ('the extra-judicial transfer of persons from one jurisdiction or State to another, for the purposes of detention and interrogation outside the normal legal system, where there is a real risk of torture or cruel, inhuman or degrading treatment').[89] The UK was, however, involved or aware of other forms of rendition ('rendition to justice', 'military rendition', 'rendition to detention')[90] and the ISC recommended that ministerial approval be sought in all cases where 'despite the use of caveats and assurances, there remains a real possibility that the actions of the Agencies will result in torture or mistreatment'.[91] It recommended also that approval never be given where there was a 'real possibility' of rendition to detention in a secret facility (on the logic that secret detention is 'of itself mistreatment').[92] Both reports contain, like most of the ISC's work, significant redactions.

Following these reports there was introduced, in 2010, the 'Consolidated Guidance',[93] setting out the principles 'which govern the interviewing of detainees overseas and the passing and receipt of intelligence relating to detainees'.[94] Publication of earlier guidance

[84] ISC (n 79) [122].
[85] ibid [117].
[86] ibid [121].
[87] ibid [125].
[88] ibid [131].
[89] ISC (n 80) [7] and [D].
[90] ibid.
[91] ibid [CC].
[92] ibid [DD].
[93] In full, the *Consolidated Guidance to Intelligence Officers and Service Personnel on the Detention and Interviewing of Detainees Overseas, and on the Passing and Receipt of Intelligence Relating to Detainees* (July 2010).
[94] Consolidated Guidance (n 93) [1].

had been promised but never carried out, though media reports suggested that intelligence personnel were told that, though they should not 'engage in any activity yourself that involves inhumane or degrading treatment of prisoners', they were not obliged to intervene to prevent mistreatment by others: 'Given that they are not within our custody or control, the law does not require you to intervene to prevent this.'[95] Though the Guidance as published outlines a strict policy ('we do not participate in, solicit, encourage or condone the use of torture or cruel, inhuman or degrading treatment or punishment for any purpose')[96] it does not preclude working with countries who engage in treatment that the UK would not. Where a 'serious risk of torture' remains notwithstanding attempts by UK personnel to mitigate it, the Guidance states that 'our presumption is that we would not proceed' and sets out the circumstances under which concerns must be passed to ministers.[97] In the lesser context of CIDT, however, no such presumption exists, and the situation is complicated by the absence in UK law of a definition of CIDT.[98] The Guidance, however, provides a non-exhaustive list of practices which 'could constitution cruel, inhuman or degrading treatment or punishment' including 'use of stress positions', 'physical abuse or punishment of any sort' and 'withdrawal of food, water or medical help'.[99]

Simultaneously to the publication the Consolidated Guidance in 2010, the question of possible UK complicity in mistreatment was made the subject of an independent inquiry under Sir Peter Gibson (then the Intelligence Services Commissioner), which was to consider 'whether, and if so to what extent, the UK Government and its intelligence agencies were involved in improper treatment of detainees held by other countries in counter-terrorism operations overseas, or were aware of improper treatment of detainees in operations in which the UK was involved.'[100] The Gibson inquiry's terms of reference therefore left no room for the consideration of any mistreatment (whether or not amounting to torture) carried out by the UK itself, rather than in which it was complicit. Given this framing, the Gibson inquiry would seem to buck the trend already identified whereby the greatest possible accountability is available only in relation to acts done by the UK and its personnel alone; in fact, as discussed in Chapter 6, the Gibson inquiry was halted in 2012 in order to permit the conduct of investigations into the possibility of bringing criminal proceedings against former and current UK government and security services personnel. The inquiry produced only preparatory conclusions, and though it was later announced that no criminal charges were to be brought (a decision which is, at the time of writing, subject to judicial review),[101] the Gibson inquiry was replaced with another conducted by the ISC, in contravention of an earlier commitment that an inquiry would be 'judge-led'.[102] And even before that downgrading, the fact that the Gibson inquiry was—unlike the Baha Mousa and Al-Sweady inquiries—not constituted under the Inquiries Act 2005, meant that it did not

[95] The full passage was later published in ISC (n 79) [47]. See also Joint Committee on Human Rights, *Allegations of UK Complicity in Torture* (2008–9, HL 152, HC 230), [71]–[77].
[96] Consolidated Guidance (n 93) [6].
[97] ibid [7].
[98] ibid [5].
[99] ibid Annex, [d].
[100] HC Deb 18 January 2012, vol 538 col 751.
[101] And in relation to which an application has been made under s 6 of the Justice and Security Act 2013.
[102] HC Deb 18 January 2012 vol 538, col 751. In announcing its responsibility for the inquiry, the ISC noted the limitations of its prior work on this and related topics, and drew attention to the new regime under which it had since begun to operate: ISC, *Detainee Inquiry—Press Release* (19 December 2013).

possess the statutory powers afforded to such inquiries, including to compel the giving of evidence or the provision of material.[103] It too, therefore, would seem ultimately to exemplify the difficulties of achieving effective accountability (or, at least, the unwillingness of doing so) where to do so would impugn the UK's foreign partners.

The question of whether the UK's co-operation with foreign partners leads to mistreatment was also considered within a third special report by the ISC, this time into the circumstances in which Fusilier Lee Rigby was murdered in 2013.[104] It expressed concern about the response of the intelligence services to the arrest of one of the killers—Michael Adebolajo—in Kenya in 2010 and what followed from it. On his return to the UK, Adebolajo alleged that he had been mistreated, with the allegations possibly relating to the actions of Kenyan count-terrorism units which work closely with the UK SIAs and for one of which—referred to by the ISC as 'Arctic'—some element of the UK government is responsible. Exactly what is the relationship between the UK and Arctic is impossible to say: the redactions within the ISC report are such that the sentence explaining the matter reads, in its published version, '[t]his unit has a close working relationship with HM Government (HMG), specifically ***, who is responsible for *** and ***.'[105] The SIAs were clear in their evidence to the ISC that the Consolidated Guidance did not apply to the specific scenario in which they interacted with Adebolajo, of whose detention they had no advance knowledge: an unidentified party is quoted as stating that 'the consolidated guidance applies when we make something happen. By definition we did not know it was going on. We could not have made it happen.'[106] It transpired during the course of the inquiry, however, that Adebolajo had been interviewed not only by the Kenyan police, but also by Arctic.[107] The ISC therefore expressed surprise that MI6 had not investigated the allegation of mistreatment in order to determine to which of the two bodies the allegations referred, and it concluded that the allegations were not adequately assessed.[108] It considered, however, that it was arguable that the 'tightly drawn' CG did not apply to the circumstances of Adebolajo's detention, and did not attempt to determine whether or not the Guidance had been complied with.[109] On the nature of the UK's obligations as regards its counterterrorism partners, the Committee expressed the view that:

> Where HM Government (HMG) has a close working relationship with counterterrorist units, they will share responsibility for those units' actions. HMG must therefore seek to ensure that the same legal and moral obligations to which HMG adheres, and guidance which they follow, also apply to such units. Where there is a possibility that an allegation of mistreatment might refer to a unit where HMG has such responsibility, then HMG must investigate as a matter of priority to establish whether the unit is involved.[110]

[103] See the discussion in Ch 6.

[104] Intelligence and Security Committee, *Report on the intelligence relating to the murder of Fusilier Lee Rigby* (HC 2014–15, 795).

[105] ISC (n 104) [467].

[106] ibid [466]. The ISC notes, however, that MI6 'had been told that a British citizen was being held in detention: therefore, they did know that "it was going on"'.

[107] ibid [467].

[108] ibid [468].

[109] ibid [466].

[110] ibid [ZZ].

On the basis of these and related observations, the Prime Minister asked the Intelligence Services Commissioner to examine the concerns raised by the ISC regarding the UK government's responsibilities in relation to partner counter-terrorism units overseas.[111] Several elements of the Commissioner's conclusion are of interest for present purposes. The first is his conclusion that MI6's evidence to the ISC inquiry was 'far from satisfactory, largely because it was based on an inadequate search for and second-hand interpretation of corporate records, as opposed to proper consultation with the individuals directly involved.'[112] On the allegation, of mistreatment, however, the Commissioner was clear in finding that Adebolajo was 'most definitely not the subject of an intelligence services conspiracy and that his allegations of mistreatment at the hands of the Kenyan authorities were probably untrue':

> Indeed, I think it highly unlikely that Mr Adebolajo was mistreated by any of the Kenyan police or intelligence units which work with HMG and I certainly do not think that he was mistreated by Arctic.[113]

Most relevant here, however, are the conclusions about the application of the Consolidated Guidance, which focuses most directly upon torture and cruel, inhuman and degrading treatment, and is, the Commissioner found, 'inconsistent and vague about its application to mistreatment taking the form of unlawful arrest or detention or procedural unfairness as opposed to torture or CIDT.'[114] Moreover, the 'one size fits all' nature of the CG was such that it was not obviously well-suited to application situations such as this one, in which 'HMG has a close and ongoing working relationship with partner counter-terrorism units overseas', for which it makes no express provision.[115] Most importantly—and contrary to the view taken by the SIAs—the Commissioner thought it 'strongly arguable' that the Guidance was engaged; having done so, he took the view that, though it was impossible to be certain as to what had and had not been done by the SIAs, there was a possibility that it had not been adhered to:

> If, as may well have been the case, SIS did not then consider the risk that he would be the subject of unacceptable standards of detention or treatment and/or the need for related assurances, this would have represented a failure properly to apply the Consolidated Guidance.[116]

Though the Guidance was not considered to be 'fundamentally defective or not fit for purpose', the Commissioner recommended that the Cabinet Office undertake a review

[111] At the same time, the Commissioner's hitherto informal oversight role in relations to the Consolidated Guidance was made formal, by the issuance of the Intelligence Services Commissioner (Additional Review Functions) (Consolidated Guidance) Direction 2014, carried out under s 59A of the Regulation of Investigatory Powers Act 2000. The Commissioner chose also to consider also allegations that the arrest and mistreatment was by or at the request of the UK government ('possibly as part of an elaborate plan to recruit him as a covert agent, informant or human intelligence source'), after these claims were put to him 'directly and in more detail by a reputable journalist who told me that they were supported by a credible and reliable 'inside' source.' Rt Hon Sir Mark Waller, *Report of the Intelligence Services Commissioner: Supplementary to the Annual Report for 2015—Concerns raised by the Intelligence and Security Committee of Parliament about the government's responsibilities in relation to partner counter-terrorism units overseas* (HC 2016–17, 458), [3.1].

[112] Waller (n 111) [3.3].

[113] ibid [6.1].

[114] ibid [19.3].

[115] ibid [19.6].

[116] ibid [6.6].

of it, in conjunction with the relevant parts of the executive and that, in the interests of transparency and accountability, it solicit contributions from relevant NGOs.[117]

Alongside this process—aimed at strengthening the Consolidated Guidance—however, a second process was underway which had the effect of weakening the oversight of compliance with it. Such oversight, as has been discussed, was carried out—first informally and later formally—by the Intelligence Services Commissioner, whose expertise on the question put him in a position to disagree with the ISC as regards the Guidance's application to Adebolajo's circumstances. The Investigatory Powers Act 2016 replaces the various commissioners with a single Investigatory Powers Commissioner (with a number of Judicial Commissioners working under him or her in order to approve certain types of warrant under the Act).[118] Adherence to the Consolidated Guidance does not, however, figure amongst the 'main oversight functions' imposed upon the Commissioner by the Act.[119] Though the Home Office said, in written evidence on the draft Bill, that the Bill implemented the ISC's recommendation that the new body (then being referred 'ISIC'—the Independent Surveillance and Intelligence Commission) take on the Commissioner's task of providing oversight of the Consolidated Guidance,[120] this was incorrect. The 2016 Act does make provision for the Prime Minister to direct the IPC to oversee 'the carrying out of any aspect of the functions of' the SIAs, their heads, or the intelligence activities of the Armed Forces or Ministry of Defence.[121] Directions may be made at the request of either the IPC or ISC,[122] and must be published unless it appears to the PM that publication would be contrary to the public interest generally or prejudicial to one of a number of specified interests, including 'national security' and 'the continued discharge of the functions of any public authority whose activities include activities that are subject to review by the Investigatory Powers Commissioner.'[123] As has been the case with the giving of Directions under RIPA (made possible by the Justice and Security Act 2013),[124] it is therefore possible for the IPC to be given formal responsibility for the oversight of certain matters without the public being aware of it.

In oral evidence to the Joint Committee on the Draft Investigatory Powers Bill the Intelligence Services Commissioner, Sir Mark Waller, mentioned amongst the areas of his oversight with which the Draft Bill did not deal the 'consolidated guidance and the application of the Guidance, which, although it is not in the Bill, will presumably have to be taken over by the oversight body that is forecast by the Bill.'[125] Perhaps this will be the case,[126] but there are no guarantees either that this will happen, or—if it does—that the public will come to know of it. It would have been preferable not only to place the requirement to oversee the Consolidated Guidance within the Investigatory Powers Act itself, but also to give

[117] ibid [21.1]

[118] Investigatory Powers Act 2016, Pt 8, Ch 1. The first IPC is Lord Justice Fulford.

[119] IPA 2016, s 229.

[120] Home Office, Written evidence on the Draft Investigatory Powers Bill (IPB0146), Annex F2.

[121] IPA 2016, s 230.

[122] ibid, s 230(3).

[123] ibid, s 230(4).

[124] JSA 2013, s 5, inserting a new s 59A into RIPA 2000.

[125] Sir Mark Waller, Oral evidence to the Joint Committee on the draft Investigatory Powers Bill (2 December 2015), Q39.

[126] See also the answer given by Ben Wallace, Minister of State for Security, in response to a question put by Caroline Lucas MP: HC Deb 2 March 2017, vol 623.

the Consolidated Guidance such a legal footing, with adherence to it made a requirement of law. As it stands, the various methods of political accountability which operate in the field of national security are mostly ad hoc, overly contingent and too frequently redefined for us to be confident that wrongdoing in this domain is dealt with properly. And, as noted above, there is a pervasive distinction between the form and quality of accountability where the wrongdoing is alleged to have been carried out by UK personnel (military or intelligence) acting alone, and where the wrongdoing appears to have taken place in conjunction with others, where the preferred mechanism is not a public inquiry but rather an inquiry carried out by the ISC. Though reformed and improved in certain ways by the Justice and Security Act, the Intelligence and Security Committee offers a potentially lesser form of political accountability than is provided by a statutory public inquiry carried out by an independent (judicial) figure, notwithstanding its access to classified material.[127]

C. International Cooperation and Access to Information

In this section, I turn from political accountability for actions done in cooperation with other states to the question of legal accountability. We have already considered elsewhere the payments made (without admission of liability) to a number of individuals who alleged that UK personnel were complicit in their mistreatment in Guantanamo bay. We have considered also the failure of the doctrine of foreign act of state to block the case brought by Abdel Hakim Belhaj, allegedly rendered to Libya by US agents acting with the involvement of MI6 and subsequent ordering of a closed material procedure in relation to the civil claim in question.[128] More than one of the criminal trials which have taken place in camera have done so in order to consider allegations about British complicity in the mistreatment of defendants abroad, primarily (in those cases) in Pakistan.[129] The secrecy of those trials has rolled over into later attempts to bring civil actions relating to the alleged mistreatment, several of which have been struck out as abuses of process (being, it has been held, attempts to relitigate claims which have already been determined), with elements of the relevant judgments redacted.[130] Nevertheless, it is in situations where the claim which is argued to constitute an abuse of process of the court follows on from litigation which was the subject of a closed hearing and resulted in a closed judgment that the problem is most acute: there, unlike in the in camera context, the claimant has no way of knowing exactly what factual issues were considered, and what specific findings made, by the relevant court in its closed judgment. The courts continue to wrestle with the question of how such scenarios should be dealt with;[131] what is clear, however, is that the effects of the initial move made in order

[127] The best account of the work and development of the ISC is Hugh Bochel, Andrew Defty and Jane Kirkpatrick, *Watching the Watchers: Parliament and the Intelligence Services* (Basingstoke, Palgrave Macmillan, 2014).

[128] Discussed in Ch 6.

[129] Discussed in Ch 5. See also the Human Rights Watch, *Cruel Britannia: British Complicity in the Torture and Ill-treatment of Terror Suspects in Pakistan* (2009) and JCHR (n 95) [6]–[9].

[130] See, on the civil side, *Amin v Director General of the Security Service* [2013] EWHC 1579 (QB) and *Amin v Director General of the Security Service* [2014] EWCA Civ 598.

[131] See, eg, *Kamoka v The Security Service* [2016] EWHC 769 (QB), an appeal against which was allowed by the Court of Appeal in later 2017 on the basis that the case 'which the appellants now wish to run is not one of

to accommodate the needs of national security and international relations—whether that takes the form of a closed material procedure or an in camera trial—do not end there, but may continue to ripple through the legal landscape for some time to come. All of these cases demonstrate, in various ways, the strength of the desire to keep details of the wrongdoing in question out of the public domain. Where national security is protected in a criminal context by the ordering of an in camera trial, a backstop is provided by the option of simply abandoning the prosecution in question. Though such a move is not possible in the context of a civil claim brought at the initiative of a private person, the government even there has the option—if it chooses to do so—of conceding the issue and so avoiding the need to disclose the material which would need to be put before a court in order for the court to resolve it.

This process of incrementally increasing the scope of secrecy within litigation runs up against its logical limits, however, where the litigation is aimed not at resolving some question about the legal rights and obligations which necessitates disclosure of sensitive material, but where the disclosure of the material is an end in itself. The point can be made most strikingly with reference to the case of Binyam Mohamed, an Ethiopian national arrested in Pakistan in 2002 and—having in the meantime been moved around a network of 'black sites'—later transferred to Guantanamo Bay.[132] Though charges were brought against Mohamed, these were later dropped and whatever was the truth about Mohamed's actions and intentions prior to his detention, that part of the CIA torture report which was later declassified suggests that the US intelligence community took the view that the plot (to build so-called 'dirty bombs') with which Mohamed was suspected of involvement was 'infeasible as envisioned'.[133] That seems a remarkable understatement. The report quotes an email as describing the CIA's view of the plot in the following, wholly farcical, terms:

> Padilla and Binyam/Zouaoui had pulled an article off a satirical web site called 'How to make an H-bomb' which is based on a 1979 Journal of Irreproducible Results article. The article was intended to be humorous and included instructions such as enriching uranium by placing liquid uranium hexaflouride in a bucket, attaching it to a six foot rope, and swinging it around your head as fast as possible for 45 minutes. While it appears that Padilla and Zouaoui took the article seriously, Zubaydah recommended that they take their (cockamamie) ideas to (I believe) [Khalid Sheikh Mohammed][134] in Karachi. It was at that point that KSM told them to focus on bringing down apartment buildings with explosives, (in other words: keep your day jobs).[135]

Mohamed was released and returned to Britain (where he had previously been resident) in 2009, having already brought a judicial review of the UK government's refusal to provide him with evidence, allegedly held by it (and by the security services), that he had been

which they were aware at the time of the earlier SIAC or Control Order proceedings' and so 'they have not had any opportunity, let alone a full opportunity to run that case.': [2017] EWCA Civ 1665, [120].

[132] Mohammed was later one of the claimants in the *Al-Rawi* case, whose nature and effects are discussed in Ch 5.

[133] Senate Select Committee on Intelligence, *Committee Study of the Central Intelligence Agency's Detention and Interrogation Program* (3 December 2014), 231.

[134] Identified as the 'the principal architect of the 9/11 attacks' by the 9/11 Commission: National Commission on Terrorist Attacks Upon the US, *Final Report of the National Commission on Terrorist Attacks Upon the United States* (2004), 145.

[135] Select Committee on Intelligence (n 133) 226fn.

subject to torture and other cruel, inhuman and degrading treatment by (or on behalf of) the US.[136] The legal form of the order sought was a *Norwich Pharmacal* order,[137] which places an innocent third party who was in some way involved in a wrong done to another person under a duty to 'to assist the person who has been wronged by giving him full information and disclosing the identity of the wrongdoers'.[138] The aim of acquiring the material was to show, in the first place, that confessions made by Mohamed should not be admissible in the military commission proceedings against him which were then anticipated. Though the documents sought were later made available to Mohamed in the context of habeas corpus proceedings in the US, by that point the High Court had delivered an open judgment on the matter from which, at the request of the Foreign Secretary (who produced a PII certificate in relation thereto), seven paragraphs describing US reports to the UK authorities of the treatment to which Mohamed had been subject in Pakistan were redacted. Having first refused (in its fourth judgment on the matter)[139] an application to restore the relevant paragraphs, the High Court ordered (in its fifth judgment)[140] their restoration to the first judgment, and refused (in its sixth)[141] to edit out certain passages from that fifth judgment. The government's position was that intelligence material passed to it by foreign states was subject to the 'control principle' whereby it could not be made public without the consent of the state which had supplied it—a principle, it was noted above, which is reflected in both the previous and current frameworks governing the Intelligence and Security Committee. To allow the material to be made public would—it claimed—result in the US re-evaluating its intelligence-sharing relationship with the UK, thus prejudicing the UK's national security. This is, we see, a classic example of how the international dimension of national security impacts upon the possibility of legal accountability even for the actions of the UK's executive itself. In its fifth judgment, the Divisional court had held that the 'control principle' was not absolute, and was—in the particular circumstances of the case—outweighed by the public interest in publication of the material. Later evidence (from both the UK and US governments) was not sufficient to establish that publication would create a real risk of harm to national security.[142]

On appeal to it (from the fifth and sixth judgments of the High Court), the Court of Appeal agreed that the paragraphs should be published.[143] It did so, however, for reasons that Adam Tomkins has described as 'rather worrying'.[144] Lord Neuberger emphasised the superior position of the executive in assessing the likely implications of publishing the information:

> As a matter of principle, decisions in connection with national security are primarily entrusted to the executive, ultimately to Government ministers, and not to the judiciary … In practical terms the Foreign Secretary has unrestricted access to full and open advice from his experienced advisers,

[136] The fullest consideration of the affair is in Adam Tomkins, 'National security and the due process of law' (2011) 64 *Current Legal Problems* 215.

[137] Named for *Norwich Pharmacal Co v Customs and Excise Commissioners* [1974] AC 133.

[138] [1974] AC 133, 175.

[139] *R (Mohamed) v Secretary of State for Foreign and Commonwealth Affairs* [2009] EWHC 152 (Admin).

[140] EWHC 2549 (Admin).

[141] EWHC 2973 (Admin).

[142] EWHC 2549 (Admin), [71]–[77] and [101]–[108].

[143] *R (Mohamed) v Secretary of State for Foreign and Commonwealth Affairs (No 2)* [2010] EWCA Civ 158.

[144] Tomkins (n 136) 239.

> both in the Foreign Office and the intelligence services. He is accordingly far better informed, as well as having far more relevant experience, than any judge for the purpose of assessing the likely attitude and actions of foreign intelligence services as a result of the publication of the redacted paragraphs, and the consequences of any such actions so far as the prevention of terrorism in this country is concerned.[145]

As such, notwithstanding the Court's evident scepticism regarding the executive's assertions of the likelihood of damage to national security,[146] the Court of Appeal would have sided with the Divisional Court's initial assessment of the balance of distinct public interests; in the reasons it gave for subsequently changing its view the Divisional Court 'gave insufficient weight to the views of the Foreign Secretary, took too dismissive a view of [representations made by the United States], did not really address the attitude of governments other than the US, and overestimated the public interest in having the redacted paragraphs published.'[147] At the relevant time, 'the value in releasing the contents of the redacted paragraphs into the public domain would simply have been insufficient to justify running a risk, even what I regard as a pretty slender risk, to national security, given that the Foreign Secretary has certified that there would be such a risk, and his opinion is not irrational and is supported by material from the highest representatives of the US, the UK's largest, longest standing and closest intelligence partner.'[148] The indirect risk to national security as mediated by international relations, that is, would—notwithstanding its slightness—have been held to outweigh the public interest considerations favouring disclosure.

Nevertheless, the relevant factual matrix had in the meantime evolved so as to undermine the Divisional Court's original conclusion and, in turn, the Court of Appeal's endorsement of it. On the same day as the Divisional Court's sixth judgment had been handed down, the US District Court for the District of Columbia gave a memorandum opinion in *Farhi Saeed Bin Mohammed v Obama*,[149] arising out of a petition for habeas corpus brought

[145] [2010] EWCA Civ 158, [131]. This passage was later cited with approval by the First-tier Tribunal in *Plowden v Information Commissioner* EA/2011/0225 & 0228 (21 May 2012), in deciding whether or not a note of a phone call between Tony Blair and George Bush in the lead-up to the war in Iraq was to be released under the Freedom of Information Act (ultimately holding that some of the record was to be disclosed). In keeping with the theme of this chapter, the relevant exception was s 27, which relates to information whose disclosure would prejudice international relations. The Tribunal noted, at [89], that the 'tenor' of the Foreign Office's case as to the interpretation of the act was that 'when it comes to the US, no information of the sort with which this Tribunal is concerned should ever be released.'

[146] 'There are, to my mind, probably two reasons why the US government and some other governments could have been genuinely concerned about the publication of the redacted paragraphs. First, it would have been an indication that the UK courts are prepared to breach the control principle not merely to protect its citizens, but in circumstances which those governments would, or at least might, regard as gratuitous; secondly, embarrassment or sensitivity because the redacted paragraphs reveal communications about mistreatment of detainees by officials of the US (and other countries). The fact that I may think that there is no force in the first reason, that I may disapprove of the second reason, and that I may not consider either reason ought even to begin to justify any reconsideration of the sharing of intelligence with the UK, are not in point. When considering whether there is a threat to national security, at least where the threat is based on a logically coherent argument, it is the reality, not the morality, that matters' [2010] EWCA Civ 158, [171]. On this last point, Lord Neuberger cites the *Corner House* case discussed below.

[147] [2010] EWCA Civ 158, [187].

[148] ibid, [191].

[149] *Farhi Saeed Bin Mohammed v Obama*, 704 F Supp 2d 1 (2009).

by a detainee at Guantanamo, in which the judge had described the treatment to which Binyam Mohamed had claimed to be subject as 'torture' and in which she had accepted that what he alleged had indeed happened. This altered the balance of interests, with Lord Neuberger noting that not only would the control principle not be infringed by the inclusion of material 'once the information contained in the redacted paragraphs was openly held to be factually correct by a US court' but, moreover, it was 'simply unrealistic to think that any government, US or otherwise, would object or take exception, on the ground that it represented the unauthorised publication of US intelligence information, to the publication of facts in an English judgment when those facts have already been published in a US judgment.'[150] This view was shared by Sir Anthony May,[151] and the effect was that the original decision of the Divisional Court was both endorsed and held to be overtaken, with the principle of open justice defended in only a limited and somewhat contrived manner.[152] Only Lord Judge CJ would have been willing to hold that the relevant paragraphs of the Divisional Court's judgments should have been published regardless. Not only did they not contain anything which was 'genuinely secret', but unless the control principle was to be treated as absolute, it was 'hard to conceive of a clearer case for its disapplication than a judgment in which its application would partially conceal the full reasons why the court concluded that those for whom the executive in this country is ultimately responsible were involved in or facilitated wrongdoing in the context of the abhorrent practice of torture.'[153] This was a much more enthusiastic defence of the principle of open justice, one which acted upon rather than suppressed the scepticism of the other judges in the Court of Appeal. It would have been preferable had this been the approach of the majority rather than the minority. In any event the decision seems to have been the correct one: though on the record comments by American officials were highly critical of the Court of Appeal's decision, an anonymous White House official told *the Guardian* that—as paraphrased by its journalists—the decision 'would not provoke a broad review of intelligence liaison between Britain and the US because the need for close co-operation was greater now than ever.'[154] The self-evident correctness of that logic might be kept in mind wherever and whenever similar threats to withdraw intelligence cooperation are made. Mohamed was later given £1 million compensation by the UK as part of the *Al-Rawi* settlement.[155]

[150] [2010] EWCA Civ 158, [203].

[151] ibid, [295].

[152] The reaction of the various parties are discussed by Hickman and Tomkins, who note that both the government and the ISC initially welcomed the decision as having upheld the control principle, but that the views of each changed 'as a direct result of representations made by US intelligence agencies.' Tom Hickman and Adam Tomkins, 'National security law and the creep of secrecy: a transatlantic tale' in L Lazarus, C McCrudden and N Bowles (eds) *Reasoning Rights: Comparative Judicial Engagement* (Oxford, Hart Publishing, 2014), 143–4.

[153] [2010] EWCA Civ 158, [57]. As Tomkins points out, however, even Lord Judge implicitly accepted that the control principle was engaged by the paragraphs, notwithstanding that the Divisional Court had held otherwise, on the basis that the control principle relates to 'secret intelligence', which the contents of the paragraphs were not: Tomkins (n 136) 240. Where this point is acknowledged, the legal basis of the resistance to disclosure of the material falls away.

[154] Daniel Nasaw, Richard Norton-Taylor and Ian Cobain, 'MI5 chief denies cover-up claims over detainees', *The Guardian* (12 February 2010).

[155] Discussed in Ch 6. The publication of the Court of Appeal's judgment, however, was overshadowed in part by a row regarding a letter sent to the court by Jonathan Sumption QC—then counsel for the Secretary of State and later the first person in more than half a century to be appointed as a judge of the UK's highest court without

In his treatment of *Binyam Mohamed*, Adam Tomkins considers responses to the Court of Appeal's decision which highlight that court's alleged acceptance of the 'control principle' (the scope of which he disputes)[156] and suggests that if the case 'is remembered only for this it will be a travesty.'[157] For our purposes, the lessons of *Mohamed* are numerous, and have little or nothing to do with the control principle. The case demonstrates (for neither the first nor last time) the fact of mistreatment by the UK's closest allies, and UK knowledge of and complicity in that mistreatment. It demonstrates also (and again) the manner in which the extent of international cooperation in the security sphere makes it plausible to claim that for the executive to do or not do this or that thing (or for the judiciary to require it to do or not do such things) would harm (or—perhaps more realistically—irritate, or embarrass) some other state would cause that state to withdraw or scale back security cooperation, leading indirectly to harm to the national security of the UK. Not only has national security evolved so as to include the security of other states, but the security of the UK is inescapably impacted by the interests of those other states: interests which are in the first place often presented as pertaining to security, but which seem in practice to range far beyond that domain, and often lapse into issues upon which courts should not (and otherwise would not) act. Adding to this is the sense that the relevant claims by the UK government—claims which are derivative of some underlying interest of another country, and which may be of greater or lesser weight—are not always made in the best of faith. As well as potentially leading to UK involvement in torture (or practices which resemble it), the internationalisation of security has simultaneously created new (if not always successful) obstacles to attempts to secure accountability for that involvement and for the primary wrongdoing itself.

It should be noted here also that though—as the *Mohamed* case shows—the *Norwich Pharmacal* order was at one point primed to emerge as a powerful tool for the exposure of the detailed wrongdoing conducted by the UK's foreign partners, its use in these circumstances was highly controversial and its availability was subsequently diminished, first by judicial determination and later by statute. In *Binyam Mohamed*, the Divisional Court (in its first judgment) held that the information which the court might order to be provided thereunder was not—as had been argued—confined to the identity of the wrongdoer, but that the courts could make orders 'specific to the facts of the case'.[158] There, the 'truly exceptional' circumstances were that the information sought was 'said to be necessary to an individual facing a possible death penalty if convicted' and it would have been difficult to justify a system of law which was willing to facilitate the provision of information

prior judicial appointment—in which the court was asked to make certain amendments to one paragraph in the draft judgment which had been distributed to the parties. This Master of the Rolls, Lord Neuberger, agreed to do. The relevant paragraph was excised of certain material, including a sentence in which Lord Neuberger observed of the security services' claim to respect human rights and denial of any knowledge of the mistreatment by the US of detainees which the UK security services had interviewed: '[I]n this case that does not seem to have been true: as the evidence showed, some security service officials appear to have a dubious record relating to actual involvement, and frankness about any such involvement, with the mistreatment of Mr Mohamed when he was held at the behest of US officials.' See the account in Tomkins (n 136).

[156] Tomkins (n 136) 243n.

[157] ibid 242.

[158] *R (Mohamed) v Secretary of State for Foreign and Commonwealth Affairs* [2008] EWHC 1914 (Admin), [133].

necessary to trace property but not to protect the life and liberty of the individual.[159] In *Omar*, the claimant—a Kenyan citizen alleged to have participated in the 'World Cup bombings' which had been carried out in Uganda in 2010—was similarly facing the death penalty if convicted. He sought a *Norwich Pharmacal* order to obtain disclosure from the Secretary of State of information regarding the alleged involvement of British intelligence services officers in his interrogation and associated mistreatment by the Ugandan security services, in order to make use of that material in proceedings in Uganda. Here, however, the use of *Norwich Pharmacal* proceedings was contested by the government, on the basis that there existed statutory regimes permitting the courts to order the provision of evidence for proceedings in overseas courts.[160] The High Court agreed that 'the statutory regime is the only means by which evidence for use in foreign proceedings may be obtained'[161] and the *Norwich Pharmacal* jurisdiction had only ever been used to that end in a small number of cases—including *Binyam Mohamed*—in which the point had not been explicitly decided.[162] The use of that jurisdiction to that end in the case before the court would frustrate a number of features of the statutory scheme and underlying treaty regime, including a provision of the Hague Convention permitting a request for assistance to be refused by the receiving state to the extent that 'the state considers that its sovereignty or security would be prejudiced thereby'.[163] And even it had taken the view that the *Norwich Pharmacal* jurisdiction could be—notwithstanding the existence of the statutory scheme, with its various exceptions and limitations—invoked to this end, the High Court would have been unwilling to undermine the position of the Ugandan courts by making the order sought, for 'the principle of comity require this court in these circumstances not to act without a request from the Constitutional Court.'[164] This decision was upheld by the Court of Appeal.[165]

Even before the decision in *Omar*, however, steps had been taken to blunt this repurposed legal tool. In the *Justice and Security Green Paper* of 2011,[166] the government indicated that it had defended seven relevant cases since 2008, and that these cases had a 'disproportionate impact on our international, diplomatic and intelligence relationships with foreign governments', with both the UK government and its foreign counterparts now having 'less confidence than before that the courts will accept the view of Ministers on the harm to national security that would result from disclosure.'[167] It asserted the necessity of rebuilding the trust of those partners that 'the range of sensitive material they share with us, and the communications on diplomatic channels, all of which take place with an understanding of confidentiality, will indeed remain confidential'[168] and suggested a number of possible legislative interventions that might be made, including the abolition of *Norwich Pharmacal*

[159] [2008] EWHC 1914 (Admin), [134].

[160] The Crime (International Co-operation) Act 2003 and the Evidence (Proceedings in Other Jurisdictions) Act 1975, which apply to criminal and civil proceedings respectively.

[161] *R (Omar) v Secretary of State for Foreign and Commonwealth Affairs* [2012] EWHC 1737 (Admin), [66].

[162] [2012] EWHC 1737 (Admin), [66].

[163] ibid, [69], citing Art 12 of the Hague Convention.

[164] ibid, [78].

[165] *R (Omar) v Secretary of State for Foreign and Commonwealth Affairs* [2013] EWCA Civ 118. See also Hickman and Tomkins (n 136) 155–6.

[166] Secretary of State for Justice, *Justice and Security Green Paper*, Cm 8194 (2011).

[167] Justice Secretary (n 166) [1.42]–[1.43].

[168] ibid [1.44].

orders against government departments and other public bodies (a solution which, it was acknowledged immediately, would 'go too far in preventing Norwich Pharmacal applications in other cases against Government in which non-sensitive material is at stake.')[169] Also rejected was the possibility of leaving the jurisdiction intact on the basis that the relevant proceedings would be subject to the statutory closed material procedure whose introduction the Green Paper also proposed.[170] To leave open the possibility of seeking a *Norwich Pharmacal* order for sensitive material would mean that:

> The UK courts [would] remain a forum of choice for speculative applicants, and Norwich Pharmacal applications for sensitive material will continue to have a disproportionate impact on the Government, primarily in terms of the risk to national security caused by disclosure and the expenditure of diplomatic capital in minimising the damage caused to international relationship.[171]

The JCHR accepted that to put *Norwich Pharmacal*, including the test to be satisfied, on a statutory footing 'would serve to increase legal certainty for both courts exercising the jurisdiction and intelligence partners'[172] but that any change should apply only to the national security context, for '[t]he case for going further has not been made out.'[173] The eventual provision made in the Justice and Security Act 2013 reflected that approach, with section 17 of the Act forbidding the courts from ordering, in *Norwich Pharmacal* proceedings, disclosure of 'sensitive information'. The limited approach taken to the reform of the *Norwich Pharmacal* jurisdiction, however, is undermined by the breadth of the definition given to 'sensitive information', which includes information:

> (a) held by an intelligence service,
> (b) obtained from, or held on behalf of, an intelligence service,
> (c) derived in whole or part from information obtained from, or held on behalf of, an intelligence service,
> (d) relating to an intelligence service ...[174]

The breadth of this definition meant that although the basic approach taken was a relatively narrow one, the 2013 Act effectively makes the 'control principle' absolute in the context of *Norwich Pharmacal* proceedings, and, in fact, goes so far as to provide an absolute exemption from disclosure for a very broadly-defined category of information.[175] Most notably—and unlike in relation to the category of 'sensitive material' which operates to frame the availability of a CMP under the 2013 Act—there is no requirement in relation to these categories that the material in question be material whose disclosure would be damaging to national security or any other vital state interest. Not for the first time, the existence of genuine problems requiring legal response was used as an opportunity to legislate

[169] ibid [2.90].
[170] See the discussion in Ch 6.
[171] Justice Secretary (n 166) [2.96]. See also Appendix A, which makes in clear and stark fashion the case that a 'loss of confidence in the UK's ability to protect sensitive diplomatic reporting would result in a gradual erosion of the Government's ability to gather the information and promote the sort of co-operation, through its diplomatic relations, that is essential to protect national security and promote the wider national interest.'
[172] Joint Committee on Human Rights, *The Justice and Security Green Paper* (2010–12, HL 286, HC 1777), [186].
[173] JCHR (n 172) [189].
[174] Justice and Security Act 2013, s 17(3). *cf* the definition of 'sensitive material' in s 6(11).
[175] Joint Committee on Human Rights, *Legislative Scrutiny: Justice and Security Bill* (2012–13, HL 59, HC 370), [86].

far beyond the confines of the issue at hand. The possibility of introducing such an absolute exemption had previously been described by the Independent Reviewer of Terrorism Legislation as 'manifestly disproportionate';[176] in reviewing the Justice and Security Bill, the JCHR recommended that the system of absolute exemption from disclosure be replaced by 'a system of certification based on the contents of the information and subject to judicial control.'[177] This was not done, and there is in the 2013 Act no requirement of balancing the difference public interests—in disclosure and non-disclosure—as takes place, most importantly, in the context of an application for PII. Rather, the regime resembles much more closely that for the use of CMP (also under the 2013 Act), though without a requirement analogous to that which applies to the making of a section 6 declaration, whereby it must be 'in the interests of the fair and effective administration of justice in the proceedings' for such a declaration to be made, and with a far broader definition of 'sensitive material'.

The range of material in relation to which the JSA's exclusion of *Norwich Pharmacal* jurisdiction applies goes, however, beyond those specified (if extremely broad) categories. A fifth category of 'sensitive information' is information which is 'specified or described in a certificate issued by the Secretary of State, in relation to the proceedings, as information which' the party who possesses it should not be ordered to disclose.[178] Such a certificate may be issued only where the Secretary of State considers that it would be 'contrary to the public interest' for the relevant party to disclose either the information, its existence, or the fact that the party possess it; disclosure fits that description where it would cause 'damage' to either 'the interests of national security' or 'the interests of the international relations of the United Kingdom.'[179] A certificate may be challenged by any party to the proceedings on the basis that 'the Secretary of State ought not to have determined, in relation to the information specified or described in the certificate' that disclosure would be 'contrary to the public interest', with the court deciding the question according to judicial review principles.[180] The proceedings within which such a challenge takes place are to be closed proceedings of the sort made generally available within the civil justice system by the 2013 Act, but with the term 'national security' read more widely than in other proceedings, so as to encompass 'the interests of the international relations of the United Kingdom.'[181] Not only, therefore, does this open-ended category have the effect that the *Norwich Pharmacal* order can be excluded even where there is no (direct) national security element to the information, but it confirms also that the legal gap between national security and international relations persists.

The availability of CMP in civil proceedings generally—and the absence, already noted, of any sort of balancing test—has its own, significant, implications for the ability of the legal process to bring to light evidence of wrongdoing. In Chapter 5, certain elements of the use to which section 6 of the JSA has been put were considered: the frequency—perhaps surprising, but perhaps also not—with which declarations have been made in the context of litigation relating to Northern Ireland, and the general unwillingness of the courts

[176] Quoted in JCHR (n 172) [171].
[177] JCHR (n 172) [97].
[178] JSA 2013, s 17(3)(b).
[179] ibid, s 17(4) and (5).
[180] ibid, ss 18(1)–(3).
[181] ibid, ss 18(3)–(6).

making such declarations to narrowly interpret the relevant statutory provisions or read in additional obstacles to the use of CMPs. In light of what has been discussed so far in this chapter, it is perhaps inevitable that one other feature is the reliance upon CMP in the context of litigation in which it is alleged that the UK has been involved in mistreatment abroad. We have already noted, above, the declaration made in the *Belhaj* litigation and the vast range of ways in which disclosure of the material at issue was considered liable to damage national security. Hickman and Tomkins,[182] in their consideration of the matter, discuss *CC and CF* (originally a control order/TPIM case, with the CMP therefore ordered under authority older and more specific than that in the 2013 Act).[183] Here the defendants alleged abuse of process as exemplified by *Bennett*,[184] where 'the court's sense of justice and propriety or public confidence in the justice system would be offended if the proceedings were not stayed.'[185]

In *Bennett*, the House of Lords ruled that a criminal prosecution might be stayed as an abuse of process where—as was assumed to be the case in relation to the defendant—the normal extradition process had been bypassed and the defendant brought into the jurisdiction against his will as a consequence of collusion between the UK police and their foreign counterparts. In *CC and CF*, the claim of an abuse of process arose from the alleged involvement of the UK in the defendants' detention and subsequent mistreatment in Somaliland (an autonomous region of Somalia which considers itself to be a state but is not recognised as such by the UK) and their unlawful return to the UK. Such involvement was neither confirmed nor denied by the Secretary of State.[186] The claim of abuse of process was rejected, but no reasons for that conclusion were given in the open judgment, in which Lloyd Jones J stated only that '[w]ith considerable reluctance' he had concluded that 'these matters cannot be addressed in my open judgment.'[187] Hickman and Tomkins summarised the effect of the decision as being that the claimants 'lost but they do not know why … [they] do not know to what extent, if at all, the British authorities were involved in their arrest, detention and deportation. They do not know even know what the Government's case is.'[188] Again: the closed proceedings here took place under specific statutory authority, prior to the enactment of the JSA 2013.[189] Hickman and Tomkins note too, however, that the specific form of the power to order a CMP within the 2013 Act was motivated by the same sorts of concerns about relations with foreign partners as motivated the limitation of the *Norwich Pharmacal* jurisdiction: they quote Kenneth Clarke MP as opposing an amendment to the Bill which would have required the balancing of interests when deciding whether or not to disclose certain material on the basis that it 'would give rise to the sort of power that promoted our allies' concerns following the *Binyam Mohamed* case.'[190]

[182] Hickman and Tomkins (n 152) 157–8.

[183] *Secretary of State for the Home Department v CC* [2012] EWHC 1732 (Admin).

[184] *R v Horseferry Road Magistrates' Court, ex parte Bennett* [1994] 1 AC 42.

[185] [2012] EWHC 1732 (Admin), [92].

[186] ibid, [132].

[187] ibid, [133].

[188] Hickman and Tomkins (n 152) 158.

[189] The control orders in question were later quashed on the basis of material non-disclosure, though this had no effect on the TPIMs which succeeded them: *Mohamed Ahmed Mohamed and CF v Secretary of State for the Home Department* [2014] EWCA Civ 559.

[190] Hickman and Tomkins (n 152) 158.

This has been borne out by the use of CMP under the JSA to prevent the disclosure of the same material as was at issue in the Somaliland case: in *CF* and *Mohammed Ahmed Mohamed* (this latter claimant being a deanonymised 'CC')[191] the High Court made a declaration under section 6 of the JSA in the context of civil claims (in tort, and for breach of the Human Rights Act) brought by the two individuals in relation to the same basic facts as had grounded their challenge to the TPIMs and control orders imposed upon them.[192] Alongside that, and separately, PII was granted in relation to other material whose disclosure (in full or even in part) the Secretary of State had certified would be harmful to international relations.[193] The case highlights an important (perhaps anomalous) aspect of the working of the JSA: because CMP is available only in relation to material whose disclosure would be harmful to national security, material in relation to which PII is granted on other grounds, such as those of international relations (material which will normally, the judge observes here, be *less* sensitive than that whose disclosure would harm national security), cannot be canvassed within the closed hearing.[194] Where PII is granted in relation to it, therefore, it is made part of neither the open nor the closed process. Two conclusions can be drawn from this: the first is that the framing of the statutory power to make a CMP declaration would appear to encompass only a limited subset of international relations material (a point already noted above). The second is that not only does the claim that disclosure of certain material might cause harm to international relations (if accepted by the court within the PII process) justify non-disclosure to public at large, but it may justify its non-disclosure to the court even within a closed process under the 2013 Act. The internationalisation of national security, and accompanying potential for complicity in unlawful or unethical acts, continues to push the evolution of the legal system, which is now in most cases capable of limiting or even negating the damage to international relations which would be caused by the doings of our foreign partners becoming known, *whether or not* that damage would lead, indirectly, to damage to the security of the UK itself. In this sense international relations is not merely an aspect of national security, but is at points elevated above it. And because the line between material which harms international relations and through it national security and that which does not is such a fine one, the executive will have considerable capacity to influence how the material is treated; whether it is disclosed in a closed hearing, or whether it is not disclosed at all.[195]

[191] The original anonymity was withdrawn as part of an effort to recapture Mr Mohamed following his much-publicised evasion of surveillance by donning a burka while leaving a mosque while on bail from charges of breaching both control orders and TPIMs in 2013.

[192] *CF v The Security Service* [2013] EWHC 3402 (QB).

[193] [2013] EWHC 3402 (QB), [59].

[194] ibid, [56]–[58]. The issue should not arise in the context of the 'specialised' CMP jurisdictions which apply in the context of, eg, TPIM proceedings, as the grounds of non-disclosure encompass material whose disclosure would be contrary to the public interest generally (rather than harmful to national security specifically). Note that the government's clarification that CMP under the JSA would not be available in relation to material whose disclosure would harm only international relations took place (at least in part) at the behest of the Joint Committee on Human Rights: JCHR (n 176) [30].

[195] The effect of this decision, it would seem, is that a case might—notwithstanding the 2013 Act—be rendered untriable by a successful PII application, for essentially the same reasons as were at issue in *Carnduff v Rock* [2001] EWCA Civ 680. See the discussion in Ch 5.

The discussion above no doubt betrays a certain scepticism as to the reality of some of the legal and practical claims which underpinned the Justice and Security Act and the idea that the US might cease sharing intelligence with the UK if it could not be assured that the intelligence in question would not be released at the behest of the court. And certainly—as we shall see again in the following section—many of the hypotheticals invoked are strained and unconvincing. The problem, however, is that the logic is on its face entirely sound. That is, once national security becomes an international endeavour, in which the UK is one of a number of states involved of collaborative enterprises (sometimes as equals, sometimes as the senior or junior partner) there is nothing fundamentally illogical about the notion that the security of the state becomes an indirect function of the willingness of those allies to continue collaborating within the domain of national security. And once we operate at this derivative level, the conceptual apparatus which operates within this area is blown apart; domestic courts can legitimately rule upon (and do rule upon) the question of whether some matter is encompassed within the statutory formulation 'national security'. Similarly, they can accept (or not) that the national security of the UK is put at risk by the withdrawal of security cooperation by a foreign state. What they struggle to do, however, is adjudicate upon the assertion of the government of a foreign state that some matter is suitably compelling that it would be justified in withdrawing intelligence or security cooperation from the UK. They cannot rule that the relevant actors are acting in bad faith; that the threat has been contrived in order to keep the matter away from the public eye; that at most what we are dealing with is a question of embarrassment—on the part of the state which carries out mistreatment, and the UK which works with it. The problem is at its most acute in those legal contexts in which there is no balancing to be carried out; no opportunity to weigh the public interest in disclosure against the asserted interest in non-disclosure. It is, therefore, to be regretted that the absence of such balancing requirements is now the norm in the national security context.

The effect of all this is that the internationalisation of national security carries in it the seed of a blanket obstruction to judicial accountability within the national security constitution. No sooner do the courts declare themselves willing (summon the courage?) to adjudicate upon such matters in relation to the UK than they are forced by the irrationality—the callousness—of the UK's foreign partners (regrettable of course, but in no way the fault of the UK which—it is repeatedly reasserted—upholds higher standards) to withdraw, this time in the name not of national security but of international security. We are left instead with inquiries, usually conducted by the Intelligence and Security Committee, whose reports are often heavily redacted and whose work can, in any event, be hamstrung by the failure of the executive to provide the necessary information. On the one occasion where this mould was to be broken—the detainee inquiry under Sir Peter Gibson—the spectre of criminal proceedings provided an opportunity to bring the inquiry to a premature end; its successor slipped back into the pattern of previous inquiries (on rendition, on the handling of detainees) by being placed in the hands of the ISC, albeit now to some degree strengthened by the Justice and Security Act. Where this international dimension is absent, the picture is less grim: the Baha Mousa inquiry and the Al-Sweady inquiries, though their outcomes were very different, could take the form they did precisely because the international dimension was not manifest—they related to the acts of British troops alone.

D. National Security and the 'Ordinary' Law

As the previous section shows, one implication of the frequency and depth of international cooperation in security matters is that there arises a need to tread carefully, based upon a fear that the UK's partners will withdraw cooperation and indirectly harm the security of the UK and its people. As national security becomes international security, that is, the freedom of action of the sovereign state is progressively limited, and those limits feed into the operation of the domestic legal order. In the previous section, that point was made with reference to the sorts of national security cooperation in which the threat to withdraw cooperation can be made (or can be hypothesised) most plausibly. It is important to understand, however, that the phenomenon in question does not respect the logic which separates the national security constitutionalism from the rest of the legal order: once the logic of international security enters the legal system, mere conceptual boundaries cannot prevent its spread. The point is illustrated most neatly by the *Corner House* case.[196] The Serious Fraud Office (SFO), a specialist prosecuting body with authority to prosecute complex fraud, bribery or corruption, carried out—over the course of several years—an investigation into allegations of bribery by BAE Systems (a major manufacturer of arms) relating to contracts for BAE to supply military aircraft to the Kingdom of Saudi Arabia. The investigation was brought to an end by the SFO in late 2006. Earlier that year, as the SFO had approached the point at which it would have access to Swiss bank accounts relevant to its investigation, attempts to convince it to drop the matter—which had already been made by BAE itself, citing in particular the effect on relations between the UK and Saudi Arabia—were stepped up, with the involvement of both the then ambassador to Saudi Arabia (Sir Sherard Cowper-Coles) and the then Prime Minister (Tony Blair) himself, and allegedly as a consequence of the personal intervention of Prince Bandar of the House of Saud. The content of these attempts at persuasion focussed upon the possible withdrawal by Saudi Arabia if the investigation was to continue, and the implications of that withdrawal for the ability of the domestic authorities to protect citizens. Using the phrase—attributed to the ambassador—which best captures not only the severity but also the tone of the warnings which were given to the Director of the SFO, 'British lives on British streets were at risk'.[197] Having several times resisted the considerable pressure brought to bear upon him, the Director eventually relented and the investigation was brought to an end, on the basis that to continue it risked 'real and imminent damage to the UK's national and international security and would endanger the lives of UK citizens and service personnel' or, as it was rather less directly put in the press release announcing the decision, because of representations which had been made 'concerning the need to safeguard national and international security'.[198]

That decision was the subject of a judicial review by Corner House, an NGO focussed upon overseas corruption and the role of the UK in combatting bribery abroad. The decision to discontinue the investigation was quashed at first instance, with the Divisional Court

[196] *R (Corner House) v Director of the Serious Fraud Office* [2008] UKHL 60.
[197] [2008] UKHL 60, [14].
[198] ibid, [22].

emphasising the damage done to the rule of law by the facts described, and formulating a principle whereby 'submission to a threat is lawful only when it is demonstrated to a court that there was no alternative course open to the decision-maker.'[199] Not only would such a principle protect the rule of law; it would also—crucially for present purposes—prevent an overly keen submission to a threat, which 'may give rise to the suspicion that the threat was not the real ground for the decision at all; rather it was a useful pretext'.[200] The Court made a similar point in considering the argument that the Director of the SFO had misdirected himself as to the meaning of the OECD Convention on Combating Bribery, which provides that investigations and prosecutions of bribery should not be influenced by—amongst other considerations—'the potential effect upon relations with another state'.[201] In noting the difficulty of distinguishing between such considerations and those of national security, the court observed that it is 'all too easy for a state which wishes to maintain good relations with another state whose official is under investigation to identify some potential damage to national security should good relations deteriorate, all the more so where that other state is powerful and of strategic importance.'[202] Ultimately, the OECD point went undecided: the claim for judicial review succeeded—the Director's decision was quashed—on the basis that both he and the government had 'failed to recognise that the rule of law required the decision to discontinue to be reached as an exercise of independent judgment' and that had not happened here, where both parties had 'concentrated on the effects which were feared should the threat be carried out and not on how the threat might be resisted'.[203] On appeal, however, there was little sense that the House of Lords shared the Divisional Court's poorly-disguised cynicism as to the plausibility of the threat to withdraw intelligence cooperation and its role in motivating the pressure brought to bear upon the Director of the SFO. Casting severe doubt on the principle identified by the Division Court (which was 'novel and unsupported by authority')[204] the House of Lords framed the issue very differently, Lord Bingham identifying as the 'right question' to be asked 'whether, in deciding that the public interest in pursuing an important investigation into alleged bribery was outweighed by the public interest in protecting the lives of British citizens, the Director made a decision outside the lawful bounds of the discretion entrusted to him by Parliament.'[205] The answer to that question was yes, and the order of the Divisional Court set aside.

The ultimate decision as to the lawfulness of the decision to bring the investigation to an end is, however, of less interest than are the broader lessons offered by the *Corner House* case. The first, and most obvious, is that in a world of intelligence sharing and intelligence cooperation, anything which impacts upon the relations between states can potentially become a security issue, with many states able to manipulate events to their advantage by threatening to withdraw such cooperation. Whatever public good a state is, within this process, effectively required to balance against that of national security is hardly likely to rival it for practical or political importance. The effect is that questions which themselves

[199] *R (Corner House) v Director of the Serious Fraud Office* [2008] EWHC 714 (Admin), [99].
[200] [2008] EWHC 714 (Admin), [101].
[201] ibid, [103].
[202] ibid, [133].
[203] ibid, [171].
[204] [2008] UKHL 60, [38].
[205] ibid.

have little or nothing to do with national security are, by virtue of their (potential) impact on international relations, nevertheless brought within the confines of the national security constitution, and so in practice in danger of being subordinated to the exigencies of national security. The second point follows directly from this. Once we recognise the significance of international cooperation within the modern national security landscape, and the possibility that it will sometimes genuinely be the case that matters which are on their face unrelated to security will nevertheless be made relevant to it by their implications for such cooperation, we must take seriously the possibility that the causal mechanism will be invoked in bad faith, as at least certain of the remarks made by the Divisional Court in *Corner House* suggest might be the case. Lord Denning once observed that '[i]n some parts of the world national security has on occasions been used as an excuse for all sorts of infringements of individual liberty. But not in England.'[206] Here, we are not dealing with individual liberties, but that does not mean that the goods at stake—the Divisional Court identifies *Corner House* as speaking to the rule of law in the form of the administration of justice—are any less urgent. The international dimension of the modern national security constitution makes claims about the indirect exigencies of national security more instinctively plausible and, in turn, more easily abused; we cannot, in such circumstances, afford to emulate Lord Denning's complacency.[207]

IV. Conclusion: The Constitutional Consequences of the Internationalisation of National Security

Though the title of this book employs the phrase 'national security' in the belief that it is the concept which best describes the phenomena under discussion, what this final chapter has attempted to show is that, to the extent it implies that the relevant issues apply to the UK alone—that the developments discussed herein can be understood within the isolated context of a single jurisdiction and a single constitutional order—that phrase is liable to mislead. Instead, the period under discussion is one in which not only has national security risen to unprecedented prominence within the constitutional order, prompting

[206] *R v Home Secretary, ex parte Hosenball* [1977] 1 WLR 766, 783. See Tomkins (n 136) 525: Government claims as to 'sensitivity, risk, and security' may 'often be exaggerated and sometimes wholly spurious'.

[207] The House of Lords gave judgment in *Corner House* in 2008. In 2011, Sir Sherard Cowper-Coles, who had been instrumental in persuading the Director of the SFO that national security considerations required him to end the investigation into BAE (and had in the meantime acted as Foreign & Commonwealth Office Special Representative for Afghanistan and Pakistan) was appointed as Business Development Director for BAE's International Operating Group. The Advisory Committee on Business Appointments—the group which makes (non-binding) recommendations regarding the post-office employment of Ministers and senior Crown Servants—made the following observations as to the appointment: 'Given that it has been 4 years since he had any involvement with BAE Systems as HM Ambassador to Riyadh, and that the appointment will be 4 months since his last day of service, the appointment was approved subject to the condition that, for 2 years from his last day of service, he should not become personally involved in lobbying UK Government Ministers or Crown servants, including Special Advisers, on behalf of his new employer.' Advisory Committee on Business Appointments, *Twelfth Annual Report 2010–2011* (2011), 51. In a neat encapsulation of the British constitution's approach to dealing with such issues—with the great and good tasked with applying non-binding rules to their peers—the report also noted that one member 'recused himself from consideration of this appointment as he is a friend of Sir Sherard.'

evolution within that order, and more generally making and remaking it in its own image. It is also one in which the limitations of national security as it has often been understood have become obvious. National security can now be recognised as what it may always have been; merely an instantiation of broader international security, in which the UK acts in concert with other states to respond to threats which are similarly international or transnational in nature. The national security constitution, therefore, encapsulates—more than any other facet of the constitution other than, perhaps, the economic—the extent to which analysis which presumes the effective sovereignty of the state is liable to miss the dynamic of constitutional evolution: both in its causes and its effects. In a number of ways, the story which this book has sought to tell is the story of a country which does not and cannot act alone in the field under discussion. What this final chapter has sought to do is to demonstrate the constitutional consequences of that fact: the blurring of the line between national security and international relations; the way in which that blurring undercuts the ability (and perhaps willingness) of the UK to consistently uphold those values it professes to place at the core of its legal and constitutional order; the manner in which it influences the spread of secrecy within the legal system; and, finally, the ability of the fundamental, crude, logic of international security to leak out of the national security constitution into the wider legal landscape. Taken together, these developments counteract and perhaps even outweigh the various positive developments described elsewhere in the book: the constitutionalisation of security is undermined, perhaps even undone, by its simultaneous internationalisation.

INDEX